THE GERMAN COOKBOOK

❧ THE ❧
GERMAN
COOKBOOK

A Complete Guide
to Mastering Authentic
German Cooking

MIMI SHERATON

Random House   New York

Design by Tere LoPrete

Drawings by Sidonie Coryn

Contents

Introduction

Good Eating, Good Drinking

(Gut Essen, Gut Trinken)

❖ ❖ ❖ ❖ ❖

Few countries in Europe can boast of landscapes more beautiful or more varied than those of Germany. By our standards it is not a large country, all in all some one hundred and forty thousand square miles within the reunified borders that include a wide variety of dialects, culinary influences, architecture, crafts, and folk and religious customs. But in this area, just a little smaller than Montana, there is every kind of terrain one finds in the temperate zone. The north German province of Schleswig-Holstein is a dramatically flat land of dune beaches, farms and windmills, picturesque fishing villages and the heather-blanketed Lüneburg Moors. Here you find the handsome old cities of the Hanseatic League—Hamburg, Bremen and Lübeck, the briny ports of the Baltic, the North Sea and the Elbe, with damp, chill climates and plenty of warm, snug inns and taverns with off-yellow walls that always seem to look sunlit. Travel from Hamburg to Cologne and the Rhine country and you are struck by the difference in the air, by the warm, soft climate of this wine-growing region, a place of green tapestry landscapes and vineyard-covered slopes. The castles looming over the river will take you back to the legends of the Lorelei and the Nibelungen, and the romantic Heidelberg will recall the whole *Gemütlichkeit* era of *The Student Prince*, set in the Schloss that rises above the town. The "iron Rhine" is another matter altogether, with its industrial cities along the Ruhr tributary—Düsseldorf and Essen, to name just two.

In southern Swabia, the Black Forest, with its pine groves and crystal-clear air, its fruit orchards and vineyards, its cuckoo-clock chalets and Badekur spas, its casinos and its game forests, is a region of Walpurgis legends and fairy tales. Here are luxurious hotels at which the crowned heads of the world took the "cures" in the latter half of the nineteenth century, and to which a less celebrated but no less devoted clientele still flocks all through the summer.

Bavaria, the largest state in West Germany, has always been the archetype, the travel-poster image that stands for all of Germany in the minds of those who have not been there. It is divided into Upper Bavaria in the south, Lower Bavaria in the north, the southern region being upper by virtue of its loftier mountain ranges. Lower Bavaria consists mainly of the mountainous Franconia and its Romantic Road—die Romantische Strasse—that runs from the baroque wine-producing city of Würzburg to the old Fugger stronghold, Augsburg. Between these two cities there is a chain of medieval towns, preserved but not restored. Of them all, the walled town of Rothenburg ob der Tauber is the most perfect set-piece, with its ramparts, towers and fortresses, castles, wrought-iron signs and fountains, and where the main hotel, the Eisenhut, is a series of antique burghers' mansions. In this area one sees a unique pattern in half-timbering, called Wild Man—wilder Mann—in which the crisscrossed arrangement of wood in the masonry looks like a wild man with arms and legs flung akimbo.

Upper Bavaria is perhaps the best-known area of Germany, with its Tyrolean overtones, its Alpine ski slopes and resorts such as Garmisch-Partenkirchen and Berchtesgaden, and the passion-play, wood-carving town of Oberammergau. Visit Hohenschwangau in the gentian-covered, snow-capped Allgäu Alps, and the view from your hotel room will undoubtedly include the towering castle of Neuschwanstein, only one of the three wild palaces of Bavaria's gourmet king, the mad Ludwig II. Munich, the capital of Bavaria, and its surroundings are dotted with black onion-dome churches whose interiors are masterpieces of the heavy German baroque style at its peak, and the area is jeweled with clear blue lakes, emerald mountainsides and lush woodlands. This is the home of Lederhosen and dirndls, gray Loden cloaks bound in green braid, and some of the world's best art museums. There is even more variety to the German landscapes: the wild forests of the eastern portion of the country, most especially in Thuringia, the gracious old university town of Hanover, the bustling business-minded Frankfurt that looks like a transplanted American town, and dozens of beautiful and historic places that I could go on listing, if space allowed me to. Each of these areas has its own customs, differing styles of architecture, distinctive dialects and special holidays.

The German cuisine is almost as varied as the terrain. Just as Bavaria passes as the archetype for the entire country, so the food of that section —the dumplings, sausages, beer, pork and cabbage dishes—represents German cooking to the outside world. Delicious though the Bavarian dishes may be, they hardly begin to give even a clue to the whole spectrum of German cooking—cooking which, by the way, is very poorly represented in the German restaurants in our own country. Unfortunately, these restaurants always seem to limit themselves to what might be considered the clichés of German cooking, and even those are rarely as well prepared as they should be. Like the architecture, art, dialects and customs, German food varies from one section to another, and tends to match the cooking of the foreign border closest to it. Eastern Germany, bordered by Austria, Czechoslovakia and Poland, flavors its dishes much as those countries do, with caraway, paprika, sour cream and dried mushrooms, and here one finds the largest dumplings, the most frequent use of sauerkraut and pork. In Alsace-bordered Swabia, on the other hand, juniper flavors the sauerkraut, as it does in the French province, game specialties abound, and potatoes and dumplings are eclipsed by the wide variety of noodle dishes, most especially the celebrated flecks of noodle dough called Spätzle. Snails are favorite appetizers, and the rich creamy cheese, bacon or onion tarts are as popular here as in neighboring Alsace and Switzerland. Wine and fruit brandies distilled from the products of local orchards are served as frequently as beer.

The Rhineland, being wine-land, features a cuisine that is lighter, less spiked with vinegar, and which puts a German accent on many dishes that were French in origin. Schleswig-Holstein, long a part of Denmark, has specialties close to those of that northern country. You see this in the lavish use of butter, eggs and cream, in their seafood and herring specialties, in the use of crab-flavored cream sauces on fish and in the way they combine meat and herring in many dishes. Whipped cream flavored with horseradish is favored here for carp and poultry sauces, as in Denmark, and here too bakery windows are full of the butter-rich yeast puff pastries which we call Danish pastry and which the Danes and Germans know as Vienna bread (Wienerbrot).

Not even the names are the same, or intelligible, from one section to the other. Ask for a "Halbes Hähnchen" in Berlin and you'll get exactly what you asked for—half a chicken; ask for it in Cologne and you will get a cheese sandwich on a small round roll that looks like a chicken breast, hence the name. A potato is a Kartoffel in the north, but an "earth apple"—Erdapfel—in the south, a direct translation of "pomme de terre." Munich's steamed pâté, Leberkäse, can almost never be found in Bremen or Lübeck, and Hamburg's briny oysters served with a slice of Cheshire cheese and a glass of red wine would shock the Berliner almost as much as it would you. The Holsteiners, by and large, think carp served with the south German sauce of beer and gingersnaps is a travesty on a fish they like with whipped cream. And the thick sauce of the Rhineland sauerbraten, made golden brown and velvety with caramelized sugar and flavored with raisins, is as different from the thin, red-wine vinegar version made in Munich as it is from an Italian pot roast seasoned with bay leaves and Chianti.

In spite of the fact that it is so badly represented in this country, German cooking has more appeal to the average American palate than the cuisine of any other foreign country. True, those of us who live in large cities, especially along the coasts, have developed a taste for Mediterranean food, but this is certainly not favored by the majority of people in the Midwest and the South. Traveling through Germany, one constantly meets American tourists from these areas who agree that the food in that country is, for them, the best in Europe. It is a preference that is easy to understand, for the German seasonings, fats and food combinations are more closely related to typical American cooking than are the wine, tomato, garlic and herb seasonings of France or Italy. Basically, Germans eat a meat-and-potatoes diet, as do most Americans. The fats used are mainly butter, lard and bacon, and the German taste for dishes that are sweet-and-sour, or for sweet condiments with meat courses, is not too strange when you consider the American predilection for pineapple and sugar on ham, cranberries and sweet potatoes and marshmallows with turkey, and all of the sweet relishes and pickles served here with hamburgers and hot dogs. Those last two are reminders of all the German dishes that have been adopted outright by Americans —not only hamburgers and frankfurters, with or without the ever-present sauerkraut, but the jelly doughnut that was first the Berliner Pfannkuchen; Boston cream pie, which in Germany is "Moor's Head"; the love of ham or bacon with fried eggs; the range of Christmas cookies and even pretzels; and the old stand-by of ladies' luncheons, creamed chicken in a patty shell, that appears in every German Konditorei as Königinpastetchen. Both German and American cuisines go better with beer than with wine; both favor gravies rather than sauces; neither uses much garlic or olive oil.

Germans have always been great traders and travelers, and thus have developed a strong taste for the foods and seasonings of other countries —always adjusted, however, to their own palates. The last time I was in Hamburg I went to see a performance of Franz Lehár's *Land of Smiles,* a typical Viennese operetta where the sentiment is as thick as Schlagobers. It tells the story of a Viennese general and nobleman whose daughter falls in love with an Oriental (Laotian, I believe) prince and ambassador. She tells her father that she plans to marry him and live in a far-off Eastern land. The father asks sadly why she has chosen a man whose home is so far away. Holding a small jade Buddha, she replies in a warbling contralto voice, "Papa, ich liebe das Exotische . . ." It struck me that this love of the exotic is certainly reflected in the German taste for food. All restaurant menus list specialties that are prepared according to the styles of Italy, Spain, India, France, Hungary, and so on. Many dishes are flavored with curry, and the aromatic spices of the East had a place in German cupboards even before the ships of the Hansa League brought them home. Any German city of moderate size has several good foreign restaurants, much frequented by local people, and food shops carry as many strange and *outré* items as do ours.

Interest in food is enormous in Germany and it is fascinating to watch people order in restaurants. There is much more careful choosing there than in our own country and diners are rarely bound by menu categories. One might start with a plate of pale pink smoked salmon and then have only an entree of creamed wild mushrooms, regardless of whether these were listed as appetizer and vegetable; a fish course may be ordered as an appetizer; and an appetizer such as cold Lobster Mayonnaise might be the entire meal.

This same practice of combining appetizers for a complete meal is now popular here and is in keeping with the trend toward smaller portions of a greater variety of foods, and our currently fashionable "grazing" method of eating. Similarly, the German use of fruits with nonsweet seafood and meat dishes anticipated France's *nouvelle cuisine* chefs, who act as though the idea they once shunned was theirs in the first place.

Although this book's main purpose is to tell you how to cook authentic German meals at home, its secondary purpose is to serve as a somewhat informal guide to anyone who would like to eat his way around Germany. Therefore it would seem convenient for you to have some idea of the daily eating schedules in that country. Hotels serve you any kind of breakfast (Frühstück) you want, but in rural homes it generally is a piece of bread, with or without butter, and a cup of coffee with milk. The only common addition is a single soft-boiled egg, and schoolchildren will probably have a hot cereal such as oatmeal or rice cooked with milk and flavored with sugar and perhaps raisins. The larger morning meal— "bread time" (Brotzeit) comes at about ten-thirty or eleven. This snack varies with the locale. In Munich it consists of Weisswurst, bread and beer, while in Cologne it would be the cheese sandwich, Halbes Hähnchen, described above. In Swabia the morning snack is the Vesper, which consists of raw bacon on sour rye bread and a glass of kirsch, a combination that is known as Strammer Max in Berlin, where it is served with Schnaps made of barley. In other parts of the country a local cured ham, bacon or wurst is served, and anywhere it might be a cream pastry or coffee cake in a Konditorei. Lunch is served at twelve. Traditionally this was the big meal of the day, with the complete meat-and-potatoes routine, and it still is in rural areas or where workers can get home for lunch. Otherwise, office workers in large cities bring lunch from home or eat in restaurants much as we do, and have their large meal at night. At about four-thirty or five the wurst stands and Konditoreien are jammed again, depending on whether one wants a hot dog and beer or cake and coffee, and seven o'clock brings us to dinner. Those who had their big meal for lunch now have a cold cheese-and-meat platter with perhaps a rather rich dessert, or a thick soup and a dessert made with eggs or fruit. Those who had a light lunch now have their large meal. Anyone awake at eleven or twelve eats again—wurst and cheese, open sandwiches, goulash soup, curry wurst, cake and coffee, according to preference and locale.

Restaurants in Germany are excellent, offering varied menus, good service and huge portions. As in Italy, there are various classifications of restaurants, though the categories are perhaps not as rigid as they once were. In the top-price bracket you find the grills, dining rooms and restaurants of the leading hotels, which, with the luxury eating places, feature food that is more Continental than German. More interesting are the typically German restaurants: the Weinrestaurant or Weinhaus that serves elegant food to go with wine and the Weinstube that does the same in a less formal, more tavernlike atmosphere. The Bierstube serves simple, inexpensive food that goes best with beer, while the Brauhaus (beer hall) does the same but usually on a larger scale. These last are owned by breweries, and since their main purpose is to sell beer, the food is hearty, inexpensive and simply prepared. Munich is the world capital of the Brauhaus, and there the Platzl, the Hofbräuhaus and the Mathaser are the most famous.

To me the one place not to miss in any German city is the town-hall restaurant, the Rathauskeller or Ratskeller. These are operated on a low-profit basis for employees of the town hall; some are simple and informal such as the one in Munich, while others get quite elegant and offer a large menu and fine wines, as does the magnificent one in Hamburg. If you find yourself in a German city and have no clue as to where you can find an authentic native restaurant, just go to the local Ratskeller—you'll rarely be disappointed. For quick snacks, there are open counters or stands known as Schnell Imbiss and the more leisurely, tempting pastry-shop restaurants, Konditoreien, that offer cakes, coffee, hot and cold sandwiches, and magazines and newspapers as well. Frankfurt's special Apfelwein inns in the old Sachsenhausen section of the city are informal and a great deal of fun.

Though each chapter of this book describes the German eating habits and preferences regarding specific kinds of foods, I should like to point out some of the outstanding features of that cuisine. The soups are superb, as are the black and rye breads, the sausages and the dumplings, the cabbage dishes and the exquisite cakes and pastries. The other area where the Germans display a real genius is in the realm of delicatessen, or Feinkost. Anyone who visits Dallmyer's in Munich will be instantly reminded that "delicatessen" is a German word, a German idea and, in this shop, a German obsession. It is made up of room after room filled with rare coffees and teas, candies and wines, crackers, breads and cakes, meats and fish. There are live crayfish in marble fountains and, at last count, the delicatessen counter included forty-two different cold fish, meat, cheese, wurst, vegetable and fruit salads, as well as garlands of sausages, chilled tins of caviar and platters of jellied eggs, meat and poultry, and fish specialties all jeweled with flecks of truffles and herbs.

No book this size could ever be an encyclopedia of German cooking, as it would take twice the number of pages to cover all the baking specialties alone. It is rather a collection of recipes for dishes some of which you already know and others you might not have come across, gathered together to give you an idea of the scope, variety and high quality of Germany's cuisine.

Obviously, the German motto *gut essen, gut trinken*—good eating, good drinking—belongs on the national coat of arms, along with the before-meal wish: *Gesegnete Mahlzeit*—blessed be your meal!

Holiday Festivals and Foods

(Festtage und -gerichte)

❌ ❌ ❌ ❌ ❌

Holidays and festivals, both civil and religious, dot the German calendar like currants in a Christmas Stollen. Many of these celebrations vary from one part of the country to the other, and change as you travel from the Catholic south and Rhineland to the Protestant north. In addi-ion, many small towns and villages have festivals honoring their own patron saints or events in local history. There are probably many more holidays than those listed here, in which a cruller is turned this way instead of that, or for which a special-color soup is served. These, however, are the most important holidays and the only ones I could find during a considerable amount of research. Both the Lufthansa and German tourist offices have been badgering their staffs for months to think of more, but with no results. If you happen to know of a feast day in Mecklenburg when everyone eats red currants dyed blue, or a special festival in Pomerania when the treat of the day is Pomeranians' tongues, I can only offer my apologies for having missed them.

January 6, which is Twelfth Night or the Feast of the Magi, is known in Germany as Dreikönigsabend—Three Kings' Eve (the cake of that name is the obvious specialty). In midwinter most of Germany celebrates Fasching, a pre-Lenten carnival that reaches its peak on Fastnacht, or what we know as Shrove or Fat Tuesday, or Mardi Gras. This masked and costumed street carnival is at its wildest in Cologne and Munich, where an anything-goes spirit prevails in unimaginable proportions. The things you are supposed to eat on that night are the fried crullers

(Fastnachtkrapfen), but I can't believe that anyone does, considering the alternate (and less caloric) enticements.

Bock beer season falls during Lent also; new spring beer and Bock-wurst sausages are the specialties for that time.

Holy Thursday, just before Good Friday and Easter, is known as Green Thursday (Gründonnerstag) in Germany. A creamed green soup made of seven spring herbs or simply of new spinach is served on that day, garnished with hard-cooked eggs that are sliced in half lengthwise and tiny meat balls lightly browned in butter and poached in the soup. Fried or poached eggs on a bed of creamed new spinach is the alternate.

Good Friday, known as Grieving Friday (Karfreitag) is the most important and solemn holiday throughout the country, in both Catholic and Protestant areas. I will never forget being in Munich one Good Friday and being told that any place I wanted to visit was "geschlossen" —closed. Never in my life have I been in a place so absolutely ge-schlossened. But the churches were open and magnificent, their altars banked with hyacinths, tulips and heavily perfumed tuberoses, and rimmed by rows of glass bowls filled with red, yellow, blue, violet, and pink and green water, each lit from behind by a single candle. Since this is a meatless fast day, various fish dishes are served but none that is especially traditional.

Easter (Oster) in Germany is the time for colored eggs, candy or cake chicks, rabbits and lambs, as it is almost everywhere else. In Bavaria, Easter breakfast includes bread that was blessed in church on the previous day, a custom one also finds in eastern Europe. Throughout Germany, bakery windows are filled with Easter bread (Osterfladen), a sweet yeast coffee cake similar to Stollen or the Italian panettone. But the most dazzling sights of all are the candy-shop windows, crammed with chocolate eggs of every size, some encrusted with almond or hazel-nut praliné, others decorated with candied violets or mimosa and sugary sprays of pussy willows—the Kätzchen which are the favorite harbingers of spring and which, incidentally, are what one receives in church on Palm Sunday (Palmsonntag) instead of palm fronds. Towering over the candy lambs, bunnies and chicks are the magnificent roosters, with heads and combs of colored marzipan, chocolate bodies and regal tails fanning out in ribbons of chocolate. If anyone can eat after all that cake and candy, the feature of the Easter dinner is ham (Osterschinken), usually served with a purée of fresh or dried green peas.

May 1, May Day (Maitag) is a day of picnics, maypoles and the woodruff-scented white wine punch, the Maibowle, or its more sophisticated counterpart, a bombe of woodruff ice and strawberries.

The end of September is the time for Munich's Oktoberfest, a bit of calendar juggling I have never quite understood, except that the festival ends in October, so perhaps that explains it. For details on the general hilarity, food and beer, see page 483.

The third Sunday in October is a church consecration day called Kirchweih. It is celebrated mostly in rural areas and is a sort of farmers'

Labor Day. If you were to visit a farmhouse on that day, you would be greeted with beer and either the Kirchkucherl or Kirchnudeln crullers or fritters, depending on which part of the country you were in.

November 11 is St. Martin's Day, Martinmas, or, in German, der Martinstag. St. Martin was the patron saint of geese, drinking and merrymaking, and his day is celebrated accordingly. By coincidence, geese are considered to be at their fattest and most succulent during this season; stuffed with prunes and apples, they are served with chestnuts, red cabbage or sauerkraut, and with big dumplings to absorb the rich gravy—a strange fate for geese on the day of their protector.

December 24, Christmas Eve (Weihnachtsabend oder Heiliger Abend) is a meatless fast day for Catholics and the specialty is carp. In Swabia it will probably be cooked with gingerbread or gingersnaps, while in Bavaria the Bohemian method prevails. Though Schleswig-Holstein is Protestant and does not observe the meatless ruling, carp is something of a tradition there also on this night and is served hot, poached, and with clouds of whipped cream and grated horseradish. Rice pudding or soufflé, or rice cooked with milk, is also something of a tradition on Christmas Eve, mostly in northern Germany. Only one portion contains an almond, and the one who receives it gets a special prize.

December 25, Christmas Day (Christtag oder erster Weihnachtstag), should be a day that honors the German talent for superb baking. Dozens of kinds of cookies, large and small cakes, fruit breads and sweet yeast breads like Dresden Stollen are all prepared for this day. Families begin baking four weeks ahead of time, during Advent, and by Christmas Eve, homes are richly scented with ginger, cardamom, anise, nutmeg, vanilla —everything, in fact, except frankincense and myrrh, which probably wouldn't taste so good anyway. All of this Christmas baking is known as Weihnachtsgebäck. In addition to cakes and cookies, a big feature of a German Christmas is the marzipan or almond paste, which is colored and shaped into fruits, vegetables, animals, angels and all sorts of Yuletide signs and symbols, as well as into the flat glazed hearts studded with citron and cherries which have been favorites of mine since I was a child, though I haven't been able to find them for years. Goose, with the trimmings described above for St. Martin's Day, is also served for Christmas dinner, along with a plum pudding which might be flambéed with rum, or covered with Vanilla or Foamy Wine Sauce.

December 31, New Year's Eve (Silvester), is again a meatless holiday for Catholics and carp is featured. In some parts of northern Germany, especially in Berlin, the fish is served unscaled and each person takes one scale and keeps it as a good-luck token for the year ahead. New Year's Eve revelry usually winds up at midnight with a hot or flaming wine punch.

The German Kitchen

(Die Deutsche Küche)

❂ ❂ ❂ ❂ ❂

This book is written on the assumption that you have had some cooking experience. I have worked on the premise that you own and use at least one of the large basic cookbooks, that you *do* know how to boil water and are familiar with the more usual recipe terminology. You may never have whipped up a soufflé, rolled up a galantine of chicken or stretched out a sheet of strudel dough, but you can be expected to produce a simple meal for your family or a few guests without danger of mishap. This means that you already know the difference between boiling and simmering, and when a recipe tells you to separate three eggs, you know you are not expected to place them in opposite corners of the room.

This also means that your cupboards contain such basic equipment as a coffee pot, water kettle, some frying pans and saucepans, a few larger pots of one sort or another and, perhaps, even a double boiler, a wooden mixing spoon or two, a set of knives and a good sharpener for them, a strainer, and standard measuring cups and spoons; and that your pantry contains such simple provisions as salt, pepper, sugar, flour.

Therefore, the lists of utensils, herbs, spices and condiments, and cooking terms in this chapter include only those things that will be especially helpful to you in preparing the German recipes in this book.

Every national cuisine has its identifying flavors. By understanding what they are and knowing how to impart them to food you are preparing, you can make the same basic preparations taste authentically German, French, Italian, Turkish, Spanish or Chinese. Almost every country has its own versions of the meat ball and the rolled meat bird, but the fat in which they are browned, the seasonings with which they are flavored, and the liquids in which they are simmered combine to produce dishes that taste entirely different. The French roulade would probably be browned in butter with perhaps a little bacon added to it, it would be seasoned with shallots and minced parsley and simmered in red wine. The Italian rollatine would be browned with garlic in olive oil, simmered in tomato sauce and flavored with basil and oregano; while the German rouladen would be browned in lard or bacon fat, flavored with sautéed onions and simmered in beef stock, water or beer—a heel of rye bread or a few gingersnaps might also be added to the sauce and there would very likely be a dash each of vinegar, sugar and sour cream in it. Similar examples could be drawn for the meat ball, or for those meat-filled packets of noodle dough that are the Italian ravioli, the German Maultaschen, the Jewish kreplach or the Chinese won-ton, as well as for hundreds of other dishes. Although all cuisines sooner or later use all of the same herbs and spices, they do so in different ways and with varying degrees of frequency. If the overwhelming flavors in German food come from caraway seeds, root vegetables, onions, paprika, vinegar and sugar, juniper and nutmeg, this does not mean that a German cook never uses garlic, basil, wine or thyme. The following list tells which herbs, spices, condiments and special ingredients are most often called for in German recipes, along with some indication of how they are used. As you read and prepare the recipes in this book, you will begin to understand the idiom of German cooking. Eventually, you should be able to make any food "taste German" and be able to plan complete and authentic German meals without any recipes to guide you.

Allspice (Nelkenpfeffer): You may buy this powdered or grind the whole kernels yourself in a spice mill. Allspice flavors many German fish and meat dishes and is used in the pickling marinades for Sauerbraten and herring.

Almonds (Mandeln): Either the blanched, untoasted, unsalted nuts—or almond extract—flavor many candies, cakes, desserts and sweet sauces. The almond paste candy, marzipan, is world-famous and goes into many cake fillings and confections. That of Lübeck is the best in Germany, if not in the world. Sweet almonds are generally mixed with a few bitter almonds in most recipes. If you cannot get the latter, use extract along with the sweet almonds. A quarter of a pound of almonds is equivalent to two-thirds to three-quarters of a cup, depending on whether the nuts are whole, slivered, chopped or grated.

Anchovies (Sardellen): Mashed with butter, these salty fish filets flavor canapés, sandwiches and such broiled fish as salmon and swordfish. They are also mixed into mayonnaise dressings used on cold fish and shellfish. Flat filets are toppings for open sandwiches and flavor many veal and lamb dishes. Surprisingly, they also go into meat dishes such as Sailor's Hash and Beef Tartar. If you use anchovy paste, allow 1 teaspoonful for 3 mashed or minced filets. If filets are extra salty, they should be rinsed in cold water and then drained before being added to a dish that is to be cooked.

Anise (Anis): These licorice-flavored seeds, whole or powdered, go into Chrismas cookies, cakes and desserts. In the latter, anise-flavored liqueurs such as anisette, or Strega, can be substituted. Whole seeds should be lightly crushed before being stirred into a batter.

Apples (Äpfel): This fruit is used as flavoring throughout Germany and is often added to soups and vegetable dishes made with cabbage, sauerkraut and potato. You may also get the same flavor by substituting cider (Apfelwein) or a dark jam, Apfelkraut, which is like apple butter. Do not use sugar with the latter.

Arrack (*see* Rum)

Basil (Basilikum): Although used mainly in Bavaria, this does appear in some soups, meat stews and sauces elsewhere in Germany. Germans rarely use pepper in a dish that contains basil.

Bay leaves (Lorbeerblätter): Used in many fish and meat soups and stews, this is especially popular with veal and lamb. Bay leaves are also used in Sauerbraten marinade.

Borage (Borretsch): This is very popular in Germany and more widely available than it is here. Its mild cucumber flavor is used to enhance salads and, of all things, cucumbers.

Candied fruits (Kandierte Früchte): Citron (Zitronat), orange peel (Orangeat), angelica (Angelika) and cherries (Kirschen) are used in many sweet yeast breads or coffee cakes, cookies, candies and puddings as well as in frozen or jelled desserts. They are often soaked until softened in a little rum or arrack.

Capers (Kapern): These spicy seeds, bottled in vinegar, should be drained, rinsed and drained again, before being added, whole or chopped, to other ingredients. They are used in many hot and cold sauces that are served with fish, shellfish or bland meats such as veal or lamb.

Caraway seeds (Kümmel): These fresh-tasting gray seeds flavor many breads, soups, meat stews, sauerkraut and cabbage dishes, a few cakes and an akvavit-like liqueur, Kümmel. They are also very good mixed into cottage cheese or butter as a sandwich or canapé spread.

Cardamom (Kardamom): When powdered, this aromatic ivory-colored pod is added to Christmas sweet breads and cookies, most especially to Lebkuchen.

Chervil (Kerbel): Used in Germany as here, mainly in salad dressings but also for Green Soup.

Chives (Schnittlauch): Used in Germany as here, chives are mainly a flavorful garnish for soups, sauces, egg dishes, vegetable salads, cottage cheese and sandwich butters. In Germany they are usually added raw, after a dish is cooked. Chives are rarely cooked.

Cinnamon (Zimt): In stick, cracked or powdered form, cinnamon flavors cakes, desserts and hot drinks. It is also used in several soups and sweet-sour sauces, especially those that have raisins.

Cloves (Nelken): Whole or powdered cloves are used in much the same way as here, except that they are added to a greater variety of meat dishes; they flavor sauces served with fish, and some vegetables.

Curry powder (Curry): This exotic Oriental spice blend is surprisingly popular in Germany. It is mixed into mayonnaise, cream sauces and tomato sauces and is a great favorite in hot or cold fish and chicken dishes, and in Curry Wurst.

Dill (Dill): Fresh dill is much preferred and almost always available in large well-stocked vegetable markets the year round. Only the fresh is used for salads; fresh or dried may flavor soups, sauces and especially cucumber dishes.

Fruit Juices (Obstsäfte): Anyone who has not sampled the superb concentrated berry juices that are so popular in Germany has a wonderful surprise in store. My favorite is the winy currant juice (Johannisbeersaft), but the blackberry (Brombeersaft), strawberry (Erdbeersaft) and cherry (Kirschsaft) are also excellent. Used separately or in combination with each other, they make very good punches or, with ice and soda, Spritzers.

Garlic (Knoblauch): This is used very sparingly in Germany and appears mainly in the food of the eastern regions. The rest of the country confines its use mainly to mutton and lamb dishes or as a seasoning in several sausages and salamis.

Ginger (Ingwer): Used for the most part as it is here, in desserts, cakes and cookies. It is also added to potted beef dishes, either in powdered form or via spicy Lebkuchen which are also used in preparing carp.

Horseradish (Meerrettich): Freshly grated horseradish root mixed with whipped cream, sour cream, cream sauce, apples or grated lemon rind is served with dozens of boiled meat and fish dishes throughout Germany. It should be sprinkled with a little vinegar or lemon juice as it is grated, or it will blacken. Since it is very peppery, grate it near an open window. Never cook horseradish; simply stir it into cooked food just before serving.

Jams and jellies (Marmeladen): Currant and raspberry preserves are often melted into sauces that are to be served with meats, especially game, and into such dishes as Hamburg Eel Soup. They are also used in preparing red cabbage, and as fillings for cakes and cookies.

Juniper berries (Wacholderbeeren): Although most popular in Swabia, these large brown berries, lightly crushed, are used in game dishes all over Germany. In Swabia they are also added to sauerkraut instead of caraway seeds, and flavor a popular white Schnaps liqueur. Juniper, by the way, is the herb that gives gin its flavor and aroma.

Lemon (Zitrone): Strips of rind, or the juice, are used in all sorts of soups, stews, sauces, meat and fish dishes, desserts and cakes. Lemon juice may be used instead of vinegar for sauces that are sweet and sour, and it flavors all of the white stews known as fricassees.

Lovage (Liebstöckel): Although pretty generally available fresh in Germany, you will probably have to buy this dried here unless you grow it yourself. Its mild carrot flavor is especially popular in soups and meat stews. One leaf of the fresh herb goes a very long way.

Mace (Muskatenblüte): Used in fish or chicken soups, stews and some white sauces, this is also a great favorite with creamed cauliflower and potato dishes.

Marjoram (Majoran): As with basil, this is mainly popular for soups and stews in Bavaria, though it does appear elsewhere in the country to a lesser degree.

Mustard (Senf): Powdered mustard is used in salad dressings in Germany as elsewhere. The real difference is in the superb prepared mustards one finds in that country. They are sweet or hot, finely or coarsely ground, light or dark, with horseradish and without. Go to a good German delicatessen or gourmet food shop and sample all of the varieties. Düsseldorf mustard is the most famous but you might find another favorite. Mustard is used in many sauces and in such cooked dishes as Mutton Pot Roast with Mustard.

Nutmeg (Muskatnuss): Used for the most part, as here, in desserts and cakes, but also very popular in creamed potatoes and potato puddings. Cream soups and sauces and bread dumplings are also flavored with this spice.

Onions (Zwiebeln): These must be considered seasonings in German cooking as they are the base of almost every soup, sauce, meat, fish and vegetable dish. They are also sautéed in fat and used as toppings for many meat and potato dishes and are served as vegetables, creamed or French-fried.

Paprika (Paprika): Sweet paprika is used in many soups, stews and sauces, more in Bavaria and Prussia than elsewhere. It is an essential ingredient in goulash and goulash soup and is also used as garnish on many dishes, as it is here.

Parsley (Petersilie): Used in Germany a great deal, in the same way as it is elsewhere. The fresh is preferable, and usually the flat Italian variety is the kind used, rather than the curly parsley. If you must use dried parsley, steep it in a little hot water first.

Pepper (Pfeffer): This is used with restraint, as food is rarely highly seasoned in Germany. The white pepper is preferred to the black because it is milder, and for one thing, will not spoil the appearance of light sauces. You may buy whole or powdered white pepper—actually the inside of the husked black peppercorn.

Poppy seeds (Mohnsamen): Used for cakes and yeast breads as well as for flavoring buttered noodles and potato puddings.

Pot vegetables, root vegetables or soup greens (Wurzelwerk oder Suppengrün): This combination is perhaps the most distinctive in the German cuisine. Countless soups and fish or meat stews and pot roasts are flavored with this group of root vegetables and greens. It includes carrot, parsley root (petrouchka), parsnip, leek, knob celery or celeriac, onion and sometimes white turnip, along with such greens as flat parsley, celery leaves and perhaps dill, though this last is likely to sour as it cooks and is better added raw as a garnish. Not all are essential at all times, but the more variety, the better. Turnip is very strongly flavored and is the root vegetable most often eliminated—especially by me.

Raisins and currants (Rosinen und Korinthen): Used, as here, in desserts and cakes, but in Germany these are also added to many sweet-and-sour sauces and meat dishes such as Rhineland Sauerbraten.

Rosemary (Rosmarin): Used almost exclusively for lamb and mutton dishes in Germany.

Rum (Rum): This flavors dozens of puddings, molded jellies and frozen cream desserts, as well as cakes and frostings. It is used interchangeably with the mellow-flavored Arabic liqueur, arrack. The latter is perhaps harder to find, so use whichever is more convenient.

Sage (Salbei): Fresh sage leaves are cooked with many eel, pork, lamb and mutton dishes and also flavor a few cheeses and sausages.

Savory (Bohnenkraut): As its name implies, this is Germany's favorite "bean herb." It is used in almost all dried and fresh bean dishes, many vegetable soups, and is an essential ingredient in Hamburg Eel Soup.

Tarragon (Estragon): Used in Germany as elsewhere, it is very popular in salad dressings and vinegar.

Thyme (Thymian): This is used in many vegetable soups and stews as well as in some sausages. As with basil and marjoram, it is found mostly in Bavaria and also in East Germany. It is an important ingredient in Goulash Soup and Hamburg Eel Soup, but then, everything seems to be an important ingredient of that Schleswig-Holstein hodge-podge.

Tomato purée or ketchup (Tomatenmark oder Ketchup): Often stirred into soups, stews and sauces just before serving to improve color. Both are also added to mayonnaise and cottage cheese dressing used for fish or fruit salads.

Vanilla (Vanille): Both the bean and the extract are used to flavor desserts and cakes. Vanilla Sugar can be used to flavor dishes also. If you use the bean, it must be cut and its seeds scraped into the food you are preparing, or a piece of the whole bean must be simmered with whatever liquid is used in the dish. One teaspoonful of vanilla extract is equal approximately to half a vanilla bean. Imitation vanilla flavor, or vanillin, is an all-around unsatisfactory substitute for the bean or its extract. There is no reason, and therefore no excuse, for ever using it.

Vinegar (Essig): This, along with its flavoring companion sugar, is used more in German cooking than in any other, primarily because of the passion for sweet-and-sour dishes. Unless otherwise stated, vinegar in a German recipe means distilled white vinegar. Lemon juice or white wine can be substituted in most cases. To get an instant sweet-sour flavor without using either vinegar or sugar, use the pickling liquid of sweet gherkins, which already contains both ingredients.

☙ / FATS (*Fett*)

Lard (Schweinefett), bacon (Speck) and butter (Butter) are the most commonly used fats in German cooking. Beef suet, or kidney fat (Nierenfett), is used in beef stews and pot roasts and in some English-style puddings. Mildly flavored oil (*Öl*) is used in dressings and for some cooking, but much less often than those above. Some olive oil is used for salad dressing, but its flavor is most "un-German."

Now, of course, the Germans have become as cholesterol-conscious as everyone else, and the market shelves are lined with bottles and tins of polyunsaturated fats, just as ours are. These, and the semi-ersatz vegetable shortenings, are fairly popular, but they are not typical of German cooking and detract from its true flavor. I have not used them in recipes, but you may substitute them as you would in any other kind of cooking. Margarine (Margarine) is used there as here, but is rarely served melted or in sauces.

Although many people in this country have a squeamish attitude toward lard, it is probably due to a bad experience with some that was of poor quality or, worse yet, not fresh. Good lard, usually purchased from a butcher, produces excellent results in cooking and baking. Avoid the kind that is treated with preservatives and needs no refrigeration.

If you use bacon that is very smoky or salty, blanch it in hot water for 5 minutes before going ahead with the recipe.

Rendered chicken, duck and goose fats (Geflügel-, Enten- und Gänse-fett, oder Schmalz) are used more in northern Germany and Swabia than elsewhere. They add a wonderful flavor to cabbage and kraut dishes, boiled or mashed potatoes. They are also popular spread on bread and sprinkled with salt and eaten as open sandwiches. To render these fats, trim fat from inside of poultry, taking much of it from the area around the throat and chest. Dice it, rinse in cold water and cook very, very slowly in a heavy-bottomed saucepan until all of the fat has melted down. If some skin is cut up with the fat, this will remain and form cracklings (Grieben), which are sometimes sprinkled on top of mashed or boiled potatoes or used in cabbage, kraut and noodle dishes. The liquid poultry fat is also sometimes mixed with melted butter before solidifying, to give it a more delicate flavor. Rendered fat can be stored for weeks in a tightly closed jar in the refrigerator. Onions may be fried with the fat when it is being rendered, but I think that they limit its use.

⚄ / STARCHES AND FLOUR (*Stärke und Mehl*)

Wheat flour (Weizenmehl) and rye flour (Roggenmehl) are used most often in baking. Wheat flour is also used to bind sauces. Potato starch or flour (Kartoffelmehl) is used in some baking, but more to bind fruit puddings or flummeries. Semolina or farina (Griess), rice or rice flour (Reis oder Reismehl), tapioca (Sago), cornstarch (Stärkemehl) and arrowroot (Mondamin) are all used for binding sauces and thickening puddings and flummery desserts.

⚄ / THE UTENSILS (*Die Geräte*)

Although no pot, no matter how costly or magnificent, ever made a good cook out of a bad one, the right equipment can make the cook's work easier and more effective. In many cases the difference between a good pot roast and a great one is the pot in which it was cooked. With that in mind, I have suggested the equipment listed below. You probably already own a good deal of it, and the rest can be filled in gradually as you need it. Though suggested here in relation to German cooking, all of the equipment is equally effective for preparing any kind of food and should be a useful addition to your kitchen. Where possible, buy professional cooking utensils, as they are more durable and practical than their high-fashion, gimmicky counterparts usually found in fancy cookware departments.

Electrical appliances: A mixer with attachments for yeast doughs, grinders, choppers, purée mechanisms and the like can be the most helpful thing in the world for German cooking. So many things are chopped, ground, puréed and blended that such a machine is as good as an extra helper in the kitchen. An electric blender would be a fairly good second choice, though there is plenty of work for both appliances in the recipes in this book. A third and most useful appliance is an electric hot tray. So many German meats, fish and vegetables must be kept hot while their sauces are prepared that this kind of tray would be a tremendous aid. With it, you do not have to heat serving platters, food stays hot at the table and the trays are usually attractively designed and sturdily built.

Pots and pans (Töpfe und Pfannen): Heavy copper cookware, lined with tin, is a superb material for pots and pans. However, good copperware is extremely expensive, and all of it is something of a nuisance to clean. If you would like one or two pieces, the most useful would be an oval-covered casserole in a 3- or 5-quart size, and a sauté pan with a cover. Enameled cast iron, the heavier the better, is the most all-around satisfactory material for any cooking—German or otherwise. It does not scorch, it holds and distributes heat evenly, and will not discolor itself or darken sauces that contain white wine, vinegar, lemon juice or egg yolk. This is an extremely important point in German cooking because so much vinegar is used. Plain black cast iron is also very good when no acids or egg yolks are to be stirred into it, and one very large skillet of this material is a great asset. Heavy cast aluminum is the next best choice as far as ordinary cooking is concerned, but again, not if acids or egg yolks are to be included in foods prepared in it. Spun aluminum, fireproof glass and the newly popular, decorative and inexpensive enameled steel are all highly unsatisfactory, as is stainless steel, with or without copper bottoms. All of these materials scorch and are poorly insulated. Heavy earthenware is good for oven cooking but is very fragile when used on the stove. It should be placed over an asbestos mat, never directly on the burner.

Casseroles, stew pots and Dutch ovens are all perfect for braising, pot-roasting and stewing. For complete explanations of these processes, and the requirements of pots used for them, see pages 75, 140. A 2-, 3-, and 5-quart casserole or Dutch oven are all very useful. If you entertain large groups, a 7- or 9-quart size would also be useful. The small round pot with the flat cover and two handles is perfect for stews. The larger, taller versions of these are also good for soups and boiled meats. If you prepare a great deal of soup often, you should have a special soup pot, since its shape enables you to cover meats and vegetables with a minimum amount of water or stock.

Stew Pot

Dutch Oven

Marmite or Soup Pot

Braising Pan

Saucepans with lids, in a wide range of sizes (from 1 pint to 5 quarts), are endlessly useful. If they have metal handles and knob lids, they can be used as oven casseroles. Wooden handles do not get hot and are therefore practical, so perhaps you should have several of each type.

Skillets and sauté pans: The one best suited for making crepes should be about 7″ in diameter. Frying and browning are best done in a pan with sloping sides. Several of these, ranging from 9″ to 12″ to 14″ in diameter, are very useful. They can also be used for omelettes, unless you are a purist about yours and want them done in a thin steel omelette pan. The straight-sided pan is best for sautéing. It is most generally useful in a 12″ size with a lid.

Fish cooker: If you serve a great deal of steamed or poached whole fish, this pot is essential (see page 104 for a description of its use). It is also good for steaming asparagus and other vegetables.

Vegetable steamer: This is very popular in Germany and does preserve color, flavor and vitamins in the vegetables it cooks.

Frying Pan or Skillet

Sauté Pan

Fish Cooker

Baking pans: It is good to have a variety, since many German cakes differ from each other only in form. They are the Kugelhupf, the mock venison saddle (or Rehrücken) mold, savarin and/or other ring molds, layer-cake pans, spring form, flan rings, cookie sheet, jelly-roll pan that is also used for yeast coffee cakes, loaf tins and muffin tins. Other useful baking accessories are the rolling pin, Springerle roller, wood blocks for such cookies as Prenten, pastry decorating tubes and cookie cutters. If you want to prepare deep-fried cakes and crullers, you will need either a deep saucepan with fry basket or an electric deep fryer. A skimmer and a deep-fat thermometer are other essentials.

Pudding and bombe molds: The covered molds are for steamed puddings; see page xxix for how they should be set in the water bath. Also used for steamed puddings or jelled deserts are porcelain molds. The round soufflé dish is used in the oven or in a water bath. Some of the bombe molds can be used for puddings. The most classic shapes are the melon, the bombe, the conical and the tiered mold.

Rehrucken Form

Kugelhopf

Spring Form and Bottoms

Savarin Ring Mold

Lining a Flan Ring with Pastry

Flan Rings

Springerle Roller

Springerle Board

Springerle Board

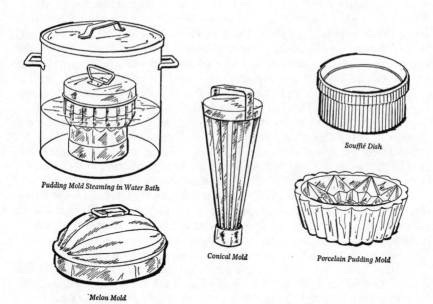

Pudding Mold Steaming in Water Bath

Conical Mold

Soufflé Dish

Porcelain Pudding Mold

`Melon Mold

Miscellaneous equipment

Spatulas: Wooden spatulas are useful for turning food when it is fry-ing, as they do not break delicate bits and pieces. The rubber spatula is essential for cleaning batter out of a bowl, for folding egg whites into batter and for scraping the sides of a blender or elecric mixer. The metal spatula is used for spreading frosting.

Food mill and food grinder, or chopper: The first is useful for puréeing fruit, potatoes and vegetables; the second for grinding meats, nuts, vegetables, etc. You will not need these if you have an electric mixer with similar attachment.

Beaters and whips: Wire whips or whisks in both small and large sizes are essential—the smaller for producing smooth sauces, the larger for egg whites. A rotary beater is fairly good for batters and egg whites; better still, of course, is an electric beater. Whisks do a superior job, however. Be sure you get very good ones, preferably made of piano wire.

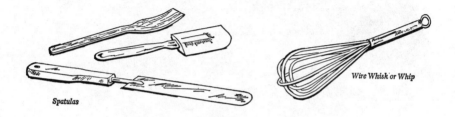

Spatulas

Wire Whisk or Whip

Large mixing bowl: This should be used for egg whites so that you will get enough air into them. Purists insist that one should have a huge copper bowl that is used for nothing else, but this is a rather costly and bulky kitchen appointment for such limited use. The bowl you use for egg whites should be absolutely free of moisture or grease, or the egg whites will not be stiff and voluminous.

Larding needles and pin: Lean meat should be larded, or it will become dry and stringy during cooking. Lard, salt pork or bacon strips can be used for this. If you prefer, strips of the fat can be tied around the meat instead of being laced through it; the results are *almost* as good.

Meat tenderizer or flattener: This helps make tough meat more tender. Large pot roasts can be beaten before being seasoned and the mallet can also be used for pounding cutlets into scallopini or Schnitzels.

Graters: The most useful of all is the four-sided grater. In some cases, electric mixer attachments can replace graters. A very small grater is for nutmeg, and a long-handled cheese grater is a most convenient gadget.

Sieves and strainers: The cone-shaped sieve with several layers of fine wire mesh is used for straining soups and fine sauces.

Brushes and basters: These are convenient for roasted meats and fish dishes. The brushes are used to apply fat to the roasting food; the bulb baster or long-handled spoon for basting with pan liquid. A small brush is used for brushing pastry or breads with melted butter, milk or beaten egg, and the same brush should never be used with strong-tasting fats or gravies. Let brushes dry in the open air after washing.

Thermometers: Besides the deep-fat thermometer, a roasting thermometer is essential. It is the best way to be sure meat will be roasted to

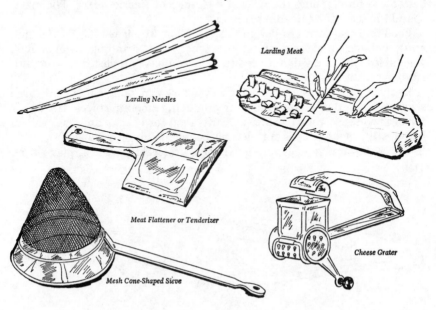

Larding Needles

Larding Meat

Meat Flattener or Tenderizer

Mesh Cone-Shaped Sieve

Cheese Grater

the desired doneness. If you make a great deal of candy or sugar confections, the candy thermometer is also essential.

In addition to the above, a ball of good strong white cotton twine and tough cotton thread are very useful in the kitchen for trussing meat roasts and poultry. Since many German dishes come directly from oven or stove to the table, several trivets are helpful too.

☆ / *COOKING TERMS* (*Worterklärungen*)

Bind (binden, oder legieren): To thicken a soup or sauce with a starch such as wheat, potato or rice flour, cornstarch, breadcrumbs, tapioca or egg yolks beaten into a little cold liquid, then stirred into the hot, not boiling, soup or sauce. In Germany, binding is done mainly with a roux, or Einbrenne, or cornstarch dissolved in a little cold water and then stirred in and simmered for a minute or two, or with egg yolk. Another popular method uses the butter-flour dumplings (Mehlbutterklösse). Knead together 1 tablespoon each butter and flour, roll into tiny balls, then drop into the soup or sauce when it is ready and simmer 2 or 3 minutes, or until properly thickened.

Blanch (blanchieren): To place an ingredient in boiling water and boil for a given amount of time, until it is partly cooked or can be skinned or peeled, depending on the purpose of blanching. This is often followed by a plunge into cold water, but follow instructions in specific recipes.

Blend (vermengen): This is a gentler method of combining foods than beating, and is done with ingredients of different textures, such as butter and sugar. It is usually done with a wooden spoon, fork or pastry cutter, or with a special slow speed on an electric mixer.

Braise (braten, oder schmoren): See page 140 for all variations and explanations.

Breading (panieren): A coating of flour and/or breadcrumbs and seasonings used to coat meat, fish or vegetables that are to be fried. Beaten egg and sometimes milk are used to first moisten the food so the breading will adhere. Breaded food should stand for about 20 minutes before being fried.

Coat a spoon: Custards, and the sauces which contain egg yolk and often cornstarch and which are cooked over hot water, must reach this thickness to be done. It simply means that if you dip the bowl of a spoon (usually wooden) into the sauce, enough will remain on it to coat the back.

Fold (unterheben): To turn gently a light and fragile mixture such as beaten egg whites or whipped cream into a heavier batter. This is best done with a rubber spatula. Although it can be done either way, it is easier to fold if the heavier batter is poured on top of the lighter one. The spatula is then drawn and turned through the mixture, starting in the center of the bowl and working to the side. The bowl is turned after each fold.

Gratiné (überkrusten): To brown the top of a cream sauce dish that is sprinkled with breadcrumbs and/or cheese and dotted with butter; this may be done in the upper third of a hot oven or in a preheated broiler.

Knead (kneten): To work dough until it is smooth, pushing it in small batches with the heel of the hand, folding over and repeating process. The amount of time necessary is indicated in specific recipes. Pastry and yeast doughs are almost always kneaded.

Lard (spicken): To lace lean meats with strips of fat so they will remain moist and tender during cooking. See page xxx for information on larding needles and methods of doing this.

Marinate (marinieren): To soak food, usually meat but sometimes fish, in a liquid that will add to the flavor or tenderness, or both, of the food itself. Marinades may be based on vinegar, lemon juice, wine, beer or, in Germany, buttermilk.

Poach (dünsten, pochieren): To simmer food just below the boiling point, in a minimum of water (that is barely enough to cover it). The cooking liquid is brought to a boil and the food added; then the pot is covered and the heat reduced. Foods are generally poached covered.

Purée (Pürée): This is a process that creates a mash (Brei, oder Mus) out of solid foods. It can be done through a sieve or a food mill, sometimes with a potato masher or ricer, with a fork or in an electric blender.

Ribbon: There is no equivalent to this in German cooking terminology, at least as far as I can tell. It refers to a batter, usually of egg yolk and sugar, that must be beaten until thick enough to form "ribbons" on the surface of the mixture when it drips from a mixing spoon.

Roux (Einbrenne): This is a thickening base for soups, sauces and stews. It is made by first melting fat in a pan, then stirring in flour and cooking to the desired color. See page 330 for the complete German use of the Einbrenne. It is one of the most important steps in that country's cooking.

Sauté (schwenken): To brown, or brown and cook, food quickly in a little very hot fat. The food may or may not be breaded, but it should be dry and the pan should not be overcrowded, or the food will steam and not brown. Pieces of food should never touch each other when being sautéed. Frying is a similar but longer process, and more fat is used.

Skim or degrease (abschöpfen oder entfetten): To remove fat and/or foam that rises to the top of soup or gravy. This is done with a large tablespoon, as necessary. To make it very easy to remove fat, a little cold water can be added to the liquid to be skimmed, to separate the fat. Or, if you have time, let the liquid chill in the refrigerator overnight and remove the solidified fat from the top.

Steam (dünsten, dämpfen): To cook in steam (usually fish or vegetables), by placing food in a covered, perforated container over boiling water. Usually an alternate to boiling, steaming takes much longer, but preserves flavor and vitamins.

Steep (Einweichen): This is what you do to leaves when brewing tea. To steep something (usually a seasoning or herb), place it in water that has been brought to the boiling point, cover the pot or kettle and remove it from the heat. Let the steeping continue until the brew is as strong as you want it to be.

Toss (anmengen): This is a lighter, gentler form of mixing, usually applied to salad greens in their dressing. The food is literally, but gently, tossed, usually with two forks or a fork and spoon, and as it lifts it also turns, until all pieces are coated with fat, dressing or whatever they're supposed to be coated with. This is done when it is important to keep the food in its original or cut shape instead of having it tear or break apart.

Water bath, or bain-marie (Wasserbad): This is a receptacle, one-third to one-half full of hot water, into which a pan, pot, bowl or pudding form is set in order to cook food or keep it hot. Water baths may be set up on the stove or in the oven. A double boiler is one version of the water bath, used for cooking sauces and custards, keeping foods hot or reheating them. See page xxix for illustration.

THE GERMAN COOKBOOK

I

Appetizers and Light Snacks

(Vorspeisen und Zwischengerichte)

* * * * *

Unlike the Mediterraneans and Scandinavians, who like their appetizer courses to consist of little bits of many things (hors d'oeuvre variés, antipasto, the Greek, Turkish and Arabic meze, and smörgåsbord), the Germans prefer to concentrate on one single dish for their Vorspeise—literally, "before food." Usually, it is a relatively expensive food item, something that will add a luxurious accent to the meal that follows, and it always has a piquant flavor that will whet the appetite. Vorspeise specialties are so delicious and so attractively arranged and garnished, that it is easy to get carried away and eat too much of this first course. Remember that portions should be large enough to take the edge off ravenous appetites, but small enough to leave room for the rest of the meal. Most of the foods served as Vorspeisen double as Zwischengerichte*—between-meal dishes that are midmorning second breakfasts, afternoon pickups or even late suppers.

The list of Vorspeisen and Zwischengerichte is a long one, and includes an enormous variety of smoked, canned and fresh fish and shellfish, meats, sliced or in salads, stuffed eggs and cheese dishes and vegetable salads. Smoked salmon and caviar, snails done in the manner of Burgundy, and Strasbourg goose-liver paté are as popular in Germany as they are in the rest of Europe, and when a German wants to splurge on an elegant all-out dinner, chances are he will begin by ordering Lobster Mayonnaise. In Germany this will be a boiled, chilled, firm and flavorful

* Also called *kleine Imbisse*, small snacks.

lobster from the waters around Helgoland, the island off the coast of Hamburg famous for these crustaceans. The lobster will be split, its meat loosened, and possibly cut, and replaced in the shell. It will be arranged on a bed of crisp green lettuce and served with a side dish of very rich mayonnaise, bread or toast and butter and a glass of dry white wine. Oysters are another specialty of Hamburg, where they are served, in small restaurants called Austernstuben, along with slices of tangy yellow Cheshire cheese and a glass of dry red wine—a most unusual and delightful appetizer or between-meal snack.

In addition to the Vorspeisen that are popular all over Germany, there are a number of regional favorites based on local specialties. Most Germans like herring, but what is a mild preference in Bavaria becomes a full-scale passion in Schleswig-Holstein, where the North Sea and the Baltic provide a superb variety of fresh herring close at hand. Cured raw hams and bacon, such as those of Westphalia and the Black Forest, are favored on their home grounds. In Bavaria, dozens of types of wursts are sliced up as appetizers, and the people of Pomerania favor a first course of their greatest local delicacy, smoked breast of goose.

Since only a small amount of food is needed for Vorspeisen, and because most of them take a great deal of time to prepare, the busy Hausfrau relies on her delicatessen for this course for ordinary family dinners. But you can be sure she has her own set of recipes for all of the popular appetizers and prefers that they be *zu Hause gemacht* (home-made) for special occasions. Although there are few delicatessens in this country that can compare with the fantastic originals existing in Germany, you should be able to find a fairly good one in any German neighborhood, or in an eastern European or Jewish section, where similar shops are known as "appetizer stores." These offer the full range of Vorspeise items, except for fresh fish and shellfish and some of the more unusual wursts that are carried only by specialty butchers.

Beautiful garnishes are important to Vorspeise platters. Slices of tomatoes, olives, capers, chopped onion or thin onion rings, chives, lettuce, sprigs of parsley and dill, radish roses, carrot curls, strips of green pepper and pimento, sections of mandarin oranges, bits of apple or pear, currant jam or Preiselbeeren, and lemon slices scored around the edges or cut in half and then twisted into butterfly shapes—these are some of the standard frills.

Many German appetizers are traditionally served with some special condiment, a particular bread, or a specific drink, and I have indicated the authentic accompaniments when appropriate.

✄ COLD APPETIZERS ✄
(*Kalte Vorspeisen*)

✄ / HERRING (*Hering*)

In addition to the many prepared herrings and herring salads available in delicatessens and appetizer stores, you can find dozens of versions in jars and cans, imported and domestic, in almost all grocery stores, gourmet food departments and supermarkets. None of these is, in my opinion, perfect as is, and many will remain hopeless no matter what you do to them, but if you shop around you should find a few brands that will respond to some doctoring. Depending on the type of herring, its sauce and its flavor, you can do a lot to these preparations by adding, as needed, sour cream, vinegar or sugar if the herring is too sweet or too sour, fresh minced dill or slivers of onions, a pinch of curry powder or a dab of prepared mustard, a slice of lemon or a few spoonfuls of white wine.

All of the herring sold in barrels for preparation at home is cured in brine and must be kept soaking in the refrigerator in several changes of cold water before you can proceed with a recipe. Salt herring is a firm fish which, as you might expect from its name, is extremely salty. It can be used interchangeably with the more expensive schmaltz herring, a softer, whiter, fatter, milder and, to my mind, far superior fish. Matjes is a name used to denote a reddish salt-cured herring that has not yet spawned. It is quite salty and richly flavored, very tender and delicate of texture. It is almost always sold in filets and is at its best chilled on ice and served with sprays of dill and hot boiled new potatoes. Bismarck is a sharply flavored herring, pickled whole in a spicy mixture of vinegar, onions, spices and lots of dried red chili peppers.

Some type of Schnaps is always served, ice-cold, with a herring course, usually a mild-flavored, potent drink similar to the Scandinavian aquavit or the Russian vodka.

✄ / HERRING SALAD (*Heringssalat*)

10 SERVINGS

1 salt herring
1 cup boiled, peeled and diced
   potatoes
1 cup diced cooked beets (canned
   or fresh)
1 large sour apple, peeled, cored
   and diced

1 small onion, minced
1 small dill pickle, minced
1 tablespoon sugar, or to taste
1 teaspoon vinegar, or to taste
1 cup sour cream
   salt as needed

Clean herring and remove head. Soak 48 hours in 2 quarts cold water, changing water 5 or 6 times. Herring must be kept in refrigerator while soaking. With a sharp pointed knife, slit herring along the backbone. Remove backbone and as many small bones as possible. Pull off blue skin carefully, without tearing flesh of fish. Dice filets. Toss herring, potatoes, beets, apple, onion and pickle together in bowl. Sprinkle sugar and vinegar over top, add sour cream and toss lightly with fork until thoroughly mixed. Taste for seasoning and add salt, sugar, vinegar or sour cream as needed. Turn into serving bowl and chill in refrigerator about 6 hours. Before serving, garnish with chopped hard-cooked eggs.

VARIATIONS

1.   This is often varied by adding ½ cup diced veal or beef and ¼ cup diced cervelat to mixture, and add a minced hard-cooked egg as well.
2.   When meat is used, beets and potatoes may be left out and ½ to ¾ cup of mayonnaise substituted for sour cream. This version is called Feiner Heringssalat—Fine Herring Salad.

✄ / PICKLED HERRING (*Marinierter Hering*)

10 TO 12 SERVINGS

4 schmaltz or salt herrings
2 large Spanish onions, peeled,
   sliced and separated into
   rings
1¼ cups white vinegar

¾ cup water
1 teaspoon sugar
1 tablespoon pickling spices
2 bay leaves

Clean herrings, remove heads and soak as described in above recipe. If you use schmaltz herring, soak 12 hours; salt herring should soak 48 hours before being pickled. Then remove and drain. It may be boned, skinned and cut in filets, as in Herring Salad, or cut it across in 1½″ slices, leaving bones in and skin on. Using a 2-quart crock, place in it alternate layers of herring and onion rings. Combine vinegar and water with sugar, pickling spices, bay leaves. (Add a pinch of salt to this only if you use schmaltz herrings.) Bring to a boil and simmer 5 minutes. Cool marinade to room temperature, and pour over herrings and onions. Cover crock and place in refrigerator for at least three days.

VARIATIONS

1. A very rich and flavorful sauce results if you use the milt (the soft, milky roe of male herrings) when making it. Sometimes the herrings you buy have milt in them, and if not, the dealer will sell them to you separately. For this recipe, get 4 milts and reduce to a pureé, either by rubbing through a strainer or by whirling in a blender. Add this to cooled marinade and pour over herring.

2. For Herring in Sour Cream, remove pickled herring from jar, drain slightly and toss with sour cream into which is mixed a little grated onion and a dash of lemon juice. Season to taste with salt and white pepper and chill a few hours before serving. Finely minced dill can also be added to the cream dressing.

☒ / ROLLMOPS

8 SERVINGS

4 *salt or schmaltz herrings*
3 *tablespoons prepared*
  mustard
8 *slivers of dill pickle*
8 *slices of Spanish onion*
1 *tablespoon capers*
1¼ *cups white vinegar*

¾ *cup water*
1 *tablespoon pickling spices*
2 *bay leaves*
2 *large Spanish onions, peeled,*
  sliced and separated into
  rings

Clean and soak herrings as described in above recipe; bone and filet as described in Herring Salad (page 6). Each herring will yield 2 filets. Pat dry and lay them skin side down. Spread tops with mustard and place crosswise on each filet one sliver of pickle, a slice of onion and sprinkle with a few capers. Roll tightly and tie with string or fasten with two toothpicks. Pack alternate layers of rollmops and remaining onions into 2-quart crock. Prepare marinade as in above recipe and pour over rollmops. Cover and refrigerate 6 to 7 days before serving.

♫ / MATJES ROLLS, HOUSEWIFE-STYLE
(Matjesröllchen, auf Hausfrauen Art)

6 SERVINGS

6 matjes filets
1 cup milk or buttermilk
6 thick round slices of apple,
  peeled

½ cup white wine
6 tablespoons Horseradish
  Whipped Cream (page 348)
3 tablespoons minced chives

Soak matjes filets in milk or buttermilk (I prefer the latter) 2 hours. Let apple slices marinate in white wine 30 minutes to 1 hour. Remove herring filets from milk and drain on paper towel. Put 1 tablespoon Horseradish Cream into center of each filet, roll and fasten with toothpick. Sprinkle top with minced chives. Set each roll on an apple slice that has been drained on paper towel and serve on individual plates garnished with a few slices of pickled beets and several gherkins.

♫ / CANNED FISH

Tuna fish or sardines in olive oil, anchovy filets, flat or rolled around capers, and the various herrings packed in tomato, mustard, dill, curry or wine sauces, are all popular Vorspeisen. They are usually served with wedges of lemons, chopped onions, or minced hard-cooked eggs, or possibly gherkins. Anchovy filets which are used as garnishes on hard-cooked egg dishes are also served separately as appetizers on buttered toast.

♫ / SMOKED FISH (Geräucherter Fisch)

Delicately flavored, golden smoked fish are favorites both as Vorspeisen and Zwischengerichte and they can be had in an enormous variety throughout Germany. Fish market and delicatessen windows are laden with open crates of smoked eel, whitefish, chunks of halibut and haddock, flounder filets, the herrings that are called Bückling, mackerel, butterfish, sturgeon and carp—all looking as though they were covered with sheets of gold leafing. One of the best smoked fish specialties in Germany is called Schillerlocken, long curled strips of shark or dogfish meat. These resemble the corkscrew curls worn by the poet Schiller, hence the name, which is, incidentally, applied for much the same reason to a cream-filled pastry horn. The fish are now available, packed in oil and canned, in many large cities of the U.S.

Smoked trout and whitings are also excellent appetizers. If you cannot get good smoked fish conveniently in your city, or if you would like to serve freshly smoked fish, you can now buy a pan made just for this purpose. Called the Swedish Smoker and available at most large department stores in major cities, this enameled steel pan is about the size of a shoebox, comes with powdered hardwood, and will smoke-cook up to 2 pounds of fish on your kitchen range within 10 minutes. You can prepare the fish early in the day and serve it cold, or smoke it after the guests arrive and serve it warm with melted butter and lemon, a most delectable appetizer perfectly suited to German menus.

✂ / SHELLFISH (*Schaltiere*)

Like most north Europeans, the Germans like their shellfish best well-chilled and au naturel. Oysters on the half-shell with lemon, the tiny North Sea shrimp no bigger than a baby's little finger, Lobster Mayonnaise as described earlier, cold crab and crayfish tails flavored with dill, lemon and possibly mayonnaise, are far and away the most popular versions of seafood. There are also, however, several shellfish salads and variations in the German cuisine as well as a few hot appetizers made from them.

✂ / SHRIMP SALAD (*Garnelensalat*)

4 SERVINGS

1 *pound medium-sized shrimp, cooked, shelled and de-veined*	*salt and pepper to taste*
1 *tablespoon minced onion*	1 *tablespoon lemon juice*
1 *tablespoon minced parsley*	½ *cup mayonnaise*
	1½ *tablespoons salad oil*

Toss shrimp with onion and parsley, sprinkle lightly with salt, pepper and lemon juice and refrigerate for about ½ hour, or until just before serving time. Add mayonnaise and trickle oil in slowly until salad has the right creamy consistency and is neither too thin nor too thick. Adjust seasoning and serve on chilled, crisp lettuce leaf.

✂ / CRABMEAT COCKTAIL (Krabbencocktail)

4 SERVINGS

1 pound cooked fresh crabmeat   4 tablespoons cognac or German
¼ cup ketchup   Weinbrand
1 cup whipped cream   few drops Worcestershire sauce

Pick over crabmeat and remove all spiny fragments. Fold ketchup into whipped cream and stir in cognac or Weinbrand and Worcestershire sauce. Fold in crabmeat and pile into sherbet or seafood cocktail glasses lined with a lettuce leaf. Garnish with shelled lobster claw or two peeled shrimp on top.

For jellied fish appetizers, see page 106.

✂ / STUFFED EGGS (Gefüllte Eier)

Stuffed hard-cooked eggs are among the favorite Vorspeisen in Germany, always made with a great deal of mayonnaise and a variety of fillings. Unless they are to be served on a tray along with other cocktail hors d'oeuvre, they are arranged on individual salad plates, garnished with lettuce leaves, tomatoes cut in eighths, thin slices of cervelat and some additional salad or mayonnaise heaped in center of plate. When used as appetizers before a meal, one egg (two halves) is a correct portion. When served as an afternoon snack, as they are in German Konditoreien, two eggs (four halves) make up the standard portion. Although a few specific recipes for stuffed eggs follow, you can obviously take off on your own and make them out of all sorts of leftover meat, fish and salads, or cream the yolks with any one of a number of finely minced herbs or seasonings.

To have the most attractive-looking hard-cooked eggs for stuffing, take very fresh eggs out of the refrigerator 15 or 20 minutes before cooking so they will not be too cold. Lower them gently into boiling water, let water come back to boiling point, then lower the flame so they will simmer. After 20 minutes pour off water and place pot under running cold water until eggs are cool. Tap egg gently to crack shell, then roll between your hands to loosen it. Peel under running cold water. To make eggs stand on the plate without rolling around, cut in half lengthwise and cut a small slice off bottom of each half to level it.

Pile filling high in egg white. For a really fancy touch, force yolk filling through a pastry bag, using a star-shaped tube.

/ *RUSSIAN EGGS* (*Russische Eier*)

6 hard-cooked eggs
3 tablespoons mayonnaise
1 teaspoon prepared mustard, or to taste
salt and white pepper to taste
optional garnishes: capers, smoked salmon or black caviar

Peel eggs and cut in half lengthwise. Remove yolks and mash thoroughly. Add other ingredients and blend well. Refill egg white with yolk mixture, and top with one or two of suggested garnishes. Arrange on individual plates as described under Stuffed Eggs, above. Standard accompaniments to Russian Eggs are salads such as crabmeat, chicken, or tongue and mixed vegetables, or any of the salads described elsewhere in this chapter.

VARIATIONS

1. For 6 eggs stuffed with smoked salmon and caviar, mash yolks with 2 slices of salmon, 2 tablespoons sour cream, 1 teaspoon grated onion, salt and pepper to taste. Fill egg whites and top with a little dab of caviar. Freshly grated horseradish can also be added to mixture.
2. For 6 eggs stuffed with goose-liver paté, mash yolks, paté and 2 tablespoons mayonnaise, salt and pepper to taste. Fill egg whites and top each with a sprinkling of finely diced truffles.
3. Other German favorites to be mixed with egg-yolk stuffing include anchovies (3 filets for 6 eggs); crabmeat salad (2 tablespoons for 6 eggs); finely minced cooked ham (2 tablespoons for 6 eggs); Roquefort cheese (about ½ tablespoon for 6 eggs and 2 tablespoons sour cream instead of mayonnaise); and black caviar (1 tablespoon for 6 eggs), 2 tablespoons sour cream instead of mayonnaise, a dash of lemon juice. You can also add a bit of grated onion. This is an excellent way to use the relatively inexpensive pressed caviar.

/ *PICKLED EGGS* (*Soleier*)

¼ cup salt
3 cups water
yellow skin of 3 onions
6 hard-cooked eggs in shells

Bring water to a boil with salt and onion skin and cook about 10 minutes, or until water turns brown. Let water cool. Crack egg shells all around but do not peel. Put eggs into bowl or jar and pour salt-water solution over them. Cover and let marinate in refrigerator at least 24 hours. Peel eggs, slice in half and serve with mustard and gherkins. For a large party, put peeled eggs, uncut, in a bowl, and let guests help themselves. These are particularly good with beer.

✲ / WURST

For a description of some of the most popular kinds of wursts, see pages 248-250. It is customary throughout Germany to have an appetizer or in-between meal composed of a platter of several wursts. Four or five varieties are generally included, with 2 slices of each per portion. Gherkins, tomato wedges, radishes, a small amount of potato, beet or cucumber salad, mustard, bread and butter are usually served along with the wursts, and if it is to be a between-meal snack, some sliced cheese may be on the platter also.

✲ / BAVARIAN WURST SALAD (*Bayrischer Wurstsalat*)

6 SERVINGS

¾ pound Regensburger knock-
    wurst (if this type is un-
    available, substitute kosher-
    style hard salami)
2 medium-sized onions, finely
    diced

2 to 3 tablespoons olive oil
2 to 3 tablespoons wine vinegar
    salt and pepper to taste
    paprika

Peel casing from wurst and slice very thinly. If the wurst is small, leave slices whole. If it is wide, cut slices in halves or thirds. Toss wurst with diced onion, olive oil, vinegar, salt and pepper. Adjust amount of oil and vinegar so that salad is moist enough, but there should be no liquid floating in bowl. Chill in serving dish 1 hour before serving, then dust top with paprika. If you like, 1 teaspoon paprika can be added to dressing and mixed in with salad. Serve with gherkins, pickled beets, rolls and butter.

�֍ / *CHEESE-WURST SALAD* (*Käse- und Wurstsalat*)

8 SERVINGS

½ *pound Swiss cheese*
½ *pound cervelat*
1 *onion, diced*
4 *tablespoons olive oil*

2 *tablespoons wine vinegar*
1 *teaspoon prepared mustard*
salt and pepper to taste

Cut cheese and cervelat in slim julienne strips from 1″ to 2″ long. Mix with onion, olive oil, vinegar, mustard, salt and pepper and toss lightly with a fork until salad is coated with dressing. Chill 1 hour in serving dish. Serve with gherkins, rolls or thin black rye bread and butter.

✖ / *HAM AND BACON* (*Schinken und Speck*)

With all of the wonderful cured raw hams available in Germany, it is no surprise to find them as favored appetizers on menus. Similiar to the Italian prosciutto in color and texture, these hams have a mild nutty flavor and are generally served witth a special bread, curls of sweet butter, gherkins and a few radishes. Westphalian ham, which you can easily find at gourmet food shops and German butchers, is usually served sliced paper-thin on little blond wood cutting boards or paddles, about 8″ long by 5″ wide. Dark Westphalian rye bread or pumpernickel always come with it, as well as a clear fruit brandy.

In the Black Forest, a similar ham called Bauernschinken—farmers' ham—is the local specialty, along with a special smoked bacon that is eaten raw. The latter is especially popular for the midmorning Vesper, the ceremonious snack that takes place throughout Swabia between 10 and 11 A.M. With the raw bacon one eats Bauernbrot, the farmers' bread that is also served with the cured ham here, and a glass of chilled Kirschwasser, or the plum brandy, Zwetschgenwasser, or a mellow, aged raspberry brandy, Himbeergeist.

Italian prosciutto or Prague ham can be substituted. In summer they are served with fresh melons or figs, as in Italy, and are also often accompanied by buttered toast and half a stuffed egg.

✖ / HAM ROLLS WITH ASPARAGUS (*Schinkenröllchen mit Spargel*)

4 SERVINGS

12 *asparagus, cooked but firm*
4 *thin slices boiled or baked
   ham*
2 *to* 3 *tablespoons mayonnaise*

2 *cups water in which asparagus
   were cooked*
2 *envelopes unflavored gelatin*
1 *teaspoon lemon juice*

Asparagus should be well drained on paper toweling and thoroughly chilled. (Retain water in which it is cooked.) Spread one side of each ham slice with mayonnaise. Lay three asparagus crosswise at one end of each ham slice. Roll ham. Each roll must then be coated with following aspic. Dissolve gelatin in ½ cup cold asparagus water. Flavor remaining water with lemon juice. Heat, remove from stove and add softened gelatin. Stir until it has completely dissolved. When mixture begins to thicken slightly, and before it sets, spoon over ham and asparagus rolls which have been arranged on a large flat dish so they do not touch each other. Place in refrigerator 1 hour or until thoroughly set. Serve on individual salad plates, on lettuce leaves. Decorate tops of ham rolls with pimento strips or chopped hard-cooked eggs. Serve extra mayonnaise on the side.

✖ / CHICKEN LIVER PATÉ (*Hühnerleberpastete*)

4 TO 6 SERVINGS

1 *pound chicken livers*
3 *tablespoons rendered chicken
   fat*

1 *medium-sized onion, chopped*
2 *hard-cooked eggs*
  salt and pepper to taste

Sauté livers in chicken fat very slowly, so that they will cook through but not brown. Remove livers and sauté onion in same fat until soft and golden, but do not let it brown. Cut up livers and hard-cooked eggs; remove onions from fat. Mix all together and put through fine blade of a food grinder twice. Mix with salt and pepper and melted fat in which liver and onions were sautéed. Pack liver mixture into a deep round bowl, chill 30 minutes and turn out on plate for serving.

NOTE

If you have cracklings (Grieben) left when you render the chicken fat, they can be ground in with this mixture.

✂ / *TONGUE SALAD* (*Zungensalat*)

6 SERVINGS

2 cups julienne of cooked
   smoked tongue
1 cup cooked elbow macaroni
1 cooked carrot, diced
½ cup cooked green peas
½ cup diced cooked knob celery

salt and pepper to taste
pinch of powdered mustard
1 cup mayonnaise
a few dashes each of olive oil
   and vinegar

Toss tongue, macaroni, carrot, peas and celery lightly together. Sprinkle with salt and pepper and dry mustard. Mix with mayonnaise and add a little oil and vinegar to achieve a smooth creamy dressing with just a slightly sharp edge to it. Chill 1 hour and serve with Westphalian rye bread.

VARIATIONS

1. When this salad is made with a smoked salami-type sausage, it is called Dänischer Salat—Danish Salad.
2. When it is made without any meat, it is called Italian Salad because of its red, white and green color scheme.

✂ / *MOCK BEEF HEAD SALAD* (*Falscher Ochsenmaulsalat*)

Literally, Ochsenmaulsalat means ox-mouth salad. To be authentic it should be made with the meat picked from the cheeks and mouth of a cooked corned beef head. Since acquiring a corned beef head and then having it boned so it will fit into a pot is a relatively complicated procedure, I suggest you make this very popular Vorspeise with pickled beef tongue instead. The authentic version is sold at most German delicatessens and sausage butchers and is always on the menu of German and Austrian restaurants.

4 TO 6 SERVINGS

1 pickled beef tongue
   water to cover
½ cup white vinegar
1 onion, minced

salt and black pepper to taste
2 tablespoons white vinegar
3 to 4 tablespoons olive oil

Place tongue in pot and cover with cold water. Add ½ cup vinegar, bring to a boil, reduce heat and simmer gently but steadily about 3 hours. Tongue is done when bones slip out easily and when tip feels tender as you press it between thumb and forefinger. Cool tongue, peel it, slice it thinly and then cut slices into slivers. Mix minced onion, salt, pepper, vinegar and oil together and pour over tongue slivers. Adjust seasoning and add more or less oil and vinegar, according to your taste. Chill until ready to serve. Pour off excess marinade before bringing salad to the table.

❧ / JELLIED CALVES' AND PIGS' FEET (*Saure Sülze*)

Jellied meats or fish are often served as appetizers in Germany. The jelly used in molding these dishes is either of two types: aspic (Aspik), made with unflavored gelatin, and Sülze, a jelly that forms naturally from the bones cooked in the stock. The piquant "sour" Sülze below is the simplest and most commonly served version of that Vorspeise. The jellied meat sausage we know as headcheese is another version of the same thing and can be purchased in many varieties at delicatessens and German butchers.

APPROXIMATELY 4 SERVINGS

2 *calves' feet*	2 *tablespoons salt*
2 *pigs' feet*	1 *large onion*
water to cover	2 *bay leaves*
1 *cup white vinegar*	10 *peppercorns*

Wash calves' and pigs' feet well in several changes of water. Place in pot with water to cover, vinegar, salt, onion, bay leaves and peppercorns. Bring to a boil and cook briskly 4 or 5 minutes, skimming surface as foam rises. Reduce heat and simmer slowly but steadily for 1½ hours. Remove feet and simmer broth for another ½ hour, or until it is reduced by ⅓ to ½ its original volume. When feet are cool enough to handle, pick meat from bones and place in mold or baking dish. Strain stock through a very fine sieve or cloth, cool and skim fat from surface. Taste for seasoning and add more vinegar if needed. Pour over meat and chill until set. To serve, unmold onto a cold platter, or simply cut portions from mold and place on individual salad plates. Garnish with pickled beets, gherkins, hard-cooked egg slices and freshly grated horseradish.

VARIATIONS

1. To make Wine Sülze, use ¼ cup white wine and ½ cup white vinegar, instead of 1 cup vinegar. When you taste stock after skimming it, flavor it with additional wine.

2. A sliced carrot, a stalk of celery and a leek can be cooked along with other ingredients in the stock. The vegetables can be discarded, or sliced and molded along with meat.

3. Gherkins, pickled beets and/or hard-cooked egg slices can be molded into the Sülze, instead of being served on the side.

4. For an even meatier Sülze, cook 1 pound lean pork along with the feet. When done, slice in thin flat slabs and place smaller bits of meat from feet on top of pork slices before pouring stock. Because the bottom slice of meat forms a small "plate," this version is known as Tellersülze; it can be molded in individual portions in any small, flat but rimmed, oval, square or round dish. A shirred-egg dish would be perfect.

✂ / MEAT SALAD (*Fleischsalat*)

This is a good appetizer to remember when you have any sort of meat leftovers.

4 TO 6 SERVINGS

3 cups diced, cold, cooked beef,
   veal, ham or tongue
2 dill pickles
1 medium-sized onion, sliced
1 tablespoon capers
1 tablespoon minced parsley
1 teaspoon prepared mustard

1 medium-sized boiled potato,
   peeled and diced
salt and pepper to taste
Marinade:
2 tablespoons olive oil
3 tablespoons vinegar
3 tablespoons cold beef stock

Mix marinade well. Toss all other ingredients together and pour marinade over them. Mix thoroughly, season to taste. Chill 2 hours and garnish with hard-cooked egg slices.

✂ / BEEF TARTAR APPETIZER (*Schlemmerschnitte*)

For Beef Tartar served as an entree, see page 141.

For each serving:

4 ounces lean (filet or sirloin)
   ground or, preferably, scraped
1 egg yolk

1 teaspoon olive oil
1 teaspoon ketchup
1 anchovy, chopped

5 *capers, chopped*
  pinch each of salt, pepper and
    paprika
  dash of Worcestershire sauce
1 *slice buttered toast, crusts re-*
    moved

½ *ounce fresh caviar (fresh-*
    pressed would be good
    here)
1 *tablespoon onion, minced*

Mix beef, egg yolk, oil, ketchup, anchovy, capers, seasonings and Worcestershire sauce together thoroughly. Spread on buttered toast and top with caviar. Serve with minced onion on the side along with a sliced gherkin. Ice-cold vodka or Schnaps is preferred with this appetizer.

❌ / CHEESE "WITH MUSIC" (*Käse "mit Musik"*)

This is a featured item in all the apple-wine taverns in the Sachsenhausen section of Frankfurt. It is usually served as a light entree but makes a very piquant appetizer, especially with cocktails. It is also an excellent midnight snack, good with beer, but best of all with apple wine or hard cider, served in blue and gray stoneware pitchers as in Frankfurt. It should be made with Handkäse, the German hand cheese, strong-smelling but delicious. If you cannot get that, use a Liederkranz that is not too runny, or a slice of Tilsit.

For each serving:

1 *tablespoon olive oil*
1 *tablespoon vinegar*
1 *slice cheese, about ½" thick,*
    2" *wide by 4" long*

1 *tablespoon minced onion*
1 *slice rye bread with caraway*
    seeds
1 *large pat of butter*

Mix oil and vinegar together and pour over cheese slice. Let it marinate an hour or two in refrigerator, turning once. Remove cheese, drain and put on a plate with minced onion on the side. Serve with bread and butter. Cheese is spread on buttered bread, topped with onion and eaten with a knife and fork.

❌ / GERVAIS, PREPARED (*Gervais, angemacht*)

Although this is served as a dessert in Germany, it seems more suitable for an appetizer. It is also excellent as a cheese spread for cocktails.

For each serving:

1 *package Gervais cheese*	1 *teaspoon paprika*
1 *teaspoon minced onion*	*salt to taste*
1 *teaspoon caraway seeds*	

Mash cheese until slightly softened. Blend in all other ingredients thoroughly. Divide in half and serve in two small mounds along with gherkins, red radishes and Westphalian rye bread and butter, and a few small pretzels.

NOTE

Although the above is very close to the Hungarian Liptauer cheese, in southern Germany that name is applied to this recipe when it is made with Camembert cheese instead of Gervais. It is known then as Camembert Liptauer, and is also served as a dessert, though it is suggested as an appetizer here.

✂ / SACHER CHEESE (Sacherkäse)

2 TO 4 SERVINGS

¼ *cup butter (½ of a quarter-pound stick)*	1 *small onion, minced*
1 *cup pot cheese*	1 *teaspoon prepared mustard*
2 *hard-cooked egg yolks, mashed*	1 *teaspoon olive oil*
	salt
3 *anchovies, mashed*	1 *to 2 teaspoons paprika*

Cream butter until soft and mash thoroughly with pot cheese to a smooth consistency. Blend in mashed egg yolks, anchovies, onion, mustard and olive oil. Season to taste with salt and paprika. Serve with chopped hard-cooked egg white and sliced gherkins, thin pumpernickel and pretzels.

✂ / BEER CHEESE (Bierkäse)

4 SERVINGS

½ *cup butter*	*dash of Worcestershire sauce*
1 *cup pot cheese*	
½ *cup Roquefort, Gorgonzola or Bleu cheese*	

Cream butter and when soft, mash thoroughly with pot cheese, Roquefort, Gorgonzola or Bleu cheese and Worcestershire sauce. Pack into crock or bowl. Chill 2 hours. Turn out onto serving platter. Serve with Westphalian rye bread, Scandinavian crisp bread or salty rye rounds.

/ *CANAPÉS*

Now that the cocktail party is an international institution, so are canapés, and in Germany you'll find them made mainly of the dishes used in larger portions as appetizers. One of the most popular is Beef Tartar, Schlemmerschnitte, served on small rounds of rye bread. Chopped Westphalian-type ham with minced onion (on white bread as well) is popular too, and the Germans love all sorts of little cornucopias filled with various things and held together with toothpicks. Smoked salmon stuffed with a dab of Horseradish Cream; salami or tongue filled with Remoulade Dressing or Italian Salad; chicken, lobster or crab salad on white bread or pumpernickel—all are popular. Caviar on buttered toast rounds, garnished with chopped hard-cooked egg; Strasbourg goose-liver paté; smoked salmon mashed and blended with cream cheese and grated horseradish on thin pumpernickel are a few other favorite cocktail items. In addition, the Germans prepare little bits of meats and cheese stuck on toothpicks, generally without any bread. A cube of Swiss cheese topped with a stuffed olive, a chunk of ham and a gherkin . . . all sorts of such tidbits are run up on a little toothpick skewer. Tiny cherry tomatoes or mushroom caps are filled with salads or patés, and the platters are beautifully ornamented with fancy cut radishes, lemon slices, gherkins, etc.

/ *SWEDISH PLATTER* (*Schwedenplatte*)

When the Germans want an assorted appetizer, they produce this platter with a nod toward Sweden and its smörgåsbord. It includes a number of the salads described in this chapter, cold sliced meat, cheese, wursts, tuna fish and sardines, a couple of kinds of herring, some pickled beets, a cucumber salad and the like.

❧ / *TOASTS AND OPEN SANDWICHES* (*Toast und Belegtes Butterbrot*)

Most German restaurants and all cafés feature a group of dishes for appetizers or light meals, known as Toast and Belegtes Butterbrot. These are really open sandwiches, usually hot when they are on toast, cold when on bread slices. When you order one of these open sandwiches, you generally get two pieces of bread, each with a different, complementary topping. If you order an open sandwich of ham or smoked salmon, the other piece of bread may be topped with sliced hard-cooked egg; and if you order chicken salad, asparagus tips with mayonnaise will probably top the accompanying bread slice. Other Belegtes Butterbrot toppings include Beef Tartar, sliced hard-cooked eggs and anchovies, wursts, cheeses, sardines with paper-thin lemon slices, sliced tongue with vegetable salad, rare roast beef with freshly grated horseradish, and many of the meat and fish salads described in this chapter.

The breads used vary with the toppings. French-style white bread and all of the German rye and pumpernickel breads are used, as are the various crisp breads, most especially for cheese. Flavored butter is often used on these open sandwiches. Let the butter soften at room temperature, then mash it with whichever flavorings you want to add: minced dill, parsley or other green herbs, caraway seeds, hot or sweet mustard, anchovy paste, pounded cooked crabmeat, shrimp or lobster, sautéed and minced mushrooms, mashed sardines, grated horseradish, grated cheese, mashed hard-cooked egg yolk, curry powder, lemon juice with a little grated rind; even finely pounded nut meats such as walnuts or toasted almonds, or powdered ginger, rum or brandy, garlic, chives or onions.

Bread Sandwiches are, as far as I know, completely German, and a favorite in rural areas. They are made of 1 slice of pumpernickel, buttered or spread with fresh lard or bacon dripping and salt on both sides, then sandwiched between 2 slices of sour rye bread. Crusts may be trimmed off or left on.

The toast that is the base for the hot sandwiches is sautéed to a crisp golden brown on both sides, then drained quickly on paper toweling. Though caviar, goose-liver paté and sardines are often served on toast, the usual toppings are more complicated. Creamed Mushrooms with or without a slice of ham or tongue, Roquefort Cheese and Apples, Ham and Asparagus au Gratin, and scrambled eggs with minced ham and chives are typical. Oriental Toast is topped with cubes of canned pineapple, a slice of mustard fruit, cooked ham and Swiss cheese, all grilled for a few minutes under the broiler. Smoked oysters or mussels with Lemon-Horseradish are elegant and unusual Toaste, and to show you how complicated things can get, the wonderful Café König in Baden-Baden even offers something called Toast Miami, topped with a pan-broiled slice of beef filet, pineapple chunks, apple slices, a few sections of mandarins or tangerines, cream sauce and the cranberry-like Preiselbeeren.

These toasts and open sandwiches are interesting and appetizing whether they begin a meal or comprise the light lunch or between-meal pickup. Leftovers are perfect for toppings, and remember that these sandwiches are always eaten with a fork and knife. Garnishes around the sandwiches include such things as gherkins, pickled beets, raw vegetables and salads, lemon slices, etc. Lettuce may be on the side, but it is never, never on the sandwich itself.

✖ HOT APPETIZERS ✖
(*Warme Vorspeisen*)

✖ / *BAKED OYSTERS, HAMBURG STYLE* (*Gebackene Austern, auf Hamburger Art*)

For each serving:

6 fresh oysters on half shell
2 tablespoons melted butter
    dash each, salt and pepper
1 heaping tablespoon bread-
    crumbs

1 tablespoon grated Parmesan
    cheese
½ teaspoon grated lemon rind
1 tablespoon butter

If you can, open oysters just before you begin to prepare them. Otherwise ask fish dealer to open them, but keep shells. Remove oysters from shell, drain on paper towel and dip in melted butter. Sprinkle with salt and pepper and roll in mixture of breadcrumbs, grated cheese and lemon rind. Put each oyster back on a shell and put small dab of butter on each. Arrange them in shallow baking pan. Place in hot oven (425°) about 10 minutes, or until golden and crusty. Serve with additional grated Parmesan on the side, toast and butter, and a glass of white wine.

⚏ / *CURRY WURST*

This is a variation of the wurst specialty sold on the street corners of Berlin. Though it is made there with a version of a Bockwurst that looks like a thick frankfurter, it is a very good treatment for cocktail sausages served in a chafing dish at a large party.

12 SERVINGS

1½ *pounds cocktail sausages*   2 *cups spicy tomato sauce*
   (wieners), or frankfurters   *curry powder*
   cut in 1½" *pieces*   *paprika*

Put wurst in tomato sauce and keep hot in chafing dish. As wurst is served onto plate, sprinkle with curry powder and paprika and spoon sauce over it. If it seems like too much bother to do this every time a guest takes a portion, add ½ tablespoon of curry powder and paprika to tomato sauce and stir in well.

⚏ / *BAKED ROQUEFORT CHEESE WITH APPLE*
(*Roquefortkäse mit Apfel, überbackener*)

For each serving:

1 *slice French bread,* ¼" *to* ½"   1 *slice Roquefort cheese to cover*
   thick   *bread*
butter   *paprika*
1 *round slice of apple,* ¼" *thick*

Fry bread in a little melted butter until it is golden brown on both sides. Sauté apple slice in butter until golden and a little soft—about 3 or 4 minutes on each side. Put apple slice on bread, top with cheese and sprinkle with paprika. Place under medium flame of broiler until cheese is bubbling and a little brown on top—5 to 7 minutes.

▓ / ANCHOVY-CHEESE TOAST (*Sardellen-Käse auf Toast*)

4 SERVINGS

4 slices white bread, toasted
6 tablespoons grated Parmesan
   cheese (approximately)
12 anchovy filets, lightly rinsed
   in water and drained on
   paper toweling

capers
minced parsley
lemon juice
butter, slightly softened

Heat oven to 425°. Cut crusts off toasted bread slices. Arrange in a shallow buttered baking dish. Sprinkle a layer of cheese on each slice of toast. Place three anchovy filets on each slice and sprinkle with a few capers, a little minced parsley and a few drops of lemon juice. Dot with butter. Sprinkle with a top layer of Parmesan cheese. Bake in upper third of oven 10 to 15 minutes, or until cheese is bubbly and light golden brown on top. If topping seems dry, or if it does not brown as it bakes, brush a little melted butter over each slice and continue baking. To serve this as canapés with cocktails, cut each slice of toast in quarters after it has baked.

▓ / HAM AND ASPARAGUS AU GRATIN (*Schinken und Spargel, überkrustet*)

4 SERVINGS

4 slices cooked ham
4 slices lightly toasted bread,
   crusts removed
1 cup thick White Sauce (page
   331)
1 cup grated Gruyère cheese

8 cooked asparagus, cut in 1″
   pieces
salt to taste
dash of cayenne pepper
paprika

Place one slice of ham on each slice of toast. While sauce is still hot, add cheese and stir until it melts. Add asparagus to sauce. Season with salt and cayenne pepper. Spoon sauce and asparagus mixture over ham slices. Sprinkle with paprika. Bake in hot over (425°) until golden brown on top. Serve with wedges of lemon.

✸ / BRATWURST IN PASTRY (*Bratwurst in Teig*)

6 TO 12 SERVINGS

1 recipe Salty Tart Pastry, page
   413, or puff pastry according
   to your favorite recipe

12 Bratwursts
2 egg yolks, well beaten

Parboil Bratwurst 5 minutes and then brown slowly and evenly in a skillet about 8 minutes. Let cool completely. Roll out dough and cut into 12 rectangular strips to fit around Bratwurst. Place one wurst on each strip of dough and roll securely. Brush dough with egg yolks. Bake in 375° oven 15 to 20 minutes, or until dough is flaky and golden brown.

✸ / RAGOUT APPETIZERS IN PATTY SHELLS

Following are several seafood and meat ragouts that are often served as appetizers or light lunches. This is an excellent way to use up leftovers. You can make your own favorite puff pastry patty shells or buy them from a bakery and heat in oven before filling them. Serve 1 filled patty shell as an appetizer, 2 if it is a main course.

✸ / ROYAL PATTIES (*Königinpastetchen*)

Once you prepare this recipe, you'll instantly recognize it as chicken à la king in a patty shell.

6 SERVINGS

2 cups diced cooked chicken
1 cup diced cooked tongue
8 to 10 canned button mushrooms,
   sliced
5 tablespoons butter
1½ tablespoons flour

½ cup hot chicken stock
lemon juice to taste
salt and pepper to taste
3 tablespoons white wine
1 egg yolk beaten
6 patty shells

Heat chicken, tongue and mushrooms in 2 tablespoons butter 5 minutes and keep warm. In another skillet, melt 3 tablespoons butter and blend in flour. Cook until deep golden. Add hot chicken stock slowly. Flavor with lemon juice, salt and pepper and white wine. Add chicken, tongue and mushrooms to sauce and heat together on low flame for 5 minutes. Remove pan from flame. Stir in beaten egg yolk and spoon into patty shells which were heated in oven.

VARIATIONS

1.   You may make this without tongue. Add a little more chicken in that case, or use diced cooked sweetbreads instead.
2.   Cooked veal can be substituted for chicken. Add 1 tablespoon capers and 1 mashed anchovy to the sauce.
3.   Creamed mushrooms are also served in patty shells. Season sauce with a little sherry or madeira.
4.   See page 203 for Fine Tongue Ragout, which can also be served in patty shells.

▓ / LOBSTER FRICASSEE (Hummerfrikassee)

6 SERVINGS

1 pound calves' sweetbreads
3 cups chicken stock
1 carrot
2 stalks celery
1 parsley root
½ knob celery
1 small leek
2 sprigs parsley
1 small can white asparagus tips
1 small can button mushrooms
2 large lobsters, 1½ pounds
    each, boiled and shelled

4 tablespoons butter
4 tablespoons flour
1 anchovy, finely chopped
1 tablespoon lemon juice
3 tablespoons white wine
3 tablespoons minced parsley
1 tablespoon minced dill
6 egg yolks, beaten with 2 table-
    spoons water
    salt and white pepper to taste
6 patty shells

Prepare sweetbreads according to instructions on page 205, but simmer just 5 minutes. Simmer stock with carrot, celery, parsley root, knob celery, leek and parsley sprigs 15 minutes, then add cut-up sweetbreads and cook 30 minutes. Drain asparagus and add 1 tablespoon of their liquid to stock. Drain mushrooms and add 1 tablespoon of their liquid to stock. Slice mushrooms and cut asparagus spears in thirds. Cube lobster meat and dice sweetbreads. Heat lobster meat, sweetbreads, asparagus and mushrooms thoroughly in hot stock. Melt butter in a small saucepan and when it bubbles, blend in flour. Let mixture cook slowly until a deep golden color. Gradually stir in 2 cups hot stock and when sauce is smooth, add chopped anchoy, lemon juice, wine, minced parsley and dill. Remove pan from flame and stir in beaten egg yolks. Season to taste. Remove lobster, sweetbreads, asparagus and mushrooms from stock and put into the hot sauce. Spoon into patty shells which have been warmed a little in the oven. Serve.

VARIATIONS

1. Substitute shrimp, crabmeat, scallops, or chunks of any cooked firm-fleshed fish for lobster.
2. If you prefer to make this without sweetbreads, add an extra half-pound of the seafood.
3. You can also make this without asparagus. In that case add 1 tablespoon capers.

CHAPTER

II

Soups

(Suppen)

Every German child knows the story of Suppenkaspar, the little boy who faded away because he refused to eat his soup. Apparently, few Germans grow up to be Suppenkaspars, for soup is one of the most important and popular courses on the national menu. Almost everyone has it once a day, and many have it twice. Soup may be the first course of a meal, or it may be the entree, in which case it will be preceded by an appetizer such as herring, sliced cold cuts or stuffed eggs, and followed by a dessert of cheese and fruit, or a sweet pudding. Cold soups are served as refreshing pickups on warm summer afternoons, and in many parts of Germany, particularly in Bavaria, the favorite midnight snack is a steaming bowlful of paprika-bright meat and potato goulash soup.

Seven or eight soups appear most frequently on the menus of German restaurants: chicken or beef broth with dumplings, noodles or rice; oxtail; goulash; cream of asparagus; split pea; and the two most elegant and expensive, cream of lobster and Echte Schildkrötensuppe—genuine turtle soup. But don't let that limited array fool you. German cooks can and do make wonderful soup out of practically everything. In addition to those made of meats, poultry, game, fish and vegetables, there are others based on nothing more than a cupful of leftover gravy or a few slices of bread. Some are made of bones or beer, fruit or chocolate, buttermilk or wine, cereals or a little flour. There are hot soups and cold, some sweet and others sour, and several both sweet and sour. Some, like the oxtail and goulash, are practically stews. Many soups are thickened with cream and egg yolks or with the browned onion-butter-flour roux which in Germany is called an Einbrenne. Even the clear golden broths (Kraftbrühe) are enriched and made more interesting with an Einlage—literally, lay-in—the dumplings, noodles and egg garnishes you'll find in the next chapter. Hamburg is famous for an eel soup that contains, in addition to eel, seemingly mismatched ingredients such as ham, dried fruits, vegetables, wine, herbs and raspberry jam, and all day long in Berlin people crowd around the island counters at Aschinger's, to eat yellow pea soup thick with potatoes, vegetables, smoked ham and wurst. Currently, kangaroo-tail soup is the Feinschmecker status symbol on restaurant menus, and French onion soup (Französische Zwiebelsuppe) has virtually become a naturalized citizen of the German cuisine. The Mock Turtle's refrain, "Soup of the evening, beautiful soup . . ." would make a fitting gastronomic national anthem for Germany.

Unusual though they may be, a few German soups, such as those made of leftover gravy, browned flour, bread and cereal, are a little too starchy or porridge-like for our taste, and I have not included them.

While no canned or packaged soup can match an expertly and carefully prepared homemade soup, there are times when such a short cut is called for, and several very good packaged dehydrated German soups are imported into this country. Those made by ETO seemed especially good to me, most notably the mushroom and the green pea with smoked bacon. As always with such products, a little doctoring goes a long way toward improving them. Some fresh herbs, a dash of cream or wine or a lump of butter, or whatever seems suited to the particular soup you are preparing, will make them even more delicious than they already are.

₰ / POT VEGETABLES OR SOUP GREENS (*Wurzelwerk oder Suppengrün*)

Wurzelwerk means root works and refers to the root vegetables and greens that lend a rich savory fragrance and flavor to German broths and soups. When a recipe calls for pot vegetables, use the selection listed below. If any items are unavailable, eliminate them; for best results, try to use them all. Add as directed in specific recipes.

1 *large carrot*
1 *stalk celery, with leaves*
1 *small knob celery root (celeriac); trim off straggly roots, peel and rinse*
1 *small parsnip, scraped and cut in half lengthwise*
1 *petrouchka (parsley root), scraped*

1 leek with most of green leaves   1 medium onion, peeled and left
    trimmed off; wash thor-   whole
    oughly under running water   3 sprigs parsley
    to remove sand

A small white peeled turnip is often included with the other soup greens; its flavor can be too powerful and pervasive, so use it at your own discretion

---

✖ HOT SOUPS ✖
(Heisse Suppen)

Whenever possible, German cooks make their soups with meat, bone, fish or vegetable stock instead of water. The following broths may be used as stocks or can be served with dumplings, noodles, egg custard cubes, rice, fried "peas" or any other Einlage which you'll find in Chapter III. If you do not have any homemade stock on hand, substitute canned or dehydrated beef or chicken bouillon, or use a meat extract for a soup that calls for beef stock. Stock can be kept for a long time, but every five days it should be brought to the boiling point and simmered for about 5 minutes, then returned to refrigerator. Always simmer stock slowly. If it cooks too rapidly, it will become cloudy.

✖ / CLEAR BEEF BROTH (Fleischkraftbrühe)

8 CUPS

½ pound beef bones, chopped   1 to 2 tablespoons butter or ren-
    in 3" to 4" pieces   dered beef fat
2 quarts water   meat extract
1½ pounds shin or neck beef
2 teaspoons salt, or to taste
    pot vegetables

Rinse bones and cover with cold water. Bring to a boil, then simmer slowly 1 hour. Add beef and salt, bring stock back to boiling point and simmer another hour, skimming foam as it rises to surface. Add all prepared pot vegetables except onion. Heat butter or fat in a small skillet, add onion, which has been finely diced, and fry slowly until deep brown. Do not let it blacken as it will then have a bitter taste. Add browned onion to soup. Simmer 45 minutes. Add meat extract by tea-spoonful until soup is a rich brown color. Remove bones and meat and strain stock through a fine sieve. Cool and skim fat from surface. Store in refrigerator until you are ready to use it. The beef can be diced and served in soup, or it can be used for salad.

VARIATIONS

1. German menus list a number of soups named for their garnishes. Liver Dumpling Soup (Leberknödelsuppe) is nothing more than a broth, usually beef, garnished with Liver Dumplings (page 61).
2. Marrow Dumpling Soup (Markklösschensuppe) is garnished with Marrow Dumplings (page 62); if it is called Fladensuppe it has the Pancake Strips described on page 60.

✂ / CLEAR VEAL BROTH (*Kalbskraftbrühe*)

Follow above recipe, substituting veal for beef. Cut total cooking time to 1½ hours. This stock is often used to cook vegetables, in which case it should be light in color. Therefore onion should not be browned before being added to soup. Just add whole onion along with other pot vegetables and eliminate butter or fat.

✂ / BONE STOCK (*Knochenbrühe*)

8 CUPS

1 *pound veal or beef bones,*   *pot vegetables*
    chopped into 3" to 4" pieces   *salt-to taste*
2 *quarts water*   *meat extract*

Rinse bones and cover with cold water. Bring to boiling point and sim-mer 1½ hours. Skim foam from surface, add pot vegetables and simmer another hour. Add salt to taste. Add meat extract a little at a time to achieve a rich color. Strain stock through fine sieve. If you want a more strongly flavored stock, fry onion until brown as described in recipe for Clear Beef Broth. And for an even stronger flavor, brown bones in a little fat before you cook them in water.

❈ / VEGETABLE BROTH (Wurzelbrühe)

6 CUPS

3 tablespoons butter or rendered   1½ quarts water
   beef or veal fat   salt to taste
  pot vegetables, all finely diced

Heat butter or fat in skillet. Add diced vegetables and sauté until deep golden color. Add to cold water, bring to a boil and simmer 1 hour. Season to taste with salt, strain through fine sieve, and refrigerate until ready to use.

❈ / CLEAR CHICKEN BROTH OR SOUP
(Hühnerkraftbrühe oder Hühnersuppe)

10 TO 12 CUPS

1 5-6 pound fowl   pot vegetables
1 veal knuckle (optional)   salt to taste
3 quarts water

Wash and singe chicken. It may be cooked whole, or quartered, depending on what you intend to do with it later. Put chicken and washed veal knuckle in cold water. Use a tall straight-sided soup pot so that water will cover chicken. Bring water to a boil, cover pot and let soup simmer slowly 1 hour, skimming foam from surface as it rises. Add pot vegetables and a couple of teaspoonfuls salt and simmer slowly another hour. Check seasoning and add more salt if necessary. Remove chicken and bone and strain soup through a fine sieve. Cool and skim fat from surface. Store in refrigerator or heat and serve. Chicken may be sliced or diced and served in soup along with one or another of the Einlagen described in the next chapter. It may also be used for salads, fricassee or pot pie. If you want a very clear, light soup, do not use veal knuckle or any other bones.

❧ / *NOODLE SOUP WITH CHICKEN* (*Nudelsuppe mit Hühner*)

Another of Germany's most popular soups, this is a combination of the above chicken soup, garnished with slices of cooked chicken and boiled noodles—either fine or wide, packaged or homemade. Sprinkle finely chopped parsley and fresh dill over soup before serving. Add some carrots, celery and peas and this becomes a complete "one-pot meal."

❧ / *CREAM OF CHICKEN SOUP* (*Hühnercremesuppe oder Königinsuppe*)

8 TO 10 CUPS

4 *tablespoons butter*	*pinch of nutmeg*
6 *tablespoons flour*	2 *egg yolks*
8 *cups hot chicken broth*	1 *cup heavy sweet cream*
salt and white pepper to taste	½ *cup white wine*

Melt butter in saucepan and when hot and bubbly, stir in flour and cook until it turns bright golden. Gradually add hot chicken broth, stirring constantly so mixture stays smooth. Season to taste with salt, pepper and nutmeg. Beat egg yolks into cream and add a little hot thickened chicken stock. Mix together and pour egg-cream mixture into remaining thickened stock that is very hot but which has been removed from flame. This can be reheated over a low flame very briefly, but be sure soup does not come to a boiling point, as egg will curdle. Check seasoning and add white wine slowly and to taste. If you prefer a slightly thicker soup, use 1 additional tablespoon flour and one more egg yolk.

Possible garnishes: sliced mushroom caps sautéed in butter, slivered salted almonds, Veal Meat Balls or cooked shrimp with asparagus.

VARIATIONS

1. For Cream of Chicken Soup with Caraway, add 2 teaspoons caraway seeds to seasonings.
2. For Cream of Chicken and Spinach Soup, cook 1 pound of spinach* with a small piece of onion in salted water. Drain and purée through a sieve. Add to soup before adding egg yolks and cream. Heat thoroughly and then thicken with eggs and cream.

* One package of frozen spinach is the equivalent.

❊ / BARLEY AND GIBLET SOUP (*Graupen- und Kleinsuppe*)

Use giblets from chicken, duck, turkey, goose or any combination of these.

8 TO 10 CUPS

4 pounds giblets (gizzards, necks, hearts, wings and feet—no livers)
pot vegetables with 2 extra carrots and 2 extra stalks celery
salt

2 quarts water, or chicken, veal or bone stock
½ cup pearl barley, washed
2 or 3 dried mushrooms, soaked and drained (optional)

Place washed giblets in 3-quart pot, along with pot vegetables and a little salt and water or stock. Bring to a boil, cover and simmer slowly 1 hour. Skim off any foam that rises to surface. Add barley and, if you are using them, dried mushrooms cut into tiny pieces or chopped. Simmer 30 minutes, or until barley is cooked. Check seasoning.

VARIATION

Turkey, Duck or Goose Soup can be made the same way, using the leftover carcass of poultry, with or without giblets. Cook carcass with vegetables and proceed. After the first hour of cooking, remove carcass, pick off meat, which you return to soup, and discard bones.

❊ / GOULASH SOUP (*Gulyassuppe*)

This is the favorite midnight snack of the Bavarians. It is served in bowls or in individual pewter casserole-porringers in the crowded Munich beer halls. To be at its best, this soup should be made the day before you intend to serve it.

4 TO 6 SERVINGS

1 pound beef (chuck, shin, neck)
2 tablespoons fresh lard or rendered beef fat, or bacon fat
1 large onion, diced
1 heaping tablespoon Hungarian sweet paprika
salt and pepper
2 tablespoons vinegar

1 tablespoon tomato paste
1 tablespoon caraway seeds
½ teaspoon marjoram
1 clove garlic
1½ to 2 quarts water
3 medium-sized potatoes, peeled and diced

Cut beef into ¾″ to 1″ cubes. Heat lard or beef fat in 3-quart saucepan and sauté onion until golden. Sprinkle with paprika and sauté a minute or two, stirring constantly over very low heat. Add beef and stir around well in paprika and onion mixture. Let meat sear and brown very slightly. Sprinkle with salt, pepper and vinegar and stir in tomato paste. Simmer 3 or 4 minutes, then add caraway seeds, marjoram, garlic and water. Bring to boiling point, cover and simmer gently 45 minutes, or until meat is almost done. Add diced potatoes and cook slowly 15 to 20 minutes longer, or until meat and potatoes are thoroughly cooked. Check seasoning and serve in deep bowls.

⬛ / SHEPHERDS' SOUP (*Hirtensuppe*)

This piquant meat and potato soup is a specialty of Lufthansa's executive chef, Edmund Dittler.

6 SERVINGS

2 tablespoons fresh lard or rendered beef fat, or bacon fat
1 pound lean stewing beef cut into ½″ cubes
1 large onion, diced
1 teaspoon salt
1 teaspoon caraway seeds

1 clove garlic, crushed
dash of paprika
3 tablespoons flour
2 tablespoons vinegar
2 quarts hot beef broth
3 medium-sized potatoes, peeled and cubed

Heat lard or fat in a 3-quart saucepan and in it sauté beef cubes and diced onion until golden brown. Add salt, caraway seeds, garlic and paprika. Sprinkle with flour. Stir and cook over low heat until flour is absorbed and browned. Sprinkle with vinegar and stir through thoroughly, still keeping heat low. Add hot broth and simmer about 45 minutes. Add potatoes and cook very slowly another hour. Serve topped with croutons and sprinkled with dill.

⬛ / OXTAIL SOUP (*Ochsenschwanzsuppe*)

6 SERVINGS

2 to 3 tablespoons fresh lard or butter
pot vegetables, diced

1 good-sized oxtail, cut into about 1″ pieces at the joints and dried on paper toweling

2 quarts water
1 large bay leaf
  pinch of thyme
5 or 6 peppercorns
3 tablespoons butter

1 small onion, finely diced or
  chopped
4 tablespoons flour
  pinch of paprika
  madeira or sherry
  salt

Heat lard or butter in 3-quart saucepan, add diced vegetables and oxtail pieces and brown slowly. Pour cold water into meat and vegetable mixture, add bay leaf, thyme and peppercorns. Bring to a boil and simmer, covered, 2 hours. Remove oxtail pieces, trim meat from bones and dice. Return diced meat to soup and discard bones. Heat 3 tablespoons butter in small skillet, add diced onion and cook until deep golden brown but not blackened. Stir in flour, blend with butter and let brown slowly to cocoa color. Ladle a cup or so of hot soup stock into this mixture gradually, stirring to keep it smooth. Then pour this Einbrenne back into soup mixture, stirring as you do so. Let soup simmer another 30 minutes. Season with paprika, wine and salt to taste.

VARIATION

Oxtail Stew: Use only 2 cups of water and 2 oxtails instead of one. Add one #2 can of tomatoes with liquid and some additional sliced carrots; a few small white onions and 4 diced potatoes can be added the last 30 minutes.

♘ / BRAIN SOUP (Hirnsuppe)

2 TO 4 SERVINGS

1 pair calves' brains
  salt
  flour
2 tablespoons butter
3 cups brain stock
2 cups water, veal or vegetable
  stock

  strip of lemon peel
  salt and pepper to taste
  lemon juice or white wine, optional and to taste
1 egg yolk beaten with 2 tablespoons sweet cream

Prepare brains as described on page 205, parboiling them just 5 minutes in 3 cups water. Strain stock and reserve. Let brains cool slightly, then cut into small pieces. Sprinkle with salt and dredge lightly with flour. Heat butter in a 2- to 2½-quart saucepan and when hot and bubbling, add brains. Sauté over moderate heat a few minutes, stirring gently until brains begin to turn golden brown on all sides. Cover pot and braise over low heat 5 minutes. Pour in strained stock along with water or stock. Add lemon peel, cover pot, bring to a boil, reduce heat and simmer 8 to 10 minutes. Season as necessary with salt and pepper, and, if you like, add a dash of lemon juice and/or white wine. Remove from heat and gradually stir in egg yolk which has been beaten with cream. Heat over very low flame but do not boil.

⚡ / GENUINE TURTLE SOUP (*Echte Schildkrötensuppe*)

This soup is almost always purchased in cans for home use in Germany. Cut any turtle meat that is in the can into bite-size pieces, return to soup and heat thoroughly but do not boil. Just before serving, add madeira to taste and garnish each portion with a very thin slice of lemon. In Germany this soup is served in white Mokkatassen—white mocha-coffee cups that are between a regular coffee cup and a demitasse in size. A standard coffee cup would do here. As the soup is very rich and also expensive, a small portion is all that is ever served.

⚡ / HERR ADAMS' TURTLE SOUP

Hans Karl Adams, one of Germany's foremost chefs, who appeared on television and operated the charming old Adams' Hotel and Restaurant in that medieval set-piece of a town, Rothenburg ob der Tauber, served the following delectable version of turtle soup. Using a canned turtle soup, cut meat into bite-size pieces, return to soup and heat thoroughly but do not boil. Remove from stove and for each pint of soup add one egg yolk that has been beaten with 3 or 4 tablespoons of heavy sweet cream. Stir in madeira to taste and garnish each portion with a tablespoonful of lightly salted whipped cream.

⚡ / CELERY SOUP (*Selleriesuppe*)

4 TO 6 SERVINGS

2 *knob celery roots (celeriac)*   *salt and pepper to taste*
4 *tablespoons butter*   *dash of nutmeg (optional)*
⅓ *cup flour*   ½ *cup cream or milk*
6 *to 7 cups water or white stock*

Peel and wash celery roots and dice. Melt butter in a 3-quart saucepan with a cover. When butter begins to bubble, add diced celery and sauté slowly until it begins to turn light golden color and softens. Stir with a wooden spoon so celery sautés evenly. Sprinkle flour over celery and stir until absorbed. Sauté until flour turns bright yellow; do not let it brown. Cover pan and braise 5 to 10 minutes over very low heat, stirring once or twice. Pour water or stock into pot. Cover and simmer slowly but steadily about ½ hour, or until celery is completely tender. Pour through a sieve and purée celery, either through a strainer or in a blender. Return celery and stock to pot and season with salt, pepper and nutmeg. Simmer 3 or 4 minutes, stir in cream, check seasoning again and simmer another few minutes. Serve with minced parsley or slivered salted almonds sprinkled on top of each portion.

❧ / CARROT SOUP (*Möhrensuppe*)

Follow above recipe, substituting 6 to 7 medium-sized carrots. Garnish with minced parsley or dill.

❧ / SOUTH GERMAN ONION SOUP (*Süddeutsche Zwiebelsuppe*)

6 CUPS

¼ pound butter	2 egg yolks
3 large onions, chopped	½ cup heavy sweet cream
½ cup flour	
1½ quarts hot veal stock or milk, preferably stock	

Melt butter in a 2-quart saucepan and in it sauté chopped onion very slowly until deep golden but not brown. Sprinkle in flour, blend and sauté to a deep golden color also. Add hot stock or milk, and simmer slowly 30 minutes. Purée through sieve. Heat thoroughly and remove from stove. Beat egg yolks into cream, add a few spoonfuls of hot onion soup, then return egg-cream mixture to soup pot and serve.

❊ / SPRING SOUP (*Frühlingssuppe*)

This soup is traditional on Holy, or Green, Thursday.

6 CUPS

4 *tablespoons butter*
3 *tablespoons flour*
1 *quart bone or vegetable stock, or water*
½ *to ¾ pound mixed greens, including spinach, watercress, lettuce, chervil and sorrel (sour grass) if you can get it, all chopped*

2 *egg yolks*
1 *cup milk*
4 *tablespoons grated Parmesan cheese*
salt

Melt butter in a 1½- to 2-quart saucepan and when hot and bubbling, blend in flour and cook until golden. Ladle in a few spoonfuls hot stock or water and when sauce is smooth, add it to rest of hot stock. Add vegetables, washed and very finely chopped, cover and simmer 10 minutes or until vegetables are cooked. Pour through a fine sieve and purée vegetables, then return to soup. Heat thoroughly and remove from stove. Beat egg yolk into milk, spoon some hot soup into egg mixture and then pour it all into soup pot, stirring vigorously. Add cheese and salt to taste. Do not let soup boil after egg yolk has been added. For a stronger flavor, sauté cut-up greens in 2 to 3 tablespoons butter before cooking them in the soup. Garnish with halves of hard-cooked eggs or tiny meat balls.

❊ / BAVARIAN VEGETABLE SOUP (*Bayrische Gemüsesuppe*)

6 SERVINGS

½ *pound cabbage, shredded*
½ *pound kohlrabi, peeled and cut into strips*
2 *carrots, scraped and cut into strips*
½ *pound string beans, French cut*
1 *cup green peas, fresh or canned*

2½ *quarts bone, veal or vegetable stock, or water in which above vegetables were cooked*
4 *tablespoons butter*
1 *medium-sized onion, minced*
4 *tablespoons flour*
salt and pepper to taste

Cook all of the vegetables separately in salted water. (If you do not have stock, use a combination of these cooking waters instead, as called for in recipe.) Pour stock or vegetable water over combined cooked vegetables. Melt butter in a skillet and fry onion slowly until golden brown. Blend in flour and cook until it too begins to brown. Add this Einbrenne to soup, stir and cook 20 minutes. Season to taste.

⧉ / ALSATIAN SAUERKRAUT SOUP (*Elsässische Sauerkrautsuppe*)

6 TO 8 SERVINGS

3 *slices bacon, diced*
1 *pound fresh sauerkraut, rinsed, drained and chopped*
1 *onion, peeled and finely diced*
3 *tablespoons flour*

7 *cups hot beef stock*
1 *small apple, peeled and grated*
1 *tablespoon caraway seeds*
salt to taste
white wine (optional)

Fry diced bacon in a 1½- to 2-quart saucepan and when rendered, sauté sauerkraut and onion in hot fat until they begin to take on color. Sprinkle with flour and stir together, add hot beef stock, grated apple, caraway seeds and salt. Simmer, covered, 20 minutes. Check seasoning and flavor with white wine if you wish to do so.

⧉ / POTATO SOUP (*Kartoffelsuppe*)

6 SERVINGS

3 *tablespoons butter*
pot vegetables, finely diced
1 *pound potatoes, preferably old ones, peeled and cut in ½" to 1" cubes*

3 *to 4 tablespoons flour*
6 *cups water*
salt
marjoram
parsley and dill, minced

Heat butter in a 2-quart saucepan and in it sauté diced vegetables until golden. Add potatoes and toss into vegetable mixture until they take on a little color. Blend in flour and cook over low heat until flour begins to brown. Pour water over vegetable mixture, add about 2 teaspoonfuls salt and marjoram. Cook 30 minutes, or until potatoes are soft, and then pour soup through a sieve and purée vegetables into it. Let soup come to a boil and simmer 5 to 10 minutes. Check seasoning and serve sprinkled with freshly minced parsley and dill.

⚒ / *YELLOW PEA SOUP, BERLIN STYLE* (*Gelbe Erbsensuppe, auf Berliner Art*)

People crowded into Aschinger's in Berlin all day long for this soup. They picked it up, cafeteria style, and carried it to one of the little round island counters, where they ate it standing up. The miracle seemed to be that no one ever spilled the soup that was so brimful in the plates—or at least no one ever did when I was there. The least expensive version of this was Erbsensuppe ohne—literally, pea soup without, meaning with no garnish. The most expensive had everything: ham, bits of bacon, slices of wurst, Spätzle or Sponge Dumplings, pages 60, 64.

6 TO 8 SERVINGS

½ pound whole dried yellow peas (if you cannot get them whole, yellow split peas will do)

2 quarts water
smoked ham bone with some meat on it, or smoked ham butt, or ½ pound smoked bacon cut in thick strips, or combine some ham and some bacon

2 tablespoons butter or 3 tablespoons rendered bacon fat pot vegetables with a large onion, all finely diced

2 tablespoons flour

2 large potatoes, peeled and cubed

½ teaspoon marjoram

½ teaspoon thyme
salt and pepper to taste

Rinse peas and soak in water to cover overnight unless instructions on package say no soaking is necessary. Put in a 4-quart pot with 2 quarts water, using whatever is left of soaking water and adding additional amount if necessary. Add ham and/or bacon and bring to a boil. Cover, reduce heat and simmer 1 hour. Heat butter or bacon fat in skillet, add diced vegetables and cook slowly until a deep golden color. Sprinkle with flour and stir until it is absorbed and browned. Add flour-vegetable mixture to soup along with potatoes, marjoram, thyme, salt and pepper.

Simmer, covered, for 1 hour, or until peas are soft enough to eat but not entirely dissolved. They should retain some of their shape. Do not strain or purée. Remove ham and/or bacon, cut into small pieces and return to soup. Discard bone if you have used one. If you want to use smoked sausage or frankfurter as a garnish, slice and heat in soup. Add Spätzle or Sponge Dumplings (pages 60, 64) before serving.

⚃ / DRIED PEA, BEAN OR LENTIL SOUP
(*Hülsenfruchtsuppe—Erbsen, Bohnen, Linsen*)

8 SERVINGS

½ pound legumes (green or yellow split or whole peas, navy or pea beans, kidney beans or lentils)
2 quarts salted water
pot vegetables, diced
3 tablespoons butter or rendered bacon fat

1 small onion, finely diced or chopped
3 tablespoons flour
salt and pepper to taste
vinegar to taste, for lentil soup

Rinse legumes and soak in water to cover overnight unless instructions on package say no soaking is necessary. (Legumes that are absolutely untreated and need to be soaked make a much better soup, but they are a little hard to find in this age of overimprovement.) Put in a 4-quart pot with 2 quarts lightly salted water, using whatever is left of soaking water and adding additional amount if necessary. Add pot vegetables. Bring to a boil, cover, reduce heat and simmer 2 hours. If you are using peas or beans, pour soup into fine sieve at this point and purée. (Lentils should be left whole.)

Melt fat in a small skillet and sauté onion. Sprinkle with flour, blend in and brown to the color of cocoa. Gradually ladle about a cup of legume stock into onion-flour-butter mixture and stir in until smooth. Pour this Einbrenne into soup pot and stir thoroughly. Add salt and pepper to taste and cook 20 minutes more. Flavor lentil soup with a little vinegar before serving.

GARNISHES AND VARIATIONS

Smoked ham, bacon and wursts can be added to all dry-bean soups. A clove of garlic may be minced and sautéed with Einbrenne for pea or lentil soup. Lentil soup may be garnished with crumbled crisp bacon and/or Spätzle, page 60. Pea and bean soups may be garnished with Spätzle, diced cooked potatoes, minced chives or parsley.

✖ / *ALLGÄU CHEESE SOUP (Käsesuppe, auf Allgäuer Art)*

This is a specialty of Bavaria's Allgäu Alps.

8 SERVINGS

4 *tablespoons butter*
4 *tablespoons flour*
2 *quarts light veal, bone or vege-*
table stock
1 *teaspoon salt*
3 *tablespoons grated Parmesan*
cheese

½ *to ¾ cup cooked elbow*
macaroni
½ *cup white wine (optional)*
minced chives

Melt butter in a 3-quart saucepan and when hot and bubbling, stir in flour. Cook gently until flour takes on bright yellow color. Do not let it turn brown. Gradually stir in hot stock, add salt and simmer 30 minutes. Add cheese and simmer 15 minutes. Add macaroni and simmer until soup is thoroughly heated. Flavor with white wine if you wish to use it. Serve with sprinkling of minced chives.

✖ / *BLACK BREAD SOUP WITH BRATWURST* (*Schwarzbrotsuppe mit Bratwürstchen*)

8 SERVINGS

4 *to 5 tablespoons butter*
4 *thin slices pumpernickel (Rus-*
sian style, rather than West-
phalian type)

8 *Bratwurst*
water to cover
8 *cups beef or veal broth*
salt to taste

Melt butter in skillet and slowly toast bread in it on both sides. Cut slices in half and place a half slice in each bowl. Simmer Bratwurst in water 15 minutes, peel off casing and slice. Place slices on top of bread. Heat broth to boiling point, simmer a few minutes, season with salt and ladle over toasted black bread and Bratwurst slices.

✸ / BLACK BREAD AND SOUR CREAM SOUP
(Schwarzbrot-Rahmsuppe)

6 TO 8 SERVINGS

8 large, thick slices dark or light
　　pumpernickel
8 cups water or beef stock
3 teaspoons caraway seeds
　salt to taste

1 cup sour cream
beef extract, if you use water

Break bread, with crusts, into small pieces. Place in pot with water or stock and caraway seeds and soak ½ hour. Cover pot, bring to a boil and simmer slowly but steadily 15 to 20 minutes. Strain through sieve, puréeing bread as you do so. Return to pot, season with salt and using a wooden spoon or wire whisk, beat in sour cream. If you made soup with water, stir in a little beef extract to give it a richer flavor. Check seasoning, heat thoroughly and serve with pumpernickel croutons.

✸ / FISH STOCK (Fischbrühe)

1½ TO 2 QUARTS

3 tablespoons butter
2 pounds fish bones, trimmings
　　and heads
1 onion, minced
1 carrot, diced
3 or 4 sprigs parsley

2 bay leaves
8 to 10 peppercorns
1½ quarts water
2 cups white wine
salt

Melt butter in a 3-quart saucepan. Add fish trimmings, vegetables and herbs, cover and braise 10 minutes. Add water and wine, a couple of dashes of salt, cover and simmer slowly 30 minutes more. Strain before using.

✸ / CREAM OF LOBSTER SOUP (Hummercremesuppe)

4 TO 6 SERVINGS

1 large live lobster (about 1½ to
　　1¾ pounds), or 2 smaller
　　ones

3 to 4 tablespoons butter
1 tablespoon minced parsley
2 tablespoons minced onion

1 *cup dry white wine*
4 *tablespoons butter*
5 *tablespoons flour*
2 *quarts hot fish stock*
1 *tablespoon butter*

½ *cup heavy sweet cream*
salt
brandy (optional)
finely minced dill

Split live lobster down the back, remove gray intestinal vein and crack claws. Cut body and tail sections into 3 pieces. Melt butter in a skillet, add lobster pieces, parsley and onion and sauté 5 to 10 minutes, or until lobster shells turn bright red. Add white wine, cover and simmer slowly 15 to 20 minutes, or until lobster meat is thoroughly cooked. Remove meat from claw and tail sections and cover with a little warm fish stock so it will stay moist. Reserve shells and body section, and sauce in which lobster was cooked.

Melt butter in saucepan; add flour, stirring and cooking slowly until mixture is bright golden. Gradually add hot fish stock, stirring constantly so that mixture is smooth. Cover and simmer 5 to 10 minutes. Crush lobster shells and body sections in a mortar or pass through food chopper, and add to hot stock along with sauce. Cover and simmer slowly 1 hour. Strain into clean 3-quart saucepan. Swirl 1 tablespoonful butter into hot soup. Add cream, season to taste, then heat but do not boil. Before serving add a dash of brandy for flavor if you wish to. Serve with diced claw and tail meat and sprinkling of fresh dill. Asparagus and crabmeat or tiny shrimp are used to garnish this, usually in Hamburg.

▓ / CREAM OF FISH SOUP (*Fischcremesuppe*)

This creamed fish soup is adapted from the heavenly original, as prepared by Sellmer's, an elegant and charming seafood restaurant overlooking Hamburg's docks and harbor, and close to the St. Pauli fish market.

4 SERVINGS

1 *pound white firm-fleshed fish*
   filets
3 *tablespoons butter*
1 *onion, minced*
2 *tablespoons flour*

1 *quart hot fish stock (this soup*
   cannot be made with water)
salt
2 *egg yolks, beaten in 2 table-*
   spoons heavy cream
lemon juice to taste

Cut fish into small pieces. Melt butter in a 2-quart saucepan, add fish pieces and minced onion and sauté 5 minutes. Dredge with flour and cook 5 minutes more, or until flour is absorbed and begins to turn pale yellow. Add hot fish stock and a couple of dashes of salt. Cover and simmer 30 minutes. Rub through a sieve into a clean pot and reheat. Remove soup from stove. Beat egg yolks into heavy cream, add a few spoonfuls hot soup and pour mixture into soup pot. Season with lemon juice and salt as needed. Cut canned white asparagus tips and small cooked shrimp are standard garnishes at Sellmer's. You can also add Fish Dumplings, page 64.

⚅ / HAMBURG EEL SOUP (*Hamburger Aalsuppe*)

This is one dish where "eating is believing." For years I read about the unlikely combination of ingredients that went into Hamburg Eel Soup, and each version sounded more improbable than the last. Finally I went to the bustling, exciting "Free and Hanseatic city" and tried it for myself. Fortunately, I did so in Weinhaus Dölle's, a handsome, impeccable old restaurant with dark oak paneling and big comfortable leather-cushioned booths, unfortunately, no longer in existence. The proprietor was very generous about giving me the following recipe for it.

8 TO 10 SERVINGS

8 to 10 *prunes*
8 to 10 *dried apricot halves*
1 *smoked ham bone (preferably a meaty one) and rind*
3 *quarts water*
2 *carrots*
1 *small knob celery root*
1 *leek*
7 *tablespoons butter*
1 *large onion*
4 *tablespoons flour*
½ *teaspoon basil*
½ *teaspoon thyme*

½ *teaspoon marjoram*
1 *teaspoon leaf savory*
  salt to taste
1 *pint white wine*
1 *large bay leaf*
6 *peppercorns*
1 *pound eel, skinned and cut into 3" pieces*
4 to 5 *tablespoons vinegar, or to taste*
1 to 2 *tablespoons raspberry jam, or to taste*

Soak prunes and apricots in warm water to cover 2 or 3 hours. Put ham bone and rind in 3 quarts cold water, bring to boiling point and simmer slowly 1½ hours. Remove rind and discard; cut meat from bone into small cubes. Let stock cool and skim fat from surface. Clean carrots, celery root and leek, and dice finely. Heat 3 tablespoons butter in a skillet and sauté vegetables slowly until they begin to soften and take on a deep golden color. Add vegetables to ham stock. Heat 4 tablespoons butter and in it sauté finely diced onion until deep brown. Sprinkle flour over this and blend in with butter, stirring over low flame until mixture is deep cocoa brown. Be very careful not to let it scorch. Add this with basil, thyme, marjoram, savory and salt to stock and simmer 15 minutes.

While stock is simmering, bring white wine to boiling point with bay leaf and peppercorns. Add eel, simmer 10 minutes and set aside. Add diced ham and drained fruits to soup, along with vinegar and 1 cup white wine in which eel was cooked. (Do not remove pits from prunes or they will get mushy.) Stir in raspberry jam. Simmer 5 to 10 minutes. Check and correct seasoning, adding salt, jam, vinegar, spices or wine as they might be needed. The soup should have a winey sweet-and-sour taste with a subtle interplay of flavors. Keep soup hot on very low light. To serve, remove eel from remaining stock and place in bottom of tureen or individual bowls and pour soup over it. Be sure that each person has a piece of eel, an apricot, a prune and a few Sponge Dumplings (page 64).

VARIATIONS

1. This soup often includes green peas, although Dölle's version did not. If you wish to use them, add 1 cup drained canned tiny green peas during last five minutes of cooking.
2. If you do not happen to have a ham bone and would like to try this soup, order 2 smoked ham hocks with rind from your butcher. Cut rind off and trim excess fat from under it. Cook rind and hock as described above.
3. You can also make this without eel, in which case it cannot be called eel soup—naturally. Make it as directed, leaving out eel, and call it Hamburg Ham Soup, or Hamburg Sour Soup. Add bay leaf to soup with other spices, and 1 cup white wine during last 10 minutes of cooking. This is an excellent way to utilize a leftover ham bone.

✵ / *HOT BEER SOUP* (*Biersuppe*)

This soup is wonderful served in mugs on a cold winter afternoon or evening.

4 SERVINGS

1 *quart light or dark beer (the dark makes a richer soup)*
1 *tablespoon butter*
2 *tablespoons flour*
1 *tablespoon sugar*
    chopped rind and juice of ½ lemon
1 *stick cinnamon*
6 *cloves*
2 *egg yolks, well-beaten with a little water*

Pour beer into a bowl and let stand at room temperature for about 3 hours, or until beer gets flat. Pour into 1½-quart saucepan and heat. Melt butter in a skillet until hot and bubbling and then stir in flour and sugar. Cook very slowly, stirring constantly until flour and sugar turn a rich caramel color. Be very careful, as sugar can burn and blacken quite suddenly. Add this to hot beer along with lemon rind and juice, cinnamon and cloves. Bring to a boil and simmer 15 minutes. Remove from stove and gradually stir in beaten egg yolks. Serve with Snow Balls (page 72).

✕ COLD SOUPS ✕
(*Kaltschalen—literally, "cold bowls"*)

✂ / BEER SOUP (*Bierkaltschale*)

4 SERVINGS

1 *cup currants*	½ *cup sugar*
hot water	1 *large lemon, sliced*
¾ *cup grated light or dark*	1 *stick cinnamon*
pumpernickel	6 *cloves*
1 *quart light beer or ale*	

Cover currants with hot water and soak 1 hour to 1½ hours. Add grated pumpernickel and beer or ale, sugar, lemon, cinnamon and cloves. Chill 2 hours in refrigerator. Taste soup once or twice while chilling to see if more sugar is needed. Remove cinnamon and cloves. Lemon slices may be left in or removed. Stir well and serve in mugs or glasses, or in cups if you plan to add Snow Balls (page 72), or zwieback or pumpernickel croutons.

✣ / WINE SOUP (*Weinkaltschale*)

4 CUPS

2 cups wine, white or red
1 stick cinnamon
1 strip of lemon peel
2 tablespoons cornstarch dis-
    solved in a little wine

2 cups water
sugar to taste
1 egg yolk

Simmer wine with cinnamon and lemon peel 10 minutes. Add dissolved cornstarch paste to 2 cups cold water and cook 5 minutes or so. Strain through sieve and add to flavored wine. Season to taste with sugar. Heat soup thoroughly but do not let it boil. Remove from stove and gradually stir in egg yolk, which has been beaten with a little cold water. Chill 2 hours before serving. Garnish with Snow Balls (page 72) or serve with Soup Macaroons (page 72) or zwieback.

✣ / BUTTERMILK SOUP (*Buttermilchkaltschale*)

4 SERVINGS

2 eggs
juice and grated rind 1 lemon
5 to 6 tablespoons sugar

1 teaspoon powdered cinnamon
1 quart buttermilk

Beat eggs well with lemon juice and rind, sugar and cinnamon. Whip buttermilk until frothy and pour into egg mixture gradually, stirring as you do so. Check seasoning and add more sugar if necessary. Chill at least 2 hours before serving. If soup becomes too thick with chilling, stir in a little more cold buttermilk. Before serving, garnish each portion with a little stewed fruit or topping of slightly sweetened whipped cream. Serve with rusks, zwieback or Soup Macaroons (page 72).

✣ / BUTTERMILK-RASPBERRY SOUP (*Buttermilch-Himbeerkaltschale*)

This soup might sound a little strange, but it is one of the most delightful coolers you could imagine on a hot summer day. The packaged pudding to use for it is Junket Danish Dessert—a currant-raspberry pudding thickened with cornstarch instead of gelatin. Served in a cup, this chilled, frothy pink soup, garnished with a few fresh raspberries when possible, makes an excellent starter for a summer meal. Served in a tall glass, it becomes a light, easy-to-take, one-course summer luncheon.

4 CUPS

1 *quart buttermilk*
1 *package Junket Danish Dessert (currant-raspberry flavor), or any other raspberry pudding you can get—but not raspberry gelatin*

2 *cups water*
⅓ *cup sugar*

Pour buttermilk into a blender or mixing bowl. Cook pudding in 2 cups water as directed on package. As soon as it is done, add to buttermilk along with sugar. Whip until completely mixed and frothy. Taste and add more sugar if necessary. Chill thoroughly 2 or 3 hours in refrigerator. Stir and add a little more buttermilk if soup has become too thick. Serve in chilled cups or glasses and garnish with fresh raspberries if possible.

FRUIT SOUPS, ❧ HOT OR COLD ❧
(*Fruchtsuppen oder Fruchtkaltschalen*)

Although fruit soups are uncommon in this country, they are extremely popular in Middle Europe and Scandinavia. They are used even in winter, when they are made with fruit juices bottled the previous summer. Either hot or cold, they have a rich winey flavor and are served before meals or as between-meal refreshers. Since our fruit tends to have much less flavor than that of Europe, we use much less water when cooking the same amount of fruit. Be sure that any fruit you use for soup is fully ripened. Too often our markets sell only underripe fruit, and this will not produce a good soup. Wait until the fruit is at the peak of its season. Early fruits generally do not have as much flavor.

When a German Hausfrau makes soup out of fruit like plums, cherries, apricots, peaches or nectarines, she usually includes a few of the stones of the fruit when she cooks it and then strains them out. The stones should be cracked before being added to the soup. To do that, wrap them in a twist of doubled or tripled cheesecloth, hold by the twisted "neck" and hit the cloth-covered stones with a hammer. The cloth prevents the pieces from scattering all over the room. The stones add additional flavor to the soup but are not absolutely essential.

✂ / *CHERRY SOUP, HOT OR COLD* (*Kirschsuppe oder Kirschkaltschale*)

4 SERVINGS

2 *pounds ripe cherries, preferably dark Bings*	1 *stick cinnamon (optional)*
6 *to 8 cherry stones, crushed (see above)*	2 *to 3 tablespoons lemon juice*
7 *cups water*	1 *long strip lemon peel*
½ *cup sugar, or to taste*	2 *tablespoons cornstarch*
	4 *tablespoons white wine*
	½ *to ¾ cup white wine*

Pit cherries over a bowl so you will not lose juice. Set aside 1 cup cherries. Cook remaining cherries in water about 20 minutes, or until completely soft. Rub through a fine sieve and return to soup. Add sugar, cinnamon, lemon juice and peel, tasting as you do so to achieve desired flavor. Dissolve cornstarch with white wine. Add this paste to soup and simmer 5 minutes. Stir so soup will remain smooth as it thickens. Remove lemon peel, and cinnamon if you have used it, add white wine to taste and check seasoning again. If the soup is to be eaten hot, it is now ready to serve. Otherwise, chill 2 hours. In either case, add some of the reserved raw cherries, coarsely chopped or cut in halves, to each portion of soup. Top with slightly sweetened whipped cream or sour cream. Serve with Soup Macaroons (page 72) or zwieback.

VARIATION

For a very tangy flavor, use ½ pound sour cherries and 1¼ pounds sweet cherries.

✂ / OTHER FRUIT SOUPS (APPLE, RHUBARB, PLUMS, APRICOTS, BERRIES, etc.)

Substitute fruit of your choice for cherries in the recipe above. You may use one fruit alone, or a combination of several. With the exception of the apple, fruit soups look most inviting when they are red, so if you plan to use apricots, nectarines, peaches or rhubarb, combine them with something else. Cherries seem to make the most satisfactory of all the fruit soups, and second place goes to soup made of the soft, ripe red Santa Rosa plums that are in season in midsummer.

Adjust the amounts of sugar and lemon according to the flavor of the fruit you use. Rhubarb soup will take at least 1 cup of sugar. Apple soup can be garnished with currants or raisins that have been soaked in a little white wine.

✄ CEREAL SOUPS ✄

There is a whole category of "soups" in Germany that are made with cereals such as oatmeal, rice, semolina or farina, buckwheat groats or kasha. To us, all of these would pass as breakfast cereals and I have not included specific recipes for them here. The cereals are cooked just as we would prepare them, either in salted water or milk. They are usually eaten hot with butter, sugar and cinnamon; or with cooked fruit compote and juice; or with raisins, chopped nuts and sugar. In some cases white wine is added to the cooking water and the cereal is then also served with fresh or cooked fruit or berries. Soups such as beef and chicken broth are often called oatmeal or buckwheat groat soup, when those cereals are served in them instead of noodles or rice.

One also finds cooked cold cereal with fruit compote served in German homes as dessert after a light entree, and some are even raised into soufflés.

A very special cereal that should be mentioned here has the rather lengthy name Dr. Bircher-Benner Schweizer Müsli—Dr. Bircher-Benner's

Swiss Muesli. It is a combination of oatmeal flakes and other grain along with chopped raisins, figs, nuts and lemon rind. It may be mixed at home, but a very good version comes already packaged under the above name. It is the invention of a Swiss nutritionist, Dr. Bircher-Benner, and is sold at health food stores and in gourmet food shops. It can be prepared as a breakfast cereal or a dessert, or can be used in making excellent cookies. Recipes are on the package itself.

III

Soup Garnishes
and Dumplings

(Einlagen, Klösschen, Klösse, Knödel, Klopse)

❌ ❌ ❌ ❌ ❌

As though German soups aren't interesting and varied enough in themselves, there are dozens of enticing little garnishes that have been devised to enhance them even further. Most of these Einlagen (lay-ins) are used with clear soups like chicken, beef, veal and vegetable broths; in a few cases, they are also added to the thicker meat and vegetable soups.

One of the main categories of soup garnishes is Teigwaren, doughwares, the noodles and noodle derivatives that are as popular throughout Germany as they are in their native Swabia. These include the ravioli-like Maultaschen, the grated flecks of noodle dough, Reibele, and tiny Spätzle, most often served with meats and gravies.

Dumplings comprise the single most important group of Einlagen, and, in addition, are also served as side dishes with meat, fish and vegetable entrees, in which case they become Beilagen—lay-bys. Dumplings are to the German cuisine what pasta is to the Italian, and, in the same way, vary in size, shape and texture, depending upon the food and flavors they must complement, and the liquid (soup, gravy or sauce) they must absorb or carry. In many cases, the same dumplings used in soups are made in larger sizes to accompany the main course. Still others, like Königsberger Klopse, *are* the main course. A few, such as those at the end of this chapter, take fruit or sweet sauces and are served as desserts or with coffee, instead of cake. Dumplings should never be served with more than one course in any given meal; if you have them in soup, do not serve any kind of dumpling or "dough-ware" with the entree or dessert.

Since most dumplings are made according to the same principles, I have grouped them all together in this chapter. Dumpling terminology can be pretty bewildering. Roughly, the main type is the Klösse or Knödel, two names that are completely interchangeable though the second is used primarily in southern Germany. A Klösschen is a small Kloss, and I have been told that anything called Klopse is made with meat, which seemed easy enough to grasp, until I remembered that a liver dumpling is always called a Leberknödel. Whatever you call them, most dumplings are composed basically of a starch (flour, semolina, potatoes, raw or cooked, bread or breadcrumbs), a liquid (water, milk or stock) and usually egg to bind the mass together. The egg may be added whole, or the yolk may be mixed in first, and later the whites, which have been beaten to a stiff snow, are folded in. This second method makes very light and airy dumplings. Some cooks like to sprinkle a teaspoonful or so of baking powder into the batter so the dumplings will rise and be light and spongy. Flavorings come by way of herbs, sautéed onions, spices, flecks of bacon or ham, bits of vegetables or vegetable purées. Dumplings are always cooked by steaming or boiling, in water, stock, soup or, occasionally, milk. A few are made of meat, fish or vegetables, and these are boiled, never fried or browned in any way.

Dumplings can be tricky to make until you have some experience with them. It is almost impossible to give an exact recipe, as no one can know the amount of moisture in your flour or potatoes, the size of your eggs, the humidity in the air on the day you plan to make them, and a number of other such variables that will affect the batter. Once you are used to handling the dough, you will be able to tell when it is of the right consistency to produce perfect dumplings.

GENERAL RULES FOR DUMPLING MAKING

1. Always make one test dumpling and cook it completely to be sure the batter is of the right consistency. If the dumpling is too soft, and falls apart, add more of your basic raw starch, or egg yolk. If it is too heavy and leaden, add more liquid, cooked ingredients such as mashed potatoes, or egg white. Cook your test dumpling before you shape the rest of your batter.

2. Knead or mix dough thoroughly so that it becomes smooth enough to handle.

3. Shape dumplings with wet hands, or between two spoons (teaspoons or tablespoons, depending on the size you want). Wet spoons by dipping into hot liquid in which dumplings will be cooked.

4. Most dumplings should be cooked uncovered. Exceptions are those that must rise: those made with yeast or baking powder. These should be cooked covered. Cook dumplings uncovered unless the recipe says otherwise.

5. Cooking liquid should be boiling when dumplings are dropped into it, but should be reduced to a simmer while they cook.

6. A teaspoonful of potato flour can be added to the cooking water to help keep the dumplings intact. Never add the flour if you are cooking the dumplings in a soup that will be served with them, as it will be too thick, cloudy and starchy to eat.

7. Remove dumplings from cooking liquid with a perforated spoon and drain them well in a colander before serving.

8. Do not cook too many dumplings at one time. There must be room for all of them to rise to the surface of the cooking liquid.

9. Dumplings used for soup garnishes should be about ½ to ⅓ the size of main-course dumplings.

10. Dumplings should be cooked just before they are to be served. The batter can be made several hours ahead of time and refrigerated until cooking time. In that case, make your test dumpling just before cooking, so you can add more starch to compensate for any moisture that might have developed. The batter for raw potato dumplings must be prepared just before cooking, or it will turn black.

OTHER SOUP GARNISHES

1. Croutons are easily made by cutting sliced bread into squares and toasting them on both sides in a skillet of hot butter.

2. Cheese croutons are made in much the same way as plain croutons, but a little grated Cheddar or Parmesan cheese is sprinkled over them while they are still in the skillet after they have browned. Cook slowly until the cheese melts and coats both sides of the toast squares. For an even shorter cut to cheese croutons, simply use Cheddar cheese bread and toast as for plain croutons.

3. Add diced or slivered chicken, meat or fish, depending on the kind of soup you are serving.

4. Use minced fresh herbs: parsley, chives or dill, or combinations of these.

5. Tiny cherry tomatoes often serve as the garnish for tomato soups. They may be used whole or cut in half, and should be added just before serving.

6. Salted almonds, slivered or split, are delicious in cream soups.

7. Add tiny shrimp or chopped shrimp to fish soups or cream of asparagus soup.

8. Cooked rice is a favorite garnish in chicken and beef broth.

9. Farina or semolina (Griess) is very popular in broths. To make Griessuppe, sauté 2 tablespoons farina in 1 tablespoonful butter until the cereal turns a bright golden color. Slowly add 1 quart of simmering beef or chicken broth and cook together for about 15 minutes, or until the cereal is done. Season with salt and a dash of nutmeg and pour in 1 well-beaten egg and let it cook up for a minute or two, as you would when making egg drop soup. Garnish with minced parsley or chives.

10. A whole raw egg yolk is often served in beef or chicken broth. Put the yolk in the individual cup or bowl and ladle the hot soup over it.

⚒ / *EGG FLAKES* (*Einlauf*)

FOR 4 CUPS OF SOUP

1 egg
1½ to 2 tablespoons flour

salt
5 cups chicken or beef broth

Beat egg with flour and a dash of salt. Pour through colander or through a perforated skimming spoon into a pot of simmering broth. Batter should be thin enough so that it seeps through holes of spoon or colander in a thin broken stream of droplets. You can speed the process a bit by stirring batter through colander with a wooden spoon. Let boil 3 to 5 minutes and serve, ladling egg flakes into individual cups or bowls along with soup. Sprinkle with parsley or chives before serving.

⚒ / *EGG CUSTARD CUBES* (*Eierstich*)

FOR 4 SERVINGS OF SOUP

2 eggs
2 tablespoons milk
  salt

1 tablespoon finely minced
  parsley

Beat eggs with milk, a dash of salt and minced parsley. Pour into a small buttered ceramic baking dish. Batter should be about 1½″ deep in baking dish. Cover baking dish with sheet of aluminum foil and set in large pan, half full of hot (not boiling) water. Simmer gently 20 to 25 minutes, or until custard is set and firm. Unmold custard onto flat plate. Cut into dice or thin strips and add to chicken or beef broth, or tomato soup, just before serving.

VARIATIONS

A dash of nutmeg or 1 tablespoon grated Parmesan cheese can be added to egg-milk batter before it is cooked. 1 tablespoon tomato sauce or 1 tablespoon cooked minced spinach that has been thoroughly drained can be added to batter for color and flavor.

✂ / *NOODLES* (*Nudeln*)

Although you can get very good egg noodles ready-made in packages, this homemade version is easy to prepare and far superior in texture and flavor, once you get the knack of handling the dough.

FOR 4 SERVINGS OF SOUP

1 *egg*	*salt*
2 *tablespoons water*	1 *to* 1¼ *cups flour*

Beat egg well with water and a dash or two of salt. Sift 1 cup flour onto floured pastry board and make a well in center. Pour beaten egg into well and gradually work in flour until dough holds together. If it remains sticky, add flour until smooth enough to handle. Knead dough 5 or 10 minutes, or until smooth and elastic. Rub a little flour onto your hands, shape dough lightly into a ball and let stand, uncovered, 10 minutes so that it will dry out. Cut dough into thirds, and with floured rolling pin, roll each section to tissue thinness.

Place dough on clean cloth and let dry 20 minutes; roll, jelly-roll fashion, and cut crosswise slices of whatever width you want the noodles to be. They are generally very thin (about ⅛" to ¼") for soup, and about ½" when used as a side dish or in puddings. Unroll slices, scatter them on clean cloth, and let dry 5 or 6 hours before you cook them. Once dry, noodles can be kept for weeks in a tightly covered jar. Boil in salted water 8 to 10 minutes, drain and add to chicken or beef broth just before serving.

✂ / *GRATED NOODLES* (*Reibele*)

FOR 4 SERVINGS OF SOUP

To make these light and delectable egg droplets, prepare noodle dough as in above recipe. When you have shaped it into a ball, let dry 30 minutes and then grate downward on coarse side of cheese grater. Do grating directly over a clean cloth and move grater so that all the Reibele will not pile up on each other. There should be one thin layer dispersed evenly over cloth. Let dry 5 or 6 hours before cooking. Do not handle while wet or they will stick together and again form one solid mass of dough. Cook in boiling salt water 3 to 5 minutes, drain through a strainer and serve in chicken or beef broth.

Reibele can be cooked in soup instead of water. Since the liquid must boil for dough to cook, the soup will become slightly cloudy. The first method is therefore preferable even though it requires an extra step.

✂ / SWABIAN "POCKETS" (Schwäbische Maultaschen)

These delicious little meat-filled pockets of dough are a specialty of Swabia, and are first cousins to the Italian ravioli, the Jewish kreplach and the Chinese won-ton. Maultaschen means "mouth pockets"— pockets of dough that you pop into your mouth. In other parts of Germany they are known as Krapfen.

FOR 4 TO 6 SERVINGS OF SOUP

Dough:
3 *eggs*
4 *tablespoons water*
1 *teaspoon salt*
4 *cups flour*

Filling:
1 *pound spinach (or 1 package frozen), cooked, finely chopped and thoroughly drained*

¾ *to 1 cup minced cooked chicken, beef or pork*
1 *onion, grated*
4 *slices white bread with crust*
½ *cup milk or water*
salt and pepper
nutmeg
4 *eggs*
1 *egg yolk beaten with 1 teaspoon water*

Make dough as on page 58. When you have rolled it into thin sheets, it is ready to be made into Maultaschen. It is not necessary for sheets to dry further. Cut into 3″ squares with a knife, or into 3″ circles with a scalloped cookie cutter or glass. Put a heaping teaspoonful of filling in center of each square or circle, moisten edges with egg yolk that has been beaten with water and fold in half to form pockets. Press edges together firmly and crimp with your fingers or with a fork. Let stand 2 hours before cooking. Boil 10 minutes in salted water as you would noodles. Drain and serve in chicken or beef broth, or with melted butter and toasted breadcrumbs as a side dish or entree. If you prefer, you can make Maultaschen a little smaller for soup.

To make filling, mix spinach and chopped cooked meat together with grated onion. Soak bread slices in milk or water, squeeze dry after 3 to 4 minutes and crumble bread into meat-spinach mixture. Add salt, pepper and nutmeg to taste and mix in eggs. Knead or mix stuffing until thoroughly blended. Stuff Maultaschen as described above.

✖ / *SPÄTZLE, SWABIAN*

MAKES ABOUT 4 CUPS Spätzle, OR ABOUT 6 SERVINGS

2¼ cups flour   1 egg, well beaten
1 teaspoon salt   ¼ to ¾ cup water

Sift flour and salt into a bowl. Add egg and mix. Add water gradually until batter is stiff but smooth. Press dough flat on a plate or floured board. With a sharp knife, scrape small pieces of dough off and drop into boiling salted water. There should be only one layer of Spätzle at a time in cooking water. Boil gently 5 to 8 minutes, or until you try a few and find them done. Remove from water with perforated spoon and drain. Spätzle may be served in pea, lentil or tomato soups, or as a side dish with meat or game. In the latter case, hot melted butter is usually poured over them just before serving. They may also be sautéed in butter until a bright golden color. Toasted breadcrumbs or grated Parmesan cheese may also be sprinkled over them.

✖ / *PANCAKE STRIPS* (*Flädchen*)

These julienne strips of golden egg crepes are also a feature of the Swabian kitchen.

FOR 6 SERVINGS OF SOUP

½ cup flour   1 teaspoon minced parsley (op-
1 egg   tional)
salt   butter for frying
½ cup water

Sift flour into a mixing bowl. Beat egg with salt and water and pour into bowl with flour. Beat until batter is smooth, thin and absolutely free of lumps. Add parsley and stir through. Melt about 1 teaspoonful of butter in 8″ skillet and when bubbling but not brown, pour in 2 tablespoons of egg batter. Tip and rotate pan so batter covers bottom in a thin even layer. Do this quickly, as batter will set almost as soon as poured. Let batter cook until golden brown on one side, turn over and brown on the other. Remove from pan and put on a rack or cloth to cool. Continue making crepes in this way until batter is used up, adding more butter as needed. Do not let pan get too hot. This amount of batter should make 5 or 6 thin 6″ crepes. When crepes are cool enough to handle, roll each one tightly, jelly-roll fashion, and cut across into thin julienne slices. To serve, put Flädchen in soup plate or cup and ladle chicken or beef broth over them.

✂ / FRIED "PEAS" (*Gebackene Erbsen*)

FOR 6 SERVINGS OF SOUP

¾ cup flour	2 tablespoons water or milk
pinch of salt	corn oil or other vegetable fat
1 egg	for deep frying

Sift flour with salt into a mixing bowl. Beat egg with water and add to flour. Beat thoroughly until mixture is smooth and free of lumps. Heat fat in automatic deep fryer or deep saucepan until it registers 375° on a fat thermometer. Drop batter in tiny balls ("peas") from tip of teaspoon into hot fat. Do not fry all the batter at one time. "Peas" should float uncrowded in a single layer. In 1 or 2 minutes they will be golden brown. Remove from fat with perforated spoon and drain on paper toweling. Fry rest of the batter in same way. Serve on top of soup after it has been ladled into individual bowls or cups. These are good in chicken or beef broth, tomato or pea soup.

✂ / LIVER DUMPLINGS (*Leberknödel*)

10 to 12 DUMPLINGS

4 small rolls or 5 slices white bread, with crusts	1 small onion
1 cup lukewarm milk	2 eggs
¾ pound beef liver or ½ pound beef liver and ¼ pound pork liver	1 teaspoon salt marjoram grated rind 1 lemon breadcrumbs, as needed
2 ounces kidney fat	1½ quarts beef broth

Break or cut rolls or bread into small pieces. Cover with warm milk and soak until milk becomes cool. Squeeze rolls to remove excess milk. Using fine blade of food chopper, grind bread, liver, kidney fat and onion together. Be sure all membranes and connective tissue have been cut out of liver. Mix in eggs, about 1 teaspoonful of salt, a generous pinch of marjoram and grated lemon rind. Add breadcrumbs, a tablespoonful at a time, until mixture can be handled sufficiently to shape into dumplings. Shape with wet hands or two teaspoons or tablespoons that have been dipped into hot beef stock. Cook one test dumpling. The liver dumplings should be done in 15 or 20 minutes. Serve in beef broth.

VARIATION

To make a main course of these dumplings, prepare as described, and when they have been removed from beef broth and drained, serve over Cooked Sauerkraut (page 276).

❇ / MARROW DUMPLINGS (*Markklösschen*)

8 DUMPLINGS

2 ounces fresh bone marrow	breadcrumbs, as needed
1 egg	1 to 1½ quarts hot beef or veal
salt	stock
nutmeg	

Scoop marrow out of bones and melt in a skillet very slowly. When it has all melted and only a little black sediment remains, strain through a fine sieve or cheesecloth. Refrigerate until marrow solidifies. Cream chilled marrow with egg, add a dash or two of salt and a pinch of nutmeg. Add breadcrumbs a tablespoonful at a time, until dough can be handled and shaped. Let mixture stand ½ hour. Using wet hands or two teaspoons dipped in hot stock, shape dumplings. Cook a test dumpling. These dumplings should be thoroughly cooked in about 10 minutes. Drain and serve in beef or veal broth.

❇ / MEAT DUMPLINGS (*Fleischknödel*)

FOR 4 TO 6 SERVINGS OF SOUP

3 tablespoons butter	1 tablespoon minced parsley
1 egg	grated rind 1 lemon
½ pound raw meat (beef, veal or pork, or any combination of these)	salt and pepper
	breadcrumbs, as needed
	1 quart beef or veal stock

Cream butter with egg until mixture is fluffy and lemon-colored. Grind meat twice through fine blade of food grinder. Work meat into egg-butter mixture along with minced parsley, grated lemon rind, salt and pepper. Add breadcrumbs, a tablespoonful at a time, until mixture can be handled and shaped. Shape dumplings with wet hands or two teaspoons dipped into boiling stock. Cook a test dumpling. Drain and serve in meat, veal or chicken broth, in any cream of vegetable soup or stew.

▓ / BIBERACH FRIED VEAL DUMPLINGS (*Biberacher Bratknödel*)

These delicate dumplings are a specialty of the Swabian town Biberach, where they are served in a beef broth. This recipe is excellent for left-over roast veal.

FOR 4 TO 6 SERVINGS OF SOUP, 8 TO 10 DUMPLINGS

½ pound ground veal, prefer-
  ably roasted but raw will do
2 tablespoons melted butter
¼ cup milk
1 egg
½ teaspoon salt
pinch of nutmeg

pinch of black pepper
1 tablespoon minced parsley
granted rind ½ lemon
1 to 2 cups cracker meal
salted water or meat stock
butter

If veal is roasted it simply needs to be finely ground and then mixed thoroughly with melted butter. If you are using raw ground meat, brown it well in butter. Mix meat and butter with milk, egg, salt, nutmeg, pepper, parsley and grated lemon rind. Gradually add cracker meal until meat mixture can be shaped into balls. Using two wet teaspoons, drop small meat balls into simmering salted water or meat stock. Simmer 5 minutes, turn off heat and let dumplings remain in hot cooking liquid 10 minutes. Remove with slotted spoon and drain thoroughly in a colander. These dumplings may be added to beef or chicken broth as they are, or, preferably, they may first be lightly browned on all sides in a little hot butter.

✂ / FISH DUMPLINGS (*Fischklösschen*)

FOR 6 TO 8 SERVINGS OF SOUP

½ pound raw white firm-fleshed   2 to 3 tablespoons breadcrumbs
    fish   1 teaspoonful minced parsley
  1 egg   grated rind ½ lemon
    salt   1½ to 2 quarts fish stock*

Grind the fish through fine blade of a food chopper. Mix in egg, salt, breadcrumbs, parsley and lemon rind. Shape into tiny dumplings with wet hands or two teaspoons dipped in hot stock. Test one dumpling by cooking for about 15 minutes. Serve with Cream of Fish Soup (page 45), with creamed vegetables, or with mushroom sauce. If you serve with sauce as a main course, make fish balls twice the size.

  * If you do not have fish stock, make a vegetable stock by cooking a stalk of celery, a carrot, an onion, a bay leaf, a slice of lemon, some salt and 6 peppercorns in 1 quart of water 15 minutes. Strain and use this stock to cook dumplings.

✂ / SPONGE DUMPLINGS (*Schwemmklösschen oder Brandteigklösschen*)

FOR 6 SERVINGS OF SOUP

½ cup water   salt
 1 tablespoon butter   2 eggs
 3 tablespoons flour

Bring water to a boil and add butter. Cook slowly until butter has melted. Mix flour with a pinch of salt and put it, all at once, into butter-water mixture. Stir over low heat until dough forms a ball and leaves sides of pan. Remove from heat and cool slightly. Beat in eggs, one at a time, until well blended. Scoop off dumplings with wet teaspoon and drop into boiling salted water or soup stock. Cook about 10 minutes or until dumplings rise to top. Serve with chicken or beef broth, pea or tomato soup.

VARIATIONS

1. To make tiny puffs for soup, put batter into pastry tube and squeeze them onto a buttered baking sheet. Bake in middle of 400° oven

about 10 minutes, or until puffs are golden brown. Just before serving, top individual bowls of soup with these.

2. This same dough can make another, lighter version of Fried "Peas" on page 61. Make batter and drop little bits of it, from tip of a teaspoon, into hot frying oil or fat.

3. To make Cheese-Flavored Dumplings, substitute ½ cup milk for water, and stir in 1 tablespoon grated Cheddar or Gruyère before adding butter. When both cheese and butter have melted, add flour and proceed.

✖ / FLOUR DUMPLINGS (Mehlklösse)

12 TO 16 DUMPLINGS

2 *cups sifted flour*	*nutmeg*
2 *teaspoons baking powder*	2 *tablespoons butter*
1 *teaspoon salt*	½ *to ¾ cup milk*

Sift together flour, baking powder, salt and nutmeg. Using two knives, or a pastry blender, cut in butter as you would when making pie crust, until mixture has texture of coarse meal. Gradually add milk and blend in with fork, until batter is the consistency of thick cooked oatmeal porridge. Drop dough with a wet teaspoon or tablespoon, depending on size you want, into boiling salted water, seasoned stock or into pot with stew, resting dumplings on top of meat and vegetables. Cover and simmer 15 minutes without removing the cover.

VARIATIONS

1. To make Caraway Dumplings, stir 2 tablespoons caraway seeds into flour, baking powder and salt after they have been sifted together. Eliminate nutmeg.

2. To make Bacon Dumplings, fry 4 slices bacon until crisp, drain on paper toweling, crumble, and add as directed for caraway dumplings. Nutmeg can be retained or eliminated.

3. To make Herb Dumplings, add 2 tablespoons minced fresh parsley, dill, chives, or any combination of these, as described above for caraway dumplings. Eliminate nutmeg.

4. If you are in a hurry, or want to make this type of dumpling on short notice, you can achieve fairly good results with Bisquick. Instructions for making dumplings are on package.

❧ / BAVARIAN BREAD DUMPLINGS (*Bayrische Semmelknödel*)

10 TO 12 DUMPLINGS

10 to 12 slices stale bread, or 8 stale rolls (about the size of Parker House rolls), with crusts	3 slices bacon, diced
1 teaspoon salt	1 small onion, chopped
1½ cups lukewarm milk	1 tablespoon minced parsley
	1 teaspoon marjoram
	2 eggs
	breadcrumbs, if needed

Cut bread or rolls, with crusts, into small pieces, put in a bowl and sprinkle with salt. Pour lukewarm milk over bread and let soak for about an hour. If there is excess milk in bowl after that time, pour it off. Fry bacon in skillet with chopped onion until bacon is almost crisp and onion is soft and golden. Toss in parsley and marjoram and sauté 3 or 4 minutes. Add bacon, onion and herbs to bread mixture. Mix eggs in thoroughly. If dumpling batter is too soft to form, add breadcrumbs, a tablespoon at a time, until batter is firm enough. With wet hands or two wet tablespoons, form a test dumpling. Drop into boiling salted water and simmer, partially covered, for 20 minutes.

❧ / TYROLEAN DUMPLINGS (*Tiroler Knödel*)

ABOUT 10 DUMPLINGS

10 to 12 slices stale bread, or 8 stale rolls of the Parker House type, with crusts	½ pound smoked, cooked sausage such as frankfurter or knockwurst, finely diced
1 teaspoon salt	minced parsley
1 cup cold or lukewarm milk	basil (optional)
½ pound smoked ham, pork or pork loin (Canadian bacon), finely diced, or	2 eggs, lightly beaten
	½ to 1 cup flour, or as needed

Dice rolls or bread with crusts. Sprinkle with salt and cover with milk. Soak 1 hour, or until all milk is absorbed. If there is any excess milk in the bowl after that time, drain it off. Do not squeeze milk out of bread.

Mix diced meat into bread along with parsley and/or basil and lightly beaten eggs. Add flour gradually until batter can be shaped. With wet hands or two wet tablespoons, shape a large test dumpling, about the size of a lemon. Drop into boiling salted water. Reduce heat and simmer 20 minutes, or until dumpling rises to the surface. Remove from cooking liquid and break open with a fork to see if it is done. Cook other dumplings accordingly. Serve with any suitable meat roast with gravy, or as a main dish on Cooked Sauerkraut (page 276). Top with Brown Onion Sauce or Sweet-and-Sour Bacon Sauce, pages 333, 338.

❊ / *BOHEMIAN DUMPLINGS* (*Böhmische Knödel*)

6 TO 8 DUMPLINGS

3 white rolls or 6 slices white bread, with crusts	*2 cups flour, or as needed*
3 tablespoons minced onion	*2 eggs*
1 tablespoon minced parsley	*1 cup milk*
2 tablespoons butter or bacon fat	*½ teaspoon salt*

Dice rolls or bread with crusts. Sauté onions and parsley in butter or fat a few minutes, over low heat, until onions begin to soften. Add diced bread and fry slowly until bread and onions are light golden brown. Set aside to cool. Make a batter by beating together flour, eggs, milk and salt. Beat vigorously until air bubbles rise in batter. Add fried bread, onions and parsley and mix well. Let stand ½ hour at room temperature. If at the end of that time the dough is too thin to shape, add a little more flour as needed. Using two wet tablespoons, shape 1 dumpling, about the size of a lemon, and drop into boiling salted water. Reduce heat and simmer 15 to 20 minutes, or until dumpling rises to surface. Break open with a fork to test for doneness. Cook other dumplings accordingly. Drain well in a colander before serving. These dumplings are served whole with melted butter and/or sautéed onions and breadcrumbs browned in butter. They may also be sliced, browned in butter and served with same toppings.

✂ / COOKED POTATO DUMPLINGS (Gekochte Kartoffelklössel)

10 TO 12 DUMPLINGS

2 pounds baking potatoes
1 to 1½ cups flour
2 eggs, lightly beaten

1 teaspoon salt
25 to 30 croutons

Cook, peel and mash potatoes the day before you intend to make dumplings. Refrigerate until needed. Before cooking, mix with 1 cup flour, beaten eggs and salt. Add more flour, a tablespoonful at a time, if necessary, until dough is smooth and can be kneaded. Knead thoroughly on floured board until smooth. Shape dumplings with floured hands or two floured wooden spoons. Press a few croutons into center of each, molding dumpling around it. Cook test dumpling. Potato dumplings should be done in 10 minutes. They are always served with meat and gravy dishes, never in soup.

✂ / RAW POTATO DUMPLINGS (Rohe Kartoffelklösse)

12 TO 15 DUMPLINGS

1 large, or 2 small, day-old rolls, with crust
1 tablespoon rendered bacon, chicken or goose fat
2 pounds raw baking potatoes
1 pound baking potatoes, cooked, peeled and mashed

1 teaspoon salt
flour or potato flour, if needed
melted butter
toasted breadcrumbs

Cut roll in small pieces and sauté until golden in hot melted fat. Drain on paper toweling. Grate peeled raw potatoes into a pan of cold water, then put grated mass into a clean cloth and squeeze out all water thoroughly. Mix grated potatoes with mashed potatoes, add salt and knead dough on a floured board. If it is too sticky to knead, sprinkle with flour, a little at a time, until smooth enough to be handled. Form dumplings with floured hands or two floured wooden spoons. Press a few toasted bread cubes into the center of each dumpling and mold dough around them. Cook test dumpling. Serve with melted butter and sprinkle with toasted breadcrumbs. Serve with main dish, never in soup.

✣ / *THURINGIAN RAW POTATO DUMPLINGS* (*Rohe Kartoffelklösse, auf Thüringische Art*)

8 TO 10 DUMPLINGS

3 *pounds baking potatoes, peeled*
1 *cup milk*
1 *teaspoon salt*
2 *tablespoons butter*

5 *tablespoons semolina* (*farina or Cream of Wheat*)
20 *to 30 croutons*

Grate potatoes into a pan of cold water and squeeze dry in cheese cloth, as described in recipe above. Bring milk to a boil with salt, add butter, and when melted, sprinkle in semolina. Cook slowly and stir, until cereal forms a ball and leaves sides of pan. Mix cereal with grated potatoes. With floured hands, shape into dumplings the size of medium potatoes. Press a few croutons into center of each dumpling. Cook a test dumpling. These dumplings should be done in about 15 minutes. Serve with melted butter and breadcrumbs. They are best with meat and gravy and are never served in soup.

✣ / *SEMOLINA DUMPLINGS* (*Griessklösschen*)

FOR 6 TO 8 SERVINGS OF SOUP;
4 SERVINGS WHEN USED AS SIDE DISH WITH MAIN COURSE

1 *cup milk*
2 *tablespoons butter*
½ *teaspoon salt*
6 *tablespoons semolina* (*farina or Cream of Wheat*)

1 *egg, lightly beaten*
nutmeg

Bring milk to a boil with butter and salt, and sprinkle in semolina. Stir over low heat until mixture forms a ball and leaves the sides of the pot. Cool 10 minutes. Add egg and a dash or two of nutmeg and mix thoroughly. Let batter stand 15 or 20 minutes. With wet hands or two wet teaspoons, shape dumplings in small rounds and cook in boiling salted water. Cook a test dumpling. Semolina dumplings should be done in about 10 minutes. For a side dish, shape dumplings with tablespoons, rather than teaspoons, and serve with melted butter and toasted breadcrumbs.

❊ / COTTAGE CHEESE DUMPLINGS (*Topfenknödel*)

18 TO 22 DUMPLINGS

⅛ pound butter	*½ pound drained cottage cheese*
2 eggs, lightly beaten	*or pot cheese*
1 to 1¼ cups breadcrumbs	*1 teaspoon salt*

Cream butter and gradually add beaten eggs. Mix with 1 cup breadcrumbs. Rub cottage cheese or pot cheese through a strainer into breadcrumbs mixture, add salt and mix thoroughly. If mixture looks too soft to mold, add more breadcrumbs until it can be handled. An additional ¼ cup is all that should be necessary, unless your cottage cheese was too wet. Let batter stand at room temperature 1 hour. With floured hands, shape into small rounds, about ¾″ to 1″ in diameter. Cook in boiling salted water about 10 minutes. Drain and serve with melted butter. These are generally used as a main course for a light lunch, or are served in the afternoon or evening with coffee. Applesauce is often served with them but you could use other fruit sauces. They are also delicious when sprinkled with cinnamon and served with a dab of sour cream.

❊ / NAPKIN DUMPLING (*Serviettenkloss*)

6 SERVINGS

¼ cup melted butter	*4 eggs*
1 small onion, minced	*¼ cup milk*
1 tablespoon minced parsley	*½ teaspoon salt*
6 stale rolls (about the size of	*butter for napkin*
Parker House rolls), diced	*water*
with crust, or 7 slices stale	*salt*
white bread, diced with	
crust	

Heat butter in a large skillet and when hot and bubbling, add onion. Sauté and stir over moderate heat until onion is golden. Add parsley and sauté a minute or two. Stir in diced bread and fry over low heat until bread is golden brown. Place in large mixing bowl, scraping all melted butter from pan into bowl. Beat eggs together with milk and salt and pour over fried bread and onions. Soak 30 minutes and then knead well together until a fairly cohesive mass is formed.

Butter center of a large white napkin and place dough on it. Bring corners up together and tie with kitchen thread. Leave some room for dumpling to expand. Lower dumpling into a large pot of boiling salted water. The dumpling should be well covered by water. Cover pot and cook about 30 minutes. Remove from water, open napkin and see if dumpling is cooked through. If not, tie it up again and continue cooking until it tests done. Unwrap dumpling and if finished, place on heated platter. Break into 6 portions with two forks; do not cut with a knife. Serve topped with hot melted butter and browned breadcrumbs, with any meat stew and its gravy. It is often served topped with a cooked mixture of about 6 or 8 peeled, quartered pears and 2 pounds string or wax beans, flavored with lemon rind, vinegar, pepper and sugar, and sprinkled with crumbled crisp bacon. Or omit onion and parsley, flavor with nutmeg and serve with hot or cold fruit compote.

NOTE

Some cooks prefer to hang the dumpling instead of lowering it all the way into the pot. To do this, knot the napkin around a large wooden spoon, then hang the spoon across the top of the pot with the dumpling going into the boiling salted water.

/ *PLUM DUMPLINGS* (*Zwetschgenknödel*)

Plum dumplings are extremely popular throughout Germany in the summertime, when little blue Italian plums are in season. They are served with coffee, or with meats as side dishes. To make them, stone each plum and put a small cube of sugar in center of each. Enclose each plum in a casing of dough and steam as you would regular dumplings. They will cook in 10 to 15 minutes. To make dough, follow the recipe for Noodles, page 58, for Thuringian Raw Potato Dumplings, page 69, or for Cottage Cheese Dumplings, page 70. Roll or press dough on floured board and cut in pieces to fit around a plum. Press edges closed and cook in salted water, then brown with breadcrumbs in hot butter. I prefer these made of noodle or cottage cheese dough, but the potato dough version is the standard in Bavaria, and very popular.

❦ / VIENNESE APRICOT DUMPLINGS (*Wiener Marillenknödel*)

These are the same as Plum Dumplings above, except that raw fresh apricots are substituted for plums. These are always made with potato dough. Use recipe for Thuringian Raw Potato Dumplings, page 69, roll out dough to ¼″ thickness, cut in squares and wrap each around an apricot that has had its pit replaced by a cube of sugar. Pinch dough closed around each apricot and simmer in lightly salted water 12 to 15 minutes. Drain when done. Toss gently in skillet with hot butter mixed with zwieback crumbs and a little sugar, until dumplings have a golden coating. Serve hot.

❦ / SOUP MACAROONS (*Suppenmakronen*)

FOR 6 SERVINGS OF SOUP

2 egg whites
¾ cup sugar
1 cup unblanched almonds,
    finely ground

grated rind 1 lemon

Preheat oven to 400°. Grease a baking sheet with a little butter and sprinkle lightly with flour, shaking off excess. Beat egg whites until stiff enough to stand in peaks. Gradually beat in sugar, and then fold in ground almonds and grated lemon peel. Using two teaspoons, scoop mixture up and place in small rounds on baking sheet, leaving about 1″ space between each macaroon. Bake in middle of oven about 15 minutes, or until macaroons are golden brown. Serve in or with wine or fruit soup.

❦ / SNOW BALLS (*Schneeklösschen*)

FOR 6 SERVINGS OF SOUP

2 egg whites
2 tablespoons sugar

dash of cinnamon
boiling soup, stock or water

Beat egg whites into stiff peaks and gradually beat in sugar. Using two teaspoons, scoop up mixture and drop in tiny balls into boiling water, stock or fruit soup. Remove at once from heat and cover pot. Let stand on back or side of stove 5 to 10 minutes, or until snowballs are swelled up and are cooked through. Sprinkle with cinnamon and serve with fruit or wine soup, or Hot Beer Soup, page 47.

❊ / STEAMED SWEET DUMPLINGS (*Dampfnudeln*)

These great dumpling clouds can be served as a main course or as a dessert. Translated literally, their name means steamed noodles, but they are dumplings nonetheless. They are also known as Yeast Dumplings (Hefeknödel) and are very popular with the farmers of south and southeastern Germany.

4 TO 6 SERVINGS, 8 TO 12 DUMPLINGS

½ envelope powdered yeast
2 tablespoons lukewarm water
1 teaspoon sugar
¼ cup butter
5 tablespoons sugar
¼ teaspoon salt
2 eggs, lightly beaten
2 to 2½ cups flour

Cooking Liquid:

1½ cups milk
½ cup water
1½ tablespoons butter
salt
1 tablespoon sugar
1 teaspoon vanilla
strip of lemon rind

Dissolve yeast in lukewarm water, sprinkle with 1 teaspoon sugar and let stand 10 minutes in warm room. Cream butter with more sugar and salt and gradually blend in eggs. Pour yeast into butter-egg mixture and stir a little. Gradually add flour and stir well until mixture is firm and forms a mass. Turn onto floured board and knead well. Put ball of kneaded dough in clean bowl, cover lightly with a cloth and place in a warm room, out of drafts. Let dough rise until it has doubled in bulk. This should take about 1 hour. Punch it down and turn onto a floured board. With lightly floured hands, shape dough into balls, about 1″ in diameter, place in floured bowl, cover lightly with a cloth and let rise again ½ hour.

To steam these dumplings, use a large heavy pot with tight-fitting lid, either a 12″ skillet, a 5-quart Dutch oven or a covered roasting pan. In it pour all ingredients for cooking liquid. Place dumplings in pot so they are not too crowded, cover tightly and simmer over very low heat 30 minutes. Do not lift cover during that time, or steam will escape and dumplings will stop rising. Dumplings are done when liquid has all evaporated and you hear the sizzling of butter in pot. They are very good with meat and lots of gravy. They can also serve as the main course all by themselves, in which case a hole is made in top of each dumpling and in it is poured a little sauce of thick black prune jam melted in browned butter. When served as dessert following a meal that consisted of a hearty one-dish soup, Dampfnudeln are often served with either Fruit Sauce (page 407) or Vanilla Sauce (page 402).

Casserole Dinners or Meals Made in One Pot

(Eintopfgerichte)

🙰 🙰 🙰 🙰 🙰

No German cookbook would be complete without a chapter on Eintopfgerichte, meals that are "made in one pot." Certainly nothing could be better suited to the crowded schedules of modern American housewives. Eintopfgerichte are essentially what we know as casserole meals, although the German version is usually cooked on top of the stove instead of in the oven. Whether they are basically soups or stews, all these dishes are complete meals, including meat or fish, one or several vegetables, and a starch such as potatoes, rice, or dumplings, cooked right along with the rest of the ingredients.

Most Eintopfgerichte are stews, in which the meat, fish and vegetables are browned and braised in oil or fat for a few minutes, then flavored with herbs and spices, brought to a boil and then simmered slowly in a small amount of liquid. The long, slow simmering is the secret of the full flavor and rich sauces in this kind of cookery, and as the dish requires little attention once everything is in the pot, the housewife is free to go about her other tasks while dinner cooks. This type of cooking also means you can economize with tougher, less expensive cuts of meat, since the long, moist cooking will render them tender and flavorful.

To cook Eintopfgerichte (or any stews) most effectively, use a heavy stew pot, casserole or Dutch oven, with a low, tight-fitting lid. Enameled cast iron is the best material for this, for reasons explained on page xxv. You should have three such pots in 2-, 3- and 5-quart sizes (see page xxvi for illustration). The food and liquid should fill the pot as completely as possible, leaving just enough room at the top so the stew will not overflow as it cooks. This will ensure even heat during cooking. If you use a very large pot, or one with a high-domed lid, much of the heat will be dissipated in the empty area. Many people prefer to cook stews in the oven, where the pot is surrounded by even heat at all times. However, top-of-the-stove cooking produces a richer gravy requiring little thickening (if any), while oven cooking tends to make for a watery gravy.

Eintopfgerichte can be prepared hours or even days in advance. They can also be frozen for future use. If you do freeze any of these one-pot meals, I'd suggest you eliminate potatoes and rice (and certainly dumplings) and cook them when you are reheating the frozen stew. Starchy ingredients tend to decompose when they are frozen and then reheated, and will make the gravy thick and pasty.

In addition to the Eintopfgerichte in this chapter, a number of soups also serve as complete meals in Germany. Usually they are preceded by an appetizer such as herring, sliced ham or stuffed eggs, or are followed by a hearty dessert like hot pudding, apple pancakes, or fruit and cheese. Chapter II has many soups that fulfill all the necessary basic requirements for a one-pot meal.

⠺ / STEWED CHICKEN WITH DUMPLINGS
(*Hühnereintopf mit Mehlklössen*)

6 SERVINGS

1 *stewing fowl, 4 to 5 pounds,*
    cut into serving pieces
chicken gizzards, excluding
    the liver
salt
3 *tablespoons butter or ren-*
    dered chicken fat
1 *small onion, diced*
3 *tablespoons flour*
½ *knob celery root (celeriac),*
    scraped and cubed, or 1
    stalk celery with leaves
2 *parsley roots (petrouchka),*
    scraped and sliced, if avail-
    able

4 *carrots, scraped and sliced or*
    diced
8 *to 10 small white onions*
8 *peppercorns*
1 *small bay leaf*
    hot water or chicken stock
    to cover
1½ *cups shelled green peas*
    lemon juice to taste
    Flour Dumplings, page 65

Rinse chicken pieces and gizzards and dry thoroughly on paper toweling. Sprinkle with salt. Heat butter in a 3-quart casserole or stew pot and when hot and bubbling, add chicken pieces, gizzards and diced onion. Sauté slowly until chicken and onion take on bright golden color. Do not let them brown. Sprinkle with flour and continue cooking until flour is absorbed and begins to take on color. Add celery root or celery, parsley roots, carrots, white onions, peppercorns and bay leaf. Cover with hot water or stock. Bring to a boil, cover, reduce heat and simmer 1 to 2 hours, or until chicken begins to come away from bones. Add green peas for last 10 minutes of cooking time. Season with salt and pepper if necessary, and add lemon juice, a teaspoonful at a time, to taste. If stew gravy is not thick enough, mix 2 tablespoonsful flour with 4 tablespoons water, reduce stew to very slow simmer and stir flour-water mixture into it. Let it cook an additional 5 minutes.

Prepare dumplings, either plain or one of the variations, and drop from tablespoon into stew pot. Be sure dumplings rest on top of chicken and vegetables and do not sink into gravy. Cover, reduce heat and steam 15 minutes. Do not remove cover during that time. Parsley or caraway dumplings are especially good with this stew.

▓ / *MEAT AND VEGETABLE GOULASH* (*Gemüsegulyas*)

4 SERVINGS

1½ *pounds stewing beef or veal* *cut into 1½″ cubes*	2 *or 3 tablespoons flour*
1 *teaspoon salt*	1 *#2 can whole tomatoes*
½ *teaspoon pepper*	1 *cup hot water or beef stock*
2 *tablespoons butter, marga-* *rine or lard*	8 *to 10 small white onions*
1 *small onion, diced*	4 *carrots, scraped and sliced*
1 *tablespoon sweet paprika*	1 *pound potatoes, peeled and* *cubed*
	1 *cup shelled green peas*

Sprinkle beef or veal cubes with salt and pepper. Heat fat in a 2-quart stew pot and brown seasoned meat in it. Add diced onion and continue cooking over low heat until onion is soft and golden. Add paprika and sauté three or four minutes. Sprinkle with flour and stir until flour is absorbed. Add canned tomatoes with their liquid, and hot water or beef stock. Cover pot, bring to a boil, then reduce heat so stew simmers gently. After 45 minutes add onions, carrots and potatoes and simmer another 30 to 40 minutes, or until vegetables are done. Add green peas for last 10 minutes of cooking time. Season if necessary with more salt and pepper and serve.

/ *WESTPHALIAN BEEF STEW (Westfälischer Pfeffer-Potthast)*

This piquant beef and onion dish is a favorite all over the Westphalian countryside. It is always classified as a one-pot meal, although mashed potatoes are customarily served with it and, of course, are made separately.

4 SERVINGS

2 pounds short ribs of beef, cut in 2″ cubes with the bones
2 pounds onions, sliced
1 large bay leaf
8 cloves
1 strip lemon peel
3 to 4 cups water
½ cup freshly grated rye breadcrumbs (approximately)
1 to 2 tablespoons capers
lemon juice to taste
salt to taste
freshly ground black pepper

Put cut short ribs, onions, bay leaf, cloves and lemon peel in a 3-quart casserole or saucepan, and pour over them 3 or 4 cups cold water to cover. Bring to a boil, cover, reduce heat and simmer slowly 1 to 1½ hours, or until ribs are thoroughly done. Remove cover and with gravy simmering, gradually but steadily stir in breadcrumbs until thickened to desired consistency. Season with capers, a dash of lemon juice, salt and plenty of freshly ground black pepper. Serve with mashed potatoes.

/ *SPANISH FRICCO*

4 SERVINGS

2 tablespoons butter or margarine
2 pounds meat cut in 1″ cubes (beef, pork, veal or lamb, or preferably a combination of three of these, but always with pork included)
2 large onions, diced
1 teaspoon salt
½ teaspoon pepper
1 tablespoon sweet paprika
1 pound potatoes, peeled and cubed
1 cup water
½ cup sour cream

Heat butter or margarine in 2-quart casserole or stew pot and in it slowly brown cubed meat on all sides. Add onion and sauté until soft and golden. Sprinkle with salt, pepper and paprika and sauté 3 or 4 minutes. Add potatoes and water, cover, bring to a boil, reduce heat and simmer slowly 1 to 1½ hours, or until meat and potatoes are thoroughly cooked. Add sour cream and stir into sauce, cover and simmer another 10 minutes. Season with more salt, pepper and paprika if necessary.

VARIATION

This is also delicious when made with pickled pork. Use 1 pound pickled pork and no other meat.

❉ / *RICE-MEAT CASSEROLE* (*Reisfleischtopf*)

4 SERVINGS

2 tablespoons butter, margarine or bacon fat
2 pounds meat (veal, beef or lamb) cut in 1″ cubes
2 onions, diced
1 teaspoon salt
½ teaspoon pepper

1 tablespoon sweet paprika
1 small can tomato sauce
3 to 4 cups water or meat stock
1 cup converted rice
2 tablespoons grated Parmesan cheese
minced parsley

Heat fat in a 2-quart stew pot or casserole and in it slowly brown cubed meat on all sides. Add onion and sauté slowly until it softens and begins to turn golden. Sprinkle with salt, pepper and paprika and sauté 3 or 4 minutes. Add tomato sauce and 3 cups of water, or stock, bring to a boil and simmer 30 minutes. Add another cup of liquid, bring to a boil and sprinkle in rice. Cover and simmer 25 to 35 minutes longer, until rice is soft and liquid is absorbed. Season to taste with additional salt, pepper and paprika, if necessary. Sprinkle with grated cheese and minced parsley before serving.

❉ / *BAKED BARLEY CASSEROLE* (*Graupeneintopf*)

4 SERVINGS

2 tablespoons butter
1 onion, diced
½ knob celery root (celeriac), peeled and finely diced

2 pounds ground meat (beef, lamb or pork)
2 cups pearl barley, washed and drained

3 to 5 cups hot meat stock	1 to 2 tablespoons grated Parme-
4 tablespoons tomato purée	san or Cheddar cheese
salt and pepper	
minced parsley	

Melt butter in a 2-quart ovenproof casserole. Sauté onion and celery root until they begin to soften and take on color. Add ground meat and stir just long enough for it to lose its bright red color, about 3 or 4 minutes should do. Add barley, stir through with meat and vegetables and cover with 3 cups hot stock. Mix in tomato purée. Cover casserole and bake in 325° oven 40 minutes. Remove cover and if barley is dry, add more stock. Cover and bake another 40 minutes. Season with salt and pepper. Before serving, sprinkle with parsley and cheese.

VARIATION

This is also delicious when made with knockwurst. Follow recipe but eliminate ground meat. Mix 4 skinned, sliced knockwursts into barley for last 40 minutes of cooking time. Slices should be about 1″ thick.

⊠ / LAMB WITH TOMATOES OR LEEKS (*Lamm mit Tomaten oder Lauchen*)

4 SERVINGS

2 pounds lean, boneless stew-ing lamb cut in 1½″ cubes	2 pounds peeled tomatoes, halved, or 2 pounds leeks, well washed and cut into 2″ pieces
1 teaspoon salt	
½ teaspoon pepper	1 to 2 cups water
2 tablespoons butter, marga-rine or lard	½ cup sour cream
3 onions, diced	2 tablespoons minced parsley
1 tablespoon paprika	
1 pound potatoes, peeled and cubed	

Sprinkle cubed lamb with salt and pepper. Melt fat in a stew pot and when it is hot, brown seasoned lamb. Add diced onion and continue cooking slowly until soft and golden. Sprinkle with paprika and sauté 3 or 4 minutes. Add potatoes, tomatoes or leeks, and water to half cover. Cover pot, bring to a boil, reduce heat and simmer slowly about 1½ hours. Just before serving, stir in sour cream and minced parsley. Heat through, season to taste and serve.

VARIATION

When mutton is used in place of lamb for this dish, it requires 15 to 30 minutes' additional cooking time.

❧ / *SZEGED GOULASH* (*Szegediner Gulyas*)

This dish originated in Szeged, a Hungarian city famous for its paprika It has become a standard dish throughout Central Europe and most of Germany.

4 TO 6 SERVINGS

2 pounds stewing pork, cut into 1¼" cubes
1 teaspoon salt
½ teaspoon pepper
2 tablespoons lard or butter
3 onions, diced
2 tablespoons sweet paprika
2 cloves of garlic
1 cup of water

1 pound fresh or canned sauerkraut
1 pound potatoes, peeled, cut in 1½" cubes or cut into ½"-thick slices
1 tablespoon caraway seeds
1 tablespoon flour
½ cup sour cream

Sprinkle pork with salt and pepper. Heat fat and in it brown pork cubes slowly on all sides. Add diced onion and cook slowly until soft and golden. Sprinkle with paprika and sauté 3 or 4 minutes. Add garlic and water, cover and simmer slowly 25 minutes. If sauerkraut is very sharply flavored, rinse once or twice and drain. Add it to the pork along with potatoes and caraway seeds. Cover, bring to a boil, reduce heat and simmer 1 hour, or until potatoes are done. Blend flour into sour cream and pour over sauerkraut and pork, shaking pot from side to side so cream will work its way through. Cover and simmer 10 minutes, or until entire goulash is thoroughly heated. Season to taste and serve.

VARIATIONS

1. Potatoes can be boiled separately in salted water and served along with this dish. Strictly speaking, it is not then a "one pot" meal, but it will be easier to reheat leftovers and the sauerkraut will be less inclined to become pasty.
2. A peeled and sliced apple can be added to the sauerkraut.
3. In Bavaria, 1 tablespoon tomato purée is mixed into and added with sour cream.

✺ / PORK CHOPS AND SAUERKRAUT
(*Schweinekotelette und Sauerkraut*)

2 TO 4 SERVINGS

4 *pork chops, about 1" thick*
salt and pepper
2 *tablespoons lard, butter or mar-*
garine
1 *medium-sized onion, diced*
2 *medium-sized green apples,*
pared and diced

1 *pound fresh or canned sauer-*
kraut, rinsed and drained
1 *pound potatoes, peeled and*
sliced ¼" to ½" thick
1 *cup hot meat stock*
½ *cup dry white wine (optional)*

Sprinkle pork chops all over with salt and pepper. Heat fat in a casserole and brown pork chops slowly on both sides. Remove chops and add diced onions and apples to hot fat. Sauté slowly until onions are soft and slightly yellow and apples have begun to take on color. Remove apple and onion mixture and reserve. Sauté drained sauerkraut in fat 5 or 10 minutes, then remove from pot. Put a layer of kraut on bottom of casserole, then a layer of apple-onion mixture, all the potatoes, then another of kraut, apples and onions and finally chops. Pour hot stock over this and wine if you are using it. Cover tightly and bake in 375° oven 45 minutes to 1 hour.

VARIATIONS

1. This casserole can also be cooked on top of stove. If you prefer that method, put pork chops between layers of sauerkraut so they will cook through. Simmer casserole about 1¼ to 1½ hours.
2. If you prefer a slightly thickened sauce, grate one medium-sized potato into kraut for last 20 or 30 minutes of cooking.
3. You can eliminate potatoes from recipe and serve boiled potatoes with it on the side.
4. This dish can be made with other meats as well, generally those that are partially or completely precooked. A parboiled smoked ham butt, a tenderized ham steak, spareribs, a piece of the smoked pork loin called Kasseler Rippchen, bacon either in thick slices or cubes, corned beef, or sausages—especially frankfurters, knockwurst or fresh liverwurst—can be cooked right along with the sauerkraut, with or without potatoes. Several meats are often cooked together and are then sliced and served in combination, in the manner of the Alsatian choucroute garnie or the Swiss Bernerplatte. In Germany, this kind of meal goes by several different names. Frankfurt is known for its Kasseler Rippchen with kraut as well as for its Frankfurter Sauerkrautplatte, which usually includes a strip of bacon, a frankfurter and a piece of the pork loin (Rippchen), along with the kraut and potato. In many parts of Germany such a dish is known as Geräuchertes mit Kraut, meaning

smoked meats with kraut, while in others it is called a Schlachtplatte, a butcher's plate. In Swabia, a Schlachtplatte generally includes Spätzle (page 60) instead of potatoes, and some Pea Purée (page 301), made with yellow peas, is mixed with it before it is served.

░ / *WESTPHALIAN BLIND HEN* (*Westfälisches Blindhuhn*)

The following two bacon-bean-and-pear casseroles are first cousins, one being a specialty in Westphalia, the other in Hamburg and throughout Schleswig-Holstein. Both can be made with bacon or ham or a combination of the two.

4 SERVINGS

½ *pound dried white beans*
1 *teaspoon salt*
½ *to* ¾ *pound thickly sliced bacon*
1 *pound string beans, cut in 1″ or 2″ pieces*

3 *carrots, scraped and diced*
2 *large apples, pared and sliced*
3 *pears, pared and sliced*
1 *pound potatoes, peeled and cubed*

Soak dried white beans overnight or parboil according to instructions on package. Cook in salted water to cover in a 3-quart casserole or stew pot about 30 to 40 minutes. Cut bacon slices into thirds, add to beans, cover and cook another 30 minutes. Add prepared string beans, carrots, apples, pears and potatoes, bring to a boil and reduce heat and simmer, covered, another 30 minutes, or until vegetables are done. Season with salt and pepper before serving.

VARIATION

To give this dish a crusty topping before serving, it can be baked a few minutes in oven after it has finished cooking. Remove cover and top with a layer of buttered breadcrumbs. Place in 400° oven 10 to 20 minutes, or until topping is nicely browned.

❧ / BEANS, PEARS AND BACON, HAMBURG STYLE
(*Bohnen, Birnen und Speck, auf Hamburger Art*)

4 SERVINGS

1 pound dried white beans
1 pound smoked bacon, unsliced
2 tablespoons butter or margarine
3 or 4 pears, peeled and cubed

1 teaspoon salt
½ teaspoon pepper
3 cups water
minced parsley

Soak dried beans overnight, or parboil according to instructions on package. Cut bacon in 1″ to 1¼″ cubes. Melt butter or margarine in a 3-quart casserole or stew pot and in it slowly brown bacon cubes on all sides. Drain beans if you have soaked or parboiled them and add to pot with browned bacon and fat. Add cut pears, salt and pepper and stir through. Add water, cover tightly, bring to a boil, reduce heat and simmer slowly 1 to 1½ hours, or until beans are done. The pears will cook apart and should be stirred through bean mixture before serving. Season with more salt and pepper if necessary and sprinkle with parsley before serving.

❧ / PICHELSTEINER MEAT (*Pichelsteiner Fleisch*)

Pichelsteiner is a favorite Bavarian stew, most often made with a combination of beef and pork, but often with veal or mutton as well, and there are even Pichelsteiners of fish or vegetables. As with bouillabaisse, there is a running argument as to what goes into this stew to make it truly Pichelsteiner. Everyone seems to agree that the root vegetables are essential, and the following recipes and variations should cover all of the versions. Pichelsteiner was the favorite Bavarian dish of the Iron Chancellor, Bismarck; the meaning of its name and its origin have been virtually impossible to track down. Whatever its origin, it is one of the most savory of "one pot" meals.

6 TO 8 SERVINGS

1½ pounds stewing beef, cut in
1″ cubes
1½ pounds stewing pork, cut in
1″ cubes
2 teaspoons salt

½ to 1 teaspoon pepper
3 tablespoons beef marrow, butter or lard (preferably marrow)
2 large onions, diced

3 *pounds old potatoes, peeled and cubed*

1 *large knob celery root (celeriac), peeled and cubed*

3 *or 4 carrots, scraped and sliced*

2 *parsley roots (petrouchka), scraped and sliced*

2 *to 3 cups hot meat stock or water*

minced parsley

Sprinkle beef and pork with salt and pepper. Heat marrow or fat in a 3-quart stew pot and when hot, add meat and diced onion. Cook over moderate heat until meat is lightly browned and onions are deep yellow. Add potatoes and vegetables, cover, and braise about 15 minutes. Add hot water or meat stock, cover, bring to boiling point, reduce heat, and let simmer slowly about 1¼ to 1½ hours. Season with more salt and pepper if necessary. Sprinkle with minced fresh parsley just before serving.

VARIATIONS

1. There are those who say it isn't Pichelsteiner unless it includes a half-head of savoy or white cabbage, a couple of dozen Brussels sprouts or a small head of cauliflower. If any of these candidates interest you, either alone or in combination, by all means add them. The cabbage should be separated into leaves, the Brussels sprouts left whole, the cauliflower broken into flowerets. Add any or all of these vegetables for last ½ hour of cooking time and follow above master recipe. I prefer Pichelsteiner without any of these strong-flavored additions.

2. Other Pichelsteiner fans like to add 1 pound peeled and quartered tomatoes or one #2 can tomatoes with liquid, 1 pound whole baby string beans, 2 sliced carrots and 2 cups shelled green peas to the stew. In this case, eliminate the potatoes and other vegetables as well as the water and stock from master recipe above. Stir in 1 cup sour cream just before serving. Purists say this becomes Tomatenfleisch (Tomato Meat) and is not really Pichelsteiner at all, but it tastes delicious, no matter what you call it.

✓ / PICHELSTEINER FISH (*Pichelsteiner Fisch*)

4 SERVINGS

2 *pounds filets of white, firm-fleshed fish, such as sole*

lemon juice or white vinegar

salt

3 *slices bacon, coarsely chopped or diced*

1 *onion, diced*

2 *carrots, scraped and diced*

½ *knob celery, peeled and diced*

2 *leeks, washed and thinly sliced*

1½ pounds potatoes, peeled and   1 to 2 cups water
    cut into ½" slices   minced parsley
1 to 2 teaspoons paprika

Rinse fish filets and sprinkle on both sides with lemon juice or vinegar, and salt. Marinate 30 minutes. Heat bacon in a 2-quart casserole. When it begins to fry and melt, add vegetables and potatoes and sauté together until they take on color and soften. Sprinkle with paprika and sauté 3 or 4 minutes. Add water and bring to a boil. Cut fish filets into large crosswise slices and add to vegetables and potatoes. Lay fish on top of vegetables and let sauce simmer rapidly, uncovered, 15 minutes. Cover pot, reduce heat and simmer slowly another 15 minutes. Sprinkle with parsley before serving.

❧ / VEGETABLE PICHELSTEINER
(*Gemüsepichelsteiner*)

6 TO 8 SERVINGS

2 tablespoons butter or margarine
2 pounds mixed seasonal vegetables to include as many of the following as possible:
  4 carrots, scraped and sliced
  4 parsley roots, scraped and sliced
  1 small knob celery root, peeled and diced
  2 leeks, well washed and sliced
  1 small cauliflower broken into flowerets

½ pound green peas
¼ pound string beans, cut into 1" pieces
¼ head white or savoy cabbage, sliced as for cole slaw
1½ to 2 pounds potatoes, peeled and sliced
salt to taste
2 cups water or stock
minced parsley

Melt butter or margarine in a 3-quart casserole or stew pot and add vegetables in layers, beginning with first four root vegetables. Sprinkle lightly with salt, add other vegetables, also in layers, and wind up with a top layer of potatoes. Sprinkle with a little salt and pour water or stock over contents of casserole. Cover tightly, bring to a boil, reduce heat and simmer slowly 1 hour, or until all vegetables are thoroughly cooked. Season with salt, if necessary, and sprinkle with minced parsley before serving. Although this makes a more than adequate main course as is, it can also be used as the vegetable course to be served with a simple entree of broiled chicken or meat.

V

Egg Dishes
and Cheese Dishes

(Eierspeisen und Käsespeisen)

❈ ❈ ❈ ❈ ❈

Eggs are extremely popular in Germany, not only as garnishes and enrichments for other foods, but for themselves. Although soft-cooked eggs in pretty porcelain cups are the only kind that appear at breakfast, from then on and for the rest of the day, the preparations become far more imaginative and varied. For second breakfasts, afternoon snacks, late cold suppers and as appetizers, Germans like stuffed hard-cooked eggs; and in the Black Forest, there is an almost endless array of egg salads.

For luncheon or dinner entrees, eggs are combined with cheese, meats, fish or vegetables to turn them into hearty main courses. As one might expect, the basic egg preparations are the same in Germany as anywhere else. Differences lie in the foods and flavorings combined with these basic egg preparations to make them interesting and different.

Raw egg yolks (rohe Eigelb) are regarded as the most efficacious morning-after cures for a Katzenjammer—the German hangover that is remarkably like our own. To make the yolks more palatable and to give them extra restorative powers, they may be whipped up with a little red wine. An egg yolk is sometimes blended with a tablespoonful of honey, then stirred into a cup of warm milk and spiked with a tablespoonful or two of brandy—a kind of warm eggnog that is a complete and exhilarating breakfast.

Both hard-cooked eggs (hartgekochte Eier) and poached eggs, called "lost" (or verlorene Eier), are served topped with cheese, mushroom or tomato sauce. One of the sauces may be spooned over them, or they may be baked in the sauce for a few minutes before serving.

Fried eggs, known as "mirror" or Spiegeleier, are favorites on German menus. Usually three are served as the standard portion and the eggs may be accompanied by fried ham or bacon, or they may be topped with a sprinkling of grated Swiss cheese that has cooked with them, or dressed with a layer of onion rings sautéed separately in butter until soft and golden.

Scrambled eggs (Rühreier), literally, "stirred" eggs, are flavored with minced fresh herbs such as chives or parsley, cheese, caraway seeds, flecks of fried bacon or cooked ham, slices of sausages or finely diced cooked vegetables. They are often served on top of slices of cold ham or tongue and are popular garnishes for such dishes as smoked eel, smoked kippers and creamed mushrooms.

French-style omelettes are as important in Germany as they are everywhere else, and they are preferred with the same foods and flavorings as described above for scrambled eggs. But German egg cookery reaches its real genius with other types of egg pancakes—called Eierkuchen or Pfannkuchen, egg cakes or pancakes. The soufflé omelette (Schaumomelett) is a favorite, and for this the stiffly beaten egg white is added to the egg yolk and flavorings, and then cooked on top of the stove, in the oven, or a combination of both. Flour is sometimes added to the French or soufflé omelettes to make them more like spongy cakes, and the German love for crepes and large, sweet, thin pancakes, with or without apples, is too well known to need elaborating here.

Soufflés (Aufläufe) are common delights on German tables, and again, the most popular versions are the same as one finds throughout Europe: cheese and ham soufflés as main courses; chocolate, chestnut, lemon and Grand Marnier soufflés for dessert. As with the rest of the egg recipes in this chapter, I have included only those combinations that seem especially German.

✂ / CHEESE (*Käse*)

Germany produces a number of fine cheeses, some of which are exported to this country. But if the German varieties are not available where you live, you will certainly be able to get all the general types, either made in the United States or imported from other countries. There is an Emmenthaler, close to a Swiss Gruyère, a fragrant semi-soft Tilsiter, a fine buttery Münster, and several hard, tangy beer cheeses. Green-herbed Sago and Italian Parmesan are often grated into German dishes to make them more savory. When it comes to ripening cheeses, Germans prefer those that are strong-tasting and very strong-smelling. Allgäuer, Limburger and the French-sounding, strictly German Romadour are among these along with hand cheese (Handkäse) that may well be the world's worst-smelling cheese. A cheese platter is a favorite dessert after a cold meal (never after a hot one), and sliced cheeses are often served as complete light meals in themselves for breakfast, lunch, mid-afternoon or late at night. Gervais and Camembert are on all restaurant menus for dessert, prepared as described on page 18.

The most popular cheese for cooking is pot cheese (Topfen) or its creamed derivative, cottage cheese (Quark). These can be used interchangeably in most recipes, as long as you allow for the difference in moisture between them when adding other liquids. Since cottage cheese is a little easier to get in this country, I have indicated it where possible in the recipes that follow. If you *can* get pot cheese, use it and add a little more of whatever liquid is called for in the recipe. Weisskäse or Kümmelkäse is cottage or pot cheese with caraway seeds added, and in the Harz mountains this is allowed to ripen in crocks until it becomes highly fragrant, to put it mildly. In Saxony, pot cheese is mixed with minced chives and onions or scallions, and is then stirred into thick sour cream to make a dressing for boiled potatoes that are served hot, with or without jackets.

There are also dozens of processed cheeses imported from Germany, many of them blended with wines, brandies, herbs, smoked ham and many other such flavorings. German processed cheeses are not any better than other processed cheese, but this may be a personal blind spot, so perhaps you should try them for yourself.

⚄ / *FRIED EGGS WITH HAM* (*Spiegeleier mit Schinken*)

Nowhere in the world can you get better ham and eggs than in Germany, and for some reason or other this dish always seems at its best in Hamburg. It is an impression that has been corroborated on five separate visits to that city, each several years apart. Ham and eggs are always fried together, pancake style, in Germany, and to do this successfully, you must let the eggs fry slowly, or they will not cook thoroughly.

1 SERVING

2 tablespoons butter
2 or 3 slices precooked ham,
    about 1/4" thick

3 eggs (the standard portion in
    Germany)
salt and pepper

Heat 1 tablespoon butter in a 9" skillet and slowly fry ham slices, turning so both sides are slightly browned. Add other tablespoonful of butter and when hot and bubbling, break eggs over ham slices. Sprinkle lightly with salt and pepper and fry slowly so that eggs will be thoroughly cooked, basting several times with the hot butter.

❧ / SWABIAN SCRAMBLED EGGS WITH ONIONS AND CROUTONS (*Schwäbische Rühreier*)

1 SERVING

1 tablespoon butter
1 slice white bread without crust, diced
2 teaspoons finely minced onion

2 eggs, lightly beaten with 1 tablespoon milk
salt and pepper

Heat butter in an 8″ skillet and slowly fry diced bread and onion until golden. Season eggs with a few dashes of salt and pepper and pour into skillet over bread and onion. Scramble egg mixture over low heat until egg is cooked as you like it.

❧ / POACHED EGGS IN MUSTARD SAUCE (*Verlorene Eier in Senfsosse*)

2 TO 4 SERVINGS

4 eggs
3 cups water
2 tablespoons vinegar
1 tablespoon butter
1 scant tablespoon flour
1 tablespoon prepared mustard

1 tablespoon sour cream
salt and pepper
nutmeg
4 slices toast
minced chives

Poach eggs in water to which vinegar has been added. When eggs are done, remove with a slotted spoon and place on warm plate. Reserve cooking water. Melt butter in small saucepan and when hot and bubbling, blend in flour and mustard. Gradually add 1 cup water in which eggs were poached, stirring constantly over low heat. Blend in sour cream, and season to taste with salt, pepper and nutmeg. Cook until sauce is smooth and thickened. Place a poached egg on each slice of toast and cover with mustard sauce. Sprinkle with chives and serve. Serve 2 eggs to a portion for an entree; 1 egg to a portion as an appetizer.

❈ / *POACHED EGGS IN HAM POCKETS* (*Verlorene Eier in Schinkentaschen*)

1 SERVING

2 *slices cooked ham cut to fit poaching cups*
1 *teaspoon butter (approximately)*
2 *eggs*
2 *slices toast, or* 1 *English muffin, split and toasted*

4 *or* 5 *asparagus tips, cooked*
4 *or* 5 *tablespoons Hollandaise, White or Cheese Sauce, pages* 341, 331, 333

The thinly sliced ham should be trimmed to fit round cups of egg poacher. Place cups in frame and bring water to boiling point. Add about ½ teaspoon butter to each egg cup, cover pan and simmer until butter melts. Line each cup with slice of ham and gently break egg over ham. Cover and poach eggs as you usually would—ideally, until whites are set and yolks still runny. Butter toast or muffin halves. Invert egg cup over each slice and let egg and ham drop onto toast, ham side up. Arrange asparagus tips around toast and spoon sauce over all.

❈ / *FARMERS' OMELETTE* (*Bauernomelett*)

3 TO 4 SERVINGS

¼ *cup diced bacon (use unsliced bacon for this)*
1 *small onion, finely diced*
3 *medium-sized potatoes, boiled, peeled and cut into small cubes*

salt and pepper
1 *tablespoon minced parsley*
5 *eggs, lightly beaten with* 2 *tablespoons milk*

Put bacon in a cold 9″ or 10″ skillet and fry slowly. When lightly browned on all sides, add onion and continue frying slowly until onion begins to soften and take on color. Add potatoes and sprinkle lightly with salt, pepper and parsley. Sauté slowly, stirring carefully with a wooden spoon or spatula so potatoes do not break apart. When potatoes begin to turn golden brown, pour egg-milk mixture into skillet. Cook over high heat and with fork move cooked edges of omelette away from sides and toward center of pan, tilting pan so that uncooked egg will run to bottom. Continue in this way until egg is completely set. This omelette may be turned over and lightly browned on the top side, or it may be folded in half and served in the manner of a French omelette, or eggs can be added to sautéed bacon-onion-potato mixture and the whole thing then baked in oven. If you prefer, this mixture can be lightly scrambled instead of being cooked as an omelette.

✂ / TYROLEAN OMELETTE (*Tiroler Omelett*)

2 SERVINGS

2 teaspoons butter
2 slices bacon, coarsely chopped
2 Bratwursts or 4 link pork sausages, sliced
¼ cup minced parsley

4 eggs lightly beaten with a dash of salt and 2 tablespoons of milk
1 large tomato, thinly sliced

Heat butter in a 9″ or 10″ skillet and in it fry bacon until it begins to turn brown. Add Bratwurst or link sausage slices and fry slowly until browned on both sides. Sprinkle with half the parsley, sauté a minute or two, then pour egg mixture into skillet. Cook over high heat, and with a fork move cooked edges of omelette away from sides and toward center of pan, tilting pan so that uncooked egg will run over to bottom. When egg is set, slide omelette onto a heated platter or divide it in half and serve on heated individual serving plates. Top with tomato slices, a light sprinkling of salt and rest of parsley.

✂ / ROYAL OMELETTE (*Königinomelett*)

This omelette is one that is served everywhere in Germany. It is a French-style omelette filled with a chicken ragout, page 25.

✂ / OMELETTE SOUFFLÉ (*Schaumomelett*)

2 TO 4 SERVINGS

4 egg yolks
2 tablespoons sugar
salt
grated rind of 1 lemon

4 egg whites
1 tablespoon butter
fruit sauce or preserves

Beat egg yolks with sugar, a dash of salt and grated lemon rind. Beat egg whites to a stiff snow and fold into yolk mixture. Heat butter in a 9″ skillet and when it begins to bubble, add egg mixture. Cook slowly until bottom of omelette is golden brown. You may cover pan until top of omelette is thoroughly cooked, or you may serve it with top slightly runny, as with a regular French omelette. You may also turn it over if you like it browned on both sides. Spread with fruit sauce or preserves. Apricot, strawberry or raspberry preserves are especially good with this. Fold in half and serve.

VARIATIONS

1. To make a Cheese Soufflé Omelette, add 2 tablespoons grated Cheddar, Parmesan or Gruyère cheese to egg-yolk mixture and eliminate lemon rind and sugar. A dash of cayenne may be added for seasoning.
2. Finely minced parsley and/or chives may be added to egg-yolk mixture, in which case you would also eliminate sugar and lemon rind and add an extra dash of salt.
3. To make a Chocolate Soufflé Omelette, stir 2 ounces cooled melted bittersweet chocolate that has been mixed with two tablespoons water into egg-yolk mixture. Eliminate lemon rind and salt and adjust amount of sugar to taste. Finish this omelette either by covering it or by putting it in 400° oven. Do not turn it over. Serve sprinkled with granulated sugar, with whipped cream or Chocolate Sauce, page 403.

/ *HAZELNUT OMELETTE* (*Haselnussomelett*)

1 TO 2 SERVINGS

3 tablespoons flour
¼ teaspoon salt
1 cup milk
1 egg yolk
1 tablespoon sugar
2 tablespoons finely ground hazelnuts
1 egg white

Mix flour and salt with milk and stir in egg yolk, sugar and hazelnuts. Beat egg white to a stiff snow and fold into egg-yolk-nut mixture. Heat butter in an 8″ skillet and when it begins to bubble, add omelette mixture. Cook slowly until lightly browned on bottom. Omelette may then be turned over and browned on other side, or you may finish it off by placing it in a 400° oven for a few minutes, or until top is golden brown. If so, be sure handle of your skillet is not plastic.

✂ / BAKED EGGS WITH CHEESE AND BACON
(Eier, auf Lothringer Art)

This dish is a wonderful hot appetizer or an entree for a light luncheon or dinner. It is also perfect for a company brunch or midnight supper. It is a convenient "meal in one baking dish" and needs only a crisp salad and some coffee, beer or white wine to make it complete.

3 TO 6 SERVINGS

butter
6 slices white bread
12 slices bacon, crisply fried and drained, or 12 slices Canadian bacon, fried and drained

6 slices Swiss cheese, cut to cover bread slices
6 eggs
6 tablespoons sweet cream
salt and pepper
minced chives

Heat oven to 375°. Butter a rectangular baking dish well, then cover bottom with bread slices, arranged side by side in single layer. Place 2 strips bacon, or 2 slices Canadian bacon, on each piece and cover with cheese slice. Break eggs over slices. Pour a little cream around yolk of each egg, sprinkle lightly with salt and pepper and bake until eggs are set, 10 to 20 minutes. Sprinkle with chives and serve. You may also prepare and serve these eggs in individual open bakers, such as shirred-egg dishes.

✂ / SOUR CREAM OR COTTAGE CHEESE PANCAKES
(Sauerrahm- oder Quarkpfannkuchen)

6 TO 8 PANCAKES

1 cup sour cream or cottage cheese
½ teaspoon salt
2 to 6 tablespoons milk

3 egg yolks
¾ cup flour
3 egg whites
1 to 2 tablespoons butter

Sprinkle sour cream or cottage cheese with salt and gradually stir in milk until mixture is consistency of heavy sweet cream. If you are using sour cream, 2 to 4 tablespoonfuls milk will be enough; cottage cheese may require 4 to 6. Beat in egg yolks and add flour, a little at a time, stirring until batter is smooth between each addition. Beat egg whites to a stiff snow and fold into cream and egg yolk mixture. Melt 1 tablespoon butter in 10″ skillet. For each pancake, drop about ½ cup batter into hot butter. Space pancakes 3 to 4 inches apart. Fry slowly until underside is golden brown and pancake begins to puff up. Turn and brown other side. Add more butter to skillet and fry remaining batter. If you have a very large skillet, melt all the butter at once and fry 6 to 8 pancakes in a single shift. These pancakes may be served as a light luncheon entree. They can be garnished with a dab of sour cream and accompanied by a crisp green salad. They are also good sprinkled with cinnamon and sugar and served as dinner dessert or with afternoon coffee.

VARIATIONS

1.   Add 1 tablespoonful sugar and grated rind of ½ lemon to batter. Sprinkle finished pancakes with sugar and serve with fresh or preserved fruit sauce.

2.   For Apple Sour Cream Pancakes, peel 1 large or 2 small apples, cut into small cubes and sauté in hot butter 3 or 4 minutes, or until apples begin to take on color. Add apple cubes to egg-yolk-cream mixture before folding in egg whites. Fry as directed in master recipe and serve sprinkled with sugar and cinnamon.

3.   Yogurt may be substituted for sour cream. Less milk will be needed in that case; 1 or 2 tablespoonfuls will do.

⚏ / *SWABIAN CHEESE SPÄTZLE* (*Schwäbisches Käse-spätzle*)

6 SERVINGS

Spätzle, page 60
1 large onion, diced
2 to 4 tablespoons butter

3 tablespoons grated Parmesan
     or Gruyère cheese
pepper

Make Spätzle. Drain well. Sauté diced onion in hot butter until golden brown. Heat an open baker or serving bowl. Place in it a layer of Spätzle, sprinkle with half the grated cheese and a little pepper; add another layer of Spätzle and then rest of cheese and a little more pepper. Top with a fairly thick layer of browned onion and butter in which it was fried. Serve at once. If you like, dish can be placed in 400° oven for a few minutes, or until cheese has melted slightly. Top with onions after you remove Spätzle from oven.

✂ / POOR KNIGHTS (*Arme Ritter*)

Literally translated, Arme Ritter means Poor Knights; it is the dish we know better as French toast, although the German version differs from our own in that it is lightly coated with breadcrumbs before being fried. For best results, buy the very best white bread you can get, unsliced, and cut it thickly by hand. In Germany, crusty white rolls are often used for this, and you will also get excellent results with the golden, braided loaf bread you can find in Central European and Jewish bakeries. Poor Knights are often served with apple slices that have been pared and lightly browned in butter.

4 TO 8 SERVINGS

3 egg yolks
2 cups milk
1 tablespoon sugar
salt
grated rind 1 lemon
8 to 10 1"-thick slices stale white
    bread, with crusts, or 6 to 8
    stale rolls, cut into 1"-thick
    slices

3 egg whites lightly beaten with
    2 tablespoons water
breadcrumbs
3 to 4 tablespoons butter
cinnamon
sugar
sautéed apple slices (optional)

Beat egg yolks with milk, sugar, a dash of salt and lemon rind. Soak bread slices in egg-milk mixture until all liquid is absorbed. Turn slices once during soaking so bread will be evenly saturated. Carefully dip each bread slice into egg-white and water mixture and then into breadcrumbs, coating slices on both sides. Heat butter in a large skillet and slowly fry bread slices, browning first on one side and then the other. Sprinkle with cinnamon and granulated sugar just before serving. Top with sautéed apple slices if you are using them. If your skillet is too small to allow you to cook all bread slices at once, fry them in two shifts. In that case, do not soak all the slices at one time. Soak and coat second batch while first is frying, or bread will become too soggy to handle.

VARIATIONS

1. For Carthusian Dumplings (Karthäuser Klösse): Use Parker House-type rolls; grate crust off each roll, then cut in half lengthwise. Flavor egg-milk mixture with ½ teaspoon almond extract or 5 grated bitter almonds. After rolls are dipped, dredge with crumbs of grated crust. If you like, slices can be studded with slivered, blanched untoasted sweet almonds. Fry as directed and while still hot, dredge on all sides with half-and-half mixture of cinnamon and sugar.

2. For Drunken Maidens or Knights (Versoffene Jungfern oder Ritter): Using Parker House-type rolls, grate crust off rolls and cut in half

lengthwise. Soak, dredge and fry. While slices fry, heat 1½ cups red wine with 1 stick cinnamon and a little sugar to taste. Pour this hot wine over fried bread slices, and serve while hot in deep dishes. To make this even more elaborate, cut bread slices can be spread on one side with a little Preiselbeeren, cranberry or currant preserves, not jelly. Sandwich coated sides together in pairs. Dip each sandwich into egg batter, dredge with breadcrumbs, and fry; soak the finished jam sandwiches with wine.

3. Plum or Prune Hot Sandwiches (Pflaumen- oder Zwetschgenbavesen): Instead of using preserves, plum or prune jam may be substituted. The bread slices are sandwiched together, dipped in egg-milk mixture, dredged and fried. They are served sprinkled with sugar and cinnamon.

✂ / BAVARIAN CHEESE PUDDING (*Bayrischer Käsepudding*)

2 TO 3 SERVINGS

3 stale rolls or slices stale bread, with crusts
1 cup water
2 tablespoons butter
3 egg yolks
8 tablespoons grated Parmesan cheese

4 tablespoons very thick sour cream
3 tablespoons flour
salt
3 egg whites
butter
breadcrumbs

Cut bread slices or rolls into small pieces and soak in ½ to 1 cup water for a few minutes and then squeeze bread as dry as possible. Cream butter and gradually mix in egg yolks. Add drained bread, grated cheese, sour cream, flour and salt and mix through thoroughly. Beat egg white to a stiff snow and fold into egg-yolk mixture. Turn into 2-quart pudding mold that has been well buttered and sprinkled with breadcrumbs. Cover and set in larger pot holding hot water that reaches about three-quarters up the side of the pudding mold. Cook ¾ hour. Unmold onto hot serving platter and sprinkle with a little more grated cheese.

/ CHEESE-SEMOLINA DIAMONDS (*Käse- und Griessrauten*)

4 TO 6 SERVINGS

- 2 *cups milk*
- ½ *teaspoon salt*
- *nutmeg*
- 2 *tablespoons butter*
- ¾ *cup semolina (farina or Cream of Wheat)*
- 3 *eggs*
- ½ *to* ¾ *cup grated cheese; Parmesan is best but you can also use Swiss or even Cheddar*

Heat the milk with salt, a dash of nutmeg and butter. When butter has melted and milk reaches boiling point, sprinkle in semolina. Cook over low heat, stirring constantly, until cereal forms a mass and leaves sides of pan. Cool. Beat 2 eggs lightly and mix into cereal, stirring until thoroughly blended. Butter 8″-square pan and spread mixture in it. You should have a layer about 1″ thick. Beat third egg lightly and brush a thick coating of it over top of cereal. Sprinkle ¼″- to ½″-thick layer of cheese over egg. Refrigerate several hours. Just before serving time, heat oven to 400° and bake semolina 10 to 15 minutes, or until it has puffed up and top is golden brown. Cut into diamonds (or squares) and serve at once with soups, stews or salads, or a glass of white wine.

/ COTTAGE CHEESE AND NOODLES (*Topfenhaluska*)

4 SERVINGS

- 1 *pound broad egg noodles*
- 1 *pound cottage cheese or pot cheese*
- 2 *cups sour cream*
- ½ *pound bacon, crisply fried and crumbled, and hot bacon fat*

Cook noodles in well-salted water and drain thoroughly. Using a deep serving bowl, put in some hot noodles, cottage cheese, sour cream, bacon crumbles and a little hot bacon fat. Continue layers in that order until bowl is full and all ingredients are used up. You should end with a top layer of bacon. (If you want to be sure this is good and hot when you eat it, heat sour cream in the top of a double boiler before you add it to noodles and other ingredients.)

☙ / *BASIC GERMAN PANCAKES* (*Deutsche Pfannkuchen*)

3 TO 4 PANCAKES; 3 TO 4 SERVINGS

½ cup sifted flour
2 teaspoons sugar
¼ teaspoon salt
4 eggs

½ cup milk
6 tablespoons butter (approximately)

Sift flour, sugar and salt together. Using a rotary beater, whip eggs until light and frothy; beat in milk. Turn flour mixture into beaten egg and, still using beater, whip until you have a smooth batter. Melt 2 tablespoons butter in a 10″ skillet, or a 12″ skillet if you can handle it, and pour in just enough batter to cover bottom with a thin layer. This should take approximately a fourth to a third of batter. As soon as you pour batter, tilt and rotate pan so batter will run over it evenly. Cook over moderate heat until pancakes are golden brown on underside; turn and brown second side. Remove to heated platter.

Continue to fry rest of pancakes in same way until batter is used up. Add 2 tablespoons butter to pan between each pancake. To keep the first pancakes hot while you make the others, arrange them in large open baking dish and place in 250° to 300° oven until you are ready for them. It's a good idea to keep oven door open so they don't bake. Put final topping on rolled pancakes when all have been made.

PANCAKE GARNISHES

1. For a simple dessert or a breakfast entree, sprinkle each crepe with a little cinnamon and sugar. Roll and brush with melted butter.
2. For a more elaborate dessert, add any preserved fruit to crepe before rolling it. Preiselbeeren, the tiny German cranberries, are excellent for this. After rolling pancakes, brush them with a little melted butter and sprinkle with a little more cinnamon and sugar. Pour a little heated rum, brandy, or any white fruit liqueur, such as kirsch, framboise or quetsch, over rolled pancakes and flambé them.
3. For Apple Pancake (Apfelpfannkuchen), sauté pared apple slices in a little butter until they soften slightly and begin to take on color. Sprinkle with cinnamon and sugar. Prepare pancake batter, and when it has set in pan, add a layer of apples and cover with a thin coating of additional batter. Brown slowly on both sides. Fold in half or roll, brush with melted butter and sprinkle with a little more cinnamon and sugar. Use 3 medium-sized apples for this amount of batter.
4. For Cherry Pancake (Kirschpfannkuchen), substitute 1 pound cherries—washed, dried, stoned and cut in half—for apple slices.

▓ / EMPEROR'S PANCAKES (*Kaiserschmarren*)

16 TO 20 PANCAKES; 8 TO 10 SERVINGS

1 *cup sifted flour*	2 *tablespoons butter, melted*
¼ *cup sugar*	½ *cup butter*
¼ *teaspoon salt*	½ *cup raisins, soaked for 30*
3 *eggs*	*minutes in a little rum*
½ *cup milk*	1 *teaspoon cinnamon*
½ *cup heavy cream*	1 *cup sugar*

Sift flour, sugar and salt together. Using rotary beater, whip eggs until light and frothy; beat in milk and cream and melted butter. Turn flour mixture into beaten egg and still using rotary beater, whip until you have smooth batter. Grease a 6″ or 8″ skillet with a little butter and when moderately hot, pour in just enough batter to cover bottom of skillet with a paper-thin layer. To do this, pour batter, then quickly tilt and rotate pan so batter runs over it evenly. Cook over moderate heat until pancake is golden brown on underside; turn and brown second side. Remove to a heated platter. Continue frying pancakes this way until batter has been used. With two forks, tear pancakes into small pieces, approximately 1″ to 1½″ squares or rectangles will do. Melt ½ cup butter in a 10″ skillet and add soaked, well-drained raisins and cinnamon. Put cut pancakes into this sauce and sprinkle with 1 cup sugar. Toss lightly over low heat so that it becomes evenly distributed. Do this quickly, as sugar should not melt but retain some of its grainy texture. Serve immediately.

VARIATIONS

1. If you like more flavor in the pancakes themselves, add a little grated lemon rind, or a few drops of rum or vanilla extract to batter. Make this addition to egg-milk mixture before stirring in flour.
2. Add ⅓ cup chopped pecans or blanched, toasted almonds to raisin-sugar-cinnamon sauce.
3. To make Apple or Cherry Schmarren (Apfel- oder Kirschschmarren), add a few thin slices of apples or a few pieces of cut, stoned cherries to batter after it has been poured into pan. Pour another very thin layer of batter over fruit. Brown on both sides, as directed, cut in strips or pieces and sprinkle with cinnamon and sugar before serving.

▓ / BASIC CREPES (*Palatschinken oder Eierpfannkuchen*)

Use the same batter as for Emperor's Pancakes, above. In Germany, crepes such as these are very popular both as desserts with sweet fillings (süsse Füllungen), or as entrees or appetizers with salty fillings (salzige Füllungen). In the latter case, sugar is not added to batter. Following are some sweet and salty fillings.

SWEET FILLINGS

1. Crepes Confiture: Spread crepes with orange marmalade that has been slightly melted. Roll and sprinkle with sugar flavored with lemon rind. You can pour a little warm rum or brandy over these and flambé them in the manner of crepes suzette.

2. Cottage Cheese Crepes (Topfenpalatschinken): Mix a filling with ½ pound cottage cheese, 4 tablespoons sugar, 2 tablespoons raisins, 1 egg yolk and ½ cup sour cream. Blend well and spread over each crepe. Roll and place side by side in open baking dish. Brush with melted butter and bake in 375° oven 10 minutes, or until cheese filling melts slightly. Serve with Chocolate Sauce, page 403.

3. Fruit-Filled Crepes: Spread crepes with applesauce well seasoned with cinnamon and sugar, or with finely diced fresh fruit such as apricots, cherries, peaches or any berries. For best results, steep cut fruit in sugar for an hour or two before adding to crepes. Chopped pineapple and nuts is another very good filling used in this way. Roll crepes and serve, sprinkled with sugar or topped with whipped cream or vanilla ice cream. You may also reverse the order: fill crepes with ice cream and top with fruit.

4. Chocolate-Filled Crepes: Sprinkle pancakes with mixture of grated bittersweet chocolate, chopped pecans, walnuts or toasted almonds and roll. Serve with Chocolate Sauce, page 403 and whipped cream.

5. Maraschino-Gervais Crepes: Spread crepes with Gervais cheese mashed with a little maraschino liqueur. Roll and serve.

SALTY FILLINGS

Be sure to eliminate sugar from batter when using these. Also, fry crepes on one side only.

1. Creamed Spinach, page 290.

2. Creamed Mushrooms, page 287.

3. Creamed chicken with or without mushrooms.

4. Biberacher-Pfannen-Duennett: To make these filled crepes that are a specialty of the Swabian town of Biberach, prepare and fry crepe batter as in Basic Crepes. Brown crepes on one side only and arrange on warm plate or surface. The filling for these is scallions, cut in ¼" to ½" pieces and then steamed for a few minutes in a little butter. Season with salt, spoon onto crepes and top with grated Sago cheese and butter. Roll crepes, heat 4 to 5 minutes in 450° oven, brush with melted butter and serve.

CHAPTER

VI

Fish

(Fisch)

With its North Sea and Baltic coastlines, and its many rivers, mountain lakes and streams, Germany has a tremendous variety of excellent fish, both fresh and salt water. Since freshness is of paramount importance, these fish are most popular on their home grounds, so that salt-water specialties originate in the areas around Hamburg and Bremen, as well as around Lübeck and other ports. Fresh-water fish specialties such as pike, trout, carp and, most especially, Rhine salmon are naturally credited to the inland regions.

The simplest fish preparations are the ones found most often on German menus, with boiled or poached, steamed, baked or sautéed versions leading all others. Melted butter, or cream, wine, mustard, Hollandaise and green sauces are favored with fish, as is natural pan gravy thickened with sour cream. I have included examples of all such preparations here, with the hope that you will realize similar fish can be prepared in similar ways. (A firm-fleshed salt-water fish such as halibut or sole can be cut into filets or slices and prepared in the same way as pike, allowing for differences in cooking time. However, a fat fish such as salmon should never be larded with bacon and baked in sour cream.)

Buttered boiled potatoes, or Fish Potatoes (Fischkartoffeln), are almost always served with fish in Germany. To prepare these potatoes, peel large boiling potatoes and scoop out balls with a potato-ball cutter. Boil in well-salted water until tender. Drain and serve with hot melted butter and minced parsley and/or dill. Steamed rice is also a fairly common accompaniment to fish in Germany, as are cucumbers, asparagus and green salad.

In addition to fresh fish, smoked fish is eaten a great deal. For descriptions of types and uses, see page 8.

As I've already said, shellfish is usually served in the simplest way possible. Shrimp, crab, lobster and crayfish are boiled, well chilled and served with mayonnaise; oysters are favored raw, and in Hamburg's Austernstuben—oyster inns—are accompanied by sliced Cheshire cheese and a glass of red wine. In addition to being served by themselves, shellfish are often added to meat, vegetable and fish dishes as garnishes. The few cooked shellfish preparations found in Germany are included in this chapter.

❆ / GENERAL FISH PREPARATIONS

1. The most exacting German cooks and housewives always purchase fresh-water fish live and cook it as soon as possible. If they must buy it a day in advance, they keep it swimming in a tub full of cold water. Kill the fish with a heavy blow on the head—a marvelous expression in German: *mit einer kräftigen Schlag auf den Kopf.* If you do not want to go to this kind of trouble, buy the fish very fresh and cook it the same day you buy it.

2. Salt-water fish is always prepared in Germany according to the "3-S System"—*säubern, sauern, salzen. Säubern,* or cleaning, means that fish is opened and eviscerated and washed under cold running water until all blood streaks and clots are removed. *Sauern,* or souring, is done by marinating the fish in lemon juice or vinegar for various lengths of time, depending on the size of the fish. This makes the fish meat white and firm. *Salzen,* or salting, may be done along with souring or after it. The fish should not be salted too heavily or too long, as it will become watery.

❆ / BOILED FISH (*Gekochter Fisch*)

The one thing you must never do to "boiled" fish is boil it; it should cook or poach at a very slow but constant simmer. The fish may be whole or cut into large chunks or thick steaks. It should be wrapped in cheesecloth so it can be removed from the stock without being broken. Start a whole fish in cold water or stock; smaller cuts can be started in boiling liquid which must then be reduced to a simmer. If you have time and patience, and want the very tenderest fish, bring cooking liquid to a boil, before or after the fish has been added depending on its size, cover pot and turn heat off completely. It will take almost twice as long for the fish to be done, but the result will be worth it.

Fish is done when its meat can be flaked with a fork. Do not let fish overcook until it falls apart.

If you cook whole or large pieces of fish this way often, it's a good idea to buy a fish cooker. The fish is placed on a perforated rack and lowered into the cooking liquid. When done, the fish is lifted out on the rack, and it is then easy to drain it. If you use a rack, no cheesecloth is necessary. Although the showiest and best fish cookers are made of tin-lined copper, they are extremely expensive; aluminum cookers are available at one-third to one-half the price and serve the purpose admirably.

To boil salt-water fish, prepare it according to the 3-S System mentioned above. Simmer it in fish or vegetable stock. A little vinegar and/or lemon slices can be added if none was used in the stock. Season stock with a pinch of sage and/or bay leaf. Do not use parsnip in vegetable stock when cooking fish.

To boil fresh-water fish, follow same procedure, eliminating the 3-S treatment unless a specific recipe indicates that you should use it.

To poach small fish or filets, lay them in a buttered skillet or baking pan and add just enough stock, white wine or water to cover them. Cover pan, let simmer slowly on stove or in oven until fish is done, usually in 5 to 8 minutes.

❧ / STEAMED FISH (*Gedämpfter Fisch*)

This is best done with whole or large pieces of fish. Place 3 or 4 tablespoons of herb or mustard butter inside a whole fish or spread on top of a cut piece. Sprinkle with minced parsley. Place fish in a pan or baking dish that can be set over another pan of hot water. Cover fish pan tightly and steam about 1 hour. If you have a fish cooker or vegetable steamer, the fish pan can be placed on the perforated rack and steamed that way; or place the fish pan over another pan of boiling water and steam it in the oven. Cover fish pan tightly and bake-steam for 30 to 40 minutes.

❧ / *BRAISED FISH* (*Gedünsteter Fisch*)

Fish may be whole or cut into portion-size pieces. Sauté some onion, celery, carrot and parsley in butter 3 or 4 minutes, then place fish on this bed of vegetables. If fish is lean, lay some bacon on top of it. Cover pan and braise over moderate heat 5 minutes. Add just enough wine, water or stock to cover bottom of pan. Cover and braise until fish is done, basting with pan juices several times and adding more stock if needed. Bind sauce with 1 tablespoon flour (for 2 cups of stock) stirred into 3 to 4 tablespoons sour cream.

❧ / *SAUTÉED FISH, MEUNIÈRE* (*Fisch, auf Müllerin Art*)

What the French call sauté meunière, the Germans call Müllerin Art, or miller's style. Lean, white firm-fleshed fish, fresh- or salt-water, are prepared this way, most often sole. Filets are generally used, although you could also use halves that are boned but not skinned, or whole small fish that are split and boned. The fish is seasoned with salt and pepper or mace or nutmeg, dredged lightly with flour on both sides and sautéed in moderately hot butter. Turn once so fish browns on both sides. The butter should be nut-brown but not black by the time the fish is done, so regulate heat accordingly. The finished fish are placed on a hot platter. Add some lemon juice to the pan, along with a little minced parsley. Bring to a boil and swirl in an extra lump of butter. Spoon over fish.

In addition to the above, one also finds breaded fried fish and broiled fish in Germany, but these are not nearly as typical. "Blue-cooked" fish, fish in aspic and fish in cream are all given elsewhere in this chapter in specific recipes. And, if I may repeat myself, the recipes for most of them are interchangeable.

�֎ / FISH IN ASPIC (*Fisch in Sülze*)

4 SERVINGS

2 pounds fish (eel, carp, salmon,
　trout)
lemon juice
Fish Stock, page 44, or Veg-
　etable Broth, page 32

2 tablespoons vinegar
1 envelope unflavored gelatin
　softened in ¼ cup cold
　water or white wine
2 cups fish stock

If small, the fish may be served whole; otherwise cut into steaks, filets or other such portion-size pieces. A whole fish may be molded with or without its skin but usually with its head. Clean and wash fish and sprinkle inside and out with lemon juice. Let stand 20 minutes, then pat dry. Poach fish in fish or vegetable stock to cover, flavoring stock with vinegar. When fish is done, remove carefully from stock, drain and lay in large shallow but rimmed dish, such as pie pan, or individual dishes. Let cool thoroughly. When gelatin has softened, add it to the 2 cups hot stock in which fish was poached. Stir until gelatin is completely dissolved. Cool until slightly thickened but not set. Pour over cool fish to cover. Chill until completely set, 1 to 2 hours.

NOTE

If you are molding a large fish such as a salmon, remove skin after cooking. Brush aspic over fish in several layers, letting each layer set before another is added. You may have to heat aspic if it sets before last layer is added. After fish has a good glaze, pour remainder of aspic over and around it. Various garnishes such as fancy lemon slices, olives, hard-cooked-egg slices, truffles, etc., can be stuck onto the aspic glazes and then covered over with another coating of aspic after they have set into place.

✖ / JELLIED FISH (*Fisch in Gelee*)

It is only necessary to use the above method, adding gelatin to fish stock, when you want fish to be molded and encased in a solid aspic. Otherwise, fish is served in a softer and, to my mind, more delicately flavored jelly formed by its own cooking liquid. To prepare this, cook some fish heads, bones and, if fish has been fileted, the skin removed from it, in water along with an onion, a carrot, some celery, pepper-corns and, if you like, a bay leaf and/or a lemon slice or two. Simmer this 30 minutes and use that stock to cook fish itself. The stock may be strained through cheesecloth or fine mesh sieve either before or after fish is cooked. When fish is done, place in a bowl or deep dish and pour strained stock over it. The vegetables may be added in slices if you like. Store in refrigerator until serving time, but for not less than 3 or 4 hours and preferably overnight. Place fish on a chilled plate with some of the jelly spooned around it. Serve at once before jelly melts. Carp, whitefish and eel are most often used this way.

---

❸ / *FISH AU GRATIN (Überkrusteter Fisch oder Überbackener Fisch)*

This is a very popular dish in Germany. Poach steaks or filets or fork-size pieces of any lean, firm, white-fleshed fish according to directions on page 103. Prepare Cheese Sauce, page 333, using Gruyère, Parmesan or combination of both. Use some of the fish stock for sauce liquid. Place cooked, drained fish in a buttered open baking dish and pour sauce over it. Top with grated cheese, breadcrumbs and dot generously with butter. Bake in upper third of oven, preheated to 450°, or place under preheated broiler until nicely browned on top and sauce is bubbling. This dish is sometimes prepared with a ring of mashed potatoes around fish; make sure that potatoes are well seasoned. Place fish in baking dish and pipe a ring of potatoes around them, forcing potatoes through a pastry tube. Cover fish and potatoes with sauce and proceed as described above. Halibut, haddock, bass, whiting and trout are a few of the fish that are very good this way.

❧ CARP (Karpfen) ❧

This dark-fleshed meaty fish is served most often during the winter months, since it tends to taste musty in warm weather. It is the traditional speciality on Christmas Eve and Sylvester, New Year's Eve. It may be prepared at that time in any of the ways that follow, though it is usually done according to the Bohemian style, page 110. It may also be stuffed and baked as described for Stuffed Pike, page 113.

Carp is at its best when young and weighing between 2 and 4 pounds.

Carp roe is a great delicacy and should be poached separately in stock that may or may not be flavored with a little white wine. The roe is served as a garnish with the fish.

❧ / *BOILED OR BLUE CARP* (*Karpfen, gekocht oder blau gekocht*)

If carp is alive just before you cook it, it may be prepared "blue"; see Blue Trout, page 115. Otherwise it can be boiled according to directions on page 103. It will take about 25 to 30 minutes for a carp to cook, depending on its size. It is done when its eyes are white and distended; if the eyes fall out, it is overcooked. Horseradish Sauce, page 336, or hot melted butter is usually served with this.

❧ / *CARP IN BEER* (*Karpfen in Bier*)

4 TO 6 SERVINGS

3- to 4-pound carp, live if possible	1 pint dark beer
carp blood, optional	10 Lebkuchen or gingersnaps, crushed or grated
vinegar	6 to 8 peppercorns, lightly crushed
salt	
4 tablespoons butter	1 bay leaf
2 onions, minced	1 strip lemon peel
1 tablespoon flour	¼ teaspoon powdered cloves

If the carp is alive, kill it with a sharp blow to the head just before cooking. Reserve blood in a little vinegar, if you want to add it to sauce. Clean carp thoroughly and cut into portion-size pieces. Sprinkle with salt and let stand 30 minutes. Heat butter in deep saucepan and when hot and bubbling, add onion. Stir and sauté slowly until onion is golden brown. Add flour, stir and sauté 5 or 6 minutes, or until flour is medium brown. Add beer and stir smooth, over low heat, with wire whisk or wooden spoon. Add Lebkuchen or gingersnap crumbs, peppercorns, bay leaf, lemon peel and cloves. Add carp to sauce. Cover, bring to a boil, reduce heat and simmer slowly but steadily until done, about 15 minutes. Add a little beer or water if sauce thickens too quickly. Remove fish pieces. Rub sauce through a strainer into clean saucepan and reheat. If you are using carp blood, add it with vinegar and heat but do not boil. Pour sauce over carp and serve with boiled potatoes.

VARIATIONS

Chopped carrot and/or leek can be sautéed with onion. Red currant jelly can be melted into sauce just before serving.

✂ / *CARP IN RED WINE* (*Rotweinkarpfen*)

4 TO 6 SERVINGS

3- to 4-pound carp, live if possible
carp blood, optional
wine vinegar
salt
½ cup butter
2 rye bread heels, or equivalent crusts
2 onions, sliced
2 tablespoons minced parsley

1 clove garlic, crushed
6 to 8 peppercorns
pinch of powdered allspice
pinch of powdered cloves
pinch of thyme
1 bay leaf
3 slices lemon
1 to 2 cups dry red wine, as needed

Prepare fish as described above. Cut cleaned carp in portion-size pieces. Salt and let stand 30 minutes. Pat dry. Heat butter in a skillet and when hot and bubbling, add fish and brown over moderate heat, turning once or twice. Using a heavy, shallow casserole, add cut-up bread crusts, onion, parsley, garlic, herbs and lemon slices. Place fish on top of vegetables. Add butter in which fish was browned, pouring it over fish. Add red wine. Cover pot, bring to a boil, reduce heat and simmer slowly but steadily until fish is done, about 15 minutes. Baste fish several times as it cooks and add more wine to pan if necessary. Remove cooked fish to a heated platter. Add blood and vinegar to sauce if you are using it, or flavor with a dash of wine vinegar or red wine. Strain sauce and heat but do not boil if blood has been added. Pour over fish and serve.

✂ / BOHEMIAN CARP (*Böhmischer Karpfen*)

4 TO 6 SERVINGS

3- to 4-pound carp
    salt
    carp head
3 cups water
    pot vegetables, page 29
¼ cup vinegar
1 bay leaf
3 tablespoons dark molasses
6 Lebkuchen or gingersnaps,
    crushed or grated

⅓ cup almonds, blanched and
    chopped
8 prunes, soaked, pitted and
    sliced
¼ cup walnuts, chopped
⅓ cup raisins, soaked and
    drained
    vinegar, if needed

After cleaning thoroughly, cut carp meat in portion-size pieces. Salt and let stand for 30 minutes. Meanwhile, cook carp head in water along with pot vegetables, vinegar and bay leaf 15 minutes. Strain stock and cool. Pat salted carp dry and add it to strained stock. Cover pot, bring to a boil, reduce heat and simmer slowly but steadily until fish is done, about 15 minutes. Remove fish to a heated platter. Add molasses, Lebkuchen or gingersnap crumbs, almonds, prunes, walnuts and raisins to fish stock. Simmer until hot and thick, stirring frequently. Season to taste, adding vinegar if needed. Pour over cooked fish.

✂ / POLISH CARP (*Polnischer Karpfen*)

This is almost the same as above recipe, with only a few exceptions. After the fish is cooked the sauce is first thickened with a dark brown Einbrenne. Heat 4 tablespoons butter and when hot, stir into it 2 tablespoons flour. Stir and sauté slowly until flour is the color of black coffee. Pour in 2 to 3 cups stock in which carp cooked and then stir in Lebkuchen or gingersnap crumbs and molasses and season with salt. No prunes or walnuts are added to this sauce; almonds and/or raisins may be.

✖ PIKE (Hecht) ✖

This excellent fresh-water fish is very firm-fleshed, meaty and not at all "fishy." As its meat is very solid and lean, it always requires added fat for cooking. In Germany, it is usually larded with bacon and cooked with sour cream. The two most famous pike preparations in that country are those of Baden-Baden and the Moselle district. Pickerel is a young pike (junger Hecht), and can be prepared the same way.

Any recipe for pike can be used for pickerel or perch.

✖ / PIKE BAKED IN SOUR CREAM, BADEN-BADEN STYLE (Badischer Hecht)

2 GENEROUS SERVINGS

2-pound pike
salt
butter
1 onion, minced
5 slices bacon, chopped
2 to 3 tablespoons grated Parmesan cheese

breadcrumbs
2 tablespoons melted butter
2 to 3 cups sour cream
white wine or fish stock, if needed

Preheat oven to 400°. The center bone of the fish should be removed, and the head cut off. The fish may be baked in one piece or it can be cut in two long filets. Wash quickly under running cold water, then pat dry. Sprinkle fish with salt and let stand 45 minutes. Rinse and dry. Butter a shallow baking dish and lay fish in it, skin side down. Sprinkle fish with onion, bacon, cheese and breadcrumbs. Pour melted butter over fish and, finally, 1 cup sour cream. Place baking dish on a cookie sheet in preheated oven. Bake 45 minutes, or until fish is done. Baste with pan juices from time to time and if pan seems dry, spoon in a little fish stock or white wine. Add 1 more cup of cream to pan (not over fish) for last 15 to 20 minutes of baking time. Remove finished fish to heated platter and serve with the sauce. If you would like more sauce than you have in pan, add a little more sour cream along with a tablespoon or two of wine or stock. Stir and heat.

VARIATIONS

Lay 2 or 3 anchovy filets, or spread a little anchovy paste, on top of fish before sprinkling with onion and other ingredients. Some minced parsley can be added to other toppings.

⊠ / PIKE FILETS IN HERBED CREAM SAUCE
(*Hecht in Rahm*)

2 GENEROUS SERVINGS

2-*pound pike, cut in filets*
　salt
　2 *tablespoons butter*
　1 *onion, minced*
　1 *tablespoon minced parsley*
　1 *bay leaf*
　½ *cup water, fish stock or white wine, or as needed*
　2 *tablespoons butter*
　3 *tablespoons flour*
1½ *cups sweet cream*

salt
generous pinch of mace to taste
6 *anchovy filets, chopped, or 2 teaspoons anchovy paste*
1 *tablespoon grated lemon peel*
1 *egg yolk beaten with 1 or 2 tablespoons cream or white wine*

Sprinkle fish with salt; let stand 30 minutes. Rinse and dry. Heat butter in a shallow casserole or deep skillet with a cover. When butter is hot and bubbling, add onion and parsley and sauté over moderate heat 2 or 3 minutes. Lay fish filets on top of vegetables, add bay leaf and enough water, fish stock or white wine to just cover bottom of pan. Cover pan and simmer slowly but steadily about 10 to 15 minutes, or until filets are done but not falling apart. Baste once or twice during cooking and add more liquid to pan as needed.

Preheat oven to 475°. Melt 2 tablespoons butter, and when hot, stir in flour. Sauté and stir over low heat for about 4 minutes, or until flour just begins to turn color. Add sweet cream and beat with a wire whisk or wooden spoon until sauce is smooth. Add strained pan juices in which fish cooked and season sauce with salt and mace. Remove finished filets very gently with slotted spatula or pancake turner and place in a shallow buttered baking dish.

Top filets with anchovies or spread with paste, then add lemon peel. Pour about two-thirds of sauce over fish. Place baking dish in a larger pan about one-third full of hot water. Using a double thickness of aluminum foil, cover fish pan and water pan completely so fish can steam. Bake this way in preheated oven 5 to 10 minutes. Add egg yolk beaten with cream or white wine to remaining sauce that is hot but not boiling. Add the egg yolk very slowly, stirring as you do so. Heat but do not boil. Pour this sauce over fish and its original sauce.

VARIATION

The fish can be steamed in its sauce on the stove, instead of in the oven. Set baking dish on rack of steamer, cover tightly and steam for 5 to 10 minutes.

❉ / MOSELLE PIKE (Mosel Hecht)

Simmer fish filets as described above. When done, place in a buttered baking dish and cover with Cheese Sauce, page 333. Use fish pan juices along with cream to make sauce and flavor with Parmesan cheese, not Gruyère. Do not use egg yolk in sauce. Sprinkle with a little more grated cheese and dot with tiny flecks of butter. Bake in 450° oven or place under broiler until top is golden brown and sauce is bubbling.

❉ / STUFFED PIKE (Gefüllter Hecht)

2 GENEROUS SERVINGS

2-pound pike
salt
2 tablespoons butter
1 onion, minced
2 tablespoons minced parsley
6 mushrooms, chopped
6 to 8 anchovy filets, chopped
⅓ cup breadcrumbs
8 to 10 small cooked shrimp, shelled and de-veined, or 1 or 2 cooked filets of firm-fleshed fish (flounder, sole, halibut, bass)

1 egg, lightly beaten
salt and pepper
lemon juice
2 slices fat bacon cut in strips for larding
½ cup melted butter
1 onion, sliced
2 tablespoons minced parsley
water, fish stock or white wine for basting
½ to 1 cup sour cream

The center bone of the fish should be removed, but the fish should not be cut in half, nor its head cut off. The fish man can prepare this for you. Wash fish quickly under running cold water, pat dry, sprinkle with salt and refrigerate 45 minutes. Preheat oven to 400°. To prepare stuffing, melt 2 tablespoons butter in skillet and when hot and bubbling, add onion, parsley and chopped mushrooms. Stir and sauté over moderate heat about 5 minutes, or until vegetables just begin to soften and brown slightly. This should be done fairly quickly so mixture does not become too wet. Mix in anchovy filets, breadcrumbs and chopped shrimp or flaked cooked fish. Toss well and then mix in beaten egg.

Rinse fish and dry again. Sprinkle inside with a little salt, pepper and lemon juice. Lard fish across back with bacon strips. Stuff with breadcrumb-fish filling and truss with small skewers or sew with kitchen thread. Spread a little melted butter on bottom of a shallow baking dish. Add fish and top with onion slices and minced parsley. Pour rest of melted butter over fish and vegetables. Put in preheated oven and bake about 45 minutes, or until fish is done. Baste frequently with white wine, water or fish stock. Add sour cream to pan (around, not over, the fish) for last 10 minutes of cooking time. When fish is done, remove vegetables and trussing and serve fish on heated platter with sauce over it.

NOTE

Bass, flounder and any other fish that lends itself to stuffing and baking can be prepared in this way.

⚭ TROUT (Forelle) ⚭

Trout is one of the most highly prized fish in Germany, especially when it comes from the crystal streams of the Black Forest. Although they are served fried, grilled or baked, trout are preferred "blue-cooked," for which a live fish is practically essential. Traditionally, this sleek sapphire fish is served in a circle, its tail tucked into its mouth. Only a live fish will snap into a curl as it is placed in boiling water. The distinctive blue color, due to the interaction of vinegar and a substance on the skin which evaporates once the fish has been killed, can also be achieved only with a live, or *very* recently, killed fish. You could have the fish killed and cleaned at the market and then take it home and prepare it at once, but if there must be more than a 10-minute delay, prepare the trout in some other way. Needless to say, frozen trout can never be cooked "blue."

In the enchanting little Black Forest town of Herrenalb, known for its Kneipp water baths and fresh-air cures, the Mönchs Posthotel catches trout to order in the flower-edged stream that runs in front of its restaurant. The fish are then prepared as follows.

❄ / BLUE TROUT (*Forelle, blau gekocht*)

6 SERVINGS

You will need 6 live trout, one for each serving. Kill the fish with a heavy blow on the head. Cut open along the stomach and clean very quickly. Sprinkle trout with vinegar and let stand 4 or 5 minutes before cooking. Bring 2 to 3 quarts water to a boil with a little salt, and 3 or 4 slices of lemon. Other seasonings which can be included are 1 bay leaf, 6 or 8 peppercorns, 3 sprigs of parsley, 1 or 2 stalks of celery and/or 1 sliced onion. When water is boiling, turn off heat and add fish. Cover pot and let stand about 12 minutes, or until fish are done. Remove fish from stock and drain well. Arrange on a heated platter or individual dinner plates.

VARIATION

For a slightly more piquant version, bend the cleaned trout in a circle, tucking its tail in its mouth. Place in a bowl and cover with hot vinegar. Cover bowl with a double thickness of aluminum foil or a plate and let stand 5 to 8 minutes. Remove the trout gently and place in the boiling water with a little of the vinegar and seasonings as described above. Turn off heat, cover pot and let stand 15 minutes, or until fish are done. Drain and serve as above.

❄ / TROUT IN CREAM (*Forelle in Rahm*)

6 SERVINGS

6 trout	3 tablespoons flour
salt and pepper	1½ cups sour cream
flour	lemon juice to taste
⅓ cup butter	meat extract or well-seasoned
1 large onion, minced	stock to taste

The cleaned trout can be cooked whole or, if they are large, cut in portion-size pieces. Sprinkle with salt and pepper and let stand 15 minutes. Dry with paper towel and dredge lightly on all sides with flour. Heat butter in a heavy skillet and when hot and bubbling, add fish. Fry over moderate heat, turning once so fish will be golden brown on both sides. When fish is done, remove it to heated platter.

Add onion to hot fat; stir and sauté over moderate heat until onion is golden brown. Sprinkle with flour; stir and sauté until flour is absorbed and just begins to take on color, about 4 minutes. Stir in sour cream and mix well. Simmer a minute or two, until sauce is smooth and thickened. Season with salt, pepper, a dash or two of lemon juice and a little meat extract or stock. Spoon over trout.

❖ / HERBED TROUT WITH WHITE WINE (*Forelle mit Kräutern und Weisswein*)

6 SERVINGS

6 trout	¾ cup fish stock or water
salt	½ cup dry white wine
⅓ cup butter	1 to 2 tablespoons flour dis-
1 onion, minced	solved in a little cold water
¼ teaspoon thyme	lemon juice, optional and to
¼ teaspoon basil	taste
1 tablespoon minced parsley	

The trout should be cooked whole, head and all. Clean thoroughly and sprinkle inside lightly with salt. Heat butter in shallow heavy casserole or deep skillet with a cover. When butter is hot and bubbling, add onion. Mix thyme, basil and parsley together and sprinkle half this mixture over onions. Cover and steam 4 or 5 minutes, or until onions begin to soften. Lay fish over onion and sprinkle top with remaining herbs. Add water or stock and white wine. Cover and simmer slowly but steadily about 15 minutes, or until fish is done. Check to see if more liquid is needed as fish cooks. Baste with pan juices once or twice. Remove fish to a heated platter and bind sauce with flour dissolved in water. Bring to a boil and simmer 2 or 3 minutes until thickened. If you prefer, you can strain sauce before binding it, but that is not really necessary. Season to taste with salt, if needed, and a little white wine and/or lemon juice, to taste.

✖ SALMON (Lachs) ✖

✖ / COLD SALMON, RHINE STYLE (*Rheinlachs mit Remouladensosse*)

Strictly speaking, you cannot have Rhine salmon unless the fish has been caught in the Rhine, but you can have Salmon, Rhine Style. This dish is one of the most welcome signs of spring in Germany.

6 TO 8 SERVINGS

Following directions for Boiled Fish, page 103, prepare 3 to 4 pounds salmon, either whole, in steaks or in chunks. Add 1 cup Rhine wine to cooking stock. Chill and serve with Remoulade Sauce, page 345. This dish is also prepared in aspic. For a really elegant buffet, the whole fish is done that way, according to instructions on page 104. Flavor stock with a little extra wine, if needed, before adding gelatin.

✖ / HOT SALMON DISHES

One also finds broiled and hot poached salmon on menus in Germany very frequently. The first is served with melted butter, or cold butter mashed with anchovy paste or cucumbers. The second is served with Hollandaise (page 341) or Dill Sauce (page 336), boiled potatoes, and that other harbinger of spring, asparagus.

❧ PERCH (Barsch) ❧

✖ / GERMAN PERCH (*Deutscher Barsch*)

6 SERVINGS

3 1-pound perch, or 2 pounds
   perch filets
   lemon juice
2 tablespoons grated onion
3 tablespoons corn oil (approximately)
½ to 1 cup fine, dry breadcrumbs

¼ cup butter
1 tablespoon butter
4 scallions, minced, or 2 tablespoons minced chives
2 or 3 tablespoons lemon juice
   salt and pepper
   minced parsley

Marinate the cleaned, washed perch in a mixture of lemon juice and grated onion 1 hour. Pat dry, brush on both sides with oil and dredge lightly in breadcrumbs. (You may prepare either whole fish or filets this way.) Heat butter in a skillet and when hot enough for bubbling to subside, add fish. Fry quickly, turning once, until golden brown on both sides. Place on a heated platter. Add 1 tablespoon butter to skillet and when hot and bubbling, add minced scallions or chives. Sauté a minute or two, then add lemon juice, salt and pepper and parsley. Let sauce come to a boil and spoon over fish.

VARIATIONS

1. Fish can also be fried in hot corn oil or vegetable shortening. If you do that, pour excess fat out of pan and add 2 tablespoons fresh butter to skillet when you start to prepare sauce.
2. The breadcrumbs can be mixed with an equal amount of grated Parmesan cheese.

❧ COD ❧

❦ / HAMBURG COD WITH OYSTERS (*Hamburger Kabeljau mit Austern*)

Vegetable Broth, *page 32, seasoned with lemon peel, allspice, bay leaf, thyme and all other vegetables indicated except parsnip*
2 *pounds codfish, cut in steaks or filets*
1 *cup dry white wine*
1 *cup fish stock*

½ *lemon, sliced*
3 *tablespoons butter*
1 *tablespoon fine breadcrumbs, or as needed*
dash of nutmeg
salt to taste
1 *dozen shelled oysters with their liquor*
soy sauce, optional and to taste

Cook vegetable stock and when it has simmered 30 minutes, bring to a boil and add fish. Reduce heat, cover pot and simmer slowly until fish is done but not falling apart, 15 to 20 minutes. Be sure water keeps simmering but do not let it boil. Remove fish, drain and cut into fork-size pieces. Combine wine and stock in a saucepan, add lemon slices and butter, and simmer gently over low heat until butter melts. Stir in breadcrumbs, simmering as you do so, until sauce is thickened. Do not add breadcrumbs in great quantities all at once, or the sauce will thicken into a porridgelike mass before you know it. Season with nutmeg and salt. Add shelled whole oysters and their liquor to simmering sauce along with cooked fish pieces. Simmer gently until oysters are plump and begin to curl, about 5 minutes. Season with a dash of soy sauce.

✂ / *POACHED COD, HOLSTEIN STYLE* (*Gekochter Kabeljau, auf Holsteiner Art*)

This Baltic specialty reaches north to become Denmark's national dish. Poach cod steaks in stock as described above. Drain well and serve with melted butter and Fine Mustard Sauce, page 341, made with fish stock. Top with chopped hard-cooked eggs and drained capers. Serve with lemon wedges and boiled potatoes.

✂ EEL ✂

✂ / *EEL IN ASPIC* (*Aal in Aspik*)

4 TO 6 SERVINGS

Using 2½ to 3 pounds of eel, cut it into 2- to 3-inch pieces. Wash and dry. Cook in salt water with vinegar and a bay leaf about 20 minutes, or until done. Remove skin from eel pieces. You may lift meat off bone in long filets, or leave eel with bone in. Strain stock in which eel cooked and prepare aspic according to instructions on page 106, using 1 envelope of gelatin for every 2 cups of stock.

✂ / *EEL IN GREEN SAUCE* (*Aal in Grüne Sosse*)

4 TO 6 SERVINGS

Prepare and cook eel as described for Eel in Aspic. Using the eel stock, prepare Green Sauce, page 336. This should be generously flavored with fresh minced parsley and dill, and fresh chervil if you can get it. If not, steep ½ teaspoon dried chervil in hot water for 10 minutes, drain and add to sauce. Serve with boiled potatoes and Cucumber Salad, page 306.

❧ / *BLUE EEL* (*Aal, blau gekocht*)

See recipe for Blue Trout, page 115; serve with Horseradish Sauce, page 336.

❧ / *EEL IN SAGE* (*Aal in Salbei*)

4 TO 6 SERVINGS

2½ to 3 *pounds eel, skinned*
salt
lemon juice
fresh leaf sage
½ *cup butter*

2 *onions, sliced*
lemon juice
1 *to* 2 *cups meat stock, or as needed*

Have eel skinned at fish market. Wash it and cut into 2- to 3-inch pieces. Sprinkle with salt and lemon juice and wrap each piece with sage leaves, tying leaves on with kitchen thread. (If you cannot get fresh sage, soak dried sage leaves until soft and sprinkle over and around fish.) Heat butter in a shallow casserole or deep skillet and sauté onion slices 5 minutes. Lay eel on top of onion. Sprinkle with a little more lemon juice, cover pan and braise 10 minutes, adding a little liquid to pan if needed to keep onions from burning. Add 1 cup meat stock, cover pan and braise another 10 minutes, basting with pan juices once or twice, and adding more liquid to pan if necessary. Remove eel and unwrap sage leaves. Serve on a hot platter with pan juices and brown butter.

✕ HADDOCK ✕

✕ / HADDOCK AND POTATO PIE, HAMBURG STYLE
(Hamburger Schellfischpudding mit Kartoffeln)

6 SERVINGS

2 pounds haddock, cleaned and
  cut in fork-size pieces
salt
2 tablespoons butter
2 onions, minced
2 pounds potatoes, boiled in
  salted water and sliced

2 egg yolks
1 cup sour cream
salt and pepper, or mace to
  taste
½ cup breadcrumbs
butter

Sprinkle haddock with salt and refrigerate ½ hour. Rinse and dry. Preheat oven to 350°. Heat butter in skillet and when hot and bubbling, add onions. Stir and sauté over low heat until onions just begin to brown. Butter a 2-quart casserole. In it arrange alternate layers starting with potatoes, then fish, sautéed onions and some of their butter. Continue until casserole is full, ending with a layer of potatoes. Beat egg yolks well and fold into sour cream until the two are thoroughly blended. Season with salt and pepper or mace to taste. Pour over potatoes. Sprinkle top with breadcrumbs and dot well with tiny flecks of butter. Bake in preheated oven 30 to 40 minutes, or until top is golden brown.

VARIATION

Use a large 3-pound smoked whitefish or an equivalent amount of smaller smoked fish such as trout. Split and bone fish and lift meat off skin with a wide-blade knife, keeping the pieces as large as possible. Proceed with recipe, substituting smoked fish for haddock. Bake about 20 minutes in preheated oven.

✳ / BAKED HALIBUT OR WHITEFISH WITH VEGETABLES (Heilbutt oder Weissfisch mit Gemüse)

4 SERVINGS

2 halibut steaks, 1" to 1½"
   thick, or 1 3½- to 4-pound
   whitefish, boned and split
4 tablespoons butter
   salt and pepper
4 to 5 slices bacon (for whitefish)

4 to 5 drained canned tomatoes
2 green peppers, seeded and
   sliced
2 large onions, sliced
   water or stock as needed

Preheat oven to 400°. Prepare fish according to instructions on page 103. Halibut should get the 3-S treatment mentioned there. White-fish can be sprinkled with lemon juice but it is not entirely necessary. Dry fish and sprinkle with salt and pepper. If you use halibut, brown lightly in 4 tablespoons hot butter. If you use whitefish, skip that step. Arrange tomatoes, peppers and onion on bottom of a large baking dish with a cover (or make a cover of a double thickness of aluminum foil). Arrange fish on this bed of vegetables. If using halibut, pour butter in which fish was sautéed over fish and vegetables. If using whitefish, mince bacon and sprinkle over fish and add 3 tablespoons butter to pan. Cover pan and bake in preheated oven about 30 minutes, basting fish with pan juices and adding water or stock if needed. Remove cover and bake for another 10 minutes, or until fish is lightly browned on top. Serve with pan vegetables and juices.

VARIATION

This dish gets a decidedly Hungarian flavor if the fish steaks are sprinkled with paprika before being browned. With whitefish, the paprika can be mixed through the sliced vegetables. Use about 1 to 2 tablespoons sweet paprika in either case and sprinkle a little more on fish after you remove cover to brown them. Stir 2 or 3 tablespoons sour cream into the vegetables and pan juices before serving and heat. Spoon over fish.

❧ HERRING ❧

❧ / GREEN HERRING (Grüner Hering)

The term "green" is applied to fresh herring that is absolutely unsalted or treated in any way. Unlike the herring sold in barrels, this fish is purchased at a fish market, not at a delicatessen or appetizing store. It tastes, looks and is prepared almost exactly like its first cousin, the mackerel, and is not salty. Fresh sardines, smelts or small herrings can be used in any recipes for green herring that follow. These can also be cooked "blue," just to show you how flexible the German gastronomic color spectrum can get. Follow directions for Blue Trout, page 115.

❧ / FRIED GREEN HERRING OR MACKEREL (Gebratene grüne Heringe oder Makrelen)

6 SERVINGS

6 1-pound fresh herrings, or 6
    baby mackerel, about 1
    pound each
salt

flour
corn oil, butter or bacon fat for
    frying

Fish should be thoroughly cleaned and heads removed. Remove center bone but leave fish in one piece, opened flat. This can best be done by your fish man. Sprinkle lightly with salt and dredge with flour. Heat fat in large heavy skillet and when hot, add fish. Fry slowly, turning once, until both sides are golden brown, 15 to 20 minutes. Onion rings and/or breadcrumbs, both browned in butter, are often served on top of fried herring or mackerel. Other sauces used include Bavarian Mustard Sauce, page 334, or red currant jelly melted in hot butter.

❧ / HERRING AND POTATO PIE (*Hering- und Kartoffelpudding*)

6 SERVINGS

Follow recipe for Haddock and Potato Pie, Hamburg Style, page 122. Substitute two salt herrings for haddock. Have them skinned, boned and cut in filets. Rinse and soak filets in cold water to cover overnight. If extremely salty, soak 24 hours and change water 2 or 3 times. Drain, pat dry and cut into fork-size pieces. Place in casserole with alternate layers of potatoes and onions and proceed with recipe. If herring still seems salty after soaking, omit salt from sour cream mixture. (To test herring for saltiness, taste it with the tip of your tongue.)

❧ / FRIED SALT HERRING, MECKLENBURG STYLE (*Gebratene Salzheringe, auf Mecklenburger Art*)

6 SERVINGS

6 salt herring, cleaned and washed
milk, for soaking
¾ cup dry white wine

3 egg yolks
1 cup flour (approximately)
½ cup butter, or as needed

Soak herrings overnight; or if very salty 24 hours, in several changes of milk. Dry with paper towel. Combine wine and egg yolks and beat until well blended. Add flour gradually until a smooth batter is formed. It should be the consistency of a medium pancake batter. Dip dried fish in batter. Heat butter in a large heavy skillet and when so hot that bubbling subsides, add herring. Fry over moderate heat, turning once so that fish are golden brown on both sides. They will be done in 12 to 15 minutes. Serve with Cooked Sauerkraut (page 276), boiled potatoes and sautéed onion rings.

✕ SOLE ✕

✕ / FILET OF SOLE WITH SHRIMP SAUCE
(Seezungenrollen mit Garnelensosse)

This is another specialty of Sellmer's, the handsome old fish restaurant that juts out into Hamburg's exciting harbor.

6 SERVINGS

1 onion, sliced
1 stalk celery with leaves
1 slice lemon
6 peppercorns
water
½ to ¾ pound small shrimp
6 sole filets
salt and pepper

1 cup fish stock
½ cup dry white wine
3 tablespoons butter
White Sauce, page 331
nutmeg, optional and to taste
white wine to taste
½ cup heavy sweet cream

Simmer onion, celery, lemon and peppercorns in 2 to 3 cups water 15 minutes. Add shrimp and simmer 5 to 8 minutes. Remove shrimp, cool slightly, shell and de-vein. Strain stock and reserve. Cut fish filets in half lengthwise so that you have 12 long strips. Sprinkle top side of each piece lightly with salt and pepper and roll jelly-roll fashion. Fasten with toothpicks. Place rolled filets, standing upright, in a deep skillet or shallow casserole. The rolled filets should be close enough to keep each other from toppling over, but they should not be crammed together.

Combine strained shrimp stock, white wine and butter in the pan. Cover tightly, bring to a boil, reduce heat and simmer slowly but steadily until fish is solidly white throughout, about 15 minutes. Remove fish to heated platter. Prepare White Sauce, using fish stock and pan juices for liquid called for. Flavor sauce with nutmeg; add shrimp and simmer 5 minutes. Season sauce with a little more white wine and stir in sweet cream. Egg yolk may be added or not as directed in sauce recipe. Heat but do not boil if egg yolk has been added. Spoon shrimp and sauce over cooked sole, allowing 2 rolls for each portion.

VARIATION

The fish rolls can be stuffed with a few whole or chopped shrimp. Place shrimp at end of fish filet and then roll. Add extra shrimp to sauce, as above.

❆ / *FILET OF SOLE IN LEMON SAUCE* (*Seezungenrollen in Zitronensosse*)

6 SERVINGS

Cut 6 sole filets in half. Sprinkle with salt and minced parsley and roll as described above. Prepare Lemon Sauce, page 339. Place fish rolls, standing on end, in buttered baking dish. Cover with sauce and bake 20 minutes in 450° oven. Fish rolls are done when they are solidly white all the way through.

❆ MISCELLANEOUS ❆ FISH DISHES
(*Verschiedene Fischgerichte*)

❆ / *FISH AND HAM ROLLS* (*Fisch- und Schinken- rouladen*)

4 TO 6 SERVINGS

2 pounds filets of white, firm-fleshed fish such as sole or bass
lemon juice

salt and pepper
4 tablespoons grated Gruyère cheese

4 to 6 thin slices baked or
    boiled ham
3 tablespoons butter

1 small bay leaf (optional)
½ cup dry white wine

Cut fish filets in half lengthwise. You should have about 12 half-slices.
Sprinkle with lemon juice and marinate 20 minutes. Pat dry with
paper towel and lay skin side down. Sprinkle top with salt, pepper
and grated cheese. Ham slices should be cut to fit fish filets as closely
as possible. Lay a ham slice on each filet and roll jelly-roll fashion.
Fasten with toothpicks. Heat butter in a low casserole or deep skillet
with a tight-fitting cover. When hot and bubbling, add fish filets and
bay leaf if you use it. Cover pan and cook very slowly but steadily
over moderately low heat 5 to 8 minutes. Add white wine, cover pot
and steam another 15 minutes, or until fish is done and just begins
to flake when you test it with a fork. Serve on heated platter with
pan juices spooned over fish. Garnish with tangerine sections and black
olives.

✵ / FISH FILETS IN BEER BATTER (*Fischfileten in Bierteig*)

4 TO 6 SERVINGS

2 pounds filets of white, firm-
    fleshed fish such as sole or
    bass
vinegar or lemon juice
⅔ cup flour
1 egg, lightly beaten
    salt

½ cup dark beer
    corn oil or other vegetable
    shortening for deep frying
    (not olive oil)

Cut filets in halves or quarters; they should be in large portion-size
pieces, but not so large that they will be hard to handle in the batter
or deep-fryer. Sprinkle with vinegar or lemon juice and marinate for
30 minutes. Pat dry and sprinkle lightly with salt. While the fish
marinates, prepare the batter. Mix flour with beaten egg and salt and
add beer. Stir with fork until batter is blended and free of lumps but
do not beat too thin. Mixture should be the consistency of a medium
pancake batter. Set wire basket into a deep-frying pan full of fat,
heated to 375°. Slip batter-dipped fish into fat, a few at a time; fry
until golden brown, 6 to 8 minutes. Remove finished filets with wire
basket and drain on absorbent paper. Fry remaining fish filets in the

same way. Be sure that temperature of the fat remains even during frying. If you do not have a wire basket and deep fryer, simply use a deep saucepan. Slip fish directly into fat and remove finished pieces with slotted spoon or pancake turner.

VARIATIONS

1.   Shrimp can be prepared almost the same way. Peel and de-vein shrimp, marinate in vinegar or lemon juice, and proceed. Shrimp that run about 16 to 18 per pound are best for this.

2.   For an even lighter batter, separate egg and add yolk with flour, salt and beer. Let mixture stand at room temperature 30 minutes and then fold in stiffly beaten egg white.

❧ / FISH AND CAULIFLOWER PUDDING (*Fisch- und Blumenkohlpudding*)

4 TO 6 SERVINGS

1 head cauliflower
water to cover
salt
2 pounds white firm-fleshed fish (salt-water fish is preferable)
4 tablespoons butter
4 tablespoons flour
2½ to 3 cups cauliflower stock

1 to 2 tablespoons grated Parmesan cheese
salt
lemon juice to taste
2 egg yolks beaten with ¼ cup cold stock
breadcrumbs
grated cheese
butter

Preheat oven to 350°. Wash cauliflower and break into flowerets. Cook in water to cover to which salt is added. Drain well when tender. Be sure that all bones and skin have been removed from fish. Break into fork-size pieces. Heat butter in a saucepan and when hot and bubbling, stir in flour. Sauté over low heat until flour just begins to take on color, about 4 minutes. Pour in 3 cups of stock in which cauliflower cooked and beat smooth, over low heat, with wire whisk or wooden spoon. Simmer 10 minutes and season with grated cheese, salt and a dash of lemon juice. Remove from heat and gradually stir in egg yolk. Butter a 6-cup soufflé dish or comparable baker and add fish and cauliflower, tossing them together lightly with a fork. Pour sauce into dish and sprinkle top with breadcrumbs, grated cheese and dot generously with butter. Bake in preheated oven about 30 minutes, or until top is golden brown.

VARIATION

Sliced boiled potatoes may be substituted for cauliflower. Four large potatoes will do for the above recipe. Use the same sauce, or a tomato sauce; in either case, topped with breadcrumbs and grated cheese.

⋈ / FISH BAKED WITH SAUERKRAUT   (*Hechtenkraut oder Fischpudding mit Sauerkraut*)

"In Fernstein the king always ate Hechtenkraut, a specialty which had often figured in the royal menus during earlier reigns. This dish was prepared in the following way. A pike was baked and then allowed to get cold. All the bones were removed, even the very smallest, and the fish was cut up into small pieces and put on one side. Sauerkraut was then cooked with a lot of finely browned onions and plenty of butter and a fireproof dish greased with butter and lined with breadcrumbs. In this, alternate layers of fish and sauerkraut were laid and the whole topped with breadcrumbs, covered with crayfish tails and sauce and browned for twenty minutes in the oven."

From *The Monarch Dines*, by Theodor Hierneis, chef to King Ludwig II of Bavaria

6 SERVINGS

2 *pounds white, firm-fleshed fish* (*pike and skate are often used for this*)	*breadcrumbs*
water or stock	2 *tablespoons butter*
salt	3 *tablespoons flour*
1 *recipe Cooked Sauerkraut, page*	2 *cups stock*
276	¼ *cup cream*
8 *slices bacon, diced*	*paprika to taste*
2 *onions, minced*	*salt to taste*
butter	*breadcrumbs*
	butter

Cook cleaned fish in stock, or in water along with some sliced onion, celery and peppercorns. When done, remove and drain. Strain and reserve stock. Cook sauerkraut according to recipe, omitting apples but using wine and caraway seeds. Cook to the "dry but juicy" stage described. Preheat oven to 375°. Sauté bacon and when it begins to melt, add onion. Stir and sauté slowly until onion and bacon just begin to brown. Butter a 6-cup soufflé dish and sprinkle sides and bottom with breadcrumbs, tapping out excess. Place a layer of kraut in dish, top with a sprinkling of diced onion and bacon, then fish, onion and bacon, kraut, and so on until dish is full. End up with a top layer of sauerkraut.

To prepare sauce, melt butter in a skillet. When hot and bubbling, stir in flour, and sauté over low heat until flour just begins to take on color, about 5 minutes. Add stock and sour cream and beat smooth, over low heat, with a wire whisk or wooden spoon. Season sauce with paprika and salt. Cook 5 minutes, or until smooth and thickened. Pour over sauerkraut and fish. Top with breadcrumbs and dot generously with butter. Bake in preheated oven 35 to 40 minutes, or until topping is well browned.

VARIATIONS

1. Sliced boiled potatoes can be added to this casserole dish. Four or five large potatoes will do.
2. Sometimes the fish is fried instead of poached. Dredge fish in egg and breadcrumbs and brown quickly in hot butter or other fat. Follow rest of recipe.

The following three recipes provide excellent uses for leftover cooked fish. The last two are also very good quick dishes, as the fish can be cooked in advance and final preparation done a few minutes before dinner.

❊ / FISH CAKES (*Fischkrusten*)

4 SERVINGS

2 *pounds cooked white-meat fish*	*salt and pepper, or nutmeg*
or salmon	1 *egg yolk*
3 *tablespoons butter*	*flour*
1 *onion, minced*	2 *eggs, well beaten*
2 *tablespoons flour*	*breadcrumbs*
1 *cup water or fish stock*	*butter or other fat for frying*

Remove all bones and skin from fish and flake or grind in food chopper. Heat butter in a small saucepan and when hot and bubbling, add onion. Stir and sauté slowly until onion is soft and bright yellow, about 5 minutes. Add flour, stir and sauté about 4 minutes, or until flour barely begins to turn color. Add water or stock and beat smooth with wire whisk or wooden spoon. Cook 10 minutes, or until sauce is smooth and thick. Flavor with salt and pepper or nutmeg. Cool sauce slightly and pour over fish. Add egg yolk and mix thoroughly. Chill fish mixture 1 to 2 hours. (If you want to prepare this for dinner and do not have much time, you can prepare fish mixture up to this point in the morning, and leave it in the refrigerator until evening.) Shape chilled fish mixture into small hamburger-like patties. Dredge lightly with flour, then dip in beaten egg and let excess drip off, then dredge with breadcrumbs. Heat fat in a deep skillet. There should be enough melted fat for fish cakes to "swim." Add fish cakes and fry over moderate heat, turning once until golden brown on both sides.

VARIATION

This recipe can also be used to make tiny fish balls for cocktails. Shape balls instead of patties and roll in flour, egg and breadcrumbs. Fry in hot deep fat (375°) 5 to 7 minutes, or until fish balls are an even golden brown. Drain on absorbent paper and serve on toothpicks with a mustard or tomato sauce dip.

✂ / FISH HASH (*Pfannenfisch*)

4 SERVINGS

4 tablespoons butter	*2 cups diced cooked potatoes*
1 onion, minced	*3 eggs, lightly beaten*
3 cups flaked cooked fish—lean	*salt and pepper to taste*
white-fleshed fish or salmon	

Heat butter in a skillet and when hot and bubbling, add onions and sauté until soft and light golden brown. Add fish and potatoes and toss together with fork. Fry slowly, turning mixture with a spatula, until fish and potatoes are an even golden brown. Pour beaten eggs into pan and cook gently until eggs are set, about 4 minutes. Cut in pie wedges.

VARIATIONS

1. Sometimes fish, potatoes and onions are fried, as described, and then are topped with fried eggs.
2. Well-soaked salt herrings, boned and diced, can also be prepared this way, as can smoked salmon that is allowed to soak in several changes of water for 6 to 8 hours. Minced chives are very good, added to the beaten egg, when you prepare this dish with salmon.

✿ / FISH SOUFFLÉ, WITH COOKED FISH (*Fischauflauf, von gekochtem Fisch*)

4 TO 6 SERVINGS

2 stale rolls or 4 slices white
    bread
1 cup water, approximately
8 to 10 anchovy filets, washed
    and drained
5 slices bacon
1 tablespoon capers, drained
2 pounds cooked white firm-
    fleshed fish or salmon (inex-
    pensive fish will do very well
    here)

3 egg yolks
1 tablespoon grated onion
1 tablespoon minced parsley
    salt to taste
3 egg whites, stiffly beaten
    butter
1 tablespoon grated cheese
    breadcrumbs

Preheat oven to 375°. Cut rolls or bread into small pieces and soak in water. Drain and squeeze out as much water as possible after bread is softened. Put soaked, drained bread through fine blade of food chopper along with anchovy filets, bacon and capers. Be sure fish is free of bones and skin. Break into fork-size pieces, or flake. Mix into bread mixture. Add egg yolks, onion, parsley and flavor with salt. Mix thoroughly but lightly. Fold in stiffly beaten egg whites, gently but thoroughly, with rubber spatula. Turn mixture into buttered 6-cup soufflé dish. Top with cheese and breadcrumbs and bake 45 minutes. Serve with Dill, Hollandaise, Mustard, or Mushroom Cream Sauce, pages 336, 341, 334, 335.

✿ / FISH PUDDING, WITH RAW FISH (*Fischpudding, von rohem Fisch*)

If you start with raw fish, this recipe gives a more solid sort of fish pudding.

4 TO 6 SERVINGS

2 stale rolls or 4 slices white
    bread
1 cup milk, approximately

2 pounds white firm-fleshed fish,
    or salmon (inexpensive fish
    will do very nicely here)

lemon juice or vinegar
salt
3 slices bacon
4 tablespoons butter
3 eggs
1 tablespoon grated Parmesan
cheese (optional)

2 tablespoons grated onion
2 tablespoons flour
salt and pepper to taste
butter
breadcrumbs

Preheat oven to 375°. Soak rolls or bread in milk and when soft, squeeze out all excess milk. Clean, wash and bone fish and grind three-quarters of it through fine blade of a food chopper. Cut rest of fish in several long strips and sprinkle with lemon juice and salt. Let stand for 20 minutes. Grind soaked, drained bread through food chopper with bacon. Cream butter in a mixing bowl and gradually work in whole eggs. Add ground fish, rolls, cheese, grated onion, flour, salt and pepper and mix thoroughly. Dry large pieces of fish and gently stir them into ground-fish mixture. Butter a 6-cup soufflé dish or pudding form. Sprinkle sides and bottom with breadcrumbs and tap out excess. Turn fish mixture into dish or form. Set in a pan of hot water and bake in preheated oven 1 hour, or until a knife inserted into the center of the pudding comes out clean. If you use a pudding form with a cover, steam in a water bath on the stove for the same amount of time. Serve with sauces indicated for Fish Soufflé, above.

✠ / CRAYFISH OR SHRIMP IN BEER (Krebse oder Garnelen in Weissbier)

Guests have to shell their own, or go without dinner, when you serve this dish.

2 SERVINGS

1½ pounds shrimp that run 14
    to 16 per pound, or 20
    crayfish tails (thawed, if
    frozen)
salt
1 tablespoon caraway seeds
4 cups Munich or Berlin
    Weissbier (if unavailable,
    use light ale)

⅓ cup butter
salt
nutmeg
6 peppercorns
strip of lemon peel

Wash shrimp or crayfish tails and cover with water. Add salt and caraway seeds. Cook at moderate simmer until done, about 10 minutes.

Remove from stock and drain. Heat beer and add butter, salt, nutmeg, peppercorns and lemon peel. When butter has melted, add drained cooked shrimp or crayfish tails. Turn off heat, cover pot and let stand 15 minutes. Serve crayfish tails or shrimp, in the shells, in deep-rimmed soup bowl with a little beer stock spooned over them.

✂ / CRAB, SHRIMP OR LOBSTER BUTTER (*Krabben-, Garnelen- oder Hummerbutter*)

Crab butter is used as a spread for canapés and open sandwiches, and as a base for white sauce. It is also melted into fish soups and is an important ingredient in Keukenragout, the savory fricassee that is a Bremen specialty. If crayfish are unavailable, or seem too expensive for such purposes, use large shrimp instead. Lobster butter can be made in the same way.

> *2 hard-shell crabs or 16 medium-* *⅔ cup butter*
> *sized shrimp, or 1 ¾-pound*   *4 cups water*
> *lobster*

Remove crabmeat, shrimp or lobster from shell. Dry shell on paper towel and with sharp knife, or meat cleaver, chop as fine as possible. De-vein shrimp if you use them. Heat butter in a skillet and when hot and bubbling, add chopped shells. Sauté over moderate heat until they turn bright red. Stir and sauté carefully as this butter will be ruined if it starts to brown. When shells are bright red, add water. Chop meat and add to pot. Cover and simmer ½ hour. Pour into deep, narrow bowl or wide-mouthed jar and chill overnight. The pieces of shell and the shellfish meat will sink to bottom; the butter will set at the top. Remove layer of butter and use as needed. The stock may be strained and used as a base for soups, sauces or for poaching fish. Use this shellfish butter instead of regular butter when making White Sauce, page 331, for fish dishes or fish soups. To make the Keukenragout referred to above, follow recipe for Chicken Fricassee, page 221, using 2 very young broilers. Use this butter as a base for sauce indicated at end. Garnish with crayfish tails or shrimp. Sliced mushrooms sautéed a few minutes in a little butter can be added also, as can some cooked asparagus tips.

✖ / MUSSELS IN DILL SAUCE (*Muscheln in Dillsosse*)

2 TO 4 SERVINGS

24 to 30 mussels
3 tablespoons butter
1 onion, minced
1 tablespoon minced parsley
½ to ⅔ cup dry white wine
3 tablespoons butter

3 tablespoons flour
1½ cups mussel stock
1 generous tablespoon minced
　fresh dill
salt and pepper

Scrub mussels with a stiff brush until free of sand, and debeard them. Heat butter in a deep pot or kettle and when hot and bubbling, add onion and parsley and sauté slowly for 2 or 3 minutes. Add the mussels and then the white wine. Cover pot, bring to a boil, reduce heat and simmer slowly but steadily for 8 to 10 minutes, or until mussels shells open. Remove mussels and drain. Strain stock and reserve. Take mussels out of shells very gently so as not to break them. Discard shells. Heat butter in 2-quart saucepan and when hot and bubbling, stir in flour. Stir and sauté slowly for about 5 minutes, or until flour begins to take on color. Add strained mussel stock. If you do not have 1½ cups, make up the difference with water, or a combination of water and white wine. Beat sauce with wire whisk or wooden spoon, over low heat, until smooth. Add dill and salt and pepper to taste. Add shelled mussels to sauce and simmer, covered, for 10 minutes. Check seasoning and serve.

✖ / HELGOLAND CRABMEAT, SHRIMP OR LOBSTER SALAD (*Helgolander Krabben-, Garnelen- oder Hummersalat*)

Helgoland—Holy Land—is a picturesque island just off Hamburg; it is the home of this excellent salad which can be served as an appetizer or luncheon entree.

2 TO 4 SERVINGS AS ENTREE;
6 AS AN APPETIZER

1 pound cooked lump crabmeat,
　or 1½ pounds small shrimp,
　cooked, shelled and de-
　veined, or 1 pound cooked,
　shelled lobster meat

1 cup cooked rice
2 teaspoons curry powder
1 cup mayonnaise
2 hard-cooked eggs, chopped
　salt and pepper

lemon juice to taste
1 *tablespoon minced parsley
and/or dill*

pinch of dried chervil (optional)

Pick over crabmeat and remove spiny pieces; or cut shrimp if they seem too large to toss; or cut lobster meat into fork-size pieces. Toss shellfish meat and rice lightly together with a fork. Stir curry power into mayonnaise and blend well. Spoon over shellfish and rice and mix lightly with a fork. When dressing is almost completely mixed into salad, add chopped egg and toss again, flavoring as you do so with salt, pepper, a dash or two of lemon juice and any of the other ingredients you want to use. Toss until well mixed. Chill for 2 hours.

※ / *LOBSTER AND CHICKEN SALAD* (*Hummer- und Hühnersalat*)

Chicken and lobster combine somewhat surprisingly in this excellent salad. Serve with chilled white wine and hot buttered toast.

4 TO 6 SERVINGS

2 *cups cooked lobster meat*
2 *cups cooked, diced white
meat of chicken
lemon juice*
¾ *to* 1 *teaspoon salt
pepper, preferably freshly
ground
pinch of curry powder (optional)*

½ *cup mayonnaise*
2 *tablespoons juice from asparagus or peas*
1 *cup cooked fresh or frozen green
peas, or* 1 *cup* 1" *tips of cooked
fresh asparagus*

Cut lobster meat into fork-size chunks. Be sure that all bits of skin, fat and cartilege are trimmed off chicken. Sprinkle with lemon juice; toss and set aside for 30 minutes. Mix salt and a dash of pepper into mayonnaise, along with curry powder and vegetable liquid. Stir until well blended. Add to chicken and lobster and toss lightly with a fork until almost completely mixed. Add peas or asparagus and toss carefully until all ingredients are well mixed. Try not to mash vegetables. If dressing seems too thin to cling to salad, bind with a little more mayonnaise as needed.

❧ / FROGS' LEGS STEW (*Froschschenkelragout*)

6 SERVINGS

24 medium-sized, or 18 jumbo-
      sized, frogs' legs
      water to cover
½ to 1 cup vinegar
      salt
⅓ cup butter
 2 tablespoons flour
 2 cups meat stock
      strip of lemon peel

      nutmeg
1 egg yolk
¼ cup sour cream
1 tablespoon capers, well
      drained
3 or 4 minced anchovy filets or
      anchovy paste (optional)

Cover well-trimmed frogs' legs with water and add vinegar. Soak 45 minutes. Remove from water, drain and pat dry with paper towel. Sprinkle with salt. Heat butter in a shallow casserole or deep skillet with a cover. When butter is hot and bubbling, add frogs' legs and fry, turning several times, so they become golden brown on all sides. Sprinkle with flour. Stir and sauté until flour is absorbed and begins to turn color, about 4 minutes. Add stock, lemon peel and a dash of nutmeg. Cover and simmer slowly but steadily about 15 minutes, or until meat is tender. Remove peel. Beat egg yolk into sour cream and add very slowly to hot, but not boiling, gravy. Season to taste with salt, well-drained capers and, if you like, minced anchovies or a dab of anchovy paste. Heat thoroughly but do not boil.

N O T E

If you use frozen frogs' legs, thaw completely before proceeding.

VII

Meat

(Fleisch)

❖ ❖ ❖ ❖ ❖

No people in the world like meat more than the Germans do, whether it is pork, beef, veal or lamb, the important thing is that it be served in enormous portions. One favorite, braised veal shank (Kalbshaxe), is served in a standard portion that looks like enough for four people. Fresh pork (Schwein) and smoked or cured ham or bacon (Schinken or Speck) are probably the most popular meats in Germany, especially if one takes into account the eastern section of the country that is now a part of the Deutsche Demokratische Republik. But veal (Kalbfleisch) and beef (Lende when it is cut from the loin; Rind when it is from any other part) are very close behind pork in popularity and appear even more frequently on upper-class restaurant menus, as they are regarded as being a little more special. Lamb (Lamm) and mutton (Hammel) are not nearly as important in the German cuisine, though a few traditional recipes have developed around them. Incidentally, the mutton in Germany is just about comparable to our lamb, as our animals are allowed to grow much larger than those in Europe. Mutton requires longer cooking than lamb and its stronger flavor seems to call for a little more garlic or other seasoning; beyond that, you may use the two meats interchangeably.

The Germans take variety meats and innards (Innereien) very seriously, and have some delectable ways of preparing them. The liver (Leber), lungs (Lungen), tongue (Zunge), kidneys (Nieren), sweetbread (Bries or Kalbsmilch), brains (Hirne) and heart (Herz) of pigs, calves, steer, lamb and sheep are considered great delicacies. So are the head, hocks, feet, tail and, in some cases, the ears and the cheeks. Baked udder (gebackenes Euter), ox palate (Ochsengaumen), calves' spleen (Kalbsmilz) and the fried blood (geröstetes Blut) of calves, pigs and chickens are all favorites, found in homes rather than in restaurants. Stomachs and intestines of various animals are used for sausage casings and to hold pudding-stuffings that are steamed. It is said that the Germans eat every part of the pig except the squeak; the same might be said of the moo and the baa and the bleat.

Recipes for many of these innards and variety meats are included in this chapter, but I have used only those ingredients that are readily available and would be more generally popular.

Although there is a great variety of meat served in Germany, there is less variety in preparation. The meat may be grilled or broiled (gegrillt), boiled (gekocht) and fried (geröstet or gebraten) or sometimes roasted. However, most meat in Germany is braised, or pot-roasted, a process which goes by a number of different names. Meat that is lightly browned and cooked with almost no added liquid is gedünstet or gedämpft; when a great deal of liquid is added, it is gebraten or geschmort; or if that braising is done in the oven it is sometimes called, again, geröstet. A braised steak is a Rostbraten. The more German cookbooks one reads, the more confused the situation becomes, and differences in the processes are virtually indiscernible when reading recipes. These terms are included here just to give you a rough idea of what to expect when you order from a German menu.

GENERAL RULES FOR BRAISING MEAT

To braise meat, brown it slowly on all sides in hot fat, sauté onions and other root vegetables in the same fat, then add liquid and cover the pot tightly. The meat should simmer very, very slowly but steadily until it is done. That is the basic braising process. Variety comes from the meat used, the kind of fat, the vegetables and seasonings, the liquid used for cooking and the additions to the gravy. Braising is usually done on top of the stove, but it can also be done in the oven. Although the latter assures an even heat on all sides, the gravy tends to be thinner and greasier and needs more skimming and thickening.

The pot used for braising is extremely important. It should fit the meat as closely as possible so that no heat is dissipated in empty spaces. It should also have a tight-fitting lid and be made of a very heavy material that holds heat and distributes it evenly. Enameled cast iron is the best material for this. An oval or round Dutch oven is best for braising. The oval shape wastes less space, since most of the meats you braise will be long and narrow, but you should also have one round Dutch oven for cuts such as brisket. A 5-quart and a 7-quart oval, plus one 3-quart round Dutch oven or casserole would be an excellent combination to own.

Since it is important that the meat does not lose its juices while braising, it should never be pierced with a fork. Have the butcher tie some string around it securely to serve as a handle for turning the meat in the pan. Also, be sure that the meat is well seared and golden brown on all sides. If it is not seared, it will lose juices; if it is seared black, the same thing will happen, as the charred covering will come off during the cooking. Meat must be cooked at a very slow simmer, or it will also lose juices. If you cannot lower the flame sufficiently to keep the sauce at a low simmer, place an asbestos mat under the pot to cut and distribute the heat. Braised meat shrinks and becomes hard and dense when its juices cook out.

Braised meats are great favorites in Germany for two reasons. In the first place they enable the housewife to use less tender, less expensive cuts of meat. Second, they provide delicious gravies to go with the boiled potatoes and dumplings that Germans love so much. I suppose we could play "which-came-first-the-dumpling-or-the-gravy?" but it hardly seems to matter; as long as they're both here, let's enjoy them.

NOTE

A long marrow bone is often added to pot roasts to enrich the gravy. Although it adds to the flavor, it tends to make the gravy very fatty. However, if you would like to add the bone, brown it first, either by roasting it in the oven or browning it in the pan fat, before you sauté the vegetables.

BEEF
(Rindfleisch)

/ BEEF TARTAR

This is a tremendous favorite in Germany, either as an appetizer or canapé topping, or as a main course. It is always an expensive item on a menu as it requires top-quality ingredients. Since nothing is cooked, sauced or seasoned, there is absolutely no margin for error, and a Beef Tartar Feinschmecker can immediately spot meat that is not as fresh or of the quality that it should be. In Germany, the meat and its condiments are always served separately and everyone mixes his own, according to his taste. This is often a ceremony worth watching.

The beef is, of course, the most important part of this dish. It should be filet or sirloin and absolutely without any fat. Ideally, this beef should be scraped, not ground. In Germany and other parts of Europe, there is a little metal knife made specially for this purpose. Here, you can try the same thing with a silver teaspoon, though it is not nearly as good. The meat is scraped so that none of the sinew or other tissue finds its way into the final result. As a second choice, use a food processor, or, a third choice, put meat through the medium blade of a grinder. It is best to grind meat for tartar yourself just before serving, so it does not have to be refrigerated. Come as close to that as you can. There is another very sound reason for grinding meat at home when you plan to eat it raw. A butcher grinds all his meat in the same chopper, pork included. There are certain to be particles of pork left in the machine, some of which may well go into your beef, along with any trichinae that the pork may contain. Since the meat will not be cooked, this is very risky business indeed.

The meat patties may be served directly in the center of a dinner plate, or from a large platter or wooden plank. The condiments can be arranged around the meat, or served in separate dishes; the second method is preferable, although the first might look better. If all of the condiments are directly on the plate, it may be difficult to exclude those one does not want. The raw egg yolk that is so traditional with Tartar looks very pretty if it is served in half an egg shell set in an egg cup. If you are sure your guests want the egg yolk, one can be nested directly in the center of each meat patty.

For each serving:

¼ to ½ *pound raw, lean scraped
    or ground meat (sirloin or
    filet)*
1 *egg yolk*
1 *tablespoon finely minced raw
    onion*
1 *tablespoon capers*
1 *tablespoon freshly grated
    horseradish (optional)*

1 *to* 2 *gherkins (optional)*
1 *to* 2 *anchovy filets (optional)*
salt, preferably coarse
*black pepper, served from a
    mill*
*toast or Westphalian-style
    pumpernickel*

Prepare meat as directed above, either by scraping or grinding as close to serving time as possible. Shape into a patty as for hamburger. Let each guest grind pepper directly onto the meat. Serve toast or bread on the side.

✂ / *STEAKS* (*Beefsteaks oder Lendenschnitte*)

Steaks from the loin (Lende) cuts are either grilled in a broiler or pan-fried in a little butter. They are then sprinkled with salt and pepper and served. In Germany, they are almost always served on large platters surrounded by all sorts of vegetables; and, generally, they are topped with some onions that have been sautéed in the butter in which the steak was fried. Béarnaise Sauce (page 342) or parsley butter is usually served on the side. Creamed or stewed mushrooms, grilled tomato halves, potatoes both boiled and French-fried and buttered carrots are often included in the arrangement. If the cook is in a more exotic frame of mind, the steaks may be topped or surrounded by mandarins (tangerines), pineapple chunks or slices, fried banana slices or any other fruit that suggests the tropics.

✂ / *STEAK SEASONING* (*Steakwürze*)

Steak is often prepared in Germany with this highly seasoned mixture in which the meat marinates for varying lengths of time, usually 1 hour for every inch-thickness of steak. A flank steak intended for London Broil should marinate 8 hours.

For a 2- to 3-pound sirloin steak:

2 tablespoons hot prepared
　mustard
2 tablespoons olive oil, or other
　vegetable oil
½ teaspoon curry powder

½ clove garlic, crushed
generous pinch of freshly
　ground black pepper
1 tablespoon brandy
1 teaspoon soy sauce (optional)

Mix all ingredients well and spread on both sides of a steak, or on chunks of meat to be broiled on skewers. For a flank steak, double the recipe. During barbecue season, when you might want to use the seasoning often, make up a jar full of it, cover tightly and store in refrigerator or in a cool cupboard. Omit garlic and mix it with sauce just before spreading it on meat, or rub meat with a cut clove of garlic before spreading sauce.

⊠ / ROAST BEEF (*Lendenbraten*)

Sirloin or filet of beef is a great favorite in Germany, although its high cost makes it a dish for only the most special occasions—so much so, in fact, that it is in the class of delicatessen. Paper-thin slices of rare roast beef are used for canapés and elegant appetizers but are main courses only in the wealthiest homes. Most often it is prepared English style (englischer Art). This is nothing more than a boned and rolled rib roast, a top sirloin or a filet rubbed with softened butter and then seared on all sides in a 450° oven about 25 minutes. The heat is then lowered to 325° and the meat is roasted 18 minutes per pound if it is to be rare; 20 minutes per pound for medium rare; 23 per pound for medium; and 28 per pound for well-done. The meat is basted with pan juices every 20 minutes. The only gravy served with this is the pan juice. The fat is skimmed off and a tablespoon of butter is swirled in. It is then brought to a boil in the roasting pan on the stove so that the coagulated juices can be scraped into the gravy with a wooden spoon. The meat is seasoned with salt and pepper after it has been sliced.

When it is not "English," roast beef in Germany is cooked with more of an eye toward gravy. It is buttered and seared in the same way, but once brown, a cup of water or beef stock is poured into pan; this is used for basting. When the roast has 30 to 40 minutes of cooking time to go, a diced onion and a cut tomato are added to pan. When meat is done, the gravy is brought to a boil in roasting pan on stove and the coagulated juices are scraped into it with a wooden spoon. It is then strained into a clean saucepan and excess fat is removed. The gravy is thickened with a little cornstarch dissolved in cold water, or ½ cup sour cream blended with a tablespoonful of flour. Salt and pepper are added to taste and gravy is heated thoroughly.

⊠ / BOILED BEEF (*Gekochtes Rindfleisch*)

8 TO 10 SERVINGS

4 to 5 pounds beef for boiling
(first-cut flanken, brisket
or chuck)
1 veal knuckle or marrow bone
(optional)

pot vegetables, page 29, left
whole or in large pieces
1 tablespoon salt, or as needed

The meat should be tied with string so that it will retain its shape. Bring 3 to 4 quarts of water to boil in a kettle. Place tied meat and bone (if used) in large soup kettle or Dutch oven and pour boiling water over it. There should be about 6″ of water above surface of meat. If you prefer, you can start to cook meat in cold water; this will give the broth a better flavor but the meat will lose some in the process. Cover pot and simmer slowly but steadily 2 hours, skimming as necessary. Add pot vegetables and simmer another 2 hours, or until meat is tender and can be pierced easily with carving fork or skewer. When meat is done, taste broth and season as needed. Slice meat onto heated platter, spoon a little soup over it and slice pot vegetables around it.

VARIATIONS

1. For broth with a stronger flavor and a slightly darker color, both bone and onion can be browned in oven before being added to soup.
2. If you want to serve more vegetables, cook them in salted water until almost done and then finish in broth along with meat.
3. Boiled beef goes by many names in Germany and neighboring Austria, depending on cut of meat used, the vegetables cooked in stock and the sauce served with it. Boiled Beef with Horseradish Sauce (Gekochtes Rindfleisch mit Meerrettichsosse) is Badisches Ochsenfleisch in Swabia. In Hanover, a few cloves are added to stock, and the sliced beef is served garnished with boiled white onions, halves of hard-cooked eggs, slices of dill pickle and mayonnaise thinned with a little caper vinegar and then mixed with capers and a little anchovy paste.
4. Corned Beef Brisket (Gepökelte Rinderbrust), or smoked corned beef brisket, is cooked in the same way as Boiled Beef. It is then sliced and served with vegetables, or with sauerkraut or cabbage.

⛝ / *POT ROAST OF BEEF* (*Rinderschmorbraten*)

8 TO 10 SERVINGS

4- to 5-pound pot roast of beef (rump, top, bottom or eye round or brisket)
bacon or salt pork for larding, if necessary
salt and pepper
flour
3 tablespoons butter, bacon fat or lard
1 large onion, sliced
1 large carrot, sliced
1 leek, sliced (optional)

1 small parsley root, scraped and sliced (optional)
½ small knob celery, peeled and diced (optional)
1 bay leaf
heel or ½ cup crusts pumpernickel or sour rye bread (optional)
water or beef stock, as needed
½ cup sour cream
1 or 2 tablespoons tomato purée (optional)

If meat is lean, it will need larding. Either you or your butcher can do this, using strips of bacon or salt pork. Have a string tied around meat to keep it in shape and to serve as a handle for turning so you don't pierce surface of meat with a fork. Rub meat with salt and pepper and dredge lightly with flour on all sides. Heat fat in a 5-quart Dutch oven or casserole. When fat is hot, add meat and sear slowly to mellow golden brown color on all sides; do not let it turn dark brown or black. This should take about 15 minutes. Remove meat and add all cut vegetables to hot fat. Sauté slowly, stirring from time to time so they soften and turn bright yellow. Return meat to pot, placing it on top of sautéed vegetables. Add bay leaf and bread and pour in about 1 cup of water or stock; there should be just about 1″ of liquid on bottom of pot. Cover with a tight-fitting lid. Simmer very slowly as described for braised meat, page 140. Turn meat several times during cooking, using string as a handle. Add more liquid to pan if necessary as meat cooks. Simmer very slowly but steadily 3½ to 4 hours, or until meat can easily be pierced with a carving fork or skewer. Remove meat to a heated platter. Strain gravy, rubbing vegetables and bread through the sieve. Return to pot, skim off excess fat. Stir in sour cream and add tomato purée if you want to use it. Check seasoning. Return meat to pot and heat thoroughly about 10 minutes.

VARIATIONS

1. You can brown the pot roast without dredging it and thicken the gravy before serving with flour dissolved in cold water, or ½ cup sour cream blended with 1 tablespoon flour. Tomato purée may be used or eliminated.
2. Smaller cuts can be used. Buy a 2″- or 3″-thick steak cut from the round or rump and pound to tenderize it. It may then be seasoned, browned and braised with vegetables in the same way as the pot roast. You will need much less water and the meat will be tender in 1 to 1½ hours of slow, steady simmering. You can flour meat before browning it, or thicken sauce with flour when it has finished cooking and been strained. To serve, cut crosswise slices of meat and serve with sauce. Prepared this way, a 2-pound slice of meat will serve four fairly generously.

/ *POTTED BEEF BRISKET* (*Gedämpfte Rinderbrust*)

8 TO 10 SERVINGS

4 pounds fresh brisket of beef
1 large clove garlic, cut in half
salt and pepper
2 tablespoons butter, bacon fat or beef drippings
2 large onions, sliced

1 *heel of sour rye bread*   *flour, if necessary*
½ *cup water or beef stock, or as*
    needed

Have brisket tied with string so it will hold its shape and be easy to
turn. Rub all sides with cut garlic clove and sprinkle with salt and
pepper. Heat fat in a Dutch oven or deep heavy skillet with a tight-fitting
lid. Place meat in hot fat and brown very slowly on all sides. This should
take about 15 minutes and meat should be golden brown. Use string as a
handle for turning meat; do not pierce its surface with a fork. Remove
meat and add onions to hot fat, sautéing slowly until soft and pale
yellow. Return meat to pot, placing it on top of onions. Add rye bread
and water or stock. Cover and simmer slowly but steadily 3 to 4 hours.
If you cannot get heat low enough to keep gravy simmering, place an
asbestos mat under pot. Add more liquid if necessary; there should be
just enough to keep onions and meat from scorching. The meat is done
when it can be pierced easily with carving fork or skewer. Remove to
heated platter. Strain gravy and return to pot. Skim off excess fat and
if necessary, thicken with 2 tablespoons flour dissolved in a little cold
water. Check seasoning. Return meat to gravy and simmer about 10
minutes. Slice meat onto heated platter and serve gravy in heated
sauceboat.

VARIATION

For a rich paprika sauce, sprinkle liberally with sweet paprika before
browning and add 1 tablespoon paprika to onions when you sauté them.
Follow rest of recipe, but eliminate rye bread and instead stir in 2 or 3
tablespoons sour cream after gravy has been strained and excess fat removed. One tablespoon flour can be mixed into sour cream before it is
added to gravy to thicken sauce.

⧅ / *RHINELAND MARINATED POT ROAST*
(*Rheinischer Sauerbraten*)

Next to frankfurters and sauerkraut, Sauerbraten is Germany's most
famous food specialty. Every cook and every province has a different
version of this dish, but in my travels, none compared to the Sauerbraten
found along the Rhine. Its distinguishing characteristics are the white
raisins and the velvety, golden-brown, sweet-sour sauce that bears absolutely no resemblance to the watery, vinegar-sharp gravy served in
German and Austrian restaurants in the United States.

5-pound rump of beef (top or bottom round can be used but they are not quite as good)

bacon or salt pork for larding
salt

3 cups white vinegar (approximately)

3 cups water (approximately)

1 large onion, sliced

2 bay leaves

8 cloves

8 peppercorns

1 tablespoon pickling spices

1 large carrot, scraped and sliced

4 slices bacon and 2 tablespoons butter, or 5 tablespoons bacon fat, kidney fat or beef drippings

2 large onions, sliced

1 bay leaf

6 cloves

2 tablespoons butter

3 tablespoons flour

2 tablespoons sugar

lemon juice to taste

½ cup white raisins, soaked in warm water

tomato purée or sour cream (optional)

Rump or round of beef should be well larded with thin matchstick strips of bacon or salt pork. This can be done by you or your butcher. Tie meat firmly with string in several places so it will be easy to turn without piercing and will hold its shape. Rub well with salt on all sides and place in deep, close-fitting glass or earthenware bowl. Combine vinegar and water and add onion, bay leaves, cloves, peppercorns, pickling spices and carrot. Bring to a boil and simmer 5 minutes. Cool marinade and pour over beef. The meat should be completely covered by marinade; if it is not, add equal amounts of water and vinegar until it is. Cover and place in refrigerator for 3 to 5 days; the longer it stands, the more piquant the roast will be, so adjust time to suit your own taste. Turn meat in marinade 2 or 3 times each day, using the string as a handle. Remove meat from marinade. Strain marinade and reserve. Dry meat thoroughly on all sides with plenty of paper toweling. The meat will not brown properly if it is wet, so dry it as much as you possibly can. Dice bacon and fry it slowly in butter in a 5-quart Dutch oven or casserole. If you prefer lard, dice it and fry instead of bacon, but eliminate butter. When fat is hot, add meat and brown slowly. Using the string as a handle, turn so meat is well seared and golden brown (but not black) on all sides. This should take about 15 minutes. Remove browned meat and add sliced onions to hot fat. Fry, stirring from time to time, until onions are deep golden brown, but not black.

Return meat to pot, placing it on top of onions. Add marinade until it reaches about halfway up sides of meat. Add bay leaf and cloves (not those used in marinade). Bring marinade to a boil, cover pot tightly with a heavy close-fitting lid, reduce heat and simmer very, very slowly but steadily 3½ to 4 hours, turning meat two or three times during cooking. Add more marinade to pot if it is needed. If you cannot lower heat enough to keep sauce at a slow simmer, place an asbestos mat under pot. The meat is done when it can be pierced easily with a long-pronged fork or skewer.

Remove meat to a heated platter and strain gravy. Skim off excess fat and return gravy to pot. Melt butter in saucepan and when hot, stir in flour and sugar. Cook over very low heat, stirring constantly until sugar mixture turns a deep caramel color. Be very careful doing this, as sugar burns all at once, and if it becomes black, you'll have to start this part of the operation all over again. Add the sugar-flour to the hot gravy and stir through briskly with a wooden spoon or, preferably, a wire whisk. Season with lemon juice to taste; gravy should have a mild sweet-sour flavor. Add raisins, which have been soaked and drained. Return meat to pot, cover and simmer 10 minutes. If sauce becomes too thick, add a little more marinade. A tablespoonful tomato purée or sour cream can be stirred in and heated through 4 or 5 minutes before serving time. The latter is used more in Bavaria than along the Rhine. The tomato purée enriches the color of the gravy. Use one or the other or neither; never both. Check gravy for seasoning. Slice meat and arrange on a heated platter and mask with a little gravy, serving the rest in a heated sauceboat.

VARIATIONS

1.   6 or 8 crumbled gingersnaps or Lebkuchen are often added to this gravy for last ½ hour of cooking. They add flavor and richness.

2.   You may change marinade to suit your own taste. Use more or less water or vinegar, depending upon how sour you like it, and you can also substitute wine for vinegar. Any dry red wine, German or otherwise, will do.

3.   If you would like to try a Sauerbraten other than Rheinischer, use same marinade and methods of cooking, but do not use sugar in the thickening and do not add lemon juice or raisins. Other vegetables such as parsley and celery roots are added and a heel of rye bread is used instead of gingersnaps in last hour of cooking. Slice vegetables and sauté them in the fat, along with onions, before adding meat.

4.   Any meat can be cooked Sauerbraten style—lamb, mutton or pork. The latter should not be larded. Veal is an exception and will not make a good Sauerbraten.

5.   For a very rich gravy, brown a marrow bone along with vegetables and cook it with meat.

▓ / *POT ROAST OF BEEF IN BEER* (*Rinderschmorbraten in Bier*)

8 TO 10 GENEROUS SERVINGS

5–pound beef pot roast (rump is best for this but you can use   *top or bottom round instead)*

salt pork or bacon for larding
1 tablespoon salt (approximately)
1 tablespoon sugar (approximately)
6 to 8 cloves
6 to 8 peppercorns, slightly
   crushed
2 teaspoons caraway seeds
6 juniper berries, slightly crushed
1 large bay leaf
1 large clove garlic, slightly
   crushed
   1 large onion, sliced

1 carrot, scraped and sliced
1 parsley root, scraped and
   sliced (optional)
3 or 4 sprigs of parsley
½ cup olive oil
2 cans dark beer
2 tablespoons beef drippings,
   butter or bacon fat
   heel of sour rye bread (optional)
1 tablespoon butter
2 tablespoons flour
   salt and pepper to taste

The pot roast should be well larded with strips of salt pork or bacon by you or your butcher. Tie meat into a compact shape with string, so that you can turn it without piercing its surface with a fork. Sprinkle on all sides with salt and sugar. Place in a deep, close-fitting earthenware or glass bowl. Add cloves, peppercorns, caraway seeds, juniper berries, bay leaf, garlic, onion and carrot slices, parsley root and parsley. Combine olive oil and beer and pour over meat. Marinate in refrigerator 10 or 12 hours, turning several times.

Remove meat from marinade. Strain marinade and reserve. Dry meat very thoroughly with plenty of paper toweling, or it will not brown. Heat beef drippings or butter in a 5-quart Dutch oven or casserole. When fat is very hot, add meat, reduce heat a little and brown on all sides, using the string for turning the meat. This should take about 15 minutes. The meat should be well seared and a deep golden-brown color, but not blackened. Drain browning fat from pot and add enough strained marinade to cover the bottom of the pan—about ½ cup. Bring to a boil, cover, reduce heat and simmer very, very slowly, but steadily 3½ to 4 hours, turning meat two or three times during cooking. The meat is done when it can be pierced easily with a long-pronged fork or skewer. If you cannot get flame low enough to keep liquid bubbling slowly, place an asbestos mat under the pot. Check during cooking to see if more marinade is needed. Add heel of rye bread during last hour of cooking.

Remove meat to a hot platter and skim excess fat from cooking liquid. Heat butter in a saucepan and in it brown flour, very slowly, stirring constantly over low heat. When flour is color of cocoa, add cupful of cooking liquid to it and stir vigorously or beat with a wire whisk, over very low heat, until mixture is smooth and about as thick as sour cream. Pour this into rest of cooking liquid, stirring it in with a wooden spoon or wire whisk. Simmer slowly and keep hot until serving time. Slice meat and arrange on a heated platter. Check gravy for seasoning and serve in a heated gravy boat.

⧙ / *BRAISED BEEF ROLLS* (*Rinderrouladen*)

6 GENEROUS SERVINGS

2½ pounds round steak, thinly
    sliced as for veal scallopini
    (about ¼" thick)
6 slices bacon, diced
2 large onions, minced
    generous handful minced
    parsley
    salt and pepper
    flour

3 tablespoons butter, bacon fat
    or kidney fat
1 onion, minced
1 carrot, sliced (optional)
1 cup water or beef stock
½ cup sour cream (optional)
1 to 2 tablespoons tomato purée
    (optional)

The round steak should be pounded to almost paper-thinness by you or your butcher. Slices should then be cut into pieces approximately 3" wide and 4" to 5" long. They may be more or less oval to rectangular in shape. There should be approximately 12 to 16 strips from 2½ pounds of meat if it has been pounded thinly enough and cut more or less as described.

Fry the bacon slowly with the minced onion and parsley until vegetables are soft but not browned. Sprinkle one side of each meat slice with salt and pepper and spread with bacon-onion-parsley mixture. Roll meat tightly and tie with kitchen string or secure with toothpicks. Dredge each beef roll in flour. Heat fat in a shallow wide fireproof casserole with a tight-fitting lid. When fat is hot, brown beef rolls lightly, a few at a time, turning so they are seared on all sides, removing them as they are done. When all the meat has been browned, add minced onion and carrot and brown slowly, about 5 to 7 minutes, stirring several times. When vegetables are golden brown, place beef rolls on top of them. Add water or stock. Cover, bring to a boil, reduce heat and simmer very slowly but steadily 1 to 1½ hours, or until beef rolls are tender. Add liquid if necessary as meat cooks. Remove beef rolls to a heated platter. Strain sauce and return to casserole. Skim excess fat from surface and stir in sour cream and tomato purée, if you are using either or both. Check seasoning, adding salt and pepper as necessary. Return beef rolls to sauce and heat thoroughly before serving.

VARIATIONS

1. A little prepared mustard can be spread on beef rolls before onion mixture.

2. For paprika sauce, add 1 tablespoon to onion and carrot as they brown in pan.

3. If you use ½ cup red wine and ½ cup water for your cooking liquid, add wine to browned onion and carrot and simmer a minute or two before adding beef rolls and water.

4. Vegetable Stuffing: Sprinkle meat slice on one side with salt and pepper, spreading with a little mustard first if you wish to. Cut a scraped raw carrot in half lengthwise and then in half again, and lay one of these quarter strips on each meat slice, along with a lengthwise quarter-strip of dill pickle and a thick slice or wedge of raw onion. Roll, tie, dredge with flour and proceed with recipe as described, adding a small bay leaf to cooking liquid.

5. Sausage Stuffing: Mix ½ pound country-style pork sausage with a generous pinch of salt and pepper, some chopped parsley and 1 medium-sized onion minced and sautéed in butter or fat. A little thyme can be added for flavor as well.

6. Hunters' Beef Rolls Stuffing (Jägerrouladen): Brown 4 tablespoons pumpernickel breadcrumbs, 1 finely minced onion and 4 slices diced bacon in a combination of butter and some of the bacon's own fat. When mixture is golden brown, mix in 4 to 6 rinsed, finely chopped anchovy filets, 3 or 4 minced sweet gherkins, 1 tablespoon chopped, drained capers, and spread this filling on lightly salted beef slices. Roll and tie beef and brown on all sides in butter. Add water or stock for cooking, as directed above, but do not use any vegetables other than onion. Thicken pan gravy with 1 tablespoon flour stirred into ½ cup sour cream. Season to taste with salt and pepper and, if you like, a little lemon juice.

⠌ / GERMAN HAMBURGER (*Deutsches Beefsteak*)

The hamburger comes from Hamburg, where it is known as Deutsches Beefsteak.

6 HAMBURGERS: 3 TO 6 SERVINGS

2 pounds ground beef (chuck and round combined in equal parts make a good mixture for this)
1 medium-sized onion
2 tablespoons minced parsley
2 eggs
2 teaspoons salt
pepper
2 tablespoons butter, melted
3 tablespoons flour
2 tablespoons butter or other fat for frying
2 onions, sliced and separated into rings

Put ground meat through fine blade of food chopper along with onion and parsley. Mix thoroughly with eggs, salt, a dash or two of pepper, melted butter and flour. It is best to mix this through with your hands, as the ingredients will be more thoroughly blended. Shape meat mixture into 6 oval patties. Heat butter or fat in a large, heavy skillet. When fat is hot (butter should not begin to brown), add meat patties. Fry until first side is rich brown; turn and brown second side. If you want hamburgers rare, fry first side 4 or 5 minutes, and second side 3 or 4. If you want hamburgers well done, fry slowly or they will be too brown by the time the centers are finished. When hamburgers are done, remove to a heated platter. Add onion rings to pan and sauté a few minutes until soft and bright yellow, but not brown. Spoon sautéed onion rings over hamburgers. If you would like a little sauce with this, pour ½ cup hot water or beef stock into pan; let it come to a boil once or twice as you stir and scrape coagulated pan juices into it. Pour over hamburgers with the onions.

VARIATIONS

1.   These hamburgers can also be made with a combination of raw ground meats: beef with pork, beef with veal, or equal parts of all three. If you use pork, hamburgers should be served well done.
2.   In Bavaria, where these meat patties are known as Fleischpfanzel, flour is not used in meat mixture. Instead, rolls or bread, soaked in water or milk and squeezed as dry as possible, are ground in with meat, and a little water is added during mixing. Use 1 large roll or 2 thick slices of bread with ingredients called for above. A little dried basil and grated lemon peel may be added along with other seasonings listed.
3.   Hamburger, Bremen Style (Bremer Beefsteak) is made by mixing 2 pounds ground beef with 2 tablespoons thick sour cream, 1 medium-sized boiled and mashed potato, 2 teaspoons salt and a dash of pepper. Shape into 6 oval patties. Slice a large onion thinly and separate into rings. Sauté rings until soft and deep yellow in butter or fat, remove to a heated platter and then fry hamburgers in same fat in which onions were sautéed. Remove finished hamburgers to a heated platter. Add ½ cup water or beef stock to frying pan and let it come to a boil once or twice as you stir and scrape coagulated pan juices into it. Season with salt and pepper. Serve hamburgers topped with sautéed onion rings and pan gravy.

▓ / *VIENNA STEAK WITH BRAISED ONIONS* (*Wiener Rostbraten*)

Another Viennese favorite that has found a home in Germany.

4 SERVINGS

4 rib steaks, ½" thick, well   salt and pepper
   trimmed   flour

3 *tablespoons butter*
2 *large onions, cut in rings or*
    coarsely chopped

1 *to* 2 *tablespoons butter, if*
    needed
1 *tablespoon flour*
½ *cup water or beef stock*

Pound steak well on both sides with wooden mallet. Sprinkle both sides with salt and pepper and dredge lightly with flour. Heat butter in large heavy skillet, preferably of iron, and when bubbling begins to subside, add steaks. Brown quickly on both sides. This should take about 6 to 8 minutes altogether for rare steak. Remove steaks to heated platter and add onions to pan. Add more butter if necessary and fry onions until they are soft and just begin to brown. Stir frequently so onions fry evenly. Sprinkle flour over browned onions and stir in over low heat until flour is absorbed. Sauté slowly 3 or 4 minutes and add stock or water. Bring to a boil twice, stirring with a wooden spoon to scrape coagulated pan juices into sauce. Season to taste with salt and pepper. Spoon onion sauce over steak.

VARIATION

Sirloin or filet mignon steaks can be prepared in same way, but they will not need any pounding.

⚄ / SWABIAN BRAISED STEAK (*Schwäbischer Rostbraten*)

6 SERVINGS

6 *small club steaks, about* 1″
    thick
¼ *pound sweet butter*
    salt and pepper
3 *medium-sized onions,*
    chopped

Cooked Sauerkraut, page 276
Spätzle, sautéed in butter, page
    60
diced fried bacon
6 *or* 8 *tiny fried Bratwurst or link*
    sausage

Pound steaks lightly, flattening them just a little. Heat butter in a large heavy skillet and when bubbling subsides, brown steaks 3 or 4 minutes on each side if you like them rare, 5 or 6 minutes for medium to medium well done. Remove to a heated platter and fry chopped onions in same butter until golden brown. Sprinkle steaks with salt and pepper and top with fried onions. Arrange sauerkraut on one side of platter and Spätzle on the other. Top the sauerkraut with a sprinkling of bacon and the sausages.

� / *ESTERHAZY BRAISED STEAK* (*Esterhazy Rostbraten*)

The Hungarian royal family gave their name to this braised steak, which is a favorite from the Danube to the Rhine.

6 SERVINGS

6 *½-pound club steaks*
   salt and pepper
6 *tablespoons butter, bacon fat*
   or beef drippings
2 *large onions, chopped*
2 *sliced carrots (optional)*

2 *stalks celery, sliced (optional)*
2 *tablespoons sweet paprika*
1 *tablespoon vinegar*
½ *to 1 cup water*
½ *to ¾ cup sour cream*

Pound steaks lightly to flatten them a little and then sprinkle on both sides with salt and pepper. Heat butter in a large heavy skillet with a tight-fitting lid and when bubbling subsides, brown steaks lightly. Remove steaks and fry onions, and any other vegetables you care to use, until golden brown. Stir over a low flame so they will brown evenly without burning. Add paprika and sauté a minute or two. Return steaks to pan and add vinegar and water. Cover pan and simmer slowly but steadily 1 hour, or until steak is tender. Add more water if necessary as meat cooks. Remove steaks to a heated platter. Strain sauce and purée vegetables through a sieve. Skim excess fat from sauce, return to pan and stir in sour cream. Check for seasoning. Return steak to sauce, heat a minute or two but do not boil.

✛ / *SAILORS' BEEF* (*Matrosenfleisch*)

4 TO 8 SERVINGS

8 *slices beef filet (tenderloin),*
   cut 1" to 1½" thickness
   salt and pepper
8 *slices bacon*
   flour
3 *tablespoons butter or lard*
1 *onion, minced*
1 *tablespoon minced parsley*

1 *tablespoon flour*
½ *cup water or beef stock*
1 *cup sour cream*
   strip of lemon peel
1 *teaspoon chopped capers*
   pinch of chervil or marjoram
4 *anchovy filets, minced (optional)*

Sprinkle filets with salt and pepper and wrap a slice of bacon around each steak, tying with string or securing with a toothpick. Dredge *one* side of each steak with flour. Heat butter or lard in a fireproof casserole or skillet with a tight-fitting lid, and in it brown floured side of each steak. Then turn and brown second side. The steak should be rare. Remove steaks and pour off most of fat, leaving just enough in which to sauté minced onion and parsley. When onion and parsley are soft but not browned, sprinkle with flour and stir a few minutes until flour is completely absorbed. Add water or stock and sour cream to casserole and stir until blended. Add all other ingredients and return meat to casserole. Cover and simmer slowly but steadily about 20 minutes, or until meat is tender.

▓ / ONION BEEF (*Zwiebelfleisch*)

6 SERVINGS

2 pounds round steak or sirloin tip
3 to 4 tablespoons butter, lard or kidney fat
6 medium-sized onions, chopped salt and pepper
¼ teaspoon marjoram

1 large clove garlic, sliced pinch of thyme
4 tablespoons vinegar strip of lemon peel
½ to 1 cup water or beef stock
3 tablespoons flour dissolved in a little cold water

The meat should be cut into thin leaf-like strips. Heat fat in 2-quart fireproof casserole or stew pot and in it fry onions slowly, stirring, until deep yellow but not quite brown. Add meat, salt, pepper, marjoram, garlic, thyme, vinegar, lemon peel and ½ cup water. Cover and simmer slowly but steadily ½ hour, adding more water if needed as meat cooks. When meat is tender, dissolve flour in just enough cold water to make a smooth paste and stir into gravy. Check seasoning and add more salt and pepper if needed.

Use boiled, roasted or braised beef for the following recipes for leftovers.

▓ / BEEF WITH EGGS (*Rindfleisch mit Eiern*)

2 SERVINGS

1½ to 2 cups beef strips
3 tablespoons butter or bacon fat
1 large onion, minced

½ cup beef stock (approximately)
2 to 3 eggs, lightly beaten
salt
2 tablespoons milk

The meat should be cut into strips about 2″ long and ¼″ thick. Heat butter in a 10″ skillet and in it sauté onion until it begins to soften and turn bright yellow. Add meat and brown lightly, stirring with a wooden spoon so that it browns evenly. Add beef stock and let simmer for a minute or two. There should be just enough stock to moisten meat and onions; they should not "swim." Beat eggs lightly with salt and milk and pour over meat and onions. Scramble eggs slowly until they reach desired degree of doneness.

❄ / TYROLEAN "ROAST" HASH (*Tiroler Geröstel*)

6 SERVINGS

7 or 8 medium-sized potatoes	*3 cups diced, cooked beef*
2 tablespoons lard or bacon fat	*salt and pepper*
2 onions, minced	

Scrub potatoes and boil in their jackets. Chill, peel and slice. Heat fat in an 11″ or 12″ skillet and in it sauté onion until it turns bright yellow. Add beef and sauté 5 to 8 minutes, or until it begins to brown; then add sliced potatoes. Season with salt and pepper and fry slowly. Turn mass over, pancake style, after about 8 to 10 minutes and brown on second side. Serve at once.

VARIATION

Beat 2 eggs lightly with 2 tablespoons milk and pour over the browned cooked hash. Cook over low heat until egg has set. Sprinkle with minced chives or parsley.

✖ VEAL ✖
(Kalbfleisch)

✖ / ROAST VEAL (Kalbsbraten)

4- to 5-pound veal roast (rump or
    leg, whole or boned and
    rolled)
4 slices bacon
    salt and pepper
4 tablespoons butter

1 small onion minced
1 small carrot, sliced (optional)
½ to 1 cup water or white wine
1 tomato, canned or fresh, cut
    in pieces
1 cup cream or buttermilk

Heat oven to 300°. The roast may be boned or not, the former being
much easier to slice. Tie bacon slices around meat. Sprinkle on all sides
with salt and pepper. Grease a rack, put it in an open roasting pan and
place veal on rack. Add butter, onion and carrot to roasting pan. Roast
slowly, allowing 30 to 35 minutes per pound of veal, using a meat
thermometer if you have one. Baste every 20 minutes with pan juices.
After an hour, or when onion and carrot have become lightly browned,
pour in enough water or wine to cover bottom of roasting pan. Add
tomato and pour cream or buttermilk over meat. Continue roasting until
meat is done. Remove finished veal to heated platter or carving board.
Strain gravy, rubbing vegetables through a sieve as much as possible.
Skim off excess fat and scrape coagulated pan juices into gravy. Gravy
may be thickened with a little flour mixed with cold water, or it may
be left clear. Check seasoning, reheat gravy and serve.

VARIATION

Some cooks prefer to brown meat in hot butter and then roast, covered.
This prevents veal from becoming dry. Add more liquid to pan if necessary during cooking but follow rest of recipe exactly.

/ *ROAST VEAL WITH KIDNEYS* (*Kalbsnierenbraten*)

Have your butcher bone a rump or leg of veal and place 2 veal kidneys with their fat on the bone cavity and then have roast tied. Roast as described in above recipe. Each slice served should have a piece of kidney in its center.

/ *VEAL POT ROAST* (*Geschmortes Kalbfleisch*)

Follow directions for Potted Beef Brisket, page 146, using a boned and rolled veal rump, leg or shoulder, or a filet. The veal should take ½ to 1 hour less cooking time than the beef. The braised filet will be done in 35 to 45 minutes.

/ *ROAST VEAL WITH ANCHOVIES* (*Kalbsbraten mit Sardellen*)

8 TO 10 SERVINGS

4- to 5-pound rump of veal, boned, rolled and tied
3 cloves garlic, cut in slivers
5 or 6 anchovy filets, cut in half
lemon juice
salt and pepper
4 strips of bacon
3 tablespoons butter
2 cups beef or veal stock
1 tablespoon flour or 2 tablespoons cornstarch dissolved in a little cold water
1 cup sour cream or sweet cream
2 tablespoons capers, drained

Heat oven to 375°. Lard veal with garlic slivers and anchovy filet pieces, tucking them into folds of meat. Rub roast on all sides with lemon juice and sprinkle with salt and pepper. The bacon can be cut in strips and larded into meat, or it can be slipped under the strings so that it covers the roast. Heat butter in a deep open roasting pan on top of stove and when butter is hot, brown veal on all sides slowly. This should take about 15 minutes. Use the string to turn meat; do not pierce it with a fork.

When the roast is brown, slip a rack under it and pour stock into pan. Roast in oven, basting every 20 minutes with pan juices. Allow about 30 minutes per pound or use a meat thermometer. Veal should be well done and white all the way through. If pink juices run out of meat when pierced, it is not done; juices must be clear and colorless. Remove finished roast to heated platter or carving board. Skim excess fat off pan juices. To thicken gravy, either stir dissolved cornstarch into it, bring to a boil and let simmer a minute or two, or do the same with flour. As you bring gravy to a boil in roasting pan, on top of stove, scrape coagulated pan juices into gravy with a wooden spoon. Finish gravy by stirring in 1 cup sweet or sour cream and letting it simmer a few minutes until hot and thick. Season with salt and pepper as necessary, then stir in well-drained capers before serving.

▨ / ROAST VEAL MARINATED IN BUTTERMILK (*Kalbsbraten in Buttermilch*)

8 TO 10 SERVINGS

4- to 5-pound veal rump, boned and rolled
bacon for larding, if necessary
2 to 3 quarts buttermilk, as needed
salt and pepper
5 or 6 slices bacon
4 tablespoons butter
piece of rind and about 1 cup of trimmings from smoked ham, preferably raw
1 large onion, diced

1 parsley root, scraped and sliced
1 large carrot, scraped and sliced
1 large bay leaf
½ teaspoon basil
½ teaspoon thyme or marjoram
2 tablespoons flour
2 cups sweet cream, milk or half-and-half
white wine to taste (optional)

The veal should be firmly tied with string. The butcher should not trim off much of the fat; if veal is very lean, lard in six or eight places with strips of bacon. Place veal in a deep close-sided bowl and cover completely with buttermilk. This will take between 1 and 2 quarts, depending on width and depth of bowl. Marinate 4 or 5 days. After 2 to 2½ days, pour off original buttermilk and replace with fresh.

Heat oven to 450°. Remove marinated veal and dry very well with paper towels, removing as much buttermilk as possible. Sprinkle meat on all sides with salt and pepper. Place a rack in an open roasting pan and cover with 3 or 4 slices of bacon. Set roast on top of rack; add butter and ham trimmings to pan. Roast meat in preheated oven 20 to 30 minutes, turning once or twice so that it will be golden brown on all sides. Baste or brush with melted butter from pan, every 5 to 6 minutes. Reduce heat to 350° and put 2 or 3 strips of bacon over top of meat. Add prepared vegetables and herbs. Continue roasting, allowing about 30 to 35 minutes per pound or until a meat thermometer reaches 175°.

(Insert thermometer after meat has browned.) Baste with pan drippings every 15 to 20 minutes. If vegetables seem to brown too quickly, add a little water to pan from time to time so they will not burn.

Remove finished meat to a heated platter and take rack out of pan. Pour off all but 2 to 3 tablespoons of fat from roasting pan. Set pan on stove over low heat. Sprinkle in flour and blend into fat. Simmer, stirring constantly, over low heat 4 or 5 minutes, or until flour just begins to turn golden brown. Pour in milk or cream, all at once, and bring to a boil 2 or 3 times over low heat. Stir constantly with a wooden spoon, scraping all the coagulated pan juices into gravy so it will be a rich brown color. Strain into a clean saucepan, pressing through as much gravy as possible. If a great deal seems to cling to vegetables, pour a little extra milk or cream through sieve and work gravy into pan. Taste gravy, adding salt and pepper as needed, and a little white wine if you care to. If gravy seems too thick, a little more milk or cream can be added. Heat thoroughly before serving.

❧ / STUFFED BREAST OF VEAL (*Gefüllte Kalbsbrust*)

4 TO 6 SERVINGS

1 *breast of veal, 3 to 4 pounds, with pocket cut for stuffing*
salt and pepper
stuffing, as below
4 *tablespoons butter*
1 *onion, minced*

½ *to 1 cup water or meat or veal stock*
1 *or 2 tablespoons flour or 2 or 3 teaspoons cornstarch dissolved in a little cold water*
1 *cup sour cream*

Rub inside of veal pocket with salt and pepper. Fill with one of the stuffings described below and sew opening or close with skewers and kitchen string. Heat butter in a Dutch oven and in it brown veal lightly on both sides. Remove meat and sauté onion in hot fat until it begins to soften and turn bright yellow. Return veal to pot, placing it on top of onion. Add just enough water or stock to keep onion from burning. Cover and simmer slowly but steadily 1½ to 2 hours, or until veal is tender. Add more liquid if necessary during cooking. Remove finished veal to a heated platter. The gravy may be strained or not, depending on your preference. Skim off excess fat and thicken with flour or cornstarch dissolved in a little cold water. Simmer a few minutes until sauce is smooth and thick. Stir in sour cream. Check seasoning, return veal to gravy and simmer together 5 to 10 minutes.

VARIATIONS

1. The veal can be dredged with flour before it is browned. In that case, you will probably not have to add any flour or cornstarch to thicken

gravy. You can also thicken gravy by stirring flour into sour cream before adding cream to gravy.

2. Omit any thickening and serve a clear pan gravy flavored with a little white wine.

3. Add 1 tablespoon sweet paprika to minced onion and sauté together. This will give a paprika-sour cream sauce gravy.

4. A little marjoram and/or thyme can be added to gravy.

5. In Bavaria a few root vegetables such as carrot, leek, knob celery and a parsley root are generally sliced or chopped, sautéed with onion and then cooked with rest of sauce.

BREAD STUFFING (*Semmelfüllung*)

3 large rolls or 6 slices bread, with crusts (about 3 generous cups bread cubes), or 3 cups seasoned bread stuffing
water or milk
4 tablespoons butter
1 onion, minced
1 to 2 tablespoons minced parsley

2 eggs, lightly beaten
salt
nutmeg
basil, optional
grated lemon rind, optional
⅓ to ½ cup breadcrumbs
1 egg yolk, if necessary

Cube bread or rolls and soak in milk or water to cover about 15 minutes. Squeeze out as much excess liquid as possible. Heat butter in skillet and in it sauté onion and parsley until soft and onion turns bright yellow. Add vegetables and all the butter in skillet to soaked bread. Mix through with fork. Add beaten eggs, salt, a dash or two of nutmeg and a little basil and lemon rind, if you want to use either or both. Add enough breadcrumbs to bind filling. If it seems very wet, beat in one extra egg yolk and a little more breadcrumbs. Pack into prepared veal breast.

HAM STUFFING (*Schinkenfüllung*)

Add ¼ pound cooked, chopped ham to above.

LIVER STUFFING (*Leberfüllung*)

Add ¼ pound ground cooked calves' or chicken liver to above.

MEAT STUFFING (*Fleischfüllung*)

Prepare bread stuffing (above), using only 1 cup bread cubes (1 large roll or 2 slices bread) and just 1 whole egg and 1 egg yolk. When sautéed onions, parsley and their butter have been added to soaked, drained bread, mix in ¼ pound ground pork and ½ pound ground beef. You may or may not need breadcrumbs; add them as needed if filling seems too loose.

✂ / *STUFFED LEG OR SHOULDER OF VEAL*
(*Gefüllte Kalbskeule oder -schulter*)

Boned leg or shoulder of veal can be stuffed and braised exactly as described for Stuffed Breast of Veal, above. Increase any of stuffing recipes by one-half as these larger cuts will require more filling. Sprinkle boned, cut side of meat with salt and pepper, spread with stuffing and roll, jelly-roll style, tying securely with string. A stuffed leg or shoulder that weighs 4 to 5 pounds boned will serve 8 to 10 people. Braise 1½ to 3 hours, or until meat is tender.

✂ / *SHOULDER OF VEAL, HOUSEWIFE STYLE*
(*Kalbsschulter, auf Hausfrauen Art*)

6 TO 8 SERVINGS

3- to 4-*pound shoulder of veal,*
  boned
  salt and pepper
1 *clove garlic, crushed*
3 *slices bacon, diced*
1 *onion, minced*
2 *carrots, sliced*
2 *canned or fresh tomatoes,*
  drained

fresh or dried basil
fresh or dried tarragon
3 *sprays parsley*
½ *cup white wine, or as needed*
½ *cup water or meat stock, or as*
  needed

Sprinkle veal with salt and pepper and spread mashed or crushed garlic over the cut top side. Roll and tie securely. Heat bacon in a Dutch oven and when it begins to melt, sauté onion until it begins to soften and turn bright yellow. Stir with a wooden spoon so that bacon and onion will sauté evenly. Remove onion and bacon and reserve. Place rolled veal in hot fat and brown slowly on all sides, using string to turn the meat. This should take about 15 minutes. Remove from pan. Return onion and bacon to pan and add carrots and tomatoes. Place meat on top of vegetables. Add a pinch of dried basil and tarragon, or tie 2 fresh basil leaves and 2 sprigs of tarragon together with parsley, if you can get fresh herbs. Add enough wine and water, half and half, to come about halfway up sides of meat. Cover and simmer slowly but steadily, turning from time to time so meat cooks evenly. Braise for about 2 hours, or until veal is tender and no pink juices run out of it when pierced. Add more wine and water if necessary during cooking. Remove finished meat to a heated platter. Strain gravy and skim off excess fat. Heat thoroughly and season to taste.

❧ / THE SCHNITZELS

No single cut of meat is more beloved in Germany than the Schnitzel—literally a slice or cutlet, and always from the veal leg. It is the same long, flat, palm-shaped cut that the Italians call scallopini, and the French, escalope. The meat is cut with the long grain, or, more exactly, at a slight diagonal to it, so that it does not fall apart when it is pounded. It is this pounding, done with a wooden mallet, that gives the Schnitzel its tenderness and delicacy. After being cut, the slice of veal is placed between several thicknesses of waxed paper and is then pounded to about ⅟₁₆″ to ⅛″ thickness. The butcher can best do this for you. If you ever have to do it yourself and have no wooden mallet, sandwich each slice of veal between waxed paper, lay on a board and flatten with the bottom side of a dinner plate.

GENERAL RULES FOR PREPARING SCHNITZELS

1. The breaded cutlets should be allowed to stand at room temperature for 15 to 30 minutes before being fried.
2. Be sure the fat is hot enough before you put the Schnitzels into it, otherwise the breading will fall off.
3. A Schnitzel should be golden brown on both sides and thoroughly cooked in 8 to 12 minutes; it should be turned only once. If it takes longer than that, it is too thick and may need to be fried twice on each side.
4. Keep finished Schnitzels hot in a low oven (250° to 275°) while the others are being fried. Never cover the fried Schnitzels, or the breading will steam and get soggy.
5. Although Schnitzels are most often fried in butter, they can also be done in vegetable shortening or lard; the latter produces the crispest, driest crust, but many people dislike its flavor. If you like lard, and can get it very fresh without any preservatives, use it for frying breaded Schnitzels.

❧ / WIENERSCHNITZEL

Vienna's Schnitzel is a standard on menus all over the world and is just as popular in Germany as in its homeland, Austria. It was, by the way, the forerunner of northern Italy's great specialty, Veal Cutlet Milanese.

3 TO 6 SERVINGS

6 *veal cutlets, pounded*
lemon juice (optional)
salt
½ *to 1 cup flour*
2 *eggs lightly beaten with 2*
tablespoons cold water

2 *tablespoons salad oil (optional)*
1 *generous cup dry, fine bread-*
crumbs
4 *to 5 tablespoons butter, lard*
or vegetable shortening

Veal cutlets may be marinated in a sprinkling of lemon juice for 30 minutes before they are breaded. Whether or not they are marinated, sprinkle with salt on both sides before breading. Measure flour onto a sheet of waxed paper or a flat plate. Beat eggs and water in wide flat bowl; beat in oil if you are using it. The oil is supposed to hold breading on securely and help to make it crisp. Measure breadcrumbs onto a sheet of waxed paper or a flat plate. Dip salted cutlets lightly into flour on both sides, and then into beaten egg. Let excess egg drip off and dredge cutlets with breadcrumbs. Let stand at room temperature 15 to 30 minutes. Heat fat in a large skillet. There should be enough in pan for cutlets to "swim." Do not crowd cutlets into pan. Do 2 or 3 at a time, or as many as you can fit into your largest skillet. Add fat if needed. Put cutlets into pan when butter is very hot and bubbling starts to subside. Fry first side slowly until golden brown. Turn over with spatula or flat turner; do not pierce with fork. By the time second side is golden brown (allow 4 to 6 minutes for each side) the cutlet should be finished. Place finished cutlets on a platter, pan or sheet of aluminum foil, in a 250° to 275° oven, so they will keep hot while the rest are being fried.

⊠ / *SCHNITZEL À LA HOLSTEIN*

Prepare fried veal cutlets as in above recipe. Serve each cutlet topped with a fried egg across which are two anchovy filets and a sprinkling of well-drained capers.

⊠ / *CHEESE SCHNITZEL* (*Käseschnitzel*)

Follow recipe for Wienerschnitzel, but mix ½ cup grated Parmesan cheese with ½ cup breadcrumbs, instead of using 1 cup breadcrumbs.

Before serving, sprinkle a little grated cheese and some paprika on top of each cutlet and top with a paper-thin slice of lemon.

✿ / "NATURAL" OR PLAIN SCHNITZEL (*Naturschnitzel*)

The cutlets for this Schnitzel dish should be a little thicker than for Wienerschnitzel—say about ¼". Sprinkle with salt, dredge one side of each cutlet with flour. Heat fat and in it brown first the unfloured side of the cutlet. Turn after a few minutes and brown the floured side. Keep finished cutlets hot in a slow oven and make the following sauce. Stir 2 tablespoons butter into skillet in which veal was fried. When it begins to bubble up, pour in ½ cup beef or veal stock, or water, and as this simmers, scrape coagulated pan juices into the sauce with wooden spoon. Flavor sauce with salt, pepper and a dash of lemon juice. If you have used water instead of stock, stir in about ½ teaspoon beef extract. Bring the sauce to a boil and pour over the fried cutlets.

Naturschnitzel will always bring back pleasant memories of a most delightful friend, Ferenc Gunczy, a dashing gentleman who was born and raised in a great, pre-World War I Viennese household. He was both a gourmet and a cook, and on one occasion, took several of us to dinner at his favorite Viennese restaurant in New York—a place, unfortunately, now out of business. Ferenc ordered Naturschnitzel and became furious when it arrived. It had, he told us, been floured on both sides and was therefore not a Naturschnitzel at all. He explained to the captain that a true Naturschnitzel is floured on one side only, the floured side being browned first. If both sides were floured, the second to be browned was certain to be soggy. The captain apologized on behalf of his cook and replaced the offending Schnitzel with the correct version. I could not be at peace with my conscience unless I gave you Ferenc's ruling on this dish.

✿ / ALMOND SCHNITZEL (*Mandelschnitzel*)

This is prepared very much like Wienerschnitzel, with the following exceptions. Dip salted cutlets into lightly beaten sour cream and then into flour and egg. Instead of using breadcrumbs for the last coating, substitute 1 cup grated, blanched almonds. Allow cutlets to stand 15 to 30 minutes and then fry in hot butter. They will probably need an extra minute or two of cooking on each side as almonds make a slightly heavier coating. Another way to serve Almond Schnitzel is to fry Wienerschnitzel and serve topped with blanched, slivered almonds sautéed in butter.

✂ / *HUNTER'S SCHNITZEL* (*Jägerschnitzel*)

Cut Schnitzels in half after they have been pounded thin. Sprinkle with salt and pepper and sauté in hot butter or bacon fat until both sides of cutlet pieces are golden brown. Remove meat and add chopped carrot, chopped onion and some minced parsley to fat. Sauté vegetables until they are soft and begin to turn golden. Return veal to pan, add a tablespoonful butter and when it bubbles, stir in 2 tablespoons flour. Stir flour through and sauté about 5 minutes. Pour 1 cup water or white wine into pan. Cover and simmer slowly about 15 or 20 minutes, or until veal is tender. Season sauce to taste. Place Schnitzels on serving platter and top each with a spoonful of vegetables and sauce. Minced celery can be added to sauce, as can 1 tablespoon of dried, soaked, chopped mushrooms.

✂ / *CREAM SCHNITZEL* (*Rahmschnitzel*)

Sprinkle cutlets with salt and pepper and cut into 2″ by 3″ pieces. Brown both sides of meat in butter and remove from pan. Pour ½ cup water into pan, scraping coagulated juices into it with a wooden spoon. Blend 1 tablespoonful flour into ½ cup sour cream and stir that into water. Return Schnitzels to sauce, cover and simmer slowly 5 to 10 minutes, or until meat is tender. Season sauce to taste with a little beef extract and lemon juice.

✂ / *SWABIAN SCHNITZEL* (*Badisches Schnitzel*)

This is Cream Schnitzel (above) served with its sauce over a mound of hot noodles or Spätzle (page 60). You will want a little more sauce. Add 1 cup water to pan and then stir in 1 cup sour cream blended with 2 tablespoons flour.

/ PAPRIKASCHNITZEL

Follow recipe for Cream Schnitzel, but sprinkle cutlets with paprika before browning and then stir 1 or 2 teaspoons paprika into sour cream sauce. Mince a small onion and sauté in a little butter until soft and bright yellow and add to veal before cooking with sour cream.

/ VEAL ROLLS OR BIRDS (*Kalbsrouladen oder Kalbsvögel*)

Follow recipe for Beef Rolls, page 151, using thin slices of veal from leg. Veal rolls need less browning and cooking time; they should be done in about ¾ hour. A little white wine can be used along with water or stock.

/ SWALLOWS' NESTS (*Schwalbennester*)

4 TO 6 SERVINGS

4 thin slices veal leg
4 slices bacon
salt and pepper
4 hard-cooked eggs
2 tablespoons butter
1 cup water
1 tablespoon flour
½ cup sour cream
1 tablespoon capers, optional
3 or 4 anchovy filets, chopped (optional)
lemon juice or white wine to taste (optional)

Veal slices should be pounded thin and cut so they are about 3" wide by 4" long. Sprinkle one side of each slice with salt and pepper and on this side lay a slice of bacon. Place one hard-cooked egg on each slice and roll meat, jelly-roll fashion, around egg. Tie with string or fasten with toothpicks. Heat butter in a pan and brown veal rolls lightly on all sides, turning gently with a wooden spoon or spatula. When brown, add water, cover and simmer slowly but steadily ¾ to 1 hour, or until veal is tender. Add more water if needed during cooking. Remove veal to a platter. Mix flour into sour cream and stir into gravy. Heat thoroughly, check seasoning, and flavor to taste with capers and/or anchovies and a little lemon juice or white wine. Cut veal rolls in half to serve; pour gravy over them or serve on the side in a heated sauceboat.

❈ / *SALZBURG VEAL CHOPS* (*Kalbsrippchen, auf Salzburger Art*)

3 TO 6 SERVINGS

2 cups thick White Sauce, page 331
lemon juice
Worcestershire sauce
2 egg yolks beaten into ¼ cup cream
6 rib or loin veal chops, about 1″ thick

2 tablespoons lard or butter
salt and pepper
6 slices smoked beef tongue
3 tablespoons grated Parmesan cheese
butter
3 tablespoons fine breadcrumbs

Heat oven to 450°. Prepare white sauce and flavor it with a dash or two of lemon juice and a few drops of Worcestershire sauce. Stir beaten egg yolks and cream into sauce after it has been removed from heat. Beat until smooth and set aside. Brown veal chops on one side only in hot lard or butter. Remove to an open baking pan, placing uncooked side up. Sprinkle with salt and pepper. Cover each chop with a slice of tongue and sprinkle with a layer of grated cheese. Dot with butter or spread a little melted butter over cheese. Sprinkle with breadcrumbs and cover each chop generously with white sauce. Bake in upper third of preheated oven 20 to 25 minutes, or until sauce is bubbling hot and deep golden brown on top.

❈ / *QUICK VEAL-PAPRIKA* (*Geschnitzeltes Kalbfleisch*)

4 SERVINGS

1½ pounds veal cutlets, as for Schnitzels
3 tablespoons butter
salt and pepper
1 tablespoon sweet paprika

1 tablespoon ketchup, or 2 tablespoons tomato purée
1 tablespoon flour
½ cup sour cream

The veal cutlets need not be pounded as thin as for Schnitzels. Cut into finger strips or small squares. Heat butter in a large heavy skillet and when bubbling begins to subside, add veal. If necessary fry in shifts; pan should not be crowded or veal will not brown. Brown quickly on both sides, over high heat and turning gently with wooden spoon or spatula. This should take about 5 to 6 minutes. Season with salt, pepper and paprika, sauté a minute or two and then stir in ketchup or tomato purée and sour cream blended with the flour. Bring to a boil and check seasoning.

✖ / SWABIAN VEAL STEW (*Eingemachtes Kalbfleisch*)

4 TO 6 SERVINGS

2 *pounds lean stewing veal cut in*
    1" cubes
salt
2 *tablespoons butter*
2 *tablespoons flour*
1 *to 2 cups veal or beef stock,*
    or water
1 *small onion studded with 4*
    cloves

1 *slice lemon, ¼" to ½" thick*
1 *bay leaf*
juice of ½ lemon, or to taste
salt and pepper to taste
½ *cup sour cream, or 2 egg yolks*
    beaten into ½ cup sweet
    cream
2 *tablespoons capers*
white wine to taste

Sprinkle veal with salt. Heat butter in a heavy 2-quart stew pot and in it brown veal lightly on all sides, turning pieces with wooden spoon so they brown evenly. Sprinkle with flour and stir over low heat until flour is absorbed and begins to turn bright yellow; this will take about 5 minutes. Add as much stock as is needed to cover veal completely.

Add onion, lemon slice, bay leaf and lemon juice. Cover the pot, bring to a boil, reduce heat and simmer slowly but steadily 1 hour, or until pieces of veal are completely tender. Add more stock if sauce becomes too thick during cooking. When veal is done, remove onion, lemon slice and bay leaf from the pot. Taste sauce and add more salt and plenty of black pepper. Up to this point this dish may be prepared ahead and refrigerated. Before serving, reheat if refrigerated. Then stir in sour cream or remove from heat and beat in egg yolks and cream. Check seasoning again, adding more lemon juice and some white wine until the flavor is quite piquant. Stir in capers and heat thoroughly a few minutes over low heat.

❊ / VEAL FRICASSEE (*Kalbfleischfrikassee*)

4 TO 6 SERVINGS

Follow recipe for Chicken Fricassee, page 221. Simmer 2 pounds stewing veal (cut in cubes or fingers) in 6 cups water along with pot vegetables (page 29) and an onion. Prepare sauce as in chicken recipe.

❊ / BRAISED VEAL SHANK (*Geschmorte Kalbshaxe*)

2 TO 4 SERVINGS

1 *large or 2 small veal shanks*
salt and pepper
flour
2 *tablespoons butter, lard or bacon fat*
1 *onion, minced*
1 *carrot, sliced*
½ *knob celery or 2 stalks celery with leaves, sliced*

1 *tablespoon paprika (optional)*
1 *to 2 cups water or stock*
¼ *teaspoon thyme*
¼ *teaspoon basil*
dry white wine to taste
1 *tablespoon minced parsley*

Sprinkle veal shanks on all sides with salt and pepper and roll in flour. Heat butter in a Dutch oven and in it brown veal shanks slowly, turning so all sides brown evenly. Remove meat and add vegetables to hot fat. Sauté until vegetables soften and begin to brown. If you wish to use paprika, sprinkle over vegetables before sautéing. Return meat to pot, placing on top of vegetables. Add enough water or stock to cover meat halfway. Add thyme and basil. Cover and simmer slowly but steadily for about 2 hours, or until veal is tender. Remove finished veal to a heated platter. Strain sauce and skim off excess fat. Check seasoning and add white wine to taste. Sprinkle with parsley just before serving. Veal shanks may be carved and portions of meat served, but usually one whole small shank is served per person. Offer gravy in a hot sauceboat.

VARIATION

Browned Veal Shank (Kalbshaxe, gebräunt): The process can be reversed, that is, the veal is cooked first and then browned, either in a pan or in the oven. The veal shanks are simmered slowly in water along with root vegetables and onion, ¼ cup vinegar and 1 bay leaf, about 2 hours or until tender. The veal shank is then allowed to cool and is rolled in flour seasoned with salt and pepper. It is then dipped in beaten egg and breadcrumbs and fried slowly in hot butter until golden brown. This is done either in a skillet or in a hot oven. The meat can be sliced from leg after it has cooked and cooled, and these slices can be breaded and fried.

✖ LAMB AND MUTTON ✖
(Lamm und Hammel)

✖ / *LAMB OR MUTTON POT ROAST WITH CUCUM-BERS (Geschmorte Hammelkeule mit grünen Gurken)*

8 TO 10 SERVINGS

1 boned and rolled leg of lamb
　　or mutton (4 to 5 pounds)
　salt and pepper
2 cloves garlic, cut in slivers
　lard or salt pork

1 cup water or lamb stock
2 large cucumbers
½ cup sour cream
　flour or cornstarch, as needed

Have roast tied with string so it will hold its shape and be easy to turn. Rub on all sides with salt and pepper. Lard meat with garlic slivers. Heat lard or melt salt pork in a Dutch oven and when hot, brown roast slowly. Turn, using string as a handle, so that meat becomes golden brown on all sides. This should take about 15 minutes. When roast is evenly browned, pour water or stock into pot. Cover tightly and simmer slowly but steadily about 2½ hours, turning meat once or twice. Check to see if more water is needed as meat cooks.

Peel cucumbers, cut into quarters lengthwise; remove seeds. Put cucumber strips in pot with meat, cover and continue braising as before about 30 to 40 minutes, or until lamb can be pierced easily with a carving fork or skewer. Stir sour cream into gravy and season as needed with salt and pepper. Cover and simmer meat and sauce another 10 minutes. If sauce is now too thin, blend 1 tablespoon flour or 2 teaspoons cornstarch into some cold water and stir into sauce. Bring to a boil and stir to keep sauce smooth. To serve, slice meat onto heated platter and top with cucumber slices and sauce. Boiled potatoes or Spätzle are good with this.

/ *LAMB OR MUTTON POT ROAST THE ORDINARY WAY (Geschmorte Hammelkeule, auf gewöhnliche Art)*

Why this should be called ordinary is more than I can tell. It is prepared in exactly the same way as the above recipe, except that the sauce is piquant, or säuerlich. Add 1 to 2 tablespoons tarragon vinegar, 2 or 3 shallots if you can get them, 1 bay leaf, 4 or 5 cloves and 6 peppercorns to cooking liquid. The cucumbers are cut in cubes instead of strips, and after cream has simmered in sauce, it is flavored with a little more vinegar or lemon juice and 1 tablespoonful mustard.

/ *LAMB OR MUTTON, GAME STYLE (Hammelbraten, auf Wildbret Art)*

Follow recipe for Sauerbraten, page 147, making the following changes: Add 1 thick slice of lemon and 8 crushed juniper berries to marinade. Do not add bread, gingersnaps or Lebkuchen to cooking liquid. After gravy has been thickened with sugar Einbrenne, flavor it with 3 to 4 tablespoons dry red wine.

/ *STUFFED BREAST OF LAMB (Gefüllte Lammbrust)*

Follow recipe for Stuffed Breast of Veal, page 161. A clove of garlic can be minced and added to stuffing, or sliced and added to gravy.

❁ / STUFFED SHOULDER OR LEG OF LAMB (*Gefüllte Lammschulter oder -schlegel*)

Have butcher bone shoulder or leg of lamb. Sprinkle with salt and pepper, spread with one of the stuffings and cook as for Stuffed Breast of Veal, page 161. Roll meat and stuffing as for a jelly roll, and tie securely with kitchen string. A clove of minced garlic and pinch of thyme and/or rosemary should be added to stuffing or gravy.

❁ / ROAST LEG OF LAMB (*Lammbraten*)

Follow recipe for Roast Veal, page 158, or Roast Beef, page 144. Add clove of garlic and a pinch of thyme and/or rosemary to gravy. Roast in 325° oven, allowing 20 to 25 minutes roasting time per pound for well-done lamb, or rely on meat thermometer.

❁ / LAMB OR MUTTON CHOPS WITH GREEN BEANS (*Lamm- oder Hammelkotelette mit grünen Bohnen*)

4 SERVINGS

4 large mutton chops or shoulder
  lamb chops
salt
4 tablespoons olive oil
4 canned tomatoes, drained and
  chopped

1 pound string beans, cut in
  1" to 2" lengths
¼ teaspoon savory
1 to 2 cups water

Trim excess fat off chops and sprinkle both sides lightly with salt. Heat oil in a stew pot or deep skillet with a tight-fitting lid. When oil begins to smoke, add chops, reduce heat a little and brown slowly on both sides. Add tomatoes and green beans along with savory. Cover pot and steam 5 to 10 minutes over low heat, stirring once or twice so there is no scorching. Add enough water to cover meat and beans completely. Cover pot and simmer slowly but steadily about 1½ hours, or until meat is tender. Add more water if needed during cooking. Skim excess fat from pan juices and season to taste with salt. For a thicker sauce, dissolve 1 tablespoon flour or 2 teaspoons cornstarch in a little cold water and stir into gravy. Bring to a boil and simmer briefly until sauce is smooth and thickened.

⚡ / *SWABIAN LAMB STEW* (*Eingemachtes Lammfleisch*)

Follow recipe for Swabian Veal Stew, page 170. Substitute stewing lamb for the veal indicated.

⚡ / *DEVILED LAMB OR MUTTON CHOPS* (*Panierte Lamm- oder Hammelrippchen*)

6 SERVINGS

6 mutton chops or loin lamb chops, boned	1½ cups breadcrumbs
hot mustard	3 tablespoons grated Parmesan cheese
salt and pepper	3 tablespoons melted butter
4 tablespoons butter, melted	

Excess fat should be trimmed from chops. Then roll and secure with skewers. Pound lightly with a wooden mallet to flatten to about ¾" thickness. Spread both sides of each chop with mustard and sprinkle with salt and pepper. Dip each chop in melted butter. Mix breadcrumbs with grated cheese and dredge buttered, seasoned chops with mixture. Broil chops under moderate heat, allowing 4 to 5 minutes for each side. They should be a mellow brown color when done. If you prefer, the breaded chops can be fried slowly in butter instead of being broiled. A little melted butter should be spooned over each finished chop.

VARIATION

Lamb shoulder chops, or lamb cutlets, cut from leg in same way that veal is cut for Schnitzels, can also be prepared in this way.

❧ / BAVARIAN LAMB OR MUTTON ROAST WITH MUSTARD (*Bayrischer Lamm- oder Hammelbraten mit Senf*)

8 TO 10 SERVINGS

1 leg of lamb or mutton, boned
    and rolled (4 to 5 pounds)
4 or 5 slices of bacon, cut in
    strips
3 tablespoons hot or sweet mus-
    tard, or as needed
salt
3 tablespoons butter or bacon fat
1 onion, minced
1 carrot, sliced

1 knob celery or 2 stalks celery,
    sliced
1 parsley root, sliced (optional)
1 leek, sliced (optional)
1 to 2 cups water or lamb stock
1 tablespoon flour or 2 teaspoons
    cornstarch dissolved in a lit-
    tle cold water
2 to 4 tablespoons sour cream
3 to 4 tablespoons white wine

This roast should be rolled and tied securely with string. You or the butcher should lard it well with thin matchstick strips of bacon. Spread all sides of meat with mustard and sprinkle with salt. Place in a glass or earthenware bowl, cover with foil or waxed paper and refrigerate 3 to 4 days.

Preheat oven to 350°. Heat fat in a roasting pan and brown meat, using string as handle for turning. This should take about 15 minutes. When meat is golden brown all over remove it and add vegetables to pan. Sauté 3 or 4 minutes over low heat and return meat to pan, placing on top of vegetables. Place meat in oven and add liquid to pan. Allow 20 to 25 minutes roasting time per pound, basting meat frequently with pan juices and adding more liquid if necessary. When meat is done, remove to a heated platter. Bring pan juices to a boil, in roasting pan, on the stove, scraping coagulated juices into gravy with a wooden spoon. Strain into a clean saucepan and skim off excess fat. To thicken the sauce, stir in either flour or cornstarch, dissolved in a little cold water. Simmer sauce until smooth and thick. Stir in sour cream until smooth and simmer a few minutes. Season sauce with salt and wine. You can also thicken sauce by blending flour into sour cream before adding mixture to sauce.

✕ HAM, PORK AND BACON ✕
(*Schinken, Schwein und Speck*)

⧉ / NÜRNBERG ROAST LEG OF PORK (*Nürnberger Schweinskeule*)

Almost anything that is dubbed "Nürnberger" has that city's famed honey cakes, Lebkuchen, among the ingredients. They lend a very mellow, rich touch to this fresh pork leg roast.

APPROXIMATELY 12 SERVINGS

1 *leg of fresh pork, boned, rolled and tied*	*butter, bacon or lard, if needed*
black pepper, preferably freshly ground	2 *cups water*
salt	½ *pound Lebkuchen, grated*

Rub tied leg of pork generously with black pepper. Place on a platter or in a bowl, cover with foil or waxed paper and keep in refrigerator 2 days. Salt roast on all sides. If the pork has a good deal of fat around it, it can brown without adding more. If the fat seems thin, heat butter, bacon or lard in a large Dutch oven or casserole and when hot, add pork. Brown well on all sides, turning with string. Do not pierce surface of meat with fork in turning. It should take about 15 minutes for meat to brown on all sides. Add water, cover pan tightly and simmer slowly but steadily 2 to 2½ hours, or until pork is tender when pierced with a carving fork or skewer.

Lay pork on rack in open roasting pan; cover top and sides with one-third of the Lebkuchen. Roast in upper third of 450° oven until crumbs turn golden brown. Baste with sauce in which pork was braised and cover with another layer of crumbs. Brown again, baste with sauce and cover with a third layer of crumbs. When this final layer has browned, pork will have a crisp golden crust around it. Serve with gravy made by adding all the braising stock to roasting pan. Mix with Lebkuchen crumbs in bottom of pan, bring to a boil, season and pour over sliced meat.

✂ / ROAST PORK (Schweinebraten)

8 TO 10 SERVINGS

5- to 6-pound roast (leg or
    shoulder)
1 clove garlic, cut in half
    (optional)
    salt and pepper
    caraway seeds
4 onions, sliced
2 carrots, sliced

½ cup water
    white wine, light beer, stock
    or water, for basting
2 tablespoons flour or 4 tea-
    spoons cornstarch dissolved
    in a little cold water
1 cup sour cream (optional)

Preheat oven to 350°. The rind should remain on pork. Rub meat on all sides with cut cloves of garlic, if you use it. Sprinkle well with salt, pepper and caraway seeds. Arrange bed of onions and carrots on bottom of open roasting pan. Lay meat on vegetables, skin side down. Add water to pan and roast in preheated oven 1½ hours, basting with pan juices and adding more liquid to pan as needed. After 1½ hours, turn meat over and score top of fat in diamond pattern. Roast for another 1½ hours, basting and adding liquid as necessary.

Remove the finished meat to a heated platter. Strain the pan juices and skim off excess fat. Add a little more wine, stock or water if there is not enough pan juice for gravy. Thicken with flour or cornstarch dissolved in water. Bring to a boil and simmer 3 or 4 minutes, or until sauce is smooth and thick. Stir in sour cream, if you are using it, and bring to a boil. Season to taste.

VARIATION

This roast can also be made with pork tenderloin, in which case it is called Jungfernbraten. A pork tenderloin weighs about 1½ pounds, so three would be needed to equal the amount in recipe. The tenderloins should be wrapped in covering of fresh pork fat. They should be roasted, covered, with vegetables and liquid, ¾ to 1 hour. The sauce may be finished with sweet or sour cream and a little red currant jelly melted into it.

✂ / ROAST PORK WITH PRUNE AND APPLE STUFF-ING (Schweinebraten mit Pflaumen und Äpfeln)

6 TO 8 SERVINGS

1 pork loin, about 5 pounds,
    boned
½ pound prunes

2 large apples, peeled and sliced
    salt
    white pepper

powdered ginger
½ cup butter
water or stock
1 tablespoon flour or 2 teaspoons cornstarch dissolved in a little cold water

1 or 2 tablespoons sweet or sour cream, optional and to taste
1 tablespoon red currant jelly, optional and to taste

Have butcher cut a pocket down one side of meat. Parboil prunes 10 minutes in water to cover. Drain, cut in half and remove pits. Combine prunes and apples. Stuff meat pocket with prunes and apples and rub outside lightly with salt, pepper and ginger. Tie meat closed with string. Heat butter in a Dutch oven or heavy casserole and when hot and bubbling, brown meat on all sides, using string to turn it. It should be golden brown in about 10 minutes. Keep heat moderate so butter does not burn. When meat is browned, add just enough water or stock to cover bottom of pan. Cover, bring to a boil, reduce heat and braise slowly but steadily about 1½ hours, or until meat is completely tender when pierced with a carving fork or skewer. Add more water or stock as needed. Baste frequently with pan juices. Remove meat to heated platter. Skim excess fat from pan juices. Thicken with flour or cornstarch, bring to a boil and simmer 2 or 3 minutes until gravy is smooth. Stir in cream and currant jelly, if you like.

VARIATIONS

1. For twice as many people, get 2 pork loins and instead of having pockets cut in them, place filling between them and tie together, one on top of the other. Proceed with recipe, allowing an extra 35 to 45 minutes cooking time. Turn roast several times during cooking.
2. You can also use stuffing for a boned leg or shoulder of fresh pork. After meat is boned, lay it out flat and spread stuffing on cut side. Roll jelly-roll fashion and tie into shape. Braise as described, adding more liquid as needed and increasing cooking time to 3 to 4 hours.
3. As an alternate stuffing, use the one for Stuffed Pork Chops, Holstein Style, page 183.

✺ / *BAVARIAN ROAST SUCKLING PIG* (*Bayrisches Spanferkel*)

8 TO 10 SERVINGS

11- to 14-pound suckling pig
salt
marjoram
caraway seeds

1 cup melted butter or bacon fat, or ½ pound sliced or unsliced bacon
1 bottle beer, preferably dark

1 to 2 cups water or stock, if
necessary
1 tablespoon flour or 2 tea-

spoons cornstarch dissolved
in a little cold water
½ cup sour cream (optional)

In Germany, suckling pig is seared in a hot oven and then roasted in moderate heat. To do this, preheat oven to 450° and after 20 minutes, reduce heat to 350°. Nevertheless I have found that pigs brown more evenly and shrink less if roasted at even, moderate temperature throughout. To do this, preheat oven to 350° and roast, following instructions below. Allow 25 to 30 minutes per pound for roasting. The meat should be white, without any pink in the juices.

Have the pig eviscerated and cleaned by your butcher. Wash it well under running cold water and pat off excess moisture with paper towel. If you do this a day or hours ahead and pig has dried, wipe with damp cloth before seasoning so moisture holds the spices onto skin. Rub inside of pig with salt, marjoram and caraway seeds. Since this pig will not be stuffed, it will sink in slightly as it roasts, so stuff body cavity firmly with crumpled aluminum foil or clean white wrapping paper. This is only necessary for appearance of pig when served. The opening along bottom of pig does not have to be trussed closed. Tie front legs forward so feet come under the head. To tie back legs forward, bring them around under body on each side. Tie securely with kitchen string so they remain in place during roasting. Rub outside of pig with salt, marjoram and caraway seeds. Cover ears and tail with greased brown paper or double thicknesses of aluminum foil to keep from burning. Prop the mouth open with a block of wood or raw potato, so that you will be able to stuff it with an apple or lemon later. Pierce skin all over with a sharp-pronged fork, a larding needle or a skewer, so fat will drain off.

Lay pig on a rack or across two long wooden inverted spoons in open roasting pan. Pour in enough water to cover bottom of pan. To keep pig well greased as it roasts, either brush it every 10 to 15 minutes with melted butter or bacon fat, or lay strips of bacon across its back and replace them as they become crisp; or rub pig with a large, unsliced chunk of bacon. Place pig in a preheated oven and allow 25 to 30 minutes per pound for roasting, using either searing or even-temperature method described above. Brush or rub with fat every 10 to 15 minutes and add more water to pan as needed. When you baste, prick skin again to keep fat draining. If pig browns too quickly, cover it with greased brown paper or a double thickness of aluminum foil and lift this cover for basting. When there is still ½ hour cooking time left, remove paper from ears and tail, and from pig itself if it has been covered. Continue roasting and baste 4 or 5 times with beer to give skin a crisp golden glaze.

To serve pig, cut trussing from legs and place pig on a large wooden carving board or platter. Remove the block or potato from mouth and put in a whole small apple or unpeeled lemon. Show whole pig at the table, but unless you are very skilled and experienced, carve in kitchen. If you want to carve it at the table, cut a circle around the neck, and cover this with a wreath of leaves or, at Christmas, holly.

In Bavaria, a very simple gravy is served with this. Skim excess fat from pan juices and add some water or stock if there is very little gravy left. Bring to a boil in roasting pan on stove and scrape coagulated pan juices into gravy with a wooden spoon. Thicken by stirring in flour or cornstarch dissolved in cold water and simmer for 3 to 5 minutes, or until sauce is smooth and thick. Sour cream can be stirred in for creamier sauce. Season as needed and serve in heated sauceboat.

⧉ / *SMOKED PORK LOIN, KASSEL STYLE* (**Kasseler Rippchen**)

This is one of Germany's most renowned specialties. Usually the town of Kassel, between Frankfurt and Hanover, is credited with its origin. Actually, it was created in Berlin by a butcher named Kassel. Today it is a specialty of Berlin and Frankfurt, though it appears everywhere in Germany. The pork loin is smoked in a strip and cooked either in a large section, or sometimes in chops. It may be cooked with sauerkraut, as in Pork Chops and Sauerkraut, page 82, or the whole strip may be boiled like Smoked Tongue, page 201. It may be boiled, cut into chops and prepared cold in aspic like Pork Chops in Aspic, page 185. For special occasions, a double strip of loin (what we would call a saddle or carré) is roasted (see recipe below). To serve, the meat is carved loose from the bone and then sliced.

⧉ / *ROAST SMOKED PORK LOIN* (**Kasseler Rippchenbraten**)

6 SERVINGS

1 uncooked smoked pork loin
   with 6 to 8 chops
1 large onion, sliced
½ to 1 cup water, as needed

1 tablespoon flour or 2 teaspoons
   cornstarch dissolved in a
   little cold water

Preheat oven to 375°. Set roast, fat side up, in open roasting pan. Surround with onion slices and add just enough water to cover bottom of pan. Roast in preheated oven 1½ to 2 hours, or until meat is tender when pierced with carving fork or skewer. Baste frequently with pan juices, adding more water to pan as needed. Remove roasted meat to a heated platter or carving board. Skim excess fat from pan juices and bring gravy to a boil in roasting pan on stove. Scrape coagulated pan juices into gravy with wooden spoon. Strain gravy into clean saucepan and thicken with flour or cornstarch dissolved in water. Season to taste and heat thoroughly.

VARIATION

Arrange pork loin as described, but add some sliced celery and carrot along with onion. Place in covered roasting or braising kettle, add ½ cup water and steam on stove 1½ hours. When meat is tender and water has evaporated, turn and brown in pan fat. Or brown it by removing rind and placing in a 425° oven in open roasting pan, basting with red burgundy wine or fruit juice.

✖ / PORK SAUERBRATEN

Follow recipe for Rhineland Marinated Pot Roast, page 147, using any boned and rolled roasting cut of pork. Red wine is often substituted for vinegar when preparing pork this way, in which case, do not use pickling spices or cloves in marinade, or any gingersnaps or Lebkuchen in gravy. A large clove of garlic can be added to wine marinade. If you also add a dozen or so lightly crushed juniper berries, you will have what is known as Roast Pork, Game Style (Schweinebraten, auf Wildbret Art). Pork needs no larding.

✖ / STUFFED BREAST OF PORK (Gefüllte Schweinebrust)

Follow recipe for Stuffed Breast of Veal, page 161, using Bread Stuffing, page 162, or the apple-raisin stuffing in recipe on following page.

❧ / *STUFFED PORK ROLLS* (*Schweinefleischrouladen*)

Follow recipe for Braised Beef Rolls, page 151. Use any stuffing indicated there except Sausage Stuffing. Braise 1½ to 2 hours. You could also use the apple-raisin stuffing below.

To make Pork Rolls Braised in Beer, substitute 1 cup dark beer for water or stock. You may add sour cream if you like, but do not use tomato purée.

❧ / *STUFFED PORK CHOPS, HOLSTEIN STYLE* (*Gefüllte Schweinerippchen à la Holstein*)

6 SERVINGS

6 *double rib pork chops*
salt
3 *baking apples, such as Rome Beauties or Northern Spies*
2 *to 3 tablespoons butter*
3 *tablespoons raisins soaked in ½ cup rum*

1½ *cups toasted breadcrumbs or small croutons*
cinnamon, optional and to taste
½ *cup water, or as needed*

Have the butcher cut a pocket in each of the chops. Preheat oven to 350°. Sprinkle outside of chops with salt. To make stuffing, peel apples, remove core and cut in ½″-thick lengthwise or crosswise slices. Heat butter in a skillet and when hot and bubbling, add apple slices. Sauté and stir over low heat until apples begin to turn golden brown and soft. They should not become completely soft or lose their shape. This should take about 6 or 7 minutes. Sauté only one layer of apple slices at a time. When all the apples are sautéed, chop them coarsely or dice. Add raisins and rum in which they soaked. Add breadcrumbs or small croutons and toss together lightly but thoroughly with a fork. Taste the stuffing and flavor with cinnamon and sugar. You can also add a little more rum if you like. The stuffing should be only slightly moist. Stuff chops with apple mixture and close with toothpicks or sew with kitchen thread. Arrange chops in a baking pan with a cover. Add just enough water to cover bottom of pan. Bake covered 30 minutes. Add more water to pan if it is needed during baking. Remove cover and bake another 30 minutes, or until chops are nicely browned and tender when pierced with a sharp-pronged fork or skewer.

❇ / PORK CHOPS WITH CURRY RICE
(*Schweinekotelette mit Curryreis*)

6 SERVINGS

6 double loin pork chops
salt
pepper
1 recipe Curry Rice, page 326
1 eating orange, peeled

½ cup raisins soaked in brandy
    or white wine
½ cup chopped toasted almonds
2 tablespoons butter

Sprinkle pork chops with salt and pepper on both sides and fry until done in a large heavy skillet. Prepare Curry Rice. Cut peeled orange in thin slices. Drain raisins and sauté, along with almonds, for 3 or 4 minutes in hot butter.

Arrange a mound of curry rice in the center of a large heated platter and sprinkle it with the raisins and almonds and the butter in which they were sautéed. Arrange pork chops on the bed of rice and garnish platter with the orange slices.

❇ / FARMERS' PORK CHOPS (*Bauernschweinekotelette*)

6 SERVINGS

6 thick loin pork chops
salt
caraway seeds
flour
3 tablespoons lard
1 carrot, scraped and chopped
½ knob celery root, peeled and
    chopped, or 2 stalks celery,
    chopped
1 large onion, chopped

1 large knockwurst, thinly sliced
3 sweet gherkins, diced
2 teaspoons caraway seeds
    salt and pepper to taste
1 cup beef stock, or as needed
1 cup drained canned tomatoes or
    3 fresh tomatoes, diced
4 large potatoes, peeled and
    sliced

Pound chops lightly. Sprinkle with salt and caraway seeds and dredge with flour on both sides. Heat lard in a large heavy skillet with a tight-fitted lid. When fat is hot, add chops and fry until golden brown on both sides. This should take about 8 to 10 minutes. Remove chops and add carrot, celery, onion, knockwurst and gherkins. Add caraway seeds, salt and pepper to taste. Return chops to pan and pour in just enough stock to barely cover them. Put a layer of potatoes on top of meat and top with tomatoes. Cover and simmer slowly but steadily about 30 to 45 minutes, or until meat is tender.

▓ / *PORK CHOPS IN ASPIC* (*Sülzkotelette*)

Served with a glass of cold light beer or white wine, these pork chops would make a wonderful summer luncheon or light dinner entree.

4 SERVINGS

strip of pork loin with 4 good chops
4 cups water (approximately), or 3 cups water and 1 cup white wine
salt
1 onion studded with 4 cloves
1 carrot, sliced
½ knob celery, sliced, or 2 stalks celery with leaves, sliced

1 small parsley root, sliced (optional)
6 peppercorns
1 bay leaf
½ cup white vinegar
1 egg white
1 egg shell, cracked
1 envelope unflavored gelatin softened in ¼ cup cold water

Cover pork in deep pot with water or mixture of wine and water. Add a little salt. Cover pot, bring to a boil, reduce heat and simmer slowly but steadily. Skim foam from surface as it rises. After about 15 minutes, add all vegetables, spices and vinegar and continue cooking slowly 1 to 1½ hours, or until meat is tender when pierced with a carving fork or skewer. It should not be falling away from bones, so do not overcook. Remove meat from stock, let cool and cut into four separate chops. Trim off excess fat.

Set pot of stock in very cold water and skim fat off as it rises to surface. Season with salt and a little more wine or vinegar, as needed. Beat egg white with crushed shell and add it with 2 or 3 tablespoons cold water to stock. Heat skimmed stock, stirring, until it comes to a boil. The egg white will coagulate and clear stock. Set pot in cold water again. When stock is cool and clear, skim off surface and strain through a fine clean cloth or a fine mesh sieve. Bring 2 cups of this clarified stock to a boil and stir in soaked, softened gelatin. Stir until gelatin dissolves completely.

Use metal cutlet molds if you have them; otherwise any sort of shallow, portion-size, square, oval or round molds or bakers will do.

Rinse molds in cold water, pour in about ½ inch of stock and refrigerate 15 or 20 minutes, or until stock has set. Arrange an attractive design, using a slice of carrot and hard-cooked egg, slices of gherkin, a small dab of grated horseradish and a little clump of parsley. Use any or all these, as you like. Arrange pattern on set stock, remembering that mold will be inverted when served and you are doing the design face down. Lay chop on jelled stock and pour enough stock over it to fill mold completely. If aspic begins to set and you cannot pour it easily, heat it again and let cool slightly, but not so much that it resets. Place filled molds in refrigerator 2 hours or until set. To unmold, loosen edges of aspic with a knife blade rinsed in hot water. If mold will not turn out, wipe the bottom with a cloth wrung out in hot water. Suggestions for garnishes are: sliced carrot, hard-cooked egg, grated horseradish, parsley.

VARIATIONS

1. Two scrubbed and split calves' feet can be simmered in stock, with vegetables, 1 hour before cooking pork. In that case you will need no gelatin.
2. The meat of chops can be cut off bone before molding. This can be served whole, or the jelled meat can be diced and served with Vinaigrette Herb Dressing, page 346. This is known as Sülzesalat.

✂ / PAPRIKA PORK STEW (*Schweinepfeffer*)

4 TO 6 SERVINGS

2 *pounds lean stewing pork*
4 *to 5 slices bacon*
4 *onions, chopped*
1 *generous tablespoon paprika*
2 *cups drained, canned tomatoes,*
    cut in pieces
3 *cups of water, or as needed*

1 *clove garlic, optional*
1 *bay leaf, optional*
2 *tablespoons flour dissolved in*
    a little cold water
salt to taste
½ *cup sour cream, optional*

The pork should be cut into large cubes, about 1½″ square. Fry bacon in a 3-quart Dutch oven or stew pot, and when all fat has been rendered, remove bacon slices. Fry pork cubes in hot bacon fat, turning with wooden spoon or spatula until meat is brown on all sides. Brown only one layer of meat at a time. Remove browned meat from pot and add onions and paprika. Sauté and stir about 4 or 5 minutes over moderate heat, or until onions begin to soften. Add tomatoes and return meat to pot. Pour in enough water to cover stew halfway. Add garlic and/or bay leaf if you use either or both. Cover pot, bring to a boil, reduce heat and simmer slowly but steadily about 1½ hours, or until meat is completely tender. Thicken gravy by stirring in flour dissolved in a little cold water. Add sour cream if you are using it. Bring to a boil and simmer 2 or 3 minutes, or until gravy is smooth and thickened.

✂ / *RHINELAND PEPPERED PORK STEW* (*Rheinländischer Schweinepfeffer*)

Along the Rhine, this same name refers to an entirely different, but no less delicious, spicy pork stew.

4 TO 6 SERVINGS

4 tablespoons butter or bacon fat
1 large onion, minced
4 tablespoons flour
2 cups water or stock, or as needed
salt
6 cloves

1 large bay leaf
4 drained, chopped canned tomatoes
2 pounds pork shoulder or other stewing pork, in 1″ cubes
white wine and/or lemon juice, to taste

Heat butter in a 2½- or 3-quart stew pot or Dutch oven, and when hot, add onion. Stir and sauté slowly until onion is barely soft and just begins to turn bright yellow. Sprinkle flour over onion; stir and sauté 4 or 5 minutes over low heat, or until flour just begins to turn color. Pour in water or stock, all at once, and stir smooth over low heat with a wire whisk or wooden spoon. Add a little salt, cloves, bay leaf and tomatoes. Simmer, covered, 10 minutes. Add cubed, unbrowned pork to cooked sauce. Cover and simmer slowly but steadily 1½ hours, or until meat is tender. Add more liquid if needed during cooking. Season to taste with white wine and/or lemon juice.

✂ / *SILESIAN HEAVEN* (*Schlesisches Himmelreich*)

From the east German province of Silesia comes this idea of gastronomic heaven. This may be served as a stew with small pieces of meat or with whole pork chops, depending on whether you want it to be a budget dish.

1 *pound mixed dried fruits such
as apple rings, pears, prune
and apricots*
2 *pounds pork cutlets, or 2
pounds stewing pork in large
pieces or one piece*
3 *tablespoons butter*

4 *tablespoons flour
salt to taste
sugar to taste
powdered cloves to taste
any of the semolina, potato or
bread dumplings in Chapter*
III

Soak fruit overnight in cold water to cover. Drain before cooking. Cover pork with water—about 5 to 6 cups should do—and simmer it, covered, slowly but steadily about 40 minutes, or until almost done. Add soaked fruit and continue simmering 10 or 15 minutes until both meat and fruit are done. If you are using stew meat and want to cut it into smaller cubes, take it out of stock and do so. Heat butter in a large saucepan and when hot and bubbling, add flour. Stir and sauté until flour begins to turn color, about 3 or 4 minutes over low heat. Pour 4 cups of stock in which meat cooked into this flour mixture and beat smooth with wire whisk or wooden spoon. Season with salt, sugar and cloves. Add pork and fruit and simmer all together until sauce is thick and everything is hot. Prepare dumplings, drain and serve on top of meat-fruit stew. You can prepare the dumpling batter while the stew is cooking.

❆ / *SOUTH GERMAN PORK CROQUETTES*
(*Süddeutsche Schweinekotelette*)

1½ *pounds lean pork, ground*
½ *pound fat pork, ground*
1 *medium onion, minced*
1 *tablespoon butter*
10 *to* 12 *anchovy filets, rinsed,
drained and chopped*
2 *tablespoons capers, drained
and chopped*
¼ *teaspoon pepper
generous dash nutmeg*

2 *slices stale pumpernickel,
grated without crusts*
2 *eggs*
3 *tablespoons sour cream*
1 *parsley root (petrouchka),
scraped and cut in small
slivers
flour or breadcrumbs, optional
butter for frying*

Mix lean and fat pork together thoroughly. Sauté minced onion in butter until very soft and pale yellow; do not let onion brown. Add sautéed onion to meat along with all other ingredients, except parsley root, flour or bread crumbs and butter for frying. This should be mixed to a very smooth forcemeat consistency. Add more sour cream or another egg if necessary to make mixture completely smooth. It is best to use your hands for this mixing as they do the most thorough job. With wet hands, shape meat mixture into small cakes, about 1″ to 1½″ thick. They should be about the size of the heart of a loin pork chop. Stick a strip of parsley root into one end of each meat cake, to imitate bone in a lamb or pork chop. You can dredge these meat cakes lightly with flour or breadcrumbs or you may fry them as they are. Heat butter in a large heavy skillet and when hot and bubbling add the "chops." Fry over moderate heat, turning once so that both sides become golden brown. They should be done in about 15 to 20 minutes. Pour butter from pan over chops to serve.

❇ / *PORK HOCKS WITH SAUERKRAUT AND SPLIT PEA PURÉE (Eisbein mit Sauerkraut und Erbsenpüree)*

This dish is a famous Berlin specialty. It is especially good at Hardtke's, a handsome old tavern-like restaurant in that city. At almost any time of day you can see groups of businessmen talking shop over vast platters of this dish, usually washed down with fiery white Schnaps and beer.

6 SERVINGS

6 *fresh pork hocks*	6 *to 8 peppercorns*
water to cover	*salt*
1 *onion*	1 *recipe Cooked Sauerkraut, page*
2 *bay leaves*	*276*
1 *tablespoon pickling spices*	1 *recipe Pea Purée, page 301*

Scrape, scrub and split pigs' feet, or have butcher do it for you. Wash well under running cold water. Place in large pot with water to cover. Add onion, bay leaves, peppercorns and salt. Cover pot, bring to boil, reduce heat and simmer slowly but steadily 3 to 4 hours, or until meat is tender and begins to come away from bone. (The hocks should remain intact, so do not cook until meat actually falls off.) Drain well. Arrange a mound of sauerkraut on a large dinner plate and place 1 hock on top of it. Serve 3 or 4 tablespoons yellow pea purée beside kraut and hocks, on same plate.

✂ / PIGS' KNUCKLES WITH SAUERKRAUT (*Schwein-knöchel mit Sauerkraut*)

6 SERVINGS

6 *pigs' knuckles*
2 *quarts fresh or canned*
 sauerkraut
1 *to 2 tablespoons butter*

1 *large onion, minced*
1 *tablespoon caraway seeds*
 dry white wine or water
 salt to taste

Scrub, scrape and wash pigs' knuckles thoroughly. Drain sauerkraut and if it is very sour, rinse in a colander once or twice. Heat butter in heavy 3-quart Dutch oven or casserole. When butter is hot and bubbling, add minced onion and sauté until transparent and begins to turn bright yellow. Add sauerkraut and caraway seeds and toss lightly with fork until onion and caraway seeds are evenly distributed. Sauté 3 or 4 minutes. Add scrubbed and washed pigs' knuckles and push them down until they are covered with about half the kraut. Add enough wine or water to just reach level of sauerkraut. Cover, bring to a boil, reduce heat and simmer slowly but steadily 3 to 4 hours. The meat on knuckles should be tender when pierced with fork or skewer. Potatoes or dumplings can be cooked right in pot along with knuckles and sauerkraut, as described in following recipe, Variation 1.

✂ / SPARERIBS WITH SAUERKRAUT (*Rippespeer mit Sauerkraut*)

6 SERVINGS

This is prepared very much like the above recipe. Use 4 pounds spareribs and 2 quarts sauerkraut. Cut ribs into individual portions and brown them in their own fat in 3-quart casserole or Dutch oven. Remove ribs and use remaining fat in pan to sauté onion and kraut. Caraway seeds may be used or eliminated. When sauerkraut is sautéed, return ribs to pot, burying them in kraut. Add enough water or juice from sauerkraut, or a mixture of both, to just cover. Cover pot, bring to a boil, reduce heat and simmer slowly but steadily 2½ to 3 hours, or until spareribs are done. A peeled, sliced apple can be added to pot about halfway through cooking. Salt to taste before serving. Potatoes or dumplings can be added to this, as described below. If you prefer, this dish can be baked after ribs have been browned and combined with sautéed onion and sauerkraut. Cover pot and bake in 350° oven 1½ to 2 hours.

VARIATIONS

1. To make this a complete, one-pot meal, potatoes or dumplings can be cooked in sauerkraut. Use 6 to 8 medium-sized brown new potatoes, peeled, and add for last 45 minutes of cooking time. Prepare Flour Dumplings, page 65, and drop them from tablespoon on top of simmering sauerkraut. Cover and cook 15 to 20 minutes, or until test dumpling is dry and spongy.
2. Sausages such as knockwurst or frankfurters, slices of ham or smoked pork chops can be added for last hour of cooking time.

✁ / *DEVILED PIGS' FEET* (*Panierte Kalberfüsse mit Senf*)

Although pigs' feet are prepared most often as Saure Sülze, page 16, and Eisbein, page 189, they are also cooked and then grilled.

6 SERVINGS

6 *pigs' feet*	3 *or 4 sprigs of parsley*
boiling water to cover	6 *or 8 peppercorns*
1 *large onion studded with 5 or*	1 *bay leaf*
6 cloves	1 *teaspoon salt*
1 *carrot, scraped and sliced*	*prepared hot mustard*
½ *knob celery or 2 stalks of*	½ *cup cooking oil, melted butter*
celery with leaves, sliced	*or lard*
1 *large clove of garlic*	½ *cup breadcrumbs*

Scrub, scrape and wash pigs' feet thoroughly and blanch in boiling water 10 minutes. Split in half, lengthwise, with a sharp knife. You can do this yourself, or your butcher can scrape and split them for you. Place feet in large saucepan or soup kettle, along with onion, carrot, celery, garlic, parsley, peppercorns, bay leaf and salt. Bring to a boil, cover and simmer slowly but steadily about 3 hours, or until meat on pigs' feet is tender when pierced with a fork or skewer. Remove feet from broth, drain and pat dry with paper toweling. Brush feet with mustard and whichever fat you are using, then roll in breadcrumbs. Arrange in a single layer in a shallow open baking pan or steel grill platter, or lay out on a double sheet of heavy aluminum foil, on the broiler pan. Broil under moderate heat, turning once or twice, until feet are crisp golden brown on all sides.

VARIATION

If it seems easier, pigs' feet can be roasted in a 450° oven instead of broiled.

❆ / EASTER HAM (Osterschinken)

A huge baked smoked ham is the feature of Easter Sunday dinners all over Germany. It may be prepared in either of the two ways that follow, or it may be baked exactly as we do Virginia ham—with cloves, brown sugar and fruit juice, beer or wine used for basting. It is also sometimes made in a much simpler way. The ham is parboiled if necessary and then baked, rind and all, without any seasoning other than pepper and served with no gravy.

❆ / MECKLENBURG BAKED HAM IN RYE BREAD CRUST (Schinken, auf Mecklenburgische Art)

Rye bread and cloves add a savory touch to this baked ham that is a specialty of the Baltic province of Mecklenburg, now part of East Germany.

16 TO 18 SERVINGS

1 smoked ham either raw or precooked, about 12 pounds
2 cups dry rye breadcrumbs

1 teaspoon powdered cloves
1 tablespoon white or brown
  sugar

If ham is raw, boil it as you usually would, until ready for glazing. If it is precooked, heat it in oven, according to instructions on wrapper, until it has 30 minutes of cooking time left. Preheat oven to 400°. The rind should be removed from ham, if it has one, and fat scored in diamond pattern. Mix breadcrumbs with cloves and sugar and pack onto scored fat. Roast on rack in preheated oven, without basting, until ham is done and crumbs have formed a golden brown crust.

❆ / HAM IN BURGUNDY (Schinken in Burgunder)

16 TO 18 SERVINGS

1 smoked uncooked ham, about
  12 pounds
water to cover
peppercorns or black pepper

crushed whole or powdered allspice
whole cloves
2 tablespoons sugar

2 *tablespoons butter*
2 *cups red burgundy*
1 *to 2 cups ham stock*

1 *tablespoon flour or 2 teaspoons*
   cornstarch dissolved in a
   little cold water
salt to taste

Taste rind of ham with the tip of your tongue. If it is very salty, soak ham overnight in water to cover. Drain off water before cooking. If it is not salty, do not soak. Place ham in a large kettle and cover completely with cold water. Cover pot, bring to a boil, reduce heat and simmer slowly but steadily 2 to 3 hours, or until tender when pierced with a sharp-pronged fork or skewer. Preheat oven to 375°. Remove ham from stock.

Cut off rind and score fat in diamond pattern. Place ham in roasting pan with a cover. Sprinkle with crushed peppercorns and allspice or rub with powdered spices. Stud with cloves. Sprinkle sugar over top of ham and dot with flecks of butter. Add wine and 1 cup ham stock to pan. Cover pan and place in preheated oven. Braise about 45 minutes, basting 4 or 5 times with wine and stock. The top of ham should be golden brown. Remove ham to a heated platter or carving board. Skim any excess fat from pan juices, bring to a boil once or twice on stove. Swirl in flour or cornstarch that has been dissolved in cold water. Simmer until gravy thickens and is smooth, about 3 or 4 minutes. Season to taste and serve.

VARIATIONS

1. If you are using precooked ham, follow instructions on package for heating in oven. When it still has 45 minutes of cooking time left, score fat and add spices, wine and water or stock. Proceed with recipe from that point.

2. If you would like a much stronger wine flavor, start with a smoked raw ham and marinate it overnight in 2 bottles of red burgundy to which you add a pinch of tarragon, sage, marjoram, a strip of lemon peel, 2 bay leaves, 6 cloves, 8 peppercorns and a sliced carrot and onion. To cook, place ham in a deep kettle and pour marinade with vegetables and spices over it. Add water until ham is completely covered. Cover pot, bring to boil, reduce heat and simmer slowly but steadily 3 to 4 hours, or until ham is tender. This ham can be served as is, or it can be glazed on top. To do the latter, cut off rind and score fat. Sprinkle fat with 2 tablespoons sugar, dot with butter and stud with cloves. Roast in 450° oven until sugar carmelizes. Strain stock in which ham cooked and thicken with flour or cornstarch dissolved in water. Use 2 tablespoons flour or 3 teaspoons cornstarch for every 3 to 4 cups of stock.

�֍ / *HAM STEAKS WITH HAZELNUT BUTTER* (*Schinkensteaks mit Haselnussbutter*)

This recipe is for ham steak or slices of leftover baked ham.

6 SERVINGS

3 *precooked ham steaks, ½″*
  thick, or 6 ½″-thick slices
  baked ham
⅔ *cup hazelnuts, roasted and*
  then finely ground

4 *to 5 tablespoons butter*
¾ *cup sweet cream*
⅓ *cup meat stock or water*
3 *tablespoons breadcrumbs*

Preheat oven to 475°. Trim fat from ham slices. Work roasted, finely ground hazelnuts into butter, forming a thick paste. Spread one-sixth of paste on each slice of ham. Arrange slices in a single layer in a buttered open baking dish that is also fireproof. Mix cream and stock or water and pour over ham slices. Bake in preheated oven about 15 minutes, or until sauce is simmering and butter melts. Sprinkle ham steaks with breadcrumbs and slide under broiler 5 or 10 minutes, or until crumbs are golden brown.

✖ / *HAM PUDDING WITH NOODLES OR MACARONI* (*Schinkenpudding mit Nudeln oder Makkaroni*)

4 TO 6 SERVINGS

¾ *to 1 pound wide noodles*
  salted water
2 *cups chopped or shredded*
  cooked ham
2 *eggs*

1 *cup sour cream*
  salt and black pepper
  butter
3 *tablespoons grated Parmesan*
  cheese

Preheat oven to 400°. Cook noodles until just tender in boiling salted water. Drain well. Toss noodles and ham lightly together with a fork. Butter a 2-quart casserole or soufflé dish and add ham and noodles. Beat eggs into sour cream with a fork or rotary beater, season with a little salt and black pepper and pour over ham and noodles. Dot well with tiny flecks of butter and sprinkle with grated cheese. Bake in upper third of preheated oven 30 to 40 minutes, or until pudding is custardy and set. If top browns too quickly, cover with a double thickness of aluminum foil.

✼ / HAM AND POTATO PIE (*Schinken- und Kartoffelpudding*)

Follow recipe for Haddock and Potato Pie, Hamburg Style (page 122), substituting sliced or diced cooked ham for the haddock. A little diced lean bacon can be added to each layer of ham, but it is not really necessary. Bake in 375° oven 35 to 45 minutes.

✼ / HAMBURGER RUNDSTÜCK I

Hamburg has two very good dishes that serve as light entrees or snacks, both of which use leftovers—ham in one case, pork in the other. Both are called Hamburger Rundstück, Rundstück being the local dialect for a small round breakfast roll. The first of these "rolls" might do us for breakfast; the second would more likely be served for lunch or a late supper.

Toast a slice of bread or half a roll. Butter it generously after it has cooled slightly, so butter does not melt. Top with several paper-thin slices of cooked smoked ham and a hot fried egg. Sprinkle with a little salt (unless ham is very salty) and black pepper.

✼ / HAMBURGER RUNDSTÜCK II

A slice of untoasted bread or half a roll is the base for this open sandwich. Top with a slice of warm leftover roast pork and plently of hot pork gravy. The leftover meat can be heated in the gravy.

❊ INNARDS AND VARIETY ❊ MEATS
(Innereien und Verschiedenes Fleisch)

▓ / BRAISED WHOLE CALVES' LIVER (Gespickter Kalbsleberbraten)

1 whole calves' liver, 3 to 3½ pounds
¼ pound bacon or salt pork, cut in strips for larding
salt and pepper
flour
¼ pound butter, diced bacon or salt pork

¼ knob celery, chopped, or 1 stalk celery, chopped
1 carrot, sliced (optional)
2 onions, minced
2 cups meat stock
¾ to 1 cup sweet cream
sugar to taste
lemon juice (optional)

The liver should be skinned. This can be done by you or your butcher. However, if you plan to keep it a day or two before cooking, do not have it skinned that far in advance; skin it yourself before cooking. Cut bacon or salt pork in strips and roll in salt and pepper. Lard liver well with these strips and sprinkle lightly on all sides with salt and pepper and dredge with flour. Heat butter or other fat in a Dutch oven and when hot, add liver. Brown slowly on all sides, turning with a wooden spoon so you do not pierce surface of meat. It should be sufficiently seared on all sides in 10 minutes. Remove liver and add vegetables to hot fat. Sauté until they begin to soften and turn golden brown, stirring frequently.

Return liver to pot, placing it on top of the vegetables. Add stock, cover and simmer slowly but steadily about 2 hours, turning liver once or twice during cooking. Check to see if more liquid is needed as meat cooks. To test liver for doneness, pierce it with a skewer; if no blood oozes out, it is done. Do not test it before 2 hours. Remove liver to a heated platter. Skim excess fat from sauce if there is any. Stir in cream and season to taste with salt and sugar. Heat but do not boil and add a few drops of lemon juice, as needed. Slice liver; serve gravy in a heated sauceboat.

VARIATION

Before larding liver, season bacon or salt pork strips with powdered allspice, as well as with salt and pepper. Prepare in same way, but use no vegetables except onions; add 2 bay leaves and ¼ teaspoon allspice to stock. When liver is half done, add a slice or two of rye bread or a rye bread heel; when finished, strain gravy, rubbing through vegetables and bread. Season with a little more allspice, salt and pepper if needed, sugar and vinegar and half a cup red wine. Eliminate cream and lemon juice.

✁ / BREADED FRIED LIVER (*Gebackene Leber*)

2 TO 4 SERVINGS

1 *pound calves', beef or pork liver, in 4 slices*	2 *eggs beaten with 2 tablespoons cold water*
milk (optional)	½ *to 1 cup fine dry breadcrumbs*
salt and pepper	3 *to 4 tablespoons butter, bacon fat or lard*
½ *to 1 cup flour*	

If you use beef or pork liver, soak in milk 1 hour. Sprinkle lightly on both sides with salt and pepper. Turn flour onto a sheet of waxed paper or a flat plate. Beat eggs with water in a wide flat bowl. Turn breadcrumbs onto a sheet of waxed paper or a flat plate. Dredge seasoned liver lightly on both sides with flour. Dip into eggs and let excess drip off. Dredge both sides of each slice with breadcrumbs. Let stand at room temperature 15 to 30 minutes before frying. Heat fat in a large heavy skillet and when hot, fry liver slowly. When first side is golden brown, turn and brown second side. The liver should be done in 8 to 10 minutes.

░ / SOUR LIVER (*Saure Leber*)

Although this may sound like some dread disease, it is really a very savory dish.

2 TO 4 SERVINGS

1 *pound calves' or pork liver,*
   in 4 slices
2 *tablespoons butter, bacon*
   fat or lard
1 *small onion, minced*
1 *heaping tablespoon flour*
1½ *cups meat stock or water*

salt and pepper
marjoram (optional)
lemon juice or vinegar to taste
sugar to taste
white wine to taste, or 3 table-
   spoons sour cream

If you use pork liver, soak slices in milk 1 hour before cooking. Cut liver into finger strips and dredge with flour. Heat fat in a skillet. When it is hot and bubbling, add minced onion and sauté slowly until it begins to soften and becomes transparent. Add liver strips dredged in flour and sauté, turning, until pieces are brown on all sides and no blood oozes from them. This will take about 5 minutes. Pour in stock, add salt, pepper and a pinch of marjoram, cover and simmer over moderate heat about 3 or 4 minutes. Season sauce with lemon juice or vinegar and, if you like, a dash of sugar, though that is not strictly necessary. Finish sauce with a little white wine or sour cream. If you plan to use wine, use lemon juice, not vinegar, for souring. Heat sauce thoroughly but do not bring to a boil. The sour cream is a Bavarian addition.

░ / SWABIAN CALVES' LIVER (*Schwäbische Kalbsleber*)

2 TO 4 SERVINGS

1 *pound calves' liver, cut in 5*
   slices
salt and pepper
½ *to 1 cup flour*
2 *generous tablespoons butter or*
   bacon fat

1 *small onion, minced*
½ *cup meat stock or water*
½ *cup sour cream*
1 *tablespoon capers*
lemon juice to taste
white wine to taste (optional)

The slices may be left whole or they may be cut in half. Sprinkle one side of each piece with salt and pepper and dredge both sides with flour. Heat fat in a large heavy skillet with a lid, and when hot, add liver and brown quickly on both sides, 2 to 3 minutes on each side should be enough. If you cannot fit all the liver into pan at once, fry in shifts.

Remove finished liver to heated platter. Reduce heat, add minced onion to hot fat and sauté until golden brown. Stir so it browns evenly. Sprinkle 2 tablespoons flour over onions; stir and sauté until flour is absorbed and begins to turn yellow. Add stock, sour cream, capers, lemon juice and white wine to taste. Season with more salt if necessary. Return liver to sauce, cover and simmer very slowly 5 minutes, stirring once or twice so that sauce does not scorch. Serve with Spätzle, page 60, and Cooked Sauerkraut, page 276.

⛁ / CHICKEN OR CALVES' LIVER WITH APPLES AND ONIONS (*Hühner- oder Kalbsleber mit Äpfeln und Zwiebeln*)

2 TO 4 SERVINGS

1 *pound chicken liver, or calves'*
   liver, cut in 4 slices
salt
2 *medium-sized onions*
2 *apples (MacIntosh, Northern*
   Spies or Rome Beauties, but
   not sour green apples)

3 *tablespoons butter*
½ *cup stock or water*
3 *to 4 tablespoons sour cream*
   (optional)

Chicken livers should be cut in half, with all connective tissue removed, then sprinkled with salt. Slice onions and separate into rings. Peel and core apples and slice into thick rings or cut into 5 or 6 lengthwise slices. Heat butter in a large heavy skillet and when hot and bubbling, add onion rings. Sauté over moderate heat, stirring frequently, so that they fry to an even golden brown. Remove to a heated platter. Add apple slices to same hot fat and sauté until they too are golden brown. Turn with a wooden spoon so the pieces do not break up. Do not let apples get too soft; they should retain their shape. This should take 6 or 7 minutes.

Remove to the platter with onions. Fry liver slices in hot butter, turning once so that both sides are brown, about 8 to 10 minutes in all. Place liver on heated platter and top with onions and apples. Pour water or stock into pan and let it boil up once or twice. As it does so, stir with a wooden spoon, scraping all the coagulated pan juices into gravy. If you like, this sauce can now be seasoned with salt and spooned over the liver; or you can stir in sour cream.

✠ / LIVER RAGOUT WITH MUSHROOMS AND ONIONS
(*Leberragout mit Champignons und Zwiebeln*)

4 TO 6 SERVINGS

1½ pounds chicken, beef or
    calves' liver, cut in 4 slices
    salt and pepper
2 large onions
½ pound mushrooms
3 tablespoons butter

2 tablespoons flour
1 cup water or meat stock
    thyme (optional)
2 or 3 tablespoons sour cream
    (optional), or red wine or
    Madeira to taste (optional)

Chicken livers should be cut in half with all connective tissue removed. Beef liver should soak in milk 1 hour and then be well dried before proceeding. Both beef and calves' liver should be cut into finger strips or squares. Sprinkle liver with salt and pepper. Slice onions thin and separate into rings. Wash mushrooms quickly under running water, dry at once in a towel and slice lengthwise, cutting right through stem. Heat butter in a heavy skillet with a lid. When hot and bubbling, add onions and sauté slowly, stirring frequently until they soften and take on a bright yellow color. Remove and reserve. Add mushrooms to hot fat; sauté and stir over moderate heat until they begin to take on color, about 3 to 5 minutes. Remove and reserve with onions. Add liver to hot fat and brown on all sides over moderate heat. When liver is thoroughly seared (about 4 or 5 minutes) return mushrooms and onions to pan.

Sprinkle with flour and stir gently until flour is absorbed. Continue sautéing for 3 or 4 minutes. Pour in water or stock and a pinch of thyme if you are using it. Cover and simmer gently but steadily over low heat. Stir from time to time so that sauce does not scorch. Simmer about 10 minutes, or until blood no longer oozes from liver and sauce is smooth and thick. Season with salt and pepper. This sauce may be served as is, or you can stir in sour cream or wine.

✠ / TONGUE (*Zunge*)

The basic preparations are the same for ox, beef, calf, pig or lamb tongue. The tongue is boiled, or more exactly, simmered, until tender and then prepared and served according to any one of the specific recipes that follow. Although ox tongue is used very often in Germany, it is difficult to get here. Beef tongue is the most popular in the U.S. as well as in Germany. The only difference between that and ox tongue is that the former is much larger, has coarser texture and a stronger flavor. Beef tongue may be had fresh, pickled or smoked. The fresh usually has to be ordered in advance, while most butchers have the other two on hand at all times. You can generally get especially good uncooked pickled tongues at kosher-style delicatessens and butcher shops. All tongues are cooked whole, with the heavy, bony throat end (Schlund) intact. This, and the skin, are trimmed off after cooking.

A beef tongue weighs between 4 and 5 pounds and will serve 6 to 10 people, depending upon the size of their appetites and the way in which the tongue is sliced. Cutting the tongue on the diagonal results in larger slices and much less waste. The Schlund is considered a choice morsel for the cook to pick over, or if it is a smoked tongue, it can be used to flavor a pea or lentil soup, just as a ham bone might. The tongues of calves, lambs and pigs are much smaller, and one would be just about enough for two people, although for hearty eaters, plan one tongue per person. These tongues are peeled and split in half lengthwise, or are sliced, depending on the way they are to be finished. They will cook in 1 to 1½ hours.

To test any tongue for tenderness, press the tip between your thumb and forefinger. If it gives easily, the meat is done. A beef tongue is usually done when the small bones slip out of the Schlund end, but test the tip to be sure. Tongue should never boil too rapidly, as it will shrink and become hard. It is easier to skin a tongue while it is warm, so it can be allowed to cool just enough to be handled. To speed this process, run the cooked tongue very quickly under running cold water; that will cool the skin but not the meat. It is a good idea to peel a tongue over a wide bowl or rimmed platter, as a great deal of cooking liquid will run out of it.

To cook a pickled beef tongue, wash it and place in a deep pot with cold water to cover. Cover pot, bring water to a boil and reduce heat to slow, steady simmer. Skim foam that rises to surface during first ten minutes of cooking. When no more rises, add 1 large whole peeled onion and 1 tablespoon mixed pickling spices. Simmer covered 2½ to 3½ hours, or until tongue tests done.

To cook a fresh or smoked beef tongue, follow procedure for pickled tongue but do not use pickling spices. Use a large onion, a bay leaf, and, if you like, any or all the pot vegetables on page 29. The onion can be studded with cloves if that flavor will blend with sauce you plan to serve.

To cook calves', lamb or pigs' tongues, which are always fresh, never smoked or pickled, follow procedure for fresh or smoked beef tongue. Cook 1 to 1½ hours, or until tender.

/ *BOILED BEEF TONGUE WITH VARIOUS SAUCES*

Fresh, pickled or smoked tongue can be boiled, peeled and sliced onto a hot platter, then served with mustard or any one of the sauces noted below. Where stock is called for in sauce, use tongue's cooking liquid. If it is too strongly flavored, combine with equal amount of water.

Fresh tongue can be prepared with a caper sauce, as described for Calves' Tongues in Caper Sauce (page 204) or with any of the hot or cold horseradish sauces in Chapter XIII.

Pickled tongue is also good with horseradish sauces, or with Brown Sauce made with madeira, page 332.

Smoked tongue is very good with Mustard Sauce, page 334, with Polish Raisin Sauce, made with either beer or madeira, page 338, or with Sweet-and-Sour Bacon Sauce, page 338.

⧉ / BRAISED BEEF TONGUE WITH SOUR CREAM (*Geschmorte Rindszunge mit Sauerrahm*)

8 TO 10 SERVINGS

1 fresh tongue, 4 to 5 pounds	½ to ¾ cup melted butter or
salt water to cover	bacon fat
¼ pound bacon cut in larding	1 tablespoon minced parsley
strips	½ to 1 cup sour cream
1 onion, minced	salt and pepper to taste
1 carrot, scraped and chopped	1 tablespoon flour or 2 tea-
1 stalk celery, chopped, or ½	spoons cornstarch, if
knob celery, peeled and	necessary
chopped	

Place tongue in a deep heavy pot or kettle and cover with water to which a little salt is added. Follow directions on page 200, but cook for only half the time indicated. Cool tongue slightly, trim and peel it. Lard generously with bacon. Preheat oven to 350°. Place chopped vegetables in an open roasting pan and place tongue on top of them. Pour melted fat over tongue.

Roast tongue in preheated oven for 45 minutes to 1 hour, or until tongue is tender and nicely browned. Add some of tongue's cooking liquid to pan from time to time as needed to keep vegetables from scorching. Baste tongue every 10 minutes with drippings and pan juices. Remove tongue to a heated platter. Strain pan juices into a clean saucepan, rubbing through as much of vegetables as possible. Skim excess fat from surface of gravy. Stir in sour cream to taste, and season. If sauce seems too thin, dissolve flour or cornstarch in a little cold water and stir into sauce. Bring to a boil and serve over sliced tongue.

✂ / *BREADED BEEF TONGUE* (*Gebackene Rindszunge*)

4 TO 6 SERVINGS

8 to 10 slices cooked tongue
    (fresh, pickled or smoked),
    ½" thick
2 eggs beaten with 2 tablespoons
    cold water

1 cup breadcrumbs
butter, lard or bacon fat

Dip tongue slices in beaten egg and let excess egg drip off. Dredge slices with breadcrumbs and let stand at room temperature 10 minutes. Heat fat in a large heavy skillet and when hot and bubbling, fry tongue slices, turning once so they become golden brown on both sides. Drain a minute or two on paper toweling.

✂ / *FINE TONGUE RAGOUT* (*Feines Zungenragout*)

8 TO 10 SERVINGS

1 fresh beef tongue cooked with
    pot vegetables, page 29
6 tablespoons butter
5 to 6 tablespoons flour
3 cups tongue cooking liquid
    salt and pepper to taste
1 to 2 tablespoons grated
    Parmesan cheese (optional)

madeira to taste
½ pound button mushrooms,
    sliced
lemon juice
2 tablespoons butter
1 recipe very small Bread or
    Meat Dumplings, pages 66,
    62

Cook tongue as directed on page 200. Peel, slice and reserve. Heat 6 tablespoons butter in a saucepan and when hot and bubbling, add flour. Stir and sauté until flour turns a deep coffee color but do not let it burn or blacken. Pour in tongue stock and beat smooth with a wire whisk or wooden spoon. Flavor sauce with salt, pepper, cheese if you want to use it, and madeira. Simmer about ½ hour. Meanwhile sprinkle sliced mushrooms with lemon juice and sauté a few minutes in 2 tablespoons butter. Mushrooms should be faintly golden and barely tender. Also prepare tiny bread or meat dumplings and drain well in colander. Add sautéed mushrooms, dumplings and tongue slices to sauce. Check seasoning and simmer 5 minutes.

VARIATIONS

Almost every housewife or chef has a different version of this. Parboiled sweetbreads cut in fork-size pieces may be simmered in the sauce and sometimes parboiled cauliflower rosettes are also included. A dash of lemon juice can be added as a final touch, and in some cases, cheese is eliminated but a dash of powdered cloves flavors the sauce. Small pieces of braised veal and/or diced smoked ham are considered musts according to some experts, while in Bavaria the sauce is finished off with some sour cream and an egg yolk or two beaten in just before serving. The finished ragout can also be turned into a buttered soufflé-type baker, sprinkled with cheese, dotted with butter and browned in the oven for a few minutes.

✂ / CALVES', LAMB OR PIGS' TONGUES IN CAPER SAUCE (*Kalbs-, Lamm- oder Schweinezungen in Kapernsosse*)

6 SERVINGS

3 calves', lamb or pigs' tongues cooked with pot vegetables, page 29	2 tablespoons drained capers white wine or lemon juice, to taste
3 tablespoons butter	anchovy paste (optional)
4 tablespoons flour	salt to taste
2 cups tongue stock	

The peeled, trimmed cooked tongues should be thinly sliced. Melt butter in a saucepan and when hot and bubbling, add flour. Stir and sauté over low heat until flour begins to take on color. Add all the stock and beat smooth with a wire whisk or wooden spoon. Add capers, white wine or lemon juice to taste, a dab or two of anchovy paste, if you want to use it, and salt as needed. Add tongue slices to sauce and simmer together over moderate heat 3 or 4 minutes.

✂ / BRAINS AND SWEETBREADS (*Hirne und Kalbsmilch*)

Brains and sweetbreads are so alike in flavor and texture that they require much the same preparation and are almost completely interchangeable in recipes. They are easy to cook, delicate in flavor, relatively inexpensive and so nutritious it's a pity Americans do not make more frequent use of them. Although all young animals have sweetbreads (a gland known as the thymus that disappears in grown animals), only those of the calf and lamb are commonly eaten, those of the former being the most popular of all. The calves' brains are again the most popular, but those of steer, lamb, sheep and pigs are also fairly commonplace on German tables—much more so in homes than in restaurants. Both brains and sweetbreads come in pairs; 1 pair (2 connected lobes) is 1 brain or 1 sweetbread—that is, the brain or sweetbread of one animal. If you are serving them as appetizers, 1 pair of sweetbreads will serve four people, as will 2 pairs of brains. For a light main course, 1 pair of sweetbreads will serve two; for heartier eaters serve 1 pair of sweetbreads per person. When serving brains as an entree, plan on 1 pair per person for light eaters; 2 pairs per person for those with larger appetites. Recipes here refer to calves' brains, 1 pair of which equals ½ a beef brain or 3 pig, lamb or sheep brains.

PREPARATION OF BRAINS AND SWEETBREADS

Both brains and sweetbreads require some cleaning and advance preparation before they are used in any of the recipes that follow. They spoil very quickly when absolutely raw, and so the following preparation should be done as soon as possible after getting them home. Once prepared, they may be kept in the refrigerator for 2 to 3 days.

Wash brains or sweetbreads quickly under running water and then soak in icy water 2 or 3 hours. The water should be changed once or twice during soaking and a little lemon juice or vinegar added with last change of water. If bowl is placed in refrigerator during soaking process, water will remain cold enough. After they have soaked, gently pull off as much of membrane and blood streaks as possible, but do not cut into the meat itself or break it into tiny bits. They may be soaked again in ice water, another hour, and then trimmed even more, or, if they seem very clean, they can now be blanched.

To blanch sweetbreads, put them in saucepan and cover well with cold water. Add about 1 teaspoon salt and the juice of ¼ lemon to water. You may also add a few slices of onions and celery with the leaves, a sprig of parsley, a bay leaf and a few peppercorns, if you wish. Any or all of these vegetables may be used or eliminated, depending on the flavor you want sweetbreads to have. Simmer, very slowly, uncovered, 15 minutes. Place in icy water a few minutes and trim off any remaining connective tissue or white tubing. The sweetbreads may now be cooked, or they may be kept in refrigerator. Usually they are pressed between two plates for 3 hours so they will flatten and fry or sauté more evenly and be more attractive when sliced and served.

To blanch brains follow same procedure as for sweetbreads, with following exceptions: Bring water to a boil with any vegetables you plan to use and then add brains, salt and lemon juice. Simmer 15 to 20 minutes, or until brains look completely white and solid. A beef brain will require 25 to 30 minutes' cooking time. Remove brains from liquid and cut away any remaining connective tissue and white tubing. Strain cooking stock and let brains cool in it. If they are to be stored a day or two, they should be covered with stock and refrigerated. As with sweetbreads, brains may or may not be flattened between two plates.

You will find varying procedures in different cookbooks for above preparations, although, basically, all are the same as to soaking, trimming and blanching. If you have never prepared these meats before, you may wonder which is correct and what will happen to you if you follow the wrong instructions. The answers are simple: all are correct and nothing will happen, even if you were to eat these meats raw, a prospect that may not sound appetizing to you but which nutritionists think is a superb idea—something to do with B vitamins, I believe. Follow whichever method seems easiest to you, but do soak in ice water and remove blood streaks before blanching (or eating raw). If you find it easier to remove membranes after blanching, then do so. If you find it easier to cut white tubing away *before* blanching instead of after, do that too.

Brains and sweetbreads freeze very well. It is a good idea to soak and remove membranes and blood streaks before freezing. Wrap in aluminum foil or freezing paper, and freeze. Thaw meat as you blanch it, but simmer 10 to 15 minutes longer, or until completely thawed and cooked. Never freeze sweetbreads after they are blanched or cooked.

&3 / FRIED BRAINS OR SWEETBREADS (*Panierte Hirne oder Kalbsmilch*)

2 SERVINGS

Two pairs of brains or 1 pair of sweetbreads should be prepared and flattened. Each half of sweetbread may be fried in one flat slab or may be cut into ½" to 1" slices. Brains should be sliced. Sprinkle with salt and pepper, dredge lightly with flour, dip into beaten egg mixed with a little cold water and dredge with breadcrumbs. Fry slowly in hot butter, turning once so that both sides become golden brown. Sprinkle with capers and serve with lemon wedges.

⚡ / CALVES' BRAINS OR SWEETBREADS WITH EGGS
(*Kalbshirne oder Kalbsmilch mit Eiern*)

2 SERVINGS

1 *pair calves' brains or*	1 *tablespoon minced parsley*
sweetbreads	*salt and pepper to taste*
3 *tablespoons butter*	4 *to 5 eggs, lightly beaten*
1 *medium-sized onion, minced*	

Prepare and parboil brains or sweetbreads as directed on page 205. Drain and dice. Sauté onions and parsley until the onion is yellow but not brown. Add diced brains or sweetbreads and fry slowly until very lightly browned, stirring gently from time to time. Sprinkle with salt and pepper. Beat eggs lightly and pour over brain-onion mixture. Scramble gently or cook as an omelette until eggs reach desired degree of doneness, generally fairly well done for this dish.

⚡ / BAKED BRAINS OR SWEETBREADS AU GRATIN
(*Überkrustete Hirne oder Kalbsmilch*)

2 SERVINGS AS MAIN COURSE,
4 SERVINGS AS APPETIZER

Prepare 2 pairs of brains or 1 pair sweetbreads, but blanch them for 15 minutes. Prepare a thick white Cheese Sauce, page 333, using 1 extra tablespoonful flour and adding egg yolk and lemon juice as directed. Cut brains or sweetbreads into fork-size pieces and stir into sauce gently. Turn mixture into a buttered shallow baking dish, or individual ramekins. Sprinkle top with a thick layer of breadcrumbs, dot generously with butter and bake in upper third of 450° oven about 10 minutes, or until top is nicely browned and sauce is glazed around edges.

⚡ / BRAINS OR SWEETBREADS IN CAPER SAUCE
(*Hirne oder Kalbsmilch in Kapernsosse*)

This is probably the easiest way to prepare either of these meats. Do advance preparation, but simmer brains or sweetbreads in water or stock 15 to 20 minutes. Strain cooking stock and use it as liquid to make White Sauce, page 331. Cut sweetbreads or brains in pieces and add to sauce. Simmer very slowly 10 minutes. Beat egg yolks and cream into sauce, as in sauce recipe, and flavor to taste with white wine, lemon juice, salt and pepper. Stir in 1 tablespoon drained chopped capers. Heat but do not boil, and serve. A few chopped anchovies or a dab of anchovy paste can be added to sauce to give more piquant flavor. The amount of sauce in recipe is correct for 2 pairs of sweetbreads or 3 pairs of brains.

✿ / BRAIN OR SWEETBREAD RAGOUT (Hirne- oder Kalbsmilchragout)

Prepare brains or sweetbreads, but simmer half the usual time. Drain, trim and cut in fork-size pieces. Use cooking stock to prepare white Mushroom Cream Sauce, page 335, adding brains or sweetbreads and mushrooms before simmering sauce 20 minutes. Thicken with egg-yolk-cream mixture, as directed, and add lemon juice and/or white wine to taste, as well as 1 tablespoonful drained capers. You can also prepare sweetbreads or brain ragout in Brown Mushroom Sauce, as on page 335. Again, prepare them but simmer half the usual time. Add with mushrooms to sauce and simmer 15 to 20 minutes, or until meat is done. Both these ragouts may be served in patty shells or on toast, as appetizers or main courses. The amount of sauce in the recipe is correct for a ragout made with 2 pairs of sweetbreads or 3 pairs of brains.

✿ / MOCK OYSTERS (Falsche Austern)

6 TO 8 "OYSTERS";
2 TO 8 SERVINGS (see below)

2 pairs sweetbreads	salt and pepper to taste
2 tablespoons butter	lemon juice to taste
1 small onion, finely minced	6 to 8 large clean oyster shells, if
3 tablespoons flour	possible, or 4 to 6 ramekins
1 cup milk	breadcrumbs
6 anchovy filets, finely minced	butter

Prepare sweetbreads and chop finely when they have cooled slightly. (It is obviously not necessary to flatten them for this recipe.) Heat butter in a skillet and when hot and bubbling, add onion and sauté slowly until it becomes transparent. Add sweetbreads and continue to sauté slowly, stirring from time to time, so that both onion and sweetbreads begin to take on color. Cover pan 3 or 4 minutes and braise. Sprinkle flour into skillet and stir until it is absorbed. Sauté 3 or 4 minutes, add milk and simmer over moderate heat 10 minutes. Stir frequently so that mixture does not scorch. The mixture should be very thick. Add minced anchovies and season as needed with salt, pepper and, if you like, a dash of lemon juice. Pack mixture into oyster shells or ramekins. Sprinkle tops with breadcrumbs and dot generously with tiny flecks of butter. Bake in upper third of 450° oven for 10 minutes, or until topping is nicely browned. Serve hot: 1 to 2 filled oyster shells as an appetizer, 3 to 4 as an entree.

⚼ / STUFFED CALF'S HEART (*Gefülltes Kalbsherz*)

2 GENEROUS SERVINGS

1 calf's heart	1 dill pickle, chopped
salt and pepper	2 tablespoons butter or bacon
marjoram	fat
2 or 3 slices bacon, blanched and	½ cup water
diced	1 tablespoon flour
1 carrot, scraped and chopped	½ cup sour cream

If possible, prepare heart without cutting it open. Using a scissors or a knife, remove all sinews and tubes from inside. If you cannot manage to do that without cutting, cut along one side toward the point and open flat. Sprinkle inside with salt, pepper and marjoram. Mix bacon, carrot and pickle together and stuff into heart. If it has been cut, sew it closed before stuffing. Sew bottom opening closed with strong kitchen thread. Heat fat in a small heavy pot with a tight-fitting lid. When hot, add heart and brown slowly on all sides. Add water, cover and simmer slowly but steadily 45 minutes to 1 hour, or until heart is completely tender when pierced with a carving fork or skewer. Turn once or twice during cooking and add more water if necessary. When heart is tender, blend flour into sour cream and stir into pan juices. Season as needed and bring to a boil, stirring until sauce is smooth and thick. Slice heart and cover with sauce, or serve sauce on the side.

/ SOUR CALF'S-LUNG STEW (*Beuschel*)

4 SERVINGS

1 calf's lung
6 cups water, lightly salted
pot vegetables, page 29
1 onion, sliced
1 slice lemon
6 to 8 peppercorns
1 large bay leaf
¼ cup white vinegar
3 tablespoons butter
3 tablespoons flour
1 teaspoon sugar
3 to 4 cups cooking stock
salt and pepper to taste

Wash lung well under running cold water. Put in a heavy pot with a tight-fitting lid and cover with 6 cups water to which you add a little salt. Add prepared pot vegetables, onion, lemon, peppercorns, bay leaf and vinegar. Cover, bring to a boil, reduce heat and simmer slowly but steadily 1½ to 2 hours, or until lung is completely tender. Drain and reserve stock. Press lung flat under a weighted plate and refrigerate several hours. When it is cold and very flat, cut into fine noodle strips. Strain stock and pour it over strips; marinate in refrigerator 24 hours.

Melt butter in a large saucepan and when hot and bubbling, stir in flour and sugar. Sauté slowly, stirring constantly until Einbrenne turns a rich brown coffee color. Do this very slowly and watch carefully, as sugar turns brown all at once and can burn suddenly. Pour 3 cups of cooking stock into Einbrenne and stir in with a wire whisk or wooden spoon, over low heat, until you have a smooth sauce. Add lung strips and season sauce with salt and pepper. If sauce becomes too thick, add more stock. Cover and simmer slowly about 30 minutes. Season with a little more vinegar if necessary. Serve with Bread Dumplings, page 66.

/ SOUR KIDNEYS (*Saure Nieren*)

4 SERVINGS

8 lamb kidneys, or 2 veal kidneys, or 2 pork kidneys
3 tablespoons butter
1 onion, minced
2 tablespoons flour
1 cup water or meat stock
salt and pepper to taste
vinegar or lemon juice to taste
sugar to taste
3 to 4 tablespoons sour cream (optional)

The coating of fat and the outside membrane should be removed from kidneys by you or your butcher. This must be done carefully so that the meat itself is not broken. Most of the extra knob of fat on kidney underside should be trimmed away as well. Cut in half lengthwise. Pork kidneys should be washed under cold running water a few minutes. This is not necessary with lamb or veal kidneys. Cut kidneys into thin, crosswise slices. Heat butter in a skillet with a cover. When hot and bubbling, add kidney slices and sauté over high heat about 3 minutes, or until kidney slices turn gray. Remove to a heated platter.

Add onion to fat; sauté and stir until it becomes transparent and takes on a yellow color. Sprinkle with flour; stir and sauté over low heat until flour is absorbed and begins to turn bright yellow, about 3 or 4 minutes. Return kidneys to pan, add stock or water, cover and simmer about 5 minutes. Season sauce with salt and pepper and flavor with enough vinegar or lemon juice to give sauce a decided sharp edge. Add a little sugar if necessary. You may serve kidneys at this point, or stir in sour cream if you want to use it.

NOTE

It is very important that kidneys do not sauté for more than 3 or 4 minutes; if they do they will become tough and leathery. It is better for them to be a little underdone as they will finish cooking in sauce.

❇ / *PALATINATE STUFFED PIG'S STOMACH* (*Pfälzer Saumagen*)

Although a pig's stomach is not the most readily available item in ordinary butcher shops, it can be had if ordered several days or a week in advance. Since this dish is such a special and typical Sunday dinner feature in the farmhouses of the Rhine Palatinate district, it seemed worth including. Naturally, the thing to drink with it is one of the golden Rhine wines of the area.

6 GENEROUS SERVINGS

1 *pig's stomach*
1 *pound ground raw beef*
1 *pound minced lean raw pork*
½ *pound streaky bacon, diced*
4 *stale rolls* (*Parker House-size*), *soaked in water and squeezed as dry as possible*
1 *pound potatoes, peeled, diced and half cooked*

2 *eggs*
1 *large onion, grated*
  salt and pepper
  melted butter or bacon fat, as needed
1 *teaspoon marjoram*

Preheat oven to 350°. Clean stomach thoroughly inside and out and wash well under running cold water. Tie one end tightly closed with kitchen string. Mix all ingredients thoroughly until you have a smooth, well-blended dough. For a perfect mixing job, use your hands. Stuff stomach with prepared filling, but do not pack it in too tightly as it swells during cooking. Tie open end tightly closed with string. Place on greased rack of open roasting pan and roast in preheated oven 2 hours. Turn once during roasting and baste frequently with pan drippings or with melted butter or bacon fat.

VARIATIONS

1.   This is sometimes cooked by boiling first in water to cover, along with some sliced onion, carrot, celery and parsley. After 2 hours it is removed from stock, placed on roasting pan, brushed with hot melted fat and browned in 400° oven.
2.   The parboiled potatoes can be grated instead of being diced.

⚄ / *KIDNEYS ON SKEWERS* (*Nierenspiesschen*)

4 SERVINGS

2 *veal kidneys, or 4 lamb kidneys*   2 *onions*
3 *tablespoons butter*   *salt and pepper*
4 *to 5 slices bacon, blanched*

Clean kidneys as in above recipe, but do not cut in half lengthwise. Cut crosswise into slices ½" thick. Heat butter in a skillet and when hot, add kidney slices. Sauté very quickly, over high heat 2 or 3 minutes. Remove slices and drain on paper toweling. Preheat broiler. The blanched bacon slices should be cut in 1½" lengths. The onions should be cut in sixths, lengthwise. Thread kidney slice, bacon slice and onion section onto metal skewers in that order, continuing until each skewer is full. Brush with melted butter in which kidneys were sautéed and sprinkle with salt and pepper. Grill in very hot broiler 7 or 8 minutes, turning so that meat and onion brown evenly. If you wish, serve on hot toast spread with herb butter.

▓ / *CALF'S HEAD* (*Kalbskopf*)

There are several interesting dishes to be made from a calf's head and all require the same basic preparation. You will probably have to order the head from your butcher several days or a week in advance. Have him clean it and remove the snout. The tongue and brains should also be taken out and cooked separately, as they require far less cooking time than rest of head. One head will serve about 12 people. In some neighborhoods, where this is very popular, it is possible to buy half a head. The head is boiled as follows, before the meat is used for any of the other dishes in this chapter.

BASIC PREPARATION FOR CALF'S HEAD

1 *calf's head, cleaned*
  water to cover
1 *large onion studded with 4 or 5*
  cloves
1 *knob celery, peeled and sliced,*
  or 4 stalks celery with tops

4 *sprigs parsley*
1 *carrot, scraped and sliced*
8 *to 10 peppercorns*
  salt

Place head in a deep pot with water to cover. Bring to boil and cook rapidly about 10 minutes, skimming surface of water as scum rises. Add all vegetables and seasoning to pot, reduce heat, cover and simmer slowly but steadily for 1½ hours. Add tongue and continue cooking about 2½ hours more, or until meat is tender and begins to fall away from bone. To cook brains, prepare as described on page 205, but use some of the liquid in which head cooked instead of plain water. The head, tongue and brains should be removed from cooking liquid, then drained and cooled. Proceed as described for specific recipes below. The stock should be strained and reserved for making soups, gravies, etc. The sliced meat of veal, tongue and brains can be made into a Sülze, as described on page 16. Substitute head meat and use cooking stock for an aspic, adding gelatin or a calf's foot so it will jell.

▓ / *CALF'S HEAD VINAIGRETTE* (*Kalbskopf Vinaigrette*)

12 SERVINGS

Prepare head, tongue and brains (see recipe above). When meat is cool enough to handle, cut it from head in long strips. Peel and slice tongue. Cut brains into fork-size pieces. While still warm, cover with a double recipe of a good vinaigrette dressing. Let stand at room temperature 2 hours and then refrigerate 1 hour before serving. This is very good as an appetizer or light entree.

❈ / BROWNED CALF'S HEAD (*Abgebräunter Kalbskopf*)

12 SERVINGS

Prepare head (page 213). The tongue and brain may be used with this or they may be cooked and reserved for other uses. Pick pieces of meat off head in long strips, and peel and slice tongue and brains if you want to prepare them this way. Dip each piece of meat in egg beaten with a little water and then dredge with breadcrumbs. Heat some butter or lard in a skillet and when hot, add breaded meat. Fry over moderately high heat, turning once so both sides are golden brown. Drain quickly on paper towel, sprinkle with salt and pepper and serve. Keep fried meat hot on a heated platter while rest of meat is cooking.

❈ / CALVES' FEET (*Kalbsfüsse*)

In addition to being made into Sülze (page 16) calves' feet are cooked the same as the head (page 213). Feet should be scraped, scrubbed, washed, blanched in boiling water 10 minutes, split and then boiled in water to cover along with vegetables and seasonings. They will be cooked in about 1½ hours, or when meat begins to fall away from bone. Drain and cool. Pick meat from bone and prepare as described for Calf's Head Vinaigrette (page 213) or Browned Calf's Head (above). Strain stock and reserve. It is excellent for making aspic dishes. Cook 2 calves' feet for 2 moderate-sized servings.

❇ MISCELLANEOUS MEAT ❇ DISHES
(*Verschiedene Fleischgerichte*)

❇ / MOCK HARE OR MEAT LOAF (*Falscher Hase oder Hackbraten*)

4 TO 6 SERVINGS

1 pound ground beef
½ pound ground veal
½ pound ground lean pork
2 rolls soaked in ½ cup milk,
    or ½ cup dry breadcrumbs
    softened in milk
1 large onion, chopped fine
1 tablespoon minced parsley
2 tablespoons butter
1 large or 2 small eggs
    grated rind of ½ lemon
    salt
    pepper or nutmeg

basil or ginger
flour
3 tablespoons butter, lard or
    bacon fat
1 onion, sliced
1 carrot, sliced
1 cup water or stock, or as
    needed
    heel or crust of rye bread
½ cup cream
2 teaspoons cornstarch or 1
    tablespoon flour dissolved
    in a little cold water

Mix ground meats together. Squeeze excess milk out of soaked rolls or breadcrumbs. Sauté minced onion and parsley in 2 tablespoons butter until soft but not browned. Put meat, rolls and sautéed onions and parsley through grinder together once. Put ground mixture in a large bowl. Add lightly beaten eggs, grated lemon rind, salt, and season with pepper and basil, or nutmeg and ginger. Shape into loaf with wet hands. Dredge meat loaf lightly on all sides with flour.

Heat fat in a stew pot or small Dutch oven and when it is hot and bubbling begins to subside, add meat loaf. Brown slowly on all sides, turning very gently so it does not break in half. It should be brown, top and bottom, in about 8 or 10 minutes. Add sliced vegetables around meat loaf, rye bread and enough water to cover bottom of

(215)

the pot. Cover pot, bring to a boil, reduce heat and simmer slowly but steadily 1 hour, basting from time to time with pan juices and adding more liquid if needed. Spoon cream over meat loaf, cover pot and braise another 20 to 30 minutes. If you want meat to have a nicely browned top, place it, uncovered, in a 375° oven for 15 minutes, after adding cream.

Remove finished meat loaf to a heated platter. Add a little water or stock to pan juices and bring to a boil in braising pan, scraping coagulated pan juices into gravy with a wooden spoon. Strain gravy into a clean saucepan and skim off excess fat. Season to taste and bind with flour or cornstarch dissolved in cold water. Finish off with a little more cream; heat but do not boil.

VARIATIONS

1. Stuffed Meat Loaf (Gefüllter Hackbraten): Follow recipe. Shape bottom half of meat loaf and lay across it 2 peeled whole hard-cooked eggs. Top with upper half of meat loaf and proceed. When meat is sliced, each portion will have a slice of egg in the center.
2. This loaf can be made without veal, in which case use 1½ pounds ground beef and ½ pound ground pork.
3. The meat can be seasoned with 2 teaspoons anchovy paste or ½ herring, ground. Use lemon rind, salt, pepper and basil, but not nutmeg and ginger.
4. Frikadellen are small hamburgers, fried in butter, made with this meat mixture.
5. This meat loaf can also be wrapped in puff pastry after being browned, and then baked in oven until done.

/ *KÖNIGSBERGER KLOPSE*

These piquant meat dumplings are served along with sauerkraut and are a favorite main course in Berlin and Prussia.

4 SERVINGS

Meat balls:

1½ *pounds ground meat (preferably ⅓ each beef, veal and pork, but always pork and one of the others)*

2 *small stale rolls or 3 slices stale white bread, with crusts*

1 *cup lukewarm water*

1 *medium-sized onion*

5 *anchovies*

2 *eggs*

1 tablespoon minced parsley
grated rind of 1 lemon
½ teaspoon salt
¼ teaspoon pepper
3 to 4 cups veal or beef broth

Sauce:

1 tablespoon butter
½ teaspoon minced onion
1½ tablespoons flour
2 tablespoons capers
2 to 3 tablespoons sour cream (optional)

Mix meat together in a bowl. Cut rolls in small pieces and soak 15 minutes in water; then drain and squeeze as dry as possible. Using the fine blade of a food chopper, grind meat, along with soaked bread, onion and anchovies. Add eggs, minced parsley, grated lemon rind, salt and pepper and mix thoroughly. *Do not taste this mixture for seasoning, as it contains raw pork.* With wet hands shape mixture into balls about the size of lemons and cook in boiling veal or beef stock. Try a test dumpling before you cook rest of batter. Cook for 15 minutes. Then melt butter in a skillet, add minced onion and let brown slowly; stir in flour. Let brown slowly until it is the color of cocoa. Add this Einbrenne to stock, stir through and let dumplings cook in this thickened sauce another 15 minutes. Add capers for last 5 minutes of cooking time. In Bavaria, sour cream is stirred into sauce just before it is served. Serve on mound of Cooked Sauerkraut, page 276.

/ *MEAT PUDDING (Fleischpudding)*

6 TO 8 SERVINGS

double the recipe for meat loaf mixture, page 215, using
4 to 5 eggs, depending on their size
water
butter
breadcrumbs

After meat mixture has been combined, work ½ to ¾ cup water into meat. To do this, pour a little water over ground meat, knead it in and add more. Then combine with rest of ingredients in that recipe.

Butter a large soufflé dish and sprinkle sides and bottom with breadcrumbs, tapping excess out before filling. Turn meat mixture into form. Set in larger pan half filled with hot water. Bake in 350° to 375° oven 1½ hours.

❧ / SAILOR'S HASH (*Labskaus auf Seemann Art*)

Literally, Labskaus (lobscouse in English) means "scow refreshment." It is a sailors' stew or hash that dates back to the days of the wind-jammers, when galleys had to be stocked with foods that were not perishable, hence the use of pickled meat and salt herring in this dish. Labskaus still appears in the "big three" cities of the Hanseatic League—Hamburg, Bremen and Lübeck, as well as in such major Hansa outposts as Bergen, Oslo, Copenhagen, Amsterdam and London. In Germany, the meat and potatoes for Labskaus are so finely ground that the consistency is close to a porridge; in Scandinavia the ingredients are cubed or diced and the results are closer to a stew. As you might expect with a dish that has such a long history, dozens of versions have developed, each avowed to be the only authentic one by its particular enthusiasts. The best Labskaus I had in Germany was in the Schiffergesellschaft in Lubeck. Again, they were kind enough to let me have this recipe along with the variations that follow it. Although Labskaus is really a family-style entree, not suitable for elegant entertaining, it would make a very unusual and tempting main course for a Sunday-brunch party.

4 TO 6 SERVINGS

2 *pounds potatoes, peeled*
water to cover
1 *to 1½ pounds corned beef or*
pickled pork
2 *large onions*
6 *to 8 white peppercorns*
¼ *cup butter*

1 *small matjes or salt herring,*
chopped
6 *to 8 anchovy filets, minced, or*
2 *teaspoons anchovy paste*
(optional)
½ *cup chopped, drained, pickled*
beets

Cook peeled potatoes in *unsalted* water to cover, until done. Drain well and return potatoes to pot. Shake back and forth gently several times over low heat until dry and mealy. Mash or purée in a food mill. Grind meat through finest blade of food chopper. Also grind onions and peppercorns. Heat butter in heavy casserole or stew pot and when hot and bubbling, add ground onion and peppercorns. Sauté over low heat 2 or 3 minutes or until mixture just begins to turn yellow. Stir in meat and continue sautéing until it loses its bright red color, but do not let it brown. Stir mashed potatoes into meat and onion mixture until well blended. Mixture should be fairly stiff. Mix in chopped herring, anchovies or anchovy paste, if you are using either, and pickled beets. Cover and simmer over low heat, adding just a little water as needed to keep mixture from scorching. Simmer 15 to 18 minutes, or until completely cooked. Season with salt and more ground white pepper if needed. Each portion should be topped with an egg fried in butter and a slice or two of sour pickle.

VARIATIONS

1. In Bremen this is prepared without any herring or anchovies added.

2. If you prefer, pickled beets can be served on the side instead of cooked with meat and potatoes.

3. You may use herring without anchovies, or vice versa, according to your taste.

4. For a slightly blander version, use plain cooked beets instead of pickled.

VIII

Poultry

(Geflügel)

❖ ❖ ❖ ❖ ❖

The German cuisine includes some excellent poultry specialties, most of which came to the country by way of eastern Europe. For some reason which I have not been able to fathom, chicken is not featured very much on the menus of German restaurants, although it is very popular in homes. Less expensive restaurants rarely have more than a chicken broth and perhaps roast or broiled chicken on the menu and often not even the latter. Nevertheless there are some delicious recipes for broilers (Brathühnchen or Brathühner), pullets or young hens (Poularde), fowls and young stewing chickens (Suppenhühner) and capons (Kapaune).

Turkey (Truthahn or Truthuhn and also called Puter or Indianer) is increasing in popularity but is far less common than it is here. Goose (Gans) is to the German table what turkey is to ours: the large bird served on the most festive occasions. It is always featured at Christmas and also on November 11, Martinmas, the day that honors St. Martin, the patron of drinking and jovial meetings. Smoked goose breast, which is purchased at sausage shops and from delicatessens, is one of the most highly prized delicacies in Germany and is available here in all German neighborhoods.

I doubt that any country has a better or wider variety of recipes for duck (Ente or Mastente, the latter meaning a large, especially well-fed duck). I doubt also that any country produces more flavorful ducks than does Germany and they are much leaner and meatier than ours.

In general Germans prefer to braise poultry rather than to roast it. Roasting may produce a crisper skin, but braising results in far more tender and flavorful meat. This is true of duck and goose and most especially of turkey. To braise poultry, prepare it as you would for roasting, stuffed or unstuffed. It may be braised whole, or quartered, though the former is more impressive when you serve it. Melt butter or some other cooking fat in a covered roasting pan and place the bird in the pan on top of the stove. Turn bird carefully as each side becomes a deep yellow color. Do not brown it and do not pierce the skin with a fork when turning. When bird is all seared, place it on a bed of root vegetables and onions, or simply onions alone, add a cup or two of hot stock or water, cover the pan tightly and place it in a moderate oven. Allow 20 to 25 minutes' cooking time for each pound of meat. Bird should be basted frequently and turned during roasting. The pan can be uncovered for the last 20 minutes of cooking time so that the breast will brown. If you have always thought that turkey was too dry, you'll find this method of cooking it a revelation.

The Germans have devised some wonderful stuffings for poultry and have borrowed others from the countries that surround them, and you'll also find they have equally ingenious recipes for giblets.

/ *CHICKEN FRICASSEE* (*Hühnerfrikassee*)

This is one of the best dishes I have ever eaten in Germany, or anywhere else for that matter. It is a relatively expensive item on the menus of the more elegant restaurants. I've never had this dish better prepared than it was at the Hotel Eisenhut in the romantic, walled, medieval village of Rothenburg on the Tauber.

4 TO 6 SERVINGS

5-pound stewing chicken, preferably a young fowl
1 *medium onion*
1 *carrot, scraped*
½ *knob celery root (celeriac), peeled and cubed, or 2 stalks of celery with tops*
1 *small parsley root (petrouchka), scraped*
2 *or 3 sprigs parsley*
5 *or 6 peppercorns*
1 *very small bay leaf*
½ *teaspoon salt*
water or chicken broth to cover, about 1 to 1½ quarts
3 *tablespoons butter*
3 *tablespoons flour*
2 *egg yolks*
¼ *cup heavy sweet cream*
white wine or lemon juice
4 *cups cooked rice*

Wash chicken and cut in quarters or halves. Put in a 3-quart soup kettle or a pot that is tall and narrow so that it will not take too much water to cover the chicken. Add onion, carrot, celery root or celery, parsley root, parsley, peppercorns, bay leaf and salt and cover with water or chicken broth. Bring to a boil and simmer slowly but steadily, uncovered, about 10 minutes. Skim foam off as it rises to surface. When foam no longer appears, cover pot, reduce heat and simmer very gently about 1¼ to 1½ hours, or until largest pieces of chicken are tender and begin to come away from bone. Remove chicken and strain soup through a fine sieve, discarding vegetables. Return 3 or 4 cups soup to pot. Skim fat from surface of soup and keep hot over low flame. Melt butter in a saucepan and when hot and bubbling, blend in flour. Sauté over low heat, stirring constantly until mixture is bright yellow. Do not let it turn brown. Gradually pour in 1 cup hot chicken broth, stirring over very low heat until sauce is smooth and thickened. Stir thickened sauce into rest of stock. Simmer about 10 minutes. Salt to taste. Beat egg yolks with cream and remove sauce from heat. Gradually stir in egg-yolk-cream mixture. Add a few dashes of white wine or, preferably, fresh lemon juice to taste.

Remove skin from chicken and cut meat from bones in large, thick slices and chunks. Put chicken into sauce and heat a few minutes, but do not let sauce boil or egg will coagulate. Turn cooked rice onto a heated serving platter. Arrange chicken pieces on top of it, and cover with sauce. You may serve extra sauce in a heated gravy boat.

Sliced mushroom caps that have been stewed 7 or 8 minutes in a little butter can be added to sauce the last few minutes of cooking time. A tablespoon drained capers and/or a tablespoon minced parsley is often stirred into sauce before serving and sometimes a dab of anchovy paste is blended in as well.

The famed Berlin Fricassee is unquestionably the most elaborate and beautiful of all. It includes diced cooked calves' tongue, diced cooked sweetbreads, tiny dumplings of veal or pike (see Meat Dumplings, page 62, or Fish Dumplings, page 64), as well as cooked crayfish tails for which shrimp can be substituted, mushrooms both wild and cultivated, and little golden crescents of puff pastry.

⚄ / ROAST CHICKEN WITH CURRY-RICE STUFFING
(*Brathühnchen mit Curryreis gefüllt*)

4 SERVINGS

5-pound roasting chicken	salt
¼ lemon	1 cup chicken broth
1 recipe, Curry Rice, page 326	2 to 3 tablespoons sweet cream
butter	

Wash chicken well, pat dry with paper toweling and rub inside with cut lemon. Prepare rice, cooking until almost done. Stuff chicken with cooked rice, and truss. Rub with softened butter, sprinkle with a little salt and place breast up on rack of small open roasting pan. Pour 1 cup chicken broth into pan. Roast in 350° oven, allowing 20 minutes for each pound of chicken. It should be done in about 1½ hours, or when chicken's legs can move easily in their sockets. Remove chicken to heated platter, bring pan juices to a boil and stir in 2 or 3 tablespoons cream. Heat a minute or two but do not boil again.

≈ / *MUNICH GRILLED CHICKEN* (*Münchner Wiesenhendl*)

Rotisserie-grilled chicken is as popular in Germany as it is everywhere else in the world these days, but in Munich it is even more of a feature than in other large cities. Every few blocks one finds a little shop that grills these chickens and sells them for take-out orders, or serves them on the premises with some potato salad, cucumber salad, pickles and such accompaniments. Münchner Wiesenhendl is the food specialty served during the October Beer Festival and the city's fairgrounds are fragrant with the scent of the buttered chickens roasting on their spits. The chickens are served split, one to a portion, with crusty rye rolls and new beer.

For each serving:

1-pound broiler, cleaned but left whole	*6 or 7 sprigs of parsley, preferably the Italian type*
salt	*melted butter*

Rinse broiler inside and out and pat dry with paper towel. Sprinkle inside with salt and stuff with parsley. It is not necessary to close vent, but it's a good idea to tie legs in place. Brush with melted butter and broil on rotisserie. Baste with butter as broiler is cooking so that it browns evenly and does not become dry. Broil slowly. Split in half to serve. If you do not have a rotisserie, you can roast a broiler, following same directions. Set oven at 375°, baste broiler frequently with butter and cook 45 minutes to 1 hour.

/ CORNISH HENS, STUBENKÜKEN STYLE

One of Hamburg's greatest specialties is Stubenküken, tiny chickens raised indoors. They are cooked lightly stuffed, then braised in butter with a little wine and stock. The stuffings vary with the cooks, but for special holidays the most elegant is of ground pork, raisins and apples, moistened with good, aged madeira. Since you cannot find real Stubenküken here, substitute Cornish hens, preferably not frozen. The new Purdue Cornish chickens are perfect.

4 SERVINGS

- *4 fresh Cornish chickens or frozen Rock Cornish hens*
- *lemon*
- *salt and pepper*
- *½ pound ground lean pork*
- *2 tablespoons butter*
- *1 cup diced, peeled cooking apple*
- *2 tablespoons raisins*
- *2 to 3 tablespoons gold madeira*
- *2 tablespoons butter*
- *2 strips diced bacon*
- *1 cup well-seasoned chicken stock*

If birds are frozen, thaw completely. If fresh, clean and singe. Rub inside with cut lemon. Pat dry, inside and out, and rub with salt and pepper. Sauté ground pork in 2 tablespoons butter, until meat begins to brown. Toss with apple, raisins and enough wine to moisten mixture slightly. Stuff hens and truss. Heat 2 tablespoons butter in a heavy Dutch oven or braising pot and sauté diced bacon until it begins to turn brown. Do this slowly so that butter does not burn as bacon is frying. Brown hens on all sides, slowly, turning frequently. When hens are golden brown on all sides, arrange them breasts up in the pot, and add 1 cup hot, well-seasoned chicken stock. Cover pot and simmer slowly but steadily 30 to 40 minutes, or until done. Baste several times during cooking, and if more moisture is needed, add additional hot stock. Remove hens to heated platter, skim excess fat from pan juices and check for seasoning, adding a spoonful or two of madeira if necessary. Spoon sauce over hens when serving.

VARIATIONS

1. The Curry Rice on page 326 also makes an excellent stuffing.
2. For a slightly stronger flavor, sauté ½ small onion, minced, along with bacon and butter. A clove of garlic can be added with stock.
3. Squabs can be used instead of Cornish hens, but their meat is considerably darker than authentic Stubenküken and more strongly flavored.

❧ / *VIENNESE FRIED CHICKEN* (*Wiener Backhuhn oder Backhendl*)

Fried chicken the Viennese way is finished in the oven, where it is baked for a few minutes so that it emerges with a crisp, dry breading. It is a standard favorite throughout Germany.

2 TO 4 SERVINGS

2 *frying chickens, cut in serving*
  pieces
lemon juice
salt
flour

3 *eggs, well beaten with a little*
  water
breadcrumbs
lard or vegetable shortening
melted butter

Chicken pieces may be skinned or left as they are. Flatten breast quarters so they will fry evenly. Sprinkle all pieces with lemon juice and let stand at room temperature 1 hour. Pat dry with paper towels. Sprinkle with a little salt and dredge well with flour. Dip into beaten egg until all sides are well coated. Dredge thoroughly with breadcrumbs. Let stand at room temperature with breading 20 minutes before frying them.

Heat lard in large skillet. Melted fat should be about 2″ deep. Sauté, turning once so that pieces become golden brown on both sides. Once chicken is brown, lower heat and fry 8 to 10 minutes on each side. Total frying time should be about 25 minutes. Arrange chicken in open baking pan. Pour a little melted butter over each piece and bake in 350° oven 10 to 15 minutes, or until breading is very dry and crusty.

VARIATION

South German Fried Chicken (Wiener Backhendl, auf süddeutsche Art): Fry chickens in same way but sprinkle with a little ginger, as well as salt and pepper, before breading, and mix breadcrumbs, half-and-half, with grated Parmesan cheese. Finished chicken should be served covered with Mushroom Cream Sauce, page 335.

❧ / *CHICKEN WITH PAPRIKA-SOUR CREAM SAUCE* (*Paprikahühner*)

Now a regular part of the national cuisine, this paprika-flavored chicken dish came to Germany via Hungary and Austria.

4 TO 6 SERVINGS

2 chickens, broilers or fryers	1 tablespoon sweet paprika
salt	2 cups chicken broth
½ cup butter	1 tablespoon flour
1 large onion, minced	1 cup sour cream

Cut chickens into serving pieces and dry thoroughly with a paper towel. Sprinkle lightly on all sides with salt. Heat butter in a large, deep skillet that has a cover. When butter is hot and bubbling, add onion and sauté slowly until very soft but just pale yellow in color. Onions should "melt" and must not brown or they will ruin delicate flavor of sauce. If they do brown, throw them out and start over. Add chicken pieces and sauté slowly, turning frequently so they become bright yellow on all sides. Do not let them brown. Sprinkle with paprika and stir through onions and chicken until all pieces are coated. Sauté 3 or 4 minutes more. Add broth, bring to a boil, cover, reduce heat and simmer until chicken is done, about 30 to 35 minutes. Check during cooking to see if more stock is needed in pan. When chicken is done, remove to a heated platter. Blend flour into sour cream and stir into sauce until smoothly thickened. Return chicken to pan, bring sauce to boil and reduce to slow simmer 5 to 10 minutes. Check for seasoning and serve with cooked noodles or Spätzle, page 60.

VARIATIONS

1. A light tomato flavor is a very pleasant addition to sauce. Use 1 cup tomato juice and 1 cup chicken stock, instead of 2 cups chicken stock.
2. There is a very good, slightly sharper version of this dish also commonly used in Germany. It is made with bacon fat instead of butter and 1 teaspoon vinegar is added to chicken just after the paprika and before liquid is poured in. Water is used for cooking liquid instead of broth or stock.
3. To make Squabs in Paprika-Sour Cream Sauce, birds should be split and then cooked the same way as chicken. They will be done in about 25 minutes.

▓ / SQUABS, GAME STYLE (*Tauben, auf Wildbret Art*)

4 SERVINGS

4 squabs	4 cups water
2 tablespoons white vinegar	salt and pepper

2 tablespoons butter
1 onion, sliced
1 carrot, scraped and sliced
1 leek, washed and sliced
¼ knob celery root (celeriac),
     peeled and diced

2 stalks celery with tops, sliced
1 parsley root, scraped and
     sliced
     piece of lemon rind
2 tablespoons flour

Clean squabs and rinse inside and out. Mix vinegar with water, bring
to a boil, cool and pour over squabs. Marinate from 2 hours to 2 days. Unless you like them very sharply flavored, 6 or 8 hours should be enough.
Place in refrigerator while they marinate. Remove squabs from marinade
and pat dry with paper toweling. Sprinkle with salt and pepper. Melt
butter in a 3-quart Dutch oven or casserole and sauté squabs a few
minutes until golden yellow on all sides. Remove squabs and add vegetables. Sauté about 5 minutes. Place squabs on bed of vegetables, add
lemon rind and 1 cup of the marinade. Bring to a boil, cover, reduce
heat and simmer about 45 minutes, or until squabs are done. Add liquid
if necessary. Remove squabs to heated platter, drain off gravy and
reserve. Leave vegetables in pot, sprinkle with flour and sauté until
flour browns. Pour gravy back into pot slowly, stirring as you do so. Let
this boil up and simmer so gravy thickens and becomes smooth. Season
to taste with salt and pepper and a little vinegar, if needed, to be sufficiently piquant. Strain sauce, heat again and serve over squabs.

⊠ / BRAISED TURKEY OR CAPON WITH NOODLE STUFFING (*Truthahn- oder Kapaunbraten mit Nudel-füllung*)

6 TO 8 SERVINGS

8- to 10-pound turkey, either a
     tom or hen will do, or 7-
     to 8-pound capon
1 pound broad egg noodles
½ cup butter
1 onion, minced
     turkey or capon liver, finely
     diced
½ pound goose-liver paté or very
     good liverwurst finely diced
1 tablespoon minced parsley
     salt and pepper
2 teaspoons sweet paprika
½ teaspoon poultry seasoning or
     sage

5 tablespoons butter
1 large carrot, scraped and sliced
2 stalks celery with tops, sliced
1 onion, sliced
1 small parsley root (petrouchka),
     scraped and sliced (optional)
3 or 4 sprigs parsley
1 bay leaf
1 clove garlic
2 cups chicken broth
1 cup sour cream mixed with 1
     tablespoon flour

Clean turkey and singe, if necessary, to remove all feathers and pin feathers. Rinse inside and out. Cook noodles in well-salted water and drain thoroughly. Melt butter in a 10″ skillet, add onion and sauté until it softens and begins to take on color. Add finely diced liver and paté or liverwurst and sauté about 5 minutes, or until liver is seared but not brown. Add noodles, parsley, salt and pepper to taste, paprika and poultry seasoning or sage. Toss lightly until stuffing mixture is thoroughly mixed and noodles are well coated with butter and seasonings.

Dry turkey inside as well as possible, stuff with noodles and truss. Be sure that legs and wings are tied firmly in place and tie extra piece of string around middle of bird to facilitate turning. Sprinkle lightly with a little salt and pepper. Melt butter in a large braising pot, Dutch oven or covered roaster. When hot and bubbling, place turkey in pan. Cook over low heat, turning frequently so that bird turns deep golden yellow on all sides. Do not let it brown. Use middle cord tied around the turkey to turn it. Do not pierce skin with a fork during turning process.

Remove turkey from pan and add sliced carrot, celery, onion, parsley root, parsley, bay leaf and garlic. Simmer vegetables in butter 3 or 4 minutes. Lay turkey on its side, on this bed of vegetables. Add 1½ cups hot chicken stock. Cover roaster and place in 350° oven 3 hours. (Capon will be done in about 2½ hours.) Turn turkey from one side to other, three or four times during cooking. Bird is done when legs move freely in their sockets. Place turkey on heated platter. Strain pan juices into clean saucepan. Discard vegetables. Swirl ¼ to ½ cup hot chicken stock into empty roasting pan and stir with a wooden spoon, scraping bottom and sides of pan. Add this to other gravy in saucepan. Simmer over low heat until liquid is reduced by ⅓ to ½. Stir in sour cream blended with flour and bring to boiling point. Season to taste with more salt, pepper and paprika if necessary. Serve gravy in heated gravy boat along with turkey.

▐▌ / ROAST TURKEY WITH VEAL-ANCHOVY STUFFING
(*Gebratener Truthahn mit Kalbs- und Sardellenfüllung*)

8 TO 10 SERVINGS

10- to 12-pound turkey	10 anchovy filets
salt and pepper	½ cup butter
5 slices bacon, diced	3 egg yolks
1 large onion, minced	grated rind of 1 lemon
½ pound veal, minced	3 egg whites, stiffly beaten
5 or 6 slices bread, moistened	butter
with a little milk	2 cups chicken stock or water

Clean turkey and singe, if necessary, to remove all feathers and pin feathers. Rinse outside and inside. Rub inside with salt and pepper. Heat bacon in a skillet and when it begins to fry, add minced onion and sauté until it turns bright golden. Add veal and stir lightly until seared. Cool. Mix veal, bacon and onions with bread moistened in milk and squeezed as dry as possible. Mash anchovy filets with butter and work in egg yolks. Add this to meat and bread mixture and stir until thoroughly blended. Season to taste with salt, pepper, and lemon rind. Add stiffly beaten egg white to mixture and stir through well. Stuff and truss turkey. Tie legs and wings firmly in place. Tie a cord around middle of bird to facilitate turning. Sprinkle turkey with a little salt and pepper and brush with melted butter. Place turkey on its side on rack of open pan. Roast 15 minutes in 450° oven, or until first side turns golden. Turn bird over so second side can take on color. Then turn bird breast side down, reduce heat to 350° and roast. Baste frequently with chicken stock and pan juices. Allow 20 minutes a pound for roasting. Turn bird on its back for last 20 minutes of cooking time. Brush breast with butter so it will brown evenly. Turkey is done when its legs move freely in their sockets.

⅔ / *ROAST GOOSE OR DUCK* (*Gebratene Gans oder Ente*)

Since both these birds are fat and should emerge from oven with a crisp skin and as lean as possible, they are handled in much the same way. Be sure that all pin feathers have been removed and that birds have been singed if necessary. Remove as much fat as possible from inside of goose or duck, especially the heavy fat that is usually found at openings. Rinse well inside and out. If you like, rub inside of bird with a cut lemon or rinse with a little brandy or white wine. Rub inside with salt and pepper and stuff.

Truss bird, tying legs and wings firmly in place. Tie extra piece of light cord around middle of bird to facilitate turning. Pierce skin around legs and wings with tines of a fork, to allow fat to drain. Place bird breast down, on a rack, in a large open roasting pan. Pour over it 1 cup boiling water. Place in middle of oven heated to 425° and turn thermostat down to 350° as soon as bird is in. Baste frequently with pan juices, skim off fat as it collects in pan and prick skin several times during roasting. For last 20 minutes of cooking time, turn bird over on its back and remove rack from pan. Baste with melted fat that has been skimmed from the pan, so that breast will brown evenly.

To serve duck, cut into quarters. Legs and wings can be cut off if you prefer or quarters can be served intact. Usually a quarter is an adequate serving.

When buying a goose for roasting, do not select one over 10 pounds.

Geese larger than that tend to be old and tough and are better for braising. There is a saying in Germany that a goose is a peculiar bird —too much for two people and too little for three. Anyone who has cooked a very fat goose will understand this at once. You may start out with what seems to be an enormous bird and find it almost hollow when you cut into it for serving. A 10-pound goose will serve four people adequately; if you're lucky and skillful at carving, you can stretch it to serve six.

When serving goose to your own family, or on any occasion where informality is acceptable, I would suggest you simply quarter and dejoint it. If you are serving it to guests and want to be a little more elegant, carve off the wings and legs and cut the breast meat into 1"- to 2"-wide crosswise slices, so that each slice is edged by a strip of crisp skin.

Do not prepare a goose for guests until you have roasted one or two for practice. It is one of the most flavorful members of the poultry family, and it is worth a little extra effort to learn to cook it perfectly.

Any of the recipes for duck in this chapter can also apply to goose, but since the latter is a larger bird, it requires longer cooking. Double the amount of other ingredients in these recipes when you prepare goose instead of the duck that is called for.

✂ / *BOHEMIAN ROAST GOOSE, APPLE-SAUERKRAUT STUFFING* (*Böhmischer Gänsebraten, Apfel- und Sauerkrautfüllung*)

4 TO 6 SERVINGS

10-pound goose
1 tablespoon goose fat
1 medium-sized tart apple,
    pared and diced
1 large onion, minced
3 pounds sauerkraut, washed
    and well drained

salt and pepper
1 tablespoon caraway seeds
½ cup dry white wine
1 large raw potato, peeled

Prepare goose according to instructions on page 229. Melt goose fat in a skillet and in it sauté diced apple and onion until they soften and just begin to brown. Stir in sauerkraut, season to taste with salt and pepper, add caraway seeds and sauté over low heat 5 to 10 minutes. Add white wine, bring to a slow boil and gradually grate in potato, stirring between additions. Cook slowly, uncovered, until mixture is fairly thick and dry. Stuff goose, truss and roast (see page 229). To serve, place goose on a carving board and untruss it. Remove stuffing and place on a large, heated serving platter. Carve goose and arrange pieces on bed of stuffing. Serve pan juices unthickened in a heated gravy boat.

VARIATION

This same stuffing is equally good with roast turkey or duck. Use same amount for 10-pound turkey; half the amount for 5-pound duck.

✖ / ADDITIONAL STUFFINGS FOR ROAST POULTRY

The amounts given will fill a 10-pound goose or turkey. Cut recipes in half for a 5-pound duck or chicken.

APPLE-CHESTNUT STUFFING (*Apfel-Kastanienfüllung*)

Poach ½ pound peeled chestnuts in a little chicken or beef stock about 15 minutes. Drain and chop coarsely. Mix with 6 large tart apples pared and cut into large cubes or slices, 2 tablespoons raisins, the sautéed and diced liver and giblets of bird and a little brandy, sugar, salt and pepper to taste. Stuff bird and roast.

DRIED-FRUIT STUFFING (*Backobstfüllung*)

Soak ½ pound dried apple rings and ½ pound pitted prunes in 1 cup warm white wine 30 minutes. Drain well and cut prunes in halves or quarters. Season with a little sugar.

POTATO STUFFING (*Kartoffelfüllung*)

Boil and peel 1½ pounds potatoes and mash while hot. Sauté diced liver with 3 tablespoons minced onion in 3 tablespoons fat removed from bird. Mix fat, onion and liver with potatoes. Season to taste with salt and pepper.

✖ / DUCK STEWED IN BEER (*Ente in Bier*)

4 SERVINGS

5-pound duck	*3 to 4 tablespoons butter*
salt	*½ cup dark beer*
marjoram	*¾ to 1 cup hot chicken stock*
flour	*1 clove garlic*

¼ *small onion*
1 *bay leaf*
  small piece of lemon rind
1 *stalk of celery*
3 *sprigs of parsley*

¼ *teaspoon thyme*
2 *tablespoons flour mixed with*
  3 *tablespoons water*
¼ *teaspoon anchovy paste*

Cut duck into serving pieces. Sprinkle lightly with salt and a little marjoram and dredge with flour. Heat butter in a 10″ or 12″ skillet with a cover. When hot and bubbling, add duck and brown well, on all sides. Pour in beer, let it sizzle up for a minute or so, then add chicken stock. Add garlic, onion, bay leaf, lemon rind, celery, parsley and thyme. Cover and simmer gently about 40 minutes, or until duck is tender. Remove vegetables, bay leaf and lemon rind. Skim fat from gravy. Stir in flour diluted in water. Stir in anchovy paste and check seasoning. Put duck on heated deep serving dish and pour gravy over it.

✂ / *POLISH DUCK RAGOUT* (*Ente Potrafka*)

4 SERVINGS

5-*pound duck*
  salt
  marjoram
3 *to* 4 *large dried mushrooms,*
  giblets
½ *onion*
4 *cups water*

½ *pound ground cooked pork*
1 *egg*
1 *tablespoon breadcrumbs*
  salt and pepper to taste
2 *tablespoons butter*
1 *cup sour cream blended with*
  2 *tablespoons flour*

Rub duck with a little salt and marjoram, and roast. Rinse mushrooms and soak 20 minutes in a little warm water. Cook giblets and onion uncovered in water and simmer slowly until liquid is reduced by half. Strain off and cook mushrooms in stock 10 minutes. Drain mushrooms and chop; reserve cooking stock. Discard all giblets except liver. Mince cooked liver and mix with pork, egg, breadcrumbs, and 1 tablespoon chopped mushrooms. Season with salt and pepper to taste. You should be able to shape this mixture into sausage rolls or balls. If it is too soft, add more breadcrumbs until it can be properly handled and shaped. Form sausage rolls about ½″ thick, or tiny meat balls if you prefer, and fry in butter a few minutes until brown. Skim fat from pan juices and add stock in which giblets and mushrooms were cooked. Stir with a wooden spoon, scraping bottom and sides of roasting pan. Stir in sour cream thickened with flour and add rest of chopped mushrooms. Bring to a boiling point, season to taste and add meat rolls. Simmer until heated through. Pour sauce into a heated, deep serving dish and arrange pieces of duck in it with meat rolls around them.

✖ / *VIERLÄNDER DUCK IN CASSEROLE* (*Vierländer Mastente im Topf*)

Vierländer, or Four Lands, is a pretty farming province in Lower Saxony, quite close to Hamburg. It is celebrated for the ducks and geese it raises, so it should be no surprise to discover that it is also responsible for this recipe. This delectable dish was perfected and given to me for use here by Lufthansa's executive chef, Edmund Dittler.

4 SERVINGS

5-pound duck	1 cucumber, peeled and sliced
salt and pepper	2 large tomatoes, skinned and
3 tablespoons olive oil	sliced
1 green pepper, sliced	1 clove garlic, lightly crushed
1 red pepper, sliced	1 teaspoon salt
1 yellow pepper	1 tablespoon paprika
1 large onion, sliced	dash of sugar

Sprinkle duck with salt and pepper and broil. If you have a rotisserie, do broiling on this, leaving duck whole and cutting into serving pieces when done. If you are using oven broiler, split duck in half, broil and then cut into serving pieces. While duck is broiling, cook vegetables. Heat olive oil in 2- to 3-quart oven proof casserole. Add balance of ingredients, stir together and sauté slowly about 10 minutes, or until vegetables have all softened. Place pieces of duck on top of vegetable mixture, cover casserole and bake in 375° oven about 15 minutes.

✖ / *SWEET-AND-SOUR DUCK-OR-GOOSE-GIBLET SOUP* (*Ente- oder Gänseklein Schwarzsauer*)

This is served as a sort of small soup or in-between course as a special family treat when a duck or goose has been cooked.

1½ pounds giblets from goose or
    duck, including neck and
    wings, and feet if you can
    get them
3 cups water
½ carrot
½ stalk celery or small piece
    knob celery
½ small onion
    salt
3 cloves

marjoram
6 peppercorns
½ pound dried mixed prunes
    and apples, soaked for 1
    hour
goose or duck blood*
1 tablespoon flour
    white vinegar
    sugar
Cooked Potato Dumplings,
    page 68 (half the recipe)

* If you cannot get goose or duck blood, make a brown roux with flour and goose fat or butter, stir it into stock and season with a little red wine.

The feet should be scalded and skinned and gizzard should also be scalded. Clean other giblets. Bring water to a boil, add giblets, vegetables, a little salt, cloves, marjoram and peppercorns. Cover, reduce heat and simmer slowly about 30 minutes or until giblets are done. Remove giblets to a heated platter and add fruit that has been soaked and drained. Simmer 10 minutes. Mix goose or duck blood with flour and stir into boiling sauce. Flavor with a little vinegar and sugar until sauce tastes half sweet, half sour. Make dumplings and place on platter with giblets and pour sauce and fruit over them. Serve in deep plates.

⚄ / FRIED CHICKEN, DUCK, GOOSE OR TURKEY LIVERS (*Gebratene Hühner-, Enten-, Gänse- oder Truthahnenlebern*)

These poultry livers are considered great delicacies in Germany. Take as many as you have (save them in freezer until you have enough to serve) and soak in milk to cover 30 minutes to 1 hour. Drain on paper toweling, sprinkle with salt and pepper and dredge with flour. Heat butter in a skillet and when hot and bubbling, add livers and fry slowly until brown on all sides, about 12 minutes. Drain on paper toweling and serve.

❧ / STUFFED GOOSE NECK (*Gefüllter Gänsehals*)

2 SERVINGS

1 *goose neck*
1 *goose liver*
1 *tablespoon minced raw bacon*
1 *roll, diced and moistened with*
   a little milk
minced parsley

grated rind of ½ lemon
salt and pepper
1 *tablespoon rendered goose fat*
1 *tablespoon minced onion*
2 *cups chicken stock*

Pull neck out of skin carefully so that skin does not tear. Rinse skin and sew one end closed. Dice goose liver. Heat bacon in skillet and when it begins to fry, sauté liver and roll until liver is seared and roll pieces have absorbed bacon fat. Sprinkle with parsley, grated lemon rind and a dash each of salt and pepper. Grind whole mixture through fine blade of a food chopper. Fill neck skin with this mixture and sew open end closed. Heat goose fat in a 1-quart saucepan, add minced onion and stuffed goose neck and sauté a few minutes until onion is soft and neck turns golden yellow. Add chicken stock, bring to a boil, cover, reduce heat and simmer slowly 1 hour. This should be served sliced, like wurst. It may be eaten hot or cold.

Game and Game Birds

(Wild und Wildgeflügel)

⧓ ⧓ ⧓ ⧓ ⧓

Germany's magnificent forests and mountain slopes are filled with an enormous variety of game, and the country's cooks certainly make the most of that natural bounty. Through the centuries, they have developed recipes that keep the meat moist, tender and full of flavor, and they have mastered a number of sauces and condiments, both sweet and tart, to complement the richness of the meat.

Although every part of Germany has its game specialties, the section most celebrated for its variety and preparations is Swabia, where the Black Forest is a lushly green, pine-scented storehouse of venison, wild boar, hare, pheasant, partridge and grouse. Swabia borders on Alsace, and as in that French province, juniper berries (Wacholderbeeren) are a favorite seasoning, especially for game dishes. Red currant jelly (Johannisbeergelee) or a compote of those tiny cousins of our cranberries, Preiselbeeren, is almost always served with game throughout Germany, as are cooked pears, pineapples or apples. Creamed Pfifferlinge, perhaps the most delicately aromatic mushroom in the world, accompany game here too, and since Swabia is Spätzle-land, those tiny flecks of dough, steamed and then sautéed in butter, are eaten with the gravy, while in Bavaria the preference is for bread or potato dumplings.

But whether you have game in the Rhineland, in the mountains of Franconia, in Munich or in the Allgäu Alps, or in one of the northern provinces, you will find it has been well hung and cooked to perfection. Because such game meats as venison, wild boar and hare tend to have a strong flavor, German cooks usually marinate the larger cuts for two or three days in buttermilk, or in a combination of vinegar, red wine, juniper berries, celery root, onion, carrots, lemon peel, thyme and crushed peppercorns. In some cases they use white wine, and in others no wine at all but a blend of three parts of water to one of vinegar; others prefer plain lemon juice with any herbs and spices that appeal to the individual cook. Smaller cuts of these meats, such as chops, filets, stew meat or cutlets, are cooked with a little wine or vinegar and most of the same seasonings. Game birds are hung but not marinated.

Since most game is lean, the meat becomes dry, stringy and tough if it is not cooked properly. It must be larded or wrapped with bacon, salt pork or sheets of fresh lard, or, if it is a stew, enough fat should be cooked in the sauce. In Germany, game is preferred stewed, roasted or braised. In the latter cases, the gravy is a combination of strained pan juices, sweet or sour cream, and a little brandy or red currant jelly stirred in just before serving.

Unless you have experience in preparing game, I would suggest you leave hanging, skinning, plucking, bleeding, cutting and boning to your butcher. Even if you bag your own, there are butchers who will prepare and store it for you, so that it is ready to marinate and cook when you get it home.

✖ GAME (Wild) ✖

✷ / HARE (*Hase*)

Hare has more flavor and usually requires marinating, while rabbit may or may not be marinated. Frozen rabbit is sold in most chain supermarkets and can be used for the recipes that follow.

�## / BRAISED HARE (*Hasenbraten*)

4 SERVINGS

1 *saddle of hare*	3 *tablespoons butter*
2 *legs of hare*	4 *juniper berries, crushed*
3 *slices bacon*	½ *cup sour cream*
2 *cups buttermilk*	1 *tablespoon flour*
salt	*lemon juice to taste*

Lard pieces of hare with strips of bacon. Marinate overnight in buttermilk. Remove meat from marinade, dry throughly and sprinkle with salt. Heat butter in a casserole and brown hare. Add ½ cup water and juniper berries, cover casserole and place in 400° oven 30 minutes. Baste meat often with pan juices. Add sour cream and roast another 15 minutes, or until meat is done. It should remain a little bit pink toward center. Bind sauce by stirring flour into it and season to taste with salt and lemon juice.

✣ / RABBIT STEW WITH CAPERS (*Eingemachtes Kaninchen*)

See recipe for Swabian Veal Stew, page 170, and follow directions, substituting rabbit (or hare) for veal. Cook a little longer if necessary, until meat is very tender.

✣ / JUGGED HARE (*Hasenpfeffer*)

Hasenpfeffer is one of Germany's most famous dishes. Like most such classics, each cook who prepares it thinks his or her method is the only authentic one. The hare or rabbit meat may be marinated in a wine and vinegar mixture, or in buttermilk; or it may not be marinated at all. If it is not, it is always cooked in a sharply flavored sauce, so the end result tastes just about the same. If you are using hare, or a rabbit that is not very young, it is best to marinate the meat. Some cooks use only the loin and rump of the hare; others insist that all parts should be used, including the cleaned head and scalded giblets.

4 TO 6 SERVINGS

1 well-hung hare or rabbit
   (about 5 pounds), cut in
   serving pieces
½ cup vinegar
½ cup water
1 cup dry red wine
1 large onion, sliced
10 peppercorns, crushed
4 juniper berries, crushed

1 bay leaf
4 cloves
½ tablespoon pickling spices
salt
4 tablespoons butter or bacon
   fat
4 tablespoons flour
black pepper, freshly ground
½ cup sour cream (optional)

Place hare or rabbit pieces and giblets in a deep bowl. Simmer vinegar, water, wine, onion, peppercorns, juniper berries, bay leaf, cloves and pickling spices 15 minutes. Cool marinade and pour over hare. Marinate in refrigerator 1 or 2 days, turning meat once or twice each day. Remove meat from liquid and pat dry. Sprinkle with salt. Heat butter or bacon fat in a casserole and when hot and bubbling, add hare pieces and giblets. Brown thoroughly on all sides and sprinkle with flour. Stir over moderate heat until flour begins to brown and is absorbed by fat. If there is excess fat, pour it off. Strain marinade and add to hare. Cover and simmer 35 to 45 minutes, or until meat is tender. Add salt and freshly ground pepper to taste. Stir in sour cream if you want to use it, and heat but do not boil.

✳ / HARE IN CASSEROLE (Hase im Topf)

This highly seasoned hare (or rabbit) casserole is well spiked with madeira, red wine and a little brandy. It is a superb dish and a specialty around Düsseldorf, where it is made with fresh pork, and in Swabia, where the cured raw ham, Schinkenspeck, is substituted.

4 SERVINGS

1 well-hung, 5-pound hare (or
   rabbit)
   brandy
½ to ¾ pound raw pork loin,
   thinly sliced, or ½ to ¾
   pound Black Forest Schinkenspeck, page 250, or ½ to
   ¾ pound Canadian bacon
salt
black pepper, freshly ground

2 cloves garlic, minced
½ to ¾ cup minced parsley
   fresh rye or pumpernickel
   breadcrumbs (approxi-
   mately 1 cup)
1 cup dry red wine
1 cup madeira
   flour and water for very stiff
   dough

Cut hare or rabbit off the bones and slice; sprinkle with brandy. Let stand at room temperature 20 or 30 minutes. An earthenware casserole is traditionally used for this, but you can substitute enameled cast iron. The casserole should be about 5″ deep, with 2- to 3-quart capacity; you should be able to arrange 3 layers of meat in it. Line bottom with thin slices of pork loin, Schinkenspeck or Canadian bacon. Then add layers in following order: hare or rabbit meat, salt and freshly ground black pepper, a little minced garlic, some parsley, a thin layer of bread crumbs and a layer of bacon slices. Continue until all ingredients are used up. The top layer should be bacon and casserole should be about ¾ full. Pour red wine and madeira into casserole, along with any hare or rabbit blood you might have. Cover casserole. Make a very stiff dough of flour and water and pack it around edge of casserole cover so that pot is completely sealed. Bake in 350° oven 2 hours. The casserole should be brought to table unopened.

VARIATION

A little paprika and thyme are sometimes added with other seasonings.

❄ / *ROAST SADDLE OF VENISON* (*Gebratener Rehrücken*)

4 TO 6 SERVINGS

1 *saddle of venison (6 to 8 pounds)*	6 *to 8 juniper berries, crushed*
1 *quart buttermilk*	4 *tablespoons butter*
¼ *pound bacon or salt pork*	1 *cup beef or veal broth*
salt and pepper	½ *cup sour cream*
	2 *tablespoons red currant jelly*

Marinate venison in buttermilk 2 days in the refrigerator. Turn the meat several times each day. Remove from buttermilk and pat dry. Lard with strips of bacon or salt pork at intervals of about 1½″ to 2″, or in the center of each chop. Rub well with salt, pepper and juniper berries. Melt butter in a roasting pan and brown venison in it on all sides. Pour beef or veal broth into the pan and roast in a 375° oven, allowing about 15 minutes to the pound if you like your venison rare, 18 minutes per pound if you like it well done; it should be pink to be at its best. Remove meat to a carving board, skim excess fat from pan juices and stir in sour cream and currant jelly. Heat for a minute or two and serve in a heated gravy boat.

VARIATIONS

1.   Instead of buttermilk, you can marinate the venison in a mixture of 3 parts water to 1 part vinegar. Cook the liquid with some sliced onion, carrot, celery, peppercorns and a bay leaf. Cool and pour over venison. Use this marinade for cooking the meat instead of the broth called for above.

2.   If a whole saddle is too much for you, use a single loin instead. (A saddle is a double loin.)

3.   To make Roast Leg of Venison (Gebratene Rehkeule) follow the recipe, but marinate 3 days instead of 2. Allow 15 minutes to each pound in a 350° oven.

4.   Venison Baden-Baden is a standard feature on German menus. It is either roast loin or leg of venison, but since Baden-Baden is in Swabia, Spätzle are served with it and the garnish is always halves of canned pears, heated (sometimes in white wine) and filled with red currant jelly.

✂ / *VENISON SCHNITZEL IN MUSHROOM SAUCE* (*Rehschnitzel in Champignonsosse*)

4 SERVINGS

4 cutlets from leg of venison
salt
mustard
flour
2 tablespoons butter or ren-
    dered bacon fat
¼ pound white button mush-
    rooms, sliced

1 tablespoon dried Pfifferlinge,
    if you can get them
    water or stock if needed
½ cup sour cream or sweet
    cream

Cutlets should be pounded slightly, but should remain about ½″ thick. If they are very large, cut in half. Sprinkle with salt, spread with just a little mustard and dredge with flour. Heat butter or bacon fat in a skillet and when hot and bubbling, add venison cutlets. Brown slowly on both sides; cutlets should be cooked in 7 or 8 minutes and should be pink inside. Then add sliced mushrooms to skillet, and if you can get them, dried Pfifferlinge which have been soaked and drained according to instructions on package. Stir and sauté slowly about 5 or 6 minutes, or until mushrooms are cooked and golden in color. Add a little water or stock if the pan is dry. Stir in sour cream, heat and season sauce to taste with salt and a dab of mustard.

/ *VENISON OR HARE ROLLS IN RED WINE* (*Reh- oder Hasenrouladen in Rotwein*)

4 SERVINGS

- 4 *cutlets from leg of venison or slices of hare*
- *salt and pepper*
- 1 *tablespoon mustard*
- 1 *tablespoon red currant jelly*
- 4 *slices bacon*
- *flour*
- *butter, lard or bacon fat*
- ½ *cup red wine*

Each cutlet should be pounded to paper thinness. If very large, cut them in half. Sprinkle each slice with salt and pepper and spread with a little mustard and currant jelly. Lay a strip of bacon on each cutlet, then roll, jelly-roll style, fastening with toothpicks or tying the roll with kitchen thread. Dredge each rolled cutlet in flour. Heat fat in a small casserole and brown game rolls on all sides. Add red wine, cover tightly, bring to a boil, reduce heat and simmer slowly about 40 minutes, or until meat is well done and tender. If you need more liquid during cooking, add a little water or broth.

/ *VENISON LIVER, HUNTER STYLE* (*Rehleber, auf Jäger Art*)

4 SERVINGS

- 2 *pounds venison liver*
- *milk and water, to cover*
- 2 *tablespoons butter*
- *salt*
- *minced parsley*
- *juice of ½ lemon*
- ¼ *to ½ cup sour cream*
- 1 *tablespoon drained capers*

The liver should come from a freshly killed deer, before it is hung. It must be wiped off and washed very well so that there is no liquid blood in it. Soak whole liver in a mixture of half water, half milk 2 hours, or until you are sure all the blood is out of it. Cut liver into ½″- to 1″-thick slices. Melt butter in a skillet and when hot and bubbling, add liver slices. Brown on both sides over moderate heat. When liver is nicely browned, sprinkle with salt, parsley and lemon juice and remove to a heated platter. Bring pan juices to a boil, stir in sour cream and blend over low heat until smooth. Stir in capers and spoon sauce over liver slices.

⧓ / *WILD BOAR IN BURGUNDY* (*Wildschwein in Burgunder*)

This recipe for wild boar cooked in burgundy wine is a German classic. In other countries it is known as Wild Boar, German Style.

6 SERVINGS

1 *rump of wild boar (about 2½ to 3½ pounds)*
1 *large onion, sliced*
1 *carrot, scraped and sliced*
1 *stalk celery with leaves thyme strip of lemon peel*
12 *peppercorns, crushed*

10 *juniper berries, crushed*
3 *cups water*
½ *cup wine vinegar salt*
6 *cloves*
2 *to 3 cups red burgundy wine*
1 *tablespoon cornstarch*

Place rump of wild boar in a bowl. Cover with sliced onion, carrot and celery and add thyme and lemon peel, peppercorns and juniper berries. Pour on water and wine vinegar and marinate in the refrigerator 3 or 4 days, turning meat once or twice each day. Remove boar from marinade, stud with cloves and sprinkle with salt. Combine marinade with the wine, bring to a boil and add boar. Cover and simmer very slowly but steadily 2½ to 3 hours, or until meat is well done and tender. Place finished boar in an open roasting pan and roast in 375° oven 30 minutes, or until well browned on all sides. Thicken sauce with cornstarch which was dissolved in a little water or red wine. Bring to a boil and simmer 3 or 4 minutes. Strain sauce through a fine sieve and serve in a heated gravy boat.

▓ / TYROLEAN GAME STEW (*Tiroler Wildragout*)

4 SERVINGS

2 *pounds of game (meat, head,
  shoulder, liver, heart, gizzard
  of venison, hare or wild boar)*
5 *cups water*
  salt
2 *or 3 tablespoons white vinegar*
2 *sprigs parsley*
1 *carrot, scraped and sliced*
1 *stalk of celery with tops, or* ½
  *knob celery, peeled and
  cubed*

1 *leek*
1 *onion*
8 *to 10 peppercorns*
4 *cloves*
1 *bay leaf*
  strip of lemon peel
4 *slices bacon*
2 *tablespoons flour*
1 *tablespoon sugar*
½ *cup red wine*
  game blood, if you have any

Clean and blanch giblets in boiling water. Cut giblets and meat up as for stew. Simmer in salted water along with vinegar, vegetables, spices and lemon peel. Keep pot well covered and cook about 1 hour, or until meat is completely tender. Dice bacon and fry in a saucepan until crisp. Remove cracklings but leave melted fat in the pan. Add flour and fry until cocoa-colored. Add sugar and sauté very slowly until it too becomes a rich caramel-brown. Be very careful doing this as sugar burns quickly. Gradually pour in 3 cups of broth in which the meat cooked. Simmer 10 minutes, stirring from time to time, until sauce is well blended and thickened. Remove meat from the rest of stock and drain. Add to the thickened sauce, along with red wine and game blood, if you have the latter. If you do not, use an extra tablespoonful of flour to thicken sauce. Season with salt and a little vinegar or lemon juice to taste. Simmer uncovered 20 minutes.

VARIATION

To make Venison Stew, Polish Style, (Rehragout, auf Polnische Art), follow the recipe but eliminate cloves. Add 2 tablespoons blanched, chopped almonds and 2 tablespoons raisins to the sauce, and flavor with a dash of lemon juice.

❊ GAME BIRDS (Wildgeflügel) ❊

✴ / PARTRIDGE WITH LENTILS (Rebhuhn mit Linsen)

4 SERVINGS

1 pound lentils
1 teaspoon salt
4 partridges (old partridges can be used for this)
  salt and pepper
  juice of 1 lemon
8 strips bacon
¼ pound bacon, finely diced

1 onion, minced
1 carrot, scraped and diced
1 stalk celery, diced
2 tablespoons tomato purée
1 cup red wine
1 cup meat stock, or as needed
  dash of vinegar (optional)

Cook lentils in salted water to cover 1 to 1¼ hours, or until *almost* done. Drain off cooking liquid by pouring lentils into a strainer; reserve both liquid and lentils. While lentils are cooking, rub partridges inside and out with salt, pepper and lemon juice. Tie 2 strips of bacon across the breast of each. Heat diced bacon in a heavy 3-quart casserole or Dutch oven, and when fat begins to melt, add onion, carrot and celery and sauté until bacon is brown and vegetables are soft and golden. Stir in tomato purée and red wine. Place partridge in casserole and turn once or twice until they are coated with sauce. Cover the casserole and place in a 400° oven 45 minutes. Remove cover, turn oven temperature down to 350° and roast 15 or 20 minutes, or until birds are brown and *almost* done. Baste with pan juices as they are browning, and if you need more liquid, add meat stock. Cut the partridges in half. Pour pan juices into a saucepan and skim off excess fat. Turn drained lentils into empty casserole and top with partridge halves.

Add about 1 cup of the liquid in which the lentils were cooked to pan juices in saucepan. Bring to a boil and simmer 5 or 10 minutes, or until sauce is blended and slightly thickened. Season with salt and pepper and a dash of vinegar if you want a slight piquancy to the sauce. Pour this seasoned sauce over the partridges and lentils. Cover casserole and simmer on top of stove, or in a

375° oven 20 minutes, or until lentils and partridges are thoroughly cooked.

✿ / *PHEASANT WITH LENTILS (Fasan mit Linsen)*

Prepare as described in above recipe. If pheasants are young and tender, cut cooking time accordingly.

✿ / *ROAST PHEASANT (Gebratener Fasan)*

For two servings you will need 1 young pheasant that was hung about 4 days. Rub bird inside and out with salt, pepper and softened butter and cover breast with 2 or 3 strips of bacon, fastening into place with toothpicks. Roast in a 350° oven 45 minutes, or until tender. Baste once or twice with melted butter. Remove bacon strips before serving. Serve with pan juices from which excess fat is skimmed.

✿ / *PHEASANT WITH WINEKRAUT (Fasan mit Wein-*
kraut)

If you have a young pheasant, roast as described in above recipe. When done, cut into halves or quarters and place on top of Wine Kraut, page 276. Bake in 400° oven 10 minutes. Pan juices from pheasant should be mixed through the kraut. If the pheasant is old, prepare in same way but roast only about 30 or 40 minutes, or until browned and about half done. Cut into quarters and cook with Wine-kraut for another 30 or 40 minutes, in covered casserole.

X

Sausages

(Würste)

☒ ☒ ☒ ☒ ☒

Germany is unquestionably the sausage capital of the world. In some parts of the country a puppet theater is known as Wursteltheater, the counterpart of our Punch is Hans Wurst, and any fun fair is dubbed a Wurstelprater. The philosophy of "an eye for an eye" is expressed here as Wurst wider Wurst, a sausage for a sausage, and the idea that everyone gets what he deserves (you made your bed, now lie in it) becomes in Germany *die Wurst nach dem Manne braten*—every man fries his own sausage. Although Munich leads all other German cities in sausage inventiveness, every section of the country has its local versions, and in the vineyard towns of the Palatinate, the Rhinelanders are especially proud of their three gastronomic W's—*Weck, Wurst und Wein*—roll, sausage and wine.

An assortment of sliced sausages, served with rolls and butter, pretzels, radishes and pickled gherkins, is equally popular in Germany as a mid-morning breakfast, a light lunch, an afternoon snack, before or after soup at dinner and as a late supper.

The frankfurter is only the beginning. This ancestor of our hot dog, created in the Main River city that also gave the world Goethe and the Rothschilds, is merely one of three hundred varieties that the German sausage maker (Wursthändler) has in his repertoire. Any sausage shop (Wurstladen) that takes itself seriously includes about one hundred types on its price lists and has between fifty and sixty different kinds of sausages on hand at all times.

These clean and sparkling shops with their garlands of white, gray, tan, red, brown and black wursts are as tempting to the eye as their wares are to the palate. Sausages vary as to their meat fillings and seasonings, their size, shape and casings, and the method of preservation used. Some are absolutely raw and fresh, others may be smoked or pickled in brine in varying degrees, still others are cooked, and many go through a combination of these processes.

A visit to a German sausage shop can be a dazzling and rewarding experience. If there is one in your town or city, don't fail to shop there and gather a sampling of its irresistible wares. The following is a very brief guide to some of the most common and delectable varieties you can choose from.

Weisswurst—white sausage—is the most delicately flavored of all sausages. It is made of veal, sometimes with a little pork added, and seasoned with salt, pepper and flecks of fresh parsley. It is slightly cured in a mild brine, and is always steamed and eaten hot. The casing is removed as it is eaten. This is the great specialty of Munich, where it is served from midnight until 11 A.M.—Brotzeit, or bread time. Purists wouldn't touch it after that hour. It comes to the table in a casserole of hot water, along with rye rolls and, if you like, a white radish and a couple of crisp pretzels. Sweet mustard is the standard condiment. Weisswurst is so delicately flavored and its meat so finely ground, it can easily be made into veal dumplings or quenelles. Simply steam the wurst, skin it, cut into ½"- or 1"-thick slices and use as a garnish for soups or stews.

Bockwurst is a small finger-size weisswurst made only in spring during bock beer time and is served with that seasonal brew. In Berlin, however, the term Bockwurst denotes a smoked red sausage, similar to our hot dog. It is made of beef, or beef and pork, and is sold the year round at late-night street-corner stands as Curry Wurst (page 23).

Bratwurst, or "fry wurst," is made mostly of pork and sometimes has a little veal added to it. The filling is coarsely ground and flavored with nutmeg, caraway, marjoram, pepper, salt and sometimes mace. The combination and degree of seasonings vary according to the taste of the sausage maker. Bratwurst is the specialty of Nürnberg, where small, thin versions called Schweinwurstel are grilled over open wood fires and served on pewter plates. It is not unusual for a patron to eat twelve to twenty-four of these grilled wursts at one sitting. Nürnberg's Bratwurst-Herzle is the most famous restaurant featuring these sausages. It has been in existence since the fifteenth century and is about as charming an old restaurant as one can imagine. In other cities of Germany, restaurants featuring these grilled sausages are invariably called Nürnberger Bratwurstglöckl. Munich's is especially good. Smoked, or geräucherte, Bratwurst, is a larger salami-like version that is steamed for about half an hour, then sliced and eaten hot or cold.

Frankfurters are smoked and cooked, and though they *can be* eaten without further heating, they are generally steamed or grilled. They may be made of beef, pork or a combination of the two, and are usually seasoned with pepper and often with garlic. In Germany a very long, thin frankfurter is also known as a Polnischer, and when this same elongated version is bright red with paprika, it is called a Debreziner, after the Hungarian town Debrecen, which is its home.

Bauernwurst looks like a large, fat frankfurter, usually made of pork; the meat is coarsely and unevenly ground. This "farmers' wurst" is smoked and should be steamed for a few minutes and then grilled. It is highly seasoned and often contains mustard seeds.

Knockwurst is a short, stubby, fat wurst that is also called a Regensburger, after the historic town which we call Ratisbon in English. It is made of beef and pork, or of beef alone, and is well seasoned with pepper and garlic. It may be steamed, but it is generally split or scored and grilled; it may also be cooked with lentils or sauerkraut.

When it comes to liverwursts, German butchers offer an enormous choice, all of which are smoked and cooked and are eaten cold. Braunschweiger is made of pork and stuffed into a natural pork casing. Zwiebelwurst is liverwurst with bits of browned onions in it. Trüffelwurst is flavored with truffles, as you might guess. Sardellenwurst contains anchovies in its pork-meat mixture. One of the best of all is Hildesheimer Streichleberwurst, which is made with calves' liver and is as good as any paté I have ever eaten. Of them all, however, perhaps the best-tasting and least known is Kasseler liverwurst, a coarse grind of pork liver and fat seasoned with garlic and herbs and absolutely wonderful when spread on rye bread. Fresh liverwurst (Frische Leberwurst) is served hot, as described on page 256.

Mettwurst, or tea wurst, is a short, stubby pork sausage, bright red in color. It is completely cooked and is spread on bread, never sliced. Hamburger Mettwurst gets an additional cooking and is served in slices. Rügenwalder Mettwurst is a small, hard salami-like version of this sausage.

Lyoner, or Fleischwurstring, "meat sausage ring," is a circular wurst very close to our own baloney in flavor and texture. It may be made of beef or pork, or both, and is lightly smoked. Though it can be eaten as it comes from the store, it is almost always steamed for 20 minutes and then served hot or cold. Fleischwurst is the same filling in a long roll, instead of in a ring.

Kolbascy is another ring-shaped sausage that originated in Poland and though similar to the Fleischwurst, it is cooked longer. Its meat is of a coarser, more uneven grind, and it contains more garlic. Kolbascy is often hung in the air and dried, in which case it is very much like salami.

Blutwurst, or blood wurst, is made of fresh pig's blood. It is sometimes sold completely cooked and smoked, and is then usually studded with bits of pork or veal tongue, diced fat and other bits of other meat. It is then called Zungenwurst (tongue wurst) or, if it is packed in a natural pork casing, Thüringer Blutwurst. Fresh blood-wurst (frische Blutwurst) is always cooked before it is served, and is eaten hot, as described on page 255.

Schinkenwurst, or ham wurst, is a wide, smoked and cooked sausage containing pieces of ham in a pork baloney filling. We know it as ham baloney.

In addition to the frankfurter, liverwurst and baloney type sausages, there are a number of smoked, cooked and dried salamis or cervelats in the German sausage collection. These are known as Dauerwürste, "hard sausages," and can be kept for months if hung in a cool place. Any mold that may develop on the casing can be wiped off with a damp cloth. These sausages are used in hot weather and are also known as "summer sausage," and are carried by hikers, campers and sportsmen on extended expeditions. They come in various sizes and with many different flavor-ings. There are tiny leathery strips called Jägerwurst (hunter's sausage) and TV wurst for nibbling in front of the Late Late Show. Touristen-wurst is a big ring-shaped salami and Bierwurst (beer sausage) and Plockwurst are among the medium-sized sticks.

Pinkelwurst is a winter specialty of northern Germany. It is a sausage made of pork fat, oatmeal and seasonings and is cooked with kale, Pinkel mit Braunkohl (Pinkel with Kale, page 274) being a favorite dish in Schleswig-Holstein.

There are also several versions of the meat, fat and spices in aspic which we group together under the name of "headcheese." These include red or white Schwartenmagen, and Sülze, which has a slight sour tang to its jelly.

Other enticing products sold in a German sausage shop include the raw, cured, ready-to-eat hams that are similar to Italian prosciutto. These include the famous Westphalian ham; Nusschinken, which de-rives its name from its smoky, nutlike flavor; Schinkenspeck, which is cured pork loin that is sliced and served like ham; Lachsschinken which is cut in pink, paper-thin slices that resemble smoked salmon, after which this meat is named; and Schwarzwalder Rauchfleisch—Black Forest smoked meat. This last is a cured bacon that is served with the rye Bauernbrot (farmers' bread) throughout the Black Forest region for the mid-morning Vesper, the little meal that is not complete without a glass of the fragrant, fiery cherry brandy Kirschwasser. (See page 13 for details on serving these hams.) Bundnerfleisch, the cured beef specialty of Switzerland, is also sold in these stores, as is the wonderful hot liver paté, Leberkäse, described in detail on page 256.

❂ / *BRATWURST SAUSAGES OR PATTIES*

Bratwurst is one of the most popular and versatile of the German sausages. Link pork sausages are first cousins to this Nürnberg original, so even if there is no German sausage shop near you, your own butcher can supply you with a close approximation, or you will find it easy to make at home, by following this recipe.

2 TO 4 SERVINGS

1 *pound pork, preferably loin with just a little fat*	*caraway seeds*
½ *pound lean veal*	1 *teaspoon salt*
nutmeg	½ *teaspoon pepper*
marjoram	½ *cup cold water*
	pork casings

Grind pork and veal together twice, using the fine blade of a food chopper. Season with a pinch each of nutmeg, majoram, and caraway seeds that have been finely ground or powdered. Add salt, pepper and cold water and mix thoroughly. It is best to knead and mix this mass with your hands to be sure seasonings are thoroughly blended into meat. Fill casings and tie off in 2½″-lengths or shape the meat into patties as you would for hamburgers. Cook according to any of the Bratwurst recipes that follow. The patties can be pan-fried in a little butter or bacon fat.

❂ / *FRIED BRATWURST* (*Gebratene Bratwurst*)

8 SERVINGS

8 *pairs Bratwurst (about 3 pounds)*	*water to cover*
	2 *tablespoons butter*

Prick sausages on all sides with a fork and arrange in a large heavy skillet with a cover. Pour water into skillet until sausages are covered. Cover skillet, bring water to a boil and simmer sausages 5 minutes. Drain off water and add butter to skillet. Fry sausages slowly in butter and turn frequently so they brown evenly on all sides. They will be thoroughly cooked in 20 minutes. These sausages may be served with apple rings or slices that have been browned in the butter in which the sausages were fried, or they may be topped with sautéed onion rings or the Brown Onion Sauce on page 333.

✂ / *BARBECUED BRATWURST, NÜRNBERG STYLE* (*Nürnberger Bratwurst*)

Grill Bratwurst over an open wood fire and you will have a very good approximation of how the Nürnberger Bratwurstglöckl is served in Germany.

Although small Bratwurst (usually called Schweinwürstl) are best for this, the larger ones will do if they are all you can get. Prick wurst on all sides with a fork and parboil for 5 minutes. Drain and brush with melted butter or cooking oil and arrange on a long-handled metal grill. The wood fire should be very hot and burning low. Place grill right on grate of the barbecue pit, or hold 5 or 6 inches away from the white hot wood if you are cooking in a fireplace that has no grate. Broil sausages, turning rack frequently so they brown evenly on all sides. Brush with oil or melted butter once or twice during the broiling. They will be done in 10 minutes if you have the small Bratwurst, 15 to 20 minutes if you have the larger ones. You can, if you prefer, broil these without parboiling them, but add about 5 more minutes to the cooking time. You can also broil them over a charcoal fire. It's not authentically Nürnberger, but they will taste delicious. Follow same directions for grilling the Bratwurst in the oven broiler.

✂ / *BRATWURST IN ALE* (*Bratwurst in Ale*)

4 SERVINGS

4 pairs Bratwurst (about 1½ pounds)
boiling water to cover
2 tablespoons butter
1 small bay leaf
2 to 3 cups ale or light beer
1 tablespoon butter

1 heaping tablespoon minced onion
2 tablespoons flour
salt and pepper
lemon and sugar (optional and to taste)

Prick Bratwurst on all sides with a fork. Place in a large skillet with a cover and add enough boiling water to cover. Cover skillet and simmer 5 minutes. Drain off water. Add 2 tablespoons butter to skillet and brown wurst quickly on all sides. Add bay leaf and enough ale to cover sausages. Cover, bring to a boil, reduce heat and simmer 25 minutes. Remove cover and let ale boil rapidly until it is reduced by almost half. Reduce heat and simmer.

Melt butter in a small skillet and sauté minced onion until golden brown. Blend in flour and sauté slowly until mixture is the color of cocoa. Add to the simmering ale and stir in until smoothly blended and thickened. Season to taste with salt and pepper, and a little lemon and sugar if you like a sweet-sour flavor.

❧ / *BAKED BRATWURST OR WEISSWURST, SWEDISH STYLE* (*Brat- oder Weisswurst, auf Schwedische Art*)

4 SERVINGS

2½ pounds potatoes
½ cup butter
salt and pepper
4 to 5 tablespoons grated Parmesan cheese
4 pairs Bratwurst or Weisswurst (about 1½ pounds)

sweet mustard (preferably flavored with horseradish)
melted butter
2 to 3 tablespoons cracker meal

Peel and wash potatoes. Slice very thinly, and as uniformly as possible. If potato slices are not all the same thickness, some will be cooked while others remain raw. Soak in cold water 5 or 10 minutes and drain thoroughly on a paper towel. Arrange potatoes in a buttered baking dish, which should be about 11″ or 12″ in diameter and about 2″ deep. Place potatoes in thin layers, topping each with a sprinkling of salt, pepper, grated cheese and dotting generously with butter. Sprinkle top layer with salt, pepper, grated cheese and dot with butter. Place in middle of 450° oven about 15 minutes.

Meanwhile, parboil sausages 5 minutes. Cut lengthwise down center of each. Fill gash with mustard. When potatoes have baked 15 minutes, place sausages on top of them. Brush sausages with a little melted butter and sprinkle with grated cheese. Sprinkle cracker meal over sausages and top layer of potatoes. Bake another 20 minutes, still at 450°, until potatoes are soft and sausages are nicely browned on top. Serve directly from baking dish.

VARIATION

For a richer, creamier version, divide only ¼ cup of butter between layers of potatoes, and pour 1 cup boiling milk over potatoes after they have been arranged in layers in baking dish. Top with parboiled, mustard-seasoned sausages at once, sprinkle with cheese and cracker meal and bake in a 425° oven 25 to 30 minutes, or until potatoes are soft and sausages are nicely browned on top.

⌘ / BERNE FRANKFURTERS WITH CHEESE AND BACON (*Berner Würstchen mit Käse und Speck*)

4 SERVINGS

8 thick frankfurters (about ¾ to 1 pound)	4 thin slices Emmenthaler or Gruyère cheese
mustard	8 strips of bacon

Cut lengthwise gash down the center of each frankfurter but be careful not to cut all the way through the bottom as the halves should not separate. Spread each cut side with a little mustard. Cut cheese slices in half and place one in center of each frankfurter. The cheese slice should run the length of the gash. Blanch bacon in boiling water 3 or 4 minutes. Drain well and wrap a piece of bacon around each cheese-stuffed frankfurter. Fasten at both ends with toothpicks. Grill in oven broiler or on a long-handled metal grill over an open wood or charcoal fire. Broil 3 or 4 minutes on each side. These frankfurters can also be fried in a skillet that has been lightly greased with bacon fat.

⌘ / FRANKFURTER OR KNOCKWURST GOULASH (*Wurstgulyas*)

4 SERVINGS

4 pairs frankfurters or knockwursts (about 1½ pounds)	1 tablespoon white vinegar
1 tablespoon butter or lard	1 cup tomato juice or meat stock
1 small onion, finely minced	¼ cup sour cream blended with 2 teaspoons flour
1 tablespoon paprika	
2 teaspoons caraway seeds	salt

Cut frankfurters or knockwursts into 1"-thick slices. Heat butter or lard in a 1½"-quart saucepan and in it sauté onions until soft and bright yellow. Do not let them brown. Add paprika and caraway seeds and sauté another 3 to 4 minutes. Add vinegar and frankfurter slices and stir over low heat until frankfurters are well coated with spices. Add tomato juice or meat stock, cover, bring to a boil, reduce heat and simmer 15 minutes. Stir in sour cream and season to taste. Heat thoroughly but do not boil.

VARIATIONS

1. Half a green pepper, finely diced, can be sautéed along with onions.
2. If you would like to make this a "meal in one pot," add 2 cups cold,

boiled cubed potatoes, just before you add the tomato juice or stock. The potatoes will heat through as wurst cooks.

❧ / *REGENSBURGERS OR KNOCKWURSTS* (*Gebratene Regensburger*)

Allow 2 Regensburgers or knockwursts for each portion. Cut sausages in half lengthwise. Halves may be separated, or cut *almost* all the way through and opened flat butterfly style. Dredge well with flour and fry in hot butter or lard. Turn once so both sides become brown and crisp.

VARIATION

To make these even crisper, cut butterfly style, dredge in flour on both sides, dip in beaten egg and coat well with breadcrumbs. Fry in hot butter or lard, turning once so both sides are well browned.

❧ / *SAUSAGE WITH SPINACH AND FRIED EGG* (*Wurst-schüsserl mit Spinat und Spiegelei*)

This is an excellent luncheon entree that is quick and easy to make.

2 TO 4 SERVINGS

4 *frankfurters or knockwursts, or* ½ *pound baloney-type wurst, unsliced*	1 *tablespoon butter* Creamed Spinach, *page 290* 4 *eggs, fried in butter*

Cut frankfurters or knockwursts into 1"-thick slices. If a baloney-type of wurst is used, cut it into 1" cubes. Prepare Creamed Spinach. Mix wurst into spinach. Fry eggs. Arrange spinach and wurst on luncheon or dinner plates and top each portion with one or two fried eggs.

❧ / *HOT BLOODWURST* (*Heisse Blutwurst*)

To heat blood wurst, bring well-salted water to a boil, turn off heat, place wurst in water, cover pot and let stand 20 minutes. Blood wurst can then be served, or it can be drained, sliced or diced and sautéed in a little butter, along with some diced or sliced onions, and/or apple slices. Serve with Preiselbeeren or cranberry sauce.

✖ / HOT LIVERWURST (*Heisse Leberwurst*)

Fresh liverwurst is heated the same way as blood wurst (above). It is either steamed, or steamed and fried with onions, and it is often served in a combination of the two: liverwurst and blood wurst, each steamed and then fried with some onions, in separate pans. The blood wurst and onions are placed in the center of the dish and a ring of liverwurst and onions is placed around that.

✖ / HOT LIVER PATÉ (*Leberkäse*)

Leberkäse is one of Germany's greatest delicacies, and though it is known and appreciated all over the country, you will come across it most often at snack stands in Bavaria. Literally translated, it means "liver cheese," but it is really a very smooth meat and liver paté with the consistency of a soft, very fine and slightly porous baloney-type sausage. It is steamed and served hot, with a little mustard and a wedge of crusty rye bread or a rye roll. Fleischkäse, should you come across the term, is almost indistinguishable from Leberkäse. It is usually a coarser blend of less expensive meat and is therefore a little cheaper to buy. Since it takes the kind of grinder used by commercial sausage butchers to get the meat smooth enough and sufficiently well blended for an authentic Leberkäse, this product is almost always purchased from sausage shops. It also requires a special steamer to cook it. However, it can be approximated at home, in case you cannot get the real thing.

2½ pounds lean pork, ground	3 eggs
1 quart ice water	1 tablespoon salt
1½ pounds pork liver	1 teaspoon pepper
1 onion	2 teaspoons saltpeter (you can
1 clove garlic	get this from a druggist)
½ pound unsliced bacon, finely diced	1 teaspoon sugar

Place ground pork on a cutting board or in a very large bowl. Gradually work ice water into meat. To do this, pour a little water onto meat and knead with both hands until water is absorbed. If you do this very slowly and carefully, you should be able to work the entire quart of water into the 2½ pounds of pork. The smoothness of the paté depends upon this operation. Grind pork liver, onion and garlic together, twice, using the finest blade of a food chopper. Mix ground pork with ground liver mixture, diced bacon and remaining ingredients. Mix well until very thoroughly blended.

Grease one or two loaf pans. Pack paté mixture in pans until each is almost full. It is not necessary to leave more than 1″ of space at the top. Brush top of meat with cold water until smooth and glossy. Set loaf pan in a larger pan of hot water. The water should come about halfway up the sides of the pan. Bake in lower third of a 350° oven 2½ to 3 hours, or until paté is cooked solid and is white throughout.

Leberkäse may be served directly from the oven or it may be stored in the refrigerator until you want to use it. It may be eaten cold, but it is much better hot. To heat, remove from refrigerator about 30 to 45 minutes before serving time. Cut off as many slices as you will need and heat in a vegetable steamer if you have one, or in the top of a double boiler that is set over simmering water about 30 minutes, or until meat slices are heated thoroughly.

VARIATION

Cut Leberkäse in 1″-thick slices and fry slowly in butter with some onion rings, until meat is brown on both sides and onions are soft and golden. Serve Leberkäse slices topped with onion rings.

XI

Vegetables and Salads

(Gemüse und Salate)

❈ ❈ ❈ ❈ ❈

Although the vegetable dishes in Germany are not the most exciting elements in that country's cuisine, they are far better than one is led to believe in German restaurants here. I have a feeling this is because American diners are used to having one or two vegetables alongside their meat and potatoes, and feel cheated if they do not. Since most German vegetable dishes are rich and complicated and require careful timing, it would seem wasteful to any frugal person to serve them merely as a garnish or Beilage—"lay-by." Therefore, in an effort to cater to this American blue-plate requirement, the chef simply adds one or two tepid, unseasoned, overcooked canned vegetables to the platter and sends it out—meat, potatoes and two vegetables.

In Germany, vegetables are taken more seriously, as they are in Italy and the French provinces. They appear only as standard accompaniments to the entree when they are especially and traditionally suited to it, such as certain cabbage and sauerkraut preparations are to certain meats and wursts. While in some international-type restaurants one is served steak or roast meat, platter style, surrounded with several vegetables as a garnish, this is an exception and not at all in keeping with the spirit of German cooking. Vegetable dishes, richly sauced, perhaps baked, fried or puffed into soufflés and puddings, are important enough to be a separate course. In rural homes they are often the dinner entree, followed by a platter of cold cuts and cheese or a rich pudding. Such an entree might consist of a single vegetable such as cauliflower or asparagus, covered with a creamy cheese sauce and browned in the oven, or it may be a huge platter of assorted vegetables—a whole cauliflower in the center surrounded by five to eight other vegetables, selected for color as well as flavor. A bowl of hot Cream Sauce, Hollandaise or Cheese Sauce might be served on the side and a few of the vegetables will be topped with breadcrumbs browned in hot butter.

The variety of vegetables served in Germany is staggering, and I don't think I will forget a 5 A.M. visit I made to the wholesale vegetable market in West Berlin just before Easter. There were literally miles of magnificent stalls decked with every vegetable we know here and many that are found only in a few foreign market sections in the United States and were therefore unfamiliar. Vegetables that were sold in large quantities were packed in net bags colored to match the vegetables themselves. Pale green cabbages were strung up in jade-colored mesh, red cabbages in amethyst sacks; yellow turnips in gold, and so on. You can be sure they all tasted every bit as good as they looked and for the most part had a much more robust, natural flavor than any we get here, unless one is lucky enough to live near small farms. The tomatoes and mushrooms were the most surprising of all, the first being sun-ripened and ruby-red, with a flavor I haven't tasted in a tomato here for at least twenty years. As for the mushrooms, there are six or eight standard varieties, any of which make our own tasteless white mushrooms seem like balsa wood.

Since Germany is a northern country, winter vegetables are extremely popular and widely used, much more so than here. All of the cabbages and root vegetables make frequent appearances on menus and there are a number of interesting ways in which they are prepared.

As you might expect with people who hate to waste anything, vegetables are cooked in extremely healthy and economical ways in Germany. They are simmered or steamed quickly in as little water as possible, and often are first braised for a few minutes in hot fat. This is the best possible way to preserve their color, flavor and vitamins. In addition, vegetable cooking water is rarely thrown away. It is thickened into a sauce with an Einbrenne, or roux, or saved for soup stock. Leftover vegetables go into omelettes, puddings or fritters, or are served as salads the next day with vinaigrette sauce or mayonnaise.

Almost any vegetable is used raw or cooked for a salad in Germany. The raw is usually sliced, cut or thinly grated, always marinated in Raw Vegetable Marinade and then sometimes finished with mayonnaise. Cooked vegetables, whole or cut in larger pieces, are covered with Cooked Vegetable Marinade while warm and then chilled. They may also be mixed with mayonnaise, depending upon your own preference and the vegetable in question. One thing in Germany that would delight any health-food addict is a Rohkostsalatplatte—a platter of assorted raw vegetables, arranged in a pinwheel pattern. This would include such things as grated beets, carrots, celery, red and/or white cabbage separately or mixed, sliced tomato, radish, some spikes of endive and a few bouquets of lettuce leaves. The vegetables may be plain, or marinated separately, and are sprinkled with minced parsley or dill. This is often an appetizer that is followed by a one-pot stew or soup entree.

❌ VEGETABLE DISHES ❌
(*Gemüsegerichte*)

The following two recipes are for general and typical preparations you can use when you want vegetables to "taste German."

❌ / STEWED YOUNG VEGETABLES (*Dünstgemüse*)

This pertains to young and tender vegetables, as follows: carrots, turnips, parsley root, parsnip, knob celery, small kohlrabi, horseradish, beets, spinach, lettuce, all cabbages, broccoli and Brussels sprouts, peas, beans, Swiss chard, tomatoes, cucumbers, squashes, peppers and mushrooms.

GENERALLY ABOUT 4 SERVINGS

2 *pounds young, small vegetables in season*
2 *to 3 tablespoons butter or minced bacon*
½ *onion, minced*
  seasonings to taste: such as minced parsley, dill, savory, marjoram, chives, nutmeg, pepper, sugar, lemon juice, vinegar, grated cheese, etc.
salt

1 *to 2 cups stock or water, as needed*
1 *to 2 tablespoons flour dissolved in a little cold water, or tiny dumplings made of 1 to 2 tablespoons butter and 1 to 2 tablespoons flour, kneaded together*
3 *or 4 tablespoons sweet or sour cream, optional and to taste*

Peel, trim and wash vegetables as necessary, and cut into suitable pieces or shapes. Heat butter or bacon in a heavy saucepan or casserole and when fat is hot, add onion. Cover and braise over low heat about 3 minutes, until onion is soft and transparent. Add vegetables, toss until well coated with fat; cover pan tightly and braise about 5 minutes, shaking pan once or twice to prevent scorching. Vegetables should have become intensely colored. Add herbs, spices or seasonings to taste. Sprinkle with salt and add about 1″ liquid to pan. Cover tightly and simmer slowly but steadily until vegetables are tender, but not too soft. Add more liquid to pan as needed during cooking. Mix flour with water to a thin paste; or knead butter and flour together and form tiny dumplings. Add either of these bindings to hot but not boiling pan juices and simmer 3 or 4 minutes, or until sauce has thickened. Check seasoning, adding what is necessary and stir in cream if you are using it. Heat but do not boil.

/ *COOKED VEGETABLES (Kochgemüse)*

This method is used on any old or tough vegetables, or any that are inclined to be scaly, stringy or otherwise fibrous. These would include cauliflower, asparagus, oyster plant, knob celery if large, leeks, or any of the large or old vegetables mentioned above.

GENERALLY 4 SERVINGS

2 *pounds vegetables*
water to cover
salt
2 *tablespoons butter*
½ *onion, minced*
2 *tablespoons flour*
1 *to* 2 *cups vegetable stock, as needed*
milk, cream or half-and-half, optional and to taste
seasonings such as minced parsley, savory, dill, marjoram, chervil, salt, pepper, nutmeg, lemon juice, vinegar, etc.

Peel, trim, wash and cut vegetables as necessary. Cook until tender in just enough boiling salted water to cover, or steam in a vegetable steamer. If necessary to cut vegetables after cooking—i.e., chopped spinach or cabbage—drain well and do so. Reserve vegetable stock. Heat butter in a 1- to 2-quart saucepan and when hot and bubbling, add onion. Sauté and stir over low heat; you may fry onion from pale yellow to golden brown, depending on the flavor you want in your sauce. Add flour, stir and sauté about 5 or 6 minutes. The darker brown you want your sauce to be, the longer you should sauté the flour. Add 1½ cups of vegetable stock. Beat over low heat with a wire whisk or wooden spoon until sauce is smooth and thick. Add seasonings and herbs. Return vegetables to sauce and simmer together 10 to 15 minutes. Check seasoning again before serving. Milk, cream or half-and-half can be stirred in just before serving. Heat but do not boil.

VARIATION

Bacon can be substituted for butter if it seems suited to the vegetable you are cooking. Olive oil can be used if you do not intend to finish the sauce with milk or cream.

/ *VEGETABLES AU GRATIN* (*Überbackene Gemüse*)

This preparation is frequently found in Germany, mostly with such vegetables as artichoke hearts, asparagus, broccoli, leeks, cauliflower, oyster plant, knob celery and parsnips, but never with leaf vegetables or seed vegetables that become watery as they cook down. The vegetable in question is cleaned, trimmed, peeled and washed as necessary and cut into suitable shapes and sizes or left whole if small enough. It is then cooked in boiling water to cover with a little salt, until tender. The vegetables are drained and the stock reserved. The vegetables are then placed in a shallow buttered open baking dish, such as a pie plate. Prepare the Cheese Sauce, page 333, or the White Sauce, page 331, using vegetable stock as liquid and finishing off with heavy sweet cream but no egg yolks. Pour sauce over vegetables, sprinkle breadcrumbs and grated cheese and dot with butter. Bake in upper third of 475° oven about 10 minutes, or until sauce is bubbling-hot and top has a nicely browned crust.

/ *VEGETABLES UNDER CRUST* (*Überkrustete Gemüse*)

4 SERVINGS

2 pounds vegetables in season, such as cauliflower, asparagus, leeks, chicory oyster plant, artichoke bottoms, etc.
salt water to cover
2 to 3 tablespoons butter
4 tablespoons grated Parmesan cheese, approximately
3 to 4 tablespoons cream
1 tablespoon tomato purée (optional)
chopped ham or smoked pork loin (Canadian bacon) (optional)

Preheat oven to 475°. Wash and cut vegetables as necessary. Cauliflower may be left whole or broken into flowerets. Asparagus may be whole or cut in 2″ lengths. Leeks should be split lengthwise if large. Remove bitter leaves from chicory and split head lengthwise. Oyster plant should be cut in finger-strips. Artichoke bottoms can be left whole. Cook until tender in just enough boiling salted water to cover. Drain well. Place vegetables in a buttered baking dish or casserole, depending on depth needed. Top with dots of butter and grated cheese. Plain cream can be poured over vegetables or it can be mixed with a little tomato purée and/or minced ham or smoked pork loin. Place in upper third of preheated oven about 10 to 15 minutes, or until vegetables are topped with a golden brown crust.

⊠ / *BERLIN VEGETABLE PUDDING* (*Gemüsepudding, auf Berliner Art*)

6 SERVINGS

½ small cauliflower, cooked in flowerets
½ cup cooked green peas
6 to 8 cooked Brussels sprouts
2 or 3 cooked kohlrabi, or 6 or 8 cooked asparagus
2 or 3 small cooked carrots
½ cup sliced mushrooms, sautéed in butter or canned

2 tablespoons butter
2 tablespoons flour
1 cup milk
salt to taste
nutmeg to taste
5 egg yolks
5 egg whites, stiffly beaten
butter
breadcrumbs

Vegetables may be fresh, frozen or canned. If raw or partially cooked, they should be completely cooked, separately, in well-salted water and then drained. Cauliflower should be in flowerets; peas whole, Brussels sprouts cut in halves or quarters, if large; kohlrabi in strips; asparagus in 1″ lengths; carrots in julienne strips or slices; mushrooms sliced. Combine together, tossing gently with a fork. Heat butter in a saucepan and when hot and bubbling, stir in flour. Stir and sauté slowly about 4 minutes, or until flour just begins to take on color. Add milk and beat smooth, over low heat, with a wire whisk or wooden spoon. Simmer sauce 5 minutes. Season with salt and nutmeg to taste, and cool completely.

Preheat oven to 350°. When sauce is cool, beat yolks lightly and stir into sauce. Add vegetables and turn gently in sauce. Fold in stiffly beaten egg whites gently but thoroughly with a rubber spatula. Butter a 6-cup soufflé dish, or comparable baking dish, and sprinkle bottom and sides with breadcrumbs, tapping out excess. Turn vegetables into baking dish. Set in pan a third full of hot water and bake in preheated oven for about 1 hour, or until pudding has risen and is completely set.

VARIATIONS

Obviously you can vary the vegetable combination in this pudding, depending on the season and what you might have as leftovers. Parboiled zucchini, cubed cooked artichoke hearts, cooked oyster plant or any vegetable that is not too moist can be included. Minced parsley and/or dill can be added to the sauce before the vegetables are stirred in, as can a little grated onion or lemon rind.

⚄ / *LEIPZIG MIXED VEGETABLES* (*Leipziger Allerlei*)

Leipzig, in the eastern province of Saxony, is a city of great cultural associations—the birthplace of Wagner and a musical center where Bach composed much of his work. It was also noted for its many booksellers and for the following mixed-vegetable combination that is served all over Germany. The Leipzig "variety" contains a combination of vegetables that may vary from season to season and from one cook to another. I do not remember ever seeing a recipe for it that did not include carrots, kohlrabi and green peas, usually cauliflower, often asparagus and, occasionally, mushrooms. Cabbage may also be used, but no other leaf vegetables are ever part of the mixture; neither are such "fruit" vegetables as tomatoes, squash or peppers. Celery and parsley roots may be included and once or twice I have been served this Allerlei with string beans in it. Now that I've said all that, I have no doubt that on your first day in Germany you will come face to face with some Feinschmecker who will insist that if it contains kohlrabi and carrots and not string beans or mushrooms, it may be an Allerlei but it's certainly not Leipziger. It's one of those dishes—along with bouillabaisse, paella and Sauerbraten. The following combination is my favorite, but you can change it to suit yourself and the season.

4 TO 6 SERVINGS

3 *small young carrots*	4 *tablespoons butter*
2 *or* 3 *medium-sized kohlrabi*	1 *large onion, minced* (*optional*)
1 *cup green peas* (*about* 1 *pound*	2 *tablespoons flour*
in shells)	1 *to* 1½ *cups vegetable stock*
½ *head cauliflower*	*salt to taste*
½ *pound asparagus* (*optional*)	*white pepper to taste*
½ *pound small white mushrooms*	*minced parsley*

All vegetables should be washed and trimmed, scraped or peeled, as necessary. Carrots should be sliced or cut in julienne strips; kohlrabi in matchstick strips; cauliflower in flowerets; asparagus in 1" to 2" lengths; mushrooms sliced and sautéed in butter 3 or 4 minutes along with a little lemon juice. Cook each vegetable separately in just enough lightly salted water. Drain well and combine all vegetable stock. Sauté mushrooms in a little butter with lemon juice but do not mix with other vegetables.

Heat butter in a saucepan or casserole; when hot and bubbling, add onion if you are using it. I find that it gives the vegetables a rich and savory touch; others think it too overpowering. If you use onion, fry slowly until it becomes golden brown, then sprinkle with flour. If you do not use onion, sprinkle flour into hot butter. Stir and sauté flour slowly about 6 minutes, or until the color of cocoa. Add 1 cup vegetable stock and stir until smooth with a wire whisk or wooden spoon over low heat. Simmer sauce 5 minutes, adding more vegetable liquid if it becomes too thick. Season to taste with salt, pepper and parsley. Add vegetables and mushrooms to sauce and heat through slowly. In northern Germany, Crab Butter, page 135, is often stirred into this sauce or used instead of plain butter for making the Einbrenne; crayfish tails or shrimp may also be added as a garnish.

✂ / ARTICHOKES (*Artischocken*)

These are usually served just as they are in the U.S.—steamed or boiled, hot or cold. To wash and prepare artichokes, cut off stem end flat, so bottoms can stand on a plate. Remove tough or spotted outer leaves and trim thistles off leaf tips. Soak in cold water 5 to 10 minutes and drain. To cook, place artichokes upright in a deep saucepan, close together so they hold each other up, but do not cram them too tightly. Add 2" to 3" boiling water to the pot, 1 tablespoon vinegar and a little salt. Cover pot and steam slowly but steadily 25 to 35 minutes, depending on size of artichokes. An artichoke is done when a leaf can be plucked out easily. Turn upside down to drain. Melted butter or Hollandaise Sauce, page 341, is served with hot artichokes. If you want to serve them chilled, use Vinaigrette Herb Dressing, page 346. Artichoke bottoms are often served as hot or cold appetizers in Germany. Cook as above and when done remove all leaves and the choke.

To prepare cold stuffed artichoke bottoms, fill with Meat Salad, page 17, piling the salad up in an attractive peak and masking it with mayonnaise. Set on a salad plate and surround with a ring of mayonnaise. Garnish with lettuce, tomatoes, pickled gherkins, etc.

To prepare hot stuffed artichoke bottoms, fill each with Creamed Mushrooms, page 287, to which you can add a little sautéed minced onion, or minced cooked ham, if you like. Top with a sprinkling of breadcrumbs, dot with butter and bake until brown in the upper third of a 475° oven.

◘ / ASPARAGUS (*Spargel oder Stangenspargel*)

This delectable vegetable is recognized as one of the most welcome signs of spring in just about every country in the Western world, and Germany is no exception. The tender, mildly flavored ivory asparagus of Schwetzingen are the most highly prized in that country, and, along with rose-pink salmon, new potatoes and the first tiny strawberries, herald the arrival of Frühling am Rhein—spring on the Rhine, usually the first place it presents itself in Germany.

The Germans like asparagus most of all with ham, but they often eat it with smoked salmon, or with one of the toppings that follow here. Asparagus also flavor many chicken and shellfish stews and salads, while leftovers are generally used for omelettes or a vegetable pudding such as the one on page 263.

To prepare asparagus, snap off tough ends with your fingers; do not cut off with a knife. Scale off any tough skin that remains near the bottom with a sharp, thin paring knife. Wash asparagus well under running cold water. The tough ends and skin can be washed and used to make a soup stock. Asparagus may be steamed or boiled in bundles, on a rack, or, if you go in for such specialized equipment, in an asparagus steamer. The simplest method is to cook them in a large, deep skillet that has a tight-fitting cover. Place washed, trimmed asparagus in boiling water to which you add a little salt and, for a real German touch, a pinch of sugar as well. Cook rapidly just 5 or 6 minutes. They should retain their bright green color and be slightly firm to the teeth, though tender when pierced with a sharp-pointed knife. Remove from water immediately with slotted pancake turner or tongs and drain before adding sauce.

SAUCES AND TOPPINGS FOR COOKED ASPARAGUS:

Melted butter, plain or with breadcrumbs browned in the butter.
Grated lemon rind may be sprinkled over the breadcrumbs.
Chopped hazelnuts or blanched, slivered almonds, browned in butter.
Hollandaise Sauce, page 341.
Fine Mustard Sauce, page 341.
White Sauce, page 331, is a great favorite in southern Germany. Use asparagus stock and milk for the liquid and flavor with nutmeg. Egg yolk, cream and lemon juice generally finish this sauce. Minced cooked ham is sometimes added, in which case the dish becomes Asparagus in Ham-Cream (Spargel in Schinkencreme).

/ *ASPARAGUS AU GRATIN* (*Überbackene Spargel*)

See Vegetables Au Gratin, page 262.

/ *ASPARAGUS UNDER CRUST* (*Überkrustete Spargel*)

See Vegetables Under Crust, page 262.

/ *DEEP-FRIED ASPARAGUS* (*Ausgebackene Spargel*)

See deep-fried vegetables, page 282.

/ *IMPERIAL ASPARAGUS* (*Kaiserspargel*)

4 GENEROUS SERVINGS

- 2 *pounds asparagus, cooked as described in above recipe*
- 3 *tablespoons butter*
- 3 *tablespoons flour*
- ¾ *cup asparagus stock*
- ¾ *cup Rhine wine*
- 2 *egg yolks beaten into ¼ cup sweet cream*
- *salt to taste*
- *sugar to taste*

Drain asparagus well and keep warm on heated covered platter. Do not leave asparagus in cooking water while you prepare sauce. Heat butter in a saucepan and when it is hot and bubbling, stir in flour. Stir until flour just begins to take on color, about 4 minutes. Add asparagus stock and beat with a wire whisk or wooden spoon, over low heat, until sauce is smooth and thick. Simmer 5 minutes, then stir in wine and mix until smoothly blended. Bring sauce to a boil once, then remove from heat. Add a little hot sauce to the egg-yolk-cream mixture, then turn that back slowly into the rest of the sauce. Stir and heat if necessary, but do not boil. Flavor with salt and sugar as needed and serve over asparagus.

✥ / BEETS (*Rote Rüben*)

Usually beets are served cold and pickled, as described on page 303. However, they are often eaten hot. To preserve their color, flavor and vitamins, they are cooked without being peeled. The leaves should be cut off, but about 2″ to 3″ of stem should be left on so beets do not "bleed" as they cook. If the leaves are young and tender they can be cooked separately in the same way as spinach. Scrub beets well with a stiff brush; wash under cold running water. Cook cleaned beets in boiling salted water to cover, until tender when pierced with a fork or skewer or, in Germany, with a knitting needle. Small beets will be done in about 30 minutes; large ones in 1 to 1½ hours. Drain and cool slightly before peeling; the skins will slip off easily. Serve with hot melted butter to which you can add some minced dill, or prepare as in the two following recipes. Allow ½ pound beets for each serving.

✥ / PURÉE OF BEETS IN HORSERADISH CREAM (*Rote Rüben in Meerrettichsahne*)

4 SERVINGS

2 *pounds beets without tops*
5 *slices lean or Canadian bacon*
　butter, as needed
2 *to 3 tablespoons freshly grated*
　horseradish

½ *cup sweet cream*
　salt to taste

Cook beets as described above, until just barely tender, about 20 to 25 minutes for small ones. Peel and grind through fine blade of food chopper. Dice bacon. If it is regular bacon, fry until rendered and lightly browned; if it is Canadian bacon, brown in a little hot butter. Add puréed beets to bacon and fat and stir. Add horseradish, cream and salt to taste. Bring to a boil once and serve.

NOTE

If you do not have fresh horseradish, use 1 tablespoon of the bottled and use sour cream instead of the sweet; add a little sugar if needed.

❧ / *BEETS WITH DILL AND SOUR CREAM* (Rote Rüben mit Dill und Sauerrahm)

4 SERVINGS

2 *pound beets, cooked as above*	*beet stock, as needed*
⅔ *cup butter*	1 *tablespoon vinegar, or to taste*
1 *tablespoon minced parsley*	½ *cup sour cream*
1 *tablespoon minced fresh dill*	*salt to taste*
1 *onion, minced*	*sugar to taste*
2 *tablespoons flour*	

Peel cooked beets and cut in thin slices or in strips. Heat butter in a shallow casserole and add parsley, dill and onion; sauté slowly 5 minutes, stirring once or twice. Sprinkle with flour; stir and sauté about 3 minutes or until flour is absorbed and faintly tan in color. Add about 1 cup beet stock and beat until smooth, with wire whisk or wooden spoon, over low heat. Flavor with vinegar and salt. Add beets, cover pot and simmer about 10 minutes. Add more liquid to pan if needed during that time. Stir in sour cream, check seasoning and add sugar if necessary. Heat until sauce is well blended and smooth.

❧ / *CABBAGE* (Kohl oder Kraut)

Both Kohl and Kraut denote cabbage in Germany, although strictly speaking they are not synonymous. Kohl is cabbage, and everything in that family is some kind of Kohl. Cauliflower is Blumenkohl, or flower cabbage; kale is Grünkohl, or Braunkohl, because it is green raw but darkens to a brownish color when cooked; common white cabbage is Weisskohl; winter cabbage is Winterkohl; red cabbage is Rotkohl, while curly, mild-flavored savoy is Wirsing. Brussels sprouts are rose cabbage, Rosenkohl; the name Kohlrabi denotes the vegetable that is half cabbage, half turnip. Kraut, literally, is a purée or concentration of any fruit or vegetable; shredded cabbage is Kraut. When shredded cabbage is pickled or sour, it becomes sauerkraut. The cabbage family is far and away the favorite vegetable group in Germany and there are an enormous number of recipes for each variety. It is so popular, in fact, that many sayings and maxims are based on it. "An old story" in Germany is "aufgewärmter Kohl" (warmed-over cabbage), and the English expression, "fair words butter no parsnips," becomes in German *schöne Worte machen den Kohl nicht fett*—pretty words do not make the cabbage fat. A person who is something of a blockhead is a Kohlkopf—cabbage head, and that is the only derogatory statement Germans ever make concerning their favorite vegetable.

❈ / SAVOY CABBAGE IN BROWN SAUCE (Wirsing)

4 TO 6 SERVINGS

1 *large head savoy cabbage*
  salt
3 *tablespoons butter*
1 *onion, minced*

4 *tablespoons flour*
2 *cups vegetable stock*
  salt and pepper to taste
  vinegar to taste

Remove tough outer leaves from cabbage. Cut head in quarters and wash well. Remove center stalk and trim off heavy spiny ribs. Bring water to a boil, add a little salt and the cabbage. Cover and simmer over moderate heat about 10 minutes, or until tender. Remove from pot and drain well, reserving cooking stock. Grind through a food chopper, or chop by hand and drain again. Heat butter in a 2-quart saucepan and when it is hot and bubbling, add onion. Sauté slowly, stirring, until onion turns deep golden brown. Sprinkle flour over onion. Continue stirring and sautéing over low heat until flour becomes color of cocoa. Do this slowly and carefully so that onion and flour do not burn and blacken. Pour in 2 cups of cabbage liquid and beat smooth with a wire whisk or wooden spoon. Season sauce with salt, pepper and, if you like, a dash of vinegar. Add chopped cabbage to sauce, cover and simmer 5 to 10 minutes.

VARIATIONS

1. For Savoy Cabbage in White Sauce, follow recipe but when cabbage has been cooked, chopped and drained, use its cooking stock to make White Sauce, page 331. Onion may be used or eliminated. Finish sauce with a dash of cream. In southern Germany, some minced fresh chives and ½ teaspoon meat extract are added to this cream sauce.
2. Any of the recipes for savoy cabbage can be applied to white cabbage, kale, broccoli or Brussels sprouts. Adjust cooking time according to type of cabbage being used. White cabbage should be shredded raw or chopped after it is cooked. Broccoli should be cooked and then chopped or cut in flowerets. Brussels sprouts may be whole if small, otherwise cut in half when raw, or chopped after they are cooked. Kale can be cooked in leaves, then chopped. Any of these can be combined or mixed with kohlrabi.

❊ / *SAVOY CABBAGE WITH KOHLRABI* (*Wirsing mit Kohlrabi*)

6 TO 8 SERVINGS

Cook, chop and drain cabbage as in above recipe. Cook kohlrabi and tender leaves, as on page 286, and chop. Combine cabbage and kohlrabi. Make either of the sauces described above for Savoy Cabbage. For the liquid, use 1 cup of cabbage stock and 1 cup of kohlrabi stock.

❊ / *BAVARIAN WHITE CABBAGE* (*Bayrisches Weisskraut*)

4 TO 6 SERVINGS

1 2- to 3-pound head of white cabbage
3 tablespoons butter or lard, or 4 slices minced bacon
1 teaspoon sugar
1 onion, minced
1 tablespoon caraway seeds
1 to 2 cups meat stock

1 to 2 tablespoons flour dissolved in a little cold water, or tiny dumplings made with 2 tablespoons butter and 2 tablespoons flour kneaded together
1 tablespoon vinegar, or to taste
salt to taste

Remove old or spotted leaves and tough center core from cabbage. Wash, drain and chop coarsely or shred thinly. Heat butter or lard or melt bacon in a small enameled Dutch oven or kettle. When fat is hot, add sugar and fry slowly until a golden caramel color. Add onion and caraway seeds, cover pan and simmer over very low heat 2 or 3 minutes. Add cabbage and toss until well coated with fat and sugar syrup. Cover and braise 5 to 10 minutes, then add stock to cover. Cook slowly, covered, until cabbage is tender, about 1 hour. Thicken with diluted flour or tiny butter-flour dumplings and simmer for a few minutes until sauce is thick. Season with vinegar and salt.

✂ / WHITE CABBAGE IN WINE (*Weisskraut als Weinkraut*)

4 TO 6 SERVINGS

1 2- to 3-pound head of white
    cabbage
4 or 5 slices bacon, minced
1 onion, minced
1 apple, peeled, cored and
    chopped

salt
½ cup meat stock
1 cup white wine or apple wine
    vinegar, optional and to taste

Remove old or spotted leaves from cabbage; wash and drain. Chop coarsely or shred thinly. Do not use core. Fry bacon slowly in an enameled Dutch oven or casserole and when golden, but not crisp, add onion and apple. Toss them gently to coat with fat, cover pot and braise 3 or 4 minutes. Add chopped or shredded cabbage, toss to coat with fat, cover and braise for 10 minutes. Sprinkle lightly with salt. Add stock and wine, cover and simmer until cabbage is tender, about 1 hour. Check seasoning, and flavor with a little more wine, or vinegar if you prefer.

✂ / WESTPHALIAN CABBAGE (*Weisskohl, auf Westfälische Art*)

4 TO 6 SERVINGS

1 2- to 3-pound head of white
    cabbage
boiling water to cover
salt
3 tablespoons rendered goose or
    chicken fat

1 onion, minced
1 cup poultry stock or water
butter-flour dumplings, page
    xxxi
salt to taste
sugar to taste

Cut cabbage in quarters after removing tough or spotted outer leaves. Wash well and chop coarsely, stem, ribs and all. Blanch with lightly salted boiling water 5 minutes, then drain well. Heat fat in a deep saucepan or casserole and when hot, add onion. Stir and sauté over low heat until onion is soft and bright yellow. Add chopped cabbage, toss to cover with fat, cover and braise about 5 to 8 minutes. Add stock or water, cover and cook 1 hour, or until cabbage is tender, adding more liquid if needed during cooking. Thicken sauce with dumplings and simmer 3 or 4 minutes until smooth and thick. Season with salt and sugar as needed.

✂ / *CABBAGE OR KALE IN WHITE OR BROWN SAUCE* (*Weisskohl oder Braunkohl in Heller oder Dunklér Sosse*)

Follow recipe for Savoy Cabbage (page 270), using whichever sauce you prefer. If you use white cabbage, cook in quarters and shred or chop it after cooking, then make sauce. Kale may be chopped or sliced in shreds after cooking.

✂ / *SWEET-AND-SOUR CABBAGE* (*Pikanter Kohl*)

Cook cabbage, cut in quarters, in boiling salted water to cover until barely tender. Cut in shreds, removing tough spiny portions. Using cabbage liquid, prepare brown sauce as described for Savoy Cabbage (page 270) and flavor with lemon juice and brown sugar, adding equal amounts alternately until the right taste is achieved (about 2 tablespoons of each should do). Add ½ cup white raisins and a few whole cloves or a pinch of powdered cloves, and simmer sauce 5 minutes. Add cooked shredded cabbage and simmer in sauce 10 minutes.

✂ / *BREMEN KALE* (*Bremer Braunkohl*)

4 TO 6 SERVINGS

2 to 2½ pounds kale	3 to 4 tablespoons raw oatmeal
4 tablespoons rendered goose or	or buckwheat groats (kasha)
chicken fat	salt
1 onion, minced	sugar to taste
water, as needed	

Remove tough stems or leaves from kale, wash well and cut in coarse shreds. Heat fat in a casserole or deep, heavy saucepan and when hot, add onion. Stir and sauté until onion becomes soft and bright yellow. Add kale, toss until coated with fat, cover and braise 5 minutes. Add about ½ cup water and sprinkle with oatmeal or groats and just a little salt. Cover and cook until kale is tender and cereal is done, about 20 to 30 minutes, depending on the age of the kale. Add more salt if needed and a pinch of sugar if kale is very bitter.

NOTE

If kale is old and strong-flavored, blanch in boiling water to cover for 10 minutes; drain well, chop or shred and proceed.

VARIATION

Pinkel with Kale (Pinkel mit Braunkohl) is a great winter specialty in Bremen and much of Schleswig-Holstein. Braunkohl is cooked the same way, cereal and all. Pinkel are small sausages that also contain either oatmeal or buckwheat groats, and are cooked right along with the kale and cereal. If you live in a city that has a German shopping section, you can probably find Pinkel there in midwinter. If not, you could brown some small pork link sausages in a skillet and then simmer them with the kale.

⌘ / RED CABBAGE, OR BLUE KRAUT (Rotkohl, oder Blaukraut)

When cooked properly, red cabbage is known as Blaukraut—blue kraut—because of the deep purple color it takes on. This is due to the hot vinegar and fat in which the cabbage is braised before water or stock is added. If you skip that initial step, the cabbage will "bleed" as it cooks and you will have the faded pink, oversoft concoction that gives red cabbage a bad name. It tastes best when made a day in advance.

4 TO 6 SERVINGS

1 2- to 3-pound head red cabbage
2 to 3 tablespoons butter, lard or minced bacon
1 tablespoon sugar
1 large apple, peeled, cored and chopped
1 onion, minced
4 tablespoons white or wine vinegar

salt
1 to 2 cups water or stock, as needed
butter-flour dumplings, page xxxi
¼ cup red currant jelly or preserved Preiselbeeren

Remove any ragged or spotted leaves from cabbage. Cut in quarters, wash and drain. Shred cabbage on cutting board, discarding core and tough ribs. Heat fat in an enameled Dutch oven or casserole. If you use bacon, let it melt but not brown. Add sugar to hot fat and sauté slowly until golden brown. Add apple and onion, cover and braise over very low heat 3 or 4 minutes. Add shredded cabbage and toss until coated with fat.

Pour vinegar over kraut and stir to mix through. Cover pot and braise slowly about 10 minutes, or until cabbage has turned "blue"—or, more exactly, bright purple. Sprinkle with salt, add 1 cup water, cover and simmer slowly 1½ to 2 hours, or until cabbage is tender. Add more liquid if needed as cabbage cooks. Thicken sauce by adding dumplings to hot but not boiling sauce. Simmer 3 or 4 minutes until thickened. Season with salt and melt in jelly or preserved Preiselbeeren.

VARIATION

Add ½ to ¾ cup minced cooked ham to fat along with apple and onion to give a very rich and mellow flavor.

⬛ / *SAUERKRAUT*

> The table was set, and I have found
> the good old German flavor.
> You greeted me, my Sauerkraut,
> With your most charming savor.

No less a poet than Heinrich Heine wrote the above ode to that most German of German vegetables—sauerkraut. If it has been badly maligned, it is due to the soggy, overcooked versions of it we get too often in German restaurants or hot-dog stands. When prepared properly and well seasoned, it is a succulent and tempting vegetable. Ideally, sauerkraut should be cooked to a stage known as "dry but juicy," the kraut itself being moist but with no soupy sauce around it. To achieve that result, sauté the sauerkraut first in hot fat, then cook very slowly in a little water or stock in a heavy casserole or Dutch oven, adding more liquid if needed. The kraut sauce can then be bound in any of the ways indicated in the following recipes. Seasonings vary from place to place; juniper is always used in Swabia, caraway seeds may be, apple and onion almost always are. When sauerkraut needs an elegant touch it gets it via pineapple, wine or even champagne.

The best sauerkraut to buy is the kind that comes in big wooden barrels and is sold in delicatessens and appetizing stores. However, sauerkraut packed in plastic bags or cans can also be fairly good, but find a brand that is not too soft. Both of these will probably be more sour, and need more washing, than the fresh barreled kraut. In addition to these recipes, sauerkraut is also eaten cold and raw—as is—as a sort of pickle relish or condiment with meat dishes.

Since sauerkraut is shredded raw cabbage that has been pickled in salt, it has a high acid content. Therefore, it is best to cook it in a glass or enameled pot—a must if you plan to add wine or vinegar.

⚅ / COOKED SAUERKRAUT (*Gekochtes Sauerkraut*)

6 TO 8 SERVINGS

*3 pounds or 2 quarts sauerkraut,
    fresh or canned
4 tablespoons rendered lard, goose
    fat or finely minced bacon,
    or butter if you prefer it
1 large onion, minced
2 medium-sized apples, peeled,
    cored and chopped
3 to 4 cups stock or water, as
    needed*

*6 or 8 juniper berries (optional),
    or 1 tablespoon caraway seeds
    (optional)
1 tablespoon flour dissolved in a
    little cold water, or 1 large
    raw potato, peeled
salt to taste*

Drain sauerkraut in a colander, pressing out excess liquid. If it is very sour, rinse once or twice in the colander until the flavor is mild; press out excess water. Heat fat or melt bacon in an enameled Dutch oven or casserole; when hot, add onion and apple and sauté slowly until golden brown. Add sauerkraut, stir until mixed with fat, cover and braise over very low heat 10 minutes. Add enough stock to half-cover sauerkraut. Add juniper berries or caraway seeds if you are using either. Cover and simmer slowly but steadily 1½ to 2 hours, or until sauerkraut is soft but not overcooked. Add more liquid to pot as needed during cooking. To thicken sauce, stir in flour blended with water and simmer 3 or 4 minutes. I find that the potato makes a richer, more flavorful thickening. It should be grated into sauerkraut the last 20 minutes or so of cooking time. Check to see if more liquid is needed as sauce thickens. Season to taste. It is a good idea to make sauerkraut the day before you want to serve it and store in the refrigerator overnight, as its flavor will improve.

VARIATIONS

1. Wine Kraut (Weinkraut): Apples and caraway seeds or juniper berries may be used or eliminated. After sauerkraut is sautéed, add ¾ cup dry white wine or apple wine and just enough water or stock to half cover kraut. Proceed with cooking, adding a dash of wine for extra flavor at the end.

2. Hungarian Sauerkraut (Ungarisches Sauerkraut): Eliminate apples and juniper berries, but use caraway seeds if you like. Sauté 1 tablespoon sweet paprika along with onion. Lard or bacon are the fats normally used for this. Cook sauerkraut. To thicken, stir 3 tablespoons flour into 1 cup sour cream and add to sauce. Stir into sauerkraut and simmer 10 minutes. Season with salt and a pinch of sugar if necessary.

3. Pineapple Kraut (Ananaskraut): This is made the same way except that it is thickened. Add 1 #2 can cubed drained pineapple to cooked kraut; stir in and heat together 15 or 20 minutes.

4. Champagne Kraut (Sektkraut): Substitute champagne for water or stock. Or the washed and drained kraut can simply be covered with champagne and cooked in it, without any fat or thickening being added. I like the sauerkraut sautéed in butter, then cooked in champagne without onion, apple or other such flavorings. You can mix ½ cup crushed, drained canned pineapple into cooked kraut and heat through before serving, or finish with an extra dash of champagne.

5. Wine Kraut, Lorraine Style (Lothringer Weinkraut): Use rendered goose fat for braising, and cook kraut in white wine without adding any other liquid. Add 8 juniper berries and 3 whole cloves. Do not bind sauce but finish with ¼ to ½ cup brandy and simmer 3 or 4 minutes before serving.

✛ / SWABIAN SAUERKRAUT–SPÄTZLE OR NOODLES (*Krautspätzle oder -nudeln*)

4 TO 6 SERVINGS

2 *pounds sauerkraut*
4 *tablespoons lard or butter*
1 *onion, minced*
½ *to 1 cup water, as needed*
¼ *pound diced smoked cooked ham or pork loin (Canadian bacon), optional*

salt and pepper to taste
¾ *to 1 pound noodles, browned in a little butter, or Spätzle, page 60, browned in a little butter*

If kraut is very sour, wash in a colander once, or even twice if necessary. Press out excess water. Heat fat in an enameled skillet and when it is hot, add onion and sauté slowly until it begins to soften. Add sauerkraut and fry over low heat, stirring with a fork, until both kraut and onion are golden brown. If dry, add water as needed. Stir in chopped ham or pork loin if you are using it. Season with salt and pepper. Cook noodles or Spätzle in salted water, drain well and toss until golden in a little hot butter. Add to the pan with sauerkraut and fry together a minute or two. Check seasoning and serve. This is very good with fried fresh liver sausage such as described on page 256, or with almost any meat that is breaded and fried.

❧ / SAUERKRAUT "STRUDEL" (*Schwäbischer Kraut-krapfen*)

4 TO 6 SERVINGS; 8 TO 12 PIECES

noodle dough, page 58
2 pounds sauerkraut
4 tablespoons lard or butter
1 large onion, minced
½ to 1 cup water, as needed
salt
¼ pound chopped or ground
 smoked, cooked ham or
 pork loin (Canadian bacon)

3 to 4 tablespoons lard or butter
 stock or water, as needed
1 tablespoon parprika (optional)
¼ cup sour cream (optional)

Prepare dough. Divide in halves or thirds and roll out in paper-thin sheets. Let dry in open air about 15 or 20 minutes; do not let dough get brittle. Rinse sauerkraut in a colander, twice if it is very sour, and press out excess water. Heat fat in an enameled casserole or Dutch oven and when it is hot, add onion. Sauté until onion is soft and bright yellow, then add sauerkraut. Cover and braise 4 or 5 minutes, then add about 1″ to 2″ water to pan. Salt lightly, cover and simmer until sauerkraut is done. Add more liquid if needed during cooking but avoid adding more than is absolutely necessary. Sauerkraut should be fairly dry by the time it is done, about 30 minutes. Drain off excess liquid and season to taste. Cool completely.

Spread the cooled, drained sauerkraut over the sheets of dough and sprinkle with the ground or chopped smoked ham or pork loin. Roll sheets carefully, jelly-roll style. Cut in pieces about 3 fingers wide, as you would for strudel. Flatten slightly with your hand so each piece has two wide flat sides. Heat butter or lard in a shallow casserole or baking dish that has a cover. Add strudel pieces, side by side in a single layer, without crowding into pan. Brown on both sides in hot fat, turning once gently with a wooden spatula. When brown, add just enough water or stock to cover bottom of pan. Cover and braise in a 375° oven or on the stove about ½ hour, or until dough bakes through. Add more liquid to pan if necessary. If you would like a sauce for this, remove finished strudel from pan to a heated platter. Stir paprika into pan juices and then add sour cream. Heat but do not boil, then spoon over strudels.

NOTE

If you would like to serve this as an appetizer, make strudels half the size; this amount will give you enough for a dozen people.

⚅ / CARROTS (*Gelbe Rüben, Mohrrüben or Karotten, depending on the particular species but used almost interchangeably*)

Steamed or boiled carrots, either whole, sliced or diced, are most often served with melted butter to which some minced parsley or dill has been added. They are also served in a White Sauce, page 331, made with their own stock, which might be flavored with a dash of sugar and again, minced parsley or dill. Onion would not be used in that sauce, nor would it be thickened with egg yolk; finish it off with a little milk or sweet cream.

Diced carrots mixed with peas, buttered or in white sauce, are also favorites in Germany; the less said about them the better, here or there.

Whole glazed carrots are attractive garnishes for roasts and pot roasts. To prepare, scrape and cook carrots in salted water. Drain well and reserve stock. For 4 or 5 carrots, melt 2 tablespoons butter in a skillet and when it is hot, stir in 1 tablespoon sugar. Sauté slowly until sugar turns a golden caramel color but do not let it burn. Add 1 cup carrot stock, stir, then add carrots. Cover skillet and simmer slowly but steadily until liquid evaporates. Shake pan frequently during cooking until carrots are evenly glazed on all sides.

⚅ / RHINE CARROTS (*Rheinische Mohrrüben*)

4 TO 6 SERVINGS

5 or 6 young carrots	2 cooking apples
water	1 cup carrot stock
sugar	salt and pepper to taste
2 tablespoons butter, or 3 slices	nutmeg to taste
bacon, minced	sugar to taste
1 large onion, minced	lemon juice to taste

Scrape carrots and cut in 2″ lengthwise slices. Cook in boiling water to cover to which a generous pinch of sugar has been added. When carrots are barely tender, drain well and reserve stock. Heat butter or melt bacon in a saucepan. When fat is fairly hot, add onion. Stir and sauté slowly until golden brown. Pare, core and slice apples and add to hot fat. Sauté over low flame 3 or 4 minutes, or until apple slices begin to turn bright yellow on all sides. Add carrots, toss gently in the fat-onion-apple mixture and add 1 cup carrot stock. Cover pot and simmer 5 to 10 minutes, or until vegetables and apples are tender and apples just begin to fall apart. Season with salt, pepper, nutmeg, sugar and lemon juice to taste.

✂ / CARROTS AND POTATOES (*Gelbe Rüben und Kartoffeln*)

Puréed or mashed carrots may be mixed with highly seasoned, creamy mashed potatoes and then flavored with nutmeg, salt and pepper to taste. Use 3 to 4 medium-sized potatoes to 5 to 6 carrots. Minced parsley can be mixed in with this just before serving, and crisp crumbled bacon can be sprinkled on top.

✂ / CAULIFLOWER (*Blumenkohl*)

This is another German favorite usually prepared in White Sauce, page 331, or Hollandaise Sauce, page 341. It is also cooked, broken into flowerets, topped with breadcrumbs and browned in the oven, as for Vegetables Under Crust, page 262, or Au Gratin, page 262. Sometimes the precooked flowerets are dipped in batter and deep-fried, page 282. It is most popular of all when cooked, drained and served with melted butter and toasted breadcrumbs, with or without a dash of lemon juice.

✂ / CAULIFLOWER AND HAM PUDDING (*Blumenkohl- und Schinkenpudding*)

4 SERVINGS

1 large head cauliflower
water to cover
salt
1½ cups coarsely ground cooked
  ham
3 to 4 tablespoons grated Parmesan cheese
butter
1 egg yolk
¾ cup sour cream

1 tablespoon grated onion
1 tablespoon minced parsley
1 tablespoon tomato purée (optional)
1 teaspoon paprika (optional)
3 to 4 tablespoons grated Parmesan cheese
3 to 4 tablespoons breadcrumbs
butter

Preheat oven to 375°. Break cauliflower into flowerets, wash and cook until tender in just enough salted water to cover. Drain well. Butter a soufflé dish, or comparable open baking dish, and add alternate layers of cauliflower and ham. Pack ham down around cauliflower pieces. Sprinkle each layer with grated cheese and dot with tiny flecks of butter. Mix egg yolk into sour cream along with onion and parsley, and tomato purée and/or paprika if you use them. Flavor with a little salt and pour into baking dish. Sprinkle with cheese and breadcrumbs and dot with butter. Bake in preheated oven 20 to 30 minutes, or until top is brown.

✣ / *STEAMED KNOB CELERY* (*Gedünstete Sellerieknollen*)

4 TO 6 SERVINGS

4 large celery knobs (celeriac)	*butter-flour dumplings, page*
3 tablespoons butter	*xxxi*
salt	*4 tablespoons sweet cream*
2 cups stock or water	*minced parsley*

Cut off thin scraggly roots and peel celery knobs, using a stainless-steel knife. Wash and cut in round slices, cubes or strips. Heat butter in a saucepan or shallow casserole and when it is hot and bubbling, add celery. Stir until all pieces are coated with butter. Cover pot and steam slowly 10 minutes. Shake pan several times so celery does not burn. Sprinkle with salt and add stock or water. Cover pot and simmer 20 to 25 minutes, or until celery is tender. Bind sauce by adding dumplings. Bring to a boil and simmer until sauce is smooth and thickened. Check seasoning and stir in minced parsley before serving.

VARIATION

The cut celery can be cooked in water without being sautéed. Then make White Sauce, page 331, using some minced onion and the celery stock as your liquid. Finish with egg yolk, cream and lemon juice or nutmeg.

/ *DEEP-FRIED KNOB CELERY, OYSTER PLANT, CAULIFLOWER OR ASPARAGUS* (*Ausgebackene Gemüse*)

4 SERVINGS; MORE IF USED ONLY AS GARNISH

2 *pounds vegetable*
water to cover
salt
1 *scant cup flour*
½ *cup milk or flat beer*
1 *teaspoon cooking oil*
salt
2 *egg yolks*
2 *egg whites*
butter, oil or vegetable shortening for frying

Wash and trim or peel vegetables as necessary. Cut asparagus or oyster plant in finger-length pieces; break cauliflower into flowerets. Leave knob celery whole if small, otherwise cut in halves. Cook vegetable in just enough boiling salted water to cover until tender. Knob celery should be cut in slices or strips when cooked. Drain well and dry with paper toweling.

Next, make a batter by mixing flour, milk or beer, egg yolks and oil. It should be the consistency of a medium pancake batter. Beat egg whites until stiff and fold into batter gently with a rubber spatula. Dip vegetable pieces into batter. Cauliflower, asparagus and oyster plant should be fried in about 2 inches of fat, enough for them to "swim." Celery slices can be done in shallower fat. Fry until golden, turning so pieces brown on all sides. Drain on paper towel.

/ *CHESTNUTS* (*Kastanien*)

Chestnuts are standard accompaniments to game, turkey, duck and goose, in Germany as elsewhere. To peel them easily, make a gash in flat side of each chestnut with a sharp-pointed knife, cutting right through to meat. Place in a skillet with olive oil or vegetable oil, allowing 1 cup for 2 quarts of chestnuts. Heat oil over moderate heat and when it gets very hot, keep shaking pan back and forth gently; fry chestnuts 3 to 5 minutes. Drain and cool until chestnut can be handled. Remove outer shell and inside skin with a sharp-pointed knife and proceed with any specific recipe.

❈ / GLAZED CHESTNUTS (*Glasierte Kastanien*)

4 TO 6 SERVINGS

1 *pound chestnuts, shelled and*   2 *tablespoons butter*
    skinned   ¼ *cup sugar*
2 *cups well-seasoned beef stock,*   ½ *cup water*
    or as needed

Cook chestnuts in beef stock to cover, until they are barely tender, about 20 minutes. Drain well. Heat butter in a saucepan and when melted, stir in sugar. Stir and sauté slowly until sugar is a rich golden brown, but be careful that it does not blacken and burn. Add chestnuts and turn in sugar mixture. Add water, cover and simmer slowly until water cooks down and chestnuts are coated with sugar syrup.

❈ / CHESTNUT PURÉE (*Kastanienbrei*)

4 TO 6 SERVINGS

2 *pounds chestnuts, shelled and*   1 *onion, minced*
    skinned   ½ *cup chestnut-beef stock*
well-seasoned beef stock to   *salt to taste*
    cover   *nutmeg to taste*
3 *tablespoons butter*

Cook chestnuts in beef stock until tender, about 25 minutes. Drain well and reserve ½ cup of the cooking liquid. Heat butter in a saucepan and when it is hot and bubbling, add minced onion. Stir and sauté slowly until onion is light golden brown. Add cooked chestnuts and ½ cup of the stock in which they cooked, cover and simmer 5 to 10 minutes, or until liquid is absorbed. Mash chestnuts with a potato masher, or for a finer purée, use a food mill. Season to taste with salt and nutmeg.

VARIATION

To make Madeira Chestnut Purée, use ½ cup wine instead of chestnut-meat stock. Onion may be included or omitted. Flavor with salt, a dash of sugar and a little more wine after mashing.

✜ / BRAISED CUCUMBERS IN TOMATO SAUCE
(*Schmorgurken in Tomatensosse*)

4 SERVINGS

3 large cucumbers
3 tablespoons butter, or 3 slices
   minced bacon
salt
½ cup water
½ cup tomato purée

2 tablespoons flour
2 tablespoons Parmesan cheese
4 to 5 tablespoons sweet cream,
   milk or half-and-half
minced parsley

Peel cucumbers, cut in half lengthwise and scrape out seeds. Cut into cubes or into 1″ to 2″ finger strips. If you are using bacon, fry in a 1-quart casserole or heavy saucepan until melted but not brown. If you use butter, heat in saucepan until hot and bubbling. Add cucumber and sauté over moderate heat, stirring, until golden brown on all sides. Do not crowd pan for this browning; do one layer at a time, remove and add the next batch. Return all cucumbers to the pan, sprinkle with salt and stir in water and tomato purée. Cover pan tightly and simmer slowly but steadily 15 minutes, or until pieces of cucumber are soft but still slightly crisp. Mix flour to a paste with 3 or 4 tablespoons water and add slowly to hot but not boiling tomato sauce, stirring as you do so. Add grated cheese, cream, minced parsley and salt as needed. Stir, cover, bring to a boil, reduce heat and simmer 3 or 4 minutes.

✜ / CUCUMBER IN SOUR CREAM AND DILL SAUCE
(*Gurken in Sauerrahm und Dillsosse*)

4 SERVINGS

3 large cucumbers
3 tablespoons butter
1 onion, minced
1 tablespoon minced fresh dill

salt
1 tablespoon flour
½ to ¾ cup sour cream

Peel cucumbers and slice in half lengthwise, and scrape out seeds. Cut cucumbers in cubes or into 1″ to 2″ finger strips. Heat butter in a 1-quart heavy saucepan or casserole. When butter is hot and bubbling, add onion. Sauté slowly and stir frequently, until soft and beginning to turn yellow. Add cucumber and dill and sprinkle lightly with salt. Cover tightly and steam over low heat about 8 minutes, or until cucumber begins to soften but is still slightly crisp. Stir once or twice during this steaming, and shake pan to keep cucumber from scorching. Sprinkle with flour and stir with a wooden spoon until flour is absorbed and just begins to turn color, about 4 minutes. Stir in sour cream, bring to a boil and season to taste.

VARIATIONS

1. Yellow squash or zucchini can be cooked the same way. Do not peel, but remove seeds. Cut into julienne strips, sprinkle with salt and let stand 30 minutes. Drain and prepare according to recipe.
2. If you like, a tablespoonful of paprika and a little vinegar can be added to the sour cream sauce. This is known as Cucumbers or Squash, Farmers' Style (Gurken oder Kürbis, auf Bauern Art).

⊠ / EGGPLANT (*Eierfrucht oder Eierpflanze*)

Most German eggplant preparations are copied from the French, the Italians or the Middle Eastern countries. The following seems more closely related to the German cuisine.

⊠ / BAKED EGGPLANT AU GRATIN (*Überbackene Eierfrucht*)

2 TO 4 SERVINGS

1 *large ripe eggplant*
salt
½ cup *flour, approximately*
3 *tablespoons butter*
2 *tablespoons salad oil*
1 *tablespoon butter*
1 *small onion, minced (optional)*
1 *tablespoon flour*

½ cup *half-and-half or light sweet cream*
1 *tablespoon grated Gruyère cheese*
nutmeg
2 *tablespoons grated Parmesan cheese*
breadcrumbs
butter

The eggplant should be very black in color, otherwise it is not ripe. Wash, dry and cut in half lengthwise, using a stainless-steel knife. Cut gashes in the white pulp and sprinkle both halves lightly with salt. Let stand at room temperature 20 to 30 minutes. Gently squeeze excess moisture from eggplant and pat as dry as possible. Dredge lightly on all sides with flour. Heat 3 tablespoons butter and the salad oil in a large skillet. When fat is hot, place eggplants in it, cut side down. Cover pan and cook 8 to 10 minutes, or until meat softens and skin begins to wrinkle. Turn and cook skin side in the same way. Be sure to keep heat adjusted to prevent scorching. Remove from pan. With a spoon, carefully scoop out pulp without tearing skin; leave a ½″ layer of pulp inside the shell. Chop pulp coarsely or dice; reserve skin. Heat 1 tablespoon butter in a saucepan and when it is hot and bubbling, add onion. Stir and sauté slowly until onion softens and just begins to turn bright yellow, about 5 minutes. Add flour, stir, and sauté 3 or 4 minutes or until flour is absorbed and begins to turn color. Add half-and-half or cream and beat smooth, over low heat, with a wire whisk or wooden spoon, until sauce is smooth and thickened. Stir in Gruyère cheese and a pinch of nutmeg. Stir and simmer over low heat until cheese has melted. Adjust seasoning to taste. Mix chopped pulp with the cheese sauce and turn into shells. Top with Parmesan, breadcrumbs and dot with butter. Place in upper third of 475° oven until top is brown; or brown under preheated broiler.

✠ / *KOHLRABI*

This is one of Germany's most popular vegetables and one of the least appreciated here, unfortunately. These jade-green globes, somewhere between cabbage and turnip in flavor, are extremely good when prepared in any of the ways included in this chapter. The leaves are edible if they are tender and in good condition and are usually added to the roots for the last 7 or 8 minutes of cooking time. Kohlrabi have a spiny, thread-like cover that must be peeled off before being cooked. As this outer skin separates itself easily from the white inner meat, the job of peeling is a simple one. If they are small, they may be cooked in halves or quarters, though usually this vegetable is cut in matchstick strips or diced. Kohlrabi are sold in bunches, usually 4 or 5 in each. Allow 2 small roots per person.

✠ / *KOHLRABI IN SAUCE* (*Kohlrabigemüse*)

Follow recipe for Leipzig Mixed Vegetables (page 264), using kohlrabi only instead of vegetables called for. Three bunches should be used for the ingredient amounts indicated.

Kohlrabi can also be prepared according to recipes for Stewed Young

Vegetables, page 260; Cooked Vegetables, page 261; Berlin Vegetable Pudding, page 263; Savoy Cabbage with Kohlrabi, page 271; or stuffed kohlrabi, page 299.

✖ / *CREAMED MUSHROOMS* (*Gedünstete Pilze*)

6 SERVINGS

2 *pounds firm white mushrooms*
4 *tablespoons butter*
½ *onion, minced*
  salt
2 *tablespoons flour*
½ *cup stock or water, as needed*

nutmeg to taste, or white pep-
  per to taste
¼ *cup sweet or sour cream, ap-*
  proximately
2 *tablespoons minced parsley*
1 *or 2 teaspoons butter*

Wash mushrooms quickly under running cold water and pat each dry as thoroughly as possible. Do not peel unless mushrooms are old and badly spotted. Slice off very bottom of stem. Slice mushrooms lengthwise, cutting through cap and stem together.

Heat butter in a saucepan and when it is hot and bubbling, add onion. Sauté and stir slowly until onion just begins to turn golden. Add sliced mushrooms, increase heat and sauté quickly, stirring gently, 3 or 4 minutes, until mushrooms just begin to brown lightly around the edges. Be sure butter is hot enough or mushrooms will become too moist. Sprinkle lightly with salt. Sprinkle with flour and sauté 3 or 4 minutes, until flour is absorbed and begins to take on color. Add about 1" of stock or water to pan, stir until blended and add a little nutmeg or white pepper. Cover and simmer slowly 5 to 8 minutes, checking to see if more liquid is needed in the pot. When mushrooms are tender, stir in sweet or sour cream and heat thoroughly 3 or 4 minutes. Add parsley and melt in the extra dab of butter. Check seasoning before serving.

✖ / *GLAZED ONIONS* (*Glasierte Zwiebeln*)

ABOUT 4 SERVINGS

1 *pound small white onions*
  water to cover
  salt
2 *tablespoons butter*

1 *tablespoon sugar*
½ *cup beef stock, or as*
  needed
  salt to taste

Peel onions and cook until almost tender in just enough boiling salted water to cover. Drain well. Heat butter in a deep skillet and when it has melted, stir in sugar. Simmer slowly until sugar is a golden-brown caramel color. Add onions and toss in sugar syrup until well coated. Pour in enough stock to cover the bottom of the pan. Cover pan and braise very slowly until onions are tender, and all the liquid has evaporated. If liquid evaporates before onions are done, add more and continue simmering. Uncover pan and sauté, shaking pan back and forth constantly, until onions are coated with the glaze. Salt if necessary before serving. These onions are more of a garnish than a vegetable and 2 or 3 are often enough for a portion.

✂ / OYSTER PLANT, OR SALSIFY (*Schwarzwurzeln*)

This delicately flavored root vegetable is extremely popular throughout Germany, and is prepared with melted butter and breadcrumbs, au gratin, fried or creamed. It is also mixed with other vegetables and added to stews. Its name in German means "black root," and that is a clue to the main problem in preparing it. Once it is scraped, this long thin snow-white vegetable turns black almost instantly. To avoid that, it must immediately be plunged into cold water that has lemon juice or vinegar added to it, or a tablespoonful or two of flour mixed in with it. Acidulate the water with lemon or vinegar and mix in the flour. Drain the cleaned and cut oyster plant just before cooking. Simmer in fresh clear lightly salted water. Always use a knife with a stainless-steel blade when cutting oyster plant. Prepare according to recipes for Cooked Vegetables, page 261; Vegetables Under Crust, page 262; deep-fried vegetables, page 282.

✂ / PARSNIPS (*Pastinaken*)

These sweet white-root vegetables are most often used to flavor soups and braised meats. However, they are also served as a vegetable. Scrape as you would carrots, or peel thinly and wash. They may be cooked whole, sliced, diced or cut in half lengthwise, though it is best to cook whole and cut them when done. Simmer in just enough salted water to cover. A whole parsnip will be done in about ½ hour. Drain when tender and serve with melted butter, with or without breadcrumbs, creamed, baked or fried, or in crisp savory cakes, as below. Allow one large parsnip for each serving.

❧ / FRIED PARSNIP CAKES (*Gebackene Pastinakepfannkuchen*)

6 SERVINGS

6 parsnips, cooked as above	salt and pepper to taste
2 eggs, lightly beaten	nutmeg or mace (optional)
1 to 2 tablespoons flour, as needed	minced parsley
	3 tablespoons butter, or as needed

Drain cooked parsnips and purée through a sieve or in a blender. Add eggs and enough flour so that cakes can be formed. Season with salt, pepper and nutmeg or mace if you use either; mix in parsley. Form small patties, about half the size of ordinary hamburgers and ¾" to 1" thick. Dredge lightly with flour. Heat butter in a large skillet. When hot and bubbling, add parsnip cakes and fry, turning once, until both sides are crisp golden brown.

VARIATION

To use as a garnish for a stew or fricassee, shape batter into small balls and fry until brown.

❧ / YOUNG PEAS WITH HAM (*Junge Erbsen mit Schinken*)

4 SERVINGS

2 pounds fresh young peas (about 2 cups, shelled)	1 tablespoon butter
½ cup water	2 slices cooked ham, ¼" thick
salt	2 tablespoons butter
sugar	minced parsley
	pepper

Shell peas and cook in water to which a pinch of salt and sugar are added. Add butter, cover pot and simmer slowly about 20 minutes, or until peas are tender but not falling apart. Drain through a sieve; reserve stock. Dice ham. Heat 2 tablespoons butter and in it fry ham quickly, stirring so that all sides are evenly browned. Toss ham and peas together gently with a fork, adding minced parsley and salt and pepper as needed. Moisten with a little vegetable stock and serve.

❂ / *CREAMED SPINACH, SALZBURG STYLE* (*Spinat, auf Salzburger Art*)

Creamed chopped spinach appears often on German menus and tables. It is usually seasoned with nutmeg, and the spinach cooking water combined with milk makes up the liquid for the cream sauce. The closer one gets to the Austrian border, the more one finds this garlic-flavored creamed spinach that is Salzburg's specialty.

6 SERVINGS

3 *pounds spinach, well washed*   *½ cup cream and ½ cup milk,*
½ *cup water*   *or 1 cup half-and-half*
   salt   ½ *clove garlic, chopped*
2 *tablespoons butter*   *white pepper to taste*
2 *tablespoons flour*   *salt to taste*

Cook washed spinach in lightly salted water until just tender, about 5 minutes. Drain very well in a colander, pressing out all excess liquid. Chop fine by hand or purée in a mill. Heat butter in a saucepan and when hot and bubbling, stir in flour. Stir and sauté over low heat for 2 or 3 minutes, then add cream and milk or half-and-half. Beat until smooth, over low heat, with a wire whisk or wooden spoon. Add chopped garlic, white pepper and simmer sauce about 5 minutes, or until smooth and thick. Mix spinach into sauce, season with salt if necessary and heat thoroughly.

VARIATIONS

1. A tablespoonful grated onion can be substituted for the garlic.
2. Both garlic and onion can be omitted and the sauce seasoned with nutmeg.
3. To make Viennese Spinach, omit garlic, add 1 tablespoon grated onion and substitute sour cream for milk and cream. Stir 1 tablespoon minced parsley into creamed spinach before simmering it with the sauce.

❧ / *SPINACH PUDDING, SOUFFLÉ OR RING* (*Spinatpudding*)

4 SERVINGS

2 pounds spinach, well washed
¼ cup water
  salt
2 small stale rolls, or 3 slices
  stale white bread
½ cup milk
2 tablespoons butter
4 egg yolks

2 tablespoons grated onion
1 tablespoon minced parsley
  salt
  nutmeg
4 egg whites, stiffly beaten
  butter
  breadcrumbs or grated cheese

Wash spinach well but do not shake water off leaves. Place in a heavy saucepan with ¼ cup water and a little salt. Cover tightly and steam about 5 minutes, or until spinach is tender. Drain very well. Soak bread or rolls in milk until soft and then squeeze out as much excess milk as possible. Put bread and spinach through the fine blade of a food chopper or chop together very finely by hand. Rub butter with a wooden spoon until creamy and then work in one egg yolk at a time. Mix grated onion and minced parsley into butter-egg-yolk mixture, then add ground spinach and bread and mix thoroughly. Season with salt and nutmeg and fold in beaten egg whites. Butter a 6-cup soufflé dish, a pudding mold or a ring mold and sprinkle sides and bottom with crumbs or cheese, tapping out the excess. Add spinach. If you are using an open soufflé dish, dot top generously with butter. For a soufflé, bake in preheated oven 45 minutes. If using a pudding mold, cover and steam in water bath 1 hour. If using a ring mold, set in a larger pan half full of hot water and bake in preheated oven until set, about 30 minutes. Serve with Cream Sauce, page 331, or Mushroom Cream Sauce, page 335.

❧ / *SWEET-AND-SOUR STRING BEANS* (*Grüne Bohnen, süss-saure*)

4 TO 6 SERVINGS

2 pounds string beans
  water to cover
  salt

1 recipe Sweet-and-Sour Bacon
  Sauce, page 338

Wash string beans. If small and tender they may be cooked whole; otherwise cut in 1″ to 2″ lengths. Cook in just enough boiling salted

water to cover until tender. Drain and reserve stock. Use stock to prepare sauce. Pour over beans and simmer together slowly for 5 minutes
before serving.

❧ / STRING BEANS WITH SAVORY (*Grüne Bohnen mit Bohnenkraut*)

4 TO 6 SERVINGS

2 *pounds string beans*	2 *tablespoons butter*
water to cover	½ *onion, minced*
salt	2 *tablespoons flour*
½ *teaspoon dried savory*	1 *cup string bean stock*

String beans should be washed and French-cut. Cook until tender in
just enough boiling salted water to cover. Add savory to pot for last
5 minutes of cooking time. Drain beans and reserve stock. Heat butter
in a saucepan and when it is hot, add onion and sauté slowly until
soft and pale yellow. Sprinkle with flour and sauté slowly about 4
minutes. Pour in stock and beat smooth over low heat with a wire
whisk or wooden spoon. Add string beans and simmer together about 5
minutes. Check seasoning before serving.

❧ / STRING BEANS, POLISH STYLE (*Grüne Bohnen, auf Polnische Art*)

4 TO 6 SERVINGS

2 *pounds string beans*	½ *cup stock*
2 *tablespoons butter, bacon fat*	1 *tablespoon minced dill*
or lard	2 *teaspoons vinegar, or to taste*
1 *onion, minced*	*salt and pepper*
2 *tablespoons flour*	½ *to* ¾ *cup sour cream*

If small and tender, string beans may be cooked whole; otherwise cut
in 1″ to 2″ lengths after washing. Cook in lightly salted water to cover
until tender, about 20 minutes. Drain well. Heat fat in a saucepan and
when hot and bubbling, add onion. Fry and stir over moderate heat
until onion is brown, but do not let it blacken. Sprinkle with flour, stir
and sauté slowly until flour turns the color of cocoa. Add soup stock

and beat smooth, over very low heat, with wire whisk or wooden spoon. Add dill, vinegar, a dash of salt and pepper and bring to a boil. Add string beans and sour cream. Stir until smoothly blended and simmer about 5 minutes. Check seasoning, adding more salt, pepper or vinegar as needed, or more stock if sauce seems too thick.

❄ / SWISS CHARD (*Mangold*)

The stalks or leaves of Swiss chard may be cooked together or separately, unless stems are very thick and tough, in which case they must cook longer than the leaves. Wash well to remove all sand. Shred leaves and slice stems thinly. Cook according to recipes for Stewed Young Vegetables, page 260, or Cooked Vegetables, page 261. The chard will take the same amount of water and cooking time as spinach. The sauce may be white or brown, as in these two recipes.

❄ / WHITE TURNIPS (*Weisse Rüben*)

6 SERVINGS

2 *pounds small white turnips*	1 *to 2 cups stock or water*
3 *tablespoons butter*	*salt*
2 *tablespoons sugar*	*butter-flour dumplings, page* *xxxi*

Wash and peel turnips and cut into round slices. Melt butter and stir in sugar; sauté over low heat until sugar turns a rich caramel color; do not let it burn or blacken. Add turnip slices, cover and braise 5 minutes. Add stock and a little salt. Cover and braise 30 to 40 minutes, until tender. Bind sauce by adding dumplings. Bring to a boil and simmer a few minutes until sauce is smooth and thick.

❄ / STUFFED VEGETABLES (*Gefüllte Gemüse*)

Stuffed vegetables, such as tomatoes, cucumbers, kohlrabi, cabbage, zucchini and peppers, are often served for dinner in German homes.

They are simple to prepare, are economical and provide a change in the standard meat and vegetable theme. The three main stuffings follow, but the variety is quite endless. All of these are very good when re-heated and so can be cooked a day or two ahead of time. If the filling does not contain meat, one small stuffed vegetable often is served as an appetizer, usually hot, but in the case of rice stuffing, sometimes cold.

BREAD FILLING (*Semmelfüllung*)

4 *stale rolls, or 5 slices stale*	2 *tablespoons minced parsley*
bread, with crusts	1 *or 2 eggs, lightly beaten*
1 *cup milk*	1 *to 2 tablespoons sweet cream*
salt	*salt to taste*
2 *tablespoons butter*	*chives, marjoram, thyme, basil*
1 *small onion, minced*	*(optional and to taste)*

Cut bread or rolls in cubes and cover with lightly salted milk. Soak 5 to 10 minutes, then squeeze out as much excess milk as possible. Heat butter in a skillet and sauté onion and parsley slowly until soft and onion is transparent. For a stronger flavor, brown onion first, then stir in parsley for a minute or two. Mix well into soaked bread. Add one beaten egg and one tablespoonful cream at a time, until mixture is moist but not too soft. Other herbs can be mixed in according to taste. Stuff vegetables according to specific recipes.

RICE FILLING (*Reisfüllung*)

1 *cup rice*	2 *cups well-seasoned meat or*
2 *tablespoons butter*	*chicken stock*
1 *small onion, minced*	1 *tablespoon minced parsley*

If rice is converted or otherwise processed, it needs no washing or cleaning. If you are lucky enough to be able to get absolutely raw rice, clean by rubbing grains until glossy between two layers of clean kitchen toweling. Heat butter in a 1- to 1½-quart heavy saucepan or casserole and when hot and bubbling, add onion. Stir and sauté over low heat until soft and yellow. Add rice and stir until well coated with butter. Stir and fry rice over low heat about 5 minutes, or until grains become glassy. Bring stock to a boil and pour over rice. Cover, bring to a boil and reduce heat until sauce is simmering very slowly but steadily. Cook until rice is tender, anywhere from 20 to 40 minutes, depending on the type you use. Add more liquid if necessary during cooking but do not raise lid too often. Do not stir rice as it cooks or it will become pasty. Rice should be tender and grains separate. Use to stuff vegetables according to specific recipes.

CHEESE FILLING (*Käsefüllung*)

1 cup breadcrumbs	6 tablespoons sour cream (ap-
1 cup grated Parmesan cheese	proximately), or 1 egg beaten
1 to 2 tablespoons minced parsley	into ½ cup milk
1 to 2 tablespoons minced chives	salt

Combine breadcrumbs, cheese, parsley and chives. Moisten to desired consistency by adding and mixing in 1 tablespoon sour cream at a time, or the egg-yolk-milk mixture. Stuffing should be moist enough to pack together lightly, but not too wet. Season with salt, and stuff vegetables according to specific recipes.

MEAT FILLING (*Fleischfüllung*)

1 pound ground raw meat (use all pork or beef, or veal in combination with either)	potato, or ½ cup raw rice
	1 small onion, finely chopped or grated
salt	1 tablespoon minced parsley
1 stale roll soaked in a little milk or water, or 1 boiled, grated	2 slices ground or finely chopped bacon, if needed

Mix meat thoroughly with salt, roll which was squeezed as dry as possible, or grated potato or rice, onion and parsley. Add bacon if meat is very lean. Stuff vegetables according to individual recipes.

VARIATION

Leftover ground meat can be used for this filling but it should be mixed with 3 or 4 slices of ground or finely chopped fat bacon to keep it from becoming dry.

❊ / *STUFFED CABBAGE* (*Gefüllter Kohl*)

Cabbage is stuffed in three different ways in Germany, always with some version of a meat filling. It may be formed into rolls, baked as a pudding with alternate layers of meat and cabbage leaves, or the head may be stuffed whole. The last method sounds much better than it looks when served. The stuffing is spooned between the leaves of green or savoy cabbage, the head is tied together and the whole thing is steamed until done. However, once you cut this apart to serve it, you have nothing but a pile of cabbage leaves with meat tumbling around them. I have, therefore, not included this version here. When preparing the filling for cabbage, rice is generally used instead of the alternate potato or bread.

1 *2-pound head of cabbage*
water to cover
salt
twice the recipe for Meat
   Filling, page 295

butter
Tomato, Anchovy or Bacon
   Sauce, pages 340, 336, 334

With a thin sharp pointed paring knife, carefully cut the core out of the cabbage head. This will loosen the leaves so they can be removed easily. Remove leaves individually as gently as you can so they do not break. Wash under running water. Stack leaves on top of each other in a deep pot, cover with water, add a little salt and cook about 10 minutes, until half done. Drain and let leaves cool slightly. Place on a board and very carefully trim thick portion of ribs off backs.

Prepare filling, using rice. Butter a baking dish with tight-fitting cover, or use a pudding mold. Place a layer of cabbage leaves on the bottom, then half the meat, another layer of cabbage, the rest of the meat and, finally, the remaining cabbage leaves. Or you could start with a layer of half the cabbage leaves, add all the meat and top with remaining cabbage which has been shredded. Cover dish or mold and set in a larger pot. Add enough hot water to come halfway up sides of dish or mold. Steam 1 to 1½ hours, until done. Serve with one of the sauces suggested above.

---

❷❸ / STUFFED CABBAGE ROLLS (*Krautwickerl oder Kohlrouladen*)

1 *3-pound head of cabbage*
water to cover
salt
twice the recipe for Meat
   Filling, page 295
3 *tablespoons butter or bacon fat*
2 *cups beef stock*

1 *small onion studded with 6*
   cloves
1 *tablespoon flour*
¼ *cup sweet or sour cream*
1 *tablespoon tomato purée*
   salt and pepper to taste

For this dish, use only the large outer leaves. Smaller inside leaves can be reserved for another use, or can be shredded and cooked along with cabbage rolls. Prepare and cook leaves as directed in above recipe. Be extra careful about trimming ribs, as it is even more important for leaves to be intact for this. Cook leaves 7 or 8 minutes. Some of the smaller ones can be cooked also, to piece out rolls should that be necessary.

Prepare filling with rice rather than potato or bread. When leaves have been drained and trimmed, lay out flat. Place 1 generous tablespoonful of stuffing at rib end of leaf. Roll from the rib end to the tip, tucking sides in as you go along. These rolls can be tied together, but if you can handle them gently, that is not strictly necessary. Heat butter or bacon fat in a deep Dutch oven or casserole and when it is hot, add rolls. Brown on all sides over moderate heat, turning very gently if they have not been tied. Add stock and onion with cloves. Cover pot and simmer slowly but steadily 1 to 1½ hours, or until meat is done. (You will have to cut through one test roll to be sure.) Remove onion from sauce. Dissolve flour in sweet or sour cream and stir into hot but not boiling sauce. Add tomato purée and simmer about 5 minutes, adjusting seasoning to taste.

VARIATIONS

1. A tablespoonful of paprika can be added to the rolls as they are browning.
2. The rolls may braise in a 375° oven instead of on the stove. Check to see if more liquid is needed in pan during baking.
3. Sweet-and-Sour Cabbage Rolls (Pikante Kohlrouladen): This unusual but not unknown version was a favorite of my grandmother's and met with unqualified success whenever she served it. I suspect it originated around Nürnberg, where Lebkuchen are so often used in cooking, or it might reflect the Rhinelanders' love of raisins and a sweet-sour sauce. Prepare and stuff cabbage leaves. It is not necessary to tie them or brown in fat. Place in a deep pot or kettle and cover completely with beef stock or water. Add the clove-studded onion, 1 bay leaf, juice of 1 lemon, 2 tablespoons brown sugar and 3 to 4 tablespoons tomato purée. Cover and simmer slowly but steadily 1 hour. Add ½ cup unsoaked raisins and 8 or 9 crushed Lebkuchen or gingersnaps and simmer again 15 minutes. Stir sauce once in a while to keep it smooth and add more stock if it seems too thick. (As an alternate to the crushed cookies, thicken the sauce with an Einbrenne made by sautéing 2 tablespoons flour until brown in 3 tablespoons butter, bacon fat or lard and adding to sauce.) Arrange cooked cabbage rolls in a single layer in an open baking pan that is at least 3″ to 4″ deep. Check sauce for seasoning, adding salt and more lemon juice and/or sugar to give a sweet-sour flavor. Pour sauce into baking pan, covering cabbage rolls completely. Bake in 375° oven 30 to 40 minutes, or until sauce is thick and rolls are browned.

✂ / CUCUMBER WITH MEAT FILLING (*Gurken mit Fleischfüllung*)

4 SERVINGS

4 *large cucumbers*	3 *tablespoons butter*
salt	1 *cup vegetable or beef stock*
lemon juice	4 *tablespoons sour cream*
Meat Filling, page 295	1 *tablespoon tomato purée*

Peel cucumbers, cut in half lengthwise and scrape out seeds and watery pulp. Sprinkle lightly with salt and lemon juice. Prepare filling. The meat may be cooked or raw; a little smoked ham or bacon can be ground in for added flavor. Stuff halves of cucumber with filling and tie tightly together with kitchen thread. Heat butter in a deep skillet or casserole and when hot, add cucumbers. Fry and turn gently until brown on all sides. Add stock, cover pan tightly and braise about ½ hour, until cucumber is tender. This can be done on the stove or in a 375° oven. Add more liquid if needed during cooking. About 10 minutes before cucumbers are done, combine sour cream and tomato purée and spoon over vegetables. Continue cooking until cucumbers are done and tops are brown with the cream glaze. Season pan juices and spoon over cucumbers when serving.

Cucumbers can also be stuffed with rice or cheese (pages 294, 295). With these fillings, sweet cream may be mixed with tomato purée and added at the end instead of sour cream.

✂ / STUFFED TOMATOES (*Gefüllte Tomaten*)

6 TO 8 SERVINGS

6 *to 8 medium-sized tomatoes,*	*grated cheese*
ripe but firm	*butter*
salt	
Rice or Cheese Filling, pages	
294, 295	

Wash and dry tomatoes. Cut lid off top and reserve. Gently scoop out seeds and juice. Salt lightly inside and out and fill with stuffing. It should not be packed in too tightly. Replace tops as lids. Butter a deep baking dish and stand tomatoes in it. Bake in preheated oven, 375° for rice, 450° for cheese. Bake 15 minutes; remove tomato lids for last 5 minutes of cooking time. If rice is used, sprinkle tops with grated cheese when you remove lids.

Tomatoes stuffed with meat can be prepared the same way, using leftover meat for the recipe on page 295 and allowing 5 extra minutes of baking time before removing tomato lids. Raw meat takes too long to cook for tomatoes, which would fall apart by the time the filling was done. If you do start with raw meat, sauté in butter or oil, then proceed with filling.

❈ / KOHLRABI WITH BREAD FILLING (*Kohlrabi mit Semmelfüllung*)

4 TO 6 SERVINGS

8 *to* 10 *medium-sized kohlrabi*	½ *to* 1 *cup vegetable stock*
water to cover	2 *tablespoons sour cream*
salt	2 *tablespoons tomato purée*
Bread Filling, page 294	1 *tablespoon flour, if necessary*
butter	

Preheat oven to 375°. Peel kohlrabi and cook whole, until tender, in boiling salted water to cover. Cut lid off top and with a teaspoon gently scoop out inside pulp, leaving a shell about ⅓" thick. Pulp may be mixed with stuffing or used for another recipe. Stuff kohlrabi and cover with lid. Dot or brush with butter and add a little butter to a deep baking dish. Set kohlrabi in dish, cover and bake 15 minutes. Add about 1" vegetable stock, cover and braise another 10 minutes, adding more stock if needed. If sauce is thin, mix sour cream with flour and tomato purée and stir into pan juices. If it does not need thickening, omit flour. Season as needed and serve over kohlrabi.

❈ / KOHLRABI STUFFED WITH MEAT (*Kohlrabi mit Fleichfüllung*)

4 TO 5 SERVINGS

8 *to* 10 *medium-sized kohlrabi*	1 *to* 1½ *cups stock*
water to cover	1 *to* 2 *tablespoons flour, as*
salt	*needed*
Meat Filling, page 295	½ *cup cream or milk*
4 *tablespoons butter*	

Prepare and cook kohlrabi as in above recipe. Reserve pulp, chop and add to filling. The meat should be sautéed until no longer red, or cooked meat should be used. Fill kohlrabi, replace lids and tie on with string or fasten with toothpicks. Preheat oven to 350°. Heat butter in a deep skillet or casserole and sauté kohlrabi over moderate heat, turning gently so they brown on all sides. Add enough stock to cover halfway. Cover and bake in preheated oven ½ to ¾ hour. For last 5 to 10 minutes of cooking time, uncover baking dish and brush kohlrabi with cream. Return to oven until brown on top. Thicken pan juices if necessary by stirring in flour that is first dissolved in a little cold water. Season as needed.

✂ / STUFFED PEPPERS (*Gefüllte Paprikaschoten*)

4 TO 8 SERVINGS

8 medium-sized green peppers
Meat Filling, page 295, or
Rice Filling, page 294
4 tablespoons butter or bacon
fat
1½ to 2 cups meat stock

3 canned tomatoes, drained and
cut up, or 3 tablespoons
tomato purée
2 tablespoons flour dissolved in
a little cold water (optional)
½ cup sweet cream

The peppers should be as perfect as possible and equal in size. Wash and dry and cut lid off top. Remove seeds and white fibers from inside shell. Rinse insides, dry and sprinkle lightly with salt. Fill to the brim but do not pack stuffing too tightly. Cover with lids. Heat butter or bacon fat in a deep casserole and stand peppers upright in hot fat. Cover pan and braise about 10 minutes, adding a little liquid to cover the bottom of the pan if the fat is burning or the peppers scorching. After 10 minutes add enough stock to half-cover peppers. Cover and simmer about 20 to 30 minutes or until almost done. Add tomatoes or purée and simmer, covered, again for 10 minutes. If sauce seems thin, stir in dissolved flour and simmer until smooth and thickened. Finish off with cream and season to taste with salt and pepper.

VARIATION

When no cream is added to sauce, peppers can be prepared with a slightly sweet-and-sour flavor. Add ½ a small bay leaf to stock along with tomatoes. Before sauce has its final simmering, flavor with about 1 tablespoon each sugar and lemon juice.

❧ / *DRIED BEANS, PEAS OR LENTILS* (*Hülsenfrüchte*)

6 TO 8 SERVINGS

2 cups white beans, yellow or
green split peas or whole
dried green peas, or lentils
(1 scant pound)
water to cover
pinch of baking soda, if
necessary
salt
1 large carrot, diced
2 stalks celery, sliced, or ½ knob
celery, peeled and sliced

1 leek, sliced (optional)
3 to 4 tablespoons minced bacon,
lard or butter
1 large onion, minced
2 tablespoons flour
vinegar to taste, for lentils
2 tablespoons tomato purée, for
white beans
pinch of marjoram, optional for
peas

If necessary, soak beans, peas or lentils overnight in water to cover with pinch of baking soda. Some dried legumes are treated so that they do not have to be soaked. Follow instructions on package. To cook, cover with water and add a little salt along with carrot and celery, and leek if you use it. Cover and cook slowly until tender but not mushy, about 45 minutes to 1 hour for treated legumes, longer for the old-fashioned kind. Heat fat in a skillet and when hot and bubbling, add onion. Sauté slowly, stirring, over low heat, until onion is a rich golden brown. Add flour and sauté until it becomes a medium brown cocoa color. Stir flour and onions into legumes, bring to a boil slowly and simmer until thickened. Check seasoning, adding vinegar to lentils, tomato purée to beans, and marjoram to peas.

White beans are always served whole. Lentils are served whole or puréed.

PEA PURÉE (*Erbsenpüree*)

Peas, whether yellow or green, split or whole, are always puréed; this should be done before adding onion-flour thickening. Stir in, heat and stir until smooth, and season to taste. Garnishes vary. You can top any of these with bits of crumbled crisp bacon or minced parsley.

The yellow purée is a standard with Berlin's Eisbein, page 189, and in Swabia with sauerkraut, fried fresh liver sausage and Spätzle. Pea purée is almost always topped with onion rings, that have been sautéed golden brown in butter, and toasted breadcrumbs. The pea purée, after being thickened, is turned out into a shallow buttered baking dish, topped with onions, melted butter and breadcrumbs and baked in a 350° oven for 20 minutes, or until there is a rich brown crust on top.

VARIATIONS

1. In some parts of Germany, 1 clove sliced garlic is substituted for onion when thickening sauce. Browned bits of garlic can also be used to top split pea purée if none is in purée itself.
2. Any of these legumes become one-pot meals if you cook frankfurter-type wurst in them. Brown the wurst first in a skillet for richer flavor. If large, such as knockwurst, slice in 1"-thick pieces; otherwise add smaller wursts whole.

✖ SALADS ✖
(*Salate*)

✖ / GREEN SALAD, OR LETTUCE SALAD (*Grüner Salat, oder Kopfsalat*)

Using any single type of lettuce, or any combination of salad greens, wash well in ice-cold water until free of sand, then dry thoroughly. Roll in clean kitchen towel and store in refrigerator crisper until serving time. If necessary, break greens into fork-sized pieces; do not cut. Place in salad bowl and cover with Raw-Vegetable Marinade (page 345). Use any of the herbs suggested there and include either sour cream or yogurt in the dressing. As an alternate dressing, use Vinaigrette Herb Dressing (page 346).

✖ / SPINACH SALAD (*Spinatsalat*)

Follow above recipe. Wash spinach well in several changes of water until free of sand. Use only very young, small-leaf spinach and serve with Raw-Vegetable Marinade (page 345).

✂ / *ASPARAGUS SALAD* (*Spargelsalat*)

Wash, trim and cook asparagus in boiling water for 3 minutes. Drain and cut into 1″ to 3″ pieces. Cover with Cooked-Vegetable Marinade (page 346) and chill before serving. Chopped hard-cooked egg should garnish this.

✂ / *RAW BEET SALAD* (*Rote-Rüben-Salat, roher*)

Wash, peel and wash again, 6 to 8 medium-sized raw beets. Grate on the fine side of a grater and mix with Raw-Vegetable Marinade (page 345) made with sour cream and seasoned with 2 teaspoons chopped or crushed caraway seeds. Marinate about 2 hours before serving. A teaspoon of drained bottled horseradish can be stirred into this.

✂ / *PICKLED BEETS OR COOKED BEET SALAD* (*Rote-Rüben-Salat, gekochter*)

Use 2 to 3 cups sliced cooked beets, home-cooked or canned. Arrange in layers in a tall narrow bowl or wide-mouthed jar, sprinkling each layer with a little salt and sugar. A layer of thinly sliced onion slivers can be placed between the layers of beets. Heat enough water or beet liquid and vinegar, half and half, to cover beets—1 cup of each should do. Sprinkle 1 tablespoon caraway seeds on top of beets and pour hot liquid over them. Marinate in refrigerator at least 24 hours, checking from time to time to see if more salt and sugar are needed. Stir gently once in a while so marinade penetrates evenly.

✂ / *LEEK SALAD* (*Lauchsalat*)

Cut off green leaves and wash all sand from 10 leeks. Cut in 2″ lengths and parboil in salted water. Drain and while hot cover with Cooked-Vegetable Marinade (page 346). Marinate 4 or 5 hours or overnight.

✠ / *RAW CARROT SALAD WITH HORSERADISH (Gelbe-Rüben-Salat mit Meerrettich, roher)*

Wash and scrape 5 or 6 carrots and a 2" to 3" piece of horseradish root, or use the bottled sauce (2 tablespoons will do). Grate carrot and mix with horseradish. Cover with Raw-Vegetable Marinade (page 345) made with sour cream and flavored with a little mustard, some minced parsley and chives. Or dress with mayonnaise, also flavored with mustard, parsley and chives.

✠ / *COOKED CARROT SALAD (Gelbe-Rüben-Salat, gekochter)*

Wash, scrape and cook whole 5 or 6 carrots. Cut in slices and cover with Cooked-Vegetable Marinade (page 346) while carrots are warm. Chill overnight.

✠ / *CAULIFLOWER SALAD (Blumenkohlsalat)*

Wash cauliflower, break into flowerets and cook until tender in boiling salted water. Drain well and cover with Cooked-Vegetable Marinade (page 346) flavored with onion and/or parsley and chives. Marinate overnight, drain and serve with mayonnaise.

✠ / *COLD STRING BEAN SALAD (Kalter Bohnensalat)*

Wash and cook 1 pound string beans or wax beans, whole or cut, in boiling salted water until tender. Drain and while warm cover with Cooked-Vegetable Marinade (page 346). Add minced onion, toss and chill 2 or 3 hours.

❉ / HOT STRING BEAN SALAD WITH BACON DRESSING (*Warmer Bohnensalat mit Specksosse*)

Cook string beans as directed above, drain and while hot toss with thinly sliced raw onion rings and Hot Bacon Dressing (page 342).

❉ / WILTED LETTUCE WITH BACON DRESSING (*Verwelkter Kopfsalat mit Specksosse*)

Wash and dry 1 head of lettuce separated into leaves. Break in fork-sized pieces and chill in refrigerator. Place in salad bowl and cover with Hot Bacon Dressing (p. 342). Serve garnished with sliced hard-cooked egg.

❉ / GREEN PEPPER SALAD (*Paprikasalat*)

Use 1 pound firm, perfect green peppers. Remove seeds and white spiny fibers; wash and dry well. Cut in thin noodle strips. Combine with 3 tomatoes that were seeded, drained and similarly cut. Marinate in Raw-Vegetable Marinade (page 345) 2 or 3 hours. Serve as is, or drain and toss with mayonnaise. Green pepper can be used without the tomato, if you prefer.

❉ / KOHLRABI SALAD (*Kohlrabisalat*)

Wash, peel and grate or shred 5 or 6 small kohlrabi. Cover with Raw-Vegetable Marinade (page 345) made with sour cream. Season with minced fresh dill and a little grated onion.

❧ / RADISH SALAD (*Rettichsalat*)

Use 1 bunch red or white radishes. Trim, wash and dry. Grate or slice thin. Prepare Raw-Vegetable Marinade (page 345) without vinegar but with 4 tablespoons thick sour cream. For black radish salad, peel radish, grate, sprinkle with salt and pepper and moisten with a little oil and white vinegar.

❧ / CUCUMBER SALAD I (*Gurkensalat I*)

Peel two large cucumbers and cut into thin slices. Arrange in layers, in a wide bowl, sprinkling each layer with salt, preferably coarse. Place another bowl on top of cucumbers and weight down. Set in refrigerator 1 to 2 hours or until all water is out of cucumbers. Drain and if very salty, rinse quickly and drain again. Sprinkle with white pepper and cover with mixture of half water–half vinegar. Season with sugar and add salt if necessary. Minced dill and/or parsley can be added, as can very thinly slivered raw onion rings. Chill at least 1 hour and serve.

❧ / CUCUMBER SALAD II (*Gurkensalat II*)

Prepare cucumbers as above. Press and drain. Cover with Raw-Vegetable Marinade (page 345) made with sour cream and flavored with dill, parsley and/or onion. Or mix with sour cream thinned with a little vinegar. For a pink color, stir a little paprika into sour cream or marinade.

❧ / *TOMATO AND ONION SALAD* (*Tomaten-Zwiebelsalat*)

4 SERVINGS

2 or 3 medium-sized ripe
   tomatoes
2 to 3 tablespoons diced onion
   salt and pepper
3 to 4 tablespoons olive oil or
   other salad oil

2 tablespoons white vinegar
   minced parsley, chives, chervil,
    borage, optional and to taste

Wash and dry tomatoes and cut into fork-size chunks. Combine with diced onion, tossing together gently with a fork. Sprinkle with salt and pepper. Mix oil and vinegar together in a bowl or shake together in a bottle; pour over tomato-onion combination. Any of the green herbs mentioned can be added but are not necessary. Let salad marinate about 30 minutes in refrigerator or in a cool corner. Mix gently once or twice during that time.

⧓ / *RAW KNOB CELERY SALAD* (*Selleriesalat, roher*)

Peel 2 large knob celery and grate directly into ½ to 1 cup sweet cream, yogurt or milk. Peel, core and dice apple and mix with celery. Prepare Raw-Vegetable Marinade (page 345), omitting any cream, and stir into celery and apple. Season with salt and lemon juice.

⧓ / *COOKED KNOB CELERY SALAD* (*Selleriesalat, gekochter*)

Wash, peel and cook 2 whole knob celery in boiling salted water until just tender. Slice and cover with Cooked-Vegetable Marinade (page 346). Marinate overnight in refrigerator. Drain and serve with mayonnaise seasoned with a little grated onion.

⧓ / *WALDORF SALAD* (*Waldorfsalat*)

This is, oddly enough, one of Germany's most popular salads and almost always on the menus of Konditoreien. Peel, wash and grate or shred 2 knob celery and cover with 1 cup sweet cream mixed with 3 tablespoons lemon juice or vinegar. Add 4 peeled, cored and chopped or diced apples, 2 tablespoons chopped, blanched almonds and season with salt and sugar to taste. Flavor with 2 tablespoons Worcestershire sauce and enough mayonnaise to bind. Chill 1 to 2 hours.

/ *WHITE CABBAGE SALAD (Weisskohlsalat)*

Quarter and wash 1 2-pound head of white cabbage. Discard core and tough ribs and shred. Sprinkle with 1 tablespoon salt, preferably coarse, and press down with weighted plate about ½ hour or until all water is out of cabbage. Drain and cover with Raw-Vegetable Marinade (page 345) made without salt or oil. Dice and fry 6 slices bacon, pour hot fat and bacon over cabbage, toss and serve without chilling. Red cabbage can be prepared in the same way.

/ *SAUERKRAUT SALAD (Sauerkrautsalat)*

Wash 2 pounds sauerkraut and drain. Chop kraut and mix with 3 tablespoons salad oil. Sprinkle with salt and 2 tablespoons minced onion. Add 2 peeled, cored chopped apples and 1 or 2 scraped and diced carrots. Moisten with 2 or 3 tablespoons vinegar. Toss and serve cold. To make Hot Sauerkraut Salad, omit the oil. Toss together and heat with 3 tablespoons melted brown butter or rendered bacon fat.

/ *RAINBOW SALAD (Buntersalat)*

Toss together lightly with a fork 3 peeled, cooked, cubed potatoes, 2 cooked, diced carrots, 1 peeled, cooked, diced knob celery, 1 cup cooked Brussels sprouts cut in quarters or halves. Sprinkle with salt and pepper and toss with 2 tablespoons white vinegar and 3 tablespoons salad oil, or use Cooked-Vegetable Marinade (page 346).

/ *RUSSIAN SALAD (Russicher Salat)*

Shred 1 raw red cabbage, 1 peeled raw knob celery, and chop 2 peeled and cored apples and 1 large dill pickle. Sprinkle with salt and white pepper and cover with a mixture of half vinegar–half water. Let stand in refrigerator overnight. Drain in a colander, sprinkle with 2 table-spoons grated horseradish, 1 chopped onion, a pinch of sugar and stir in 1 to 2 cups sour cream.

⊠ / *GRAPE AND OLIVE SALAD* (*Weintrauben-Olivensalat*)

Using green or purple grapes, cut in halves and remove seeds. Slice green olives that are stuffed with pimento, add to grapes and sprinkle with lemon juice, olive oil, sugar and pepper—no salt. Use 1 cup whole olives to a 1½-pound bunch of grapes.

Potato, Noodle and Rice Dishes

(Kartoffel-, Nudel- und Reisgerichte)

❈ ❈ ❈ ❈ ❈

✂ POTATOES (Kartoffeln) ✂

"All that meat and no potatoes" would be as lamentable a situation to the average German as it was to the lyricist of that American song hit of the 1940s. Although they have a passion for dumplings and a predilection for noodles, the dietary staple of the Germans is potatoes, and they have dozens and dozens of tempting ways to prepare them. One is often served two kinds of potatoes at the same meal, and even the Swabian Spätzle and noodles live in a state of peaceful co-existence with potatoes—so much so, in fact, that Swabian cooks often make noodles out of potatoes (see page 320).

Besides being used in soups and stews, as side dishes, salads and entrees, potatoes serve as thickening agents in cooking other dishes. Raw grated or cooked mashed potatoes are used in this way, and potato flour or starch is a popular substitute for cornstarch or tapioca. You can buy this product in almost any supermarket in the United States.

In Germany you will most often be served fried, boiled or steamed potatoes. The last two are usually cooked in their jackets, both for nutrition and flavor, and may be served peeled or unpeeled. In either case they will be dry and fluffy, never soggy and waxy, as they are well dried over heat after being cooked and drained (see recipes that follow below). Germans also love such international potato dishes as French-fries, shoestring potatoes, waffle-fried potatoes, potato chips and pommes soufflées. Leftover boiled potatoes are added to omelettes or salads, and extra mashed potatoes may be fried the next day, pancake style, in a little butter.

The most important rule of etiquette when eating boiled potatoes in Germany is that they must be broken with a fork, never, never cut with a knife. Doing so marks you as a boor and an illiterate, just the way cutting spaghetti with a knife does in Italy.

✂ / *SALT POTATOES* (*Salzkartoffeln*)

One of the most commonly served potato dishes in Germany, these are simply potatoes that have been washed, peeled, quartered and boiled until tender in well-salted water. They should be drained through a colander as soon as they are done, returned to the empty pot and placed over low heat. Shake pot back and forth gently several times until potatoes are thoroughly dry and mealy.

GARNISHES FOR SALT POTATOES

1. Melted butter with minced parsley, dill, chives or caraway seeds.
2. Breadcrumbs browned in butter.
3. Browned butter.
4. Minced onion, browned or lightly sautéed in butter.
5. White Sauce, plain, or seasoned with mustard, minced parsley, chives or dill, or with bits of cooked ham or bacon, pages 331 through 334).
6. White Onion Sauce, page 333.

✂ / *POTATOES IN JACKETS* (*Schalenkartoffeln*)

Potatoes that are to be boiled in their skins must be well scrubbed so that the dirt does not penetrate as they cook. Both brown and red new potatoes, and medium-sized old potatoes, are cooked in jackets in Germany. New potatoes are eaten jackets and all, though often a narrow strip of skin is pared off around the middle of each before cooking. Old potatoes cooked in their jackets are generally peeled before being served and it is these that are used for potato salad and other such dishes.

Unpeeled potatoes may be boiled or steamed and the cooking water may be completely unseasoned, or flavored with salt, caraway seeds or both. Potatoes must be drained through a colander as soon as they are done. Return them to the empty pot and place over low heat. Shake pot back and forth gently several times, until potatoes are well dried and mealy.

❧ / SNOW POTATOES (*Kartoffelschnee*)

Old potatoes are best for this. They should be scrubbed clean and cooked in their jackets. Peel while hot and put through a potato ricer or food mill. Season with salt and a generous lump of butter before serving, or top with breadcrumbs and/or onion rings that have been sautéed in butter.

❧ / MASHED POTATOES (*Kartoffelbrei*)

Cook unpeeled potatoes. Peel while hot and mash well with a potato masher. Work in 1 cup hot milk and 1 to 2 tablespoons butter for 2 pounds of potatoes. Season with salt, pepper or nutmeg. Serve at once or keep warm by placing pot in a larger pan filled with hot water. Onion rings, or breadcrumbs lightly browned in butter, may be used as toppings for mashed potatoes.

To make Baked Mashed Potatoes, mix 2 egg yolks into mashed potatoes and turn into a buttered baking dish or soufflé dish, top with sautéed onion rings, browned breadcrumbs, or both, brush with melted butter and bake in 450° oven 5 or 10 minutes, or until topping is nicely browned. To make a creamier version, whip potatoes with a litttle more milk, using a wire whisk or a rotary beater.

❧ / *HEAVEN AND EARTH* (*Himmel und Erde*)

A favorite dish with sautéed liver, roast lamb or mutton, this is simply mashed potatoes mixed with warm, well-seasoned applesauce, salt, and enough sugar and vinegar to give it a slight sweet-sour tang. Pour brown butter over this before serving.

❧ / *GERMAN FRIED POTATOES* (*Bratkartoffeln*)

This is perhaps the best-known potato dish in Germany; to the rest of the world it is a classic.

6 SERVINGS

7 or 8 medium-sized old potatoes	*2 tablespoons butter, lard or*
salt	*bacon fat*

Wash and peel potatoes. They are usually cut in very thin slices, but they may be cubed instead or cut into sticks as for French-fried potatoes. Sprinkle them with salt. Heat fat in an 11″ or 12″ skillet that has a tight-fitting cover. When fat is hot and bubbling, add potatoes and cover. Steam slowly but steadily 15 to 20 minutes, shaking pan back and forth several times during cooking. Potatoes should turn a deep yellow color as they cook. Remove cover and dry for another 10 minutes, turning potatoes once or twice with a wooden spatula so that they become brown on top and bottom.

VARIATIONS

1.   Diced onions are sometimes sautéed and cooked along with potatoes.
2.   Cold boiled, peeled potatoes, cut in thick slices, can also be fried in butter or bacon fat, with or without diced onion. Follow recipe, but do not cover pan. Turn from time to time with wooden spatula so potatoes brown evenly.

❇ / *PAPRIKA POTATOES WITH PARSLEY*
(*Paprikakartoffeln mit Petersilie*)

6 SERVINGS

7 or 8 medium-sized potatoes
⅓ cup butter
salt

2 tablespoons parsley
1 teaspoon sweet paprika

Wash and pare potatoes and cut into cubes. Heat butter in a large skillet and add potatoes. Cover skillet and fry potatoes very slowly, shaking the pan from time to time so they will not stick. Turn gently several times during cooking so potato cubes brown on all sides. Cook about 15 minutes, or until potatoes are tender. Sprinkle with salt, parsley and paprika and toss lightly. Serve at once.

VARIATIONS

1.　If you would like a little sauce with these potatoes, add ½ cup buttermilk or sour cream with the salt, paprika and seasonings.
2.　A little minced onion can be sautéed and cooked along with potatoes.
3.　Caraway seeds and/or thyme or basil can also be added for seasoning.

❇ / *BACON POTATOES* (*Speckkartoffeln*)

6 SERVINGS

7 or 8 medium-sized potatoes
salt
water

¼ pound bacon, finely diced
1 medium onion, minced
salt and pepper

Wash and peel potatoes and cook whole until tender in well-salted water. Drain through a colander as soon as done and return to empty pot. Place over low heat and shake pot back and forth gently several times until potatoes are thoroughly dry and mealy. Cool potatoes and slice. Fry bacon slowly with minced onion. When both are golden brown, add potato slices to pan and fry slowly until lightly browned. Season with salt and pepper and serve.

✂ / *CREAMED POTATOES* (*Niedernauer Kartoffeln*)

6 SERVINGS

7 or 8 medium-sized potatoes
2 tablespoons butter
  salt and pepper
3 eggs

1 cup cream, sweet or sour
1 to 2 tablespoons minced chives
  or parsley

Boil potatoes in their skins and peel while hot. Let cool a little, then cut into cubes. Melt butter in a large skillet and when it is hot and bubbling, add potatoes. Sprinkle with salt and pepper and fry slowly until potatoes are golden brown. Beat eggs into cream, add minced chives or parsley and pour over potatoes. Cook slowly, uncovered, until sauce is thick and smooth and set. Do not boil after adding eggs. Check seasoning and serve.

VARIATION

In Swabia, minced onion and parsley are added to the hot butter and sautéed 2 or 3 minutes before potatoes are added.

✂ / *POTATOES IN HORSERADISH CREAM SAUCE* (*Meerrettichkartoffeln*)

6 SERVINGS

⅓ to ½ root horseradish,
  depending on size
1 cup milk
7 or 8 medium-sized potatoes
2 tablespoons butter
1 medium-sized onion, minced

3 tablespoons flour
½ cup water
1½ cups milk
  sugar
  salt
  minced parsley

Wash and peel horseradish root and grate into 1 cup milk; let stand 20 to 30 minutes as you proceed with rest of recipe. Scrub potatoes and boil in their jackets. Cool until you can handle them, then peel and slice. Do not chill. Melt butter in an 11″ or 12″ skillet and in it sauté onion until it turns bright yellow. Sprinkle with flour. Stir over low heat until flour is absorbed and turns bright yellow. Slowly stir water into butter-flour mixture, then add 2 cups milk, stirring constantly over low heat. Add grated horseradish and milk in which it soaked to the hot cream sauce. Stir over low heat until smooth and thickened. Season to taste with a little sugar, salt and parsley. Add potatoes to sauce and simmer 5 or 10 minutes until thoroughly heated.

� / SOUR POTATOES (*Saures Kartoffelgemüse*)

6 SERVINGS

7 or 8 medium-sized potatoes	vinegar to taste
2 tablespoons butter	1 bay leaf
1 large onion, minced	2 cloves
3 tablespoons flour	thyme
3½ cups beef or veal stock	sugar
salt	

Cook potatoes in jackets. Cool until you can handle them, then peel and slice. Do not chill. Heat butter in an 11″ or 12″ skillet and in it fry onions slowly until they are brown, but not black. Sprinkle with flour. Fry slowly, stirring constantly, until flour is absorbed and turns a deep cocoa color. Gradually add meat stock, stirring over low heat until sauce is smooth and thickened. Add salt, a dash of vinegar, bay leaf, cloves and a pinch of thyme. Simmer uncovered 20 minutes, or until sauce is fairly thick. If it becomes too thick, add more stock or a little water as needed. Remove bay leaf and cloves and add potatoes to sauce. Check seasoning and add a pinch of sugar if needed. Simmer 5 or 10 minutes until potatoes are thoroughly heated.

✶ / CARAWAY POTATOES (*Kümmelkartoffeln*)

6 SERVINGS

18 to 24 small new potatoes, red or brown	1 to 2 tablespoons caraway seeds
	salt
2 tablespoons butter, melted	

Scrub potatoes and cut in half lengthwise. Do not peel. Dip the cut side of each half in melted butter and sprinkle with caraway seeds and salt. Set halves, cut side down, in a buttered baking dish. Pour melted butter over each one. Bake about 30 minutes in 400° oven, or until potatoes are completely tender. Sprinkle again with a little salt and serve.

✖ / POTATO CROQUETTES (*Kartoffelkroketten*)

6 SERVINGS

7 or 8 medium-sized potatoes
3 tablespoons butter
2 eggs, lightly beaten
2 tablespoons grated Parmesan
  cheese
1 tablespoon salt (*approximately*)
½ teaspoon nutmeg (*approximately*)

flour, as needed
2 eggs, beaten with 2 tablespoons water
fresh breadcrumbs
fat for deep-frying (lard or
  vegetable oil)

Scrub potatoes, cook unpeeled and peel while hot. Purée in a food mill or rub through a sieve. Add butter, 2 eggs, grated cheese and mix well. Season with salt and nutmeg to taste. Work flour into potatoes, a tablespoon or two at a time, until you can form croquettes—sausage-shaped rolls about 1½″ in diameter and 2″ to 3″ long. Dip each roll in egg-water mixture and roll in breadcrumbs until well coated on all sides. Heat fat in deep fryer. When it registers 375° on a fat thermometer, add croquettes, four or five at a time, and cook each batch until they are a deep golden brown. Drain on paper towel before serving. If you prefer not to deep-fry these, shape potato-flour mixture into hamburger-like patties and fry in 1″ hot fat. Drain on paper towel and serve.

✖ / POTATO PANCAKES (*Kartoffelpuffer, oder Reiberdatschi*)

6 SERVINGS

7 or 8 medium-sized old potatoes
1 large onion
  starch from potato water
2 eggs, separated
2 tablespoons flour, potato flour
  or cracker meal

1 tablespoon salt
1 teaspoon white pepper
  lard or vegetable shortening for
  frying

Peel potatoes and keep in cold water until ready for use. Potato pancakes must be made just before they are to be eaten; they cannot be grated in advance as they will blacken very quickly. Grate potatoes and onion into a bowl and drain in a strainer, pressing out as much liquid as possible with your hands or with a wooden spoon. Reserve liquid and let it settle. Pour away potato liquid but do not throw away the starchy sediment that has settled at the bottom of the bowl; this should be returned to the potato-onion mixture. Mix potatoes with egg yolks, flour, salt and pepper. Beat egg whites stiffly and gently fold into potatoes. Heat fat in a skillet so that you have a depth of 1″ when it is melted. Drop potato mixture into hot fat—about 2 tablespoons per pancake—and fry, turning once so pancakes are a deep golden brown on both sides. Drain on paper towel.

VARIATIONS

1. Potato pancakes are often made without onion. At other times apple is added for flavor, an unusual and delicious touch. Grate 1 large peeled apple into potato mixture, with or without onion, and proceed.

2. Add 2 tablespoons minced parsley to drained potato mixture.

3. Instead of making small pancakes, German housewives often make a huge pan-size cake and serve one to a portion, usually as a luncheon or supper dessert-entree, after a first course of soup, a vegetable casserole or a sausage platter. If a 10″ skillet is used, this mixture will give 4 or 5 large thin pancakes. Usually onion is omitted and so is pepper. The finished pancake is sprinkled with granulated sugar or, sometimes, cinnamon.

4. A somewhat simplified version can be made by baking pancakes, all at once, in the oven, a dish known as Kartoffelkuchen (Potato Cake). Prepare potatoes with or without onion and/or apple. Put 3 or 4 tablespoons vegetable shortening or lard in an 8″-square cake pan and place on moderate heat until fat is quite hot. Turn mixture into pan and pour a little more melted fat over the top. Bake in a 425° oven about 45 minutes, or until potato mixture is very brown and crisp on top. Turn onto serving platter and cut into squares. This method is a little easier to handle when you have guests, as it saves you from having to fry individual pancakes just before dinner is served.

❧ / *POTATO SOUFFLÉ* (*Kartoffelauflauf*)

6 SERVINGS

7 or 8 medium-sized potatoes	onion and 2 tablespoons
3 tablespoons butter	minced parsley
3 eggs, separated	butter
salt	breadcrumbs
nutmeg or 3 tablespoons grated	

Scrub potatoes and boil in their jackets. Peel and purée in a food mill or mash well while hot. Potatoes should cool completely before proceeding. For best results, cook, peel and mash a day ahead of time and store in refrigerator. Cream butter until lighty and fluffy and work in egg yolks, salt and a dash of nutmeg, or grated onion and parsley. Mix into mashed potatoes, beating well until smoothly blended. Taste and add more salt if needed. Beat egg whites until stiff and fold into potato mixture, using a rubber spatula and working very gently. Pour into buttered soufflé dish that has been sprinkled with breadcrumbs on the bottom and sides. Bake in 375° oven about 45 minutes, or until soufflé has risen and is nicely browned on top.

❖ / STUFFED POTATOES (*Gefüllte Kartoffeln*)

6 SERVINGS

6 *Idaho potatoes of uniform size*	2 *tablespoons butter or bacon fat*
stuffing (see below)	1 *cup meat stock*

Wash and peel potatoes. Cut a slice, lengthwise, off one of the flat sides of each potato. Reserve cut-off slice to be used as lid. Scoop out potato until you have a pocket about the size of an egg, or just a little larger. Be careful not to cut through the sides or bottom. Fill with one of the stuffings. Place "lid" on each potato and tie in place with string. Heat fat in a fireproof-ovenproof baking dish and brown potatoes on all sides. Pour stock into pan; cover, and bake in 425° oven about 45 minutes, or until potatoes are done. Baste from time to time with pan liquid. Untie string and serve with Tomato Sauce, page 340, or Caper Sauce, page 204, using beef broth.

STUFFINGS FOR POTATOES

1.   Mince 3 slices bacon and sauté 3 tablespoons minced onion in hot fat 3 or 4 minutes. Add ¼ pound sauerkraut and sauté until limp and golden. Season with salt, pepper and caraway seeds.

2.   Sauté 3 tablespoons minced onion in a little butter until onion is soft and bright yellow. Mix with finely diced or slivered cooked sausage such as baloney or salami, or with country sausage meat that has been lightly sautéed with the onion. Season with salt, a little mustard if you use cooked sausage, or thyme or marjoram if you use raw country sausage.

3.   Saute ½ pound chopped mushrooms in a little butter, along with 2 tablespoons minced onion. Season with salt, pepper and minced parsley, 1½ tablespoons breadcrumbs and mix in 1 well-beaten egg to form a smooth paste.

✂ / POTATO NOODLES (*Kartoffelnudeln oder Schupfnudeln*)

A close relative of the Italian gnocchi, these noodles, browned in butter, are served as an entree with a crisp green salad, as a light lunch or supper entree.

6 SERVINGS

6 Idaho baking potatoes	1 tablespoon salt
1 egg	2 to 3 cups flour, as needed
1 egg yolk	butter

Scrub potatoes and boil in their jackets. Peel and return to empty pot. Place pot over low heat and shake back and forth gently several times until they are dry and mealy. Mash, using a potato masher, or purée through a food mill. For best results, potatoes should be cooked and mashed a day before you intend to make the noodles. Store in refrigerator. Mix potatoes with egg, egg yolk and salt and blend well. Mix flour into potato mixture until smooth enough to be handled and kneaded. It will take between 2 and 3 cups of flour, depending upon the moisture in the potatoes and eggs. Knead dough until smooth on a floured pastry board. Shape into a long roll and slice into flat lengthwise strips. Cut again into slim ribbon-like strips. Fry in hot butter 10 or 12 minutes, or until noodles are golden brown on all sides.

VARIATION

To make Potato Patties (Kartoffelkücherl) prepare the same dough and shape into a roll about the thickness of a cucumber. Cut round slices, each about ½″ to ¾″ thick. Fry in hot butter, turning once so they become golden on both sides.

✂ / HOT POTATO SALAD WITH BACON (*Warmer Kartoffelsalat mit Speck*)

6 TO 8 SERVINGS

6 to 8 boiling potatoes	½ to ¾ cup vinegar
water to cover	½ to ¾ cup beef stock
salt	salt and white pepper
¼ pound bacon, diced	sour cream, optional
1 onion, minced	minced parsley

Boil potatoes in their jackets in lightly salted water to cover. Do not overcook or potatoes will fall apart in salad. Peel while hot and cut in thin slices. Fry bacon in a saucepan and when golden but not yet brown or crisp, add onions. Sauté slowly until onions become transparent but not golden. Remove from heat and carefully pour in combined vinegar and stock. Do this carefully so the liquid does not cause the hot fat to splutter. Bring to a boil and pour over sliced potatoes. Using a wooden spatula, gently lift potatoes a little so dressing runs over them evenly. Fold in a couple tablespoons of sour cream if you like, or serve without it. Sprinkle with minced parsley.

/ *COLD POTATO SALAD* (*Kalter Kartoffelsalat*)

6 TO 8 SERVINGS

6 to 8 boiling potatoes
water to cover
salt
1 medium onion, minced
1¼ cups beef stock
5 to 6 tablespoons white vinegar
4 to 5 tablespoons salad oil
prepared mustard (optional)
white pepper
½ cup mayonnaise or sour cream (optional)

Cook unpeeled potatoes in boiling salted water to cover. Do not overcook or they will fall apart in salad. Peel while hot and slice thinly. Place in bowl and add minced onion. Bring beef stock to a boil with a little salt and the vinegar. Pour over potatoes and marinate until almost all liquid is absorbed, about 20 to 30 minutes. Pour excess liquid off and gently fold in oil, mixed with mustard if you want to use it. Flavor with pepper. Cool salad slightly and serve as is, or fold in mayonnaise or sour cream. Usually it appears without either.

VARIATIONS

All kinds of interesting things flavor this salad in Germany. You may add more vinegar, or you can use dry white wine throughout instead of vinegar. Minced green herbs are often added—especially parsley and chives—and so are chopped cucumber, diced peeled apple or diced cooked knob celery. Leftover meats can be chopped or slivered, as can any kind of smoked ham, tongue or wurst. Chopped anchovies or salt herring, or dill pickle, is sometimes added.

✕ NOODLES (Nudeln) ✕

Noodles and noodle "dough-wares" (Teigwaren) are served often everywhere in Germany and most especially in Swabia. Generally they are boiled, drained and mixed with melted butter or bacon fat. They are seasoned with salt, pepper or nutmeg, paprika and poppy seeds, minced dill or parsley, crumbled cooked bacon or diced cooked ham, or a little sautéed minced onion or celery. The seasoning added depends upon the food that will be served with the noodles. Some more unusual additions are brown butter, buttered breadcrumbs, and cottage or pot cheese either of which may or may not be thinned down with a little sour cream.

Thin noodles are among the preferred garnishes for chicken, veal or beef soup; noodles, wide or thin, are molded into rings to be filled with suitable stews, generally those that are seasoned with paprika.

Sweet noodle puddings or soufflés are equally popular for desserts and entrees, or as side dishes with meats such as tongue in raisin sauce or roast pork; and cold leftover noodles are mixed into nutmeg-flavored omelettes by frugal German housewives.

If you would like to make your own noodles for the recipes that follow, the recipe for the dough is on page 58. Otherwise use any good brand of packaged egg noodles that are available in several widths.

✂ / NOODLE SOUFFLÉ (Nudelauflauf)

This soufflé is usually served as a hot dessert after a light first course. When served with coffee it is a very good replacement for cake, and it is a delightful entree when you have guests in for a late Sunday breakfast in winter.

4 TO 6 SERVINGS

3 cups milk
2 teaspoons salt
strip of lemon peel

½ pound wide or narrow egg
noodles
4 tablespoons butter

½ *cup sugar*
3 *egg yolks*
½ *cup raisins soaked in a little*
   rum
½ *cup chopped pecans, walnuts*
   or almonds (optional)

dash of cinnamon or vanilla to
   taste
grated rind of ½ *lemon*
3 *egg whites, stiffly beaten*
butter

Heat milk with salt and lemon peel. When it boils, add noodles, cover and simmer steadily until tender but firm. Set pot in a sink or pan filled with cold water and keep there until noodles and milk are cool. Milk will thicken and should be almost completely absorbed by the time the mass has cooled. Cream butter and sugar until light and fluffy. Add egg yolks, one at a time, beating well between each addition. Add to the cooled noodle-milk mixture. Mix in raisins, which were soaked and drained, and nuts if you are using them, cinnamon or vanilla or both, according to your taste, grated lemon rind and a little more salt or sugar if you think either is needed. Beat egg whites to a very stiff snow and fold gently into mixture, using a rubber spatula and working quickly so that egg whites do not lose their airiness. Turn into a 2-quart soufflé dish that has been well buttered on the sides and bottom. (The baking dish may also be sprinkled lightly with sugar or breadcrumbs after it has been buttered if you like a stiff crust around the soufflé.) Bake in 375° oven 45 to 50 minutes, or until top is a deep golden brown and filling is set but slightly custardy.

VARIATIONS

To make Apple-Noodle Soufflé, or Cherry-Noodle Soufflé, add ¾ to 1 cup peeled, cubed apples, or stoned, halved cherries to the noodle mixture. Roll fruit lightly in a little flour before adding it. Nuts and raisins may be used or eliminated.

❧ / *MACARONI OR NOODLES WITH HAM AND MUSHROOMS* (*Makkaroni oder Nudeln mit Schinken und Champignons*)

4 SERVINGS

1 *pound elbow macaroni, or 1*
   pound spaghetti broken into
   small pieces, or 1 pound
   wide noodles
water

1 *tablespoon salt*
½ *pound cooked ham, minced*
   (approximately)
½ *pound sliced mushrooms,*
   sautéed in butter

salt to taste
nutmeg
¾ cup sour cream

2 eggs, lightly beaten
buttered breadcrumbs
grated parmesan cheese

Cook macaroni or noodles in rapidly boiling well-salted water and drain through a colander. Toss minced ham and lightly sautéed mushroom slices into noodles; add a little more salt if necessary and a generous pinch of nutmeg. Mix sour cream and beaten eggs together and stir through mixture. Butter a 2-quart baking dish and sprinkle with breadcrumbs on all sides. Turn mixture into baking dish and sprinkle generously on top with buttered breadcrumbs and grated cheese. Bake in 400° oven 10 or 15 minutes, or until topping is nicely browned and the cream and eggs are set.

VARIATIONS

1. You can use just ham *or* mushrooms.
2. Any cooked-meat leftovers can be substituted for the ham; smoked tongue is especially good.
3. Minced dill is a very pleasant addition, but if you use it, eliminate nutmeg.
4. This same dish can be made with macaroni or noodles alone, without any meat or mushrooms. In this case, add some grated cheese to the macaroni mixture; sweet cream may replace sour cream if you prefer it.

✂ / BAVARIAN TOMATO SPAGHETTI (*Bayrische Tomatenspaghetti*)

4 TO 6 SERVINGS

1 pound spaghetti
water
1 tablespoon salt
1 tablespoon butter or bacon fat
1 small onion, finely minced

1 small can seasoned tomato sauce
3 to 4 tablespoons grated Parmesan cheese
1 to 2 tablespoons minced parsley

Cook spaghetti in rapidly boiling salted water and drain well through a colander. Heat butter or bacon fat in a skillet and in it sauté minced onion until it softens and begins to take on color. Add tomato sauce and simmer 7 or 8 minutes, uncovered, until sauce thickens a little. Pour sauce over hot drained spaghetti, season to taste with more salt and half of the grated cheese. Sprinkle the rest of the cheese and the minced parsley on top of spaghetti when it is in the serving dish.

✖ RICE (Reis) ✖

Rice is often served in Germany, either steamed or boiled, and always very dry and fluffy. Whichever way it is cooked, it is drained and set to dry in a warm oven for a few minutes. It is then seasoned with a generous lump of butter, salt, pepper or nutmeg, sometimes with grated cheese or capers, minced parsley or sautéed mushroom slices; very often a little well-seasoned tomato sauce is stirred into it just before it is served. Some cooks prefer to sauté the rice in a little hot butter until the grains become glassy, at which point they pour in some hot water or stock, add a small onion studded with 3 or 4 cloves, cover the pot and let the rice simmer slowly until it is tender. (Rice should never be stirred while it is cooking or it will become mushy.)

Italian risotto (called, in German, Risotto or Gedünsteter Reis) is very often served, and rice rings filled with some sort of stew or gravy and meat dish appear on all restaurant menus. Rice is a favorite addition to chicken and beef broths and is also the basis for some of the country's most tempting and famous desserts, hot as well as cold.

✄ / RICE RING (Reisrand)

4 TO 6 SERVINGS

5 cups water	salt
2 cups converted long-grain rice	nutmeg or pepper to taste
2 teaspoons salt	minced parsley (optional)
2 tablespoons butter	melted butter or olive oil

Boil water in a saucepan, then add rice and salt. Cook according to instructions on package. This will give about 5 cups of cooked rice, which is what you will need to fill the mold. When rice is tender, dry and fluffy, toss in butter with a fork, add salt if needed and nutmeg or pepper to taste. Toss in minced parsley if you want to use it. Coat inside of a 8″ ring mold with melted butter or olive oil. Be sure that all sides are well greased. Pack hot cooked rice into mold, pressing it firmly into place with the back of a tablespoon. Set in a warm place for 8 to 10 minutes. (I have found the most effective way of doing this is to heat the oven to 250°, turn off the heat, place the rice-filled mold in oven and leave door open for the 8 or 10 minutes.) Invert mold on a serving plate and lift mold off rice.

⬛ / CURRY RICE (*Curryreis*)

4 SERVINGS

1 *tablespoon butter*	1 *teaspoon curry powder*
2 *tablespoons minced onion*	2 *to 3 cups hot chicken broth,*
1 *cup converted rice*	*well seasoned*

Melt butter in a 1-quart saucepan that has a cover. Sauté onion in butter until it softens and turns pale yellow. Add rice and curry powder. Toss together and sauté slowly for about 5 minutes. Add 2 cups hot chicken broth, bring to a boil, cover, reduce heat and simmer slowly for 20 to 25 minutes, or until tender. Do not let rice overcook or it will become pasty. Add more of the hot stock as needed during cooking. The stock should be absorbed by the time the rice is done.

⬛ / RICE PANCAKES (*Reispfannkuchen*)

4 SERVINGS

1 *cup converted long-grain rice*	4 *egg yolks*
2½ *cups milk*	2 *tablespoons sugar*
salt	*(approximately)*
1 *tablespoon butter*	2 *tablespoons cracker meal*
1 *small stick cinnamon, or* ½	*(approximately)*
teaspoon vanilla	4 *egg whites, stiffly beaten*
strip of lemon peel	*butter*
½ *cup raisins*	*breadcrumbs*
½ *cup chopped pecans,*	
walnuts or almonds	
(optional)	

Cook rice in boiling milk to which was added a dash of salt, butter, cinnamon or vanilla and a strip of lemon peel. When rice is tender, add raisins and nuts; let mixture stand until slightly cooled. Beat 4 egg yolks into rice mixture along with sugar to taste and enough cracker meal to give consistency of thick cottage cheese. Fold in beaten egg whites. Melt butter in a skillet and sprinkle bottom of pan with a thin layer of breadcrumbs. Batter may be poured in by tablespoonfuls to make small pancakes, or all at once to make a single large pancake. Fry slowly until golden brown on underside. Sprinkle top side with breadcrumbs; turn and brown second side. Sprinkle with fine granulated sugar and a little cinnamon.

XIII

Sauces

(Sossen)

✠ ✠ ✠ ✠ ✠

Anyone who is trying to avoid sauces and gravies will certainly have his work cut out for him in Germany. Hardly any fish, meat or vegetable dish comes to the table without this final embellishment, and, as a rule, these sauces are as hearty and substantial as the rest of that country's fare. As in all Europe, it is considered very bad form (downright sinful, in fact) to leave any sauce on the plate; the wide array of dumplings, potato and noodle dishes and breads are used to absorb every last drop of these velvety concoctions.

Cold fish, meats and salads are always accompanied by some version of mayonnaise or a vinaigrette dressing; whipped cream is often folded into the former, sweet or sour cream into the latter. Hot and cold fruit or wine sauces, piquant dressings flavored with capers or caraway, anchovies or herring, sauces made with bacon and others spiked with beer, all are popular throughout the country. The most typically German of all are sweet-and-sour sauces, a tantalizing interplay of contrasting flavors arrived at through the judicious use of sugar, lemon juice, vinegar or the pickling liquid of sweet gherkins. Many sauces included here, such as the basic white and brown, hollandaise, béarnaise, tomato, remoulade, mayonnaise, etc., are, of course, the standard European classics. But since they are always found on German menus, and since many of them are changed in some way to make them more suited to the German palate, this book would be incomplete without them.

Most German sauces resemble what we think of as gravies, and are thickened and enriched with flour, egg yolks and sweet or sour cream. They are usually quite a bit thicker than those we are used to, and I have adjusted the recipes slightly with that in mind. If you find they are still too thick to suit you, increase the amount of liquid called for, or decrease the flour. If you use 1 cup of liquid, 1 tablespoon of butter and 1 tablespoon of flour, you will have a thin sauce; 1½ to 2 tablespoons of each make a medium sauce; 3 tablespoons of each result in a thick sauce.

A wire whisk is the most practical utensil you can have for making sauces that are smooth and free of lumps. Always use a saucepan large enough to allow room for beating without having the sauce spill over the sides. A 6-cup (1½ quarts) saucepan is a good size for making 2 to 3 cups of sauce. Use a heavy-bottom saucepan to prevent scorching, preferably one made of porcelain, enameled cast iron or tin-lined copper. Aluminum or uncoated iron will darken or discolor sauces that have egg yolks, wine or vinegar in them; this is especially true when making white sauces but it is best to abide by this rule for any sauces you might make.

Let the flour sauté in the fat for close to 5 minutes so it will not have a raw flavor when added to the sauce. Do this over a very low heat, stirring constantly; remove pan from heat once in a while to prevent burning. Hot sauces generally taste better if a little extra butter is melted into them just before serving. Sour cream, lemon juice, vinegar, wine and horseradish should be stirred into the sauce for the last few minutes of cooking time, and should not be boiled. Add fresh herbs after sauce is finished cooking, just before serving.

Any of the sauces here that do not have egg yolk in them can be made in advance and reheated before serving. If you make a sauce an hour or two before serving time, you can simply leave it at room temperature. Reheat slowly over a low flame or in the top of a double boiler. If you want to make a sauce the night before you will serve it, store it in the refrigerator and reheat slowly. A reheated sauce may need a little seasoning added, or additional liquid to thin it down. If a sauce is to have egg yolk added to it, and if it must be made in advance, add the egg yolk after it has been reheated, beating it in as described for Variation 2 in the White Sauce recipe on page 331.

Sweet dessert sauces are not included in this chapter. They can be found in the one that follows, on pages 402 through 408.

✕ HOT SAUCES ✕
(*Warme Sossen*)

❈ / *MELTED BUTTER* (*Zerlassene Butter*)

This is about the only clear "sauce" I ever came across in Germany, except when an occasional slice of roast meat was served in its own pan juices. Hot melted butter is most often served on fish or vegetables and it may be flavored with minced parsley, chives or other herbs, a dab of prepared mustard or some anchovy paste and a dash of lemon juice.

Brown Butter (Braune Butter) is also served very often on steamed or sautéed fish, or with such vegetables as steamed asparagus, cauliflower, spinach and Brussels sprouts. Brown butter slowly over very low heat, or it will burn and blacken. Capers, with or without a dash of lemon juice, are often added.

❈ / *THE EINBRENNE*

This is the basis of almost every German sauce and is used also as thickening for soups and vegetable cooking liquids. It is exactly what the French call a roux. Flour and fat (usually butter) are blended together, cooked and then mixed with the liquid that is to be thickened. When butter and flour are sautéed to a very pale yellow, the result is a white or light (weisse or helle) sauce; when it is done to a medium tan color it is a medium brown (mittelfarbene) sauce; when it is browned to a deep cocoa color and brown stock is added, it is a dark (braune or dunkle) sauce.

The feature that makes this classic roux taste typically German, however, is the use of finely minced onion sautéed with the butter and flour. If it is a light sauce, the onion is added to the hot butter, sautéed until pale yellow and then the flour is sprinkled in. If it is a dark sauce, the onion is usually added when the flour is half brown so it will not blacken and taste bitter. Though in northern Germany one finds these sauces made without onion fairly often, it is practically unthinkable in Bavaria and in most of southern Germany to make an Einbrenne without it.

✂ / *WHITE SAUCE* (*Helle Sosse*)

2 CUPS

4 tablespoons butter
1 small onion, finely minced
4 tablespoons flour
2 cups cold milk or white stock,
    or 1 cup each (depending

upon the food to be served
    with the sauce)
salt and black or cayenne
    pepper to taste

Melt butter in a 6-cup saucepan. When hot, add minced onion and sauté, very slowly, stirring constantly, until onion is soft and pale yellow. Sprinkle flour into butter, stir and sauté, slowly, about 5 minutes, or until flour begins to take on a pale yellow color. If it seems to fry too rapidly, remove pan from heat for a few seconds. Pour in cold milk or stock, beating sauce with a wire whisk until smooth and well blended. Cover and simmer over low heat 10 minutes. Season to taste before serving.

VARIATIONS

1. Onion may be omitted if you think its flavor will spoil the food to be served with the sauce.
2. To make an especially rich and luxurious sauce, thicken sauce with egg yolks. Beat 2 yolks into ½ cup cold heavy sweet cream and gradually stir into this about ½ cup of hot white sauce. When blended, turn back into saucepan with rest of sauce. Heat for a few seconds but do not boil. Check seasoning and serve.
3. A dash of lemon juice or dry white wine and 1 tablespoon drained capers improve this sauce greatly, and are quite a good touch if it is to be served with a fish, chicken or veal dish.

✂ / *MEDIUM BROWN SAUCE* (*Mittelfarbene Sosse*)

Follow recipe for White Sauce (above), but sauté onion until it begins to take on a light golden-brown color. Add flour and sauté slowly until it turns cocoa tan. Use white or brown stock, not milk, as the liquid. This sauce is often flavored with 1 tablespoon well-drained capers, white wine, lemon juice and sugar.

✂ / BROWN SAUCE (*Dunkle Sosse*)

2 CUPS

4 *tablespoons butter*
4 *tablespoons flour*
1 *small onion, finely minced*

2 *cups cold brown stock*
salt to taste

Melt butter in a 6-cup saucepan and in it sauté flour slowly, stirring constantly until it begins to brown. Add finely minced onion, sauté a few seconds until onion begins to brown and flour has become a deeper brown. Stir in cold stock all at once, beating with a wire whisk until smooth and well blended. Cover and simmer 30 minutes. Season to taste.

VARIATIONS

1. Crushed caraway seeds or 1 minced dill pickle and a dash of vinegar are often added just before serving. If pickle is used, also add a little sugar to taste.
2. Two or 3 tablespoons sweet cream and/or same amount of burgundy or madeira may be stirred in just before serving.

✂ / BROWN SAUCE WITH SUGAR (*Dunkle Sosse mit Zucker*)

2 CUPS

4 *tablespoons butter*
4 *tablespoons flour*
1 *tablespoon sugar*
2 *cups water, meat or vegetable stock*

1 *bay leaf*
4 *peppercorns*
salt to taste

Melt butter in a 6-cup saucepan and in it sauté flour slowly, stirring constantly until medium brown. Add sugar, sauté and stir until mixture is deep coffee color. Be very careful that sugar does not burn as this can happen very suddenly. Stir in cold water or stock, beating with a wire whisk until smooth and well blended. Add bay leaf, pepper-corns and salt to taste. Cover and simmer slowly 25 to 30 minutes. This is an excellent way to darken sauces made with the cooking liquid of stews and pot-roasted meats such as Sauerbraten.

❧ / *CHEESE SAUCE (Käsesosse)*

Follow recipe for White Sauce, page 331, using milk as the liquid. Stir in 2 generous tablespoons grated Gruyère or Parmesan cheese and heat (do not boil) a few seconds more. Cheese may be added in same way to a sauce thickened with egg yolks. Add cheese before egg yolks and cream have been stirred into hot sauce.

❧ / *WHITE ONION SAUCE (Helle Zwiebelsosse)*

Follow recipe for White Sauce, page 331, using 3 medium-sized onions finely minced. A dash of sugar may be added if necessary and a little extra cream just before serving. If you would like this to be an extra fine sauce, press it through a sieve and reheat before adding final dash of cream.

❧ / *BROWN ONION SAUCE (Dunkle Zwiebelsosse)*

Follow recipe for Brown Sauce, page 332, using 2 medium-sized onions finely minced. Just before serving, season with salt, sugar and a little vinegar and/or red wine. This can also be made using 3 tablespoons bacon fat instead of butter. It is then flavored with a dash of vinegar and served over boiled potatoes. If a little beer makes up part of cooking liquid, this becomes an excellent sauce for fried Bratwurst.

✖ / MUSTARD SAUCE (*Senfsosse*)

Follow recipe for White Sauce, page 331, using stock as the liquid. Add 2 tablespoons sharp German mustard to sauce for last 5 minutes of cooking time. Finish with a dab of butter. Serve with fish, asparagus or cauliflower.

✖ / BAVARIAN MUSTARD SAUCE (*Bayrische Senfsosse*)

Follow recipe for Medium Brown Sauce, page 331, and when it has simmered 10 minutes, add 1 tablespoon sharp German mustard, a dash of sugar and 1 small dill pickle, finely minced. Simmer 5 to 10 minutes more and finish off with a dash of apple wine and/or cream.

This is especially good with fried herring, as well as with pork or tongue.

✖ / HAM OR BACON SAUCE (*Schinken- oder Specksosse*)

Add ½ to ¾ cup cooked minced ham, or fried minced bacon to basic White Sauce, page 331, and simmer 5 minutes. Minced parsley can also be added just before serving. This is excellent with vegetables, chicken or potatoes.

✖ / TOMATO CREAM SAUCE (*Tomaten-Rahmsosse*)

Follow recipe for White Sauce, page 331, and simmer 10 minutes. Add 1 small can seasoned tomato sauce and simmer 15 minutes. Season with salt, sugar and a dash of lemon juice.

✂ / *MUSHROOM CREAM SAUCE* (*Champignonsosse*)

Follow recipe for White Sauce, page 331, and add ¼ pound mushrooms sliced and lightly sautéed in butter about 5 minutes. Simmer 20 minutes. This sauce may then be thickened with the egg-yolk-cream mixture and flavored with a dash of lemon juice after sauce has been removed from heat.

✂ / *BROWN MUSHROOM SAUCE* (*Dunkle Champignonsosse*)

Prepare Brown Sauce, page 332, and add to it ¼ pound mushrooms, sliced and lightly sautéed in butter 5 minutes. Simmer 15 minutes and season to taste with salt, a dab of butter and a little madeira.

✂ / *LOBSTER OR CRAB SAUCE* (*Hummer- oder Krabbensosse*)

Add 1 cup cooked, diced lobster meat or 1 cup crabmeat, cooked and picked-over, to basic White Sauce, page 331, and let it simmer. Season with a little madeira and 1 tablespoon paprika. Proceed to thicken with egg-yolk-cream mixture, if you want to. For a stronger shellfish flavor, the raw, diced crab or lobster meat can be cooked right in sauce, but in that case simmer for 15 minutes, or until shellfish meat is thoroughly cooked. Serve over steamed fish, boiled chicken, cauliflower or asparagus. This sauce can also be made with Crab Butter, page 135.

✂ / *HORSERADISH BREAD SAUCE* (*Semmelkren*)

2 *soft rolls or 4 slices white bread,*
  with crusts
2 *cups cold meat stock*
2 *tablespoons milk*

2 *tablespoons finely grated fresh*
  horseradish
1 *generous tablespoon butter*
salt to taste

Cut bread into small pieces and soak in cold stock until it falls apart completely. Cook over moderate heat and let it come to a boil; simmer 5 to 10 minutes, or until a smooth, thick sauce results. Stir in remaining ingredients and heat 2 or 3 minutes, but do not boil. Serve with boiled beef or tongue.

✃ / HORSERADISH SAUCE (*Meerrettichsosse*)

Follow recipe for White Sauce, page 331. Use beef stock and a little milk, adding to it grated pulp of ¼ fresh horseradish root. Stir through, heat but do not boil. Season with salt, sugar and/or lemon juice, if you think it necessary. A little heavy sweet cream can be swirled in just before serving. Serve with boiled beef, tongue or chicken.

✃ / ANCHOVY SAUCE (*Sardellensosse*)

Follow recipe for White Sauce, page 331, using stock instead of milk. Add 8 anchovy filets, rinsed in cold water and pounded to a paste. Simmer 5 minutes. A dash of cream and lemon juice can be added before serving. This is a wonderful sauce with steamed fish, boiled potatoes or veal. It is also sometimes made with Medium Brown (page 331) instead of White Sauce. If you prefer this slightly stronger flavor and deeper color, sauté the Einbrenne until flour turns to light cocoa color. Add brown stock, simmer and add anchovy paste. Capers and lemon juice are often added, especially if sauce is to be served over roast veal.

✃ / GREEN OR DILL SAUCE (*Grüne Sosse oder Dillsosse*)

Follow recipe for White Sauce, page 331, and just before serving add 3 tablespoons finely minced fresh green herbs such as Italian parsley, chives or dill, or any combination of these.

/ *CURRY SAUCE* (*Currysosse*)

3 CUPS

- 4 *tablespoons butter*
- 1 *small onion, finely minced*
- 4 *tablespoons flour*
- 2 *medium-sized tart apples, peeled and diced*
- 1 *to* 1½ *teaspoons curry powder*
- 1 *cup hot stock (chicken, veal or beef, depending on the food to be served with the sauce)*
- 1 *scant cup hot milk*
- *salt to taste*
- 4 *tablespoons sour cream*
- 3 *to* 4 *tablespoons dry white wine*

Melt butter in a 6-cup saucepan and in it sauté onion slowly until soft and pale golden in color. Sprinkle flour into butter and sauté, stirring constantly over low heat, until flour is pale cocoa color. Add diced and peeled apples, sprinkle with curry powder and sauté together for 2 or 3 minutes. Stir in hot stock and milk. Cover and simmer slowly 15 to 20 minutes, or until apple is soft enough to mash. Strain sauce through a fine sieve and return to pan. Season to taste with salt, sour cream and white wine. Heat for a few seconds but do not boil. This is excellent with boiled chicken and rice, or with grilled pork or lamb chops.

/ *BEER HORSERADISH SAUCE* (*Bier-Meerrettich-Sosse*)

ABOUT 1½ CUPS

- 2 *tablespoons butter or bacon fat*
- 2 *tablespoons flour*
- 1 *cup dark or light beer (dark gives the sauce a richer flavor and better color)*
- 2 *tablespoons grated horseradish root*
- *salt, prepared sharp mustard, pepper to taste*
- 2 *egg yolks*
- ½ *cup water or sweet cream*
- *sweet cream or sour cream (optional)*

Melt butter in a 1-quart saucepan and in it sauté flour until medium brown. Gradually stir in cold beer, beating as you do so to keep sauce smooth. Simmer 10 minutes. Add grated horseradish, salt, mustard and pepper and mix well. Sauce may be kept hot over low heat, but do not let it boil again. Beat egg yolks into cold water or sweet cream. Add slowly about ½ cup of the hot sauce to egg-yolk mixture, and when blended, turn this back into rest of the sauce. Stir and heat, but do not boil. If you mixed egg yolks with water, sauce may be finished with a tablespoonful or two of sweet or sour cream. Well-drained bottled horseradish sauce can be used for this, but in that case do not add any cream and season with a little sugar.

❧ / POLISH RAISIN SAUCE (*Polnische Rosinensosse*)

2 TO 3 CUPS

2 tablespoons bacon fat	1 strip of lemon peel
2 tablespoons flour	1 bay leaf
2 cups cold beef stock	cinnamon, lemon juice or
½ cup grated stale gingerbread or gingersnap crumbs	vinegar, red wine
¼ cup raisins	salt and sugar to taste
1 small onion studded with 2 cloves	

Heat bacon fat in a 6-cup saucepan and in it sauté flour slowly, stirring constantly until it is deep coffee color. Gradually add cold beef stock, beating well between each addition with a wire whisk, so that sauce remains smooth. Stir in grated gingerbread or gingersnap crumbs; add raisins, onion studded with cloves, lemon peel and bay leaf and simmer very slowly 30 minutes. Season as suggested. Sauce should have a very even half-sweet, half-sour flavor.

VARIATIONS

1. You can also add about 18 or 20 blanched slivered almonds and 1 to 2 tablespoons red currant jelly.
2. If you would like to serve this sauce with steamed carp, use ½ cup beer and 1½ cups beef stock for cooking liquid. Season as suggested, including red wine and almonds.
3. If you use madeira as the wine seasoning, this becomes an excellent sauce for baked ham.

❧ / SWEET-AND-SOUR BACON SAUCE (*Specksosse, süss-saure*)

ABOUT 1 CUP

5 slices bacon, diced	1 cup water or stock
1 large onion, minced	3 cloves
4 tablespoons flour	salt, vinegar and sugar to taste

Fry bacon in a skillet until half cooked. Add minced onion and sauté slowly until bacon is brown and onion is deep golden. Remove bacon and onion and reserve. Sprinkle flour into bacon fat. Sauté slowly, stirring constantly, until mixture is light brown. Add cold water or stock, stirring constantly, so that sauce remains smooth. Return fried bacon and onion to sauce. Add cloves and simmer 20 minutes. Add salt to taste and season with vinegar and sugar until sauce has an even half-sweet, half-sour flavor. Serve over poached or hard-cooked eggs, or over string beans.

VARIATIONS

Add ½ cup raisins to sauce and serve over boiled tongue, steamed or stuffed cabbage.

✲ / DRIED MUSHROOM SAUCE (*Schwammerlsosse*)

ABOUT 1 CUP

½ ounce dried mushrooms
½ cup hot water
1½ cups water or beef stock
1½ tablespoons butter

1½ tablespoons flour
salt and pepper to taste
1 to 2 tablespoons sour cream
  (optional)

Soak mushrooms in ½ cup hot water 20 minutes. Drain water off and chop mushrooms. Cook slowly 25 minutes, or until tender, in water or beef stock. Melt butter in a 1-quart saucepan and in it sauté flour until medium brown. Add stock in which mushrooms were cooked, beating constantly to keep sauce smooth. Cook sauce with mushroom pieces 5 to 10 minutes and season to taste with salt and pepper. Stir in sour cream if desired, and heat 3 or 4 minutes, but do not boil.

✲ / LEMON SAUCE (*Zitronensosse*)

1½ TO 2 CUPS

rind of 1 large lemon
1½ cups water
3 tablespoons butter
3 tablespoons flour
lemon juice to taste
salt to taste

sugar to taste
white wine, optional and to
  taste
1 egg yolk
2 tablespoons sour cream

Using a very sharp paring knife, cut rind from lemon in paper-thin strips, taking none of the white zest along with the peel. Add to water, bring to a boil and simmer, covered, 10 minutes. Strain and reserve liquid. Heat butter in a 1-quart glass or enameled saucepan and when it is hot and bubbling, stir in flour. Sauté over low heat 3 or 4 minutes, or until flour just barely begins to take on color. Pour in strained stock and beat smooth over low heat with a wire whisk or wooden spoon. Simmer slowly about 5 minutes until sauce is smooth and thick. Flavor with lemon juice, salt and, if necessary, sugar. A little white wine can be added to taste. Beat egg yolk in sour cream and add gradually to hot, not boiling, sauce. Heat for a minute or two but do not boil. Serve over poached salmon or any steamed fish, or with boiled chicken.

⧱ / TOMATO SAUCE (*Tomatensosse*)

1½ CUPS

3 tablespoons butter or bacon fat
1 small onion, minced
2 tablespoons flour
2 tablespoons tomato paste, or ¾ cup unseasoned tomato purée, or 3 to 4 canned

tomatoes, well drained and chopped
1 cup water or stock
salt and pepper to taste
sugar, if needed

Heat butter in a 1-quart saucepan and when hot and bubbling, add onion. Sauté and stir over low heat until onion is soft and bright yellow but not brown. Stir in flour and sauté until flour begins to turn color, about 4 minutes. Stir in tomato paste, purée or tomatoes and water or stock. Beat with wire whisk or wooden spoon over low heat until sauce is smooth. Cover and simmer slowly 20 minutes, or until thickened. Season to taste with salt, pepper and, if needed, a little sugar. If canned tomatoes are used and you want a very smooth sauce, rub through a fine sieve after cooking and reheat.

NOTE

This sauce can be seasoned wtih thyme, marjoram, savory or garlic, depending on the food it is to complement.

❧ / HOT CURRANT SAUCE (*Warme Johannisbeerensosse*)

ABOUT 1 TO 1½ CUPS

2 tablespoons butter	4 tablespoons red currant jelly
2 tablespoons flour	port wine, salt and sugar to
1 cup water, stock or pan gravy	taste

Melt butter in a 1-quart saucepan and in it sauté flour until medium brown. Stir in cold water or stock, or cooled pan juices from a roast. Beat constantly as you add liquid so sauce becomes smooth. Simmer 10 minutes. Add red currant jelly and simmer 5 to 10 minutes, or until jelly has melted. Season with port wine, salt and sugar.

❧ / HOLLANDAISE SAUCE (*Holländische Sosse*)

1 CUP

¼ pound butter	salt and white pepper to taste
4 egg yolks	Worcestershire sauce, optional
1 to 2 teaspoons lemon juice	and to taste

Divide butter into 4 equal parts. Place egg yolks in top of a double boiler and add 1 portion of butter. Stir quickly and constantly, over hot but not boiling water, until butter is melted. Use a wire whisk or wooden spoon for beating. Add second portion of butter, and as it melts, the third, and so on, until all the butter has been melted and worked into egg yolks. The water in the lower part of the double boiler must never come to a boil and the mixture should be beaten or stirred constantly. Remove pan from hot water, beat for another minute or two and add lemon juice, salt and pepper. In Germany, a little Worcestershire sauce is often added to this sauce. Put pan back over the hot (but still not boiling) water. Heat and stir for another minute or two and serve. If sauce curdles as you are cooking it, add 1 or 2 tablespoons boiling water and beat until smooth. Always make this sauce just before it is to be served.

VARIATION

Fine Mustard Sauce (Feine Senfsosse) is made by stirring 1 tablespoon prepared sharp mustard into finished Hollandaise Sauce.

❖ / *BÉARNAISE SAUCE*

1½ CUPS

This is made like Hollandaise (above), except that herb-flavored vinegar is substituted for lemon juice. Prepare vinegar well ahead of time so that it will be cool before you start making the sauce. Simmer ½ cup wine vinegar with 1 tablespoon each minced shallots or scallions and tarragon and 2 peppercorns, slightly crushed. Simmer uncovered over low heat until vinegar is reduced to about 2 tablespoons. Strain and cool. Beat cooled, flavored vinegar into 3 egg yolks and using ½ pound butter, proceed with recipe. A sprinkling of chopped tarragon and/or parsley can be added before serving. If you do not have fresh herbs, use half the amount dried. If you cannot get fresh *or* dried tarragon, use tarragon vinegar and simmer it down with the minced shallots.

❖ / *HOT BACON DRESSING* (*Warme Specksosse*)

    6 *slices bacon, diced*   ½ *teaspoon salt*
    ¼ *cup vinegar, or to taste*   ¼ *teaspoon pepper*
    1½ *tablespoons sugar, or to taste*

Fry diced bacon slowly in a skillet until crisp. Do not drain off fat. Add vinegar, sugar, salt and pepper, heat to boiling point and stir constantly. Check seasoning and add a little more sugar, vinegar or salt as needed. Pour while hot over warm cooked string beans or warm sliced boiled potatoes. This amount of dressing is enough for a salad of 1 pound potatoes, or 1 pound string beans. Never chill this dressing, as the bacon fat will solidify.

COLD SAUCES AND SALAD DRESSINGS
(*Kalte Sossen und Salatsossen*)

❧ / *MAYONNAISE*

Although mayonnaise is thought to be a very tricky thing to make, it is actually quite easy to do successfully if just a few simple basic rules are remembered. The oil and egg yolk should not be colder than room temperature, and both should be as nearly as possible of the same temperature. Take eggs out of refrigerator, separate yolks and place in a bowl 20 to 30 minutes before using them. If oil is very cold, set bottle in warm water until chill is off. Do not use more oil than egg yolks can absorb—½ to ¾ cup of oil is all you should try to beat into a single egg yolk. Do not add too much oil at once, especially in the beginning. If you want to store mayonnaise in refrigerator, beat in 1 to 2 tablespoons boiling water after it has been made. If mayonnaise should curdle (the egg yolk and oil separate), drop a fresh egg yolk into a warm bowl, beat lightly with a little salt and a drop of vinegar or lemon juice, and then gradually beat in the curdled mayonnaise.

ABOUT 1½ CUPS

2 *egg yolks*
½ *teaspoon salt*
pinch of white pepper
½ *teaspoon dry mustard*
1 *to 2 teaspoons lemon juice or vinegar*

1 *to 1½ cups olive oil or salad oil, or a combination of both*
2 *tablespoons lemon juice or vinegar*
1 *to 2 tablespoons hot water*

Rinse a large porcelain, glass or stainless-steel mixing bowl in hot water and dry thoroughly. Drop egg yolks in, add salt, pepper, mustard and a little lemon juice or vinegar and beat well. Using a bottle or any narrow-necked pourer, or a teaspoon, drop oil very, very slowly into egg mixture, beating with a wire whisk between each addition. Do not add more oil before the previous addition is absorbed. Add a little lemon juice or vinegar from time to time to keep mixture workable. When dressing has reached consistency of sour cream, add oil in a thin stream, beating as you do, until desired consistency is reached. Continue adding lemon juice or vinegar to taste. Check for seasoning, and if you plan to store mayonnaise, beat in hot water.

VARIATIONS

The list of flavorings used in mayonnaise in Germany is almost endless. Holsteiner Mayonnaise is mixed with 1 cup slightly sweetened whipped cream and then flavored with a dash of lemon juice and tomato ketchup. Mayonnaise "Alter Schwede," Old Swede, is mixed with about 4 tablespoons thick applesauce and a teaspoonful grated horseradish, and is then served with cold boiled beef, roast pork or herring filets. Some mayonnaise is spiked with a little orange juice; others are mixed with crushed, drained canned pineapple, and one is mixed with some mashed banana and lemon juice. Mayonnaise flavored with fruits or chopped nuts is served with cold poultry, game dishes or fruit salads, while mayonnaise flavored with a little anchovy paste, some minced chives and capers is a favorite with hard-cooked eggs or cold chicken slices. All amounts given here are meant to be used with the amount of mayonnaise made by following the basic recipe on the preceding page—about 1½ cups.

▓ / *POT CHEESE MAYONNAISE* (*Topfen Mayonnaise*)

2½ TO 3 CUPS

1 cup pot cheese (or cottage cheese, well drained)
1½ cups mayonnaise
salt and pepper to taste

anchovy paste, ketchup, capers, minced chives, parsley to taste

Rub pot cheese or very well-drained cottage cheese through a fine sieve and mix through with prepared mayonnaise. Season to taste with salt and pepper. Serve as sandwich or canapé spread or with fruit salads, hard-cooked eggs or cold tongue. Season, if you like, with one or more of the final ingredients suggested.

/ *REMOULADE SAUCE* (*Remouladensosse*)

ABOUT 1½ CUPS

- 1½ *cups mayonnaise, page 343*
- ½ *small onion, finely minced*
- 1 *tablespoon finely minced parsley*
- 2 *tablespoons capers, finely chopped*
- 1 *mashed anchovy filet (optional)*
- *salt, pepper, prepared mustard to taste*
- 2 *small sour gherkins, finely chopped*
- 1 *tablespoon mixed green herbs —chervil, tarragon, parsley, chives*

Mix mayonnaise with all ingredients listed. Season to taste, adding salt, pepper or mustard if needed.

VARIATION

A mashed hard-cooked egg yolk is often mixed into the mayonnaise with the rest of the ingredients.

/ *RAW-VEGETABLE MARINADE* (*Rohe-Salat-Marinade*)

ABOUT ½ CUP

- 2 *to 3 tablespoons white vinegar, wine vinegar or lemon juice*
- ½ *teaspoon salt, or to taste*
- *pinch of sugar, or to taste*
- 1 *tablespoon finely minced onion*
- *one or more green herbs, such as borage, chives, chervil, dill, tarragon or parsley, to taste*
- 2 *to 3 tablespoons olive oil or salad oil, or 4 to 6 tablespoons sour cream or yogurt for salads of raw root vegetables such as beets, carrots, knob celery, etc.*

Combine all ingredients except oil or yogurt and shake well in a bottle or mix in a bowl. Pour over prepared raw vegetables and let stand at room temperature about 15 minutes. Add oil, yogurt or cream and toss into salad lightly. Chill, check seasoning and serve. When green salads are prepared, the oil is usually tossed in before the rest of the marinade.

VARIATIONS

1. When marinade is prepared with oil, some mayonnaise is often mixed with the salad after it has marinated.
2. Melted butter or bacon fat (both warm but not hot) are sometimes substituted for oil.

✺ / COOKED-VEGETABLE MARINADE (*Gekochte-Salat-Marinade*)

ABOUT 1 CUP

4 to 6 tablespoons white or wine vinegar or lemon juice
½ teaspoon salt, or to taste
pinch of sugar, or to taste
½ to 1 cup vegetable or white meat stock

1 tablespoon minced onion
one or more green herbs, such as borage, chives, chervil, dill, tarragon or parsley, to taste
3 to 4 tablespoons olive or salad oil

Combine all ingredients except oil and shake well in a bottle or mix in a bowl. Pour over hot cooked vegetables and let stand at room temperature 15 minutes, unless otherwise stated in specific recipes. Add oil, toss lightly through salad and again let stand at room temperature about 30 minutes.

✺ / VINAIGRETTE HERB DRESSING (*Vinaigrette-Kräutersosse*)

ABOUT 1 CUP

6 tablespoons olive oil or salad oil
2 tablespoons vinegar
2 tablespoons dry white wine
1 tablespoon prepared mustard
½ small onion, minced
2 small gherkins, drained and and chopped

1 tablespoon capers, drained and chopped
2 hard-cooked eggs, finely chopped
salt to taste
1 tablespoon minced parsley

Combine oil, vinegar, wine and mustard in a bottle and shake vigorously until well blended. Or place in a bowl and beat well. Combine onion, gherkins, capers and hard-cooked egg in a bowl and pour dressing over them. Season with salt and stir in parsley. Chill slightly.

/ *HORSERADISH* (*Meerrettich*)

Horseradish is one of the favorite flavorings for hot and cold sauces throughout Germany. It is popular with meats, poultry and fish dishes. Usually fresh horseradish root is used. It must be peeled and grated and as it is very tough, it requires a very sharp steel grater. It can also be grated in an electric blender after it has been peeled and cut into small pieces. As horseradish blackens quickly, it should be cut with a stainless-steel knife and sprinkled with lemon juice or vinegar, or stirred into a sauce as soon as possible after being grated. Grate near an open window, as horseradish is very peppery.

Bottled prepared horseradish-vinegar sauce is a substitute for the freshly grated root in some cases. It has been suggested in those recipes where it is usable, but should always be pressed free of excess vinegar. No additional vinegar is needed when the bottled sauce is used, and you may have to use a little extra sugar.

/ *VINEGAR HORSERADISH* (*Essigkren*)

This is a homemade version of what you usually buy bottled; once you've tried it, you'll probably never revert to the store-bought version.

6 tablespoons finely grated fresh horseradish
white vinegar, as needed
salt to taste
sugar to taste
stock, if needed

(If the horseradish is unusually strong and you want it milder, grate and rinse with hot stock; drain well and proceed.) Place grated horseradish in a bowl and add vinegar, a tablespoon at a time, until mixture reaches consistency of bottled horseradish sauce. Flavor to taste by adding salt and sugar, a little at a time. Stir and taste between additions. Chill well before serving. If kept in a tightly closed bottle or jar, this will keep for weeks in the refrigerator.

⚡ / APPLE HORSERADISH (*Apfelmeerrettich*)

2 apples, peeled and grated
½ horseradish root, peeled and
    grated

lemon juice, salt and sugar to
taste

Grate apple and horseradish, toss together and sprinkle with lemon juice so they will not darken. Season with salt and more lemon juice and sugar, until sauce has an even half-sweet, half-sour taste. It should be the consistency of thick bottled horseradish sauce. If bottled horseradish is used, use 6 tablespoons for 2 apples, but be sure excess moisure has been pressed out. Use no lemon juice and season with salt and sugar.

⚡ / LEMON HORSERADISH (*Zitronenmeerrettich*)

½ horseradish root, peeled and
    grated
grated peel of 1 lemon

lemon juice, salt and sugar to
taste

Toss grated horseradish and lemon peel together and season with lemon juice, salt and sugar until sauce has an even half-sweet, half-sour taste. If you use bottled horseradish, press out excess moisture and mix with grated lemon peel, but no lemon juice.

⚡ / HORSERADISH WHIPPED CREAM (*Meerrettich-Schlagrahm*)

ABOUT 1 CUP

1 cup heavy cream, stiffly
    whipped
1 tablespoon lemon juice
½ horseradish root, peeled and

grated (about 3 to 4 table-
spoons)
salt, white pepper and sugar to
taste

Whip cream until stiff and stir in lemon juice. When mixture is consistency of thick sour cream, grate in horseradish. Season with salt, white pepper and sugar. Serve with hot or cold boiled beef, poultry or steamed fish. If using bottled horseradish, press out moisture and omit lemon juice.

VARIATION

Frozen Cream Horseradish is served in Schleswig-Holstein and, just across that border, in Denmark. Prepare as described, then freeze in ice-cube tray of refrigerator. Just before serving, scoop the sherbet-like mixture into a chilled sauce boat.

✠ / *CUMBERLAND SAUCE* (*Cumberlandsosse*)

1 SCANT CUP

peel of 1 orange
peel of 1 lemon
juice of 1 orange
juice of ½ lemon
5 *tablespoons red currant jelly*
pinch each cayenne pepper and ginger
5 *tablespoons port, madeira or dry red wine*
2 *teaspoons prepared sharp mustard*
sugar to taste

The peel of the orange and lemon should be cut from fruit in paper-thin shavings and these should be cut again into the thinnest possible julienne slices. Blanch cut peel in boiling water 5 minutes to remove bitter oils, then drain. Combine strained juice of orange and lemon with the blanched fruit peel. Melt currant jelly over some hot water and mix with citrus peel and juice, cayenne pepper and ginger, wine and mustard. Season with sugar. Beat well and chill thoroughly. Serve with roasted game and ham.

VARIATION

This sauce is sometimes made thicker and sharper by adding 1 tablespoon freshly grated horseradish. In that case, use dry red wine and only half the amounts of orange and lemon juice. Omit cayenne pepper and ginger.

✿ / JUNIPER-MUSTARD GAME SAUCE (Wacholdbeeren-Senf Wildsosse)

3/4 TO 1 CUP

3 hard-cooked egg yolks
1 tablespoon prepared sharp
   mustard
½ cup olive oil or salad oil

1 tablespoon vinegar
10 juniper berries, finely crushed
   salt and pepper to taste

Rub hard-cooked egg yolks through a sieve. Blend with prepared mustard and gradually stir in oil and vinegar alternately, beating well between each addition to keep the sauce smooth. Stir in crushed juniper berries and season with salt and pepper. This sauce has a sharper, richer flavor if it is made 5 to 10 hours before it is to be used. If made a day or two in advance, check seasoning to see if it has become too sharp, in which case beat in a little more oil and another sieved hard-cooked egg yolk.

✿ / MUSTARD DILL SAUCE (Senf-Dillsosse)

Follow above recipe, but substitute lemon juice for vinegar, omit juniper berries and season with ½ tablespoon minced fresh dill. Serve with herring or smoked fish.

✿ / PREISELBEEREN

Although most of the fruit compotes are served as condiment sauces with meat courses in Germany, I have included them in the following chapter on desserts. However, this one is strictly a condiment sauce, and so seems more logical here.

This is far and away the most popular fruit sauce in Germany and is almost always served with game, pork, turkey, etc. Preiselbeeren are smaller, darker cousins of our cranberry, and though they can sometimes be found fresh in this country, they are scarce and expensive.

On the other hand, excellent preserved Preiselbeeren compotes, jams and conserves are available in jars and crocks, both in German markets and in gourmet food shops. Swedish lingonberries are an almost exact substitute, if they are easier to get. Use the preserves as they are or mix with a little lemon and/or orange juice. If you like, they can be melted slightly over hot water, seasoned with white wine and/or the fruit juices and rechilled.

XIV

Desserts

(Süsspeisen, oder Nachspeisen)

☒ ☒ ☒ ☒ ☒

Whether you call them sweet foods (Süsspeisen) or after foods (Nach-speisen), anyone must pronounce German desserts as rich, luscious and completely irresistible. In Germany, the most interesting desserts appear in homes rather than in restaurants, the latter relying mainly on the ice cream concoctions, stewed fruits and such international regulars as Crepes Suzette and Baked Alaska.

In addition to the desserts here, all sorts of fruits and flavorings, such as coffee, chocolate, pumpernickel crumbs, cinnamon and grated lemon rind, rum and citron, are often whipped into cottage cheese, chilled and served. Flavored whipped creams, frozen or half frozen, are also favorites. The most persistent flavors in German desserts are of apples, cherries, macaroons, pumpernickel crumbs, rum, arrack, vanilla and lemon rind, and almost everything ends up in a cloud of whipped cream. If there seems to be a great many rice and apple desserts here, it's because there are so many in Germany.

Two related types of desserts that are very popular in Germany are the gelatins (Süsse Sülze oder Gelee) and the puddings or flummeries (Flammeri oder Grütze). Both consist of such liquids as fruit juice, wine, milk or buttermilk with various flavorings. The first type is set with unflavored gelatin. The second is thickened with a starch such as potato flour, rice, farina or semolina, or cornstarch. The gelatins are very much like our packaged Jell-O desserts; the flummeries are closer to our packaged chocolate or vanilla puddings. Although you might not think these worth the effort, considering the final effect, you will find the homemade versions have a much richer flavor than the packaged variety. Packaged-gelatin and flummery desserts are, of course, used by German housewives when they are pressed for time. These German products are imported into this country and, I think, have a slight edge over our own in both flavor and texture. If you live near a German neighborhood and can get them, you might like to try them and decide for yourself.

Sometimes it is difficult to tell an entree from a dessert in Germany without a program—which in itself says something interesting about that country's eating habits and its national sweet tooth. And as you can see from the Index, there are many desserts elsewhere in this book.

✖ HOT DESSERTS ✖
(*Warme Süsspeisen*)

✖ / PUDDINGS AND SOUFFLÉS (*Puddinge und Aufläufe*)

By our standards, all of these desserts are more puddings than soufflés. Although all are lightened and raised by beaten egg white, they contain very heavy ingredients and do not have the airy, cloudlike quality we associate with soufflés. The real French soufflés, consisting mainly of a sauce base, flavoring or filling, and beaten egg white, are served in Germany and are called by their French names.

As for the Puddinge and Aufläufe, the main difference between them is in the method of cooking. A pudding is steamed in a covered mold. It should be buttered and may be sprinkled with sugar or crumbs, depending on the specific recipe. It should never be more than two-thirds full, as the pudding must have room to expand. Once covered, the mold should be set in a large pot of water (see page xxix). The water should come between halfway and two-thirds up the sides of the mold. The larger pot is then covered and the pudding steamed until it is completely set. The lid can be removed carefully during cooking so that the pudding can be tested. Let the pudding stand 5 minutes or so when it is done, and then invert it onto a serving platter. If you are serving sauce with it, pour a little over the pudding and the rest into a sauce boat. An Auflauf consists of the same ingredients as a pudding, but it is baked in a soufflé dish or comparable open baking dish. This may be set in a pan of water, depending on the specific recipe. To serve, simply spoon the pudding directly out of the baking dish and cover with sauce.

Usually, the same filling indicated for a pudding mold can be baked in a buttered soufflé dish that is then set in a pan half full of hot water. However, the molded pudding makes a far more festive appearance. To complicate things further, I must tell you that it is also possible to turn the filling into a buttered sugar- or crumb-sprinkled soufflé dish or porcelain pudding mold, and then to steam it in a covered pot half full of water, on the stove instead of in the oven. This will give a moist, light, unbrowned pudding.

It is best to serve any of the puddings after a light meal rather than a heavy one. They also make excellent and impressive replacements for cake, served with coffee. In Germany they are usually served after a one-pot main course, or a soup, or a platter of cold cuts.

⟨⟩ / RICE PUDDING OR SOUFFLÉ (*Reisauflauf*)

6 to 8 servings

¾ cup converted rice
water
3 cups milk
pinch of salt
strip of lemon peel
3½ tablespoons butter

4 egg yolks
⅓ cup sugar
⅓ cup raisins
4 egg whites, stiffly beaten
butter

Cover rice with water and cook 5 minutes. Drain and add rice to milk, along with salt, lemon peel and butter. Cover and cook very slowly in top of double boiler until rice kernels are tender but not so overcooked that they lose their shape, about 1 to 1½ hours. Cool when done. Beat egg yolks and sugar together until mixture is thick and pale yellow. Add, with raisins, to cooked rice mixture and stir through gently with a wooden spoon. Preheat oven to 350°. Beat egg whites to a stiff snow and fold into cold rice-egg-yolk mixture. Use a rubber spatula and fold whites in gently but thoroughly. Butter a 2-quart soufflé dish, or comparable baking dish, and turn rice into it. Dot generously with butter and bake about 45 minutes in preheated oven. When done, pudding should be fairly high, with the custard completely set; the top should be a light golden brown. Serve with Vanilla Sauce or Fruit Sauce, pages 402, 407.

VARIATIONS

1.   Apple-Rice Soufflé (Apfelreisauflauf): Peel, core and slice 1 pound cooking apples that are not too sour. Prepare rice. Turn half into baking dish, then add apples. Sprinkle with 2 tablespoons sugar, dot with butter and cover with remaining rice.
2.   A little powdered cinnamon, nutmeg or vanilla extract can be mixed in with the rice.

✂ / *TAPIOCA PUDDING OR SOUFFLÉ* (*Sagoauflauf*)

Follow above recipe, substituting same amount of tapioca for rice. Use old-fashioned tapioca for this, not the "minute" variety. Soak overnight and cook as for rice.

✂ / *FARINA PUDDING* (*Greisspudding*)

6 TO 8 SERVINGS

2 *cups milk*	1 *to* 2 *tablespoons ground al-*
2 *tablespoons butter*	*monds or other nuts*
strip of lemon peel	1 *to* 2 *tablespoons raisins or*
1 *teaspoon salt*	*currants*
½ *cup farina*	*rum or arrack, optional and to*
4 *egg yolks*	*taste*
¼ *cup sugar*	4 *egg whites*

Heat oven to 350°. Scald milk and add butter, lemon peel and salt. When butter has melted, sprinkle in farina, stirring constantly. Cover and simmer slowly but steadily 15 to 20 minutes, or until cereal forms a thick mass and leaves sides of pan. Cool. Remove lemon peel. Beat egg yolks with sugar until thick and lemon-colored. Stir in almonds or nuts, raisins or currants and flavor with a few drops of rum or arrack, if you want to use either. Add to cooled cereal and stir through thoroughly. Beat egg whites until they form stiff peaks and are glossy. Fold lightly but thoroughly into the cereal-egg-yolk mixture. Butter a 2-quart soufflé dish or straight-sided casserole. Sprinkle sides and bottom evenly with sugar and tap out excess. Turn batter into baking dish. Set dish in a larger pan half full of boiling water. Bake pudding in this water bath

1 to 1½ hours, or until a knife blade inserted in the pudding comes out clean. Serve with Fruit Compote, page 367.

✖ / BAKED BREAD PUDDING WITH NUTS OR POPPY SEEDS (*Semmelauflauf*)

4 SERVINGS

4 stale rolls with crusts, thinly sliced, or 5 slices stale white bread
¾ cup lukewarm milk
3 tablespoons butter
½ cup sugar
2 egg yolks
grated rind of ½ lemon

⅔ cup almonds, walnuts or hazelnuts, shredded or chopped, or ⅔ cup poppy seeds
⅓ cup raisins
¼ to ½ teaspoon cinnamon to taste
3 egg whites, stiffly beaten

Put roll or bread slices in a bowl and cover with milk. Soak until milk is absorbed. Cream butter with sugar until light and fluffy, then gradually beat in egg yolks; add grated lemon peel and blend well. Add soaked bread, nuts or poppy seeds and raisins to egg-yolk batter and mix together thoroughly. Flavor with cinnamon. Beat egg whites until stiff and fold into bread mixture, gently but thoroughly, using a rubber spatula. Butter a 4- to 5-cup soufflé dish and turn mixture into it. Place in 450° oven and immediately turn down to 350°. Bake 30 to 45 minutes.

VARIATION

Cherry or Apple Bread Soufflé (Apfel- oder Kirschenauflauf): Substitute 1 pound peeled, cored, chopped apples or 1 pound washed, dried, pitted and chopped cherries for nuts or poppy seeds. Use raisins with the apples, if you like, but do not use them with cherries. You can use ¾ pound of cherries with ⅓ cup chopped blanched almonds. When made with cherries, this pudding is called, in German, Kirschenmichel.

✖ / BEGGARMAN'S APPLE OR APPLE AND BLACK BREAD PUDDING (*Apfelbettelmann oder Apfel-Pumpernickelauflauf*)

It's difficult to understand why this succulent pudding should be called "Beggarman's Apple," since it is a fragrant dish worthy of any table. It is a perfect dessert to serve after a course of delicatessen or a thick

German soup. It is also an excellent lunch or light dinner served with some cold milk or hot coffee.

6 SERVINGS

½ cup raisins
4 tablespoons dark rum
1½ cups finely grated pumper-
    nickel breadcrumbs
¾ cup sugar
1 teaspoon cinnamon
4 tablespoons butter
    water or white wine, if
    necessary

4 or 5 cooking apples (Rome
    Beauties or Northern Spies
    are perfect for this)
½ cup chopped pecans or
    walnuts
¾ cup seedless green grapes (op-
    tional)
2 tablespoons butter

Heat oven to 350°. Butter a 1½-quart soufflé or pudding dish. Soak raisins in rum about 20 minutes. Mix breadcrumbs with sugar and cinnamon and sprinkle with rum that has been drained off raisins. Melt butter and stir into breadcrumb mixture. The butter should be evenly distributed through the mixture, which should be as moist as wet sand. If it is too dry, sprinkle with water or white wine. Peel, core and slice apples lengthwise. Slices should be about ⅛″ to ¼″ thick. Place about one-third of breadcrumb mixture in greased baking dish. Follow with half of apples, then sprinkle with soaked raisins, chopped nuts and grapes, if you are using them. Add another layer of breadcrumbs, apples, raisins, etc., ending up with a thick layer of crumbs. Dot well with butter. Bake in middle of preheated oven about 30 minutes, or until apples are tender when pierced with a fork and crumb topping is crisp and brown. Serve with plain or whipped sweet cream.

☒ / SWABIAN BREAD PUDDING (Schwäbischer Ofenschlüpfer)

The name Ofenschlüpfer means "oven sneak"—why, I can't imagine.

6 SERVINGS

6 stale rolls, about the size of
    Parker House rolls, sliced,
    or 7 thick slices stale white
    bread
butter
½ cup raisins

1 pound cooking apples, not too
    sour, peeled, cored and
    thinly sliced, or 1 pound
    ripe small blue plums,
    peeled, stoned and cut in
    half

1 *tablespoon sugar*   2 *tablespoons sugar*
1 *teaspoon powdered cinnamon*   3 *to 4 tablespoons flour*
3 *tablespoons butter*   2 *to 3 cups milk*
3 *eggs*

Preheat oven to 375°. Butter a 6-cup soufflé dish or comparable baking dish and arrange half the rolls or bread slices as a bottom layer. Toss raisins together with sliced apples or plums, 1 tablespoon sugar and cinnamon. Place over bread slices and dot with half the butter. Top with rest of bread slices. Make batter by beating eggs with sugar and flour and adding milk until mixture is consistency of thick sweet cream. Pour over bread and apples, dot with rest of butter and bake 1 hour, or until pudding is completely set and golden brown on top. Serve with sweet cream or Vanilla Sauce, page 402.

✤ / FRANKFURT CHOCOLATE PUDDING (*Frankfurter Pudding*)

There are at least a dozen versions of hot steamed chocolate pudding in Germany; this is one of the best and richest.

8 SERVINGS

¼ *pound plus 1 tablespoon*   1½ *cups grated, unblanched*
  butter   *almonds*
⅔ *cup sugar*   3 *tablespoons white bread,*
5 *egg yolks*   *pumpernickel or zwieback*
3 *ounces melted semi-sweet*   *crumbs*
  chocolate   5 *egg whites stiffly beaten*
1 *tablespoon rum, or 2 table-*   *butter*
  spoons strongly brewed   *sugar*
  black coffee

Cream butter with sugar until light and fluffy. Gradually beat in one egg yolk at a time until thoroughly blended. Stir in melted chocolate along with rum or coffee; add almonds and crumbs. Fold in stiffly beaten egg whites gently but thoroughly, using a rubber spatula. Butter a melon mold and sprinkle inside with sugar, tapping out excess. Turn filling into mold, which should be about two-thirds full. Cover and set in water bath that comes two-thirds up the sides of the mold. Steam 1 to 1½ hours, or until pudding is completely set, and let stand for a few minutes after it is done. Uncover and invert onto serving platter.

✸ / *MOOR IN A SHIRT* (*Mohr im Hemd*)

After discovering how many different desserts go by this one name throughout Germany and Austria, I found myself asking, "Will the real Moor in the Shirt please stand up?" It covers concoctions that are hot, cold, molded or simply spooned into glasses. In every case there is one part of the dessert that is dark—the chocolate, usually, or pumpernickel breadcrumbs that represent the "moor." This is covered or topped by a white sauce, vanilla ice cream or whipped cream—the "shirt."

The Frankfurt pudding (above) is one of the more common versions of Moor in a Shirt, though it is steamed in a tall conical mold rather than in the melon shape. Prepare the filling as directed and after the "moor" is unmolded, cover with White Rum Sauce, page 406, and top with a "turban" of whipped cream.

In Bremen, Moor in a Shirt refers to a sherbet glass half full of cooked cherries or red berries, topped with a layer of pumpernickel breadcrumbs that have been mixed with sugar and cinnamon or grated chocolate, or both. This in turn is topped with a "shirt" of vanilla-flavored whipped cream. To confuse things completely, this is also called, in Bremen, Food of the Gods, or Götterspeise, a name you will also find for the frozen dessert on page 400. (There are as many Foods of the Gods as there are Moors in Shirts.)

In Bavaria and Austria, the local version is Moor's Head (Mohren-kopf). It is made up of a chocolate-frosted cream puff filled with vanilla-flavored whipped cream.

Chocolate pudding made in individual custard cups and then un-molded and topped with a vanilla sauce and/or whipped cream also becomes Moor in a Shirt. I'm sure there are even more desserts known by that name, but, luckily, I haven't found them. If you've been wondering what to call a scoop of chocolate ice cream covered with whipped cream or marshmallow sauce, why not Moor in a Shirt?

✸ / *RHINE MERINGUE PUDDING* (*Rheinischer Bund*)

4 SERVINGS

3 *egg yolks*
½ *cup sugar*
2 *tablespoons cornstarch*

1 *to* 1½ *cups apple wine, white wine or apple juice, or combination of white wine and apple juice*

juice and grated rind of ½
   lemon
15 to 20 small crisp bitter macaroons, such as Italian amaretti, crushed
3 to 4 tablespoons candied
   citron (optional)

3 egg whites
¼ cup sugar
   blanched slivered or split almonds
   confectioners' sugar

Preheat oven to 400°. Beat egg yolks with sugar until mixture is very thick and pale yellow. Stir in cornstarch, wine or apple juice, lemon juice and grated rind. Set over hot, not boiling, water which does not touch the bottom of the mixing bowl. Stir until mixture is thick enough to coat a wooden spoon. Stir in macaroon crumbs and pour into 9″ pie plate. Sprinkle with citron, and cool. Beat egg whites and as they thicken, gradually beat in sugar until snow stands in stiff glossy peaks. Spread meringue over egg-yolk mixture. Sprinkle with almonds and confectioners' sugar. Bake in preheated oven a few minutes, or until meringue is golden brown and pudding is hot all the way through.

VARIATIONS

1.   Crumbs can be eliminated from mixture if you prefer a consistency closer to custard than to cake. Or use crushed anise biscuits instead of macaroons.
2.   Again, if you like a custard consistency, set pie plates over, not in, a pot half full of hot water and bake in oven 10 to 15 minutes.

✄ / BERLIN COFFEE PUDDING (*Berliner Kaffeeauflauf*)

6 SERVINGS

4 tablespoons butter
⅓ cup sugar
6 egg yolks
1 cup almonds, blanched and
   grated
½ cup double strength black
   coffee

⅔ cup fine breadcrumbs
6 egg whites, stiffly beaten
   butter
   sugar

Cream butter with sugar until light and fluffy, then gradually beat in egg yolks until well blended. Add almonds. Soak breadcrumbs in coffee, adding more if necessary until all coffee is absorbed. Turn into egg-yolk mixture and mix thoroughly. Fold in stiffly beaten egg whites gently but thoroughly with a rubber spatula. Butter a 6-cup pudding mold and sprinkle on sides and bottom with sugar. Turn filling into mold, cover and place in water bath that comes two-thirds up the sides of the mold. Steam 1 hour. Serve with Foamy Coffee Sauce, page 405.

⣙ / *VIENNA WINE PUDDING* (*Wiener Weinkoch*)

4 TO 6 SERVINGS

4 egg yolks
⅓ cup sugar
  pinch of salt
  juice and grated rind of 1
    lemon
  pinch of powdered cinnamon
  pinch of powdered cloves
1 teaspoon baking powder
4 egg whites, stiffly beaten
  scant ½ cup bread or zwie-
    back crumbs
¾ cup blanched almonds, grated
  butter

Sauce:

1 cup white wine
  strip of lemon peel
4 cloves
2 tablespoons sugar
1 stick cinnamon

Preheat oven to 450°. Beat egg yolks with sugar and salt until mixture is thick and pale yellow. Beat in lemon juice, grated rind, cinnamon, cloves and baking powder. Turn stiffly beaten egg whites on top of egg-yolk mixture and sprinkle with crumbs and grated almonds. Fold all together gently but thoroughly, using a rubber spatula. Turn into a well-buttered soufflé dish or 8" to 9" Kugelhupf pan, depending on the shape you want; set in 450° oven but immediately turn it down to 375°. Bake 35 to 45 minutes, or until pudding is high and top is golden brown.

If you prefer, you can turn this into a pudding mold that is buttered and sprinkled on sides and bottom with bread or zwieback crumbs. Cover and place in water bath that comes two-thirds up the sides of the mold. Steam 1 hour. Unmold pudding or Kugelhupf pan. If you use a soufflé dish, spoon pudding out of it. To prepare sauce, heat wine and steep (do not cook) with lemon peel, cloves, sugar and cinnamon. Strain and pour hot over hot pudding.

✸ / ALMOND OR HAZELNUT SOUFFLÉ (*Mandel- oder Haselnussauflauf*)

4 TO 6 SERVINGS

½ cup zwieback crumbs
2 to 3 tablespoons rum or arrack
5 tablespoons butter
½ cup sugar
4 egg yolks
1 cup blanched almonds or un-

blanched hazelnuts, grated
or finely chopped
grated rind of ½ lemon
5 egg whites, stiffly beaten
butter
sugar or zwieback crumbs

Preheat oven to 450°. Moisten crumbs with rum or arrack. Cream butter with sugar until light and fluffy and gradually work in egg yolks. Add soaked crumbs, grated nuts and lemon rind and mix well. Fold in stiffly beaten egg whites gently but thoroughly with a rubber spatula. Butter a 4- to 5-cup soufflé dish and sprinkle side and bottom with sugar or crumbs. Turn filling into dish and place in 450° oven which you immediately turn down to 375°. Bake 30 to 45 minutes, or until soufflé is high, puffy and golden brown on top. Serve with Foamy Wine Sauce or Foamy Hazelnut Cream, page 405.

VARIATION

If you prefer, you can steam this as a pudding. Follow recipe, using hazelnuts or walnuts, 1 cup sugar, 6 egg whites and ⅔ cup zwieback or breadcrumbs. Butter a pudding mold and sprinkle sides and bottom with grated nuts. Turn filling into mold and steam in water bath, as illustrated on page xxix, 1 hour.

✸ / COTTAGE CHEESE SOUFFLÉ (*Quarkauflauf*)

4 SERVINGS

1 pound cottage cheese
½ cup sugar
3 tablespoons flour
3 egg yolks
½ cup raisins

grated rind of ½ lemon
pinch of salt
4 egg whites, stiffly beaten
breadcrumbs or sugar

Preheat oven to 400°. If cottage cheese is very wet, drain through a sieve. If there is a little excess liquid, do not drain. Rub cheese through a fine sieve. Mix with sugar, flour and egg yolks until well blended. Stir in raisins, grated lemon rind and salt. Fold in stiffly beaten egg whites, gently but thoroughly, with a rubber spatula. Turn mixture into well-buttered soufflé dish that is sprinkled on sides and bottom with bread-crumbs or sugar. Place in 450° oven which you immediately turn down to 375°. Bake 35 to 45 minutes, or until soufflé has risen and top is golden. Serve with Fruit Sauce or Fruit Compote, pages 407, 367.

✷ / APPLE SOUFFLÉ (*Apfelauflauf*)

4 TO 6 SERVINGS

4 to 6 apples, approximately 1½ pounds (for best results use Northern Spies; avoid apples that are either too sweet or too sour)
½ cup sugar
1 cup water
3 egg yolks

⅔ cup zwieback crumbs
½ cup raisins
½ cup blanched almonds, grated
½ teaspoon cinnamon
grated rind of ½ lemon
3 egg whites
zwieback crumbs

Preheat oven to 400°. Pare, core and slice apples. Place in saucepan with water, cover and simmer slowly until apples cook down to a thick mass. Mix in sugar and cool. Beat egg yolks with crumbs, raisins, almonds, cinnamon and lemon rind until batter is thoroughly blended. Whip egg whites to a stiff snow and fold into egg-yolk mixture. Do this lightly and carefully, using a rubber spatula, so that yolk and white are well blended but whites do not lose their airiness. Turn into a 2-quart soufflé dish that has been buttered and sprinkled with zwieback crumbs on all sides. Bake 35 to 45 minutes. Serve with Vanilla Sauce or Foamy Wine Sauce, pages 402, 405.

✷ / PUNCH SOUFFLÉ (*Punschauflauf*)

2 TO 4 SERVINGS

3 egg yolks
1¼ cups sugar
1 teaspoon lemon juice
⅓ cup rum or arrack
1¼ cup zwieback crumbs

½ teaspoon baking powder
grated rind of ½ lemon
4 egg whites
sugar

Preheat oven to 375°. Mix egg yolks, sugar, lemon juice, rum, crumbs, baking powder and lemon rind until thoroughly blended. Whip egg whites to a stiff snow and fold into egg-yolk mixture. Do this lightly and carefully, using a rubber spatula, so that yolk and white are well blended but whites do not lose their airiness. Turn into a 2-quart soufflé dish that has been well buttered and sprinkled with sugar on all sides. Bake 35 to 45 minutes. Serve with Vanilla Sauce, page 402.

✂ / *SOUR CREAM SOUFFLÉ* (*Sauerrahmauflauf*)

2 SERVINGS

3 egg yolks
1 tablespoon sugar
½ cup very thick sour cream
1 tablespoon and 1 teaspoon
   flour
¼ teaspoon salt

grated rind of ½ lemon, or ½
   teaspoon vanilla extract
3 egg whites
butter
sugar

Preheat oven to 400°. Beat egg yolks with sugar until foamy and lemon-colored. Blend sour cream with flour, salt and lemon rind or vanilla. Mix sour-cream mixture into egg yolks and sugar. Beat egg whites to a stiff snow and fold into mixture. Pour into a buttered 1-quart soufflé dish and bake 20 minutes, or until set. Serve with Fruit Sauce or Fruit Compote, pages 407, 367.

VARIATION

This soufflé also goes well with a roast meat course. To serve it that way, eliminate sugar and lemon rind or vanilla. Use ½ teaspoon of salt, a dash of pepper and serve with browned butter and grated cheese.

✂ / *KARLSBAD SOUFFLÉ* (*Karlsbader Auflauf*)

3 TO 4 SERVINGS

6 egg yolks
2 tablespoons cornstarch
2 tablespoons sugar
½ teaspoon salt

nutmeg
2 cups milk, scalded
6 egg whites
sugar

Preheat oven to 350°. Beat egg yolks with cornstarch, sugar, salt and nutmeg until well blended. Beat into scalded milk that has cooled slightly and cook batter over low heat, stirring constantly until it reaches the consistency of thick cream. Remove from heat and stir until cool. Whip egg whites to a very stiff snow and fold into the cooked mixture. Do this lightly and carefully, using a rubber spatula, so that batter will be thoroughly mixed but egg whites will not lose their airiness. Turn into a 2-quart soufflé dish that has been well buttered. Using a sifter, sprinkle a covering of granulated sugar over the top. Bake 20 to 30 minutes, or until icing is shiny and soufflé is well puffed. Serve with Vanilla Sauce or Fruit Sauce, pages 402, 407.

VARIATION

This same soufflé, made without any sugar in the batter and with no sugar topping, but seasoned instead with a little more salt and a dash of nutmeg, is often served in Germany along with Creamed Spinach, page 290, or Mushroom Cream Sauce, page 335, as a luncheon entree.

⅔ / *SALZBURGER NOCKERL*

These golden soufflé egg puffs are a specialty of Salzburg, the pretty Austrian town so full of Mozartiana. It is easy to see why they have become popular throughout neighboring Germany; they are featured on restaurant menus throughout the country and most especially in Bavaria. Serve them as a dessert, a light luncheon, as a special treat for afternoon guests or for a late supper. They are good with coffee, even better with a glass of chilled dry white wine, and absolutely elegant with champagne.

4 NOCKERL; 2 TO 4 SERVINGS

3 *egg yolks*	5 *egg whites*
1 *teaspoon flour*	1 *heaping teaspoon sugar*
grated rind of ½ lemon (op-	1 *tablespoon butter*
tional) or nutmeg (optional)	

Preheat oven to 425°. Mix egg yolks and flour thoroughly in a large bowl. Add lemon rind or nutmeg if you want to use either. Beat egg whites to highest, stiffest snow possible, sprinkle with sugar and beat together a minute or two. Turn egg whites into bowl that contains the egg-yolk mixture and fold together with a rubber spatula. Do this carefully and lightly so that yolk and white will be thoroughly mixed but egg whites will retain their stiffness. Put butter in a 9" or 10" porcelain or glass pie plate or open baker and heat in oven 2 or 3 minutes, or until butter melts.

Tilt and rotate dish until bottom and sides are well coated with butter. Using a large serving spoon, pile four big cloudlike masses of batter in baking dish. It does not matter if they touch each other; it is customary to break them apart for serving. Place in middle of oven and bake 10 minutes. Nockerl should be very lightly browned on top and centers should be moist but not runny. Serve at once with fine granulated sugar and Vanilla Sauce, page 402.

❇ / APPLE-SAUCE MERINGUE (*Apfelreisberg*)

4 TO 6 SERVINGS

1½ *cups raw rice*
3 to 4 *cups milk, as needed*
  pinch of salt
  strip of lemon peel
¼ *cup of sugar, or to taste*
1 *generous tablespoon butter*
1 *pound of apples, not too sour*

2 to 3 *tablespoons butter*
  sugar
⅔ *cup red or black currant preserves or apricot preserves*
3 *egg whites*
½ *cup sugar*
  sugar

Wash rice. Heat 3 cups of milk with salt, lemon peel, sugar and 1 tablespoon butter. When it comes to the boil, stir in rice. Cover and simmer slowly until rice kernels are tender; do not let them get too soft. Add more hot milk during cooking if mixture thickens too quickly. Do not stir rice as it cooks. By the time it is done, all liquid should be absorbed. Check flavoring and add more sugar if needed.

Peel and slice apples. Sauté in butter 5 or 8 minutes, turning with a wooden spatula. Apples should be pale golden brown on both sides but they should not get too soft. Melt preserves in a saucepan over very low heat and simmer slowly until thick, about 3 to 5 minutes. Butter a 10″ to 12″ fireproof baking dish, and turn half the rice into it. Cover with apple slices and spread with thickened preserves. Cover with rest of rice. Preheat broiler. Beat egg whites and as they thicken, gradually add sugar. Beat until whites stand in soft, shiny peaks. Spread egg whites over the apple slices and sprinkle lightly with sugar. Place under preheated broiler 3 to 5 minutes, or until top of meringue is browned.

✖ COLD DESSERTS ✖
(Kalte Süsspeisen)

✖ / FRUIT COMPOTES (Fruchtkompotte)

Stewed fruits of all kinds are served not only as desserts in Germany, but as accompaniments to meat dishes as well. If they are served with meat, they may or may not have a little vinegar added to give them a sharp edge. As desserts, they may be topped with whipped cream, or may themselves be the toppings for various puddings and cold creams.

Although stewed dried fruits such as prunes, apricots, apples, etc., are the same in Germany as they are anywhere else, they are used in slightly different ways. They are often served as sauces on cooked hot breakfast cereals, or on dessert puddings. In addition, they may be desserts in themselves, with or without whipped or plain sweet cream, sour cream or yogurt. They also make a most unusual appearance on the dinner table as side dishes for such meats as duck, goose, turkey, pork or ham. In that case they are always flavored with wine, lemon juice or vinegar, and sometimes with cloves and/or cinnamon.

To retain its color and flavor, fresh fruit should always be poached or stewed in a sugar syrup. You must always be sure you cook fruit only until barely tender; otherwise it will fall apart and be less attractive to serve. Flavorings such as lemon or orange peel, vanilla bean, whole cloves or stick cinnamon are cooked with the syrup. Wine and lemon juice are generally added after the fruit has cooked. Liqueurs, rum and brandies are always added after the fruit has finished cooking. The fruit should be cooled in the syrup. Usually fruit is peeled, and it may be cooked whole, quartered, halved or sliced, depending on size and your preference. You can also mix various kinds of fruits in a compote. Berries make wonderful compotes but should never actually be cooked; place them in the hot syrup along with any flavorings you want to add. They can then be cooled right in the syrup and served. Always select ripe, perfect fruit or the compote will not have a good appearance or flavor.

SUGAR SYRUP

Cook ¾ cup sugar in 2 cups water for 5 to 10 minutes, or until mixture forms a sugary syrup. This mixture will do for most of the fruit compotes here; where other proportions are necessary, they are given for specific recipes.

✂ / APPLE COMPOTE (*Apfelkompott*)

8 SERVINGS

2 cups sugar syrup, see above
    rind of ½ lemon, cut in strips
8 medium-sized cooking apples,
    not sour

white wine and lemon juice, or
    vanilla extract, optional and
    to taste

Prepare syrup with lemon peel. Peel and core apples. They may be left whole or cut into halves, quarters or thick slices. Poach in syrup 5 to 8 minutes, or until barely tender. Flavor to taste with wine and/or lemon juice, or vanilla. Cool in syrup.

VARIATIONS

1. Apples can be spiced with a stick of cinnamon or a few cloves if you use wine and/or lemon juice. Add either spice to water and sugar as it cooks to a syrup. Rum or arrack can be used for flavoring instead of wine or vanilla.
2. You can poach apples in sugar syrup made with white wine instead of water. In that case, do not use vanilla flavoring; add a little more white wine and lemon juice to taste after apples have cooked.
3. To prepare Stewed Apples with Anise Seeds, follow recipe, cooking the apples whole or halved in the sugar syrup along with lemon peel, a stick of cinnamon and 2 teaspoons anise seeds. Flavor with white wine and cool in the syrup, from which you remove cinnamon but not the anise.
4. To give any apple compote a red coloring, add strawberry or raspberry syrup after the fruit has cooked. Either of these berries may be added to apples after cooking and served with them.
5. Quince (Quitten) can be prepared same as apples, but cook twice as long and flavor with more sugar, as needed.

❦ / *STEWED PEARS* (*Birnenkompott*)

Pear compote is prepared the same way as Apple Compote (above), except that vanilla is never used as flavoring. Instead, use either lemon peel and juice *or* 1 stick of cinnamon added to the sugar syrup as it cooks. White or red wine may be added for flavoring later.

❦ / *CHESTNUTS WITH APPLES OR QUINCE* (*Kastanien mit Äpfeln oder Quitten*)

ABOUT 8 SERVINGS

1 *pound chestnuts*
3 *tablespoons butter*
½ *cup beef broth or water*
1 *pound cooking apples or quince*

peel and juice of 1 lemon
½ *cup water*
3 *tablespoons sugar, or to taste*
  white wine, optional and to taste

Peel chestnuts (see page 282). Melt butter in a saucepan and add chestnuts. Toss until chestnuts are coated with butter, then add broth or water. Cover and simmer gently over low heat 20 to 30 minutes, or until chestnuts are tender. Wash, core, peel and cut apple into eighths, lengthwise. Add with rind and juice of lemon to water and sugar. Simmer gently about 5 minutes, or until water becomes syrupy. Remove lemon peel and add cooked, drained chestnuts; flavor with white wine, if you like, and chill. This may be served as a dessert or with such main courses as roast chicken, goose, duck or turkey, roast ham or pork.

❦ / *STEWED RHUBARB* (*Rhabarberkompott*)

6 SERVINGS

2 *pounds rhubarb*
1 to 1½ *cups sugar*
1 *cup water*

strip of lemon or orange peel, or
½ *strip vanilla bean or 1 teaspoon vanilla extract*

Wash rhubarb. If young and tender, do not peel; otherwise strip off tough stringy coating. Cut in ½″ to ¾″ pieces. Place in pot and sprinkle with sugar. Add lemon or orange peel, vanilla bean or extract. Cover and simmer slowly 5 to 10 minutes. Rhubarb should be tender, but do not overcook or pieces will lose their shape. If you use vanilla extract, stir it in now to taste; otherwise remove citrus peel or vanilla bean. Taste to see if more sugar is needed; if so, stir in while fruit is hot so it will dissolve. Chill thoroughly before serving.

VARIATIONS

1. White wine can be substituted for water, in which case use no vanilla.
2. Whole strawberries can be added to the hot cooked compote.

✂ / STEWED GOOSEBERRIES (*Stachelbeerkompott*)

6 SERVINGS

1½ to 2 *pounds gooseberries*	¼ *vanilla bean, or* ½ *teaspoon*
1 *cup water*	*vanilla extract, or* ½ *stick*
1½ *cups sugar*	*cinnamon*

Wash, pick over and clean gooseberries. Bring water and sugar to boil for 5 minutes, or until a syrup is formed. Add vanilla bean or stick cinnamon to sugar syrup as it cooks. When liquid is syrupy, add gooseberries and simmer about 5 minutes, or until done. If you are using vanilla extract, add it now; otherwise remove cinnamon or vanilla bean. Chill and serve.

✂ / STEWED CURRANTS (*Johannisbeerkompott*)

6 SERVINGS

Prepare syrup, using 1 cup water and 1½ cups sugar. Pour over 2 pounds red or black currants that have been cleaned and picked over. Chill and serve.

✂ / *SPRING COMPOTE* (*Frühjahrskompott*)

4 SERVINGS

2 *cups water*
1 *cup sugar*
2 *pears, peeled, cored and quar-*
   tered
8 *apricots or peaches, peeled,*
   stoned and cut in half

1 *pound gooseberries, cleaned*
   and picked over
1 *pound ripe cherries, washed,*
   stoned and cut in halves
white wine, to taste

Prepare a syrup by cooking liquid and sugar 5 minutes. Add pears, simmer about 5 to 7 minutes, or until just tender, and remove with a slotted spoon. Place in a glass serving bowl. Add apricots or peaches to hot syrup and cook 3 or 4 minutes, or until just tender, and, with a slotted spoon, remove to bowl. Cook gooseberries in syrup, then add to serving bowl. Place a top layer of uncooked cherries on top of other fruit. Add a little white wine to taste. Simmer syrup until quite thick and cover fruit with it. Chill and serve.

VARIATION

Obviously, you can vary the fruits you serve this way. Just be sure you cook each separately, as cooking times differ; you should have separate layers of each fruit in the glass serving bowl.

✂ / *AUTUMN COMPOTE* (*Herbstkompott*)

This is prepared like the Spring Compote above, except that the fruits used are melon balls, 1 pound small blue plums, 1 large apple, 1 peach and 1 pear. Honeydew melon or cantaloupe are very good for this, allowing a 1½-pound melon for this recipe. The sugar syrup should be cooked with a stick of cinnamon. Cook melon balls first 3 or 4 minutes, then place as bottom layer in serving bowl. The peeled, cored and sliced apple and pear can be cooked together. Peel plums by first blanching and then slipping off skins. Cook whole without stoning and use for top layer. Flavor remaining syrup with white wine and cook until thick; pour over fruit and chill.

⧓ / STEWED DRIED FRUIT IN WHITE WINE
(*Trockenobstkompott in Weisswein*)

8 SERVINGS

2 *pounds mixed dried fruits*
1 *cup water*
1 *cup white wine*
½ *to ¾ cup sugar*

2 *slices of lemon studded with*
  3 cloves each
lemon juice and white wine to
  taste

Follow instructions on package as to whether or not fruit needs soaking. The best dried fruit is that which is purchased in bulk and does not have sulphates added; they need overnight soaking. Place soaked or unsoaked fruit in a heavy saucepan with water, wine, ½ cup sugar and clove-studded lemon slices and simmer until done. If more sugar is needed, add as necessary. When fruit is done flavor with lemon juice and more white wine. Chill thoroughly before serving. Although lemon slices are not served with the fruit, they are usually stored with it. This compote tastes best when made a day or two in advance.

VARIATIONS

1. If you prefer, cloves can be eliminated and a stick of cinnamon added with or without the lemon slices.
2. Raisins or dried figs can be added. Do not cook them. Add to fruit bowl and cover with hot syrup.

⧓ / BERRY COMPOTES (*Beerenkompotte*)

ABOUT 4 SERVINGS

Wash and pick over 1 quart ripe blackberries, raspberries, strawberries or blueberries, or use any combination of these that you like. Prepare sugar syrup by combining and boiling 1 cup water and ½ to ¾ cup sugar, depending on the sweetness of the fruit. Place berries in a bowl and cover with boiling syrup. If you like, the fruit can be flavored with some white wine, brandy or any of the fruit liqueurs such as kirsch, maraschino, Grand Marnier or Curaçao. Chill and serve.

✤ / *CHERRY, PEACH, APRICOT OR PLUM COMPOTE* (*Kirschen-, Pfirsich-, Aprikosen-, oder Mirabellenkompott*)

4 TO 6 SERVINGS

- 2 *pounds fruit*
- *sugar syrup*
- *flavorings, according to fruit used*

Wash fruit. Cherries should not be peeled. To peel peaches, plums or apricots, blanch in boiling water 2 or 3 minutes, then slip skins off. Leave whole or cut in half. If you do the latter, remove pits. Cook in hot syrup 5 to 8 minutes, or until tender. When cooking cherries or plums, use ½ stick cinnamon when cooking sugar syrup. Peaches may be flavored with cloves cooked in the syrup or ½ vanilla bean. Apricots are usually cooked with a plain syrup. White wine may be used with any of these.

✤ / *FRUIT SALAD WITH HONEY AND WINE* (*Fruchtsalat mit Honig und Wein*)

4 TO 6 SERVINGS

- ¾ *cup white wine*
- 3 *tablespoon honey*
- 3 *tablespoons chopped nuts*
- 1 *large apple*
- 1 *large ripe pear*
- 2 *ripe peaches*
- 3 *ripe apricots*
- 1 *cup strawberries, or 3 or 4 ripe plums*

Mix wine and honey together and stir in chopped nuts. Wash, peel and core fruit as necessary and cut in thin slices. If strawberries are large, cut in half, otherwise leave whole. Combine all fruit in a large glass serving bowl and pour dressing over them. Toss gently with wooden spoon until dressing is mixed through fruit. Chill several hours before serving.

VARIATION

You can obviously add or substitute other fruits and berries here. Fresh cubed pineapple, nectarines or any ripe berries would be good. Do not use citrus fruits, however.

❧ / LEMON COMPOTE (*Zitronenkompott*)

4 SERVINGS

4 *large perfect lemons*	¼ *cup slivered blanched almonds*
½ *cup fine, quick-dissolving gran-*	*or pistachio nuts*
ulated sugar	2 *tablespoons Maraschino*

Carefully cut all peel and thick white underskin off lemons. Using a very sharp, thin knife, cut lemons into paper-thin slices. Place in a glass serving bowl or in individual glass dishes and sprinkle with sugar, nuts and liqueur. Chill in refrigerator 1 to 2 hours before serving. This is excellent as a garnish for grilled pork, ham or fish.

❧ / SUMMER FOUR-FRUIT COMPOTE (*Sommer-Vierfruchtkompott*)

This compote and marmalade are extremely popular throughout Germany. The first is served as a dessert or condiment; the second is used as a filling for layer cakes and the jelly doughnut that is the Berliner Pfannkuchen.

1 *pound ripe black bing cherries*	1 *quart raspberries*
1 *pound sour cherries*	1½ *cups sugar*
1 *quart red or black currants*	4 *cups water*

Wash, clean and remove stems, leaves, etc., from fruit. Cherries may be left unstoned, or stoned and cut in half. Simmer sugar and water together 5 minutes, or until a syrup is formed. Put cherries and currants in syrup and simmer about 5 minutes. Pour into a large bowl and add raspberries. Flavor with white wine, if you wish. Chill before serving.

VARIATIONS

1. To make Summer Four-Fruit Marmalade (Sommer-Vierfruchtmarmelade), follow the same process but use 3 pounds sugar and 1½ cups water. Remove stones from cherries and simmer all fruits together, raspberries included, stirring several times until mixture thickens. Pack in sterilized jars and seal as you normally would, or use within a week or two without preserving.
2. Other four-fruit combinations used in Germany are raspberries, strawberries, currants and gooseberries; and, in fall, small blue plums, apples, pears and elderberries. Vary the amounts of sugar depending on whether you want to make a compote or marmalade, and according to

tartness of fruit. Berries should be cooked together with the other fruits for marmalade, but not for compote.

�֎ / APPLESAUCE (*Apfelmus oder Apfelbrei*)

Although a recipe for this is hardly necessary, it is such an important item on German menus, it seemed a good idea to point out a few things about making it. Do not use apples that are too sour and do use apples that have red skins. (Macintosh apples make superb applesauce.) The skins should be cooked with the fruit, as they add to color, flavor and vitamin content of sauce. Apples should be washed, quartered and cored, then cooked in as little water as possible, about ½ cup water to 1½ pounds fruit. Add a strip or two of lemon peel and ¼ cup sugar, cover pot and simmer until fruit just begins to fall apart. Do not overcook. Purée through a sieve and flavor with more sugar as needed. Other flavorings that can be added include lemon juice and/or white wine, which are especially good if the sauce is to be served with meat or some other main course. If you like, a few cloves or ½ stick cinnamon may be cooked with the apples, or the sauce may be flavored with powdered cloves or cinnamon. Vanilla is also used as flavoring, in which case do not use wine, cinnamon or cloves. Raisins or currants are often added to the hot cooked applesauce. Serve hot, warm or cold.

If it matters, there is really a difference between Apfelmus and Apfelbrei. The first is as described above, with the fruit puréed through a sieve. In the second version, the cooked sliced apples are not puréed but are served in the syrup. However, the slices always fall apart and the result looks like lumpy applesauce. Very good sauce can also be made by baking whole unpeeled apples in 1″ or so of water until just tender, and then puréeing and seasoning them.

If you buy applesauce already made, add flavorings as described.

✖ / BAKED MARZIPAN APPLES (*Überbackene Marzipanäpfel*)

4 SERVINGS

4 baking apples, preferably Rome Beauties
5 tablespoons marzipan (almond paste)
1 to 2 tablespoons rum

2 tablespoons currants
butter
1 to 2 cups dry white wine
4 tablespoons apricot jam

Heat oven to 375°. Wash and dry apples. Core and pare one-third way down. (Do not cut all the way through the bottom of apple when you are removing core.) Using a fork, mash marzipan with enough rum so that it softens. Work currants into softened marzipan. Place a small pat of butter in the hollowed core of each apple and then stuff with marzipan filling. Top with an additional dab of butter. Set apples in a baking dish 3″ to 5″ deep. They should be placed close enough to keep them from toppling over, but should not be crammed together. Pour in enough wine to come about one-third up the sides of the apples. Bake 25 to 30 minutes, or until apples are tender all the way through when pierced with a fork or skewer. They should be light golden brown on top. While baking, apples should be basted once or twice with the wine. Remove apples to serving dish. Pour remaining wine from baking dish into a saucepan. Stir in apricot jam and simmer slowly until melted and liquid is reduced to a thick syrup. This should take about 10 minutes. Keep flame low and stir constantly so that the sugar in the jam does not scorch. Spoon this apricot glaze over apples, a little at a time. Repeat until all the glaze has been used and each apple has a shiny golden coating. Let set in a cool place (but do not refrigerate) 1 to 2 hours.

✂ / APPLE SNOW (*Apfelschnee*)

ABOUT 6 SERVINGS

2 *pounds semi-tart cooking apples*	1 *tablespoon rum or arrack, or vanilla to taste*
2 *egg whites*	*orange and/or lemon juice, optional and to taste*
½ *to ¾ cup sugar*	

Wash and dry apples thoroughly. Do not peel or cut. Place in oven in open baking pan with just an inch or so of water on the bottom. Bake at 400° until apples are tender but not falling apart, about 25 to 30 minutes. Cut apples, remove cores and purée through a food mill. If you want to use a blender, remove peel as well as core. Chill apple purée along with any juice that collects. While apple is chilling, beat egg whites to a stiff snow, gradually adding a few tablespoons sugar as the whites thicken, until they are stiff and shiny. When apple purée is thoroughly chilled fold into egg whites, adding rum, arrack or vanilla, sugar and, if you like, a little orange and/or lemon juice for additional flavor. Fold together thoroughly until no lumps of egg white appear, then beat vigorously until foamy. Turn into a glass serving bowl or individual sherbet glasses and chill 3 or 4 hours.

VARIATIONS

VARIATIONS

1. One-quarter cup whipped cream can be folded in along with egg white, but in that case use no orange or lemon juice.
2. To make Witches' Snow (Hexenschnee), mix in ½ cup apricot preserve with the egg white. Flavor with 1 tablespoon rum and no fruit juice.

⚞ / *STRAWBERRY SNOW WITH WHIPPED CREAM* (*Erdbeerschnee mit Schlagsahne*)

4 TO 6 SERVINGS

1 pint fresh ripe strawberries, washed and hulled
2 egg whites

½ cup sugar, or to taste
¼ cup heavy cream, whipped
vanilla to taste

Rub washed, hulled berries through a fine sieve or purée in a blender. Mix with unbeaten egg white and sugar and beat vigorously until mixture forms shiny stiff peaks. Using a rubber spatula, fold whipped cream into strawberry mixture and flavor with vanilla. This may be chilled or served at once.

VARIATION

Fresh ripe raspberries may be substituted or combined with strawberries.

⚞ / *GELATIN DESSERTS* (*Süsse Sülze oder Gelee*)

This is the basic recipe for gelatin desserts, along with variations for specific flavors. It is important to remember that dissolved gelatin will begin to set immediately when added to cold liquid. If possible, always add it to a liquid that is slightly warm, otherwise the gelatin will become lumpy and stringy. Should that happen, heat the whole thing over a low flame until gelatin melts, but do not boil. If it is necessary to stir gelatin into an unwarmed liquid, at least try to have it at room temperature, and stir constantly as you add it. Any of these gelatin desserts become frothy and snowy if they are whipped well with a rotary beater when they are half set. Return to bowl and chill until completely set. The gelatin will then be almost like a mousse.

2 to 3 envelopes unflavored gelatin
½ cup cold water
1 quart liquid (fruit juice and/or
   purée, wine, milk or buttermilk)

½ to 1 cup sugar, depending
   on other flavors
juice of 1 lemon
vanilla, or other flavoring, to
   taste

If you prefer a soft jelly, use 2 envelopes gelatin; if you would like a stiffer consistency, or if you want to mold the dessert, use 3. Soften gelatin by soaking about 5 minutes in cold water. Set over hot water until completely dissolved. While the gelatin is melting, heat very slightly whichever liquid you are using, just enough to remove any chill. Stir in sugar, lemon juice and other flavorings. Stir dissolved gelatin into this liquid. Pour into a large glass serving bowl, individual dessert glasses or a chilled, rinsed 4- to 5-cup mold. Chill until set, about 5 hours. If you use a mold, dip into hot water a second or two, wipe dry, loosen edges of the gelatin with a pointed knife and invert onto a chilled serving plate.

VARIATIONS

1. Fruit Gelatin (Obstsülze): Use 1 quart cooked juice and/or purée of such fruits as strawberries, blackberries, raspberries, red or black currants or ripe cherries. You may buy these juices bottled or prepare them yourself. To do the latter, start with 1 quart ripe fruit (remove stones from cherries) and cook with 1½ cups water about 10 minutes, or until all juice is out of fruit. Purée through a strainer or in a blender. Measure fruit and juice (including cooking liquid) and if you do not have a quart, make up the difference with water, white wine or a combination of both. If you use frozen berries, you will need 4 ten-ounce packages. Thaw and purée. Less sugar is needed with frozen fruit. Flavor fruit gelatins with lemon juice and white wine instead of vanilla. You may combine berry juices for this also.
2. Wine Jelly (Weingelee): For liquid, use 3 cups white or red wine and ½ cup water. Flavor with ½ to 1 cup sugar and 2 tablespoons rum or arrack. Use lemon juice but not vanilla.
3. Punch Jelly (Punschgelee): For liquid, use 2 cups white wine, 1 cup strongly brewed tea, ½ cup orange juice and ¼ cup lemon juice. Flavor with ¾ to 1 cup sugar and 2 tablespoons rum or arrack. Do not use vanilla.
4. Buttermilk Jelly (Buttermilchspeise): Use 1 quart buttermilk for liquid. Mix with ¾ cup sugar, 2 tablespoons heavy sweet cream or sour cream and 2 to 4 tablespoons rum or arrack to taste, and a little lemon juice. Or you can omit rum, arrack and lemon juice and flavor with vanilla. To make Yogurt Jelly, substitute 1 quart yogurt for buttermilk and beat with a fork until thin.

5. Chocolate Jelly (Schokoladengelee): Prepare 1 quart cocoa, flavoring it to taste with sugar and vanilla. Stir in gelatin as directed.
6. Tri-Colored Jelly (Dreifarbengelee): This striped dessert should be prepared in individual parfait-type glasses. Each layer is a different gelatin. Use white buttermilk jelly, chocolate jelly and a red wine or fruit jelly. Fill each glass one-third of the way with one jelly and chill until set. Then a second layer of another gelatin mixture that is cool but not set. Chill until second layer sets. Pour in third layer of cooled but unset gelatin and chill until set again.

✿ / AMBROSIA CREAM (*Ambrosiacreme*)

6 TO 8 SERVINGS

1 envelope unflavored gelatin	1 teaspoon vanilla extract
¼ cup cold water	juice of ½ lemon
2 cups sour cream	1 tablespoon rum
¾ cup sugar	2 egg whites, stiffly beaten

Soak gelatin in cold water 5 minutes or until soft. Set over hot water until completely dissolved. Beat sour cream with sugar until light and foamy. Beat in vanilla, lemon juice and rum, and stir in dissolved gelatin until well blended. Chill until mixture begins to thicken but is not set. Fold in stiffly beaten egg whites, gently but thoroughly, with a rubber spatula. Turn into a chilled, rinsed glass serving bowl or individual dessert glasses and chill until set. Top with whipped cream and crumbled macaroons.

✿ / COTTAGE CHEESE AND FRUIT CREAM (*Topfenfruchtcreme*)

4 SERVINGS

1 envelope unflavored gelatin	vored with a little fruit juice or stewed fruit syrup
¼ cup cold water	
1 pound pot cheese or well-drained cottage cheese	lemon juice, optional and to taste
3 tablespoons butter	2 cups fresh fruit cut in pieces, or whole berries, fresh or frozen, or well-drained stewed fruit cut in spoon-size pieces
¾ cup sugar	
2 egg yolks	
2 cups milk, which may be fla-	

Soak gelatin in 3 tablespoons cold water about 5 minutes or until soft. Place over hot water until dissolved. Rub pot cheese or cottage cheese through a sieve. Cream butter with sugar until fluffy, then gradually beat in 1 egg yolk at a time until mixture is smooth and creamy. Add sieved cheese and milk, plain or flavored with fruit juice, beat until well blended and thickened, then stir in dissolved gelatin and a little lemon juice if you want to use it. Chill until thickened and add fruit in a layer. This will sink in slightly as the mixture sets. Chill 3 or 4 hours or overnight.

⅔ / MILK RICE OR MILK TAPIOCA (*Reisbrei oder Sagobrei*)

4 TO 6 SERVINGS

½ cup converted rice or old-
　　fashioned tapioca
1 quart milk
pinch of salt

1 tablespoon butter
4 tablespoons sugar
¼ cup raisins, optional

Cook rice in milk with salt and butter, very slowly until kernels are tender but have not lost their shape. If you have patience, do this in the top of a double boiler. It will take 1½ to 2 hours but will be worth it. The mixture should be very thick and can be stirred several times during cooking. When done, flavor with sugar and add raisins if you are using them. This may be served hot or cold. If you use tapioca, soak first as directed on package, then prepare as for rice, but do not add butter.

VARIATIONS

1. Stewed sliced apples, without their juice, can be stirred into rice and served with it, hot or cold. The apple-rice mixture can also be turned into a buttered pie plate, sprinkled with sugar and then glazed under the broiler. When apples are added to this, it is known as Apfelreis.

2. Similar milk-starch desserts (Brei oder Mus) are also made out of oatmeal (Haferflockenbrei), semolina or farina (Griessbrei), zwieback (Zwiebackmus) and just plain flour (Mehlbrei). Substitute for the rice the same amount of raw (not parcooked) oatmeal, semolina or farina, 8 small zwieback broken in pieces or 8 heaping tablespoons flour. Do not use butter with the oatmeal. The oatmeal is especially good when it has raisins in it and is chilled. Any of these could be also served for breakfast.

/ *STUTTGART APPLE-RICE (Stuttgarter Apfelreis)*

10 SERVINGS

- 1 *pound rice*
- 3½ *to 4 cups milk*
- ⅔ *cup sugar*
- ¼ *vanilla bean, or 1 teaspoon vanilla extract, or to taste*
- 1 *quart water*
- 1 *pound sugar*
- *juice of 1 lemon*
- *strip of rind from 1 lemon*
- 10 *medium-sized cooking apples, preferably Rome Beauties or similar apples that are not too sour*
- 5 *tablespoons raisins or chopped brandied fruits*
- ½ *cup rum or arrack, or to taste*
- 1 *envelope unflavored gelatin softened in 3 or 4 tablespoons cold water, or ½ cup red currant jelly*

Wash rice and cook until tender in milk along with sugar and vanilla bean. All milk should be absorbed by the time rice is done; if mixture thickens too quickly, add more milk. Do not stir rice as it cooks. When done, kernels should be tender but should not lose their shape. If vanilla bean was used, remove it; if using vanilla extract, add it to taste now. Let rice cool. Mix water with sugar in a large wide pot or deep skillet. Cook slowly 5 to 10 minutes, or until a syrup is formed. Add lemon juice and rind. Peel and core apples but do not cut them. Fill core of each with a few raisins or chopped brandied fruits. Place whole apples in syrup, cover and poach slowly until just tender, about 8 to 10 minutes. Be careful that apples do not overcook and fall apart. Remove apples carefully with slotted spoon and cool. Remove lemon peel from syrup.

Flavor syrup with rum or arrack; mix 1 cup of it into rice. Pour rice into a wide glass serving bowl and chill. Add softened gelatin or red currant jelly to remaining hot syrup and stir until completely dissolved. Let cool slightly until syrup just begins to thicken but is not set. If it does set, heat slightly until melted. When apples are cool, mask with thickened syrup. Keep spooning or brushing syrup onto apples until a thick glaze covers each. Place glazed apples in the center of the rice. To serve, spoon one apple and a scoop of rice onto individual dessert plates.

/ *RICE TRAUTMANNSDORFF (Reis Trautmannsdorff)*

This elegant and creamy molded rice dessert is named for the Trautmannsdorffs, a prominent Austrian family in the days of the Hapsburg empire. It is a great favorite all over Europe, whether known by its German name, or by its French name, Riz à l'Imperatrice—Empress Rice. It may be shaped in a ring mold, a high round bombe or, handsomest of all, in a tiered and fluted mold.

ABOUT 8 TO 10 SERVINGS

1¼ cups converted or raw rice
1 cup water and 2½ cups light
    cream or half-and-half, or
    3½ cups milk
    generous pinch of salt
½ vanilla bean, or 1½ tea-
    spoons vanilla extract
2 envelopes unflavored gelatin
½ cup cold water
¾ cup fine, quick-dissolving
    granulated sugar

2 tablespoons maraschino liqueur
3 cups heavy cream, whipped
2 cups mixed candied fruits,
    such as citron, orange and
    lemon peel and candied
    cherries, soaked in kirsch or
    maraschino liqueur or
    brandy and drained

Wash rice well and drain thoroughly in a strainer. Place in a large saucepan along with water and cream or milk, vanilla bean, if you are using it, and salt. (If you use vanilla extract, do not add it yet.) Simmer, covered, over very low heat or in top of double boiler, stirring every once in a while as rice cooks. Cook until tender but not overdone— about 15 to 20 minutes for converted rice; 25 to 35 for raw rice. If vanilla extract is being used, stir it in now. If you used the bean, remove it at this point. Let rice cool to lukewarm in the milk. Do not drain. Soak gelatin in cold water about 5 minutes, or until soft. Set over hot water until completely dissolved, stirring frequently. Stir into lukewarm rice mixture, along with sugar and maraschino liqueur. Chill about 15 minutes, or until mixture thickens. Beat cream until stiff and turn onto top of mixture. Sprinkle with 1 cup of the soaked, drained candied fruits and fold them in together, gently but thoroughly, using a rubber spatula. Rinse an 8- to 10-cup bowl-shaped bombe, or tiered fluted mold or 2 ring molds, and fill with rice mixture. Chill 5 to 7 hours in refrigerator. To unmold, dip mold quickly into hot water, dry and turn onto a chilled platter. Decorate with remaining candied fruit.

VARIATIONS

1. If you prefer, mix all the candied fruits into rice and use none for decoration. Or this mold can be made without any candied fruits at all.
2. Whole strawberries and whipped cream can be used as garnishes with or without the candied fruit mixed into the rice.
3. One-quarter cup raspberry or strawberry juice can be stirred into the cooked rice to give it a pink color. Maraschino may be used or omitted in that case.

4. To give the dessert a glossy sheen, rinse the empty mold with milk and sprinkle it on sides and bottom with granulated sugar before filling. This makes for a prettier effect, but it is a little more difficult to unmold.

✂ / FLUMMERY (*Flammeri*)

6 TO 8 SERVINGS

1 *quart milk*	½ *cup cornstarch*
generous pinch of salt	½ *cup cold milk, approximately*
strip of lemon peel	2 *eggs, separated*
½ *cup sugar, or to taste depend-*	*raisins or other flavorings, as*
ing on other additions	*described under Variations*

Mix milk with salt, add lemon peel and sugar and scald but do not boil. Dissolve cornstarch in cold milk until a smooth paste and stir into hot milk. Bring to a boil once, stirring almost constantly and simmer a few minutes until a thick mass. Remove lemon peel. Cool slightly and quickly beat in one egg yolk at a time. Beat egg whites until stiff and fold into milk-egg-yolk mixture along with raisins or other flavorings. Turn into rinsed serving bowl, mold or individual dessert glasses and chill for several hours, or until completely set.

VARIATIONS

1. Vanilla Flummery (Vanilleflammeri): Substitute ½ vanilla bean or 2 teaspoons vanilla extract for lemon peel. If you use the bean, cook with the milk. If you use extract, add it to hot milk with cornstarch.
2. Chocolate Flummery (Schokoladenflammeri): Prepare 3 cups cocoa, flavoring it with sugar and vanilla to taste. Follow recipe, adding diluted cornstarch to hot cocoa. You can fold in ½ cup chopped blanched almonds along with the beaten egg white if you want to.
3. Coffee Flummery (Kaffeeflammeri): For liquid use 3 cups milk mixed and heated with 1 cup very strong black coffee.
4. Caramel Flummery (Karamelflammeri): When milk is hot, and before you add cornstarch, stir in caramel syrup. To prepare it, heat ½ cup granulated sugar over very low heat until it turns golden brown; watch carefully as sugar tends to burn all at once. When brown, stir in ½ cup water and bring to a boil, stirring constantly until a syrup is formed. Add to milk and proceed. Omit lemon peel, but flavor with vanilla if you like.

⚡ / FRUIT PUDDING (*Obstgrütze*)

6 TO 8 SERVINGS

1 quart fruit juice and/or thin
    purée of such ripe berries as
    strawberries, red or black cur-
    rants, raspberries, cherries,
    cranberries; or apricots, fresh
    or dried
strip of lemon peel

½ to 1 cup sugar, or as needed,
    depending on sweetness of
    fruit
½ cup cornstarch
½ cup water or white wine
    lemon juice and/or white
    wine to taste

Use bottled fruit juice, or prepare it according to directions on page 378. If you use dried apricots, soak, cook and then purée through a sieve, then mix with cooking liquid. If you have less than a quart of purée and liquid, make up the difference with water, white wine or a combination of both. Remove lemon peel before straining or puréeing. Dissolve cornstarch in water or wine and stir into hot fruit juice. Return juice to pot and sweeten to taste with sugar as needed. Simmer until sugar dissolves completely, then stir in dissolved cornstarch. Bring to a boil slowly, stirring until mixture is clear and thick. Simmer 3 to 5 minutes. Flavor with lemon juice and/or white wine. Pour into glass serving bowl or individual dessert glasses and chill until set.

VARIATIONS

1.   Red Fruit Pudding (Rote Grütze): This could probably be considered Germany's national dessert. It is a fruit pudding, made as described, using a combination of red currant and raspberry juices, half-and-half. Again, start from the fruit itself, or use bottled juices.

2.   Rhubarb or Gooseberry Pudding (Rhabarber- oder Stachelbeergrütze): Using 3 pounds of rhubarb or gooseberries, prepare as shown on pages 369, 370. When cooked, rub through a fine sieve or purée in a blender. This should make 1 quart of compote. Place in a pot, simmer a few minutes with a strip of lemon peel or apple peel and flavor with more sugar, if needed, and 4 or 5 tablespoons white wine. Dissolve cornstarch in water or wine and stir into hot fruit. Bring to a boil slowly and simmer 3 to 5 minutes, or until clear and thickened. Chill for several hours in a glass serving bowl or dessert glasses.

⁝⁝ / SIMPLE CUSTARD CREAM (*Einfache Creme*)

6 GENEROUS SERVINGS

3 egg yolks
⅓ to ½ cup sugar, depending
on other flavorings used
4 tablespoons cornstarch
4 cups cold milk, or white wine
or sweet fruit juice (such
as apple juice)

flavorings such as vanilla, or
lemon peel, or grated chocolate or nuts, or caramel, or
strong coffee, or kirsch or
maraschino
3 egg whites, stiffly beaten

Beat egg yolks with sugar until thick and pale yellow. Beat in corn-starch and gradually stir in milk, wine or fruit juice along with any flavoring you are using. Place over hot, not boiling, water that does not touch the mixing bowl. Heat and stir until mixture is thick enough to coat a wooden spoon. Beat egg white into *hot* egg-yolk mixture. This can be served hot or chilled. If you want it chilled, you can beat it again until frothy, just before serving, or serve as is. It can also be chilled in individual serving cups.

VARIATIONS

1. Vanilla Cream (Vanillecreme): Use milk, flavor it with ¼ vanilla bean that is removed when custard has thickened, or with 1 teaspoon vanilla extract. This can have a little arrack added and 2 or 3 tablespoons whipped cream can be folded in with egg whites. Baked or stewed whole apples can be placed in a wide glass serving bowl and covered with this cream and all chilled together. This is known as Vanilla Apples (Vanil-leäpfel). When cream is poured hot over mixed fruit compote with a little rum, the result is Tutti-Frutti Cream (Tutti-Frutticreme).
2. Chocolate Cream (Schokoladencreme): Use milk, 3 ounces of semi-sweet chocolate, that is melted and stirred into the custard mixture, and a little vanilla to taste. Use 1 or 2 egg yolks but 3 whites.
3. Caramel Cream (Karamelcreme):Use milk and add caramel syrup. To make this, heat ⅓ cup sugar slowly in a heavy-bottomed skillet or saucepan until golden brown. Pour in ½ cup water and simmer 5 minutes until a syrup is formed. Stir into warmed milk-egg-yolk mixture. Beat 2 or 3 tablespoons whipped cream into custard along with egg whites.
4. Wine Cream (Weincreme): Use 1 quart white or apple wine, 3 tablespoons lemon juice and a strip of lemon peel. Pour hot custard over pieces of leftover dry cake, such as pound cake or crisp macaroons, and chill before serving.
5. Kirsch, Maraschino or Rum Cream (Kirsch-, Maraschino- oder Rum-creme): Use 4 tablespoons kirsch, maraschino or rum and a little

vanilla to taste. Stir liqueurs or rum in after custard has thickened and before adding egg white.

6.   Hazelnut Cream (Haselnusscreme): Place ¾ cup hazelnuts on a baking sheet and roast in hot oven for a few minutes until skin flakes. Place between two towels and rub skin off. Cool nuts and grate. Add nuts to egg-yolk-sugar mixture along with the milk.

7.   Coffee Cream (Kaffeecreme): Use 3 cups milk and 1 cup black coffee brewed double strength. Use a little more sugar if necessary and beat 2 or 3 tablespoons whipped cream into custard with egg whites.

✲ / ROYAL CREAM (*Königscreme*)

6 TO 8 SERVINGS

3 *egg yolks*
⅓ *cup sugar*
¼ *vanilla bean, or ½ teaspoon vanilla extract*
2 *cups milk*
1 *level tablespoon cornstrach dissolved in a little cold water*
1½ *tablespoons (envelopes) unflavored gelatin softened in ½ cup cold water*

½ *to ¾ cup coarsely chopped or diced rum or brandied fruits or brandied cherries*
⅓ *cup raisins, soaked until soft in a little white wine*
1 *cup heavy cream, whipped*
3 *egg whites, stiffly beaten*
corn oil for mold
sugar

Beat egg yolks and sugar together until thick and pale yellow. Place in top of double boiler with vanilla bean or extract, milk and cornstarch. Heat and beat almost constantly over hot, not boiling, water that does not touch the upper pan. Do this until mixture is thick enough to coat a wooden spoon. While cream is thickening, set softened gelatin over hot water until melted, then mix into thickened egg-yolk mixture. Stir in drained fruit and raisins. Cool until mixture thickens. Fold in whipped cream and then egg whites. Use a rubber spatula and be sure that whites and cream are well blended into the egg-yolk mixture. Brush inside of a 6-cup metal or porcelain mold with corn oil and sprinkle on sides and bottom with sugar, tapping out excess. Pour cream into mold and chill 5 or 6 hours, or overnight, until completely set. To unmold, dip mold quickly into hot water, dry and invert onto chilled serving platter

---

♘ / *JELLIED CREAM OR UNCOOKED, STIRRED CREAM (Roh- oder Kaltgerührte Creme)*

6 SERVINGS

1 envelope gelatin
¼ cup cold water
3 egg yolks
½ to ⅔ cup sugar
flavorings such as lemon juice
and rind, or orange juice
and rind, or berry purée,
or crushed canned pine-

apple and juice, slightly
warmed over hot water or
at room temperature
1 to 1½ cups liquid such as wine,
fruit juice and/or fruit purée
3 egg whites, stiffly beaten
1 cup heavy cream, whipped

Soften gelatin in cold water and set over hot water until completely dissolved. Beat egg yolks with sugar 30 minutes by hand, using a wire whisk or rotary beater, or about 12 to 15 minutes with an electric mixer. The mixture should be very, very thick and almost white in color. Stir dissolved gelatin into warmed flavoring. Beat into egg-yolk-sugar mixture. Gradually add whichever liquid you are using, beating constantly. Chill until mixture begins to set. When cold and thickened, fold in whipped cream and beaten egg whites, gently but thoroughly, using a rubber spatula. Pour into glass serving bowl and chill until set.

VARIATIONS

1. Lemon Cream (Zitronencreme): This dessert is a great favorite of mine, whether it is called cold lemon soufflé, cold lemon pudding or Citronfromage. This version is slightly more lemony than the one on page 390, which is creamier. Either is delightful after a large meal and could be used as the filling in an open baked pie shell. The mixture could be turned into the shell, chilled and covered with whipped cream. Use 1 cup white wine for liquid. Use grated rind and juice of 2 lemons for flavoring. Beat ⅔ cup sugar into egg yolks.
2. Orange Cream (Apfelsinencreme): Use 1 cup white wine for liquid and juice of 3 oranges with grated rind of 1 for flavoring. Use ½ cup sugar.
3. Pineapple Cream (Ananascreme): Use 1 cup canned pineapple juice for liquid with ½ cup white wine. Use 1 #2 can of drained, crushed pineapple for flavoring. Use 1½ tablespoons (envelopes) unflavored gelatin. Do not make cream with fresh, uncooked pineapple or it will not set.
4. Wine Cream (Weincreme): Use 1¼ cups white wine. No other flavoring is needed, but if you like, you could add a little lemon juice or arrack.

❧ / SOUR CREAM MOUSSE (*Sauerrahmcreme*)

6 SERVINGS

2 cups sour cream
1 cup sugar
1 tablespoon rum or arrack
vanilla, optional and to taste

1 envelope unflavored gelatin
¼ cup cold water
1 cup heavy cream, whipped

Beat sour cream with sugar, rum or arrack and vanilla until thick and frothy. Soften gelatin in cold water about 5 minutes, then set over hot water until completely dissolved. Beat quickly into sour-cream mixture, which should have lost its chill. (If it hasn't, set over hot water 2 or 3 minutes.) When gelatin is thoroughly beaten into cream, turn mixture into a glass serving bowl and chill until set.

❧ / STRAWBERRY CREAM (*Erdbeercreme*)

6 SERVINGS

1 quart ripe strawberries
½ cup sugar, or to taste, depending on sweetness of berries
1 cup milk
1 envelope plus 1 teaspoon unflavored gelatin

¼ cup cold water
1 cup heavy cream, whipped
2 egg whites, stiffly beaten

Wash, hull and dry strawberries. Purée through a sieve or in an electric blender. Beat sugar into berry purée until it is sweet enough. Pour in milk and mix thoroughly with purée. Soften gelatin in cold water and then set over hot water until completely dissolved. Beat quickly into milk-purée mixture, which should be at room temperature or a little warmer. (If it is not, set it over hot water 2 or 3 minutes.) When gelatin is well blended with milk mixture, chill. When thickened and just beginning to set, fold in whipped cream and beaten egg whites, gently but thoroughly, using a rubber spatula. Turn into a glass serving bowl and chill until set.

❧ / *BAVARIAN CREAM, OR FINE MOLDED CREAM*
(*Bayrische Creme, oder Feine Abgeschlagene Creme*)

8 TO 10 SERVINGS

4 egg yolks
⅓ to ½ cup sugar, depending on
   other flavorings
2 cups liquid such as milk, wine
   or sweet fruit juice
flavorings such as lemon juice
   and grated rind, or vanilla
   bean or extract, or grated

chocolate, or grated nuts, or
coffee, or caramel syrup, or
rum, arrack or liqueurs
2 envelopes unflavored gelatin
½ cup cold water
3 to 4 egg whites, stiffly beaten
½ to 1 cup heavy cream,
   whipped

Beat egg yolks with sugar until very thick and pale yellow. Stir in liquid along with flavoring and set over hot, not boiling, water. The water should not touch the bottom of the mixing bowl or upper pan. Beat over hot water until mixture is puffy and thick enough to coat a wooden spoon. Soften gelatin in ½ cup cold water about 5 minutes and then set over hot water until completely dissolved. Stir into warm custard mixture, blending thoroughly. Chill until well thickened but not set. Meanwhile, whip cream and beat egg whites to stiff but still shiny peaks. Fold cream into cooled, thickened custard and then fold egg whites in. Do both gently but thoroughly, using a rubber spatula. Turn into a glass serving bowl and chill until set. This can also be molded in a rinsed bombe form.

VARIATIONS

1.   Vanilla Bavarian Cream (Vanille Bayrische Creme): Use milk for liquid. Add ½ vanilla bean to egg-yolk-milk mixture and then remove from cooked custard. Or stir 1½ teaspoons vanilla extract into the thickened custard.

2.   Nesselrode Cream (Nesselrodercreme): Use milk as liquid and same flavoring as for Vanilla Bavarian Cream. Stir ½ cup grated blanched almonds into thickened custard. Place 12 to 15 small crisp bitter macaroons into a glass serving bowl and moisten with a little kirsch or rum. When thickened cream has been mixed with whipped cream and egg white, pour over macaroons and chill until set. If you prefer, soaked, crushed macaroons can be stirred through the custard with the almonds. Chill until thick, then fold in cream and egg whites and chill again until set.

3.   Peach or Apricot Bavarian Cream (Pfirsich oder Aprikosen Bayrische Creme): Prepare Vanilla Bavarian Cream. Cut four large stewed, drained peaches or 6 apricots in halves, slices or quarters and place in bottom of glass serving bowl. After thickened cream has been mixed

with whipped cream and egg whites, pour over fruit and chill until set.

4. Chocolate Bavarian Cream (Schokoladen Bayrische Creme): Use only 3 egg yolks and 3 ounces of semi-sweet chocolate. Melt chocolate over hot water, or grate without melting. In either case, stir into egg-yolk-milk mixture as it cooks to custard. Stir frequently so chocolate blends into custard. Use 1½ cups milk, 4 egg whites and ½ cup whipped cream.

5. Coffee Bavarian Cream (Kaffee Bayrische Creme): Use 1½ cups milk for liquid and 1 cup coffee brewed double strength for flavoring. Coffee should be black. Add more sugar if necessary as custard cooks.

6. Hazelnut or Almond Bavarian Cream (Nuss oder Mandel Bayrische Creme): Use ½ cup hazelnuts or almonds. If you use almonds, blanch and slip skins off. If you use hazelnuts, roast in the oven until skins begin to flake, then rub off between two kitchen towels. Grate or crush finely and cover with 2 cups hot, not boiling, milk. Steep 15 minutes. This milk will be the needed liquid. Beat into egg-yolk-sugar mixture along with grated nuts.

7. Wine Bavarian Cream (Wein Bayrische Creme): Use 2 cups white wine for liquid and juice of ½ lemon for flavoring.

8. Lemon Bavarian Cream (Zitronen Bayrische Creme): Use 2 cups milk for liquid, and juice of 1 lemon and grated rind of 2 lemons for flavoring.

9. Punch Bavarian Cream (Punsch Bayrische Creme): For liquid, use 1 cup white wine and juice of 2 oranges and 1 lemon. Flavor with 3 or 4 tablespoons rum after custard has thickened. Stir in 2 envelopes dissolved gelatin. Use 3 egg yolks and whites and 1 cup cream, whipped.

❇ / COLD CHOCOLATE-SEMOLINA PUDDING (*Kalter Schokoladenpudding*)

ABOUT 6 SERVINGS

1 *quart milk*	2½ *ounces grated semi-sweet*
⅓ *cup sugar*	*chocolate or chocolate bits*
1½ *tablespoons butter*	½ *cup semolina or farina*

Combine milk, sugar, butter and grated chocolate or chocolate bits in a heavy-bottomed saucepan. Heat slowly until chocolate is completely melted. Stir frequently to keep sugar from burning and to distribute chocolate evenly through milk. Sprinkle semolina or farina into boiling milk, reduce heat and simmer until cereal is done and mixture has become a thick mass. Turn into a rinsed 6-cup mold and chill about 3 hours, or until thoroughly cold and solid. To unmold, loosen edges with a knife, invert onto a chilled platter and gently shake and twist the mold as you lift it off the pudding.

VARIATION

Chopped nuts or cherries, fresh or canned, can be mixed into semolina after it has cooked.

ICE CREAMS AND FROZEN DESSERTS
(*Eis und Gefrorene Nachspeisen*)

Restaurants and Konditoreien feature many ice cream specialties on their menus, to be served after or between meals. Few of them are as simple as a dish of unadorned ice cream. It is more probable that the cream will be sliced from a mold or bombe, or served as an Eisbecher, literally an "ice cap," or what we call a coupe or sundae. In either case, there will usually be more than one flavor of cream and a dazzling combination of toppings, especially for the Eisbecher. These will include fruits, nuts, liqueurs, crumbled macaroons, bits of chocolate, real or candy coffee beans, nougat, praline and, always, whipped cream for the finale.

This section includes some examples of the Eisbecher and bombes that are most popular in Germany. They can be made with commercial or homemade cream. As German ice creams do not differ from those of any country, just use your favorite recipe for French-type ice cream —that is, ice cream made with a cooked custard and not containing any cornstarch or flour.

/ *ALMOND NOUGAT SUNDAE* (*Krokantbecher*)

Fill chilled parfait or sherbet glass with almond or other nut ice cream. Sprinkle with chopped or powdered praline, page 396, crushed bitter macaroons, a little Curaçao and top with sweetened whipped cream.

/ *HAWAIIAN SUNDAE* (*Hawaiibecher*)

Fill chilled parfait or sherbet glass with pistachio ice cream. Top with chilled crushed pineapple, fresh or canned, rum, crushed or diced macaroons, toasted almonds and sweetened whipped cream.

/ *BLACK FOREST SUNDAE* (*Schwarzwaldbecher*)

Fill chilled parfait or sherbet glass with vanilla ice cream. Top with chilled stoned, halved cherries (fresh or canned, but not maraschino), chopped walnuts, a little kirsch, chocolate sauce and sweetened whipped cream.

/ *ROYAL SUNDAE* (*Königsbecher*)

Fill chilled parfait or sherbet glass with a layer each of vanilla ice cream and lemon ice. Top with mixed candied fruits such as citron, angelica, orange and lemon peel and candied cherries. Add a little cassis liqueur and sweetened whipped cream and serve with macaroons or slices of pound cake.

✿ / *TUTTI-FRUTTI SUNDAE* (*Tutti-Fruttibecher*)

Fill chilled parfait or sherbet glass with strawberry ice cream or raspberry sherbet. Top with mixed fresh fruits and/or berries that have been marinated in a little sugar, rum and kirsch 2 hours. Top with sweetened whipped cream.

✿ / *STRAWBERRY SUNDAE* (*Erdbeerbecher*)

Fill chilled parfait or sherbet glass halfway with vanilla or strawberry ice cream. Fill glass with cut fresh strawberries that have been marinated in a little sugar and kirsch 2 hours. Top with sweetened whipped cream.

✿ / *ICE CREAM BOMBES AND MOUSSES* (*Eisbomben*)

These decorative molded desserts lend a festive touch to any dinner party and are quite simple to prepare. To start with, you may use homemade or commercial ice cream or sherbets, or you may make a mousse mixture such as those on the following pages. (Unless you have a crank ice cream freezer, these are the best sort of ice creams to make at home, since they require no stirring and, if properly covered, never form ice splinters.)

You will need special bombe molds with tight-fitting lids (see page xxix for illustrations). Though originally the name "bombe" referred to the spherical shape of the molds, they now come in tiers, melon forms and towering conical shapes. A bombe with a 4- to 5-cup capacity will serve 4 to 8 people, depending on the toppings you use and the appetite of your guests. The cream for the filling should be softened just enough so it can be packed into the mold with the back of a tablespoon. It should not liquefy. If it becomes too soft while you work with it, freeze it again until solid before resuming. Line the mold with a 1" shell of your first cream. Cover and chill until hardened, then add a second shell of a different-color cream or sherbet. Cover and chill until hardened again. Fill the center hollow with a third color cream or sherbet, or with flavored whipped cream or fruit purée. Cover and chill until completely set. If you prefer, the mold can be filled in three horizontal bands. Always stand mold, lid side up, in the freezer.

If you do not have a freezer, bury the mold in a pail packed with 3 parts ice to 1 part rock salt.

To prevent water from seeping into the bombe, cover cream with a sheet of buttered waxed paper before fixing the lid in place. Then butter the edges of the lid itself. Bury in ice up to the buttered edge of the lid. Freeze 2 or 3 hours, or until hard.

To unmold a bombe, dip it, lid side up, in very hot water for a second or two. Dry and remove cover. Loosen edges with a knife and invert onto a chilled serving platter. Garnish with whipped cream and fruit or nuts. To serve, cut in long wedges.

A bombe should always be well filled with cream. It is perfectly all right to open the mold when you want to check to see if the cream has frozen to the right consistency.

/ *VANILLA BOMBE* (*Vanillebombe*)

6 SERVINGS

5 egg yolks
¾ cup sugar
2 cups light cream
2 teaspoons vanilla extract
3 cups heavy cream, whipped

Beat egg yolks with sugar until mixture is thick and pale yellow and then beat in the light cream. Place bowl over hot but not boiling water; water should not touch the bottom of bowl. Heat and stir until mixture thickens enough to coat spoon. Let mixture cool; then add vanilla; fold in whipped cream gently but thoroughly with a rubber spatula. Rinse a 5-cup chilled bombe mold with cold water and add mixture. Cover tightly and freeze about 4 hours.

/ *CHOCOLATE BOMBE* (*Schokoladenbombe*)

4 TO 6 SERVINGS

1 cup semi-sweet chocolate bits, or the equivalent amount of any good bittersweet chocolate.
1 cup milk
4 egg yolks
⅓ cup sugar
1 teaspoon vanilla
3 cups heavy cream, whipped

Chill a 4-cup bombe mold 1 hour before filling. Place the chocolate bits in a saucepan with milk and set over a pan of boiling water until chocolate has melted completely. Stir until milk and chocolate are smoothly blended; set aside to cool. Beat egg yolks well, along with sugar and vanilla, and stir in cooled chocolate-milk mixture. Put back over a pan of simmering (not boiling) water, or directly over very low heat; cook, stirring constantly, until mixture thickens and coats a wooden spoon. Set aside to cool. While chocolate mixture is cooling, whip cream stiffly. When mixture is completely cooled, fold in whipped cream with a rubber spatula; work in lightly, quickly but thoroughly, otherwise there will be lumps of white cream frozen into the midst of the chocolate. Rinse the chilled mold and shake out excess water. Turn chocolate filling into mold and place cover on tightly. Place in freezer about 5 or 6 hours, or until filling is solid but still creamy. You should be able to just barely pierce it with a sharp pointed knife.

⬠ / *LEMON BOMBE* (*Zitronenbombe*)

4 TO 8 SERVINGS

3 *cups lemon ice or sherbet*
2 *tablespoons candied fruits*
2 *cups heavy cream, whipped*

1 *egg yolk*
sugar to taste
rum or arrack to taste

Let lemon ice soften just enough so you can mix it with candied fruit. Pack mixture into a chilled and rinsed 4- to 5-cup bombe, until half full. Chill until set. Beat cream until stiff. Add egg yolk after cream is half stiff and flavor with sugar and rum or arrack to taste. Fill rest of mold with whipped cream and freeze about 4 hours, or until completely firm.

⬠ / *ALMOND-PRALINE BOMBE* (*Krokantbombe*)

4 TO 6 SERVINGS

Praline:

2 *cups sugar*
⅔ *cup blanched almonds,*
   chopped
4 *cups heavy cream, whipped*

Bombe:

2 *egg yolks*
2 *tablespoons maraschino liqueur*
   scant 2 cups sugar, or to taste

TO MAKE PRALINE:

Heat sugar slowly in a heavy-bottomed saucepan and when melted, stir in almonds. Cook slowly, stirring frequently, until syrup and almonds are rich golden brown. Pour onto a buttered flat pan and cool until hard. Then chop into small pieces.

Beat egg yolks, liqueur and sugar into whipped cream. Fold in chopped-nut praline. Turn mixture into a chilled, rinsed 4- 5-cup bombe. Cover and freeze until set, 2 or 3 hours.

✣ / WHIPPED-CREAM FRUIT BOMBE
(*Schlagrahmbombe mit Früchten*)

4 TO 6 SERVINGS

2 cups cut-up stewed or frozen and thawed fruit, such as peaches, apricots, cherries or sour cherries, canned crushed pineapple or any berries

8 to 10 crushed crisp bitter macaroons

3 tablespoons rum, arrack, kirsch, orange liqueur or maraschino

4 cups heavy cream, whipped confectioners' sugar to taste

Fruit may be cut in small dice, crushed or, if small, left whole. Drain well and do not use any of the compote syrup. Moisten crushed macaroons with liqueur. Whip cream and when it begins to thicken, beat in sugar, a little at a time, to taste. Fold cream into fruit and crumbs. Turn into a chilled and rinsed 5-cup mold. Cover and freeze until set, about 2 to 4 hours.

✣ / BUTTERMILK-RUM BOMBE (*Rumeisbombe, oder Zitteleis*)

6 SERVINGS

1 quart thick buttermilk or sour milk

2 tablespoons rum

1 to 1¼ cups sugar

1 teaspoon vanilla

6 to 8 crisp bitter macaroons, finely diced

2 ounces milk chocolate, chopped or finely diced

Beat milk with rum, sugar and vanilla until thick and foamy. Add sugar gradually, until milk is as sweet as you like it. Fold in diced macaroons and chocolate. Turn into a chilled an rinsed 5- to 6-cup mold and freeze until set.

❧ / MAY BOMBE (*Maibombe*)

4 TO 8 SERVINGS

½ recipe Woodruff Ice, below	½ cup strawberry purée made
2 cups heavy cream, whipped	from fresh or frozen berries
sugar to taste, if needed	a few drops red food coloring

Prepare ½ recipe for ice and freeze until almost hard. Chill a 4- to 5-cup bombe, rinse with water and shake out excess. Pack ice on bottom and around sides of bombe, forming a shell about ¾″ thick. Work very quickly as ices should not get soft enough to liquefy. Using back of a tablespoon, press ices firmly against sides of mold. Freeze until hard. Whip cream until stiff, flavoring with a little sugar as it begins to stiffen. Stir in strawberry purée and food coloring. (If you use frozen berries, do not add sugar to the cream.) Mix well. Fill center of bombe with strawberry-whipped cream. Cover cream with a sheet of waxed paper and then put lid on tightly. Freeze about 4 hours, or until completely firm.

VARIATIONS

1. To make a Strawberry Vanilla Bombe, substitute 2 cups homemade vanilla ice cream (Vanilla Bombe, page 394) for the ice.
2. Raspberries can be substituted for strawberries.

❧ / WOODRUFF ICE (*Waldmeistereis*)

ABOUT 1 QUART

1 cup sugar	1 orange, peeled, seeded and
1 cup water	thinly sliced
3 cups white wine or, preferably,	juice of 1 orange
apple wine	juice of 2 lemons
1 bunch woodruff, fresh or dried	

Simmer sugar and water together about 5 minutes or until they form a syrup. Cool and add wine. If woodruff is fresh, wash, clean and remove roots and dead leaves and dry. Place fresh or dried woodruff in a glass or porcelain bowl and cover with wine and sugar syrup mixture. Add slices of orange and marinate for ½ hour if you use fresh woodruff, 1½ hours if you use dried. Add juice of orange and lemons and strain mixture, removing woodruff branches before you do. Freeze in an ice cream freezer if you have one. Otherwise use refrigerator trays in freezer or ice-cube unit. Using a rotary beater, whip sherbet after the first hour or when it is half set. Whip again every half hour or as soon as ice crystals form. Do this until ice is solidly frozen.

✠ / CURRANT ICE (*Johannisbeereis*)

6 SERVINGS

1 quart ripe currants, black or red
2 cups water or wine
½ tablespoon unflavored gelatin
¼ cup cold water
1 cup sugar, or to taste
white wine to taste, if berries were cooked in water

Wash currants and pick over carefully. Cook in 2 cups water or wine, covered, simmering 5 to 7 minutes, or until berries are soft enough to mash. Purée through a sieve. Soften gelatin in ¼ cup cold water and set over hot water until completely dissolved. Bring currant purée to a boil with sugar, stirring constantly over low heat until thickened. Flavor with wine. Stir in dissolved gelatin. Cool slightly, then pour into refrigerator trays and place in freezer. When stiff but not hard, turn into a chilled mixing bowl and beat with a rotary beater until snowy. Return to freezer in tray or bombe mold and freeze until hard.

✠ / PRINCE PÜCKLER'S BOMBE (*Fürst-Pückler-Bombe*)

If you wanted to present dinner guests with the dessert most often served on special occasions in Germany, this festive-looking ice cream bombe would be the best possible choice. Any restaurant that takes itself at all seriously lists it on its menu and German families order whole Pückler bombes from their favorite Konditorei, as a treat to be served at home after Sunday dinner. It was named after Hermann Ludwig Heinrich Pückler, a Silesian soldier and author who received the title of prince (Fürst) from the king of Prussia in 1822. The prince was both a gourmet and a cook, and this dessert was his invention. With its three layers of chocolate, vanilla and strawberry or raspberry ice cream, it was undoubtedly the inspiration for the chocolate, vanilla and strawberry ice cream bricks that have become standards here.

The three flavored creams that make up the layers of this bombe are each prepared separately and added to the mold after the previous layer has set in the freezer. Allow about 1½ to 2 hours from the time you begin to prepare it until the mold is finally placed in the freezer. The three fillings can all be made up at once and then added to the mold as each layer freezes; I prefer to make up each filling just before it is needed. For the filling (see below) use a 6-cup metal bombe mold with a very tight-fitting cover. Its general shape should be tall, narrow and straight, or slightly flared out toward the bottom. It may be plain, fluted or tiered. At first glance, you might not think this is enough dessert for 8 to 10 people, but it is extremely rich and one long slim wedge is ample for one person. If you are serving a very light meal and if you have invited guests who have an inordinate taste for sweets, you might have to make a little more of each filling and use an 8-cup mold.

1 to 1½ cups coarse macaroon crumbs (18 to 24 small macaroons; they should be small,	crisp bitter macaroons, such as the Italian amaretti)
	2 to 3 tablespoons rum or arrack

To prepare crumbs, grind macaroons coarsely in a blender or food grinder; or put them in a paper bag, close the bag securely and roll the macaroons with a rolling pin, turning the bag over once or twice so they are evenly crushed. Place crumbs in a bowl and sprinkle with rum or arrack, mixing so that all crumbs are evenly moistened.

Chocolate Filling:

Prepare ½ recipe for Chocolate Bombe, page 394.

Vanilla Filling:

Whip 1¼ cups heavy cream and flavor with 1 to 2 teaspoons vanilla and 1 tablespoon confectioners' sugar. Whip sugar and vanilla into stiffened cream.

Strawberry or Raspberry Filling:

Whip 1¼ cups heavy cream and when it begins to stiffen, beat in 1 tablespoon confectioners' sugar. When stiff, fold in 2 tablespoons strawberry or raspberry purée. Make this with fresh berries or by thawing and draining frozen fruit. Purée in a blender or through a strainer. If you use frozen fruit, you might like a little less sugar, so taste as you go along. To this mixture add a few drops red food coloring and mix through lightly but thoroughly.

To Assemble the Bombe:

The mold should be chilled for 1 hour before you start to fill it. Rinse and shake out excess water. Begin by turning the chocolate filling into the mold. Add a ¼″ to ½″ layer of macaroon crumbs. Cover and place in freezer 30 to 40 minutes, or until crumbs are set. Remove mold, uncover and add the vanilla filling and another layer of crumbs. Cover and replace in freezer, again 30 to 40 minutes, or until crumbs have hardened. Remove mold, uncover and fill with raspberry or strawberry cream. If you have crumbs left, and if you would like to, add a third layer after the pink cream. That is not usually done although it makes a nice base. Cover mold and set in freezer 6 to 8 hours, or until ice cream is solid. You should be able to just barely pierce it with a sharp pointed knife.

VARIATIONS

1.   If it seems too much trouble to make the chocolate filling, use chocolate-flavored whipped cream instead. Whip 1¼ cups heavy cream, beating in 1 tablespoon confectioners' sugar as cream stiffens. Stir in ⅓ cup semi-sweet chocolate bits which have been melted over a pan of hot water and then cooled.

2.   To make this the easy way, mold with ready-made, slightly softened ice cream. Prepare macaroon crumbs. Buy 1 pint chocolate ice cream, 1 pint vanilla ice cream and 1 pint strawberry ice cream. Chill the mold. Let chocolate ice cream stand at room temperature until just soft enough to be pressed into mold; do not let it turn liquid. Rinse mold and shake out excess water. Fill with softened ice cream, packing it down hard into mold. Sprinkle with macaroon crumbs and chill. When set, let vanilla ice cream soften, pack it into mold, top with another layer of macaroon crumbs, cover and freeze again until set. Follow this procedure with strawberry ice cream. Let completed mold chill 5 to 6 hours.

3.   You can devise your own version of this dessert by using any combination of ice cream or whipped-cream flavors that you like.

❦ / FOOD OF THE GODS (*Götterspeise*)

Whether you prepare it with pumpernickel or macaroon crumbs, this is a luscious dessert that looks elegant but is easy to make.

*1 generous cup stale pumper-
    nickel or macaroon crumbs
    (use crisp bitter Italian maca-
    roons, amaretti, for this; 14
    to 15 will give right amount
    of crumbs)*

*2 tablespoons rum
3 cups heavy cream, whipped
2 egg yolks
2 to 3 tablespoons confectioners'
    sugar*

Chill a 4-cup mold in freezer 1 hour. Sprinkle crumbs with rum and stir until evenly and thoroughly moistened; set aside. Whip cream, beat in yolks and sugar and fold into rum-soaked crumbs. Rinse mold and turn cream and crumb mixture into it. Cover top with waxed paper and set in freezer about 6 hours; cream should be solid but creamy; it should not be frozen hard. At first this might not look like enough for 6 to 8 people; but it is extremely rich and one can rarely finish a larger portion. It is a first cousin to the Italian tortoni, which is always served in tiny paper cups. If you prefer, you can mold this dessert in the same way and serve individual portions.

VARIATIONS

1. This same mixture of whipped cream, rum and pumpernickel crumbs can be served unfrozen, heaped in a sherbet or parfait glass. In that case, omit egg yolk.
2. Whether served frozen or unfrozen, you can combine ½ to ⅔ cup grated bittersweet or milk chocolate with ¾ cup crumbs and fold that into the cream.

---

❸ / *ROMAN ICE PUNCH* (*Römischer Eispunsch*)

This is Germany's elegant answer to the ice cream soda.

For each serving:

*½ to ¾ cup orange or lemon ice
1 tablespoon arrack or mara-
    schino liqueur
½ pint chilled champagne (pref-*

*erably German Sekt)
orange or lemon peel (op-
    tional)*

Place orange or lemon ice in a chilled highball, iced tea or ice cream soda glass. Pour arrack or maraschino over ice and mix gently with a spoon. Fill glass to brim with chilled champagne and serve with a spoon and straw. If you like, a strip of orange or lemon peel can be added as a garnish.

❈ DESSERT SAUCES ❈
(*Süsse Sossen*)

❇ / WHIPPED CREAM (*Schlagrahm*)

Whipped cream mixed with grated chocolate, pumpernickel crumbs, sugar and cinnamon is heaped into parfait or sherbet glasses, chilled and served as dessert in Germany. Various fruits such as ripe berries are prepared in the same way. Finely powdered espresso coffee, liqueurs such as maraschino, puréed cooked chestnuts and rum or arrack are also combined with sugar, and sometimes vanilla, as flavorings for whipped cream. For detailed instructions and further variations, see Flavored Whipped Cream, page 475.

❇ / VANILLA SAUCE (*Vanillesosse*)

2½ CUPS

2 cups milk	¼ cup sugar
½ vanilla bean or 1 teaspoon vanilla extract	2 teaspoons cornstarch
3 egg yolks	2 egg whites, stiffly beaten (optional)

In the top of an enameled double boiler, scald milk with vanilla bean. If you use extract, scald milk, then stir extract in. Beat egg yolks with sugar and cornstarch until light and frothy. Pour vanilla-flavored milk into egg-yolk mixture slowly, stirring vigorously as you do so. Pour mixture back into top of double boiler and set over hot, not boiling, water that does not touch the upper pan. Cook over simmering water, stirring constantly, until sauce becomes custardy and thick enough to coat a wooden spoon. If you would like a foamy sauce, beat egg whites into hot custard until frothy. Serve hot or cold.

VARIATIONS

1. Chocolate Sauce (Schokoladensosse): Add 3 ounces semi-sweet chocolate, grated, to egg-yolk mixture before it cooks to custard. Use only 2 egg yolks. Use vanilla flavor with the chocolate. Three tablespoons cocoa can be substituted for chocolate, in which case, add a little extra sugar.
2. Caramel Sauce (Karamelsosse): Use 1½ cups milk and ½ cup caramel sauce. To make this, melt ⅓ cup sugar in a heavy saucepan until it turns rich golden brown. Pour in ½ cup water and simmer about 5 minutes, or until mixture becomes syrupy. Cool and stir into heated milk.
3. Arrack Sauce (Arraksosse): Stir 2 to 3 tablespoons arrack into custard after it has thickened.
4. Extra rich sauces can be made by using 1 cup cream with 1 cup milk instead of 2 cups milk. Or you can beat 2 or 3 tablespoons whipped cream into the hot custard, with or without the stiffly beaten egg white.

∷ / *LEMON SAUCE* (*Zitronensosse*)

2 CUPS

3 egg yolks	½ cup white wine
½ cup sugar	juice of 2 lemons
grated rind of 1 lemon	2 egg whites, stiffly beaten (optional)
1 tablespoon cornstarch	
1 cup milk	

Beat egg yolks with sugar, lemon rind and cornstarch until mixture is light and frothy. Do this in top of an enameled double boiler. Combine milk, wine and lemon juice and beat into egg-yolk mixture. Set over hot, not boiling, water that does not touch the upper pan. Cook over simmering water, beating constantly, until mixture is custardy and thick enough to coat a wooden spoon. If you want this sauce to be foamy, beat in egg whites after custard has been taken off heat. Serve hot or cold.

✂ / ALMOND SAUCE (*Mandelsosse*)

ABOUT 2½ CUPS

2 cups milk
⅓ cup blanched, grated almonds
1 tablespoon cornstarch
4 tablespoons sugar

1 egg yolk
2 or 3 drops almond extract, to taste
1 egg white, stiffly beaten

Combine milk and almonds, heat, cover and steep about 10 minutes. Beat cornstarch, sugar and egg yolk together in top of an enameled double boiler until mixture is light and frothy. Beat in warm almond-milk with grated nuts. Place over hot, not boiling, water that does not touch the upper pan. Cook over simmering water, stirring constantly, until mixture is thick enough to coat a wooden spoon. Flavor with extract and beat in egg white after custard has been removed from heat. Serve hot or cold.

✂ / WHITE WINE ZABAGLIONE (*Weinchaudeau*)

Weinchaudeau and Weinschaum are closely related, the first being either a sauce or a dessert in itself, while the second is always a sauce. Both are very similar to the Italian zabaglione. Chaudeau refers to the warm water over which the custard cooks; Schaum refers to the foamy consistency of the finished sauce. The only difference between the two is the amount of egg yolk and cornstarch that is used in the latter.

6 TO 8 SERVINGS

6 egg yolks
⅓ cup sugar

1½ cups Moselle wine

In the top of a large enameled double boiler, beat egg yolks with sugar until thick and pale yellow. Set over bottom pan that is a third full of cold water. Start heating water and keep beating egg yolk and sugar, gradually pouring in white wine. By the time water is simmering, custard should be thick, frothy and hot. Be careful that water does not boil, or egg will stick to pan. Spoon into parfait glasses or whiskey-sour glasses. This can also be served cold. Set pot in bowl of ice and beat until custard is thick and cold. Serve in the same kind of glasses.

⚝ / *FOAMY WINE SAUCE* (*Weinschaumsosse*)

ABOUT 2 CUPS

2 egg yolks
1 whole egg
½ cup plus 1 tablespoon sugar
1 teaspoon cornstarch

1 cup white wine such as Moselle
1 teaspoon lemon juice
2 egg whites, stiffly beaten

In the top of an enameled double boiler, beat egg yolks, whole egg, sugar and cornstarch until light and frothy. Gradually beat in wine and lemon juice. Set over hot, not boiling, water that does not touch bottom of upper pan. Cook and beat constantly, until mixture is thick enough to coat a wooden spoon. Remove upper pan from hot water and beat in egg whites. Serve hot. To serve cold, place upper pan in bowl of ice after egg white has been folded in and beat until thick.

⚝ / *FOAMY COFFEE SAUCE* (*Kaffeeschaumsosse*)

ABOUT 2 CUPS

1 cup strongly brewed black coffee
2 egg yolks
¼ cup sugar

1 heaping teaspoon cornstarch
2 egg whites, stiffly beaten
¼ cup heavy cream, whipped

In top of an enameled double boiler, mix coffee with egg yolks and sugar; then beat in the cornstarch. Set over hot, not boiling, water that does not touch bottom of upper pan or bowl. Cook and beat until thick enough to coat a wooden spoon. Remove from heat and mix in egg whites and whipped cream until mixture is light and frothy.

⚝ / *FOAMY HAZELNUT CREAM* (*Hasselnusscremesosse*)

ABOUT 2 CUPS

¼ cup sugar
2 to 3 tablespoons coarsely chopped hazelnuts
1 cup water
½ cup cold milk

2 egg yolks
1 heaping teaspoonful cornstarch
sugar to taste
rum to taste
2 egg whites, stiffly beaten

Place sugar in heavy-bottomed saucepan over low heat until golden brown, shaking often so it does not burn. Stir in chopped nuts until coated with sugar. Add water and simmer until mixture is smooth and syrupy, about 5 minutes. Beat in milk, egg yolks and cornstarch; place over hot, not boiling, water that does not touch the upper pan. Cook and beat until mixture is thick enough to coat a wooden spoon. Remove from heat, flavor with sugar and rum to taste and beat in egg whites.

⊠ / WHITE RUM SAUCE (*Weissrumsosse*)

ABOUT 1 CUP

½ cup water
⅔ cup sugar

4 egg whites, stiffly beaten
1 to 2 tablespoons light rum

Simmer water and sugar in heavy saucepan 5 minutes or until a syrup is formed. Stir in egg whites and flavor with rum.

⊠ / HOT RED WINE SAUCE (*Warme Rotweinsosse*)

2 CUPS

2 cups red wine
⅓ to ½ cup sugar
2 strips of lemon peel
2 cloves

small stick of cinnamon
rum, optional and to taste
1 teaspoon cornstarch dissolved
  in a little cold water, optional

Simmer red wine with sugar, lemon peel, cloves and cinnamon about 5 minutes. Do not boil. If you like, the sauce can then be flavored with rum. For a thin sauce, strain and serve hot. If you would like it slightly thickened, stir dissolved cornstarch into hot sauce and simmer another minute or two, or until thickened.

⊠ / FRUIT SAUCES (*Fruchtsossen*)

Fruit sauces are used a great deal over almost every kind of dessert in Germany—puddings, ice creams, jelled creams, whipped cottage cheese, rice molds and hot fruit fritters. The sauce may be hot or cold and is almost always made of red fruit or berries such as cherries, raspberries, strawberries or currants. Any of the fruit compotes on pages 367 through 373 are served as sauces, hot and cold.

The simplest fruit sauce is heated sweet red fruit juice that is poured over hot puddings. This may or may not be thickened with cornstarch, depending on the preference of the individual cook. As you can see below, these sauces may be based on fresh or bottled fruit juices and/or purées or on fruit jams and marmalades.

✳ / FRUIT SAUCE (*Fruchtsosse*)

ABOUT 2 CUPS

2 cups fruit juice such as rasp-
    berry, strawberry, cherry,
    plum or red currant, or 4
    tablespoons fruit preserves or
    marmalade with 2 cups water,
    or 1 cup fruit purée with 1
    cup water

strip of lemon peel
½ cup sugar, or to taste
2 teaspoons cornstarch dissolved
    in a little cold water,
    white wine or fruit juice
lemon juice and/or white
    wine to taste

Bring fruit juice, or preserves and water, to a boil with lemon peel and sugar to taste. You will need less sugar with the preserves than with the juice. Stir in dissolved cornstarch, bring to a boil and simmer 2 or 3 minutes, or until sauce is thick and clear. Flavor with lemon juice and wine to taste. If you use fruit purée, from fresh or frozen fruit, cook water and lemon peel and when it is boiling, stir in dissolved cornstarch. Simmer 2 or 3 minutes until thick, then stir in purée and flavor with sugar, lemon juice and wine to taste. Serve hot or cold.

✳ / COLD RASPBERRY OR STRAWBERRY SAUCE (*Kalte Erdbeer- oder Himbeersosse*)

2 CUPS

1 to 1½ pints ripe strawberries
    or raspberries

¼ to ⅓ cup sugar
½ cup white or red wine

Wash berries; hull strawberries. Purée through a sieve or in an electric blender and beat in sugar and wine.

⊠ / SAUCE OF DRIED APPLES OR APRICOTS (*Sosse aus getrockneten Äpfeln oder Aprikosen*)

½ *pound dried apples or apricots*	1 *tablespoon cornstarch dissolved*
water to cover	*in a little cold water (op-*
strip of lemon peel	*tional)*
⅓ *to* ½ *cup sugar to taste*	*lemon juice to taste*

Soak dried fruit in water to cover for several hours. Simmer in same water along with a strip of lemon peel until fruit is soft. Remove peel and purée fruit through a sieve or in an electric blender. Flavor purée to taste with sugar and simmer 3 or 4 minutes. If you want a slightly thickened sauce, stir dissolved cornstarch into hot sugared purée and simmer 2 or 3 minutes. Flavor with lemon juice. Serve hot or cold.

⊠ / PRUNE SAUCE WITH ALMONDS (*Pflaumensosse mit Mandeln*)

½ *pound prunes*	*prune cooking liquid*
water to cover	⅓ *cup slivered blanched almonds*
strip of lemon peel	*sugar to taste*
1 *tablespoon butter*	*rum to taste, or powdered*
1 *tablespoon flour*	*cinnamon to taste*

Soak and cook prunes in water to cover, with lemon peel. Remove pits from cooked prunes; chop or dice finely. Reserve cooking liquid. Melt butter in a saucepan and when it is hot and bubbling, stir in flour. Sauté and stir over low heat until flour just begins to turn color, about 3 minutes. Pour in prune cooking liquid and beat until smooth with a wire whisk, over low heat, until sauce is smooth and thick. Stir in prunes and almonds and simmer 10 minutes. Flavor with sugar and rum or cinnamon.

CHAPTER

XV

Baking

(Backwerk)

Here I must begin by admitting defeat. I could never do justice to the variety of German cakes, tortes, pastries, cookies and sweet yeast-dough coffee cakes in a book this size, and in fact, those recipes deserve a volume all their own. There are the scores of baked items for which Germany is famous, plus dozens of other regional and holiday specialties that are equally good if less well known to the outside world. Dresden's Stollen is the citron- and currant-studded sweet yeast bread we know, but there are at least six other kinds of Stollen in Germany. The same is true of the strudel varieties, the apple or crumb Kuchen, and the cream-filled honey-and-nut-encrusted beehive cake, the Bienenstich. There are even six different ways to make an authentic Nürnberger Lebkuchen, the spicy honey cookies that are sent all over the world at Christmas from the city of Albrecht Dürer the painter, Hans Sachs the Meistersinger, and Tannhäuser the Minnesinger.

Many cakes and cookies that have different names are made of the same dough and taste identical, but the difference, and therefore the interest, is in their shapes and trimmings. I have tried to effect a compromise and have included some of the cakes, cookies and Christmas specialties that are German trademarks, plus a few you might not have come across before. I have also tried to give a sampling of the various types of German Gebäck.

The Germans, along with their first cousins the Austrians, are unquestionably the world's best bakers and their showcases are the Konditoreien. These attractive and comfortable shops are a cross between bakeries and coffee houses. You may buy their wares to take home, or they can be served to you with coffee (or other beverages) at tables. Newspapers and magazines hang on racks and you can read as you relax and enjoy whatever cake (or, more likely, cakes) you have selected. It is dazzling to step into one of these places and be greeted by spotless glass shelves and cases lined with scores of cream-filled, fruit-topped, nut-and-chocolate-encrusted, cinnamon- and sugar-rich cakes, tarts and cookies, large and small, crisp or fluffy, intricate or simple, and all lusciously, exquisitely fattening. Invariably eyes prove bigger than stomachs, but it's easy to see why, for never has it been more difficult to make a choice. Trying to get a complete list of these cakes and cookies is even more impossible. I remember going into the wonderful Café Kranzler in Frankfurt and deciding that surely their cases must contain the complete German baking repertoire (excluding seasonal and holiday specialties of course), and so I made a list. Several days later in Baden-Baden I went into the equally wonderful and even more charming Café König, to be greeted by another huge array that repeated only about a dozen items I saw in Frankfurt. I had similar experiences in Munich, traveling between the Café Feldherrnhalle, the Glockenspiel and Germany's most respected Konditorei, the Kreutzkamm, whose Christmas specialties are now boxed and flown to department stores all over this country by Lufthansa.

Although every Konditorei has its own way of categorizing cakes on its menu (small cakes, large cakes, cream cakes, fruit tortes, yeast cakes, fruit yeast cakes, cheese yeast cakes, fruit tarts, cheese tarts, house specialties, dessert cakes and on and on and on), they are generally divided as follows:

Schmalzgebäck, or "fat baked," refers to deep-fried cakes such as doughnuts and crullers, that may or may not include yeast in the dough. Hefeteig is yeast dough. Blätterteig is puff pastry, or "leaf dough," and Hefeblätterteig is yeast puff pastry. Backpulverteig is batter that contains baking powder; it is also known as Rührteig, or "stirred dough." One of the best and best-known of German doughs is the sweet tart pastry Mürbteig that is the basis of many tarts, especially those that contain fruit. Brandteig is what we know as choux paste or cream puff dough. Torte is a little more difficult to define because its meaning has become obscured. At its broadest it is taken to mean any round cake; at its narrowest it is a cake that includes neither fat, starch nor leavening. It is commonly used to denote relatively flat, richly flavored, slightly chewy cakes as opposed to the high and fluffy raised cakes we see most often here. Biskuitteig, or biscuit dough, makes a dry, spongy cake. Cookies are, in German, "small baking," or Kleingebäck, while the huge assortment of Christmas specialties are grouped under the heading of Weihnachtsgebäck or Weihnachtsbäckereien. The term Dessertgebäck cover scores of small pastries, individual tarts, tiny cake rolls filled with butter or whipped cream and crisp little lacy waffles sandwiched together with liqueur-flavored creams—all the sorts of things you might expect to find on the dessert pastry tray of a restaurant in heaven. There are more terms and categories, but these are the major ones and with them you should be able to find your way through a Konditorei menu—usually a sixteen- to thirty-two-page booklet complete with table of contents.

Except for the small pastries, few of these cakes are ever served as desserts. Fruit, cold puddings and ice cream creations are usually taken after meals, while the cakes, tortes and tarts are reserved for between-meal snacks.

There is one cake in Germany that cannot be made properly at home, but I feel you should know about it in case you happen to be near some good German Konditorei, such as Café Geiger in New York. It is called the tree cake—Baumkuchen—a sort of light poundcake with an almond flavor. This is made on a special horizontal revolving tube. Many layers of batter are poured on, each one baked before the next is added. The cakes stand on end and are anywhere from 2 to 5 feet tall. They may be iced with chocolate or white frosting and are sliced horizontally in thin half-round shavings. Each slice shows its rings of batter that look very much like the rings of age on a crosswise cut of a tree trunk. Baumkuchen is understandably expensive—about $4 or $5 a pound, but worth it. As far as I'm concerned, it's the best cake in the world.

None of this includes the breads—another craft for which the Germans have a real genius. The sour-dough ryes, the dark pumpernickels, either of the smooth, thinly sliced square Westphalian type or the big round loaves of coarse bread made in East Germany, the snowy white breads with golden crisp crusts and wonderful rolls made of rye flour and caraway seeds, these are just a few of the varieties you'll find in Germany. Munich's special "bricklayers' loaves," Maurerlaibe, are rye rolls that are just about the best I've ever tasted. Because bread baking is a rather specialized branch of baking, I have not included any bread recipes in this book. However, a few of what the Germans call Salzgebäck, or "salt baking" (as opposed to the sweet), follow here.

✖ SALT BAKING ✖
(*Salzgebäck*)

Salt baking covers all the crisp little twists and crackers the Germans make to go with soups as well as the small meat- vegetable- or onion-filled turnovers, similar to the English savories. The two crackers below are excellent with soup or can be served by themselves with drinks. The Swabian bacon, onion and sauerkraut cakes included are all fragrant, mouth-watering specialties to be eaten with wine or beer as light meals, in the manner of the Swiss onion tart, the Italian pizza or the French pissaladière, to which they are related. All of these can be cut in small slices, wedges or squares, to be served warm with cocktails. Salty Tart Pastry can also be served in similar ways.

❧ / CHEESE CRACKERS FOR SOUP (*Käsegebäck*)

FOR 8 SERVINGS OF SOUP

2 tablespoons flour
2 tablespoons grated Cheddar or
    Parmesan cheese
½ teaspoon salt

½ teaspoon paprika
1 tablespoon butter
1 egg yolk beaten with 1 tea-
    spoon water

Mix flour, cheese, salt and paprika together in a bowl and cut in butter with two knives or a pastry blender, as you would for pie crust. Mixture should have texture of coarse meal. Knead dough until it holds together and chill in refrigerator ½ hour. Roll dough out on a floured board, using a floured rolling pin. It should be about ¼″ thick. Cut into ovals, circles or strips, using a knife, a small glass or a cookie cutter. Brush with egg-yolk mixture and bake in 350° oven about 15 minutes, or until crackers are lightly browned.

❧ / CARAWAY POTATO STICKS (*Kümmel-Kartoffelstangen*)

ABOUT 50 STICKS;
ENOUGH FOR ABOUT 6 PEOPLE

1 large baking potato, ⅓ to ½
    pound in weight, boiled and
    cooled
¼ pound stick of butter
1 to 2 cups flour

1 egg
salt
beaten egg
coarse salt
caraway seeds

Preheat oven to 375°. Potato should be peeled and grated or very finely mashed. It should be completely cool. Cut butter into tiny pieces and blend with mashed potato on a floured pastry board. Add 1 cup flour, egg, a pinch of salt and mix well. Keep adding more flour, a little at a time, until mixture is not sticky and can be rolled. Roll out dough on a well-floured board, using a rolling pin that is also dusted with a little flour. Dough should be about ¼″ thick. Cut into long thin strips, about ⅓″ wide by 2″ long, or in any other shape you like. You can also then twist the flat strips corkscrew style. Brush strips or twists with beaten egg and sprinkle with coarse salt and caraway seeds. Arrange on unbuttered cookie sheet and bake in middle of oven 15 to 20 minutes, or until sticks are a pleasant golden brown. Cool and serve.

❧ / SALTY TART PASTRY (*Salziger Mürbteig*)

2 to 2¼ cups flour	½ cup butter
1 teaspoon baking powder	1 whole egg
1 teaspoon salt	2 tablespoons sour cream
flavorings to taste, paprika, curry powder, nutmeg	

Prepare dough as for Rich Tart Pastry (page 427), using either kneading or stirring method. Chill dough, roll out, cut into squares, circles or diamonds or form twists, and chill again. Brush with beaten egg yolk and sprinkle with such toppings as coarse salt, caraway seeds, poppy seeds, grated Parmesan cheese or slivered unsalted almonds. Bake on ungreased sheet.

❧ / HAM POCKETS (*Schinkentaschen*)

12 TO 16 POCKETS

1 scant cup flour	salt
½ cup butter (¼ pound)	2 cups shredded, chopped or coarsely ground ham
¼ pound pot cheese or well-drained cottage cheese	1 egg, lightly beaten

Place flour in a bowl or on a wooden board. Cut butter into small pieces and then cut into flour with two knives, a pastry blender or rub in with fingertips. Mixture should reach consistency of coarse meal. Mix in cheese and a little salt. Knead dough on a floured board until smooth enough to roll. Do not handle it so much that it becomes greasy-looking. Using a floured rolling pin, roll dough on a floured board until it is paper-thin. Cut in 3½″ to 4″ squares. Preheat oven to 400°.

Place a mound of ham in the center of each square. Bring corners of square up toward center and pinch seams closed with your fingers or crimp with a fork. Arrange pockets on an ungreased baking sheet and brush with beaten egg. Bake in preheated oven about 20 minutes, or until pastry is crisp and golden. These are very good hot cocktail appetizers or excellent light entrees.

✂ / SWABIAN SAUERKRAUT CAKE (Schwäbischer Sauerkrautkuchen)

1 recipe Basic Yeast Dough, page 444, without sugar or lemon peel and with 3 cups flour

3 pounds sauerkraut

½ cup lard, rendered bacon fat or butter, or 8 slices fat bacon, diced

1 small onion, diced

salt and pepper

1 to 2 tablespoons caraway seeds (optional)

2 tablespoons flour

3 tablespoons milk

2 to 3 tablespoons sour cream

Prepare dough. When it has risen once, punch it down and roll out to fit a cookie sheet or jelly-roll pan and let rise again in a warm place about 15 minutes. Preheat oven to 400°. Meanwhile prepare filling. If sauerkraut is salty or sour, rinse once or twice in a colander under running water. Press out as much water as possible. Chop kraut finely. Heat fat or fry diced bacon in a large enameled iron- or tin-lined copper skillet. When hot, add onion and sauté slowly until it begins to turn light golden brown. Add sauerkraut, salt, pepper and caraway seeds and toss until kraut is mixed with fat. Cover and steam 10 or 15 minutes, or until kraut is soft. Shake pan several times to prevent sticking and stir once or twice. Mix flour into milk to form a thin paste and stir into hot, not boiling, kraut. Simmer a minute or two until thickened, then stir in sour cream. Season to taste. Spread on top of the raised yeast dough and let rise another 15 minutes. Bake in 400° oven about 45 minutes, or until dough is crisp and brown and filling is baked into it.

❊ / *STUTTGART OR SWABIAN ONION TART* (*Stuttgarter oder Schwäbischer Zwiebelkuchen*)

Both Swabia and Stuttgart claim this onion tart. By either name it is delicious.

1 *recipe Basic Yeast Dough, page*	*salt to taste*
444, without sugar or lemon	1 *to 2 tablespoons caraway seeds*
peel and with 3 cups flour	1 *tablespoon flour*
6 *to 8 large onions*	¾ *cup sour cream*
2 *tablespoons butter*	2 *small eggs, lightly beaten*
4 *slices bacon, diced*	

Prepare dough. When it has risen once, punch it down and roll out to thickness of between ¼″ and ⅓″, to fit an oiled cookie sheet or jelly-roll pan. Set in a warm place to rise about 20 minutes. Meanwhile prepare filling. Chop onions finely and measure off 4 cupfuls. Heat butter and fry diced bacon in it slowly 3 or 4 minutes. Add onions, salt and caraway seeds; stir, cover and steam a few minutes, or until onions have melted and are soft and yellow, not brown. Shake pan and stir several times to prevent scorching. Sprinkle flour over onions and stir in until absorbed. Mix sour cream with eggs and stir into onion mixture. Cook slowly over very low heat, stirring, a minute or two, or until mixture is thick and well blended. Season to taste. Spread on top of dough and allow to rise another 15 minutes. Bake in 400° oven 30 minutes, or until dough is crisp and brown around edges and onion mixture has set into it.

VARIATION

Onion Tart is sometimes made with Salty Tart Pastry, page 413, instead of yeast dough. (You can even make it with your favorite pie crust or pie crust mix, but omit any sugar.) This is a little quicker, though the yeast dough tastes better. Prepare dough, set aside. Cook onions in butter and bacon, as described, and when they are soft and yellow, season with salt and caraway seeds and stir in flour. When it is absorbed, stir in 1 whole egg and 1 egg yolk beaten into ½ cup sweet or sour cream. Simmer a few minutes until thick, then pour into two 9″ pie tins lined with dough. Bake in 400° oven 30 minutes, or until crust is done and crisp and top is golden brown.

⚄ / KURLÄNDER BACON TART (Kurländer Speckkuchen)

4 TO 6 SERVINGS

1 recipe Basic Yeast Dough, page
   444, made without sugar or
   lemon peel
7 slices bacon, or ⅓ pound
   Canadian bacon
1 small onion
1 tablespoon minced parsley

1 tablespoon breadcrumbs
   (optional)
salt to taste
1 egg white, beaten
1 egg yolk, beaten
1 or 2 tablespoons grated Parmesan cheese (optional)

Prepare dough. When it has risen, punch it down and cut off two-thirds. Roll this out to about ¼″ thickness, to fit an oiled cookie sheet or jelly-roll pan. Roll remainder of dough to fit same pan but leave it on the board and cover lightly with a kitchen towel. This second sheet will be much thinner than the first. To prepare filling, grind bacon once through fine blade of a food chopper, then put it through again with onion and parsley. Mix with breadcrumbs if you want mixture to be very dry and a little stiff; otherwise omit crumbs. Taste and add salt if necessary. Spread filling over dough on baking sheet and cover with the thinner sheet of dough. Seal edges by pinching together and moistening with egg white. Brush top with egg yolk and bake in preheated 350° oven about 30 minutes, or until dough is crisp and golden.

VARIATIONS

1.   Individual tarts can easily be made with this recipe. Divide dough in half and roll out in two ¼″-thick sheets. Cut circles with a glass or cookie cutter; you may make these any size you wish, depending on whether they are to be served with cocktails, as appetizer at table or as entrees. Place a mound of filling in the center of half the circles, then cover with other circles. Pinch edges closed with a little egg white. Place on an oiled baking sheet and bake about 30 minutes in a preheated 350° oven. If you like, a little grated cheese can be sprinkled on top of each for last 10 minutes of baking time.

2.   If you happen to have any chicken, duck or goose cracklings (Grieben, page xxiv) left from fat you have rendered, crumble them and mix into filling for an especially savory touch.

✕ TORTES ✕
(Torten)

✕ / BISCUIT TORTE (Biskuittorte)

This dry, light cake is the basis for all sorts of layer cakes, round and square, and is also cut and split to form many of the little iced, individually portioned petit-four-type cakes that line the shelves of Konditoreien. It can also be baked in a jelly-roll pan, filled with cream or jam and then rolled.

8 eggs, separated	⅔ cup sifted cornstarch
2 cups fine granulated sugar	1 teaspoon baking powder
grated rind of 1 lemon	(optional)
⅔ cup sifted flour	1 tablespoon sugar

Preheat oven to 250°. Beat egg yolks with 2 cups sugar and lemon rind until mixture is very thick and pale yellow. Sift flour and cornstarch together. If you want to be doubly sure that your cake will rise, use baking powder, though you will have a better cake without it. If you do use it, sift it in with flour and cornstarch. Beat egg whites and as they begin to thicken beat in 1 tablespoon sugar. Continue beating until whites stand in stiff but glossy peaks. Turn egg-yolk mixture into whites and sprinkle with flour-cornstarch mixture. Using a rubber spatula, fold together gently but thoroughly, until no traces of egg white or flour show. Butter and flour an 8″ to 9″ spring form or square pan. Turn batter into it and bake in preheated oven about 1 hour. Cake is done if it springs back to shape when you press it with your finger. Cool in pan 15 minutes, then turn cake out onto rack and cool completely. Split into two or three layers, which can be sprinkled with fruit juice, rum, arrack or lemon juice before they are filled and iced. Sandwich together with fruit marmalade or jelly, or any of the butter creams on page 480. Top with butter cream or icing.

VARIATIONS

1. Punch Torte (Punschtorte): Prepare torte in a round spring form a day before you want to serve it. Store, lightly covered, overnight.

Cut cake in half to form 2 layers. Mix ½ cup rum with 1½ tablespoons sugar, ¼ cup water and 2 tablespoons lemon juice. Moisten layers with this and sandwich together, after spreading apricot marmalade or currant, sour cherry, raspberry or strawberry jam or jelly between them. Coat sides and top with Punch Icing, page 478.

2.   Butter Cream Torte (Buttercremetorte): Bake torte and after storing overnight, cut into layers. Flavor layers by moistening with fruit juice and/or arrack and sugar or maraschino. Prepare any of the butter creams on page 480 and use between layers and on top of cake. Top with nuts, fruit or chopped praline (Krokant), page 396.

3.   Pineapple Torte (Ananastorte): Prepare torte in round spring form and when cool, cut in two layers. Fill with gelatin-stiffened whipped cream (page 476), softening the gelatin in pineapple juice. Fold 1 cup drained, crushed or cubed canned pineapple into cream and spread between layers. Top with sweetened whipped cream and decorate with rings or half-rings of canned pineapple.

░ / NUT TORTE (Nusstorte)

8 eggs, separated	1 tablespoon sugar
1½ cups sugar	butter
1 teaspoon vanilla extract or 1 tablespoon rum	flour
1½ cups shelled hazelnuts, walnuts or blanched almonds, coarsely grated	rum- or vanilla-flavored whipped cream

Preheat oven to 350°. Beat yolks with 1½ cups sugar and vanilla or rum until mixture is pale yellow and thick enough to "ribbon." Do not grate nuts too finely. If you prefer, they can be crushed by being placed in a paper bag and then rolled with a rolling pin. Turn bag over several times so nuts are evenly crushed. Walnuts and hazelnuts need not be blanched but almonds should. Beat egg whites and as they begin to thicken, add 1 tablespoon sugar; beat until whites stand in stiff but glossy peaks. Turn into a large wide bowl unless they are already in one. Stir 2 or 3 tablespoons of the beaten whites into the yolk mixture. Pour yolk mixture over whites and sprinkle with grated nuts. Using a rubber spatula, fold mixtures together, gently but thoroughly. There should be no traces of whites or nuts showing. Butter two 9" layer cake pans or an 8" or 9" spring form and sprinkle lightly with flour, tapping out excess. Bake in 350° oven about 1 hour, or until cake springs back to shape when you press it down with your finger. Cool in pan until cake shrinks away from sides. Invert on rack to cool completely. If you have made cake in a spring form, cut into layers. Fill and top with rum- or vanilla-flavored whipped cream.

VARIATION

Nut Roll (Nussrolle): Prepare batter but spread onto an 11″ by 16″ jelly-roll pan covered with a buttered sheet of paper. Bake until done and cool in pan. Cover with a slightly damp towel and chill for several hours or overnight. Place two large overlapping pieces of waxed paper (the seam should run lengthwise) on a pastry board and sprinkle with confectioners' sugar. Turn cake over onto sugar and peel off waxed paper carefully. Spread with whipped cream flavored with vanilla or rum, or with Butter Cream (page 480), using nuts. Roll cake gently, jelly-roll style, using the waxed paper to lift it. Wrap paper snugly around roll and chill 1 to 2 hours before serving. Sprinkle more sugar on top of roll before lifting it onto serving board or plate.

✂ / *BLACK BREAD-SPICE TORTE* (*Schwarzbrot-Gewürztorte*)

2 cups very dry dark pumpernickel breadcrumbs
½ cup red wine or red fruit juice such as currant or raspberry
2 tablespoons rum
8 eggs, separated
1¼ cups sugar
¾ cup grated unblanched almonds, hazelnuts, walnuts or pecans
1 teaspoon powered cinnamon
¼ teaspoon powdered cloves
4 tablespoons candied orange peel and citron, finely chopped
grated rind of 1 lemon
1 tablespoon sugar
butter
breadcrumbs
rum or arrack
red currant jelly or apricot marmalade
Punch Icing, page 477
candied fruit

Preheat oven to 350°. Soak crumbs in wine or fruit juice mixed with rum. Separate eggs. Beat yolks with 1¼ cups sugar until mixture is very thick and pale yellow. Add soaked, undrained crumbs, nuts, spices, candied fruit and lemon rind and mix together well. Beat egg whites and as they thicken, add 1 tablespoonful sugar gradually. Continue beating until whites stand in stiff but glossy peaks. Turn egg-yolk-breadcrumb mixture onto whites. Using a rubber spatula, fold together gently but thoroughly until no whites show. Butter a 9″ spring form or Kugelhupf mold and sprinkle with breadcrumbs on bottom and sides, tapping out excess. Turn batter into pan and bake in preheated oven about 1 hour. Cake is done when it springs back to shape if you press it with your finger. Cool 10 or 15 minutes, re-move cake from pan and continue cooling on rack. Cut through mid-dle to form two layers. Sprinkle top of each layer with rum or arrack. Spread a layer of jelly or marmalade between the two layers, sand-wich together and cover tops and sides with icing. Decorate with candied fruit. If possible, store in refrigerator a day or two before serving, as the cake will ripen and taste better.

❖ / MERINGUE TORTE (Schaumtorte)

This is the most elegant dessert torte served in Germany and Austria. Whether you make it with layers or a shell or meringue, it is filled with sweetened whipped cream and, usually, strawberries, though you could use any other fresh berries or fruit in season. If meringues are thor-oughly dried in oven, they keep for several days to a week; cover them loosely with a kitchen towel or any airy cotton cloth. Add filling just before serving.

6 to 8 egg whites (¾ cup)
2 teaspoons vinegar, or ¼ tea-spoon cream of tartar
¼ teaspoon salt
1 teaspoon vanilla
2 cups fine granulated sugar

3 cups sweetened whipped cream that has been mixed with sliced strawberries, whole raspberries or cut fresh fruit such as peaches, bananas or pineapple, in season

Let egg whites stand at room temperature 20 minutes before beating, so they will not be too cold. Add vinegar or cream of tartar, salt and vanilla and beat until whites begin to form soft peaks. Gradually add sugar and continue beating until whites stand in stiff, dry peaks.

This torte may be formed in either of two ways. The first is the sim-pler: two solid layers of meringue with the filling in between; if you like, the whipped-cream mixture can be divided in half and used as filling and topping. The second method—one solid bottom layer topped by rings to form a hollow shell—is showier if a little more intricate to assemble. To form the two solid layers, you will need either two 9″ layer-cake-pan bottoms, as from a spring form or flan ring, or one very large baking sheet. The pans may be buttered and lightly sprinkled with flour or covered with sheets of waxed paper. If you use a baking sheet, trace two 9″ circles on it. Using half the meringue for each, spread evenly to the edge of each circle. To form the fancier hollow shell, you will need two large baking sheets, buttered and floured or covered with waxed paper. Trace two 9″ circles on each baking sheet. Spread one solid layer of meringue to the edges of one circle. Put the remaining meringue in a pastry bag that is fitted with a large fluted or plain tube.

Pipe rings of meringue, 1″ high and 1½″ wide, around the edges of two circles. Around the edge of the fourth circle, pipe a ring of kisses (small mounds) that touch each other to form a complete closed circle.

Meringues should dry out rather than bake. They must remain snowy white and not brown at all. Bake in the slowest possible oven (200° to 250°) 40 minutes, or until crisp and dry. Cool and peel off waxed paper or slide off baking pans. If you have made two layers, spread half the whipped-cream filling between them. Cover top and sides with remaining filling and decorate with berries or fruit. To form the hollow shell, place the solid bottom layer on the serving dish and stack the two plain rings on it. Fill with sweetened cream and fruit and top with the circle of kisses. Garnish with whole berries or fruit slices.

/ *PISCHINGER TORTE*

Since I like very thin, crunchy cakes in preference to those that are very high and floury, this one is a great personal favorite. In addition to being absolutely delicious, it is one of the simplest to prepare, since it is more a matter of assembling than baking. It is made with layers of big, round crisp sugar wafers, similar to the French gaufrettes. These are called Carlsbad Leaves—Karlsbad Oblaten—and are sold in packages not only in German food stores but in the gourmet shops of department stores all over the country.

SERVES 8 TO 10

1 package Karlsbad Oblaten
1 recipe Butter Cream Filling, page 480, using chocolate
1 recipe Dark Chocolate Icing, page 479
whipped cream (optional)

Unwrap Oblaten and discard any that might be crushed. Prepare filling and spread between layers of Oblaten. Stack them on each other and chill in refrigerator several hours or, preferably, overnight. Several hours before serving, cover top and sides with icing and chill until icing is hard. Serve with or without whipped cream.

/ *MOCK SADDLE OF VENISON* (*Falscher Rehrücken*)

This cake is a favorite in Swabia as well as in neighboring French Alsace. Form is even more important than content with this cake, for it is shaped to imitate a saddle of venison—Rehrücken—a specialty in both of those game-loving regions. The cake itself is a chocolate torte, sometimes made with potato flour or potato, other times as an authentic butterless, flourless torte. What you must have is the correct Rehrücken pan—a long, ribbed, half-round aluminum form that looks like a miniature Quonset hut. After the cake is baked, cooled and iced it is studded with whole, halved or slivered blanched almonds that imitate the strips of lard that would spike real venison meat.

5 eggs, separated	⅓ cup grated dark semi-sweet
2 whole eggs	chocolate
½ cup sugar	1 tablespoon sugar
½ teaspoon cinnamon	butter
2 tablespoons mixed candied	breadcrumbs
citron and orange peel,	Dark Chocolate Icing, page
finely chopped	479
¾ cup grated unblanched	blanched almonds, whole,
almonds	halved or slivered for garnish

Preheat oven to 350°. Beat egg yolks, whole eggs and ½ cup sugar until mixture is very thick and pale yellow. Add cinnamon, candied fruit, nuts and chocolate. Mix until thoroughly blended. Beat egg whites and as they begin to thicken, add 1 tablespoon sugar. Continue beating until whites stand in stiff but glossy peaks. Pour chocolate mixture onto whites. Using a rubber spatula, fold together gently but thoroughly until no whites show. Butter one 11″ Rehrücken pan, an 8″ loaf pan or an 8″ spring form, depending on the shape cake you want. Bake about 45 minutes, or until cake springs back to shape when you press it with your finger. Cool in pan 5 or 10 minutes then invert onto rack and cool completely. When cold, cover with icing and stud with 3 rows of almonds, lengthwise.

❇ / CHOCOLATE POTATO TORTE (*Schokoladen-Kartoffeltorte*)

3 to 4 medium-sized baking po-	2 cups sifted flour
tatoes (or 1¾ cups cooked,	1 cup ground unblanched
riced potatoes)	almonds
4 eggs, separated	¾ cup butter
2 ounces (squares) bitter	1⅔ cups sugar
chocolate	2 teaspoons vanilla extract
½ teaspoon baking powder	1 tablespoon sugar

If possible, boil and peel potatoes a day ahead of time so they can dry out a little. If not, be sure they are thoroughly cold before you rice them or they will stick together and be difficult to blend evenly into batter. Purée potatoes through a food mill, sieve or ricer. Measure off 1¾ cupfuls and set aside. Preheat oven to 350°. Separate eggs so whites will not be too cold when you beat them. Melt chocolate over hot water. Add baking powder to flour and sift again, together, onto a sheet of paper.

Add nuts to flour and gently toss together with a fork until thoroughly blended. Cream butter with 1⅔ cups sugar until light and fluffy. Beat in egg yolks and when blended, beat in melted chocolate, potatoes and vanilla. Whip egg whites and as they begin to stiffen, beat in 1 tablespoon sugar. Continue beating until whites stand in stiff but glossy peaks. Beat 2 or 3 tablespoons of the stiffened egg whites into the chocolate batter to lighten it. Turn egg whites into a wide roomy bowl, unless they are already in one. Turn chocolate batter onto egg whites, and sprinkle with flour-nut mixture. Using a rubber spatula, fold egg whites, chocolate batter and flour together, gently but thoroughly. There should be no traces of flour or egg white showing.

If you would like to use this batter for Mock Saddle of Venison, bake in buttered Rehrücken form. Ice and decorate accordingly. Otherwise, bake in two unbuttered 9″ layer-cake pans or in an 8″ spring form. Cool in pan, invert onto rack until completely cold. If you have used spring form, cut cake into two layers. Layers may be filled with whipped cream, jam or chocolate butter cream.

☙ / *PRINCE REGENT TORTE* (*Prinzregententorte*)

¼ *pound butter*	*Butter Cream Filling, page* 480,
1¼ *cups sugar*	*using chocolate*
2 *whole eggs*	*apricot marmalade and Hard*
2 *eggs, separated*	*Chocolate Icing, page* 479, *or*
1¼ *cups flour*	*raspberry jam or currant jelly*
1 *tablespoon sugar*	*and Lemon or Rum Icing, page*
butter	478
flour	

Preheat oven to 350°. Since you need 8 to 10 thin layers, baked separately, you will have to bake this in shifts. Prepare all the batter at once, then keep in a warm spot in the kitchen until all layers are done. They should be baked in the lower third of oven, so do not attempt to place them all in at one time. Cream butter with 1¼ cups sugar until very fluffy. Work in whole eggs and egg yolks until very well blended.

Place the measured, sifted flour in a sifter or larger strainer. Beat egg whites and as they begin to stiffen, beat in 1 tablespoonful sugar. Continue beating until whites stand in stiff glossy peaks. Pour egg-yolk mixture onto whites and sift flour on top. Using a rubber spatula, fold together gently but thoroughly until no traces of egg white or flour show.

Butter and flour one or two 9″ round bottoms of a spring form or flan ring. You do not need the sides. Spread 2 to 3 tablespoons batter on each as evenly as possible. Try to avoid thinning batter near edges or they will burn. Bake in preheated oven 8 to 10 minutes or until light golden brown. Remove to a board and cool while you bake the next batch. When all layers are baked and completely cold, spread on one side with butter cream filling and on the other with apricot marmalade. Stack them up so that there is marmalade and cream between each layer. There should be nothing on the bottom side of the bottom layer and marmalade should top the top layer. Cover top and sides with Chocolate Icing. Or spread with red jam or jelly and cover with Lemon or Rum Icing.

✂ / LAYER CAKE (*Schichttorte*)

This is a name one finds often on the menus of Konditoreien. Literally it *is* a layer cake and can be filled with any number of fillings and icings. The above cake is really a Schichttorte. You could use the same recipe, making anywhere from 6 to 10 layers, depending on thickness, and fill and ice them with flavors other than chocolate. Butter Cream flavored with vanilla (page 480) with Lemon Icing (page 478) is one favorite combination, as is a filling of thick, dry applesauce flavored with raisins, chopped almonds and citron, also with Lemon Icing. Obviously, the combinations are endless. All of these can also be layered, filled, cut in individual squares and then iced and decorated with nutmeats, candied fruits, etc.

✂ / BLACK FOREST CHERRY CAKE (*Schwarzwälder Kirschtorte*)

This unusual blend of chocolate, cherries, kirsch-flavored whipped cream and shaved chocolate is a specialty throughout Swabia. There are almost endless variations on the theme and this version is one of the best. It comes from the Café Harzer in Herrenalb, where it is served with a small glass of iced kirsch.

2 *chocolate layers, as on pages* 421-422	*bing cherries, stewed or canned*
kirsch	1 *recipe gelatin-thickened whipped cream, flavored with kirsch, page 476*
1 *recipe Butter Cream Filling, using chocolate, page 480*	
2 *cups stoned and halved black*	*Chocolate Curls, page 476*

Bake two round layer cakes—from the above recipes or one of your own favorites. Or buy two unfrosted layers in a bakery. Moisten both layers liberally with kirsch. Prepare cream filling and spread all of it on top of one layer. Drain cherries well and place half of them on top of butter cream, gently pressing into it. Top with second layer. Prepare whipped cream and flavor well with kirsch. Arrange on top of top layer, heaping cream in swirls and mounds as you spread it on. Garnish with remaining cherries and shaved chocolate. This can be served at once or it can be chilled for an hour or so in refrigerator.

✖ PASTRIES ✖
(*Feingebäck*)

✖ / CREAM PUFF PASTRY OR CHOUX PASTE
(*Brandteig*)

YIELDS ABOUT 24 MEDIUM-SIZED CREAM PUFFS

1 *cup water*	1 *tablespoon sugar*
pinch of salt	1 *cup flour*
½ *cup butter*	4 *large eggs*

Combine water, salt, butter and sugar in a 1-quart heavy-bottomed saucepan. Bring to a boil and simmer until butter melts completely. Put through a sifter, shake flour into liquid in saucepan. Cook over low heat, stirring constantly and vigorously until mixture forms a mass and leaves sides of pan. Remove from heat and beat in eggs, one at a time. Be sure one egg is thoroughly blended before you add the next. Cool and bake or deep-fry, according to specific recipes.

❦ / CREAM PUFFS, ÉCLAIRS OR WREATHS
(*Windbeutel, Éclairs oder Kränze*)

1 recipe Cream Puff Pastry, above
1 egg yolk, beaten
2 cups sweetened cream flavored
    to taste
2 cups sliced strawberries or
    cherries (optional)

confectioners' sugar, or 1 recipe
    Custard Filling, page 480,
    and Hard Chocolate Icing,
    page 479

Prepare pastry and let cool completely. To make puffs, drop batter from two teaspoons or two tablespoons, depending on the size puffs you want, onto a buttered baking sheet. To shape éclairs or wreaths, put batter in a pastry bag fitted with a large plain round tube and force batter out into strips or circles about 1" to 1½" wide. Éclairs should be about 3½" long and wreaths any size you like, usually 3" in diameter.

Brush wreaths or puffs with yolk; eclairs may be brushed with egg if they are not to be iced. Bake in 375° oven about 20 minutes, or until puffed up and golden brown. Turn heat off and leave puffs in oven another 10 minutes. Split in half through the middle while still warm. Cool before filling. Puffs and wreaths are usually filled with whipped cream which may or may not have chopped cherries or strawberries in it. If fruit is used, cream is flavored with a little kirsch or maraschino. Dust tops of puffs with confectioners' sugar. Éclairs may be filled with whipped cream and frosted with chocolate or simply dusted with sugar. Usually they are filled with custard and iced with chocolate. Mocha cream filling and icing are also popular for éclairs. Obviously you can use any of the fillings with any of the shapes.

❦ / RICH TART PASTRY (*Mürbteig*)

Covered fruit pies as we know them are oddities in Germany. Instead, open tarts filled with fruit, fruit preserves or cheese are made in many varieties. The pastry for them is, perhaps, Germany's greatest contribution to gastronomy. Mürbteig, literally, "mellow dough," is tender and crisp, buttery and sweet, and good enough to be cut into cookie shapes and eaten without any topping or filling at all. In addition, it does not get soggy, a great advantage for tart shells that are to hold fruit. But perhaps its greatest claim to fame is its simplicity, for it is quick and easy to make and almost foolproof to handle. Because it is such an important and basic German baked specialty, I have given several versions of it, all of which can be used for your favorite pies. Each recipe will yield one 9″ pie shell, with some dough left over for lattice strips, if you want them. It is best to bake this tart in ungreased spring form or flan ring, since the loose bottom makes it easier to remove the finished pie. Leftover strips of dough, twisted together, are formed into a ring to edge the pie and prevent sides from shrinking.

This tart shell is usually filled before being baked. It should be placed low in the oven so that it sets before it absorbs fruit juices and becomes soggy. When a custard or liquid is to be poured over the fruit, you can half-bake the crust in advance, but that is not strictly necessary. If you feel safer doing so, line the ungreased form with the pastry and prick the bottom with a fork. Fill the shell about halfway with dried beans, to keep it from buckling as it bakes. If edges shrink down, press them back into place with a fork or your finger. Place in the middle of a preheated 350° oven 10 minutes. Crust should just begin to turn golden but should not be crisp or brown. Discard beans and fill shell before or after it has cooled. Continue baking with filling 20 to 30 minutes, or according to specific recipes.

Mürbteig can be kept for several days in the refrigerator if it is wrapped in waxed paper; roll out and fill just before baking. A ring or pan lined with unbaked dough can be wrapped in foil and frozen. It is perhaps most convenient and practical to freeze the dough in disposable, inexpensive heavy-aluminum-foil pie tins. Fill and bake *without* thawing.

Mürbteig made only with egg yolks is richer in color and flavor but more fragile than that made with whole eggs. Strictly speaking, baking powder is not used in this pastry, but some people add a little to make the dough flaky, especially if it is to be baked on a sheet instead of in a ring, thereby resulting in something closer to a Kuchen, or cake.

It is a good idea to experiment with the various types of Mürbteig, to see which you like best and find most convenient to handle. Flavorings and sugar can be varied to suit the filling you want to use.

✁ / *RICH TART PASTRY I*

2 to 2¼ cups flour
pinch of salt
⅓ cup fine granulated sugar
⅔ cup butter
1 egg, lightly beaten
1 tablespoon water, milk or
    white wine

2 teaspoons grated lemon rind
1 tablespoon rum, arrack or
    brandy (optional)
⅓ cup finely grated unblanched
    almonds or other nuts (optional)

❄ / RICH TART PASTRY II

2 to 2¼ cups flour
    pinch of salt
⅓ cup sugar
¾ cup butter
2 egg yolks
1 to 2 tablespoons milk or white
    wine

2 teaspoons grated lemon peel
1 tablespoon rum, arrack or
    brandy (optional)
⅓ cup finely grated unblanched
    almonds or other nuts (op-
    tional)

❄ / RICH TART PASTRY III

2 to 2¼ cups flour
    pinch of salt
⅓ cup sugar
¾ cup butter
2 raw egg yolks or 2 raw egg
    whites
2 hard-cooked egg yolks,
    mashed

1 to 2 tablespoons milk or white
    wine
2 teaspoons grated lemon peel
1 tablespoon rum, arrack or
    brandy (optional)
⅓ cup finely grated unblanched
    almonds or other nuts (op-
    tional)

The procedure is identical for all of these mixtures. Sift flour with salt and sugar onto a board or into a wide bowl. Cut very cold butter into small pieces and quickly work into flour mixture, using two knives, a pastry blender or, preferably, your fingertips, until mixture looks like fine meal. Combine all liquid ingredients and whichever flavorings you are using. Nuts can be mixed into dough or sprinkled on top of it before filling, or not used at all. Whether you use raw egg yolks or whites in the third version depends on the result you want. The yolks give a richer, more fragile crust; the whites produce one that is less brittle. Make a well in center of flour and gradually work flour and liquid together, using a fork or your fingers, until dough sticks together in a ball. Add a little extra flour if dough is too sticky to handle, a little more water, milk or wine if it is too dry and crumbly. Using the heel of your hand, and working very quickly, knead ball of dough on a lightly floured board. Do this twice, then reshape ball, wrap in waxed paper and chill. Do the kneading quickly so butter does not melt and give dough a dark, greasy look. When dough is well chilled and no longer sticky, it is ready for rolling. Place on a lightly floured board and roll with a floured rolling pin. Or roll between two sheets of waxed paper. Fit into ungreased spring form or flan ring (see sketch on page xxviii) and chill again 30 minutes to 1 hour before filling and baking.

VARIATIONS

1.   To make flaky, slightly raised crust, sift 1 teaspoonful baking powder in with flour, sugar and salt.

2.   To make dough that can be baked on a sheet instead of in a round form, use the whole-egg recipe (I) with 3 cups flour, 2 teaspoons baking powder and 1 teaspoon powdered cinnamon in addition to the other ingredients. Topped with fruit or cheese and baked, this can be cut into portion strips or squares.

3.   The batter above is known as gebröselter, or crumbled, Mürbteig. If it seems easier, and if kneading seems a problem to you, the process can be changed a little. To do this, cream butter with sugar and mix in eggs (cooked and raw), flavorings, rind and nuts if you use them. When light and fluffy, place in well made in flour mixture and blend ingredients together, using a fork or your fingers, adding water, milk or wine only if needed to make dough stick together in a smooth ball. Wrap in waxed paper and chill 2 or 3 hours. Roll out and bake in the same way as crumbled Mürbteig. This latter method is called gerührter, or stirred, Mürbteig.

⛬ / APPLES IN NIGHTGOWNS (*Äpfel im Schlafrock*)

8 SERVINGS

1 *recipe* Rich Tart Pastry, *page* 427	2 *teaspoons cinnamon*
8 *small, not too sour, cooking apples*	2 *to* 3 *tablespoons citrus or quince marmalade, melted*
3 *tablespoons sugar*	*egg white or milk*
¼ *cup raisins or chopped nuts*	1 *egg yolk, beaten*
	confectioners' sugar

Prepare pastry, chill, then roll out to about ¼" thickness in a single sheet. Cut into squares, each of which is large enough to wrap around 1 apple. Chill. Preheat oven to 400°. Core and peel apples and set 1 in center of each dough square. Mix sugar, nuts or raisins, cinnamon and marmalade and place a little of mixture in core of each apple. Cover apples with dough, envelope-style, or bring corners of square up toward center to form a peak. Seal edges with egg white or milk. Set on ungreased baking sheet or pan and brush with beaten egg yolk. Bake in preheated oven 10 minutes, then lower heat to 350° and continue baking 20 to 30 minutes, or until crust is golden brown and crisp. Cool and serve sprinkled with confectioners' sugar. Can also be served hot.

✸ / CHEESE TART (*Käsekuchen mit Mürbteig*)

1 recipe Rich Tart Pastry, page 427	5 eggs, separated
1 pound pot cheese (not cottage cheese)	⅓ cup raisins
¼ pound butter, melted	pinch of baking powder
1 cup hot, not boiling, milk	6 tablespoons flour, approximately
⅔ cup sugar	1 tablespoon sugar
grated rind of 1 lemon	1 egg yolk, beaten

Prepare pastry, chill, roll and fit into 9″ spring form, bringing dough to full height of rim. Chill well before filling. Preheat oven to 350°. Rub pot cheese through a very fine sieve. Mix with hot melted butter, milk, ⅔ cup sugar, lemon rind, 5 egg yolks, raisins, baking powder and enough flour to make a thick mixture. Beat egg whites and gradually add 1 tablespoon sugar. Continue beating until they stand in stiff but glossy peaks. Stir 2 or 3 tablespoons beaten whites into cheese mixture to lighten it. Turn mixture onto whites. Using a rubber spatula, gently but thoroughly fold mixture together until no whites show. Turn into unbaked tart shell and brush top with beaten egg yolk. Bake 1 hour, brushing with more yolk once or twice during baking. Cool in pan, then slide off spring-form bottom onto serving plate.

✸ / SWABIAN APPLE OR PLUM TART (*Schwäbischer Apfel- oder Zwetschgenkuchen*)

1 recipe Rich Tart Pastry, page 427, flavored with rum, lemon rind and grated almonds	½ cup thick sour cream or sweet cream
	1 tablespoon rum
2 pounds not too sour cooking apples or small blue plums powdered cinnamon	½ cup raisins or currants, soaked in rum and drained, or ½ cup slivered blanched almonds
¼ cup sugar	melted butter
3 eggs, separated	1 egg yolk, beaten
4 tablespoons sugar	

Prepare pastry, chill and roll to fit spring form, forming sides about 2½″ to 3″ high. Chill well. Preheat oven to 350°. Peel, core and slice apples. Plums are not peeled, but they are cut in halves or quarters and are stoned. Twist strips of leftover dough to make a ring on top of pastry. Brush bottom of pastry with melted butter and top of ring with beaten egg yolk. Arrange apples or plums on dough and sprinkle with cinnamon and ¼ cup sugar. Bake 20 minutes. Mix egg yolks with 4 tablespoons sugar until thick and pale yellow. Beat in cream and rum. Beat egg whites and as they being to thicken, add sugar. Continue beating until whites stand in stiff but glossy peaks. Fold into egg-yolk mixture, gently but thoroughly, using a rubber spatula. Sprinkle raisins, currants or almonds over fruit and cover with egg mixture. Continue baking 20 to 30 minutes, or until custard is set and filling is golden brown on top.

VARIATION

At Kreutzkamm's in Munich, apples are cut in halves instead of being sliced. The result is quite attractive. Peel and core apples and cut in halves. Score round side with a fork or knife. Arrange in a single layer in 2″-deep pie shell, round side up, and proceed.

✂ / *BAVARIAN APPLE OR PLUM CAKE* (*Bayrischer Apfel- oder Zwetschgenkuchen*)

Follow recipe for Swabian Tart (above), but when apples or plums are in shell, sprinkle with sugar, cinnamon, raisins and almonds and dot with butter. Brush twisted ring of dough with egg and bake for 35 to 40 minutes in 375° oven. Raspberry or apricot jam can be spread on bottom crust or over apples, and again, apples may be sliced or cut in rounds.

✂ / *GOOSEBERRY TART* (*Stachelbeerkuchen*)

1 *recipe Rich Tart Pastry, page 427, using 1 teaspoon baking powder*	1 *tablespoon sugar*
	⅓ *cup heavy cream*
	1 *tablespoon cornstarch*
1 *quart gooseberries, washed and picked over*	1 *tablespoon melted butter*
	¼ *cup grated blanched almonds*
1 *cup sugar*	*confectioners' sugar*
2 *egg yolks*	

Prepare pastry. Chill, roll and line a spring form or flan ring. Chill and top with twisted ring of leftover dough. Fill with gooseberries and sprinkle with sugar. Bake in 350° oven 20 minutes. Beat yolks with 1 tablespoon sugar until thick and pale yellow. Mix with cream, cornstarch, melted butter and nuts. Pour over gooseberries and continue baking about 15 to 20 minutes, or until crust is golden brown and fruit is done. Sprinkle with confectioners' sugar.

/ *RASPBERRY OR STRAWBERRY SNOW PIE (Himbeer- oder Erdbeerschaumkuchen)*

- *1 recipe Rich Tart Pastry, page 427*
- *1 egg yolk, beaten*
- *1 quart strawberries or raspberries*
- *½ cup sugar*
- *4 egg whites*
- *1 tablespoon sugar*
- *½ cup whipped cream*

Prepare pastry and bake in a spring form or flan ring, after brushing dough with beaten egg yolk. Cool completely. Wash and hull berries and divide in 2 equal quantities. Half the berries will go into shell as they are, the rest will be mixed with egg snow. If berries for pie shell are large, cut in half. Sprinkle with sugar and let sit 15 to 20 minutes, then place in baked, cooled pie crust. Beat egg whites and as they thicken, add 1 tablespoon sugar and continue beating until they stand in stiff but glossy peaks. Remaining berries may be finely cut or puréed. Fold into egg snow gently but thoroughly with a rubber spatula, then spread over sugared berries. Chill 2 hours before serving.

/ *CRUMB-TOPPED FRUIT TART (Obstkuchen mit Streusel)*

- *1 recipe Rice Tart Pastry, page 427*
- *1½ to 2 pounds plums, cherries or apples*
- *¾ cup flour*
- *⅓ cup sugar*
- *pinch of cinnamon*
- *4 tablespoons butter*

Prepare pastry, chill. Line a flan ring, chill again and brush with a little melted butter. Wash, peel and stone fruit as necessary. Plums should not be peeled; cherries may or may not be stoned and cut in half. (Some claim they have more flavor with stones in, but it seems like a bother when it comes to eating.) Brush unbaked pastry shell with a little butter and place fruit in it. Mix flour, sugar and cinnamon thoroughly. Cut butter in small pieces, then, with you fingertips, rub into dry mixture until you have fine crumbs. More butter can be added if mixture is too fine. Sprinkle over fruit and bake in 350° oven 30 to 40 minutes, or until crust and crumbs are golden brown.

⚅ / *FRUIT TART WITH WHIPPED CREAM OR CRUMB TOPPING (Obstkuchen mit Schlagrahm oder Streusel)*

1 *recipe Rich Tart Pastry, page 427*
melted butter
1 *egg, lightly beaten*
2 *pounds not too sour cooking apples or small blue plums, or 1 quart berries, or 4 cups grapes, or 3 large oranges, or 4 bananas, or 3 to 4 cups cherries, sour cherries, gooseberries, sliced red plums,* *apricots, peaches or pineapple (cooked as for compote and drained well, page 367)*

2 *cups whipped cream, or crumb topping made with*
$\frac{3}{4}$ *cup flour*
$\frac{1}{3}$ *cup sugar*
$\frac{1}{2}$ *teaspoon cinnamon*
$\frac{1}{2}$ *to* $\frac{3}{4}$ *cup butter*

Chill dough, roll out to fit spring form or flan ring and place twisted dough strips, around the edge. Chill 1 hour. Before filling pie shell, brush bottom with melted butter and rim with beaten egg. (Apples and plums should be placed in unbaked pie shell.) Peel, core and slice apples, or stone plums and slice. Place in shell, sprinkle with granulated sugar and cinnamon and bake in 350° oven 45 minutes to 1 hour. Top with whipped cream.

For other fruits, prepare pie shell and bake according to directions on page 426 in 350° oven 30 to 45 minutes, or until crisp and golden brown. Cool and fill with raw whole berries or grapes; sliced oranges or bananas; or any of the cooked, drained fruits indicated.

The apple or plum tart can be topped with whipped cream or crumbs. Whipped cream should be added after pie has baked and cooled. To make crumbs, combine dry ingredients, then rub butter in with your fingertips until crumbs form. If mixture is too dry and mealy, add more butter; if crumbs are too large, add more flour and sugar. Sprinkle over apples or plums before baking.

VARIATIONS

1. Chopped nuts can be sprinkled on bottom of pie shell before fruit is added in either of these versions.
2. In making a pie filled with grapes, berries, oranges, bananas or pineapple, you can brush the bottom of baked shell with $\frac{1}{2}$ cup melted apricot, raspberry or currant jam or marmalade. Fill with fruit and brush with 1 cup of glaze.

✂ / LINZER TORTE (*Linzer Torte*)

Although this is usually known as Linzer Torte, it is really a pie filled with raspberry preserves. The Oblaten, or wafers, are those thin white papery leaves that are used on top and bottom of nougat candy. They can be purchased at a bakers' supply company, at some fine gourmet shops, or from your local baker if he is co-operative enough to sell you some. If you cannot get them, brush the pie bottom with several layers of beaten egg white.

Dough:

2½ cups flour
2½ cups sugar
½ pound (1 cup) butter
½ teaspoon cinnamon
   pinch of powdered cloves

½ pound almonds, shelled and
   grated but not blanched
1 egg

Filling:

1 layer Oblaten, or 1 egg white,
   lightly beaten

2 to 3 cups raspberry preserves or
   jam
1 egg, lightly beaten

Prepare dough, as on page 427, using grated almonds and spices in it. Chill 30 minutes. Roll out to fit a 9″ to 10″ spring form and line pan with dough. Cut leftover dough into strips for lattice topping and edge. Chill 1 hour. Cover bottom of dough with wafers or brush with beaten egg white. If you use egg white, let it dry about 5 minutes. Spread jam into pie shell, filling almost to top. Arrange lattice strips over top, edge with twisted strips of dough and chill. Brush edges and strips with beaten egg and bake in 350° oven about 45 minutes, or until dough is crisp and light golden brown. Spoon a little more jam into spaces between lattice strips when pie has cooled.

✂ / RICH TART PASTRY STRUDEL OR HUSSAR STRUDEL (*Mürbteig- oder Husarenstrudel*)

Dough:

2½ cups flour
¾ cup butter
¼ cup fine granulated sugar
   pinch of salt

2 egg yolks or 1 whole egg
2 tablespoons milk
2 tablespoons white wine
1 teaspoon rum

Filling:

1½ pounds not too sour cooking
    apples
1 to 2 tablespoons lemon juice
¼ cup sugar
1 teaspoon cinnamon
½ cup raisins

½ cup chopped unblanched al-
    monds or other nuts
melted butter
1 egg white, lightly beaten
1 egg yolk, lightly beaten
confectioners' sugar

Prepare dough (page 427). Chill and roll into a rectangle measuring about 15" by 20". Dough should be rolled very thin. Peel core and slice apples thinly. Sprinkle with lemon juice and toss gently with sugar, cinnamon, raisins and almonds. If apples seem very sour, add a little more sugar. Brush top of dough with melted butter. Place filling in a row lengthwise down center of dough. Fold narrow sides over filling, brush with egg white and fold one long side over, brushing with egg white. The last long side is simply folded over to close strudel. Chill 1 hour. Preheat oven to 350°. Brush top of dough with beaten egg yolk and bake on ungreased sheet about 45 minutes, or until dough is crisp and light golden brown. Cool and sprinkle with confectioners' sugar.

✂ / *STRUDEL DOUGH* (*Strudelteig*)

The only tricky part in making strudel is stretching the dough to a sheer pliable sheet. Practice several times before you plan to serve it to guests. Once you master the art, you'll be able to serve one of the best and most famous desserts that ever came to Germany via Austria and Hungary. (Ideally, strudel dough should have no holes in it. As a precaution against them, it's a good idea to remove all rings, especially those with stones that might cut through dough as your hands slip under to stretch it. I have even heard of people cutting their fingernails before making strudel, but if you keep your hands clenched in a fist with your thumbs tucked in, this should not be necessary. If the dough does tear, ignore the holes; do not attempt to patch them.)

1½ cups flour
¼ teaspoon salt
2 tablespoons corn or peanut
    oil, or any other mildly
    flavored cooking oil but
    not olive oil
2 tablespoons vinegar

1 egg, beaten
½ cup lukewarm water, approxi-
    mately
1 cup melted butter
2 cups breadcrumbs, browned
    in butter
(for fillings, see recipes below)

Sift flour into a bowl or onto pastry board. Make a well in the center. Combine salt, oil, vinegar and beaten egg and pour into well. Using fingertips or a fork, work flour into liquid, gradually adding water as needed to make a soft, sticky dough. Knead vigorously on a lightly floured board, scraping dough off board as necessary with a knife. As you knead, keep lifting dough and slapping it against the table, raising it and bringing it down hard for about 15 minutes, or until the dough has been slapped down onto the board 100 or 115 times. By this time it should be elastic, smooth and no longer sticky. Rinse a bowl in very hot water, dry thoroughly and sprinkle lightly with flour. Shape dough into a ball, place it in bowl, brush top with oil and set to rest 30 minutes in a warm corner of the kitchen.

Cover a large table with a pastry cloth or with a tablecloth that hangs over the edges. Sprinkle with flour, especially in center of cloth. Place dough in center, sprinkle top with flour, and with a floured rolling pin, roll into a large square, as thin as possible. Turn dough several times during rolling so it does not stick to cloth. Remove all jewelry and coat hands with flour. Slip tightly closed fists under dough, and working from center, begin to stretch it with a hand-over-hand motion. Work toward edges. Move around table so dough will be evenly stretched toward all sides. It should become as thin as tissue paper. Let sides of stretched dough hang down over edge of table. If dry spots appear in dough as you work, brush with oil to keep them supple. Trim off thick edges of dough with scissors and let sheet dry slightly 10 minutes. Do not let it become brittle. Before filling, brush melted butter onto entire surface of dough. Sprinkle with breadcrumbs.

Place filling in a row along one end of sheet of dough. Fold side flaps of dough over filling and brush with melted butter. Roll strudel, starting from filling end and using the cloth to help lift and turn dough, as you would for a jelly roll. The last roll of dough should flip the strudel onto a greased baking sheet or jelly-roll pan. Turn into a horseshoe if too long for pan. Bake in preheated 350° oven about 1 hour. Brush several times with melted butter. Strudel is done when dough is crisp as parchment and golden brown.

⚃ / APPLE STRUDEL (Apfelstrudel)

1 recipe Strudel Dough, above	melted butter
¾ cup finely chopped walnuts or hazelnuts	¾ cup raisins or currants
	grated rind of 1 lemon
2 pounds apples, peeled, cored and sliced	1 teaspoon cinnamon
	½ to ¾ cup sugar

Prepare dough. Sprinkle chopped nuts over breadcrumbs. Place sliced apples in a strip along dough. Brush apples with melted butter and sprinkle with raisins or currants, lemon rind, a little cinnamon and sugar; the amount of sugar you use depends on the sweetness of the apples. Roll dough and bake.

VARIATION

In Bavaria ¼ to ½ cup sour cream is usually spread over stretched dough after it has been brushed with melted butter. The nuts and bread-crumbs are sprinkled on after the cream. This gives strudel filling a wonderfully rich and velvety consistency.

✿ / PLUM, CHERRY OR RHUBARB STRUDEL (*Zwetschgen-, Kirschen- oder Rhabarberstrudel*)

1 recipe Strudel Dough, page 435
3 to 4 tablespoons thick sour cream (optional)
2 cups breadcrumbs, browned in butter
4 cups stoned cherries, or 4 cups

young rhubarb, cut in ½" to 1" pieces, or 4 cups sliced, stoned small blue plums
melted butter
½ to ¾ cup sugar
powdered cinnamon
grated rind of 1 lemon

Prepare dough. If you are using sour cream, spread it over butter, and then sprinkle breadcrumbs. Fill with cherries, rhubarb or plums; sprinkle with sugar and cinnamon; roll and bake.

✿ / CHEESE STRUDEL (*Topfenstrudel*)

1 recipe Strudel Dough, page 435
⅔ cup butter
¾ cup sugar
4 egg yolks
grated rind of 1 lemon
1 pound pot cheese, rubbed through a sieve

½ cup raisins soaked in 2 table-spoons rum
½ cup sour cream, approximately
4 egg whites, stiffly beaten
½ cup milk
melted butter

Prepare dough. To make filling, cream butter with sugar until light and fluffy, then gradually beat in egg yolks. Mix until thick and pale yellow. Add lemon peel, pot cheese, rum-soaked raisins and just enough sour cream to bind mixture into a coherent mass. Fold in stiffly beaten egg whites, gently but thoroughly, using a rubber spatula. Place filling on dough, roll and bake. When dough is beginning to turn golden brown, spoon milk over it, brush with melted butter and continue baking until crisp and golden brown.

✖ / POPPY SEED STRUDEL (*Mohnstrudel*)

1 recipe Strudel Dough, page
   435
½ pound poppy seeds
1 cup milk
⅓ cup sugar and 2 tablespoons
   honey, or ½ cup honey
1 teaspoon powdered cinnamon

1 tablespoon rum
¾ cup crushed almonds or walnuts (optional)
½ cup raisins
2 or 3 tablespoons breadcrumbs
   melted butter

Prepare dough. Wash poppy seeds under running hot water and drain well. Grind twice through finest blade of a meat chopper. Combine ground poppy seeds with milk, sugar and honey or just honey, and simmer until a thick mass. Stir in cinnamon, rum, nuts if you use them, raisins and enough breadcrumbs to absorb any liquid that may be left. Add seasoning if needed. Fill, roll, brush with melted butter and bake.

✖ / TYROLEAN STRUDEL (*Tiroler Strudel*)

1 recipe Strudel Dough, page
   435
⅔ cup butter
½ cup sugar
4 egg yolks
   juice and grated rind of ½
   lemon
1 tablespoon rum
½ cup raisins

½ cup chopped dried figs
½ cup chopped, stoned dates
1 cup stoned, coarsely chopped
   prunes
¾ cup chopped nuts
4 egg whites, stiffly beaten
½ cup milk
   melted butter

Prepare dough. Cream butter with sugar until light and fluffy, then gradually work in egg yolks. Beat until mixture is thick and pale yellow. Add all other ingredients except egg whites and melted butter and milk and mix until well blended. Fold in stiffly beaten egg whites. Fill, roll and bake. After 20 minutes, pour milk over strudel and add a little more melted butter. Continue baking another 20 minutes, or until dough is crisp and golden brown.

❊ DEEP-FRIED PASTRIES ❊
(*Schmalzgebäck*)

To fry in deep fat correctly you need a deep saucepan, a slotted spoon for removing the cakes as they brown and, the most important piece of equipment of all, a fat thermometer. Without the latter, your cakes will be underdone or burned. If you have an electric deep fryer that is controlled by a thermostat you need no thermometer. Corn or peanut oil, lard or any of the canned white solid vegetable shortenings are best for deep frying.

❊ / *BERLIN JELLY DOUGHNUTS OR SHROVE TUESDAY CAKES (Berliner Pfannkuchen, Bismarcks, Fastnachtkuchen oder Faschingskrapfen)*

The jelly doughnut may very well be the single most popular piece of pastry in the United States. It is a direct descendant of the Berliner Pfannkuchen. These cakes are usually made throughout Germany on Shrove Tuesday, or Fastnacht, and are called Fastnachtkuchen. They may be made with or without jam. They are also sometimes named after Bismarck, a favorite hero of the Prussian Berliners.

ABOUT 30 TO 34 DOUGHNUTS

1 envelope dry powdered yeast
water
1 teaspoon sugar
1 cup milk
⅓ cup butter
¼ cup sugar
1 teaspoon salt
grated rind of 1 lemon

3 egg yolks
3 to 4 cups flour
oil or melted butter
1½ cups apricot jam or Four-Fruit Marmalade, page 374
fat for deep frying
Vanilla Sugar, page 475

Soften yeast in a little water according to instructions on package, adding a little sugar to speed the process, if you like. Let stand in a warm place until bubbly. Scald milk. Cream butter with sugar, salt and lemon rind. When blended, add scalded milk and stir until butter melts. When cooled to lukewarm, mix in egg yolks and 1 cup flour and dissolved yeast. Add remaining flour gradually until dough is soft and light but smooth and not sticky. Knead on floured board until elastic and smooth. Shape into ball and place in floured bowl. Brush top of dough with oil or melted butter, cover with thin kitchen towel and set to rise in a warm draft-free corner of kitchen. Let rise 1 hour, or until double in bulk. Punch down and roll on floured board to ¼" thickness and cut rounds with a 3" cookie cutter. Put a generous dab of marmalade or jam in center of half the circles, then top each with a plain circle of dough. Pinch edges together with a little water or egg white.

Cover with towel and let rise about 45 minutes, or until again double in bulk. Heat fat to 365° and deep-fry doughnuts a few at a time, keeping fat temperature constant. Fry about 3 minutes on first side, then turn so second side can brown. Remove with slotted spoon and drain on absorbent paper. When cool, dredge with sugar.

VARIATIONS

1. These are sometimes made without any filling. In that case it is not necessary to roll dough. After it has risen, punch down and pinch off pieces about the size of limes. Let rise again until double in bulk and fry.
2. Fill doughnuts with jelly after they have been fried. Either roll out dough to ½" thickness or pinch off pieces, let rise and fry. When cool, fill by splitting and spooning jam into them, or squirt jam in through a long-necked pastry tube.
3. Bohemian Crullers (Böhmische Krapfen) are made just like unfilled doughnuts but in long narrow rolls instead of rounds. Shape by pinching off dough, then rolling between hands.

❁ / BAVARIAN CHURCH FESTIVAL DOUGHNUTS
(*Bayrische Kirchweihnudeln oder Kirchweihküchel*)

These are traditionally served on Kirchweih. Although they are called "Nudeln," to us they are more like doughnuts or crullers.

1 *envelope dry powdered yeast*	4 *tablespoons butter, cut in*
¼ *cup warm water*	*small pieces*
¼ *cup sugar*	¼ *cup sour cream*
pinch of salt	¼ *cup milk, scalded*

4 to 5 cups sifted flour
1 egg
   oil or melted butter
1 cup raisins or currants, washed,
   drained and chopped

grated rind of 1 lemon
fat for deep frying
confectioners' sugar

Dissolve yeast in warm water according to instructions on package. Combine sugar, salt, butter and sour cream. Scald milk and while still hot, pour into butter mixture. Stir until butter is dissolved. Cool to lukewarm. Stir in 1 cup sifted flour and yeast and mix well. Set aside until mixture is bubbly. Add egg. Gradually work in as much of remaining flour as you need for a light but smooth dough. Turn onto floured board and knead until dough is smooth and elastic and forms blisters. Shape into a ball, place in a lightly floured bowl and brush top of dough with oil or melted butter. Cover with a thin kitchen towel and set in warm draft-free corner until double in bulk, about 1 to 1½ hours.

Dredge choped raisins or currants lightly in the flour and toss together with grated lemon rind. Punch dough down and knead in raisins and lemon peel, working very quickly so dough is not handled too much. Let dough rest 10 minutes. Break off small pieces of dough and roll between your hands to form round "noodles" about 3″ long. Lay on a floured board, cover with a thin kitchen towel and let rise about 45 minutes, or until almost double in bulk. Heat fat in deep fryer to 365°. Drop noodles in a few at a time. When they have cooked about 3 minutes, take a pair of scissors and cut a cross in the unfried top of each. Turn and fry until both sides are golden brown. Remove with slotted spoon and drain on paper toweling. Serve warm, sprinkled with confectioners' sugar.

✂ / *REGENSBURG CRULLERS* (*Regensburger Brandteigkrapfen*)

1 recipe Cream Puff Pastry, page
   425
1 tablespoon sugar

1 teaspoon vanilla
oil or fat for deep frying

Prepare pastry. As you beat in the 4 eggs, add the sugar and vanilla. Heat fat until thermometer registers 365°. Drop batter from two teaspoons, to form tiny crullers, into hot fat. Do not fry all of batter at once, as crullers must have room to rise to the surface. Check thermometer to see that temperature of fat remains constant. Turn crullers so they brown on all sides. They should be done in about 4 minutes. Remove with slotted spoon and drain on paper towel. Serve cold with confectioners' sugar, or hot with Hot Red Wine Sauce, page 406, and/or confectioners' sugar.

❧ / LITTLE CUSHIONS (*Polsterzipfel*)

3 tablespoons butter	2¼ cups sifted flour
⅓ cup sugar	1½ teaspoons baking powder
2 eggs	fat for deep frying
1 teaspoon vanilla	1 egg white
3 tablespoons rum	confectioners' sugar
¼ teaspoon powdered cinnamon	

Cream butter with sugar until light and fluffy. Add eggs, one at a time, beating well between additions. Mix in vanilla, rum and cinnamon. Sift flour again, together with baking powder. Mix into butter-egg mixture until batter is fairly stiff and smooth enough to roll. Add a little more flour as needed. Turn dough onto floured board, and using a floured rolling pin, roll to a thickness just under ¼". Using a pastry cutter, cut squares in any desired size, brush edges with egg white and fold in half diagonally to form a triangle. Heat fat in deep fryer to 370° and fry "pillows" a few at a time, turning so they are golden brown on both sides. Drain on paper toweling and serve warm sprinkled with confectioners' sugar. Leftover scraps of dough can be cut in strips and deep fried in irregular shapes.

VARIATION

In Austria, a little jam is usually put on each square before it is folded.

❧ / RUFFLES (*Strauben*)

1 recipe Cream Puff Pastry, page 425	fat for deep frying
2 tablespoons sugar	Lemon Sugar, page 475

Prepare pastry. Fill pastry tube or cookie gun with mixture or use a large funnel. Heat fat to 365° and press pastry through bag, gun or funnel, snipping off curled lengths every 2". Let strips fall into hot fat. Turn so pieces brown on both sides, about 5 minutes in all. Remove with slotted spoon and drain on paper towel. Cool and sprinkle with sugar.

The following recipes are only a few of the many fritters, or Küchel, so often served as dessert in Germany. There are also many thin deep-fried waffles made in Germany in the shapes of roses, tongues and dozens of other things, but these require irons not generally available here.

✿ / FRITTER BATTER (Küchelteig)

1 egg yolk	⅔ to ¾ cup flour
pinch of salt	1 tablespoon melted butter
½ cup white wine or dark beer	1 egg white, stiffly beaten
2 tablespoons sugar	

Beat egg yolk with salt, wine or beer and sugar. Gradually add flour and beat until mixture is consistency of thin paint. Stir in melted butter. Let stand about 30 minutes, then fold in stiffly beaten egg white. Use batter immediately after adding egg white. Proceed as in specific recipes.

✿ / APPLE FRITTERS (Apfelküchel)

4 TO 6 SERVINGS

1 recipe Fritter Batter, above	fat for deep frying
4 large not too sour apples,	confectioners' sugar, or Foamy
peeled, cored and cut in 2"-	Wine Sauce, page 405, or
thick slices	Vanilla Sauce, page 402

Preheat fat to 365°. Prepare batter, adding egg whites just before dipping fruit. Dip fruit slices in batter one at a time until well coated. Let excess batter drip off. Fry a few slices at a time, turning once so they are golden brown on both sides. Remove from fat with slotted spoon, drain on paper towel and continue frying other fruit slices until all are done. Serve with sugar or either of the two sauces indicated.

✿ / OTHER FRUIT FRITTERS

Sliced and peeled peaches, nectarines, canned pineapple, bananas sliced in half lengthwise and then cut in 1" to 2" lengths, all can be used for fritters. The fruit may be sprinkled with a little sugar and rum or brandy and marinated for a few minutes. Giant strawberries, washed and hulled, are also very good dipped in batter and fried.

⊠ / LOCKSMITHS' APPRENTICES, OR PRUNE FRITTERS (*Schlosserbuben*)

1 recipe Fritter Batter, above
½ pound prunes, soaked until soft
15 to 20 blanched almonds

½ cup grated bittersweet chocolate
¼ cup sugar

Prepare batter. Remove pits from soaked and drained prunes, doing as little damage to the prunes as possible. They should remain in one piece. Stuff each stoned prune with a blanched almond and restore to prune shape. Dip in batter and fry. Drain on paper toweling and while hot, dredge with a mixture of grated chocolate and sugar. Serve warm.

✖ YEAST BAKING ✖
(*Hefegebäck*)

⊠ / BASIC YEAST DOUGH (*Hefeteig*)

MAKES 2 LARGE COFFEE CAKES

2 packages dry powdered yeast
½ cup warm water
½ cup butter, softened
½ cup sugar

1 teaspoon salt
grated rind of 1 lemon
1 cup milk, scalded
2 cups flour

4 *egg yolks*
1 *whole egg*
2 *to 3 cups flour*

fruits or nuts, according to
  recipe
melted butter
flour

Dissolve yeast in warm water according to instructions on package. Combine butter, sugar, salt and lemon rind in a bowl. Scald milk and pour into bowl. Stir until butter has melted. Cool to lukewarm. Add 2 cups flour and the yeast, and mix well. Set aside in a warm corner until mixture becomes light and bubbly. Stir in egg yolks and whole egg and gradually beat in 2 to 3 cups flour until you have a soft, light smooth dough. Turn onto a floured board and knead until dough is smooth and elastic and forms blisters. Shape in a ball, place in a clean floured bowl and cover with a thin kitchen towel, and set in a warm draft-free corner to rise until doubled in bulk, about 1 to 1½ hours. Punch dough down and knead in any candied fruits, nuts, etc., called for in the specific recipe. If nothing is being added, knead lightly anyway. Let dough rest 10 minutes, then shape as desired and bake according to specific recipe.

✠ / RICH YEAST DOUGH (*Feine Hefeteig*)

Follow above recipe but use 10 egg yolks, ¾ cup butter and ½ cup milk instead of amounts called for.

✠ / CRUMB COFFEE CAKE (*Streuselkuchen*)

½ *recipe Basic Yeast Dough*
  (*above*) *made with 3 to 4*
  cups flour

melted butter

Crumb Topping:

1½ *to 1¾ cups flour*
¾ *cups sugar*
1 *teaspoon cinnamon*
¼ *pound butter, melted*

Prepare dough, and after it has risen, been punched down and rested, roll or pat out to finger thickness (about ½") to fit a buttered 10" by 15" or 11" by 16" jelly-roll pan. Brush dough with melted butter. With a fork, mix ingredients for topping until you form little lumps—in German, Klümpchen, which sound more colorful somehow. If mixture is too fine and mealy, add more melted butter. If clumps are too large, add more flour. Sugar and cinnamon can be adjusted to taste.

Sprinkle crumbs generously on buttered dough. Let rise until almost double in bulk. Bake in preheated 350° oven 30 to 45 minutes, or until cake is done and crumbs are golden brown.

✷ / BUTTER COFFEE CAKE (*Butterkuchen*)

Make ½ recipe Basic Yeast Dough (page 444) and prepare as for Crumb Coffee Cake, above. Brush with melted butter, dot generously with butter and sprinkle with ⅓ to ½ cup granulated sugar and ¾ to 1 cup coarsely chopped or slivered almonds. Let rise, and bake as for Crumb Coffee Cake (above).

✷ / CINNAMON COFFEE CAKE (*Kaneelkuchen*)

Make ½ recipe Basic Yeast Dough (page 444) and prepare as for Crumb Coffee Cake, above. Brush with melted butter and sprinkle with ½ to ¾ cup sugar mixed with 2 or 3 teaspoons cinnamon. Let rise, and bake as for Crumb Coffee Cake (above).

✷ / FRUIT COFFEE CAKE (*Obstkuchen*)

Make ½ recipe Basic Yeast Dough (page 444) and prepare as for Crumb Coffee Cake, above. Brush dough generously with melted butter and top with 2 pounds raw cherries, currants, rhubarb, peaches, apples or blue or red plums, stoned, peeled and sliced as necessary. You should have about 3 cups of fruit. Sprinkle fruit with a little granulated sugar and cinnamon, or with Crumb Topping (above). Let rise about 30 minutes, then bake in 350° oven about 1 hour. Serve warm or cold.

✷ / CHEESE COFFEE CAKE (*Käsekuchen*)

Make ½ recipe Basic Yeast Dough (page 444) and prepare as for Crumb Coffee Cake (above). Let rise until dough puffs up. Top with cheese filling: Cream 2 tablespoons butter with ⅓ cup sugar and gradually mix in 2 egg yolks. Mix in 1 pound pot cheese (not cottage cheese) that has been rubbed through a sieve. Add 3 tablespoons flour and ½ cup milk or cream. Add just enough flour and milk to form a light but coherent mass. Mix in ½ cup raisins and grated rind of 1 lemon. Beat 2 egg whites with 1 tablespoon sugar until they stand in stiff but glossy peaks. Using a rubber spatula, fold gently but thoroughly into cheese mixture. Spread filling onto dough and brush with beaten whole egg. Bake in 350° oven 30 to 45 minutes or until golden brown. If you like, the filling can be flavored with a little rum, brandy or vanilla. Mix into egg-yolk mixture before folding in whites.

✂ / ROLLED COFFEE CAKE (*Wickelkuchen*)

For 2 large cakes, prepare 1 recipe Basic Yeast Dough, page 444. Make ½ recipe if only 1 cake is needed. Each filling is enough for 2 cakes.

Roll out dough into 2 squares about ¼″ thick. Brush with melted butter. Cover with filling and roll jelly-roll style. Put each roll in a buttered 8″ or 9″ loaf pan or a ring mold. Let rise until double in bulk. Brush with beaten egg yolk or melted butter and bake in 350° oven 45 minutes to 1 hour. Sprinkle with confectioners' sugar or glaze with a thin layer of melted apricot preserves or jam.

POPPY SEED FILLING

Wash and grind ½ pound poppy seeds in a poppy-seed grinder or an electric blender. Mix with 1 cup milk, 3 tablespoons butter and ⅔ cup sugar or ½ cup honey and grated rind of 1 lemon. Cook until thick. Half a cup raisins and/or nuts can be folded into this, if you like.

RAISIN-NUT FILLING

Combine ¾ cup raisins or currants, ⅔ cup sugar, 2 teaspoons cinnamon and 1 cup chopped or grated hazelnuts. Dot dough with 3 tablespoons butter, cut in tiny flecks. If you like, add 3 tablespoons chopped candied citron and/or orange peel.

❧ / NUT WREATH (*Nusskranz*)

Prepare a Rolled Coffee Cake (above), using the Raisin-Nut Filling. Butter two ring molds and sprinkle liberally with slivered unblanched hazelnuts or almonds. Place the two rings of dough in pans, let rise until doubled in bulk and bake in 350° oven 45 minutes to 1 hour. Cool in pan, invert onto rack and when completely cold, dust with sugar or glaze with melted apricot jam.

❧ / SNAILS (*Schnecken*)

24 LARGE OR 48 SMALL

2 *packages dry powdered yeast*
½ *cup warm water*
½ *cup sugar*
½ *teaspoon salt*
½ *cup butter*
1 *cup milk or sweet cream,*
  scalded
1 *cup flour*
2 *egg yolks*

1 *egg*
4 *cups sifted flour*
  melted butter
1¼ *cups brown sugar*
⅓ *cup currants*
1 *tablespoon cinnamon*
½ *pound pecans, shelled and*
  coarsely chopped

Dissolve yeast in warm water according to instructions on envelope. Combine sugar, salt and butter. Scald milk and while hot, pour over sugar-butter mixture. Stir until sugar is dissolved and butter melts. Cool to lukewarm. Add flour, the yeast, egg yolks and egg and mix lightly until well blended. Add sifted flour gradually, mixing in well between additions. Add enough flour for a light dough that is not sticky.

Turn onto floured board and knead until the dough is smooth, elastic and forms blisters on surface. Gather dough in a ball and place in lightly floured bowl. Brush top with melted butter, cover with a thin kitchen towel and set in a warm draft-free corner to rise until double in bulk, about 1 to 1½ hours. Punch dough down, turn over in bowl and let rise again until double in bulk. Brush 24 large or 48 small muffin tins with melted butter, placing about 1 teaspoon butter in each large muffin cup, ½ teaspoon in each small one. Combine brown sugar, currants and cinnamon. Spoon a little into each muffin cup and sprinkle with chopped pecans. Use about half the nuts and cinnamon mixture. Punch dough down and divide in half. Roll each half out to about ¼" to ⅓" thickness in a rectangular shape. Brush with melted butter and sprinkle with remaining sugar-cinnamon mixture and chopped pecans. Roll lengthwise jelly-roll style, as tightly as possible. Pinch last edge tightly closed. Cut in 1″ slices. Place each slice, cut side down, in prepared muffin tins. Cover with a towel and let rise until double in bulk. Preheat oven to 375°. Bake about 20 minutes, or until golden brown. Remove from tins at once and cool upside down on rack.

❉ / HONEY BEE CAKE (*Bienenstich*)

1 recipe Basic Yeast Dough,
  page 444
½ *cup milk*
⅓ *cup butter*
⅔ *cup sugar*
1 *cup slivered blanched al-*
monds, or peanuts with
  husks removed
1 *recipe Custard Filling, page*
  480
butter for pan

Prepare dough. After it has risen and been punched down, roll or pat out in a circle or square to about ¾″ thickness. Place on a buttered baking sheet. Let rise until double in bulk. For topping, heat milk with butter and stir in sugar and nuts. Cook over low heat until mixture is smooth and milk is absorbed. Cool and spread on dough. Bake in 350° oven about 30 minutes, or until cake is a rich, glossy golden brown. Prepare filling. When cake has cooled completely, cut in half through middle to form two layers. Spread bottom layer with filling.

❉ / CHRISTMAS FRUIT BREAD (*Hutzelbrot*)

1 *pound dried prunes*
1 *pound dried pears*
1 *pound dried figs, or ½ pound*
  dried figs and 2 pounds
  pitted dates
½ *pound walnuts, shelled*
½ *pound almonds, shelled but*
  not blanched
¼ *pound candied citron*
¼ *pound candied orange peel*
2 *envelopes yeast*
½ *cup warm water*
1 *cup lukewarm water in which*
  fruit cooked
10 *cups sifted flour, approxi-*
  mately
¼ *cup sugar*
1 *teaspoon cinnamon*
½ *teaspoon powdered cloves*
1 *tablespoon anise seeds,*
  crushed
1 *teaspoon salt*
  almonds split in half or
  slivered
  citron for decoration

Follow instructions on package as to soaking and cooking of prunes and pears. Cook only until barely tender; drain and reserve cooking liquid. Remove stones from prunes and chop them and pears into large pieces. Chop figs, walnuts, almonds, citron and orange peel finely. Combine all fruits and nuts. Dissolve yeast in warm water according to instructions on envelope. Mix 1 cup of warm liquid in which prunes and pears cooked and mix with 1 cup flour, sugar and the dissolved yeast; add cinnamon, cloves, anise seeds and salt. Gradually work in remaining flour and beat hard until dough blisters and comes away from sides of bowl. Shape dough in a ball, place in a lightly floured clean bowl, cover with a thin kitchen towel and set in a warm draft-free corner to rise about 1 to 1½ hours, or until doubled in bulk. When dough has risen, mix in all fruits and nuts; let dough rise again 45 minutes to 1 hour, or until almost double in bulk. Divide dough in half and form round or oblong loaves. Place on buttered, floured baking sheet. Decorate top with halves of almonds and citron and bake in 400° oven about 1 hour, or until loaves are a deep golden brown. Brush with a little more of the fruit liquid while hot.

⚄ / DRESDEN STOLLEN (*Dresdner Stollen*)

Although there are many versions of Stollen in Germany, this is the most famous and generally regarded as the best.

1½ cups raisins	2 tablespoons rum
1 cup chopped citron	2 cups flour
1 cup chopped candied orange peel	4 eggs, lightly beaten
½ cup rum	5 to 7 cups flour
2 envelopes dry powdered yeast	6 to 8 slivered blanched bitter almonds, or 1 teaspoon almond extract
½ cup lukewarm water	1½ cups chopped blanched almonds
1 tablespoon sugar (optional)	melted butter
2 cups milk	granulated sugar
1 cup sugar	confectioners' sugar, preferably vanilla-flavored
2 teaspoons salt	
1⅓ cups butter	
grated rind of 1 lemon	

Combine raisins, citron and candied orange peel and soak in rum 1 hour. Drain and reserve rum. Dissolve yeast in warm water according to instructions on package, using a little sugar to speed the process if you like. Scald milk with sugar, salt and butter. When the butter has melted, stir in lemon peel, rum and almond extract if you are using it. Cool mixture to lukewarm. Add yeast and 2 cups flour. Mix well and set in warm draft-free corner about 15 to 30 minutes, or until dough blisters. Stir in lightly beaten eggs and gradually mix in 5 to 7 cups flour until dough is soft and light but not sticky. It should be smooth enough to be handled.

Dry soaked fruit and dredge lightly with flour. Turn dough onto a floured board and knead, gradually working in fruit, almonds, and bitter almonds if you use them. Knead dough until it blisters and is smooth and elastic. Gather in a ball and place in a lightly floured bowl. Brush with melted butter. Cover loosely with a thin kitchen towel and set in warm draft-free corner about 1 hour, or until it has doubled in bulk. Punch dough down and cut into 3 equal pieces. Set aside to rest 10 minutes. Roll or flatten each third of dough into an oval ¾″ thick. Brush top of each with melted butter and sprinkle with a little sugar. Fold each lengthwise, not quite in half, so that edges are within ½″ to 1″ of meeting; pinch closed. Place loaves on a buttered baking sheet or jelly-roll pan. Brush with melted butter and place in warm, draft-free corner again so they can rise until doubled in bulk, about 1 hour. Preheat oven to 425°. Bake loaves 10 minutes, then turn heat down to 350°. Bake about 45 minutes, or until loaves are crisp golden brown. Brush with butter and sprinkle generously with confectioners' sugar while warm. Cool and sprinkle with more sugar before serving.

VARIATIONS

1.   Use any candied fruits you like in this Stollen—angelica, cherries, etc. You can also use half raisins, half currants, in which case use white raisins instead of black.

2.   Saxon Stollen (Sächsischer Stollen) is made the same way except that no nuts or fruit, other than black and white raisins, are used.

3.   For Poppy Seed Stollen (Mohnstollen), omit all fruits, using almonds only. When dough is rolled into flat ovals, brush with melted butter and fill with: ¾ pound poppy seeds, ground and simmered in 1 cup milk 5 minutes with 1 cup white raisins, ¾ cup chopped candied citron, ½ cup sugar, ½ teaspoon cinnamon, 1 tablespoon rum and a few drops of rosewater. Mix well until pasty; divide in thirds and spread one-third onto one side of each oval of dough. Fold and bake.

✂ / *BREMEN LOAF* (*Bremer Klöben oder Klaben*)

The Bremer Loaf, or Klöben, is that city's answer to Dresden's Stollen. It is said so many Klöben are made in Bremen each Christmas, there are more than enough to last until Easter. This rich, heavy white fruit cake will keep for months if it is well wrapped, preferably in a brandy-soaked cloth. It makes a wonderful Christmas gift if your family doesn't eat all you make before you can give them away.

½ pound chopped citron
½ pound dried currants
1 pound raisins
 rum or brandy
2 envelopes dry powdered yeast
½ cup lukewarm water
2 tablespoons sugar (optional)
½ cup milk
1 teaspoon salt
¼ cup sugar
1 cup butter

1 teaspoon rosewater
 pinch of powdered cinnamon
 grated rind of 1 large lemon
1 egg, lightly beaten
6 to 7 cups flour
¾ cup slivered blanched
 almonds
 melted butter
 sugar

Combine fruits and raisins and soak in rum or brandy 1 hour. Dissolve yeast in water according to instructions on package, adding a little sugar to speed the process if you want to. Scald milk with salt, sugar, butter and fat. When butter and fat have melted, remove from heat and stir in rosewater, cinnamon and lemon rind. Cool to lukewarm and add dissolved yeast mixture. Stir well. Beat in egg and 1 cup flour. Set aside in warm corner 15 to 30 minutes until mixture is bubbly. Sift 5 cups flour onto a board and make a well in the center. Pour yeast mixture into well and gradually work ingredients together, adding more flour if necessary to make a dough that is light and soft but not sticky. Drain, dry and flour fruit and raisins. Turn dough onto a floured board and knead, gradually working in floured fruits and almonds. Knead until dough blisters and is smooth and elastic. Place in a lightly floured bowl and brush top of dough with melted butter. Cover with a thin kitchen towel and set in warm draft-free corner about 1 hour, or until dough is double in bulk.

Although this is usually made in one huge loaf, you can divide dough in half to make two smaller ones. Punch dough down and turn onto a floured board. Flatten or roll into an oval (or two ovals if you have divided dough) about 1" thick. Brush top with melted butter, sprinkle with a little sugar and fold lengthwise, not quite in half, as for Stollen in above recipe. Place on buttered baking sheet or jelly-roll pan and brush with melted butter. Place in warm draft-free corner again and let rise until doubled in bulk, about 1 hour. Preheat oven to 375° and bake about 1 hour, or until a deep brown. Brush with melted butter while still warm. This may be served with or without confectioners' sugar on top.

❧ / EASTER BREAD (Osterfladen)

1 envelope dry powdered yeast
¼ cup warm water

½ cup milk
⅓ cup butter

1 *tablespoon sugar*
1 *teaspoon salt*
4 *to* 4½ *cups sifted flour*
2 *egg yolks*

1 *whole egg*
melted butter
flour
1 *egg yolk, beaten*

Soften yeast in water according to directions on package. Scald milk. Combine butter, sugar and salt in a bowl and add scalded milk. Stir until butter has melted. Cool until lukewarm. Add 1 cup flour and dissolved yeast to butter mixture and stir well. Beat in egg yolks and egg. When well mixed, gradually beat in remaining flour, or as much of it as you need to form a soft but not sticky dough. Turn dough onto a floured board and knead until it blisters and is smooth and elastic. Shape into a ball, place in a lightly floured bowl and brush top of dough with melted butter. Cover with a thin kitchen towel and set in a warm draft-free corner 1 to 1½ hours, or until dough has risen and is double in bulk.

Punch dough down and let rest 10 minutes. Form a round loaf and place on a buttered, lightly floured baking sheet. Cover with a thin towel and let rise again about 45 minutes, or until almost double in bulk. Score surface of risen dough in a crisscross pattern, using a knife or fork tines, but do not cut too deeply. Brush with beaten egg yolk. Place in 400° oven 10 minutes, then turn heat down to 350° and continue baking about 50 minutes, or until crust is deep golden brown.

VARIATIONS

1. To make two small breads instead of one large, divide dough in half before shaping into rounds.
2. This is sometimes made without any eggs at all, which produces a whiter, breadier loaf. If you prefer it that way, follow recipe, using same amount of flour and sugar but with 1½ envelopes of yeast, 1 tablespoon salt, ¼ cup butter and 1½ cups milk.

✠ / *THREE KINGS' BREAD* (*Dreikönigsbrot*)

1 *recipe Basic Yeast Dough, page*
    444, using ⅓ *cup sugar,* ½
    teaspoon salt and ⅓ *cup*
    butter
1 *blanched almond*
melted butter

2 *to* 3 *tablespoons granulated*
    sugar
powdered cinnamon
½ *cup chopped walnuts, hazel-*
    nuts or unblanched al-
    monds

Prepare dough. When it has doubled in bulk, punch down and knead again, adding the single almond. Let rest 10 minutes. Form a round loaf, cover with a thin kitchen towel and let rise in a warm draft-free corner about 1 hour, until doubled in bulk. Score surface of loaf in a crisscross pattern, using a knife or fork tines. Brush with melted butter and sprinkle with sugar, cinnamon and nuts. Bake in a 400° oven 10 minutes, then reduce heat to 350° and continue baking 45 minutes to 1 hour, or until golden brown on top. The single almond means good luck for the coming year to the person who finds it in his slice of bread.

⚌ / *TURBAN CAKES*

Cakes baked in the Kugelhupf form, page xxviii, are very popular in Germany, Austria and Alsace. They may be simple sand cakes like the one on page 457, marble cakes, poundcakes, such as the Napfkuchen (also called Health Cake, or Gesundheitskuchen), or they may be made of a rich yeast dough as the classic Kugelhupf. The Kugelhupf is the original cake to be baked in this high, round, fluted center-tube mold, a shape created after the Turks were defeated at the gates of Vienna in 1683. The Viennese bakers who helped defend their city during the siege created this victory cake, modeling it after the sultan's turban.

⚌ / *TURBAN OR HEALTH CAKE* (*Napfkuchen oder Gesundheitskuchen*)

4 cups sifted flour	7 eggs, separated
4 teaspoons baking powder	1 cup lukewarm milk
1 cup butter	3 tablespoons sugar
grated rind of ½ large lemon	butter for pan
1 heaping cup sugar	flour or breadcrumbs for pan

Preheat oven to 350°. Measure 4 cups sifted flour and sift again with baking powder; put back into sifter or large strainer and set aside. Cream butter with lemon rind and sugar until light and fluffy, then gradually beat in egg yolks, two at a time until mixture is well blended. Pour milk in gradually, beating well after each addition. Whip egg whites, and as they begin to thicken, add sugar, a little at a time. Continue beating until whites stand in stiff but glossy peaks. Stir 3 or 4 tablespoons beaten egg white into egg-yolk mixture to lighten it. Turn whites onto yolks and sprinkle all flour mixture on top. Using a rubber spatula, fold together, gently but thoroughly, until there are no traces of flour or egg whites. Butter a 9″ or 10″ Kugelhupf pan and sprinkle with flour or fine breadcrumbs, tapping out excess. Turn batter into form and bake about

1 hour. Cake is done when it springs back to shape if pressed down with your finger, or if a straw inserted in the center comes out clean. When done, remove from oven and invert pan, standing it on the tube on a cake rack. After about 45 minutes, run a knife between the rim of the cake and the pan and tap cake out. Continue cooling on rack.

VARIATIONS

1. Two teaspoons vanilla extract or 2 tablespoons rum may be added for flavor. Mix in with egg yolks and milk. If you use vanilla, omit lemon rind.
2. To give this an almond flavor, stir ¾ cup grated, unblanched almonds and 1 teaspoon almond extract into egg-yolk-milk mixture.
3. Turban Cake with Poppy Seeds or Caraway Seeds (Napfkuchen mit Mohn oder Kümmel): Stir 1 cup washed, freshly ground poppy seeds, or whole caraway seeds, into egg-yolk-milk mixture.

✖ / KUGELHUPF (*Kugelhopf or Kugelhupf or Gugelhopf or Gugelhupf—take your pick*)

1 recipe Basic Yeast Dough, page 444, or 1 recipe Rich Yeast Dough, page 445
grated rind of 1 lemon
½ cup black raisins or currants
½ cup white raisins
¾ cup mixed candied citron and candied orange peel

½ cup rum or brandy
butter for pan
½ cup coarsely chopped or slivered nuts or almonds (optional)
melted butter
vanilla sugar

Prepare dough. While it rises, combine grated lemon rind with fruits and soak in rum or brandy about 1 hour, or until dough is finished rising. Drain well. Punch dough down and knead fruit into it, working as quickly as possible so dough is not handled too much. Butter a 10″ Kugelhupf form and sprinkle top and sides with nuts if you are using them. Place dough in pan, cover with a thin kitchen towel and set in a warm draft-free corner to rise about 45 minutes, or until almost double in bulk. Brush top with melted butter and set in preheated 400° oven 10 minutes. Then turn heat down to 350° and continue baking about 35 minutes, or until top of cake is deep golden brown. Invert pan over a rack, standing it on the tube, or cool in upright pan. Tap cake out onto rack after 30 minutes and sprinkle with sugar. It is best to keep this cake 24 hours before cutting it, as its flavor will improve. Sprinkle with more sugar before serving.

VARIATIONS

You can add more, or eliminate all, candied fruit peel, according to preference. If you eliminate candied fruit, use more raisins and/or currants. Slivered almonds can be kneaded into the dough with whichever fruit you want to use.

✖ CAKES ✖
(*Kuchen*)

✖ / QUICK COFFEE CAKE (*Blitzkuchen*)

¼ cup sugar	½ cup sugar
⅓ cup flour	2 teaspoons baking powder
½ cup chopped almonds or walnuts	pinch of salt
	⅓ cup butter
1½ teaspoons cinnamon	2 eggs
1½ tablespoons butter	½ cup milk
2 cups sifted flour	1 teaspoon vanilla

Preheat oven to 375°. Combine ¼ cup sugar, ⅓ cup flour, chopped nuts and cinnamon. Melt butter and mix into dry mixture with your fingertips or a fork until you have crumbs. If mixture is too fine, add more butter. If crumbs are too large, add more flour. Add more sugar or cinnamon to taste. Set aside. Sift 2 cups flour again, together with sugar, baking powder and salt. Cut butter in small pieces and add to dry ingredients, working it in with a pastry blender or your fingertips until mixture is the consistency of coarse meal. Beat eggs well and mix with milk and vanilla. Make a well in the center of the dry ingredients and pour liquid in. Stir together gradually, mixing only enough to moisten flour mixture, but not so much that the whole thing breaks down and becomes liquid. Butter and flour a 9″ round layer-cake pan or an 8″ square pan. Turn batter into it. Sprinkle crumb topping over cake and bake about 25 minutes. To test, insert straw or toothpick into center of cake. If it comes out clean, cake is done. Serve warm or cold. Cut portions right out of pan.

VARIATIONS

1.   Simple Fruit Coffee Cake (Einfacher Obstkuchen): Almost all the yeast coffee cakes on pages 444 through 448 can also be made with this quick baking-powder dough. To top with fruit, prepare batter and arrange in square pan or spread onto a buttered baking sheet, pressing the dough in to form an edge 1½" high. Batter should be about ½" to ¾" thick. Brush with melted butter. Top with layer of peeled, cored and sliced apples, or washed, dried, stoned and quartered apricots or small blue plums, or cherries that are stemmed, washed and dried. Cherries should not be stoned, since if they are cut, the juice will make the cake soggy. Bake in 350° oven about 30 minutes, or until dough is done. Sprinkle with granulated sugar while hot. Do not sugar fruit before it is baked.

2.   To make Apple or Plum Crumb Cake (Apfel- oder Zwetschgen-streuselkuchen) follow recipe, topping fruit with crumbs before baking.

3.   To make Apple Meringue Cake (Apfelschaumkuchen) this simple way, spread dough onto buttered baking sheet, form a rim with dough and brush with melted butter. Beat 3 egg whites to a stiff snow with ½ cup sugar. Fold in 5 to 6 apples, thinly sliced, ½ cup raisins and ½ cup chopped nuts. Spread over dough and bake in 350° oven about 35 minutes.

⠶ / SAND CAKE OR TORTE (*Sandkuchen oder Sandtorte*)

Whether this is a torte or a cake is open to argument. By any name almost everyone agrees it is richly flavored poundcake that keeps for weeks. Its name is derived from its sandy texture, due mostly to the use of cornstarch. If you like a slightly less sandy texture, use half flour, half cornstarch. Although baking powder does not really belong in this cake and does make it dry out faster, many people use it to be sure the cake will rise enough and be light. I prefer it without baking powder, but you may use it if you want to be on the safe side.

2 *cups (1 pound) butter*	1 *tablespoon sugar*
2 *cups sugar*	2¼ *cups cornstarch*
5 *whole eggs*	1 *teaspoon baking powder*
4 *eggs, separated*	(*optional*)
grated rind of 1 lemon	*butter*
4 *tablespoons rum or arrack*	*flour*
2 *teaspoons vanilla*	*Vanilla Sugar, page 475*

Melt butter and chill until it has again become solid. Preheat oven to 375°. Cream butter with sugar until light and fluffy, then gradually work in 5 whole eggs and 4 yolks. Add grated lemon rind, rum or arrack and vanilla and beat 30 to 40 minutes by hand, or about 10 with an electric mixer. Mixture should be very thick, almost white and about the consistency of frozen custard. Beat egg whites, and as they thicken, add 1 tablespoon sugar gradually and continue beating until whites stand in stiff but glossy peaks. Take 2 or 3 tablespoons beaten whites and stir into yolk mixture to lighten it. Turn yolks onto whites, or whites onto yolks. Put cornstarch and baking powder, if you use it, in a sifter and shake over whites or yolks. Using a rubber spatula, fold mixtures together gently but thoroughly until there are no traces of whites or flour.

Butter and flour a 9" or 10" Kugelhupf form, or 2 small or 1 large loaf pan. Pour batter into pan and bake 1 to 1¼ hours, or until cake is done. To test, insert toothpick in center of cake; if it comes out clean, cake is done. Cool 15 minutes in pan, then invert onto rack and continue cooling. Sprinkle with Vanilla Sugar and serve thinly sliced. Keep cake 24 hours before cutting, as this improves its flavor. Store in refrigerator, lightly covered with foil or waxed paper.

VARIATIONS

1. Sand Cake with Almonds (Sandkuchen mit Mandeln): When cake is half baked sprinkle with ¾ cup granulated sugar and ¾ cup slivered or coarsely chopped unblanched almonds. If you like, sugar can be mixed with a little cinnamon.

2. Spice Sand Cake (Gewürzsandkuchen): When you are creaming butter, sugar and eggs, add a pinch each of powdered cinnamon, cloves, cardamom and grated rind of 1 lemon. Omit vanilla but use rum. If you like, you can add 2 or 3 tablespoons mixed citron, candied angelic and orange peel, in which case add a pinch of cream of tartar to egg whites as you beat them.

✕ / *FRANKFURT WREATH* (*Frankfurter Kranz*)

This is one cake that appears in almost every Konditorei in Germany.

scant ½ cup butter (about 7 tablespoons)
¾ cup sugar
3 eggs
grated rind of ½ large lemon
¾ cup sifted flour
⅓ cup cornstarch
2 teaspoons baking powder

1½ recipes Butter Cream Filling, page 480
praline, or Krokant, made with 1 tablespoon butter, ¼ cup sugar and 1 cup blanched, chopped almonds or hazelnuts

Preheat over to 350°. Cream butter with sugar until light and fluffy. Add eggs, one at a time, beating well between each addition. Mix in grated lemon rind. Sift flour again together with cornstarch and baking powder. Gradually stir in butter-egg mixture until thoroughly blended. Butter and flour a ring mold and tap out excess flour. Pour batter into pan. Bake in lower half of oven 45 minutes to 1 hour, or until cake is done. A toothpick inserted in the center should come out clean. Cool in pan until cake shrinks away from sides. Invert cake onto rack and cool completely. While cake is cooling, prepare filling. To make praline, or Krokant, place butter and sugar in a frying pan, over low heat, and stir until sugar is melted and light golden brown. Stir in nuts and pour onto a buttered flat plate. When cold and hard, crack into small pieces.

Cut cake into 3 layers. Spread about 1 cup of cream filling onto bottom and middle layers, saving enough to cover outside of cake. Stack layers and spread rest of filling on top and all sides. Sprinkle Krokant on top and sides. This cake is best if it is kept in the refrigerator 24 hours before being served.

※ / *SWABIAN RUM CAKE* (*Schwäbischer Bund*)

¾ *pound butter*	1¼ *cups flour*
1 *scant cup sugar*	1¼ *cups cornstarch*
6 *eggs, separated*	1½ *cups water*
½ *cup blanched almonds, grated*	3½ *tablespoons sugar*
½ *cup raisins or currants*	1 *tablespoon rum, or to taste*
juice and grated rind of ½	*Lemon Icing, page 478*
lemon	¾ *cup slivered toasted almonds*
3 *tablespoons sugar*	½ *cup candied fruit*

Preheat oven to 350°. Cream butter until soft and gradually work in sugar and egg yolks. Mix 30 minutes by hand or 15 minutes by electric mixer. Add almonds, raisins or currants and the juice and grated rind of lemon, and mix lightly. Beat egg whites and when they begin to thicken, gradually beat in sugar. Continue beating until whites stand in soft peaks and are glossy. Turn whites onto egg-yolk-butter mixture and sprinkle flour and cornstarch on top. Using a rubber spatula, fold whites, flour and cornstarch into batter gently but thoroughly until there are no lumps of egg white and no grains of flour or cornstarch. Butter a ring-mold cake pan, turn batter into it and bake 1 hour. To test cake, press center with finger; if it springs back into shape it is done. Cool cake 5 to 10 minutes in pan, then turn onto rack to cool completely.

Heat water and in it dissolve 3½ tablespoons sugar; flavor with rum. Add more sugar if needed and stir until dissolved. Pour liquid into a serving bowl that is large and wide, so the cake can be placed into it.

Gently set cake in bowl with rum sauce and leave it there until it absorbs all liquid. Do not attempt to turn cake as it will be very fragile when soaked. Cover top of cake with icing and sprinkle with toasted almonds and candied fruits.

/ *WESTPHALIAN CHERRY CAKE* (*Westphälischer Kirschkùchen*)

- *3 tablespoons butter*
- *⅔ cup sugar*
- *2 eggs, separated*
- *1¼ cups flour*
- *pinch of salt*
- *2½ teaspoons baking powder*
- *½ cup milk*
- *1 teaspoon vanilla*
- *3 cups raw pitted fresh cherries, or 1½ cups canned cherries, well drained*

Preheat oven to 350°. Cream butter with sugar until light and fluffy. Add one egg yolk, beat in well, then add the other. Sift flour 3 times with salt and baking powder. Add flour and milk, alternately and gradually, to butter mixture, beating well between additions. Stir in vanilla. Beat egg whites until they stand in stiff but glossy peaks. Using a rubber spatula, fold into egg-yolk batter, gently but thoroughly. Butter an 8″ spring form or layer-cake pan. Put fruit in bottom and pour batter over it. Shake pan gently from side to side and stir batter gently by drawing a fork through it, so it works down between the cherries. Bake 35 to 40 minutes.

VARIATION

Fresh stoned and quartered apricots, or cooked small blue plums that are stoned and cut in half, can also be used for this cake.

/ *CHOCOLATE CHERRY CAKE* (*Brauner Kirschkuchen*)

- *½ cup butter*
- *¾ cup sugar*
- *3 eggs, separated*
- *2 whole eggs*
- *2½ ounces (squares) semi-sweet chocolate, grated*
- *¼ cup fine cracker crumbs*
- *¾ cup grated, unblanched almonds*
- *1 tablespoon sugar*
- *½ pound fresh cherries*
- *butter*
- *flour*
- *confectioners' sugar*

Preheat oven to 375°. Cream butter with sugar until fluffy. Gradually beat in 3 egg yolks and 2 whole eggs, beating well between additions. Add grated chocolate, cracker crumbs and almonds and mix lightly. Beat egg whites with tablespoon sugar, until they stand in stiff but glossy peaks. Fold into first mixture, gently but thoroughly, using a rubber spatula. Butter a layer-cake pan and sprinkle with flour, tapping out excess. Turn batter into pan and top with cherries. (They should be whole, uncut and unstoned, but if that seems like too much bother to eat, pit them.) Bake 40 minutes. When cake is cold, slip it out of pan and sprinkle with confectioners' sugar before serving.

▓ / ROYAL CAKE (*Königskuchen*)

½ *pound (1 cup) butter*	*pinch of salt*
1 *scant cup sugar*	½ *to 1 cup milk, as needed*
4 *eggs*	1½ *cups raisins, all brown and*
2 *tablespoons rum or arrack*	*white mixed, or ¾ cup*
juice and grated rind of ½	*white raisins and ¾ cup*
lemon	*dried currants*
4 *or 5 crushed bitter almonds,*	½ *cup candied citron, chopped*
or 1 teaspoon almond ex-	¼ *cup candied orange peel,*
tract	*finely chopped*
4½ *cups sifted flour*	*butter*
4 *teaspoons baking powder*	*fine breadcrumbs*

Preheat oven to 350°. Cream butter with sugar until light and fluffy. Beat in eggs one at a time, until well blended. Mix in rum or arrack, lemon juice and rind and almond extract if you are using it. Sift flour again, together with baking powder and salt. Add flour and milk, alternately and gradually, to butter and egg, mixing well between additions. Do not add too much milk. The batter should be firm and heavy and should tear in pieces when dropped from a spoon. Fold in raisins and other fruit and bitter almonds if you are using them. Butter a loaf pan and sprinkle with breadcrumbs on sides and bottom, tapping out excess. Turn batter into pan and bake in lower half of oven about 1¼ to 1½ hours. Cake may be cooled in tin and then removed, or you may keep it in tin and slice off portions.

VARIATION

This recipe makes a heavy, moist cake, similar to the English tea cake. If you would like it to have a drier, grainier texture, use 3¾ cups flour and ¾ cup cornstarch instead of 4½ cups flour. Sift cornstarch along with flour, baking powder and salt.

✖ / BISHOP'S BREAD (*Bischofsbrot*)

Ideally, the amounts of flour and sugar should each be equal to the weight of the eggs. The measurements given are therefore necessarily approximate, based on the weight of 6 large Grade A white eggs.

6 large eggs
2 cups sugar
3½ cups flour
½ cup almonds, blanched and
  slivered
½ cup dark raisins or currants
½ cup white raisins
¼ cup candied citron, finely
  chopped

¼ cup candied orange peel,
  finely chopped
grated rind of 1 lemon
butter
flour or breadcrumbs
confectioners' sugar, or Chocolate Icing, page 479

Preheat oven to 350°. Beat eggs with sugar 30 to 45 minutes by hand, 15 to 20 minutes in an electric mixer. The mixture should be almost white in color and thick enough to ribbon. Sift in flour, add all nuts, fruits and lemon rind and stir until thoroughly blended. Butter a loaf pan and sprinkle with flour or fine breadcrumbs. Turn batter into it and bake 1 to 1¼ hours. Cool and sprinkle with confectioners' sugar or cover with icing.

✖ / LITTLE HORNS (*Hörnchen*)

These little pastries are stand-bys in Germany. They are among the dozens of little twists and curls and rolls with names such as snails (Schnecken), rose cakes (Rosenkuchen) and windmills (Windmühlen), made of Basic Yeast Dough, page 444, or, sometimes, Rich Tart Pastry, page 427. Prepare dough or pastry. Roll out to a thickness just under ¼″, and with a pastry cutter, brush with melted butter and cut triangles. The fillings may be a little marmalade, a mixture of raisins or currants and cinnamon with sugar, or chopped hazelnuts with sugar and enough sour or sweet cream to bind the mixture. Place filling in a dab just below base side of triangle and roll toward point. Yeast dough horns should rise until double in bulk. Bake dough horns on buttered and floured baking sheet. Bake pastry horns on unbuttered sheet. Brush tops with beaten egg yolk. Bake in 350° oven 20 to 25 minutes, or until dough is crisp and golden. Cool and sprinkle with powdered sugar.

CHRISTMAS CAKES AND CANDY
(*Weihnachtsgebäck und -konfekt*)

In addition to the cookies that follow, there are several other Christmas cake or bread recipes in the yeast section of this chapter. They are: Bremen Loaf, page 451, Dresden Stollen, page 450, Christmas Fruit Bread, page 449.

✲ / CINNAMON STARS (*Zimtsterne*)

ABOUT 40 COOKIES

3 egg whites
½ pound fine quick-dissolving granulated sugar
3 teaspoons powdered cinnamon
1¾ to 2 cups grated unblanched almonds

½ teaspoon almond extract
finely ground nuts or fine granulated sugar for pastry board

Preheat oven to 300°. Beat egg whites, and as they begin to get foamy, gradually beat in sugar. Continue beating until whites stand in very stiff peaks. They should retain the mark of a knife blade. Set aside ½ cup of whites to coat cookies. Sprinkle whites with cinnamon and almonds, and add almond extract. Stir together gently but thoroughly. Mixture should be heavy and fairly solid. Add more almonds if it is too sticky to be rolled out. Sprinkle pastry board with nuts or sugar and roll out dough to about ¼″ thickness. Cut into star shapes with a cookie cutter. Place on greased baking sheet and spread a little of the beaten egg white on each cookie. Bake about 30 minutes. Cookies should be golden brown and slightly chewy.

✸ / SPRINGERLE, SPEKULATIUS AND PRINTED COOKIES

Square or rectangular cookies with a design printed on them in relief are among Germany's most famous Christmas cookies. It is said that these date back to pagan times when, during a winter festival, people had to sacrifice animals to the gods. The poor, having no animals they could afford to slaughter, made token sacrifices by way of cookies with animal forms on them. Eventually all sorts of designs were used besides animals: fruits, human figures in fancy dress, etc. Springerle, Spekulatius, Frankfurter Prenten, Albert Cakes, Nürnberg and Munich "marzipan" are a few of the better-known variations on this theme. For Springerle designs, impressions are made with a decorated board or a rolling pin that makes many cookies on a single sheet of dough. Spekulatius forms are smaller, individual designs, one to a wood block. You may use them interchangeably, and if you can find antique boards of this type, you should be able to get some beautifully sculptured cookies.

✸ / SPRINGERLE

ABOUT 75 COOKIES

4 eggs	5½ cups flour
2½ cups fine, quick-dissolving granulated sugar	about ¾ cup anise seeds, for pan
grated rind of 1 lemon	

Beat eggs with sugar 30 minutes by hand, or 10 minutes in an electric mixer. Mixture must be almost white, and thick enough to ribbon. Add lemon rind. Sieve flour into mixture gradually, stirring well between additions. Dough should be thick enough to knead. Add more flour if necessary. Knead dough on floured board until shiny. With a floured rolling pin, roll out dough to ¼″ to ½″ thickness. Flour a Springerle board or rolling pin, and press or roll design on dough. Cut squares apart. Grease a baking sheet and sprinkle liberally with anise seeds. Place cookies on baking sheet and let dry uncovered, at room temperature, 24 hours. Bake in preheated 250° oven until pale golden but not brown, 15 to 20 minutes.

✳ / *SPEKULATIUS*

ABOUT 30 COOKIES

½ *pound butter*
1 *pound sugar*
2 *eggs*
   grated rind of 1 lemon
4½ *cups flour*

2 *teaspoons cinnamon*
½ *teaspoon powdered cloves*
¼ *teaspoon powdered cardamom*

Cream butter with sugar until light and fluffy. Add eggs one at a time and beat well between additions. Mix in lemon rind. Sift flour with spices and stir gradually into butter-egg mixture. Chill dough overnight. Roll out dough on lightly floured board with a floured rolling pin. Dough should be about ⅛″ thick, or the thickness of a table-knife blade. Flour a Spekulatius block, Springerle board or rolling pin, and press design into dough. Cut squares apart and place on a greased baking sheet. If you would like cookies to have a glaze, brush with beaten egg white and sprinkle with sugar. Bake in preheated 350° oven 10 to 15 minutes, or until light golden.

✳ / *FRANKFURT PRINTS* (*Frankfurter Prenten oder Printen oder Brenten*)

ABOUT 24 COOKIES

1 *pound blanched almonds*
1 *pound sugar*
4 *tablespoons rosewater*

1 *egg white*
6 *tablespoons flour*
1 *teaspoon baking powder*

Grate almonds as finely as possible and mix with sugar and rosewater. Place in heavy-bottomed saucepan over very low heat. Cook and stir until mixture is dry; do not let it brown. Sprinkle inside of ·a clean bowl with sugar and turn almond paste into it. Cover with a kitchen towel and leave in a cool place 24 hours. Mix egg white and flour with almond paste and knead together on floured board until smooth enough to roll. Add more flour if necessary. Roll dough to ⅛″ thickness.

To be authentic, these cookies must be made with a Prenten form. Unlike the Springerle forms and Spekulatius boards, these are designs that are completely outlined in silhouette, not set in square shapes. If you cannot get them, use a Springerle form, but try to follow the relief outline with a sharp pointed knife and remove the solid background around the design. If that seems like too much trouble, just bake the printed, unsilhouetted cookie. Flour whichever form you are using and press design into dough. Cut cookies apart. Heat a cookie sheet, grease it and let it get cold. Arrange cookies on sheet and let dry uncovered, at room temperature, 24 hours. Bake in 300° oven until light golden—about 15 to 20 minutes. Cool and sprinkle with a little more rosewater.

✥ / FRANKFURT BEGGARMEN (*Frankfurter Bettelmännchen*)

ABOUT 30 COOKIES

½ pound almonds, blanched and grated	1 egg white
½ pound sugar	1 tablespoon flour
2 tablespoons rosewater	½ cup blanched almonds, split in half
scant ½ cup sifted confectioners' sugar	3 tablespoons sugar
	2 tablespoons rosewater

Prepare almond paste with sugar and rosewater, as in above recipe. Let dry overnight. Mix almond paste with confectioners' sugar, egg white and flour. Knead together until dough is smooth and shiny, adding a little more flour if necessary, then shape into small round balls. With the heel of your hand, flatten balls into cakes with a diameter of about 1½″. Heat a baking sheet, grease it and let it get cold. Arrange cookies on sheet and decorate with three half almonds on each. Let cookies dry uncovered, at room temperature, overnight. Bake in 350° oven about 15 minutes until light golden brown. Mix sugar with rosewater and simmer over low heat 5 minutes, or until thick and syrupy. Cool slightly and spoon on top of cookies after they have cooled.

✥ / PEPPER NUTS (*Pfeffernüsse*)

ABOUT 115 COOKIES

2 eggs	grated rind of 1 lemon
¾ cup dark brown sugar	1 tablespoon citron, finely chopped
¾ cup white granulated sugar	

1 *tablespoon candied orange*
peel, finely chopped
¼ *cup grated unblanched*
almonds
1 *teaspoon powdered cinnamon*
½ *teaspoon powdered cloves*
½ *teaspoon powdered allspice*

¼ *teaspoon powdered cardamom*
¼ *teaspoon black pepper*
generous pinch of baking soda
3 *heaping cups flour*
rum or arrack
confectioners' sugar, or White
Icing, *page* 479

Beat eggs with brown and white sugar 1 hour by hand, or 15 minutes in electric mixer. Mixture should be very thick and pale in color. Add grated lemon rind, candied fruit, almonds and spices and mix well. Sift flour together with baking soda and mix into egg-sugar batter. Knead dough on floured board until smooth. Shape into long rolls of about 1″ in diameter, and cut in ½″ to ¾″ slices. Arrange on greased cookie sheet and let dry uncovered, at room temperature, overnight. Turn cookies over just before baking in preheated 300° oven 20 minutes, or until they test done. Sprinkle warm cookies with rum or arrack and roll in confectioners' sugar while warm. Sprinkle with sugar again before serving. If you want to ice these cookies, moisten with rum or arrack and cool completely, then spread icing on cookies. Pepper nuts keep almost forever if stored in a tightly covered container.

❧ / ANISE DROPS (*Anislaibchen*)

ABOUT 85 COOKIES

4 *eggs*
1¼ *cups sugar*
3 *cups sifted flour*

1½ *tablespoons anise seeds,*
lightly crushed

Beat eggs with sugar about 30 minutes by hand or 10 minutes in electric mixer. Mixture should be almost white and thick enough to ribbon. Sift flour again and add it to egg batter, a little at a time, working in well between additions. Mix in anise seeds. Heat a baking sheet and grease. Let pan get completely cold again. Drop dough from a teaspoon onto sheet, leaving an inch or so of space between each. Let dry uncovered, in a warm room, overnight. Bake in preheated 300° oven until light golden, about 20 minutes.

✠ / WHITE HONEY SPICE CAKES (*Weisse Lebkuchen*)

ABOUT 40 COOKIES

5 eggs
1 pound sugar
½ cup unblanched almonds,
    grated
½ cup mixed citron and candied

orange peel, finely chopped
grated rind of 1 lemon
4½ cups sifted flour
1½ teaspoons baking powder

Beat eggs with sugar until mixture is thick and pale yellow. Mix in almonds, candied fruits and lemon peel. Sift flour again together with baking powder. Stir into egg mixture gradually, blending well between additions. Dough should be fairly stiff and not sticky. Turn onto lightly floured board and knead until smooth. Shape dough into finger-thick rolls, then cut in 1″ slices. Grease a baking sheet, arrange cookies on it and let dry uncovered, at room temperature, overnight. Bake in preheated 300° oven until cookies are light golden brown, about 20 minutes.

✠ / ELISE'S SPICE CAKES (*Elisenlebkuchen*)

ABOUT 40 COOKIES

5 eggs
1 pound dark brown sugar
1 pound grated unblanched al-
    monds
½ cup citron, chopped
½ cup candied orange peel,
    chopped
1 tablespoon cinnamon

½ teaspoon powdered cloves
½ teaspoon powdered cardamom
½ teaspoon powdered nutmeg
grated rind of 1 lemon
Round Oblaten, page 434
Egg White Icing or Choco-
    late Icing, page 477, 479

Beat eggs and sugar until mixture is thick. Fold in almonds, candied fruits, spices and lemon rind. Stir well. Spread in mounds on wafers. Place on greased baking sheet and let dry uncovered, in a warm room, overnight. Bake in preheated 300° oven about 30 minutes, or until golden brown. Cool completely and brush cookies with icing.

VARIATION

This is sometimes made with 1 pound fine granulated sugar. Use a little more candied fruit and add 1 tablespoon rum.

✠ / *NÜRNBERGER HONEY SPICE CAKES* (*Nürnberger Lebkuchen*)

ABOUT 30 COOKIES

3 eggs
¾ cup sugar
1 pound honey
½ cup grated unblanched
    almonds or filberts
½ cup mixed citron and candied
    orange peel, chopped
1 teaspoon cinnamon
½ teaspoon powdered cloves

1 cup strong black coffee or
    milk
4½ cups flour
1½ teaspoons baking powder
    Egg White Icing or Hard
    Chocolate Icing, pages
    477, 479, or Lebkuchen
    Glaze, below

Beat eggs with sugar until mixture is thick and pale yellow. Add honey, nutmeat, candied fruit and spices, then coffee or milk (the first makes a darker, richer cookie; the other makes a pale golden one with a mild flavor) and mix well. Sift flour with baking powder and gradually stir into batter. Blend thoroughly. Grease and flour a baking sheet or jelly-roll pan and spread out dough, to about ½" thickness. Bake in preheated 400° oven about 12 minutes, or until golden brown. If you are using Egg White Icing or Lebkuchen Glaze, brush on cookies immediately. If you use Chocolate Icing, spread on cold cookies. When cold, cut into rectangular cookies.

Lebkuchen Glaze:

Mix ⅓ cup confectioners' sugar with 1½ tablespoons cornstarch. Sprinkle with ½ teaspoon almond extract and a little rum or lemon juice. Mix in hot water, a tablespoonful at a time, until you have a thick, smooth paste. Spread on warm cookies. If mixture cools and thickens as you work with it, stir in more hot water.

✠ / *SIMPLE HONEY SPICE CAKES* (*Einfache Lebkuchen*)

ABOUT 50 COOKIES

2 cups honey
5½ cups flour
¾ cup grated unblanched
    almonds
1 teaspoon cinnamon
½ teaspoon powdered cloves

¾ cup mixed candied fruits
    (orange, lemon and citron
    peel)
½ teaspoon baking powder
    Egg White Icing, page 477

Heat honey until thin; do not boil. Mix in all other ingredients except icing. Turn onto floured board and knead until smooth, adding a little flour if necessary. Roll with a floured rolling pin to ½″ thickness. Grease and flour a baking sheet and lay rolled dough on it. Bake in pre-heated 350° oven about 20 minutes. Spread with icing while hot; cool before cutting into rectangles.

✖ / *HONEY SPICE TORTE* (*Lebkuchentorte*)

This is a somewhat unusual version of the traditional honey spice cookies, and a little more elegant to serve to guests. Though it is served mostly around Christmas, there is no reason why it could not be eaten at any time of the year.

¾ cup butter	1 cup sugar
½ pound honey	1½ teaspoons baking powder
grated rind of 1 lemon	4½ cups flour
2 teaspoons powdered cinnamon	2 eggs
1 teaspoon powdered cloves	1 cup milk
½ teaspoon powdered cardamom	butter
1 tablespoon rum	flour

Preheat oven to 350°. Melt butter and honey together over low heat until honey is thin; do not boil. Blend in spices, rum and sugar. Sift baking powder and flour together. Beat eggs and milk together. Gradually stir in flour and egg-milk mixture, alternately, beating well between additions. Butter and flour a 9″ spring form and turn batter into it. Bake about 1 hour. Remove spring-form sides while cake is hot. Cool. Dust with confectioners' sugar or spread with Powdered-Sugar Glaze, page 477.

✖ / *VANILLA PRETZELS* (*Vanillebrezeln*)

ABOUT 24 PIECES

1 cup butter	1 egg yolk, beaten with 1 tablespoon milk
¾ cup fine, quick-dissolving granulated sugar	chopped blanched almonds
2 tablespoons Vanilla Sugar, page 475	sugar
1 egg	Sugar Icing (optional), page 478
2½ cups flour	

Cream butter with sugar and Vanilla Sugar until light and fluffy, then beat in egg. Add flour gradually, stirring well between additions. Mix until dough is smoothly blended. Chill 3 hours. Preheat oven to 350°. Shape dough into long thin rolls and cut in 3″ lengths. Twist into pretzels. Arrange on lightly greased baking sheet. Brush cookies with egg-yolk-milk mixture. Sprinkle with almonds and sugar if you want to use them. Bake about 12 minutes, or until cookies are done. If you have not used almond-sugar topping, cooled pretzels can be covered with icing, or they can be left plain.

/ *LITTLE ROGUES, OR JAM CIRCLES* (*Spitzbuben*)

ABOUT 40 COOKIES

2 recipes Rich Tart Pastry, page 427, without almonds in dough
vanilla (optional)
granulated sugar
about 2 cups apricot, strawberry or raspberry jam

Preheat oven to 350°. Prepare pastry. Flavor it with a little vanilla if you like. Chill and roll out on floured board as thin as possible. Cut out rounds with a scalloped cookie cutter, about 2″ in diameter, and with a plain round cutter or glass, 1″ smaller, make hole in center of half the cookies, to form rings. Bake all cookies about 15 minutes on an ungreased baking sheet, or until crisp and faintly golden brown. While rings are still hot, dust them with sugar. Spread bottom rounds with a generous layer of jam and place rings over them.

/ *HAZELNUT MACAROONS* (*Haselnussmakronen*)

ABOUT 2 DOZEN COOKIES

2 egg whites
1 cup confectioners' sugar, sifted
1 tablespoon lemon juice
1 cup hazelnuts, coarsely ground
1 teaspoon powdered cinnamon
24 whole hazelnuts

Beat egg whites until they stand in stiff but glossy peaks. Sprinkle confectioners' sugar and lemon juice over whites, then carefully fold in ground nuts and cinnamon. Grease a baking sheet. Drop macaroons onto sheet with two teaspoons. Set a whole hazelnut in the middle of each. Let stand uncovered at room temperature, overnight. Preheat oven to 350°. Bake macaroons 15 to 20 minutes.

⚡ / ALMOND MACAROONS (*Mandelmakronen*)

Follow above recipe, using ¾ cup granulated sugar, ¾ cup grated unblanched almonds, ½ teaspoon almond extract and grated rind of ½ lemon. (Do not use cinnamon or lemon juice.) Dry 5 or 6 hours before baking.

⚡ / FRIEND OF THE HOUSE (*Hausfreunde*)

ABOUT 36 PIECES

3 eggs
1¼ cups sugar
¾ cup coarsely chopped hazel-
    nuts
½ cup chocolate bits or
    chopped semi-sweet
    chocolate

3 cups flour
½ teaspoon baking powder
¾ cup raisins
1 egg yolk, beaten

Preheat oven to 350°. Beat eggs and sugar until pale yellow and thick enough to ribbon. Add nuts and chocolate. Sift flour together with baking powder and mix gradually into egg mixture. Flour raisins lightly and stir into batter. Grease a baking sheet and spread dough on it in 2 or 3 long loaves about ⅓" to ½" thick and about 3" wide. Brush tops with beaten egg yolk and bake 35 to 45 minutes. Cut into 1" to 1½" slices while hot.

VARIATION

Chocolate is sometimes left out of this, as are raisins, so feel free to make changes if you wish. Also, half the nuts can be mixed into the dough and the other half can be sprinkled on loaves before they are baked.

✂ / *ALMOND PASTE* (*Marzipan*)

This is Germany's most outstanding contribution to the confectioners' art. Finely ground almonds, bound with egg white and flavored with sugar, are shaped into all sorts of beautiful little fruits, vegetables and figures that are colored, frosted and decorated at Christmastime. Lübeck's marzipan is the world's best, though that of Odense in Denmark does run a close second. You can buy prepared marzipan in block form, in German food shops and gourmet food departments, and mold it yourself. You can also buy some of the candies already formed and colored, but these are harder to get in good quality unless you are near a German confectioners' shop, such as there are in New York's Yorkville.

If you cannot get the block marzipan, prepare your own according to the following recipe. Instructions follow for shaping forms and designs. Chocolate-covered marzipan is also available, but the uncoated almond paste is far better, in my opinion.

✂ / *MARZIPAN PASTE* (*Marzipanmasse*)

Prepare as described for Frankfurt Prints, page 465. When dry, knead with 2 whipped egg whites, and add confectioners' sugar until paste is smooth enough to shape.

✂ / *ALMOND PASTE POTATOES* (*Marzipankartoffel*)

Prepare marzipan. Shape into small balls (potatoes) and roll in unsweetened cocoa or powdered cinnamon.

✂ / *ALMOND PASTE STRAWBERRIES* (*Marzipanerdbeeren*)

Prepare marzipan. Shape into strawberry forms. Color with red food coloring and prick with toothpick all over surface to imitate strawberry texture. Green leaves can be made with candied mint, or you can buy fake strawberry leaves in confectioners' shops.

✤ / QUINCE CANDY (*Quittenkonfekt*)

2 pounds quince	grated rind of 1 lemon
3 cups sugar	¼ teaspoon cinnamon
¾ cup grated unblanched almonds	confectioners' sugar

Cut quince and cook in a little water until soft. Cool in covered pot. Purée through a strainer or food mill and mix with sugar. Simmer over low heat about 15 minutes, or until mixture is thick. Fold in almonds, lemon rind and cinnamon and mix well. Chill. Cut or roll in desired shapes and dredge with a little confectioners' sugar. Place between sheets of waxed paper for storing.

✤ CAKE TRIMMINGS ✤
(*Kuchengarnitur*)

Confectioners' and granulated sugar, flavored with vanilla bean, orange or lemon peel, are very useful to have on hand for baking. They lend a fragrant final touch to cakes, pies and cookies and can also be used in recipes calling for vanilla, lemon or orange flavoring, when you want to keep liquid ingredients to a minimum or for easier blending. Confectioners' sugar is the most useful of the two, although certain German cakes, such as Berlin Jelly Doughnuts, are sometimes dusted with granulated sugar. It is very simple to prepare these in advance, to have them on hand when you need them.

✿ / VANILLA SUGAR (*Vanillezucker*)

4 cups confectioners' sugar 1 vanilla bean, 7" to 9" long

Put sugar in a 1- to 2-quart jar that has a tight-fitting screw-on lid. Cut vanilla bean so it fits into jar and push down into sugar. Cover tightly and store 3 days to 1 week before using. This keeps indefinitely and does not need refrigeration. Replenish sugar as it is used. Vanilla bean is good as long as it is fragrant. Granulated sugar can be flavored in the same way.

✿ / ORANGE OR LEMON SUGAR (*Orangen- oder Zitronenzucker*)

4 oranges or 6 lemons 2 cups confectioners' or granulated sugar

Grate rind of oranges or lemon on finest side of metal grater. Do this carefully so you do not include any of the white skin, or zest, that is between the rind and the fruit. Stir into sugar with a fork until well blended. The sugar will pack together and look slightly moist. Pack sugar into a jar that has a tight-fitting lid. Cover tightly and store in refrigerator. Let stand 2 or 3 days before using. This will keep indefinitely.

✿ / FLAVORED WHIPPED CREAM (*Aromatischer Schlagrahm*)

When whipping cream, be sure the cream and the mixing bowl are cold, especially in hot weather. Otherwise the mixture will turn to butter in a split second. On a very hot day, whip cream in a bowl that is set in a bed of ice. Use heavy sweet cream for whipping. If you want the cream sweetened, use 1 to 2 tablespoons fine, quick-dissolving granulated sugar to 1 cup cream. Start to beat cream and as it thickens, add sugar and continue beating until whipped. Use at once or store in refrigerator. Whipped cream can be made up to 3 hours ahead of time.

To make Vanilla Whipped Cream (Vanilleschlagrahm), add sugar plus 1 teaspoon vanilla extract after cream has begun to thicken.

To make Rum, Brandy, Kirsch or Maraschino Whipped Cream, add 1 to 3 tablespoons of whichever flavor you are using to the cream as it thickens. Also add sugar, adjusting amount to suit sweetness of the liqueur you are using.

To make Chocolate Whipped Cream (Schokoladenschlagrahm), add 2 tablespoons sifted cocoa or 3 tablespoons finely grated bitter-sweet chocolate. Adjust sugar to taste. Vanilla can be added along with the chocolate, or some rum or a little very strong black coffee if you prefer.

To make Coffee Whipped Cream (Kaffeeschlagrahm), add 1 tea-spoon powdered instant coffee or instant espresso coffee. Sweeten to taste. A little coffee liqueur is also good added to this, about 1 tea-spoon to a cup of cream.

⬛ / WHIPPED CREAM THICKENED WITH GELATIN (*Schlagrahm mit Gelatine*)

This is a useful recipe when you want to prepare the cream a day ahead of time, or when you want to use it for the filling of a layer cake or roll that is made a day in advance. Soften 1 scant teaspoonful powdered unflavored gelatin in 1 tablespoon of cold water, or in any liqueur you want to use to flavor the cream. Set over hot water until gelatin dissolves. Whip 1½ cups heavy sweet cream, adding sugar, dissolved gelatin and a little more liqueur or flavoring as needed when cream begins to thicken. Chill until ready to serve, or spread on cake or cake roll and store in refrigerator until serving time.

⬛ / CHOCOLATE CURLS (*Schokoladenspäne*)

Dark bittersweet chocolate grated on the coarsest side of a metal grater can be used to decorate the tops and sides of cakes. For thicker curls of chocolate, melt 1 cup dark semi-sweet chocolate bits or 3 ounces semi-sweet baking chocolate (Baker's German Chocolate is very good for this) over hot water. Butter a flat, rimmed 10″ dinner plate and pour chocolate onto it. When firm but not brittle, "shave" the surface with a knife; the chocolate will peel off in curls.

❊ / POWDERED-SUGAR GLAZE (*Puderzuckerglasur*)

2 cups confectioners' sugar   flavoring to taste
6 tablespoons hot water

Sift sugar twice and place in mixing bowl. Add hot water gradually, one spoonful at a time. Keep stirring until sugar is dissolved
and icing is smooth and glossy. For flavoring add 1 tablespoon rum,
arrack, strong black brewed coffee, lemon juice or orange juice with the
first two or three spoonfuls of water. Spread on cooled cake or cookies
with a metal spatula. More sugar or water can be added to achieve
a smooth, glossy consistency.

❊ / EGG WHITE ICING (*Eiweissglasur*)

2 egg whites   1 tablespoon lemon juice
1¼ cups confectioners' sugar,
    sifted

Whip egg whites until they stand in stiff peaks. Add sugar and lemon
juice and continue beating until thick and glossy. Spread on cake or
cookies with a metal spatula.

❊ / PUNCH ICING (*Punschglasur*)

1½ cups confectioners' sugar   1 tablespoon orange juice
1 tablespoon hot water   1 tablespoon rum or arrack
1 tablespoon lemon juice

Sift sugar twice and place in mixing bowl. Stir in hot water and
flavorings and mix until smooth and glossy. Spread on cooled cookies
with metal spatula. To spread this on large cakes or tortes, beat 1 extra
tablespoon hot water and a stiffly beaten egg white into the flavored
sugar mixture.

✖ / LEMON, ARRACK, RUM OR KIRSCH ICING
(Zitronen-, Arrak-, Rum- oder Kirschglasur)

Follow above recipe, using 1 to 2 tablespoons hot water and adding 2 tablespoons lemon juice, arrack, rum or kirsch for flavoring.

✖ / COFFEE ICING (Kaffeeglasur)

1½ cups confectioner's sugar   4 tablespoons very strong black cold brewed coffee

Sift sugar twice and place in bowl. Stir with cold coffee until smooth and glossy and spread on cookies or cake with metal spatula. If you prefer, use 2 tablespoons instant coffee with the sugar and add 2 to 4 tablespoons hot water as needed.

✖ / SUGAR ICING (Zuckerglasur)

Cook I cup fine granulated sugar with ½ cup cold water until mixture spins a thread. Spread on hot cookies.

✖ / COCOA GLAZE (Kakaoglasur)

1 cup fine granulated sugar   8 tablespoons water
½ cup cocoa   1 tablespoon butter

Sift sugar together with cocoa, add water and cook in heavy-bottomed saucepan until mixture spins a thread. Remove from heat and stir in butter. Stir until mixture is smooth and thick. Spread on cooled cakes or cookies.

✖ / DARK CHOCOLATE ICING (*Schokoladenglasur*)

4 ounces dark semi-sweet choco-
late (use chocolate bits or
Baker's German Chocolate)
¼ cup butter

Melt chocolate over hot water until dissolved. Chocolate should not get too warm, so remove as soon as dissolved. Cut butter into small pieces and stir into chocolate until melted. Spread while warm over cooled cake with a metal spatula.

✖ / HARD CHOCOLATE ICING (*Feine Schokoladenglasur*)

3 ounces semi-sweet chocolate
⅔ cup sugar
5 tablespoons water
1 teaspoon vanilla

Combine all ingredients in a heavy-bottomed saucepan and cook over moderate heat, stirring constantly with a wooden spoon. Do this until mixture is smooth and all chocolate is melted. Remove from heat and continue stirring until a film forms on icing. Spread on cake at once and place in warm oven, which will give icing a glaze.

✖ / WHITE ICING (*Weissglasur*)

3 cups fine granulated sugar
½ cup light corn syrup
¾ cup water
3 egg whites
flavoring to taste

Combine sugar, syrup and water in a heavy-bottomed saucepan, and cook, stirring, over moderate heat about 10 minutes. Syrup should form a ball when dropped in cold water, or measure 245° on a candy thermometer. Beat egg whites until stiff but glossy and pour syrup in very slowly, in a thin stream, beating constantly as you do so. (An electric mixer is by far the best piece of equipment for doing this.) Add 1 teaspoon vanilla, *or* 1 tablespoon lemon juice and the grated rind of 1 lemon, *or* 2 tablespoons rum or arrack, *or* 1 tablespoon orange juice and the grated rind of ½ an orange, *or* 1 teaspoon almond extract. Continue beating until frosting forms stiff peaks. Spread immediately on cooled cake with a metal spatula.

✂ / BUTTER CREAM FROSTING OR FILLING
(Buttercreme)

6 egg yolks, lightly beaten	½ teaspoon cornstarch
¾ cup granulated sugar	1¼ cups softened butter
½ cup water	flavoring to taste

Set beaten egg yolks aside at room temperature. Combine sugar, water and cornstarch and cook over low heat until sugar dissolves. Bring to a boil until mixture forms a soft ball when dropped in cold water, or a candy thermometer registers 238°. Pour boiling hot syrup into egg yolks in a very thin stream, beating constantly and vigorously as you do so. (Use an electric beater if possible.) Continue beating until light and fluffy. Continue beating until mixture starts to cool, then set aside to cool completely. Beat softened butter into cooled cream, adding flavorings such as 3 to 4 tablespoons rum, arrack, kirsch or fruit liqueurs, *or* 1 tablespoon vanilla, *or* 2½ ounces melted semi-sweet baking chocolate, *or* ½ cup grated hazelnuts, *or*, for a mocha flavor, 1½ ounces melted semi-sweet baking chocolate and 2 teaspoons instant coffee blended into 2 teaspoons boiling water. For cocoa butter cream, beat in 4 tablespoons cocoa and Vanilla Sugar (page 475) to taste.

✂ / QUICK BUTTER CREAM (Einfache Buttercreme)

1 package flavored pudding— vanilla, lemon, almond, coffee or chocolate	½ cup milk
	1½ cups milk
¼ cup sugar	1 cup butter, at room temperature

In a bowl, combine pudding powder and sugar, and blend with ½ cup milk. Bring the 1½ cups milk to a boil, turn down heat and add pudding mixture. Bring to a boil again, stirring constantly. Cool pudding, stirring frequently so no skin forms. Beat the butter with cooled pudding mixture. (Butter and pudding should be cool, not cold, or filling might curdle.)

✂ / CUSTARD FILLING (Vanillecreme)

4 egg yolks	1¼ cups milk or half-and-half
½ cup sugar	1 teaspoon vanilla or small
3 tablespoons flour	piece of vanilla bean

Beat egg yolks with sugar until thick and pale yellow. Mix flour in lightly until blended. Scald milk with vanilla bean if you are using it. If you are using extract, add it later. Pour scalded milk into egg-yolk mixture, slowly in a thin stream, stirring as you do so. Turn mixture into a saucepan and cook over low heat, stirring constantly. Remove from heat as soon as cream reaches boiling point; do not boil. Add vanilla extract if you are using it, or remove bean. Cool and stir before using. Brush with a little melted butter to prevent skin from forming. This filling can be used for éclairs, Honey Bee Cake, or whenever you want an egg custard filling.

VARIATIONS

1. Chocolate Custard Filling: Stir 2 squares of melted dark baking chocolate into cream after it has cooked but before it has cooled. Use vanilla with the chocolate and 5 egg yolks instead of 6.
2. Rum Custard Filling: Instead of vanilla, stir 2 tablespoons rum into custard after it has cooked.
3. Almond Custard Filling: Add 1 teaspoon almond extract to custard, instead of vanilla. Crushed bitter macaroons (Italian amaretti) can also be added for interesting texture and an almond flavor. Use about 8 macaroons.

/ *JAM GLAZES* (*Geleeglasuren*)

Melted jam glazes are often used between layers or on sides and tops of cakes that may or may not be covered with additional icing. If you use a jam or preserves, rub through a sieve. That step is not necessary for jelly. Heat in a heavy-bottomed saucepan until jam or jelly is bubbling and thin. Flavor to taste with brandy, kirsch, rum, arrack, apple wine or any fruit liqueur. One cup of jam or jelly will be enough for three 9-inch layers. Apricot and orange jam or marmalade, currant jelly and strawberry and raspberry preserves are most commonly used in this way. Damson plum preserves are also very good flavored with rum.

Prosit!

❊ ❊ ❊ ❊ ❊

Gut Essen—good eating—is only half the German formula for good living; one should not forget its most important corollary, Gut Trinken—good drinking. Not that anyone could forget it while traveling through Germany. From the midmorning bread time (Brotzeit) to the midnight goulash soup or wurst, you are reminded by the much-repeated national toast, Prosit!* You hear it everywhere, in all the various classes and categories of restaurants: at the rough-and-ready street-side quick-snack stands; in the fine restaurants, in the Weinkeller, the Weinstube and the Weinhaus; in the Bierkeller, the Bierstube and the Brauhaus; in dining cars and theater lobbies and bars. It tells you that two or more convivial Germans are wishing each other well with a shot of fiery ginlike Schnaps; a great stein of cold, foamy beer; a green-stemmed, round-bowl Schoppen of fruity, aromatic golden wine or a bell-shaped glass of warming German brandy, Weinbrand.

Beer is, of course, the beverage most closely associated with Germany and is as good a starting point as any. Although primarily a product of Bavaria, it is the "liquid bread" of all the land, from the Rhine to the Tyrolean Alps, from the North Sea to Lake Constance. Beerlike beverages were brewed as far back as Egyptian times, but beer as we know it was first produced in the Middle Ages by the monks (Mönche) of Munich's Tegernsee monastery. From then on, that city was off and away toward becoming the beer capital of the world, a distinction it still holds. Munich also invented the Brauhaus, the

* Pronounced more like Pros't; rhymes with "post."

brewery-operated restaurant that features simple, hearty, inexpensive food to go along with the real business at hand—beer drinking. This city abounds in these huge, raucous, lively halls and boasts Germany's most famous: the Hofbräuhaus, where gray stoneware mugs with the bright blue initials HB are among the tourist's favorite souvenirs; and the world's largest beer hall, the Mathaser, run by the Löwenbräu brewery. Here some seven thousand people can be, and often are, seated at once and there are times when every one of them seems to be holding the identical stein of beer and singing the same currently popular um-pah-pah song. Certainly no beer festival can match Munich's Oktoberfest, which runs for the last two weeks in September, a tradition since 1810, when it was begun as the celebration of a royal wedding. Now it celebrates the arrival of the first Märzenbier, the new beer brewed the previous March. Ten thousand people can be served in each of seven tents set up on the fairgrounds by the city's leading breweries—seventy thousand people in all, each night for two weeks. The air sizzles with barbecuing chicken, fish and Bratwurst, and rings with the music of big brass bands and carnival screams, all ending in what must be the biggest municipal Katzenjammer (hangover) in the world.

But beer is serious business here too and has been since 1487, when the dukes of Bavaria laid down the first purity laws requiring that beer be brewed only from barley, malt, hops, yeast and water. These laws are strictly adhered to today, not only in Bavaria but throughout Germany. For though Munich is the most famous beer city, it is not the only one. It shares honors with Hamburg, Bremen, Berlin, Dortmund, Kulmbach, Nürnberg, Würzburg and several others. Almost all of these beers are imported into this country, and the closer you live to a well-stocked German delicatessen, the better your chances of sampling them. When in Germany, it's a good idea to try these special local brews on their home grounds, just as you would drink the vins du pays when traveling through France.

Besides differing as to locale, German beers are divided into *helles* and *dunkles*, light and dark, called sometimes, in Bavaria, Schankbier (light) or Starkbier (stout). In addition, there is white beer, Weissbier, an alelike brew made of wheat. This beer is not aged, has a slightly sour tang and cannot travel, so is always consumed locally. It can usually be found in such large German sections as New York's Yorkville. In Germany, the best-known Weissbier is that of Munich and Berlin. The first may be served plain or with a slice of lemon; the second is often served "mit Schuss"—with a generous dash of currant, raspberry or strawberry syrup. Because this beer is especially strong, it is served in especially enormous glasses, usually in the shape of a footless boot, or in a stein. Bock beer is a seasonal special available during the Lenten season. It is the new beer brewed the previous fall. A special white veal sausage, Bockwurst, is made and named for this beer and is served steamed, with hot mustard, big salty pretzels and white radishes, along with the bock beer.

Though some pilsner beer is brewed in Germany, none of it is exported. What we get, and what the Germans drink mostly, is lager, or "stored," beer. This is a heavy, malty, bottom-fermented beer originally devised so it could withstand travel and thus be sold outside the brewmaster's local area. To be at its best, German beer should be served at 45° Fahrenheit, just a little warmer than we usually drink our beer. It should be placed in the refrigerator 2 to 4 hours before serving time and should stand at room temperature for 15 minutes before it is opened and poured. If the beer is a little too warm, pour it into a cold, wet glass; otherwise pour it into a warm, dry glass.

As for the glass itself, the most classic German types are so well known they are almost clichés. The ceramic steins, whether in the half-pint, pint or one-quart Masskrug, do add something to the flavor of the beer, and if you want to be absolutely authentic, you can buy some in German neighborhoods. The thick ceramic walls retain the temperature better than glass, and the handles are comfortable to hold. Otherwise, almost any glass will do as long as it is *not* a pilsner type. This is possibly the worst glass for beer, since it tapers in exactly the wrong direction. The perfect beer glass narrows toward the top in a sort of tulip shape, so that it holds the head. German glasses used in bars and restaurants always have the assay line an inch below the rim, indicating where the head should begin. To achieve the right amount of head (beer should have one or it looks and tastes dead), start pouring beer against the side of the glass. Halfway up, raise the bottle high and pour directly into the center to form the head.

As you can see from the recipes scattered through this book, beer is a fairly important ingredient in cooking and is also whipped up in hot and cold soups and drinks. Egg in your beer or beer in your egg is often a reality in Germany. In addition, many northern German cities favor a special combination of a pint stein of beer taken as a chaser with one of the barley (Korn) or juniper gins, Schnaps. The Berlin Molle, the Hannover Lütje Lager, the Hamburg Lütt un Lütt and, in Lübeck, the Holstein beer with Korn are such boilermaker combinations. One finds similar combinations in Amsterdam (gin and beer) and Copenhagen (akvavit and beer); evidently the damp northern clime requires stronger spirits to chase the chills.

If German beer has only the *helles* and the *dunkles* to confuse you, German wine has many more differences to worry you—fewer than the French perhaps, but much more than the Italian. However, since these are such absolutely delightful wines, it's worth just a little extra trouble to learn about them. For all practical purposes, German wine is white wine, the few reds being unworthy of export or places of honor on fine restaurant menus. Although these whites come from three or four different sections of the country, they all have a related flavor and it is hard to mistake a German wine for anything else, unless it is Alsatian or Austrian. German wines can best be described as aromatic and fruity. Though this full-bodied

flavor is most pronounced in Rhine wines, it is found in more delicate degrees in all the wines of that country.

Properly selected, these wines are delightful with food, provided
you serve them with those lighter German dishes that are free of
vinegar. (Sauerbraten and most other such dishes belong with beer,
not wine.) They are very pleasant sipped by themselves in a garden
or on a terrace during a hot afternoon, and can also be used for
punches. Like all white wines, they should be stored in a cool dry
place and served well chilled. Whether you do this in a refrigerator
or in an ice bucket, the wine should be served at between 50° and
55° Fahrenheit, though in Germany many prefer it close to 60°.
Since German wine bottles have long necks and are filled right to the
cork, turn them upside down for the last ten minutes of cooling
time if you use an ice bucket; otherwise the wine in the bottleneck
will not cool.

You need have only one type of glass for German wines. It should
be a stemmed goblet and should be held by the stem so the hand
does not warm the wine. Ideally, the glass should be narrow,
straight-sided and tapered toward the top in a sort of tulip shape to
catch the bouquet. Rhine wine glasses, though beautiful, are not
very practical to own, since the tall stems make them fragile and
difficult to store and they are not really suited to the wines of the
Moselle. If you want a special "German" wine glass, buy the Schoppen. It is available in all German neighborhoods and many department stores and is very decorative and practical. Actually, it is
used in Germany for wine ordered by the glass rather than the bottle,
"ein Schoppen" being comparable to a carafe in France. But they
will be anything but "ordinaire" on your table, and with their green-
roped stems and glint of gold trimming, are quite handsome.

As a general guide, the Rhine wines are deep golden in color,
very aromatic, fruity and slightly sweet, while Moselles are clear,
light golden in color with a pronounced greenish cast. Their aroma
is gentle and their flavor drier than the Rhines: if anything they
might be called less "German"-tasting, the Rhines being the arch-
types. All Rhine wine comes in long-necked brown bottles; all Moselles
in green, so that even if the label falls off you cannot go astray. Franconian wines come in fat round squat bottles.

The best way to learn about wines is to drink them, not read about
them, and being set adrift in a sea of wine terminology is only slightly
less bewildering than to be put down in the midst of the Hampton
Court maze. Still, a few pointers will be useful to start you off and
I promise to keep it brief. For one thing, find a reliable wine dealer and
let him guide you through the German vineyards, bottle by bottle. Jot
down the names or keep the labels of those you like and just keep ordering them. The subject is clearly and explicitly covered in *Wine*, by
Hugh Johnson, published by Simon and Schuster. Although this book
deals with wines of many countries, its German section is complete,
well-written and includes details on regions, labels and good years.

Although more elaborate and expensive, the *World Atlas of Wine*, by the same author and publisher, offers additional facts as well as stunning and clarifying illustrations.

Anyone who looks at a wine map of Germany will see that the vineyards are all pocketed off in the southwestern corner of the country, in that misty, balmy region nestled around the Rhine. All German wines are, in one sense, Rhine wines, but since no one would let you get off that easy, they have been further subdivided according to the part of the Rhineland and tributaries from which they come. Here are the main wine-growing areas, along with some of the most famous vineyard towns in each.

The Rheinhessen: This is that section of Hesse that nestles around the Rhine, in a triangle between Bingen, Mainz and Worms. Its most famous Hochheim, the town that gave England its adjective "hockish" for all German Rhine wines, Martinsthal, Walluf, Eltville, Rauenthal, Kiedrich, Erbach, Hattenheim, Steinberg, Oestrich, Winkel, where the great glory is the Schloss Vollrads, Johannisberg, with its famed Schloss Johannisberg, and Geisenheim. The Rheingau, which is one long slope of vineyards, is also known as the Weingau and is one of the most picturesque sections of the country. Its wines are well suited to red roasts, cheese, lobsters and oysters.

The Rheinhesse: This is that section of Hesse that nestles around the Rhine, in a triangle between Bingen, Mainz and Worms. Its most famous wine is the "Milk of the Blessed Virgin," Liebfraumilch, a wine that can be superb but which too often means a blend of inferior qualities. Buy it only when it is on a shelf in the liquor store and sold at a respectable price; a bargain version sold from an open crate on the floor of the liquor store is certain to be inferior. The best bear the labels of Blue Nun, Hanns Christof, Crown of Crowns, Glockenspiel, Madrigal and Madonna. Hesse produces more export wines than any other section of Germany, and among the important towns of the region are Laubenheim, Bodenheim, and Nackenheim, agreed by experts to be one of the best towns, with such top vineyards as Gunderloch-Lange, Gunderloch-Usinger and Staatsweingut Nackenheim; Nierstein, another top town, with dozens of vineyards of which the four leaders are Schmitt, Heyl zu Herrnsheim, Senfter and Staatweingut Niersteiner. Oppenheim, Dienheim, Worms and Bingen are the other towns of this area. Rheinhessen wines are very good with poultry, cheese and white roasts such as lamb or veal.

The Rhenish Palatinate: Almonds and chestnuts grow in this almost Mediterranean climate, just next door to France. Here along the hot southern border runs the German Wine Road, also known as the Pfalz or Rheinpfalz. It reaches from Kallstadt to Neustadt and its best vineyards are found in the towns of Bad Dürkheim, Wachenheim, Forst, Deidesheim, Ruppertsberg and Königsbach. Poultry with chestnuts, cheese or white meat are good with these wines.

The Central Rhine: This is a secondary wine-growing area, reaching from Kaub and Bingen to Bonn. The wine is fairly good with oysters, lobsters, poultry and white meat.

The Moselle-Saar-Ruwer: Known collectively as Moselle wines, these are, in my opinion, the best German wines, and, in fact, the best white wines in the world. They are grown around the banks of the three rivers, the Moselle, the Saar, the Ruwer, and labels generally bear all three names. The most famous Moselle wine towns are Piesport, Bernkastel, Graach, Wehlen, Zeltingen, Erden, Brauneberg and Kesten. Along the Saar, the great vineyards are in Wiltingen, Oberemmel, Ayl and Ockfen, while along the Ruwer are Maximin Grünhaus, Eitelsbach and Kasel. In the district of Trier, halfway between the Ruwer and the Saar, Avelsbach produces some excellent wines too. Moselle wines are superb with fish or fowl and many connoisseurs consider them too good to drink except by themselves.

The Nahe: This is a small wine section on a river tributary running just between the Moselle and the Rhine, from Bingen to Duchroth. The big growing and shipping center is Bad Kreuznach, where the wizard Dr. Faustus once taught. The wines are full of wizardry too and are said to be equally good with rare beef, fish, fowl and hors d'oeuvre.

Franconia: This is the beautiful mountainous section of Germany close to the Romantic Road of medieval walled towns. Called Stein wines, Franconia wines come in fat round bottles known as the Bocksbeutel or Boxbeutel, the goat's bladder. Most of Franconia's wines come from the Main valley and are dry, earthy and less fruity than other German wines. Franconian wines were Goethe's favorites and a few are available in this country. Some of the top vineyard towns in the region are Castell, Escherndorf, Frickenhausen, Homburg, Hörstein, Iphofen, Kleingenberg, Nordheim, Randersacker, Roedelsee, Schloss Saaleck, Veitschoechheim and Würzburg, where the true Stein type comes from.

Baden: These wines are grown in the Swabian mountain slopes centered around Baden-Baden and Freiburg; not many of them are exported. They are very much like Alsatian wines in character. Fine Baden wines are shipped by Freiherr von Neveu, Graf Wolff-Metternich and Schloss Staufenberg.

Red Wines: The red wines of the Ahr Valley, Ingelheim, Dürkheim and Assmannshäuser, can be enjoyed if you happen to be traveling through those sections in Germany; otherwise, forget the reds and stick to the whites. If you are serving meat that demands a red wine, do as the Germans do and buy a French wine.

Before 1971 German wine labels had a dazzling number of demarcations denoting various aspects of quality, and although numerous, their meanings were clear, precise and easily remembered. In 1971 the change in German wine laws resulted in a labeling procedure far more confusing to all but students of German wines. There are still vintage wines, with good years such as 1966, 1967, 1969, 1973 and the exceptional 1971 always denoted. Other than that, the regrouping and consolidating of vineyards, although reducing them in number from 30,000 to 2,700, resulted in less precise designations. Regrouped into a larger unit known as a Grosslage (big vineyard), wine bearing a formerly respected vineyard name may now come merely from another vineyard in the area given the prominent vineyard's name.

The Weinbaugebiet (or, simply, Gebiet) is the largest land area designated, and refers simply to the main wine-growing regions described above—Moselle-Saar-Ruwer, Rhenish Palatinate, etc. The Bereich is a new subdivision, a district in the overall Gebiet. The Einzellage is the narrowest, most specific of geographical designations in the new law, as it refers to a single vineyard. The best German wines will declare an Einzellage location on their labels. The Grosslage is a name used by a grower who may blend two or more Einzellage wines. Obfuscation reigns here because there is no way to tell if the vineyard is a pure Einzellage wine from a single vineyard, or an Einzellage blend from a Grosslage. Since the law does not allow a label to contain a Grosslage designation, one can only hope an indignant wine-buying public will force this aspect of the confusing law to be changed.

Besides regions, the most important standard for judging German wines is the Oeschle scale, or the percentage of sugar in proportion to the wine's total volume. The more natural sugar (or strength), the better. In lesser-quality wines some sugar may be added to make up for nature's lack.

Tafelwein, or table wine, most of which is consumed in Germany, is the lowest level of quality. Sugar may be added to this; it may be blended not only with other German wines, but also with imported wine if that does not exceed 25 percent of its total volume. Tafelwein labels may or may not indicate a Grosslage district.

Qualitätswein bestimmter Angaugebiete (more simply written as Q.b.A.) is a quality wine from a designated area but which has had sugar added to reach a minimum strength. This wine must pass a test for quality, and a test number appears on its label. It may also be Erzeugerabfüllung, or estate-bottled, and must come from a single wine-growing region.

Qualitätswein mit Pradikat (Q.m.P.) denotes a quality wine with outstanding features, and is more simply called Prädikatswein. It is used to describe wines naturally sweet with no sugar added. It is the level of sugar that denotes a further delineation in quality of Prädikatswein.

Kabinett (73 degrees Oeschle) is the minimal in this category.

Spätlese (85 degrees Oeschle) refers to late-harvested grapes that have had time to develop a little more sugar.

Auslese (95 degrees Oeschle) is a later, riper picking of selected bunches of grapes.

Beerenauslese (125 degrees Oeschle) refers to selected grapes picked still later than the Auslese, and so, much riper.

Trockenberrenauslese (150 degrees Oeschle) is made from grapes that have dried on the vine and which are, in effect, raisins. This results in a satiny, heavy, sweet wine, far more suited to desserts and after-dinner drinking than to table use.

There are other designations, of course, but those above are about as many as you need to make a reliable selection.

Three special German wines are Sekt, or champagne, Eiswein and apple wine (Apfelwein). The first is a sparkling wine (Schaumwein), pleasant by itself and excellent in punches. It is not nearly as good as the French, since it is considerably sweeter, but it is much better than almost any we produce. Eiswein, or ice-wine, is superb, expensive and a real wine-drinking experience. It is a product of a few rare years when an early frost covers the vineyards and freezes the ripe grapes. The wine produced is sharp, crystal-clean in taste, with an edge the Germans call "steely." Anyone interested in unusual wines should sample this. Apple wine is a specialty in Frankfurt and the surrounding regions and is rarely exported. If you plan to visit that city, be sure to spend at least one evening in an apple wine inn in the old Sachsenhausen section of the city. Here the mild white wine (something between hard cider and Rhine wine) is served in blue and gray stoneware pitchers. The inns are very gay and noisy with community singing, and simple food such as spit-roasted chicken, beef tartar and Cheese "with Music" (page 18) are served. In winter the action takes place indoors, and you share long sawbuck tables with other guests; in summer the gayety moves outside to the garden.

Remember that it takes a great deal of time and effort to produce good German wines and the demand for them far exceeds the supply. Therefore, they are expensive wines, with few bargains among them, so expect to get exactly what you pay for.

Beer, wine and Schnaps make up the German drinking triumvirate, for the most part. All Schnaps is fiery, clear and white, very much like gin, akvavit or vodka. Those made of barley (Korn) or juniper, such as Steinhager, Schinkenhager, Doornkaat, Danziger Goldwasser, and Korn are usually taken before a meal, especially with ham, herring, smoked salmon or anything salty, oily or fat. They are also taken, as indicated previously, along with a beer as a between-meal pick-up or warmer. However, there are also a number of white liqueurs, also known as Schnaps, which are taken before, after or between meals. These are all delightful and are made from pears (Birnenschnaps), raspberries (Himbeergeist), plums or prunes (Zwetschgengeist or Pflaumenwasser), juniper (Wacholder), strawberries (Erdbeergeist) and the specialty of the Bavarian Alps, Enzian, a strong golden liqueur made of mountain gentians. I found all of these absolutely delightful and fortunately several brands of each are imported to this country. Birnenschnaps was especially good as a between-meal drink or dessert. Finally, the Germans produce a very acceptable brandy, called Weinbrand, or "burned (distilled) wine." The best, Asbach-Uralt, made along the Rhine, is widely distributed in the United States and well worth trying.

What is there left to say but Prosit?

❇ / MAY WINE OR WOODRUFF BOWL (*Mai- oder Waldmeisterbowle*)

1 large bunch fresh woodruff, or
   ½ cup dried woodruff
3 bottles dry white wine, preferably Moselle, well chilled

½ cup sugar, or to taste
   strawberries or orange slices
   (optional)

If you are using fresh woodruff, wash well and pick off wilted leaves. Place in punch bowl, sprinkle with sugar, pour in 1 bottle of wine and marinate in refrigerator 30 minutes. If you use dried woodruff, place in punch bowl, sprinkle with sugar, add 1 bottle of wine and let stand at room temperature 2 hours. After woodruff has marinated, whether in the refrigerator or at room temperature, add the remaining chilled wine and keep in refrigerator until serving time. Ladle into punch cups with a strawberry or two, or half an orange slice, as a garnish.

VARIATION

Substitute 1 bottle champagne for 1 of the Moselles; or use 1 bottle Moselle, 1 bottle dry red wine and 1 bottle champagne.

❇ / "COLD DUCK" ("*Kalte Ente*")

This is the original of the now popular bottled wine drink. Classically, it is made with white wine and German champagne. The spiral of lemon peel, cut with the top of the lemon left on to be hung over the side of the punch bowl, is the "cold duck" that inspired the drink's name. The homemade version is an elegant far cry from the insipid bottled version.

2 tablespoons lemon juice
3 tablespoons sugar
   peel of 1 lemon, cut in a
     spiral, with top of lemon
     left on as a sort of "head"

2 bottles Moselle wine, well
   chilled
1 bottle dry champagne (Sekt),
   well chilled

Chill a glass punch bowl thoroughly in refrigerator or by filling it with ice. When it is cold, put lemon juice in it and dissolve sugar in the juice. Rub the spiral of lemon peel around sides of bowl and leave peel in bowl, hanging top end over edge. Pour wine over peel and let stand, in refrigerator, 15 to 20 minutes. Add chilled champagne. Serve in glass punch cups, each of which has 1 or 2 small ice cubes in it. If you like a greater sparkle, add a glass of club soda.

❁ / PEACH OR STRAWBERRY BOWL (*Pfirsich- oder Erdbeerbowle*)

Follow above recipe, substituting 1 quart hulled, slightly crushed strawberries, or 12 peeled and sliced peaches. Adjust amount of sugar to tartness of fruit.

❁ / TURKS' BLOOD (*Türkenblut*)

1 bottle Moselle wine, well
    chilled

1 bottle sparkling burgundy, well
    chilled

Chill a glass punch bowl and pour into it the wine. Add burgundy and serve.

VARIATION

Although not strictly authentic a half-slice of orange or a whole strawberry makes a pleasant garnish for individual servings.

❁ / CUCUMBER BOWL (*Gurkenbowle*)

2 cucumbers, peeled and sliced
3 ounces maraschino liqueur or
    Curaçao

3 bottles dry red wine
1 orange, thinly sliced (optional)

Put cucumber slices in punch bowl and sprinkle with maraschino or Curaçao. Let stand 15 minutes. Pour wine in and chill 2 hours. Remove cucumber slices with a slotted spoon, squeeze punch out of them and back into bowl. Check seasoning and add more liqueur if needed. If you are using orange slices, marinate with the rest of ingredients or add as garnish to individual punch cups just before serving.

VARIATION

If you would like this to be a sparkling punch, substitute 1 bottle champagne or club soda for 1 bottle red wine.

/ HOT RED WINE PUNCH (*Heisser Rotweinpunsch*)

peel and juice of 4 oranges
juice of 1 lemon
1 cup sugar
2 cups strong tea
1 bottle dry red wine
½ cup rum or arrack

Slice orange peels into thin strips; place in enameled 2-quart saucepan with sugar. Rub sugar and orange peel together until sugar takes on slight orange tinge. Add orange juice, lemon juice, tea and red wine to sugar and orange peel. Heat to boiling point, but do not boil. Add rum and serve in cups or toddy glasses.

VARIATIONS

1. Tea can be omitted, in which case use only half the amounts of lemon juice, orange juice and peel.
2. Two or 3 cloves and a small stick of cinnamon can be simmered with this punch.

/ HOT WHITE WINE PUNCH (*Heisser Weissweinpunsch*)

Follow above recipe, substituting white wine for red. This also may be made with or without tea. The following two flaming wine bowls are both considered New Year's Eve punches—Sylvesterpunsch. At midnight the lights are dimmed and the burning sugar flames blue as guests raise their cups and toast each other with the traditional "Prosit Neujahr"—a Happy New Year.

/ FLAMING WINE PUNCH (*Krambambuli*)

2 bottles dry red or white wine
1 cup granulated sugar
1 pound cube sugar
½ cup dark rum or arrack, heated
1 bottle champagne (Sekt)

Heat, but do not boil, the two bottles of wine. Pour into a heavy porcelain bowl. Add granulated sugar and stir until dissolved. Place a sieve or metal rack over the bowl. Heat rum or arrack and moisten cubes of sugar with it. Place sugar in sieve or on rack and set a match to it. As the sugar burns, slowly pour more rum or arrack over it to keep it burning. The sugar will melt down into the wine. Since this is a rather showy spectacle, it's a good idea to perform it in full view of your guests. Add champagne after sugar has melted and serve in punch cups.

❈ / FIRE-TONG PUNCH (*Feuerzangenbowle*)

Originally, this punch took its name from the fire tongs that held the flaming loaf sugar over the bowl. You're welcome to try the recipe that way if you like (if you can get loaf sugar), but be ready for a great and sudden splash. It's a lot simpler and safer to use cubes of sugar in a sieve or on a rack.

2 *bottles red wine*	*juice of 1 lemon*
1 *cup sugar*	*juice of 1 orange*
6 *cloves*	½ *pound cube sugar*
1 *strip of orange peel*	1 *cup rum or arrack, heated*
2 *slices of lemon*	

Heat wine with sugar, cloves, orange peel and lemon slices. Do not boil. Pour into heavy porcelain punch bowl. Add juice of lemon and orange and stir gently. Soak sugar cubes in heated rum or arrack and place in strainer or on rack over punch. Set a match to the soaked sugar and as it flames, gradually pour more heated rum or arrack on to keep it burning. When sugar has all melted into punch, serve in punch cups.

❈ / SPICED WINE (*Glühwein*)

2 *bottles red wine*	3 *or* 4 *slices lemon, each studded*
1 *cup sugar*	*with* 3 *or* 4 *cloves*
1 *stick cinnamon*	

Heat all ingredients together until they reach the boiling point, but do not boil. Pour into glasses or mugs and serve.

✂ / HOT TODDY (*Heisser Grog*)

1 cup water
2 tablespoons sugar

½ cup rum or arrack
juice of 1 lemon

Heat water and in it dissolve sugar. Pour into glass or mug, add rum and lemon juice and serve.

✂ / HOT EGG TODDY (*Heisser Eierpunsch*)

1 cup water
1 tablespoon sugar
juice of ½ lemon

2 egg yolks
2 tablespoons water
3 tablespoons rum or arrack

Heat water and in it dissolve sugar. Add lemon juice. Beat egg yolks with water and gradually stir into hot water. Add rum or arrack and serve.

✂ / HOT EGGNOG (*Hoppel-Poppel*)

3 egg yolks
6 tablespoons sugar
1 teaspoon vanilla, or to taste

1 quart hot milk
1 cup rum

Beat egg yolks with sugar until light and foamy. Add vanilla and very slowly pour in hot milk, beating constantly as you do so. Add rum, stir, and serve in cups or mugs.

✂ / HOT EGG BEER (*Heisses Eierbier*)

2 cups white or light beer
strip of lemon peel
3 tablespoons sugar

4 egg yolks
1 cup milk

Heat beer with lemon peel and sugar. Bring to boiling point, but do not boil. Beat egg yolks with milk. Add a little of the hot beer to the egg yolk mixture and when smoothly blended, turn back into rest of the beer. Beat over *very* low heat until thick and foamy. Serve in cups or mugs.

Following are a few non-alcoholic beverages.

⚡ / STRAWBERRY MILK (*Erdbeermilch*)

2½ cups fresh strawberries	2 cups milk
2 to 3 tablespoons sugar, or to taste	¾ cup heavy sweet cream, lightly whipped
juice of ½ lemon	fresh strawberries for garnish

Wash strawberries well and rub through a sieve or purée in a blender. Add sugar and lemon juice and beat into purée. Gradually pour milk into fruit mixture, beating constantly with a rotary beater or a blender. The sweet cream should be whipped so that it is thick and foamy but should not stand in peaks. Beat half-whipped cream into fruit-milk mixture. Chill 1 to 2 hours, or until drink is ice-cold. Serve from a pitcher into 6-ounce glass tumblers or cups. Garnish each serving with a whole berry. This is very good as cold lunch or summer soup.

VARIATION

Frozen strawberries can be used for this, but they should be thawed thoroughly and well drained of excess liquid. One small package will do for this but use less sugar, as frozen berries are already sweetened.

⚡ / BUTTERMILK WITH BLACKBERRIES (*Buttermilch mit Brombeeren*)

2 cups fresh blackberries	2 cups buttermilk
2 tablespoons honey	

Wash blackberries well and rub through a sieve or purée in a blender. Beat honey into purée and pour buttermilk in gradually, beating constantly with a rotary beater or a blender. Check seasoning and add more honey if necessary. Chill thoroughly in refrigerator and serve in glasses or soup cups. This is a wonderful cold luncheon for summer and is equally good as a cold soup, though it may be a little sweet for the latter.

❉ / CHOCOLATE SOUP (*Schokoladensuppe*)

2 1-ounce squares semi-sweet
   chocolate
1 quart milk
   pinch of salt
1 tablespoon sugar, or to taste

1 teaspoon vanilla or 1 small
   stick cinnamon
2 egg yolks or 1 tablespoon cornstarch, beaten in 2 tablespoons sweet cream

Melt chocolate in top of double boiler. While it is melting, simmer, but do not boil, milk with salt, sugar and vanilla or cinnamon stick. Combine melted chocolate and seasoned milk. Check to see if more seasoning is needed. Beat egg yolks with a few tablespoons cold water, if you use them. Remove hot chocolate from heat and pour egg yolks or cornstarch in very slowly, beating all the time with a wire whisk. If you use cornstarch, simmer 2 or 3 minutes; if egg yolks, heat slightly without letting it boil. Serve in cups, mugs or bowls.

❉ / HOT FRUIT PUNCH (*Heisse Fruchtbowle*)

1 quart concentrated juice of
   such fruits as apples, red
   currants, black currants,
   cherries, blackberries, etc.

4 thin slices lemon
1 stick cinnamon
2 cups hot strong tea
   sugar to taste

Heat fruit juice to boiling point with lemon slices and cinnamon. Simmer very slowly, but do not boil, about 4 or 5 minutes. Add hot tea and sugar to taste. Serve with a lemon slice garnishing each punch cup or mug.

English Index

German Index

MIMI SHERATON traveled throughout Germany over a two-year period to gather authentic material for this book, which has become the classic in its field, and she has since been back many times to keep it up-to-date. She is, arguably, our foremost restaurant critic, and, because of her candor, the most controversial and respected. Longstanding food critic for *The New York Times, Time,* and *Condé Nast Traveler,* she has traveled all over the world gathering information on food, crafts, and interior design for publications such as *Vanity Fair, Esquire, Vogue, Mademoiselle,* and *Town & Country.* She is now a contributing editor to *New Woman.* She won a JCPenney–University of Missouri prize for journalism for articles in *New York* magazine and a Front Page Award for work in *The New York Times.*

Born in Brooklyn and a graduate of New York University, where she received a degree in journalism and marketing, Ms. Sheraton studied interior decorating at the New York School of Interior Design, and cooking in various places, including Le Cordon Bleu in Paris, and with private teachers in Bangkok, Istanbul, and Beirut. For many years she was on the staff of *Seventeen, Good Housekeeping,* and *House Beautiful.*

Ms. Sheraton loves to photograph foreign food markets, and collects exotic cookware and junk antiques. She and her husband live in a Greenwich Village town house. In addition to four New York City restaurant guidebooks, she wrote *The Seducer's Cookbook, Visions of Sugarplums, From My Mother's Kitchen,* and *City Portraits,* a travel guide to sixty of the world's great cities. She also served as the historical foods consultant on *The Horizon Cookbook.* Her latest cookbook, *The Whole World Loves Chicken Soup,* received both the James Beard Foundation Award and the Julia Child/IACP Award.